International Law
for Seagoing Officers

International Law
for Seagoing Officers

FOURTH EDITION

Burdick H. Brittin
A.B., J.D.

NAVAL INSTITUTE PRESS
Annapolis, Maryland

Library of Congress Cataloging in Publication Data

Brittin, Burdick H.
  International law for seagoing officers.

  Bibliography: p.
  Includes index.
  Supt. of Docs. no.: D 201.2:(4)
  1. International law. I. Title.
JX3110.B6815 1981   341   81-607005
ISBN 0-87021-304-0   AACR2

Printed in the United States of America

To Trudi
who has more than tolerated the
growing pains of all four editions
and
Peter, Michael, and Christopher
to whom the gauntlet is tendered

Contents

Foreword

The publication of a fourth edition of this book is eloquent testimony to its usefulness to seagoing officers as well as to others in the United States and abroad whose business or interest lies in the oceans and foreign lands. The appearance of the fourth edition is timely, for, as the author states in his preface, the past twenty-five years have seen a profound and ever-accelerating change in the law of the sea. Rapidly expanding claims by coastal states over ocean space have had an impact on traditional freedoms of maritime movement, and the old alliance between peace-keeping power, global peacetime mobility of military forces, and a universal system of ocean law has been disintegrating.

Renewal of the law of the sea under terms appropriate to the present remains an essential task of the Third United Nations Conference on the Law of the Sea, and one in which all nations have a major stake. As the author correctly observes, the conference has produced a consensus on a regime for navigation. A widely accepted system of international law for the oceans is within the grasp of the world community. If, as I confidently hope, the labors of the conference should be crowned with success, a new vista of peaceful, fruitful use of the oceans would open up. This book, with its emphasis on emerging ocean regimes affecting navigation, will be an invaluable tool for all whose business or interest pertains to the oceans and foreign lands beyond.

September 1980

Elliot L. Richardson
Ambassador at Large
Special Representative of
the President for the
Law of the Sea Conference

Preface

This enlarged edition covers a twenty-five-year period of evolution of the law that governs man's use of the world's oceans. In 1956, when the first edition was published, I certainly did not visualize historically tested precepts changing so much and so rapidly that a fourth edition would be necessary only two and a half decades later. Indeed, if my recollection of history is correct, the quarter-century just ended saw more change than any other. Before that time, the cadence of the law's development was almost measured. Assuredly, there were periods of experimentation and rather abrasive testing of conflicting views but, in balance, the march forward was slow and relatively predictable.

In 1973, when the Third Law of the Sea Conference began to grapple with its charter to reexamine the entire body of sea law and to create a new regime for mining the resources of the deep seabed, it became apparent that one of the realities to be dealt with was the new, insistent, coordinated voice of well over a hundred developing countries. By the time the great mass of issues had been thoroughly debated and compromises had been reduced to initial drafts and then to treaty language (1978–80), it was clear that the views of the developing countries had helped produce many dramatic changes.

As this edition goes to press, some issues, primarily those related to the seabeds, have not been resolved, but the leadership of the conference forecasts final resolutions probably by 1981. While these seabed issues are indeed important, they are not of direct concern to the users of this text because they will have but peripheral and secondary impact on navigational regimes. As it was in the earlier editions, navigation over, on, and under the oceans is the primary focus of this book. While there is a degree of hazard in publishing this fourth edition before completion of the treaty negotiations, I believe the articles that set forth the navigational regime, as well as those that address other ocean uses that affect navigation, can be characterized as final. The history of the conference, as noted in this text, supports this view. At this writing, customary practice throughout the world plus the mutuality of the opinions expressed by the representatives at the conference lead to the conclusion that the norms for navigation developed at the conference will be, in fact, those practiced at sea in the years to come.

The usefulness of the present edition is that, like its predecessors, it is a simplified text on a complex subject. It is not a lawyer's law book, rather it is an aid for those whose profession or interest is related to the seas and those who come in contact with foreign countries either in an official or unofficial capacity.

When Dr. Liselotte B. Watson, my coauthor for the last two editions, succumbed to the beauty of the Strait of Juan de Fuca, she moved there forthwith. While I appreciated her reasoning and was envious, I knew that professionally I would sorely miss her renowned expertise in the fields of jurisdiction over persons and related matters. The success of the prior editions can certainly be attributed to the many contributions she made, not to mention the quiet and pleasant harassment she focused on my maintaining an energetic schedule of work. Although the geographic distance proved too great for her to cooperate with me again, the content and personality of this volume reflects her earlier participation.

It was rewarding to have previous editions translated into several languages. Resulting comments by many foreign experts, coupled with those of U.S. authorities, served as a valuable guide in the preparation of this edition.

I was encouraged to undertake this fourth edition by Admiral James L. Holloway III, USN, former Chief of Naval Operations, and General Louis H. Wilson, Jr., former Commandant of the Marine Corps. Both showed their support of the effort by submitting incidents, which I have incorporated into the text.

I must gratefully acknowledge the suggestions and recommendations of many experts from the Navy Department, the State Department, the academic world, the scientific and legal communities, and men of the sea who reviewed various parts of the manuscript during the drafting stage. The following ladies and gentlemen warrant special mention: Ambassador Thomas Clingan, professor of law at the University of Miami and a U.S. delegate to the Law of the Sea Conference, and Captain Bruce Harlow, JAGC, USN, then director of the Navy Department's International Law Division, both of whom shared their knowledgeable perspectives of ocean uses with me; Ambassador Morris D. Busby, Deputy Assistant Secretary of State for Ocean and Fisheries Affairs, Dr. James A. Storer, director of the Office of Fisheries Affairs, Norman A. Wolf, director of Marine Science and Technology Affairs, Brian S. Hallman, Office of Fisheries Affairs, and B. Tucker Scully, Office of Ocean Affairs (with specific emphasis on the Antarctic region), all from the State Department, who contributed their expertise to my various drafts; Lieutenant Susan Gillette, JAGC, USN, who was a primary contributor to the chapter on sovereign states and their diplomatic representatives; Captain Harold J. Sutphen, USN, of the Politico-Military Policy and Current Plans Division of the CNO's office, whose numerous thoughtful suggestions made the text more readable; Commander William L. Schachte, Jr., JAGC, USN, head of the Law of the Sea Branch of JAG's International Law Division, who advanced several helpful suggestions; Leonard R. Raish, a Washington attorney who is an expert in international communications law, and Joseph J. Hahn, a scholar on space law, both of whom made in-depth contributions; Commander George P. Wisneskey, USCG, chief of the Rules of the Road Branch, at Coast Guard Headquarters, who contributed his time and his highly specialized expertise; Melvin A. Conant, president of Conant and Associates and an expert on international resources, who aided in the preparation of material on seabed resources; John Dugger of the Department of Energy who did the same thing for issues concerning the continental shelf; William Utz, executive director of the National Shrimp Congress, and August Felando, president of the American Tunaboat Association, who added to the text substantive thought involving fisheries.

Because of heightened interest in the subject, the expanding body of law pertaining to the conduct of war or armed conflict and its effect on its victims has received considerably more attention in this edition. Thus, chapters 9 and 10 have been considerably expanded. Full credit and appreciation must go to Commander J. Ashley Roach, JAGC, USN, head of the Law of Armed Conflict Branch of JAG and a member of the U.S. delegation to the U.N. Conference on Prohibitions or Restrictions on the Use of Certain Conventional Weapons, Geneva, 1979, whose work and deep interest permeate the new text of those chapters. Indeed, the resulting comprehensive treatment accorded this field of International Law is the product of Commander Roach's substantive knowledge. Helpful and thoughtful suggestions in this area were made by Professor Charles L. Cochran, of the Political Science Department, U.S. Naval Academy.

The ready cooperation of Rear Admiral William O. Miller, JAGC, USN, and his successor as Judge Advocate of the Navy, Rear Admiral Charles E. McDowell, JAGC, USN, facilitated the completion of the task. Captain William R. Palmer, JAGC, USN, director of the Navy's International Law Division, also gave me useful advice and cooperation. George Taft, of the Law of the Sea Office in the Department of State, also was most helpful.

Many of the changes in emphasis and additions contained in this edition are the result of comments by people affiliated with the Naval Academy, the Coast Guard Academy, the Naval War College, and other institutions having an interest in ocean affairs.

The exacting work of updating the glossary and extensive index was done by Christa Conant; her thoroughness and skill are much appreciated. Preparation of the manuscript for submission to the publisher was cheerfully and accurately carried out by Laura Love Yates, who sacrificed much of her free time in the endeavor.

Editing and proofreading of the text before its submission to the publisher was accomplished with a high degree of precision by Christopher Mark Brittin; his task was hazardous in that he is a son of the author. Mary Veronica "Ron" Amoss, editor, Naval Institute Press, contributed much to the success of the third edition; most fortunately for me, she has contributed her marked professionalism to this edition also. The pleasure of working with her is a constant.

And finally, one of the most pleasant, helpful, and rewarding circumstances connected with the preparation of this fourth edition was the action taken by Attorney Edmund L. Walton, Jr., in permitting me to use space in his law office in McLean, Virginia, to work on the draft. To my joy, that saved me from having to do the long commute between Great Falls and downtown Washington; the cheerful environment served as an incentive to me to get the project completed.

Indeed, I am indebted to many. I trust that whatever errors were found in the prior editions have been eliminated. If the text serves to increase the appreciation that those whose career relates to the oceans and foreign lands have for the significance of International Law, its mission has been achieved.

Some years ago I wrote:

> The seas are ancient, yet they are new.
> Their regimes are immutable, yet they are fragile.
> They are catalysts for progress, yet platforms for discord.

I believe that statement is still valid. How man conducts his ocean affairs under the regimes that emerge from the Third Law of the Sea Conference is going to determine whether the seas will be a platform for discord or a catalyst for progress. In brief, the global ocean can serve as a splendid servant to the world community, but only if that community respects it and its processes and the rights and duties imposed on ocean users by nature and by International Law.

Great Falls, Virginia   Burdick H. Brittin
September, 1980

International Law
for Seagoing Officers

1 Scope and Sources

Physically our world remains the same size, but as man increases his technical knowledge and mutually shares his ideas and ideals, we witness a world of ever decreasing dimensions.

B.H.B.

INTRODUCTION

The scope of the subject we are going to explore and study here is as broad as the world itself. Some newspaper headlines indicate the diversity of the matter concerned:

UN CALLS CONFERENCE ON LAW OF THE SEA

JAPAN SEEKING PEKING TRADE

MOSCOW-BONN PACT: A HISTORIAN'S ASSESSMENT

COMMANDOS TAKE INITIATIVE
EVEN IN RESTRAINED LEBANON

BRAZIL EXTENDS ITS TERRITORIAL SEA TO 200 MILES

U.S. DOUBTS HARASSMENT OF BERLIN TRIP

PERUVIANS ATTACK U.S. FISHING BOATS

CAIRO EMPHASIZES PEACE WITHOUT FORMAL TREATY

THE MIDEAST: VIEWS FROM 3 CAPITALS

RED ARMY GENERAL AFFIRMS
SOVIET RIGHT OF INTERVENTION

Although the sample headlines relate to subjects seemingly foreign to one another, there is a common thread that ties them together. That thread is the fact that two or more countries are trying to solve a problem.

We can broaden our scope and approach the subject from another angle by considering some of the routine events that are so commonplace as to go unnoticed by most of us.

If you want to mail a letter to a friend in Switzerland, you first buy a U.S. stamp at the local post office and pay for it in U.S. money. En route to Switzerland the letter may cross the territory of Great Britain, Belgium, and France. The postal authorities in these countries undoubtedly assist in speeding the letter on its way. Two questions are apparent: What authority or arrangement permits a letter to cross the borders of various countries? Do the post offices of the other countries get any monetary reimbursement from the U.S. postmaster general for the work they do in helping to deliver a letter from the United States, and, if so, who determines how much is their equitable share? The same two questions might well be asked about a telephone call or cable to a distant country.

Assume that a Brazilian training ship comes to Annapolis or King's Point for a three-day rest-and-recreation visit. As the midshipmen come down the gangway and set foot on U.S. soil, no one is there demanding their passports. Further, if you were to ask them about their passports, they probably would tell you that they had none. Under what authority or understanding do we permit a foreigner to enter our territory without a valid passport?

If you look over the training ship, you will notice that she carries running lights precisely the same as those in use on our own ships. A query to one of the visitors will show that he knows that when two ships meet at sea both are obligated to turn to starboard. As a matter of fact, the Rules of the Road are as familiar to him as they are to you. If you question him a little more, he will undoubtedly state that not only do Brazilian and U.S. ships follow the Rules of the Road, but the ships of all countries feel a positive obligation to do so. Why is this true?

If you have not already traversed the Panama Canal, the odds are that you will do so sometime. The engineering history of that tremendous canal and the story of how the United States acquired the rights to build it are classics in their field. Those rights, ceded in the early part of this century, have a bearing on the jurisdiction over and operation of the canal today.

The scope of the subject we are about to explore and study can also be gleaned from some of the words and phrases used:

continental shelf	chargé d'affaires
blockade	International Court of Justice
innocent passage	territorial sea
immunity	reprisal
comity	hot pursuit
de facto	extradition
neutrals	protocol
visit and search	sovereignty
thalweg	visas
Security Council	deep seabed
asylum	contiguous zone
exclusive economic zone	transit passage

You are undoubtedly familiar with many, if not all, of these terms. If you are familiar with even a few of them, you will recognize the fact that the subject of this text is not restricted to a narrow field. As you proceed through this text, you will learn that these words, and many more of like import, have significant shades of meaning that a mariner cannot afford to ignore.

Thus far we have touched briefly on heterogeneous questions and sub-jects. We have sampled newspaper headlines that report routine events with a foreign flavor, and some words that have a familiar ring. It should be apparent that the focal point here lies in the fact that all these items have something to do with foreign countries. Not only do they pertain to foreign countries, but, more specifically, they involve *relations* between countries. Countries can no more escape having relations with other countries than people living in the same small town can escape some form of relationship with one another.

Before the Industrial Revolution the necessity for countries to have relations with one another was minimal. All types of communication were poor, and most of the simple needs of a community of that day were satisfied by its own particular skills and land. The technological advances of the modern era, and in particular of the twentieth century, abruptly changed the mode of living throughout the world. No longer did it take weeks to go from Paris to Rome or to send a communication from one of those cities to the other. In the former case, it is now a matter of hours; in the latter, it takes but a few seconds. The demands of modern living require that products be obtained from all over the world. The jet airplane will continue to make the world still smaller. When we speak of making the world smaller we can only mean that, in contrast to the past, relations between countries have grown, and will continue to grow, more complex. In other words, countries have become more interdependent. This fact is inescapable. As we have already seen, it forces itself on us in many ways every day.

If there must be relations between countries, there must be some over-riding authority or "rules of the game" to control them. Without such rules, and binding ones at that, we could liken international relations to an Army-Navy football game without referees, sidelines, goal posts, an agreed num-ber of players, and a specified type of ball and field. In essence, if it were not controlled by rules, it would no longer be a game. In the field of internation-al relations, the absence of authoritative rules would produce a similar free-for-all, which in more formal language is termed *anarchy*.

The rules that control relations between countries and their source are the subjects of this text. The rules and their application are collectively called *International Law*.

DEFINITIONS

Let us first take a look at the word *law*. Webster defines it, in part, as:

All the rules of conduct established and enforced by the authority, legislation, or custom of a given community or other group.

Black's *Law Dictionary* provides a more precise definition:

That which is laid down, ordained, or established. A rule or method according to which phenomena or actions co-exist or follow each other.

A system of principles and rules of human conduct, being the aggregate of those commandments and principles which are either prescribed or recognized by the governing power in an organized jural society as its will in relation to the conduct of the members of such society, and which it undertakes to maintain and sanction and to use as the criteria of the actions of such members.

Turning the pages in the dictionaries, we see how they define the word *international*. Webster says:

1. Between or among nations: as, an international treaty. 2. Concerned with the relations between nations: as, an international court.

Black says:

The word "international" is a generic term pertaining to relations between nations, and, when applied to business or transactions of private character, it imports dealings of some sort in matters or with people of different nations.

The two words, *international* and *law*, standing apart give us a flavor of what they mean when they are joined together. However, let us marry them correctly into the phrase *International Law* and see how they are defined. Webster says:

The system of rules generally observed and regarded as binding in the relations between states.

Black defines the phrase as:

The law which regulates the intercourse of nations; the law of nations. The customary law which determines the rights and regulates the intercourse of independent states in peace and war.

The system of rules and principles, founded on treaty, custom, precedent, and the consensus of opinion as to justice and moral obligation, which civilized nations recognize as binding upon them in mutual dealings and relations.

To contract these basic definitions to a rather dangerous simplicity, we can say that the phrase *international law* means law that is applicable to relations between countries, as distinguished from law that governs the internal matters of a particular country.

International Law is divisible into two distinct categories. Public International Law, which is the subject of this book, pertains to the body of law governing relations between independent sovereign states. In contrast, private International Law regulates relations between individuals in separate states: it does not deal with relationships between sovereign states and, consequently, is not covered in this text.

THE U.S. GOVERNMENT AND INTERNATIONAL LAW

It has been said that International Law is a static science, that it is not vital and moving, and that individual countries apply it only when and if such application is to their advantage. In the preceding introductory statements we have tried to indicate that this approach is not valid.

How does the U.S. government feel about the validity and importance of International Law? The makers of the Constitution appreciated its significance fully, for they incorporated in that document the explicit directive that treaties form part of the supreme law of the land. (As will be discussed later, treaty law is a major part of International Law.) The Supreme Court also specifically declares the validity and importance of International Law. In the *Paquete Habana* case (175 U.S. 677,700), the court, reiterating a principle that has been constant since the organization of that body, said: "International Law is part of our law, and must be ascertained and administered by the courts of justice of appropriate jurisdiction, as often as questions of right depending upon it are duly presented for their determination."

The following address made by Secretary of State Dean Rusk at the University of Georgia on 4 May 1968 is also indicative of our government's position. In light of the major international problems facing the world at that time, a significant feature of the speech is the conclusion reached by Secretary Rusk.

Each year at this time we as a nation pause to consider the impact of law upon our lives and the efforts we must make if the family of man is to achieve, an ordered society based upon justice and peace. We celebrate law as liberator—law, which expands the range of freedom by making it possible to predict with reasonable assurance the conduct of others. Law is the guardian of the presumption of good faith which is the cement which holds our society together. It permits us to pursue our own eccentric orbits with the minimum risk of collision with each other. In international affairs the steady consolidation of the rule of law is the alternative to the law of the jungle and is an essential condition, in this nuclear age, for the survival of man.

When we turn our attention to domestic problems, the role of law is clear. Our own country has long been attuned to the intellectual concepts of equal justice and opportunities for all citizens. They are embedded in the very foundation of our legal system.

On the world scene, the role of the law is often less clear. Unused as we are to a legal system functioning without police or a courthouse, we tend to view law in the international framework as more of a hope than a reality.

I think, however, that the law plays a vastly more important role in world affairs than occurs to most people. Just as the law provides us with the ultimate objectives at home, it provides international goals to which we must bend our national efforts. Law forms the basis for collective action by which nations guard the peace. It knits together countries in an ever-stronger fabric of agreements about common policies and goals. Finally, it provides the tools with which mankind can deal with the utterly new problems we encounter on the earth and in space around it.

In examining any legal system, the most sensitive point of departure is its basic constitutional structure. The community of nations has a constitution— the United Nations Charter. In its very first article, the charter announces as a purpose of the organization: "To maintain international peace and security, and to that end: to take effective collective measures for the prevention and removal of threats to the peace, and for the suppression of acts of aggression or other breaches of the peace."

This, then, is one of the basic tenets of our international structure.

This is a purpose firmly supported by the United States because we believe world order cannot exist without collective security. This purpose has not changed with the coming and going of political events in the United States or with the ever-shifting pattern of developments on the world scene. It has represented a basic continuity in American foreign policy that has applied regardless of who has been President and regardless of which party has controlled the Congress. . . .

Today, the ability of nations to act in concert to preserve peace is gravely challenged. I believe the challenge can be met succcessfully. One basis for my optimism is the pervasive role the law has been playing in developing and strengthening world order.

All too often, we view the world as a group of independent countries each pursuing its own policies and following its own interests, like so many stars hurtling through space away from one another. However, this explosive view of world politics neglects to take into account the important ways nations have tied themselves together and continue to do so.

The United States belongs to more than 70 international organizations and institutions and each year takes part in approximately 600 multilateral international conferences. Most of these conferences receive little or no attention in the general news media.

Before 1945, the United States was a party to some 1,300 international agreements with other countries. Since that time, we have entered into 4,000 more. Our annual catalog, *Treaties in Force*, discloses that we have agreements with over 150 other countries and international organizations. We and others have decided on joint action on subjects ranging from fisheries to post offices, from the control of epidemics to collisions at sea.

This compilation indicates the degree to which this country has tied its economy, its defenses, and its political outlook to the concept of community action. This multitude of agreements, even those treating rather prosaic subjects, represents the roots that bind us tightly to the fertile soil of world order. It is healthy, I believe, that the countries of the world show signs of recognizing that, no matter how much they wish to live alone, they must live together.

The ever-expanding network of international arrangements comprises what Sir Wilfred Jenks has called "the common law of mankind."

A major share of the activity of the Department of State is concerned with the quiet business of ordering and facilitating the affairs of men that reach across international frontiers.

From the above evidence it must be concluded that the U.S. government looks to the body of International Law for the solution of basic problems that face it on the international scene. International Law is part and parcel of the routine business of conducting international affairs in the U.S. Department of State; it is recognized by the United States and, indeed, the world community as indispensable to orderly relations.

MARINERS AND PILOTS AND INTERNATIONAL LAW

Granting that every country must have relations with othe countries, that International Law is the instrument used in maintaining and conducting such relations, and that the United States attaches the utmost importance to International Law, of what concern is it to those whose profession is that of the sea or of the air?

It is a popular misconception that International Law has to do only with heads of nations, legislatures, courts, and diplomats. In part this idea is correct, but in large measure it is erroneous: everyone who comes in contact with a foreign country, officially or otherwise, uses International Law whether he knows it or not. For those whose profession is related to the sea or the air—be it the Navy, Coast Guard, National Oceanic and Atmospheric Administration, Merchant Marine, Air Force, or civilian aviation—the importance of International Law cannot be overemphasized.

John Paul Jones was fully aware of the close relationship between professional men of the sea and International Law. In delineating the most desirable qualifications for a naval officer, he wrote almost 200 years ago:

> The naval officer should be familiar with the principles of International Law . . . because such knowledge may often, when cruising at a distance from home, be necessary to protect his flag from insult or his crew from imposition or injury in foreign ports.

Evidence that it is still important for a naval officer to be familiar with International Law is provided by Article 1124 of *U.S. Navy Regulations*:

> Persons in the Department of the Navy, in their relations with foreign nations, and with the governments and agents thereof, shall conform to international law and to the precedents established by the United States in such relations.

Today's *Navy Regulations* contain some sixty articles related directly to the science of International Law. In the following chapters, which examine the substantive rules of law, there will be many references to and discussions of these articles. International Law is so important to the U.S. Navy that, as a naval officer prepares himself for high rank, he is obliged to make himself as familiar with it as possible. Correspondence courses are widely used in this connection, and the subject receives more and more emphasis in promotion examinations for senior officers. Officers selected to attend the Naval War

College will find that not only are they required to take advanced studies in International Law but that the college itself is actively engaged in research on the subject.

The Naval War College publishes the results of its research annually in *International Law Situations*, which is more familiarly called the "Blue Book." When the U.S. Navy needed a new operating manual on the law of naval war, the Naval War College guided the preparation of *Law of Naval Warfare* (NWIP 10-2).

Within the Navy Department the Judge Advocate General has an International Law Division, whose primary function is to solve the day-to-day problems of a navy that operates on a continuous basis throughout the world. In carrying out these duties, legal officers work closely with officers from the Strategy, Plans, and Policy, the Fleet Operations, Readiness, and Navy Command Center, and the Politico-Military Policy and Current Plans divisions of the Office of the Chief of Naval Operations. It is through this close liaison that operating policy and strategic plans reflect the navy's historic adherence to the principle of International Law. As noted elsewhere in the text, this same division of the Judge Advocate General's office is also active in the formulation of new aspects of International Law as they relate to the navy.

The following comments by Vice Admiral B. L. Austin, USN, also show the importance with which the navy views International Law. In light of the position the admiral held on the Joint Staff, his comments are significant.

> The degree of respect for and adherence to International Law varies among nations. As a nation sincerely striving for a world in which honest differences can be settled peacefully, International Law is a consideration in much of our day to day handling of politico-military matters.
>
> During the period that I was Director of the Joint Staff of the Joint Chiefs of Staff (1956–1958) many of the tasks that confronted the Joint Chiefs of Staff dealt with major problems of our relationships with foreign countries and our rights and duties in foreign lands, in the air and on the sea. Many of those problems were of great complexity. Frequently several aspects of International Law came into play in arriving at recommended position papers or policy decisions for the Joint Chiefs of Staff. It was essential that such recommended positions or policies fall within the dictates of International Law. To accomplish this end, all of the departments within Defense processed the proposals through their International Law divisions.
>
> In order to better equip my office to handle immediate and urgent problems, I took the necessary measures to have an officer specially skilled in International Law assigned. This proved to be advantageous for it provided the officers in the Joint Staff, all of whom had a broad knowledge of International Law, with someone who had a specialized skill in that field. As such, open discussions of the problem at hand became a practical reality wherein rapid recommended policy decisions could be established—and established within the law of nations.

I would like to take this opportunity to note that while one is a junior officer International Law might appear to be remote and tenuous. I have not found that to be the case, for as one goes up the ladder in grade, he is expected to know more and more about International Law and how it affects our Navy at sea and in foreign lands in both peace and war.

HISTORICAL BACKGROUND

The first consciousness of International Law came with the emergence of separate communities, or states, whose creation stemmed from geographic or economic factors. These early state-communities developed laws for *internal* conduct based on the moral code prevailing at the time. The principles growing out of the moral code on a *national* basis were used by the rulers as a guide in their conduct of relations with other state-communities. At first, the rules were based on the personal interpretation of the rulers, but they gradually became defined, gained public support, and acquired a "traditional" character as concrete rules of general conduct. This development gave birth to feelings of common interest and of a "community of nations." International Law had begun. Many of the rules of today date back to these early times.

Around 1400 B.C. the pharaohs of Egypt and rulers of nearby areas had agreements or treaties that dealt with the recognition of individual sovereignty; they also had arrangements for the handling of refugees and immigrants. In 500 B.C., the Indian Code of Manu went into the details of warfare and attempted to establish norms—admittedly without much success—for the treatment of prisoners of war and the use of poison and other inhumane weapons. The city-states of Greece, such as Athens and Sparta, were so limited in area that in some ways they were economically dependent on each other. Thus, during the Greek era there was a relatively keen awareness of a community of interests between sovereign groups. With this awareness came growth in the scope of the rules between nations and many of the rules of International Law in force today can be traced back to those propounded by the Greek city-states:
1. Precise treaty law—methods of negotiation, interpretation, and conditions of termination.
2. Principles of international arbitration.
3. The immunity of ambassadors.
4. The right of asylum.
5. The rights and duties of aliens.

The Twentieth Century

By the time the twentieth century began, the law of nations had expanded successfully in many areas. It had passed the tests of time and experience and was generally accepted without question. International traffic in slaves and commercialized vice had all but ceased to exist. Questions involving the health of the peoples of the world had been met with joint sanitation measures. Administrative procedures and agencies had been set up to permit the transmission of mail and messages throughout the world. The adjective *free* had become accurately descriptive of the seas of the world, and canals connecting great oceans had been opened for international trade. Individuals and their property could move about freely in many foreign lands, and foreign vessels could expect to receive the same treatment as home-flag vessels. Persons who fled to a foreign country after committing a crime were returned to the country in which they committed the crime upon presentation of a request to the proper authorities.

The scope of International Law at the beginning of the twentieth century was broad and effective. The examples given in the preceding paragraph show that the subjects it covered were matters of mutual convenience. Agreement as to what the law should be in such matters was relatively easy to obtain. More vital subjects, such as sovereignty and the right of existence and self-defense, were cloaked behind a shield of national "policy" not to be tampered with by the outside world. Each state was free to determine its own line of conduct on these sensitive matters. If it agreed by treaty to a set course of action, then found the results were not to its liking, a state would unilaterally judge, usually on the grounds of sovereignty, that it was no longer bound. This vital gap in the scope of International Law was the basic problem that confronted members of the world legal community as they entered the twentieth century. It is a problem for which the world is seeking a solution in the United Nations and in all the other agencies interested in the question of war or peace. The measure of success obtained thus far will be discussed in the following chapters dealing with the substantive law.

SOURCES

Where can one find International Law? In one respect it is similar to the common law, which is the basis of our legal system in the United States. One cannot go into a book store or law library and get books that spell out the whole body of common law, for it is unwritten law based on custom, usage, and the decisions of courts. In large measure, International Law is also unwritten law.

CUSTOM

As noted in the brief historical summation, relations between states developed on a plane of abstract principles of conduct reflecting the moral and ethical standards of the day. As these abstract principles were applied more and more, the various states became used to them and eventually accepted them as standards of conduct between themselves. When a state attempted to diverge from the standard or norm, other states would point out that the practice or usage had been in effect for a long time and should therefore be adhered to. Eventually, by dint of usage, custom was recognized by states as an obligation instead of a matter of voluntary compliance. Today, obligations that have grown out of custom are known as *customary law*. It is worthy of note that customary law does not refer only to what has happened in the past. It is actively growing today. An example of this fact is the expanding law of space which is taking cognizance of the increasing use of satellites.

PUBLICISTS

Scholars and lawyers interested in the field of International Law have, through the centuries, put down in writing the rules and customs that were in force in their day; such writers are known as *publicists*. They performed a valuable service, for they helped to crystallize common concepts and practices. A few went beyond that point and included in their treatises not only the existing rules but also comments on the application of ethical and moral standards that they felt should have been acknowledged as part of the law. Undoubtedly the most famous of all publicists was Hugo Grotius, whose treatise *De jure belli ac pacis* (The Law of War and Peace), published in 1625, earned for him the title of "Father of International Law." His work is still considered a primary source of law. Another publicist, Emmerich von Vattel, published his treatise *Droit des Gens* (The Law of People) in 1758. The excellence of his work was evidenced by the fact that national courts cited it in making decisions, diplomats quoted it in negotiations, and foreign offices used it as a primary reference book.

The words of the U.S. Supreme Court in the *Paquete Habana* case provide an example of how the works of publicists, or commentators, are used:

> Where there is no treaty, and no controlling executive or legislative act or judicial decision, resort must be had to the customs and usages of civilized nations; and, as evidence of these, to the works of jurists and commentators, who by years of labor, research, and experience, have made themselves peculiarly well acquainted with the subjects of which they treat. Such works are resorted to by judicial tribunals, not for the speculations of their authors concerning what the law ought to be, but for trustworthy evidence of what the law really is.

Since World War II the United Nations has been actively collecting and consolidating the effective law between nations. Article 13 of its charter declares that the organization shall initiate studies and make recommendations for the purpose of encouraging the progressive development of international law and its codification. In this respect the United Nations International Law Commission, which does the codifying, is strengthening the law in the same manner as did the earlier publicists. For example, the commission's draft restatement or codification of the law of the high seas, published in 1956, formed the basis for the five conventions on the Law of the Sea, negotiations being completed in 1958 and 1960.

COURT DECISIONS

Other sources of International Law are the decisions of international tribunals and courts. Rulings laid down by these bodies in specific cases are cited as precedents for the laws in question. Domestic courts in the United States follow the same law of prior decision: common law. At the present time the International Court of Justice, sitting at The Hague, is the foremost permanent tribunal for the adjudication of international claims and problems that arise between sovereign states. In a limited sense it can be likened to the U.S. Supreme Court.

Another type of international tribunal whose decisions lead to the growth of International Law is the arbitration court or board. These decision-making bodies come into existence when two or more countries have a conflict of claims or interest and agree to be bound by the findings of a court or board formed for the specific purpose of settling the dispute. Arbitration boards are among the most successful devices for settling international claims, just as the same device has been found of great value in settling management-labor problems in the United States.

Finally, the decisions of various national courts, including admiralty, prize, and consular courts, contribute to the body of the law. It must be acknowledged, however, that because they are national, these courts tend to reflect the local interpretation of the general principles of the law. Thus, although their decisions are treated with respect on the international scene, their opinions are not considered as authoritative as the judgments of international tribunals.

INTERNATIONAL INSTRUMENTS

International Law is also to be found in international instruments, collectively, more commonly referred to as international agreements. They are divided into three categories: conventions, executive agreements, and treaties. Despite the fact that in modern usage the terms are used interchangeably, they can be defined as follows:

Conventions

A convention is a pact or agreement between several states in the nature of a treaty; the term is usually applied to agreements for the regulation of matters of common interest, such as postage or the protection of submarine cables, but not to such matters within the sphere of politics.

Executive Agreements

Whereas a treaty is a compact between the United States and another country and must be approved by a two-thirds vote of the Senate, all other international compacts that are exclusively within the power of the executive branch of the U.S. government are executive agreements.

Treaties

A treaty is an international agreement embodied in a single formal instrument (whatever its name, title, or designation) made between entities, both or all of which are subjects of International Law possessed of international personality and treaty-making capacity, intended to create rights and obligations, or to establish relationships, governed by International Law. When the agreement is between two states, it is a bilateral treaty; when it is between three or more states, it is a multilateral treaty.

A convention is the end-product of an agreement by representatives of several countries on some special economic or social problem. Unlike a treaty, whose function, in part, is to regulate conflicting claims, a convention deals with matters of interest to a large number of countries wherein the establishment of rights, obligations, and procedures would operate to the general good. We have conventions dealing with safety of life at sea, protection of trademarks, and the handling of international mail. It is beyond the scope of this text to enumerate the vast number of fields wherein conventions play a daily part in the governing of international trade and social intercourse. Suffice it to say that they are a major source of International Law. The term *convention* is also used for treaties between two countries on such subjects as fisheries which are traditionally covered by conventions.

Treaties and agreements are sources of law, for they bind countries together just as, under national law, a contract binds the seller and purchaser of an automobile. While they create obligations on the part of the signatory countries, they do not affect other countries. As in the case of extradition treaties, however, when the majority of states sign bilateral treaties, the cumulative results are treated as part of the body of International Law. Treaties and agreements usually cover the vital areas of international intercourse, such as political commitments, common military defense interests, and the settlement of territorial claims.

Today treaties are regarded as primary sources of International Law. The twentieth century might well be looked upon as a period when nations, realizing the complexity and vastness of the ties between them, attempt to regularize those ties by means of treaties. The inception, negotiation, and coming into force of a treaty or an agreement, as well as the many subsidiary documents growing out of them, are discussed in Chapter 12.

Article 914 of *U.S. Navy Regulations* is pertinent in regard to the importance of treaties:

> On occasion when injury to the United States or to citizens thereof is committed or threatened in violation of the principles of international law or in violation of rights under a treaty or other international agreement, the senior officer present shall consult with the diplomatic or consular representatives of the United States, if possible, and he shall take such action as is demanded by the gravity of the situation. In time of peace, action involving the use of force may be taken only in consonance with the provisions of the succeeding articles of these regulations. The responsibility for an application of force rests wholly upon the senior officer present. He shall report immediately all the facts to the Secretary of the Navy.

The connotation of the above article is obvious. Before an officer goes to a foreign country, he must know the main features of the treaties between the United States and that country.

DIPLOMATIC CORRESPONDENCE

Another source of International Law is diplomatic correspondence. These letters or documents are frequently declaratory of a state's position in regard to a problem; the document may be a letter of instruction to a diplomatic agent or an advancement of a proposition to another state. Many such documents are published: the Department of State's *Foreign Relations of the U.S.* as well as various White Books and White Papers, are examples. These documents afford a valuable source of information regarding the attitude of states towards problems or unsettled questions. When many states use this method of stating the same opinion on a problem, this consensus can, over a period of time, receive international sanction as declaratory of the principle involved. In brief, a consensus of several states, as shown in their diplomatic correspondence, can point to what is the actual law on a given issue.

2

Sovereign States and their Diplomatic Representatives

One [fundamental principle] is the perfect equality and entire independence of all distinct states. Relative magnitude creates no distinction of right; relative imbecility, whether permanent or casual, gives no additional right to the more powerful neighbor; and any advantage seized upon that ground is mere usurpation.

Case of Le Louis, High Court of Admiralty, 1817

The progress of modern civilization is marked by no circumstance better than by the institution of diplomatic missions between the different powers.

American Jurisprudence, Vol. 16

INTRODUCTION

In the preceding chapter International Law was defined as the law that governs relations between nations or states. It is different from national law, which is concerned with relations of individuals with one another or with their government.

The words *nation* and *state* have already been used here. International Law is often called the Law of Nations, and we find *nation* used in such titles as League of Nations and United Nations. There is no need to give elaborate definitions of the words *state* and *nation* because in this text they are used interchangeably. When we talk about a *country*, we stress territory and think of physical boundaries as we see them on a map. The word *nation* places emphasis on people and their supposed blood ties, common language, customs, and religion. The word *state* stresses the authority or the government of a geographical entity. All three of these interpretations are involved in discussing a sovereign state as a subject of International Law.

A state that is subject to International Law has both rights and duties under that law. When the average person speaks of the rights and duties of a state, he is usually referring to internal matters, such as the government's right to tax or duty to protect its citizens. Although taxation and the protection of individuals have their place in International Law, this text is limited to a discussion of rights and duties that are matters of International Law because they involve the relations of states with one another.

Some states are members of the international community, as the large body of nations is sometimes called; others are not. What, for example, is the difference between a state like France and a state like Maryland? In his textbook on International Law, Charles G. Fenwick offers this definition of the former type of state:

> As understood in international law, a "state" is a permanently organized society, occupying a fixed territory, and enjoying within the borders of that territory freedom from control by any other states, so that it is able to be a free agent before the world.

This status as a free agent before the world is what makes France a member of the international community and subject to International Law. Maryland does not enjoy that status and is, therefore, not a member.

Reference is often made to sovereign states. *Sovereignty*, as noted in *American Jurisprudence*, "in its full sense, imparts the supreme, absolute and uncontrollable power by which an independent state is governed." The traditional doctrine of sovereignty included the right of a state to be the judge of its own case and to resort to war when it deemed that to be necessary: today, the doctrine is less broad. Many states have accepted restrictions on their freedom to act. For example, members of the United Nations have had their right to resort to war limited by that organization's charter. As a British jurist, J. G. Starke, noted, "it is probably more accurate today to say that sovereignty of a State means the residuum of power which it possesses within the confines laid down by international law." This restricted sovereignty in International Law is what is meant whenever the concept is mentioned herein.

Sovereign states enjoy all the rights conferred by International Law and incur all the duties and obligations imposed by it. The rights include the sending of diplomatic representatives to other sovereign states; the conclusion of treaties with other states on matters of their own choosing; the admission and expulsion of aliens; the granting of privileges to their diplomatic envoys by other countries; and sole jurisdiction over crimes committed within their own territories. Some of the correlative duties are: abstention from performing acts of sovereignty within the territory of another state, such as using the air space or land of another state without the latter's consent; prevention of their agents or subjects from committing acts that violate another state's independence or territorial supremacy; and nonintervention in the affairs of another state. Thus it is a breach of International Law for a state to send its agents into another state to apprehend persons accused of violating the laws of the former (e.g., the Eichmann case): such an act violates the other state's independence and territorial supremacy.

Intervention means dictatorial interference with the will of the state affected. Anything less than this is not intervention. Legitimate intervention is recognized in the following instances: collective interference under the United Nations charter; protection of the lives and rights of the intervening state; self-defense against the danger of an armed attack; interference in the affairs of an entity under the dominion of the intervening state; and the commission of a gross breach of International Law by the state that is the object of interference.

As the subjects of common interest among nations increase in number and international agreements are concluded on a broad range of topics, the realm of affairs that fall into the category of dictatorial interference will shrink.

In order to be sovereign, a state must have territory. Sovereignty and territory go together, as do rights and duties. The legal problems arising from a sovereign state's possession of territory are considered in detail in another chapter. Only a few of the basic points involved will be mentioned here.

A state's territory must be well enough defined for other members of the international community to be able to determine the areas over which it exercises sovereign jurisdiction. Countries gain and lose territory in various ways, but their sovereignty is not affected thereby. The size of the territory is of no importance; small as well as large countries are sovereign. Examples of how small a state's territory can be are Barbados, Tuvalu, and Kiribat.

That International Law regards the possession of territory as essential to sovereignty was made clear when Italy annexed Rome in 1870. At that time many jurists claimed that, although the pope sent and received diplomatic envoys, he did not have sovereignty because he had no territory. On 11 February 1929, by treaty with Italy, Vatican City was constituted as the territory of the Holy See. Vatican City is neutral and inviolable, a status that was respected by all the participants in World War II.

RESTRICTIONS UPON SOVEREIGNTY

The sovereignty of some members of the international community is subject to certain restrictions, most of which have been imposed by treaty, affecting the relations of those states with other states. Although in such cases certain rights inherent in the general concept of sovereignty have been curtailed, the states concerned are still considered sovereign states in the technical sense. The following discussion should help to clarify this point.

NEUTRALIZED STATES

Neutralization is a status of permanent neutrality, usually imposed by treaty. A neutralized state agrees not to wage war, except in self-defense, and not to enter into any agreement that would put it under obligation to participate in war. Countries that are parties to neutralization treaties agree to respect the status of the neutralized state—in particular, the inviolability of its territory. The best-known neutralized state is Switzerland, which was neutralized by the Congress of Vienna in 1815 and has succeeded in maintaining that status. Belgium, first neutralized in 1831, has not been equally fortunate. The Treaty of London in 1839 declared that Belgium should be an independent and perpetually neutralized state. Although this treaty obligation was still in effect at the outbreak of World War I, Germany violated it by invading Belgium on the grounds of "state of necessity." After the war, the Treaty of Versailles formally abrogated the neutralization of Belgium. In the face of German expansion after 1933, however, Belgium succeeded in obtaining pledges of neutrality from France, Great Britain, and Germany, only to be invaded again by Germany in 1940. Austria declared its permanent neutralization by a constitutional federal statute on 26 October 1955. However, this declaration did not become valid in International Law until it was recognized by the other members of the world community.

Laos became neutralized pursuant to a unilateral statement of neutralization of 9 July 1962 and the Thirteen Power Declaration made in Geneva on 23 July 1962 guaranteeing this status. The thirteen powers included Great Britain, France, the People's Republic of China, the United States, and the Soviet Union. However, since a change of government in 1975, Laos has aligned itself closely with Vietnam and against China. Officials of the new government have made statements inconsistent with neutralization, and the U.S. government no longer recognizes Laos as a neutralized state.

A neutralized state may become a member of the United Nations. Under Article 48 of the U.N. charter the Security Council may exempt such a state from the duty of assisting the United Nations in any enforcement action taken pursuant to its charter. Despite this provision, Switzerland has not joined the United Nations. She joined the League of Nations on the understanding that she would not be forced to participate in any military action or to permit the passage of foreign troops through or the preparation of military enterprises on her territory. The language of Article 48 of the U.N. charter, however, does not guarantee such broad exemptions in specific terms. Austria has become a member of the United Nations.

NEUTRAL STATES

Neutralized states should not be confused with *neutral states.* The former enjoy a status of permanent neutrality assumed by treaty and guaranteed by other powers; or, as in the case of Austria, by unilateral declaration recognized by other states. In contrast, neutrality is achieved by nonparticipation in a given war, and may be relinquished any time the state concerned wishes. The only rights to which a neutral state is entitled are those granted to neutrals in time of war by the general principles of International Law. It is interesting to note that the Scandinavian countries remained neutral in both world wars, although in the second some were invaded and occupied by Germany.

DEPENDENT STATES

Suzerainties

Suzerainty is of historical interest only. The term was originally used to describe the relationship between a feudal lord and his vassal, the lord being the suzerain. This form of dependence disappeared with the feudal system. Later, the term *suzerainty* came to be applied to a form of international guardianship whereby one state (the suzerain) acted for another (the vassal) in foreign affairs. The vassal state was half-sovereign because it maintained internal independence but, because it was considered a part of the suzerain state, any treaty concluded by the suzerain bound the vassal, unless there were specific exemption. Also, a war of the suzerain became a war of the vassal.

Protectorates

Another form of dependence is the *protectorate*, which also permits the protected state complete internal autonomy but places its foreign relations in the hands of another power. This relationship is usually created and defined by treaty. Unlike a suzerainty, a protectorate retains some international personality as a subject of International Law. For instance, the head of government of a protectorate enjoys jurisdictional immunity in the courts of the protecting state and probably in the courts of other states, too *(Mighell* v. *Sultan of Johore* [1894] 1 Q.B. 149). A protectorate is not considered just part of the protecting state (*see* Advisory Opinion of the Permanent Court on the *Nationality Decrees in Tunis and Morocco*, Series B, No. 4). Therefore, treaties concluded by the protecting state do not, ipso facto, bind the protected state. Similarly, a protected state is not automatically a party to a war in which the protecting state is engaged. A state may be under the protection of more than one state, in which case the protection is exercised jointly.

In recent years, the following protectorates have acquired full sovereignty and independence: Morocco (1956), Sudan (1956), Tunisia (1956), Ghana (1957), Federation of Malaya (1957), and Guinea (1958). Acceptance of these new members of the world community by other nations is evidenced by their admittance to membership in the United Nations. The gradual trend towards independence became more and more evident in the developments of the 1960s, and in particular among the colonial dependencies and trust territories of the African continent. Since 1960 more than fifty states have gained independence and most of them have joined the United Nations.

British Commonwealth Nations

The British Commonwealth of Nations enjoys a unique status in International Law. It consists of forty independent countries, fifteen dependencies, the West Indies Associated States, and Brunei. The independent members have evolved from dependent colonies of Great Britain to become sovereign states. Great Britain and the other thirty-nine independent member states enjoy complete sovereignty in their internal and external affairs. The West Indies Associated States are self-governing and are in voluntary association with Britain, which is responsible only for the conduct of their foreign affairs and defense. They have the right to proceed unilaterally to full independence once certain procedural requirements have been satisfied. Pursuant to a 1971 agreement between the sultan of Brunei and Great Britain, the latter is responsible for Brunei's external affairs. The sultan's government is responsible for internal affairs. Brunei is expected to become independent in 1983.

All commonwealth countries recognize the queen of England as head of the commonwealth, but only fourteen of them recognize her as head of state: Great Britain, Canada, Australia, New Zealand, Jamaica, Barbados, Mauritius, Fiji, the Bahamas, Grenada, Papua New Guinea, the Solomon Islands, Tuvalu, and St. Lucia. Association with the commonwealth is voluntary and members may disassociate themselves, as Ireland and Pakistan have done. At most, the bond between the members of the British commonwealth is an ideological one, based on common origin, history, law, and economic interests. More than half of the nations that emerged as independent during the 1960s had been part of the British commonwealth.

Relations between the commonwealth nations and other nations are governed by International Law, as are practically all the relations between the independent members. The Kashmir dispute between India and Pakistan that arose when the latter was a member of the commonwealth was submitted to the Security Council of the United Nations, rather than to commonwealth arbitration, as prescribed by the Imperial Conference of 1930.

Mandates and Trust Territories

Two other forms of dependence have been of great importance since World War I—mandates under the League of Nations and trust territories under the United Nations.

A *mandate* was a form of international guardianship over territories that had belonged to the nations defeated in World War I. Germany lost its colonies in this manner, and Turkey also lost some of its territories. Since the territories involved were not considered sufficiently advanced for self-government, they were placed under the mandate of the League of Nations, which entrusted them to "mandatory states." These states administered them under written agreements, or mandates, they entered into with the league. A mandated territory was not owned by the mandatory state. The latter could not annex or dispose of mandated territory without the consent of the Council of the League of Nations.

Mandates were grouped according to their ability to govern themselves. The most advanced group, which included the former Turkish provinces of Syria, Lebanon, and Iraq, acquired sovereignty and independence within a relatively short time. Others, such as the former German colonies, remained mandates until World War II. Some of the territories in the Pacific that were German colonies before World War I are of particular interest to the United States because they were placed under Japanese mandate by the League of Nations and are now trust territories of the United Nations under U.S. administration.

In 1945 Article 77 of the charter of the United Nations introduced a system of *trust territories*. This system was applied to former mandated territories, to territories detached from states defeated in World War II, and to territories relinquished by the states that had been exercising sovereignty over them. Although the charter does not require that mandatory states place their mandates under the trusteeship system, all the Allied mandatory powers, except South Africa, agreed to do so. In an advisory opinion on the status of Southwest Africa delivered in 1950, the International Court of Justice held that South Africa had no legal obligation to conclude a trusteeship agreement with respect to Southwest Africa, now known as Namibia. However, the court held that South Africa could not unilaterally alter the status of her mandated territory. A change of status could be effected only with the consent of the United Nations. According to the court, South Africa was still bound by her obligations under the covenant of the League of Nations and the mandate agreement, and the league's supervisory functions had passed to the United Nations. In a second opinion, rendered in 1966, the court held that enforcement of the terms of the mandate was a matter of institutional action by the United Nations. That same year the United Nations revoked South Africa's mandate, a decision that South Africa refused to accept.

In the spring of 1977 the United States, Great Britain, West Germany, France, and Canada, began discussions with South Africa and the Southwest Africa People's Organization (SWAPO) in an effort to resolve the conflict over Namibian independence. These negotiations produced an agreement between SWAPO and South Africa to end hostilities and give Namibia independence and majority rule through U.N.-supervised elections. South Africa later expressed concern over certain aspects of the U.N. secretary general's report on implementation of the proposals and decided, in defiance of U.N. directives, to hold elections in Namibia in December 1978.

The five Western powers regard the elections as void. At this writing it remains to be seen whether U.N.-sponsored elections will ever take place. A grant of independence to a government headed by officials elected in South African-sponsored elections is not likely to be recognized by the international community.

Under the trusteeship system, the United Nations transfers the administration of territories whose inhabitants "have not yet attained a full measure of self-government" to certain countries. The ultimate goal of trusteeship is independence and self-government. The rights and duties of the administering authority are embodied in agreements between it and the United Nations. Trustee countries are responsible to the United Nations and report annually to the Trusteeship Council on the progress and development of the territories under their administration.

On 1 January 1960 the Cameroons, under French administration, became the first territory to emerge from the trusteeship system as an independent state. The last remaining trust territory is that of the Pacific islands administered by the United States. All the rest of those created after World War II became independent states during the 1960s and 1970s, in accordance with the mandate of the United Nations.

Trust Territory of the Pacific Islands

By agreement between the United States and the Security Council of the United Nations, responsibility for the former Japanese-mandated islands in the Pacific was transferred to the United States in 1947. This trusteeship differs from the others in that the area it covers is the only one designated "strategic."

Article 82 of the U.N. charter provides that a trusteeship agreement may designate a strategic area or areas to cover all or part of the territory in question. Article 83 of the charter states that all U.N. functions relating to such strategic areas, including establishment of the terms of the trusteeship agreement, are to be exercised by the Security Council. The United States is not the sovereign of the Pacific Islands but, as the administering authority, has been granted the right to pass all laws and regulations necessary to carry out its obligations under the trusteeship agreement. Because the territory has been designated "strategic," many of the obligations of the United States are tempered by security considerations.

Immediately following World War II, these islands were administered by the U.S. Navy which brought law and order to the area after the Japanese surrender. Only after a sound administration had been established was governmental responsibility transferred to U.S. civil authorities. The navy retains responsibility for the security of the area.

In the mid-1970s the United States initiated negotiations aimed at providing self-government for the Micronesians in the trust territory. By a separate action in January 1978, the Mariana Islands, as the result of a plebiscite held in 1975, took a major step towards becoming the Commonwealth of the Northern Mariana Islands. At this writing, negotiations with representatives of Micronesia are focused on ensuring Micronesian control over the internal affairs of the islands and a consultative arrangement between Micronesia and the United States concerning foreign affairs. Defense and security of the area would be the responsibility of the United States for a minimum of fifteen years. The goal is to complete the negotiations by 1981.

When the Trust Territory of the Pacific Islands ceases to exist, trust territories, like suzerainties, will be of historic interest only.

Special Jurisdiction

Until recently there was in the Ryukyu Islands, including the large island of Okinawa, and in other lesser chains, a form of administration that was neither a mandate nor a trusteeship.

By Article 3 of the peace treaty that terminated World War II and restored Japanese sovereignty, Japan granted to the United States "the right to exercise all and any power of administration, legislation and jurisdiction over the territory and inhabitants of these islands, including the territorial waters." The territory referred to in this article consists of the Ryukyu, Bonin, Volcano, Amami, and Marcus islands. In spite of the sweeping authority granted by Article 3 of the peace treaty, these islands were not U.S. possessions nor were they under U.S. sovereignty. They were Japanese islands temporarily administered by the United States. Under this arrangement, Okinawa became a major forward base of the United States.

The Amami Islands were the first to be returned to Japan. The Volcano, Bonin, and Marcus islands were returned in June 1968 and the Ryukyus on 15 May 1972.

Free Association

A new form of state is evolving in the Pacific area, i.e., a nonindependent state that is in *free association* with an independent state. Two examples are Niue Island and the Cook Islands, which are in free association with New Zealand. Under this negotiated arrangement, they retain their sovereignty but have ceded certain rights of administration and protection to New Zealand.

Non-Self-Governing Territories

Non-self-governing territories are territories that have not been placed under the trusteeship system. Chapter XI of the U.N. charter requires that member states that administer such territories ensure the political, economic, educational, and social advancement of their inhabitants. Administering states must transmit to the secretary general of the United Nations statistical and other technical information concerning economic, social, and educational conditions in the territories they administer. The U.N. General Assembly appointed a Committee on Information from Non-Self-Governing Territories, whose function is to examine the information submitted and make recommendations concerning the social and economic conditions in these territories.

ACQUISITION OF SOVEREIGNTY

GENERAL

Sovereignty having been defined earlier in this chapter, the various ways of acquiring that status should be examined.

A colony may break away from the mother country and establish itself as an independent state; the United States was formed that way. On the other hand, a country may grant independence to its territories and permit their existence as sovereign states; familiar examples are the British dominions, which gradually became fully independent sovereign states as members of the British Commonwealth of Nations. A former U.S. territory, the Philippines, became a sovereign nation by a similar grant of independence on 4 July 1946. Another example is Cuba, which acquired sovereignty after the United States recognized its independence and demanded that Spain give up its claim to sovereignty there.

Another way in which sovereignty may be acquired is by treaty or agreement. An example worthy of notice is Austria, which was incorporated into Germany in 1938, and restored to full sovereignty by the State Treaty of 15 May 1955. Also, Sudan became a sovereign state by a treaty signed in 1956 between Great Britain and Egypt.

RECOGNITION

A state consists of a clearly defined territory and people who owe allegiance to a government that is presumed to be capable of exercising control over them and acting and speaking for them. Where the creation of a new state is concerned, another factor to be considered is the attitude of other sovereign states towards the new legal entity. States may, however, and in fact do exist regardless of recognition: Article 9 of the charter of the Organization of American States provides that "the political existence of the State is independent of the recognition by other States." Although admission to an international organization can constitute recognition, the U.S. view is that membership in the United Nations does not, in itself, do so.

New States

Recognition is mainly an instrument of policy. No state is obliged to recognize a new state. This, however, does not mean that the new state does not exist, nor does it mean that the new state is at liberty to act towards the nonrecognizing state as it wishes: it must observe International Law. One result of nonrecognition is that it leaves the citizens of the one state without protection in the other.

When a new state has been created by revolution or the breaking-away of a colony, recognition by the mother country has usually led to recognition by other countries, although sometimes the order of recognition was the reverse. In the case of the Philippines, recognition preceded the formal confirmation of independence, because the Philippines became a full member of the United Nations before acquiring full sovereignty.

New Governments

Quite different from the recognition of a new state as a political entity is the recognition of a new government in an already-established sovereign state. On the principle of self-determination, a change of government is an internal matter and does not affect a country's status as a member of the international community. As long as changes in government are the outcome of decisions made by the people, in keeping with their constitutional processes, they are of no concern to the outside world.

Recognition under International Law is based on a new government's ability and willingness to carry out its obligations and to acknowledge the binding force of treaties entered into by its predecessor. This test has gradually come to have definite political implications.

U.S. Position

The U.S. position on recognizing new governments has undergone considerable change since Thomas Jefferson declared in 1792: "It accords with our principles to acknowledge any government to be rightful which is formed by the will of the nation substantially declared." Later, the United States narrowed this criterion and required that a new government should be capable of "protecting American interests." In 1923, when justifying the refusal of the United States to recognize the Soviet government following the 1917 revolution, Secretary of State Charles Evans Hughes declared: "The fundamental question in the non-recognition of a government is whether it shows ability and a disposition to discharge international obligations."

The frequent political upheavals in Latin-American countries and the lack of uniformity in granting and withholding recognition of new governments in that region have pointed to the need for a codification of rules for the procedures. However, because it is difficult to separate the political elements from the legal aspects of this problem, no rules have so far been developed. One doctrine has it that approval or disapproval of a new government should not be a criterion for recognizing it. Another holds that recognition should be dependent solely on objective tests, such as the effectiveness and stability of the new government and its ability to fulfill international obligations. Although the People's Republic of China was admitted to the United Nations on 25 October 1971, the United States did not formally recognize it until 1 January 1979.

Belligerency or Insurgency

Recognition of belligerency in an insurrection acknowledges the fact that the insurgents have attained sufficient success to create a status more akin to war between countries than to internal revolution. This kind of recognition, therefore, gives definite advantages to the insurgents. For one thing, the Rules of War become applicable and that gives the insurgents the rights and duties of belligerents, rather than those of rebels. The recognizing state then assumes the rights and duties of a neutral in its relationships with the insurgents. On the other hand, withholding recognition of belligerent status from insurgents may amount to aiding their enemies, since, without it, they have no status in International Law. In a case of serious internal strife, both recognition and the withholding of it obviously have political implications of intervention on one side or the other.

Recognition of insurgency does not have the same effect as recognition of a state of belligerency. It may, however, bring certain laws into effect within the country granting recognition. Thus, in the Cuban insurrection against Spain, which began in 1868, the United States refused to recognize a state of belligerency, but repeatedly proclaimed that a state of insurrection existed. This contention, according to a decision of the U.S. Supreme Court, brought into operation the U.S. Neutrality Act then in force.

WITHDRAWAL OF RECOGNITION

Most authorities insist that when a state withdraws its recognition of a state or government it must at the same time recognize another state or government. This theory is based on the premise that the entity from which recognition is withdrawn does not become a vacuum.

Withdrawal of recognition frequently signifies no more than does a breach of diplomatic relations with a country whose government no longer meets the requirements essential to friendly international cooperation. But there is one important difference. Withdrawal of recognition nullifies the prior recognition and therefore releases the no-longer-recognized government from treaty obligations it assumed with the withdrawing state while it was recognized: in other words, treaties between the two governments are no longer in effect. A breach of diplomatic relations, on the other hand, merely suspends the operation of any treaty between the two governments that requires diplomatic relations for its effectiveness. Extradition treaties fall into this category. Severance of diplomatic relations affects neither the existence nor the validity of treaties. This fact may have been responsible for the decision of the United States to break diplomatic and consular relations with Cuba on 3 January 1961, rather than withdraw the recognition that had been granted the Castro government on 7 January 1958. When diplomatic relations were severed, the United States made it clear that it considered the treaty granting the United States the right to the base at Guantánamo Bay to be in full force. Both countries have been scrupulous in fulfilling their obligations under this treaty.

LOSS OF SOVEREIGNTY

GENERAL

The only way a state can lose its sovereignty is by its own extinction as a subject of International Law. There have been instances of a state making itself extinct. Texas did this when it incorporated itself into the United States. More commonly, however, a state becomes extinct because it is annexed by another country. The world has seen many annexations, the most notable involving Austria, which was annexed by Germany in 1938 and did not regain its sovereignty until 1955. The Baltic States lost their sovereignty when they were annexed by the Soviet Union in 1940, although the United States does not recognize the loss.

SUCCESSION

Closely associated with the acquisition and loss of sovereignty is the question of the succession of a state to the rights and duties of another state. When one state is completely swallowed up by another, a distinction must be made between the rights and duties that were vested in the former *state* and closely associated with its existence and those that are vested in the *territory* of the state. Generally, the succeeding state does not take over the rights of the extinct state that arise out of political treaties. Thus, treaties of friendship and commerce, which represent reciprocal rights between two countries, do not remain in effect under the succeeding state. However, property rights, such as title to public property, remain vested in the new sovereign. Most treaties of cession carry a provision to that effect.

There is no clear rule governing the assumption of an extinct state's obligations. Some succeeding states have assumed them, others have refused to do so. Willingness to assume obligations is a factor that other states consider in determining whether or not to accord recognition.

RIGHTS AND DUTIES OF STATES

FUNDAMENTAL RIGHTS

Certain rights and duties are inherent in sovereignty and form the basis of a state's relations within the international community. Specific rights, such as jurisdiction over territory, water, and persons, and those applicable in time of war, and duties, such as respecting the territory of a neighboring state, will be discussed in separate chapters because of their importance. Rights and duties, as discussed here, are interdependent. For example, the right of one state corresponds to the duty of other states not to interfere with that right.

Some rights have become so closely associated with the concept of sovereignty that they are referred to as *fundamental rights*. Further, some of them are so closely related to each other that the possession of one implies possession of the other. For example, the right of independence carries with it the right of freedom from interference or intervention, and the right of existence is closely related to the right of self-defense.

Like many other concepts in International Law, all these fundamental rights have undergone changes in interpretation, in order to keep abreast of changes in foreign policies, particularly changes in relationships between states in the international community. For example, absolute sovereignty has been restricted by the prohibition against waging war, except in self-defense.

In spite of the preoccupation of all sovereign states with these fundamental rights and the importance of finding generally acceptable definitions, efforts towards codifying them and incorporating them into a declaration have been made only within the community of American states. Codification was first attempted in 1916, and drafts were submitted at regional conferences in 1927 and 1928. When the charter of the Organization of American States was adopted in 1948, it was signed by all the American republics and has since been ratified by all of them. This document, therefore, represents agreement by a large group of nations on what they consider to be the fundamental rights of states. Although the agreement is valid only among the member nations of the organization, the fact that the organization is a regional agency within the United Nations gives added weight to the codification.

Equality

Equality, as the word is used in Article 6 of the charter of the Organization of American States and in the charter of the United Nations, is interpreted as equal rights of a substantive nature, equal access to international courts and organs of arbitration to protect or enforce these rights, and an equal voice in the creation of new rights and duties and the restriction of established ones.

It does not necessarily mean that all states have the same rights and duties. The United States has by treaty, for example, rights to maintain military bases in many foreign territories—rights that other countries do not have.

Domestic Affairs

Even inside their own territories, states are bound by accepted international standards of humanity and the recognized rights of individuals. When a state treats a part or the whole of its population in a manner that shocks other states, it is not living up to international standards of humanity, and thereby provides legitimate grounds for intervention in its internal affairs. Actions contrary to the accepted standards of humanity include dispossession or extermination of groups of people for political reasons. Although a state can generally exercise its sovereignty in dealing with its own nationals within its own territory, it is doubtful whether outright violations of individual rights will remain immune from some form of intervention by other states.

Foreign Affairs

A state has the right to determine the kind and extent of diplomatic intercourse it wishes to conduct with other states. Since foreign relations and diplomatic representation are a function of sovereignty, a state that chooses to dispense with them may well be said to have set itself apart from the international community. Modern communications and increasing awareness that states must have relations with other states in order to exercise their rights make it obvious that isolation is a thing of the past. A state has the right to enter into treaties with other nations on matters of common interest, as long as such treaties do not violate the principles of International Law or commitments to other states.

Existence and Self-Defense

To members of the armed forces of the United States, the most important sovereign right is that of existence and the closely related one of self-defense. The right of self-defense in face of attack is well established. Equally well established is the concept that, in the face of imminent danger, a state need not wait for an attack before exercising its right to act in self-defense. Any activity that may be construed as creating a threat to its existence or security gives a state the right to take adequate measures for self-defense. A state's buildup in armament or fortifications that appears out of proportion to normal defense levels has been considered sufficient grounds for other states to build up their own defense. Such action is based on the principle that the right of a state to continued existence includes the right to take all measures necessary to ward off potential danger. In other words, the right of self-defense includes the right to prevent attack. The right to wage war in self-defense is recognized by the United Nations, but a preventive war is not considered a war waged in self-defense and is, therefore, illegal.

DUTIES

In International Law a state has as many duties as it has rights, since for each right there is a corresponding duty. The duty to honor obligations embodied in treaties, the duty to observe rules of warfare, and many other duties are discussed elsewhere in the text. Only the duty to protect aliens is discussed here.

Protection of Aliens

With few exceptions, resident aliens enjoy the same rights as the citizens of the state in which they reside. Their property rights are usually protected and they have access to the courts to enforce claims. Furthermore, they are protected against discriminatory acts of the state not warranted under International Law. When an alien has a grievance against an individual, he has recourse to local courts. When he is arbitrarily denied justice, the state of which he is a national has the right to lodge a diplomatic protest in order to protect him while he is in the foreign country.

DIPLOMATIC AFFAIRS

THE RIGHT OF LEGATION

The right of a state to send representatives to other states for the purpose of carrying on diplomatic negotiations and to receive representatives from other states for the same purpose is known as the *right of legation*.

Since earliest recorded times, nations have exchanged diplomatic missions or legations. However, the practice of keeping permanent legations in foreign countries is of comparatively modern origin. No state has an inherent right to have a permanent legation in another nation, nor, conversely, is it required to receive envoys from another nation. The right of legation means only that a nation may send and receive envoys. Exercise of the right depends on mutual consent. The United States today, for example, has no permanent legation in several countries of the Soviet bloc and does not receive permanent envoys from them, but it could do so, if it wished.

On the other hand, conditions in the modern world are such that the reception of legations could be said to be an almost indispensable prerequisite to membership in the international community. It is difficult to see how, in a world where even the most self-sufficient nation is growing more and more dependent on trade with other nations, the international community could function without exchanges of diplomatic missions. Permanent legations are, therefore, fixed institutions in every major capital city.

DIPLOMATIC AGENTS

As exercise of the right of permanent legation became more and more common, a need arose for a new class of government official—the diplomat. The most important member of this class is, of course, the chief of mission, or minister. He is the official who is accredited to the foreign nation by the sending nation, and all acts on behalf of the latter are done officially in his name. A mission may be composed of a number of officials having diplomatic status, including secretaries, counselors, military attachés, and commercial attachés.

Vienna Convention on Diplomatic Relations

By the beginning of the nineteenth century, practices with regard to the denomination of the ranks of ministers varied so greatly and controversies as to their relative ranks were so frequent, that it became necessary to settle the matter by treaty. At the Congress of Vienna in 1815 and the Congress of Aix-la-Chapelle in 1818 it was agreed that all signatories of the treaties there concluded would limit themselves to four ranks of ministers and, with certain variations, those rules remained in effect for more than a century.

Because of the importance of diplomatic relations and the status of diplomatic personnel, the United Nations directed the International Law Commission to prepare a code or treaty to incorporate the rules recognized by most nations. The final draft of the treaty drawn up by the commission was submitted to the General Assembly of the United Nations, which convened an international conference at Vienna in the spring of 1961. All 104 nations that were then members of the United Nations were invited to attend, and 81 of them participated. After extensive discussion, the final text of a treaty, the Vienna Convention on Diplomatic Relations of 14 April 1961 was adopted and signed by 45 nations, including the United States. During the period in which the convention remained open for signature, many more countries signed. For those countries that had ratified it, the convention came into force on 24 April 1964, and, by June 1971, 94 nations were parties to it.

Although the U.S. Senate gave its advice and consent to ratification on 14 September 1965, the United States did not become a party until 13 December 1972. In the interim the United States recognized the provisions of the convention as pronouncements of customary International Law and therefore considered itself bound by them.

On 30 September 1978 Congress enacted the Diplomatic Relations Act (P. L. 95-393, 92 Stat. 808), which brings U.S. legislation concerning the status and rights of foreign diplomats into line with the provisions of the Vienna Convention. The act repealed previous U.S. statutes, which granted protection broader than that required by International Law as set forth in the Vienna Convention.

Classification of Heads of Mission

Article 14 of the Vienna Convention replaces the four ranks of ministers previously recognized as "heads of mission" with three classes: ambassadors or nuncios and other heads of mission of equivalent rank accredited to heads of state; envoys, ministers, and internuncios accredited to heads of state; and chargés d'affaires accredited to ministers for foreign affairs. The convention states that, except as concerns precedence and etiquette, there shall be no differentiation between heads of mission by reason of their class. The class to which heads of missions are to be assigned is determined by agreement between states.

An ambassador is considered to be the personal representative of the head of his own state. The special honors to which he is therefore entitled vary from state to state, but invariably include the right to be addressed as *Excellency*. A chargé d'affaires is the lowest rank of a head of mission and must be distinguished from a chargé d'affaires *ad interim*. The latter is an officer of a diplomatic mission appointed to act during the temporary absence of the head of mission.

Classification of Members of a Mission

The members of a mission fall into three categories: diplomatic staff, administrative and technical staff, and service staff. The diplomatic staff, of which the head of mission is a member, hold diplomatic rank and are therefore entitled to more immunities and privileges than are members of the other two staff categories. Members of the service staff are persons who perform domestic functions, such as maids, chauffeurs, and so forth.

Appointment and Certification by the Sending Government

International Law has no rules governing the personal or professional qualifications of persons appointed as envoys to a foreign country; each country determines such matters according to its own domestic laws. By custom, however, a nation is not required to receive a particular person who may be appointed to fill a ministerial post.

The requirement that a state, before appointing a head of mission, inquire of the receiving state whether the intended appointee would be acceptable is incorporated in Article 4 of the Vienna Convention. The receiving state is free to refuse a person it considers unacceptable and does not have to give a reason for its refusal. The consent of the receiving state to accredit a certain person as head of mission is called *agrément*.

There are certain restrictions on the nationality and number of members a mission may contain but, by and large, the sending state is free to appoint the staff members of its choice. One important exception to this freedom is that the receiving state is permitted to require that the names of military attachés be submitted for approval before they are appointed. No doubt, this exception has been made because military attachés have intelligence functions, and the receiving state has a right to guard its own security interests. In practice, few states insist on advance submission of the names of military attachés, and most of those that do require only that they be given an opportunity to approve the senior attaché. Optional procedures like this are based largely on reciprocity: for example, the United States requires advance approval of military attachés sent to this country only when the other state does so.

The appointment of an individual is confirmed by his credentials, or *letter of credence*. This letter is usually a request that the head of the receiving state give full faith and credit to matters presented in the name of the accrediting government by its representative. If the minister is to have any special negotiating task, he may in addition be given a document called *full powers*, which will delineate his authority to speak for his nation.

Upon his arrival in the country to which he is appointed, a minister presents a copy of his letter of credence to the Ministry of Foreign Affairs. That ministry then secures for him an audience with the head of state, to whom he presents his original sealed letter of credence. A head of mission takes up his functions when he has presented his credentials or when he has notified the receiving state of his arrival and a true copy of his credentials has been presented to the Ministry of Foreign Affairs. A minister who is a chargé d'affaires follows much the same procedure, except that his formal audience is with the Secretary for Foreign Affairs.

FUNCTIONS AND DUTIES OF DIPLOMATIC MISSIONS

Article 3 of the Vienna Convention lists the following functions among those to be performed by a diplomatic mission:

(a) representing the sending State in the receiving State;
(b) protecting in the receiving State the interests of the sending State and its nationals, within the limits permitted by International Law;
(c) negotiating with the Government of the receiving State;
(d) ascertaining by all lawful means conditions and developments in the receiving State, and reporting thereon to the Government of the sending State;
(e) promoting friendly relations between the sending State and the receiving State, and developing their economic, cultural and scientific relations.

This article specifically recognizes that diplomatic agents are frequently called upon to perform consular functions.

The most important function of a diplomatic agent is to represent his country in diplomatic negotiations. An envoy is the official spokesman of his country in the nation to which he is accredited. However, his communications must always be carried out through the organ of the host government charged with cognizance over foreign affairs—the Foreign Office or, as it is called in the United States, the Department of State. The negotiating function of an envoy does not consist solely of making treaties. It includes such matters as extraditing criminals, protecting citizens, presenting diplomatic claims, and acting as a channel for a myriad official communications between his government and the government to which he is accredited.

Besides acting as official spokesman for his country, the minister has the duty of reporting to his government any occurrence in the country where he is stationed that might affect the interests of his home state. To assist him in carrying out this task, he is generally assigned specially trained attachés from other departments of his own government. A large U.S. diplomatic mission, for example, may have assigned to it several military attachés, a commercial attaché, an agricultural attaché, and perhaps others.

In addition to the above strictly diplomatic functions, the domestic laws of many countries require their envoys to perform certain duties that are not purely diplomatic but are nevertheless necessary to preserve the interests of the country abroad. Many of these duties are of a type that ordinarily fall within the cognizance of consuls but have been given to diplomatic agents by some countries. Among these diverse tasks are the recording of births and deaths of citizens residing in the country to which the agent is accredited and the legalization of citizens' signatures on official papers.

PRIVILEGES AND IMMUNITIES OF DIPLOMATIC AGENTS

On the morning of 4 November 1979, hundreds of Iranian "students" demonstrated outside the U.S. embassy in Tehran. They chanted anti-American slogans and, obviously enjoying the endorsement of the de facto leader of Iran, Ayatollah Khomeini, finally broke through the gates. Inside the compound, they took control of the chancery and subsidiary buildings, blindfolded about sixty members of the embassy staff, bound their hands, and made them sit on the floor. The condition for the release of the hostages was the return to Iran of the ex-shah, who was in the United States to receive treatment for cancer. The detention of the confined hostages and the occupation of the embassy was to be for a protracted period.

The above case serves as a blatant example of disregard for the fundamental norms of diplomatic immunity accepted by the civilized countries of the world. The "students" who attacked the U.S. mission were not political adventurers; they were citizens of a state that maintained diplomatic relations with the United States. Their invasion of the embassy violated a principle of diplomatic immunity respected by even the most radical governments.

The term *diplomatic immunity* is well known. But what is its exact meaning? Is it a personal immunity of the diplomat? What are its limits? Does it attach only to the chief of legation or do the people in his retinue enjoy it? What is the reason for granting it? The subject is an extensive one, and for that reason a word of caution is appropriate at this point. Because of the broad nature of diplomatic immunity and the necessity for brevity in the present text, it is possible to treat it only in a general way. Generalizations are subject to exceptions and refinements; therefore, the following paragraphs should be viewed as nothing more than a rough guide to a complicated subject.

Earlier it was pointed out that an envoy is the direct representative of his state. He is charged with the performance of important and sometimes delicate missions on behalf of his government. To perform them, he must reside in a foreign country that might be antagonistic to his own. In many cases he must travel through other foreign states to reach the country to which he is accredited. If, therefore, he is to perform his functions, he cannot be subject to the legal and political interferences that an average citizen of his country may encounter while in a foreign land. His communications with his home government must also be free from interference, and his mind must be at ease as to the safety of his retinue and the members of his family who accompany him. Obviously, if an ambassador ran the risk of being held liable in a court suit for any of his actions, considerations of personal safety or convenience might influence his performance of his duties.

International Law has developed a body of rules, most of them customary and now codified in the Vienna Convention, designed to ensure that diplomatic envoys have the freedom necessary for the unrestricted performance of their duties. These rules also ensure the safety and dignity of the minister, grant to his domicile, his retinue, his family, and his official communications the utmost protection from interference by the state to which he is accredited, and establish certain privileges commonly known as *diplomatic immunities*. These privileges are not personal to the officials who enjoy them but are accorded to the state they represent. The immunities show a recognition of the sovereignty of that state and provide the means whereby its agents may freely carry out their duties in equally sovereign nations.

The above explanation of diplomatic immunity and the reason for its existence make the enormity of the action taken by the "students" in Tehran readily comprehensible. Further reinforcement is provided by the fact that on 5 December 1979 the U.N. Security Council, by unanimous vote, called on Iran to release the hostages immediately.

Freedom of Transit

When an envoy's journey to the seat of the foreign government to which he is accredited requires that he transit a third country, it is customary for that country to grant him the right of innocent passage through its territory. This is a limited right, however, and does not allow him to linger in that country or to enjoy the privileges of a diplomat therein. Article 40 of the Vienna Convention states that the third country shall grant the passing diplomat inviolability and such other immunities as may be required to ensure his transit and his return. These immunities vary according to the mode of transportation and the time a diplomatic officer may have to spend in transit.

As noted, the right of transit is not an absolute right. At the Vienna Convention, the United States emphasized the rights of a state to deny the transit, or to impose certain conditions on it and remove persons who violate them. These restrictions were not incorporated into the text of the convention, but they are implicit in the right of a state to require a transit visa as a condition to permitting passage. Permission would not normally be granted if the country of transit were at war with either the sending or receiving state. In this event, safe-conducts are sometimes granted.

Inviolability of Person

The person of an envoy is inviolable. The receiving government is obligated not only to treat him with respect in its official dealings with him, but to protect his person from violation or embarrassment by any source whatever while he is within its territorial limits. The U.S. Congress, like the legislative bodies of many other nations, has translated this unwritten International Law into written domestic law by passing statutes imposing a maximum penalty of three years' imprisonment on anyone who violates the law of nations by assaulting, striking, wounding, imprisoning, or in any other manner offering violence to the person of an ambassador or a minister. In the case of assault with a dangerous weapon, the maximum penalty is imprisonment for ten years. In cases where U.S. envoys have been assaulted or offended, the U.S. government has uniformly pressed upon the foreign government the need to take prompt measures to punish the offender.

Inviolability of Domicile

Closely related to the inviolability of an envoy's person is the inviolability of his residence, which is called an *embassy* or a *legation*. The official residence of any envoy used to be considered exterritorial, which is to say that it was to be treated as though it were actually outside the territory of the receiving state. This concept meant that the embassy and every person and thing within its confines were beyond the jurisdiction of the receiving state, and out of it grew the right of an envoy to grant asylum within his official residence to fugitives from justice.

Today, both the concept of exterritoriality and the right to grant asylum are in disrepute. The current doctrine appears to be that it is not the exterritoriality of his domicile that shields an envoy and all inside the domicile, but the reverse. Out of his inviolability grows the inviolability of his domicile and its contents. Actually, his domicile enjoys only a limited inviolability. It is immune from the jurisdiction of the receiving state only insofar as the protection of the envoy and the independence of his mission are concerned. Should an envoy, for example, shield a fugitive murderer within his embassy, the receiving state could take whatever measures were necessary to capture the fugitive, and the envoy's government would have no legal basis for protest.

The inviolability of the envoy's residence and his right to grant asylum to persons subjected to political persecution is evidenced by the case of Cardinal Mindszenty, who was granted asylum in the U.S. embassy in Budapest, Hungary, after the Hungarian revolt in 1957.

How far an embassy's right to inviolability can be carried was demonstrated when the Soviet embassy in Ottawa, Canada, caught fire. The Soviet diplomats, standing on the right of inviolability of the embassy, prevented Canadian firemen from entering and putting out the blaze. Strictly speaking, they were within their rights. They finally yielded to the persuasion of the Canadian Department of External Affairs, but by that time it was too late and the building was destroyed.

Jurisdictional Immunities

An envoy, while within the receiving state, is entitled to certain immunities from the jurisdiction of the receiving government and its political subdivisions. Such immunities include freedom from criminal jurisdiction and freedom from subpoena as a witness in a civil or criminal trial (Articles 31 and 34). An envoy also enjoys immunity from civil and administrative jurisdiction and from taxation, except in certain specified instances when he acts as a private person rather than as a representative of the sending state.

Today, it is a settled rule of International Law that a receiving state does not have the right, under any circumstances whatever, to prosecute an ambassador for violation of its criminal laws. Even if a diplomatic envoy should conspire against the receiving state, the only right that state has is to expel him.

The privileges enjoyed by an envoy do not mean that he may act without any restraints whatever. Indeed, because of his freedom from ordinary restraining influences, he is expected to act with the utmost decorum and to conform to the highest standard of behavior. If he continually breaks the law of the receiving nation, the sending government may be asked to recall him, or the receiving state may declare him *persona non grata* and demand his removal.

Immunity from civil suit means that an envoy may not be held liable for actions committed by him or in his behalf. For example, if he is alleged to have failed to pay a debt to a department store or to have negligently injured someone in an automobile accident, he may not be sued in a court. Many countries have enacted positive laws in respect to this unwritten tenet of International Law. The Diplomatic Relations Act passed by Congress on 30 September 1978, for example, provides that any action brought against an individual entitled to diplomatic immunity shall be dismissed. However, the act is noteworthy in that it requires foreign diplomats to carry automobile liability insurance and, in cases where diplomatic immunity may be invoked, allows an injured party to sue the insurance carrier directly.

The fact that diplomatic officers cannot be sued does not, of course, absolve them from the payment of debts and settlement of claims. Clearly showing their concern for the fact that a diplomat's immunity might deprive a creditor or injured person of his recourse to the courts, the participants in the Vienna Convention resolved that, wherever possible without impeding the performance of a mission's functions, immunity should be waived. If this cannot be done, the sending state is obliged to see that all debts are paid and all claims are settled.

An envoy's freedom from subpoena as a witness in a court action has, on occasion, come into conflict with the immunity that provides for his personal inviolability. This situation would exist, for example, if an ambassador were assaulted. In such an event, it would be the duty of the receiving state to punish the offender adequately and promptly. Obviously, the testimony of the ambassador might be essential to securing a conviction in the criminal trial.

In many countries such a problem is solved by the diplomatic agent making depositions and sworn statements before authorized personnel of the embassy and of the receiving state, and having them submitted to the courts in accordance with the laws of the receiving state.

Waiver of Immunity

The preamble to the Vienna Convention states expressly that diplomatic officers are granted immunity for the benefit of states, not of individuals. Consequently, only the sending state has the right to waive immunity. An ambassador cannot take it upon himself to decide whether his immunity or that of a member of his staff can be waived without injury to the interests of the state he represents. He must ask his own government for a determination. This requirement applies whether the immunity to be waived involves criminal jurisdiction, civil jurisdiction, or appearance as a witness. Waiver must always be express and in writing. A separate waiver is necessary for the execution of any judgment that may have been rendered against a diplomatic officer by a court of the receiving state.

Waiver of jurisdiction in a criminal action ends, as a practical matter, the diplomatic status of the person who is on trial. Such waivers are extremely rare, and diplomatic officers who have committed offenses in the receiving state are usually either recalled by the sending state or declared *non grata* and expelled by the receiving state.

Most civil actions against diplomatic officers arise out of claims resulting from traffic accidents. Adequate insurance and prompt settlement of claims where insurance coverage is insufficient usually obviate requests for waiver of immunity.

Exemption from Taxes and Customs Duties

Diplomatic agents are exempt from all direct taxes, fees, customs duties, and social security payments (Articles 33, 34, 35). Consequently, they are not subject to income taxes, excise taxes on telegrams, telephone calls, transportation tickets, and so forth, or to sales taxes. On the other hand, they generally do have to pay a tax that does not fall on them directly. For example, an automobile manufacturer includes in his selling price any excise tax to which he is subject, and a diplomat would ordinarily be required to pay the full price, including the hidden tax. A diplomatic agent would also be required to pay so-called charge or rate taxes levied to defray the costs of furnishing services such as water, sewage, and garbage disposal.

Diplomatic agents are not required to pay customs duties on articles they import for their own use and that of their household. This exemption applies not only to when they first enter the receiving state to assume their functions, but also thereafter.

Their personal luggage is exempt from inspection "unless there are serious grounds for presuming that it contains articles not covered by the exemptions . . . or articles the import or export of which is prohibited" by the laws of the receiving state. For instance, the luggage of a diplomatic agent is not exempt from inspection if there is serious reason to suspect that he is engaged in smuggling. Cases of diplomats attempting to engage in the large-scale smuggling of narcotics into the United States are well known. The Vienna Convention specifies that inspection must be conducted in the presence of the diplomat or his authorized representative.

Immunities of Persons other than Ambassadors

Members of the official household, or retinue, of a diplomatic mission and their families are generally entitled to the same immunities as the chief of the mission. Practices vary slightly from country to country and depend to a large extent on reciprocity.

Each embassy furnishes the Foreign Office of the receiving state with a list of the members of the ambassador's retinue and the members of their families who are entitled to immunities. The Foreign Office uses these lists to compile a Diplomatic List, which is published and furnished to police, judicial, and other authorities in the capital.

Much less extensive immunities are granted to members of an embassy staff who are not diplomatic agents. For example, members of what are termed administrative and technical staffs enjoy the same immunity from criminal jurisdiction as do diplomatic agents, but their immunity from civil and administrative jurisdiction covers only their official acts. For example, if while on their own business, they were responsible for a traffic accident, they would be immune from criminal jurisdiction only: they would not be immune from civil jurisdiction, such as a damage suit, if the damage were not covered by insurance.

General Louis H. Wilson, Jr., USMC, when commandant of the Marine Corps, provided the following description of the ambiguous status of embassy security guards. As can be seen, it is well to know the status of security guards on foreign soil.

> In the more than thirty years the Marine Security Guard Program has been in existence the diplomatic status of the Marines serving at the various embassies has never been positively determined. In most cases the Vienna Convention on Diplomatic Relations sets forth the immunities available to the individual members of embassy staffs. The specific form of immunity applicable to each individual under the Treaty depends upon the position of that individual. In the ordinary case, the Marine Security Guard is considered, at least by the United States Government, as a member of the Technical and Administrative Staff of the embassy, and under the terms of the Vienna Convention would expect to be immune from all criminal jurisdiction of the host state and from civil jurisdiction in the case of acts performed while on official duty.

> Although seemingly explicit, the principles of the Convention have not been uniformly applied. First, not all nations hosting United States Embassies are parties to the Vienna Convention. Second, several party states are signatories with reservation. Third, regardless of participation in the Vienna Convention, several states do not recognize Marine Guards as members of the Technical and Administrative Staff. Fourth, in those states not parties to the Vienna Convention and not recognizing the Marine Guard as a member of the Technical and Administrative Staff under the principles of customary international law, the military guard is without diplomatic protection and may be subject to the civil and criminal laws of that state subject only to bilateral agreements, such as a Status of Forces Agreement.

> Highlighting the uneven handling of the Marine Security Guard diplomatic status throughout the world have been several incidents in recent history:

> a. In 1977 a Marine Security Guard shot and killed an Egyptian security guard within the American Embassy compound in Cairo. Egypt is a party to the Vienna Convention with Reservation; there is no Status of Forces Agreement. The Reservation to the Convention is that Egypt will not be bound by paragraph 2 of Article 37 which gives diplomatic immunity to members of the Administrative and Technical Staff. In this case the

Marine was permitted to leave the country and was tried by court-martial. Thus, the case was handled as if the Marine had diplomatic immunity even though Egypt does not recognize immunity for members of the Administrative and Technical Staff.

b. In 1978 a Marine Security Guard killed an American citizen in Morocco, not within recognized Embassy grounds. Morocco is also a party to the Vienna Convention with Reservation; no Status of Forces Agreement exists. The Moroccan Reservation is the same as the Egyptian. In this case, Morocco intended to prosecute the Marine according to Moroccan law. The international law issue raised in this case was whether or not Morocco recognized any form of diplomatic immunity for the Marine Security Guard, or whether Morocco considered him a member of the Technical and Administrative Staff of the United States Embassy and thus, because of the Reservation, not within the umbrella of immunities provided by the Convention. Additionally, there was the issue regarding whether Marine Security Guards should be considered as a separate class of persons entitled to immunity under customary international law. The issues were never resolved. As a result of diplomatic negotiations, Morocco permitted military authorities to transport the Marine to the United States where he was subsequently tried and convicted by court-martial.

The third category of embassy employees, the service staff, includes those who carry out domestic functions, chauffeurs, the private servants of the diplomatic agents, and so forth. They have even less immunity than do administrative and technical staffs. Whatever immunities they do enjoy are based largely on custom and reciprocity.

Military Attachés

As far as International Law is concerned, military attachés are no different from any other high-ranking members of an envoy's official household. They enjoy the same immunities and protection as an ambassador. They are of especial interest in a text of this nature, however, and a few comments on their functions are appropriate.

Until the attaché system was unified, U.S. naval attachés were selected and assigned by the secretary of the navy, subject to the approval of the secretary of state. Since that time, naval and military attachés have been assigned by the Department of Defense. The senior attaché is called the defense attaché, the others assistant defense attachés. They are still selected by their service and subject to its orders, and they perform the same functions as they did in the past. In performing their duties, military attachés are subject to the direction of the head of mission and responsible to him for their personal conduct. They form an integral part of the ambassador's staff.

The primary duty of a military attaché is to collect information of intelligence value and forward it to the Department of Defense and to his service. He may also have certain ceremonial and honorary duties assigned to him by the head of mission and may be charged with protecting the rights of U.S. servicemen who have committed offenses in a foreign country and are subject to trial by a foreign court. Status-of-forces questions, into which category such protection matters fall, are covered in detail in Chapter 8.

TERMINATION OF MISSION

The most common way for a mission to come to an end is by recall of the envoy, which may come about as a result of his resignation, his assignment to a new post, or some similar event. In such cases the sending state notifies the receiving state that the functions of the diplomatic agent have come to an end (Article 43). Although his mission ends at that time, the envoy continues to enjoy diplomatic privileges until he has returned home.

A recall may also result from the receiving state advising the sending state that its envoy has become persona non grata. This situation has most frequently occurred when an envoy has used his position to meddle in the political affairs of the receiving state or has used the diplomatic domicile as a headquarters for espionage or some equally objectionable activity (Articles 44 and 9).

Of course, the outbreak of war terminates a diplomatic mission in an enemy capital. If diplomatic relations have not been severed by the time war breaks out, the members of the mission are escorted to the border of the receiving state. If it is not possible for them to depart immediately, they are entitled to protection by the receiving state until their exchange can be arranged.

Changes in the form of the sending government sometimes result in a diplomatic mission being terminated. If the sending state ceases to exist, either through voluntary merger into another state or through conquest, its missions abroad end. The overthrow of the sending government by revolution usually suspends rather than terminates its diplomatic missions in foreign capitals. In the interim, members of missions continue to enjoy full privileges, though not the right of representation. Assuming that the new government is recognized, new letters of credence are issued, and the envoy's diplomatic precedence is not impaired.

The death of an envoy naturally ends his mission. Further, where the envoy's government is monarchical, the death or abdication of the monarch has traditionally been held to end the mission.

CONSULAR AFFAIRS

During World War II a medical officer in the navy was serving in the South Pacific when his father died. In the settlement of his father's estate, he had to execute some legal papers requiring authentication. Obviously there was no U.S. court within thousands of miles, and the nearest consul was perhaps as far away. Nevertheless, the officer was able to have the papers authenticated by the Senior Officer Present Afloat (SOPA), and the authentication was honored in the court that was settling the estate.

By what authority did the SOPA act? The answer is to be found in Article 0642 of *U.S. Navy Regulations*:

> The senior officer present afloat, when upon the high seas or in any foreign port where there is no resident consul of the United States, has the authority to exercise all powers of a consul in relation to mariners of the United States.

This power has been conferred by act of Congress.

Today, with rapid communication and transportation facilities available and U.S. consular offices within reach of virtually anywhere, it is extremely rare for naval officers to be called upon to act as consular officers. Nevertheless, such occasions can still arise, particularly in matters relating to merchant seamen in foreign ports. Therefore, since even the most junior naval officer might find himself the SOPA, it is important that all naval officers have some knowledge of the functions, duties, and privileges of consuls. The provisions applicable to the performance of these functions are to be found in the Department of State's *Foreign Affairs Manual*.

VIENNA CONVENTION ON CONSULAR RELATIONS

As in the case of diplomatic relations and the status of diplomatic agents, the United Nations early recognized that, in order to ensure uniformity of practice, long-established rules on consular relations would have to be codified. The procedure was much the same as in the case of the Convention on Diplomatic Relations. After a final draft text had been approved, a conference was convened in April 1963. The result was the Vienna Convention on Consular Relations which was signed on 24 April 1963. For the nations that had ratified or acceded to it, the convention came into force on 19 March 1967, and for the United States on 24 December 1969. By June 1971, forty-five nations were parties to this convention.

The Convention on Consular Relations covers such general matters as the establishment of consular posts, consular functions, and the status of consular officers. Details of a consul's functions are normally spelled out in bilateral agreements between individual countries. This practice is specifically recognized in Article 73 of the convention which states: "Nothing in the present Convention shall preclude States from concluding international agreements confirming or supplementing or extending or amplifying the provisions thereof." Therefore, practices depend on the extent of consular relations between two countries and agreements concerning them.

Classes of Consuls

Article 9 of the convention designates four classes of heads of consular posts: consuls-general, consuls, vice consuls, and consular agents. States are free to fix the designation of consular officers other than heads of posts. Consuls-general normally head a large consular district or supervise several small ones. Consuls are appointed for small consular districts or port cities.

Appointment of Consuls

As in the case of diplomatic agents, International Law has no requirements as to the qualifications of a person appointed consul, nor does it require any nation to admit consuls of other nations. Commercial necessity, however, almost requires that nations engaged in significant mutual trade exchange consuls.

In most cases the exchange of consuls between nations is provided for either in a bilateral treaty of commerce and navigation or a bilateral consular treaty or convention. The first type of treaty is a general one regulating all commercial relations between the signatories. The second type, which is coming more and more into use, is concerned only with consuls.

The actual appointment of a consul is made through a commission, or patent, issued to the individual by his government. When the appointee presents this document to the receiving state, assuming he is acceptable to that state, he is granted what is known as an *exequatur*, or authority to act in the receiving state.

FUNCTIONS OF CONSULS

Since consuls are not diplomatic agents and are appointed chiefly in the interests of commerce, industry, and navigation, most of their duties are governed by the domestic law of the sending state.

By an act of Congress of 1792, U.S. consuls were authorized: to receive protests and declarations of American captains, masters, crews, passengers, and merchants; to care for American ships stranded in their consular districts; to relieve distressed seamen and to require masters of American ships, under penalty of a fine, to convey such seamen to their homes with no charge, provided they work for their passage; to require the masters of ships that may be sold abroad to pay their men's passage back to the United States; to authenticate copies of documents; and, finally, to take charge of and settle estates of Americans who die abroad and have no legal representative there. Since 1792 the laws and regulations governing the duties of U.S. consuls have changed. Many functions have been added, perhaps the most significant being very considerable duties in connection with the issuance of passports and visas. Changes in commercial practices and usages have caused some aspects of a consul's duties to assume more importance than others. Today, for example, many U.S. consulates are more important to the United States for their commercial and political reporting than for their performance of traditional consular functions. In general, however, the essential nature of consular duties has not varied radically from that laid down in the statute of 1792.

Article 5 of the Vienna Convention on Consular Relations lists thirteen groups of activities that are generally recognized as consular functions. These include the ones listed above. A consul may even be authorized, with the consent of the receiving state, to perform diplomatic acts in countries where the sending state does not maintain a diplomatic mission. His consular status is not affected by the exercise of such functions, and he is not entitled to diplomatic privileges and immunities.

A consul's dealings with the receiving state are not usually carried on through that state's Foreign Office. They are carried on directly with officials of the executive or judicial branch of the receiving government, or with private persons within his consular district.

PRIVILEGES AND IMMUNITIES OF CONSULS

Although the privileges and immunities of consuls are not as extensive as those of diplomatic agents, the Vienna Convention on Consular Relations provides for a great number of rights which in many respects closely resemble diplomatic immunities.

The receiving state does not have criminal jurisdiction over acts performed by a consul in the exercise of his official functions. It does, however, have jurisdiction over acts performed otherwise. In the event he committed a serious offense, not in the performance of his duties, he would, upon decision by competent judicial authority, be subject to arrest and detention pending trial (Articles 41 and 43). The convention lists numerous other privileges and immunities, including exemption from taxes and customs duties; inviolability of the consular building and archives; and the right to display the national flag and coat of arms on the consular building.

TERMINATION OF CONSULAR OFFICE

A sending state may terminate the functions of a consul by recalling him, and a receiving state may terminate them by withdrawing his exequatur. In any case, the receiving state is obligated, even in the event of armed conflict, to grant the necessary time and facilities to enable a consul and his family to depart with their property. The receiving state must, even in the event of war, protect the consular premises, the property of the consular post, and the consular archives. This protection and certain of the functions of the departing consul are usually entrusted to a third state, which must be acceptable to the receiving state.

INTERNATIONAL LAW GOVERNING
DIPLOMATIC AND CONSULAR RELATIONS

The codifications governing diplomatic and consular relations that have been discussed in this chapter have given the nations of the world an invaluable source of the law as recognized by the majority of states. The practices and procedures of states that have not yet become parties to the two Vienna conventions vary only slightly from those set forth in the conventions.

3

Territory—Land

Fundamental to the territorial principle are two opposing impulses; there is the urge to intrude on the property of one's neighbor, and the urge to avoid it.

Robert Ardrey

GENERAL

It is the duty of an officer exercising command to respect territorial sovereignty, not only at sea but in the air and on land as well. In order to carry out this obligation faithfully, he must, of course, know the territorial limits of the authority of other states. He may have charts or maps that graphically portray the boundaries of the area in which he is operating, and generally he can rely upon these aids in determining the limits of his sphere of action. He may even have specific instructions as to the limits of territorial authority of the state involved. Suppose, however, he is operating in an area where many states have made conflicting claims of sovereignty; or suppose he is operating an aircraft over seas dotted with innumerable, minute, coastal islands, which may or may not be inhabited. How is he to proceed in such cases?

It is the purpose of this chapter and of Chapters 4 and 7 to discuss some of the more important aspects of the International Law of territory, including the nature of territorial authority, the boundaries of states, how a state can acquire and lose territory, and the law of dominion over air and space.

THE NATURE OF TERRITORY

In International Law, the *territory* of a state is that part of the globe—surface, subsurface, air, and water—which is subject to its sovereignty. Within that territory, the authority of the state concerned is supreme. A state that has no territory is not, in any legal sense, a state at all. Granted, the territory may be minute, as in the cases of Vatican City and the Principality of Monaco, but the possession of some territory is a requisite of international statehood.

The fact that a state has sovereignty over a part of the globe known as its *national territory* does not mean that it owns the land in question. Sovereignty must be distinguished from ownership. Sovereignty means the right and power to govern; ownership is a property right in the land itself.

ACQUISITION OF TERRITORY

International Law recognizes the following ways in which a sovereign state may acquire new territory: occupation, cession, annexation, prescription, and accretion.

OCCUPATION

The method of territorial acquisition that we know today as *occupation* was born in the Age of Discovery, but its present maturity was achieved only during the last century. The discovery of the New World near the end of the fifteenth century found the European community of nations without a universally recognized principle of law to apply to the territorial claims that followed in the wake of each discovery. The attempt by Pope Alexander VI to divide between Spain and Portugal the undiscovered as well as the discovered territory of the New World, was disregarded by less-favored nations, despite the political and religious power of the pope. Unhonored, too, were claims advanced on the grounds of mere discovery; that is, discovery in the sense of sighting a land previously known to exist. Something more seems to have been required even in those early times. In short, a valid claim required that the discoverer perform a symbolic "taking of possession." This symbolic act generally consisted of no more than the navigator going ashore and "taking possession" in the name of his sovereign, but the gesture was regarded as virtually indispensable. For example, one of the bases for England's claim to most of the North American continent was provided by the first voyage, in the late-fifteenth century, of John Cabot, who anchored off the coast of North America, somewhere between Halifax and Labrador. He probably spent no more than a few hours on shore and saw no more than a few hundred miles of the continent as he coasted eastward on his return voyage to England. However, in those days, even such limited reconnaissance constituted acceptable grounds for a claim of territorial sovereignty.

Within the two following centuries, colonization of the New World advanced to the point where claims based on a symbolic taking of possession could no longer withstand the pressures generated by the conflicting claims of various nations. The law of territory had developed to the stage where it was recognized that more concrete action was required to establish a valid claim to a newly discovered area. Discovery and symbolic taking of possession provided only an imperfect title. That such an imperfect, or inchoate, title had a degree of validity in acquisition of territory in later days is witnessed by the Guano Act, a U.S. statute of 1856. This act provided the method by which jurisdiction over the so-called guano islands could be established. These small, unclaimed, uninhabited islands in the Pacific Ocean contained valuable guano deposits, and the U.S. claim to them was based on the symbolic act of "taking peaceful possession." At this writing, in recognition of the decreasing interest of the United States in these islands, most U.S. claims over them have been relinquished. The above exception did not change the development of the law requiring concrete evidence to establish a valid claim. Title had to be perfected by *occupation*, which could take the form either of actual settlement of the claimed area or of subjection of the area to the control of the claimant's government. As the continent of Africa was opened by European colonization, the same general rules were applied to claims asserted there.

Also during that period the law entered its final stage of development. The key to the validity of a claim of sovereignty became *actual occupation*, not original discovery and taking of possession. Although the point is controversial, it would appear that today mere discovery and symbolic taking of possession would not confer upon the claimant nation even imperfect title or right of priority to perfect a claim of sovereignty by actual occupation at a later date. Effective and actual occupation is now generally considered a prerequisite for a valid, legal claim.

Antarctica

Until recently there remained one vast, largely unexplored continent which, at least in the view of the United States, had not been brought under the sovereignty of any nation. That continent was Antarctica.

Many nations had made territorial claims in the Antarctic region, but none of them were recognized by the United States. Some of these nations, notably those of South America, advanced their claims on the basis of proximity to Antarctica. Others, harking back to the Age of Discovery, made extensive territorial claims based on discovery and the symbolic taking of possession. Certain nations advanced claims on a novel theory which was a combination of the archaic doctrine of discovery and the so-called sector theory used by Russia and Canada for asserting claims in the Arctic region.

The sector theory involved using the full width of areas within which discoveries or explorations had been made to produce an east-west arc. The pie-shaped sector which this arc and the two terminal longitudinal meridians enclosed to the South Pole formed the area claimed. The sector was then assigned to a political subdivision of the claimant nation, a subdivision that faced the sector concerned. Using this theory, Great Britain laid claim to three large "dependencies" and assigned their administration to New Zealand, Australia, and the Falkland Islands. France laid claim to Adélie Land and assigned it to the government of Madagascar, which is fully 5,000 miles away.

Still other nations, although making no territorial claims in the Antarctic region, indicated to the United States that they regarded themselves as having priority to perfect claims in certain sections of the Antarctic by actual

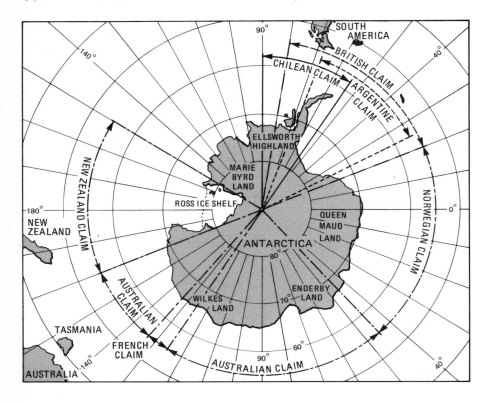

Territorial Claims in Antarctica

occupation. These claims were based on discoveries and explorations made under the flags of the nations concerned.

Despite the distinguished achievements of Admiral Richard E. Byrd and other American explorers in the Antarctic, the United States made no territorial claims in the area.

U.S. Position on Antarctic Claims

The reason for the United States not advancing a claim was best expressed by Secretary of State Charles Evans Hughes, who said in 1924:

> It is the opinion of the Department that discovery of lands unknown to civilization, even when coupled with a formal taking of possession, does not support a valid claim of sovereignty unless the discovery is followed by an actual settlement of the discovered country. In the absence of an Act of Congress, assertive in a domestic sense of dominion over Wilkes Land, this Department would be reluctant to declare that the United States possessed a right of sovereignty over the territory.

On the other hand, the United States has always been careful to inform other nations making claims to sovereignty over the Antarctic that it does not admit that mere discovery or exploration, unaccompanied by actual occupancy or use, vests any measure of jurisdiction in any claimant nation.

In view of the large amount of disagreement as to rights and claims in the Antarctic, is it possible to state any conclusions as to what principles of law may be applied? It would appear that the traditional concept of occupation has as much validity for application to Antarctica as it has had in any other unoccupied area. The difficulty is not in the doctrine itself, but in the climate and geography of the region and in the advances that have been made in communication and transportation since the Age of Discovery. In these days of rapid and efficient transportation and communication, mere discovery or exploration and the symbolic taking of possession are not enough to vest sovereignty in a nation, even if the land claimed is as forbidding and uninhabitable as Antarctica. Nor does the additional act of assigning a geographical sector to a political subdivision for government give any greater validity to a claim, unless there is an actual exercise of control over the area. On the other hand, since the land is—at least at the present stage of technical advancement—apparently habitable only on a marginal basis, something less than permanent settlement of the area should suffice.

It would appear, therefore, that if a nation should occupy a particular area of Antarctica and exert some measure of actual control over it, that nation could justly claim to have acquired that portion of the continent as its own. Because of the extensive explorations it has made and the knowledge it has gained in the area, the United States is probably in a better position than is any other nation to perfect a claim to certain parts of Antarctica by occupation.

The Antarctic Treaty of 1959

The importance of Antarctica was highlighted by the intensive scientific work carried out there during the International Geophysical Year (1957–1958). At the height of these activities, more than forty research outposts were in operation. This was a joint effort on the part of twelve countries: Argentina, Australia, Belgium, Chile, France, Japan, New Zealand, Norway, South Africa, the United Kingdom, the Soviet Union, and the United States. While the scientific findings of this effort have been invaluable to mankind, the economic potential that could be realized through new technological advances, including atomic power, has not been overlooked. Nor has the strategic importance of Antarctica been overshadowed. From the standpoint of geography alone, Antarctica should eventually become the crossroads for the countries that lie in the southernmost latitudes.

In recognition of these facts, on 3 May 1958 the United States invited eleven other countries to join it in a treaty to preserve Antarctica as a continent for scientific research and to prevent its becoming a battleground. In announcing the proposed treaty, President Dwight D. Eisenhower said that it was "directed at insuring that this same kind of cooperation for the benefit of all mankind shall be perpetuated" after the conclusion of the International Geophysical Year on 31 December 1958. The significance of the U.S. invitation being manifest, it is quoted here in full:

> I have the honor to refer to the splendid example of international cooperation which can now be observed in many parts of the world because of the coordinated efforts of scientists of many countries in seeking a better understanding of geophysical phenomena during the current International Geophysical Year. These coordinated efforts of the scientists of many lands have as their objective a greatly increased knowledge of the planet on which we live and will no doubt contribute directly and indirectly to the welfare of the human race for many generations to come.
>
> Among the various portions of the globe where these cooperative scientific endeavors are being carried on with singular success and with a sincere consciousness of the high ideals of mankind to which they are dedicated is the vast and relatively remote continent of Antarctica. The scientific research being conducted in that continent by the cooperative efforts of distinguished scientists from many countries is producing information of practical as well as theoretical value for all mankind.
>
> The International Geophysical Year comes to a close at the end of 1958. The need for coordinated scientific research in Antarctica, however, will continue for many more years into the future. Accordingly, it would appear desirable for those countries participating in the Antarctica program of the International Geophysical Year to reach agreement among themselves on a program to assure the continuation of the fruitful scientific cooperation referred to above.
>
> Such an arrangement could have the additional advantage of preventing unnecessary and undesirable political rivalries in that continent, the uneconomic expenditure of funds to defend individual national interests, and the recurrent possibility of international misunderstandings. It would appear that if harmonious agreement can be reached among the countries directly concerned in regard to friendly cooperation in Antarctica, there would be advantages not only to these countries but to all other countries as well.
>
> The present situation in Antarctica is characterized by diverse legal, political and administrative concepts which render friendly cooperation difficult in the absence of an understanding among the countries involved. Seven countries have asserted claims of sovereignty to portions of Antarctica, some of which overlap and give rise to occasional frictions. Other countries have a direct interest in that continent based on past discovery and exploration, geographic proximity, sea and air transportation routes and other considerations.
>
> The United States for many years has had, and at the present time continues to have, direct and substantial rights and interests in Antarctica. Throughout a period of many years, commencing in the early eighteen hundreds, many areas of the Antarctic region have been discovered, sighted,

explored and claimed on behalf of the United States by nationals of the United States and by expeditions carrying the flag of the United States. During this period, the Government of the United States and its nationals have engaged in well-known and extensive activities in Antarctica.

In view of the activities of the United States and its nationals referred to above, my Government reserves all of the rights of the United States with respect to the Antarctic region, including the right to assert a territorial claim or claims.

It is the opinion of my Government, however, that the interests of mankind would best be served, in consonance with the high ideals of the Charter of the United Nations, if the countries which have a direct interest in Antarctica were to join together in the conclusion of a treaty which would have the following peaceful purposes:

A. Freedom of scientific investigation throughout Antarctica by citizens, organizations and governments of all countries; and a continuation of the international scientific cooperation which is being carried out so successfully during the current International Geophysical Year.

B. International agreement to insure that Antarctica be used for peaceful purposes only.

C. Any other peaceful purposes not inconsistent with the Charter of the United Nations.

The Government of the United States is prepared to discuss jointly with the governments of the other countries having a direct interest in Antarctica the possibility of concluding an agreement, which would be in the form of a treaty, for the purpose of giving legal effect to these high principles. It is believed that such a treaty can be concluded without requiring any participating nation to renounce whatever basic historic rights it may have in Antarctica, or whatever claims of sovereignty it may have asserted.

It could be specifically provided that such basic rights and such claims would remain unaffected and no new claims made by any country during the duration of the treaty. In other words, the legal status quo in Antarctica would be frozen for the duration of the treaty, permitting cooperation in scientific and administrative matters to be carried out in a constructive manner without being hampered or affected in any way by political considerations. Provisions could likewise be made for such joint administrative arrangements as might be necessary and desirable to insure the successful accomplishment of the agreed objectives.

The proposed treaty would be deposited with the United Nations and the cooperation of the specialized technical agencies of the United Nations would be sought. Such an arrangement would provide a firm and favorable foundation for a continuation of the productive activities which have thus far distinguished the International Geophysical Year; would provide an agreed basis for the maintenance of peaceful and orderly conditions in Antarctica during years to come; and would avoid the possibility of that continent becoming the scene of international discord.

In the hope that the countries having a direct interest in Antarctica will agree on the desirability of the aforesaid high objectives, and will work together in an effort to convert them into practical realities, the Government

of the United States has the honor to invite the Government of . . . .
to participate in a conference for this purpose to be convened at an early date
at such place as may be mutually agreeable.

Accept, Excellency, the renewed assurances of my highest consideration.

On 1 December 1959, in response to the above proposal, the eleven
nations concerned joined the United States in signing a treaty which, in
effect, "freezes" the territorial claims that had previously been made, insofar
as they relate to the specific activities provided for under the treaty. Such
claims are neither given increased stature nor diluted by the terms of the
treaty. Other significant features of the treaty include the preservation of the
continent, in recognition of its relatively fragile environment; the exclusion
of military activity, except that military personnel and equipment may be
used for scientific research; the banning of nuclear explosions and of dumping radioactive wastes; and the granting to the signatories of the right to send
inspectors anywhere they wish on the continent at any time.

The Antarctic Treaty applies to the zone south of sixty degrees south
latitude, including all ice shelves. It does not prohibit any state from exercising rights granted by International Law with regard to the high seas within
that zone. There is, however, disagreement as to which waters south of sixty
degrees south latitude are, in fact, high seas. States whose territorial claims in
Antarctica are "frozen" by the treaty of 1959 claim that sovereignty over
territory carries with it jurisdiction over offshore areas, including the continental shelf and two-hundred-mile fishery or economic zones. States that
neither claim nor recognize sovereignty in Antarctica take the position that
there is no national jurisdiction over the marine areas around the continent
and that all these waters are high seas.

For the text of the Antarctic Treaty of 1959, *see* Appendix A.

Antarctic Offshore Resources

Significantly, Article 4 of the Antarctic Treaty of 1959, which specifies
the activities that may take place in a cooperative manner, does not cover the
exploration or exploitation of resources.

In the period since the treaty was concluded, particularly in the past few
years, commercial-scale exploitation of fishery resources in Antarctic waters
has become a real possibility. Scientific research has indicated that these
waters may offer a significant source of protein in a protein-hungry world.
Opinions on this point vary, but in October 1978 the highly respected
publication *Australian Fisheries*, reported:

> Some scientists say that the Southern Ocean is capable of yielding an
> annual seafood harvest of about 140 million tonnes—twice the present world
> catch and more than 1,000 times greater than Australia's.

And this 140 million tonnes relates only to krill—a Norwegian word meaning smallfry and which, for the sake of quick description, relates primarily to the tiny shrimp-like *Euphausia superba*.

The figure is enormous but even that fades to a kind of insignificance compared with the krill's total biomass of at least 1,000 million tonnes, according to some scientific estimates, none of which, however, are precise.

Then there are fish, squid, seals, whales, penguins, lobsters, and other creatures with a total mass which may approach even that of krill.

Nobody really knows.

As the possibility of the existence of this vast resource developed, so did the recognition of its vulnerability to uncontrolled exploitation. The principal cause of this vulnerability is that there are short, simple food chains in Antarctic waters, mostly based on krill. Consequently, in 1977, the Antarctic Treaty Consultative Parties determined that an international convention to provide for the effective conservation of Antarctic marine living resources was required, and went to work to produce one. They have had to contend with their own differing legal views over maritime jurisdiction—claimants asserting their right to 200-mile zones and non-claimants disputing that right.

The draft convention rests upon the same sort of compromise on jurisdiction as is contained in the Antarctic Treaty. It establishes a system for the effective management of fishery resources which both claimants and non-claimants can interpret as consistent with their legal positions and without giving up those positions. The convention, which will be distinct from but consistent with the Antarctic Treaty of 1959, will apply not only to the full scope of the Antarctic marine ecosystem in the area covered by the treaty of 1959, but in significant areas north of it as well.

If the parties succeed in creating an effective conservation system, they will have set an important precedent; they will have proved that states with differing legal and political views can cooperate to manage shared resources and prevent their depletion to the detriment of all.

Success in this area is particularly important in light of the fact that the question of how to deal with possible future activities with regard to mineral resources in Antarctica has also emerged. If that challenge can be met, Antarctica is likely to remain a unique area of international cooperation. The negotiations were successfully concluded in May 1980.

The Moon

The advent of the space age has raised possibilities heretofore deemed exceedingly remote. Man has been to the moon—and, much later, he will travel to the planets. The possible status of these remote pieces of territory is pointed out by an authority on the subject, Philip Quigg:

Will the moon and planets be other Antarcticas? Certainly no claim of national sovereignty on the moon would be recognized and a legal claim would be extremely difficult to establish. Effective occupation by one country seems highly unlikely. The sector principle by which Antarctica has been divided into so many slices of political pie is inapplicable to a sphere. And in a land without seas one cannot claim sovereignty on the hinterland principle by which so much of the Western Hemisphere was claimed by the European Powers. And, having no modern equivalent in authority of Pope Alexander VI, who arbitrarily divided the New World between Spain and Portugal at the end of the fifteenth century, we must foresee the possibility that one day the Soviet Union and the United States will assert conflicting claims on the moon. Indeed the President's Science Advisory Committee is already concerned that some foolish gesture of nationalism, such as the explosion of an atomic bomb on the moon, will contaminate the oldest of Earth's satellites before scientists can examine its natural environment.

Though most responsible opinion holds that the moon will be of little military significance, earth dwellers would feel exceedingly uncomfortable if one of the major Powers established control there. Precisely because of its limited military potential, it might be possible and desirable to place the moon under international control. This could be accomplished without reference to more complex questions of sovereignty in space. Though certain risks are involved in taking political action where there are so many unknowns, they seem on the whole less awesome than alternative lines of development. Fifty years of exploration of Antarctica have done nothing to reduce the desirability of internationalizing that continent, yet political developments in that half-century have vastly complicated the task. ("Open Skies and Open Space." *Foreign Affairs,* October 1958.)

On 14 September 1959 a rocket fired by the Soviet Union struck the moon. It was the first object sent from the earth to another cosmic body. The rocket contained, in addition to scientific instruments, metal pennants that bore the Soviet coat of arms. When queried as to the significance of the Soviet pennants, the U.S. State Department issued the following statement:

The placing of national insignia would not of course constitute a sufficient basis to found a claim of sovereignty over unoccupied land masses.

In the case of celestial bodies there is also a question as to whether such bodies are capable of appropriation to national sovereignty.

If so, acts beyond the placing of national insignia which would be adequate to found a claim of sovereignty in the case of such a body would have to be determined.

All of these questions will be the subject of serious discussion before their resolution becomes necessary as a result of human settlement and exploitation of resources of celestial bodies. (14 September 1959.)

An announcement by Soviet authorities gave, in essence, the same response regarding possible territorial claims in the lunar region where the rocket fell; no territorial claim will be made, it stated.

Floating Ice

On 16 July 1970, an American was shot and killed on an ice island identified as T-3, sometimes called Fletchers Island and, at that time, located 192 miles due west of Ellesmere Island. The victim was a member of a 19-man U.S. weather team residing on that floating ice island. The interesting legal point raised by this incident was who had jurisdiction over the offense. Canada could not claim it, inasmuch as the ice island was not in its jurisdictional waters. Without any precedent to guide it, the U.S. Department of Justice defined the ice island as a "vessel on the high seas" and prosecuted the defendant on that basis. Perhaps the United States could have based its right to jurisdiction on the facts that it had such right over the persons involved and that no other sovereign state had it over the area in question.

CESSION

The second way in which a nation may acquire territory is *cession* by another sovereign nation. The title acquired by this means derives its validity from that of the ceding nation. Necessarily, therefore, ceded territory must already have been "occupied" in the sense of International Law. Otherwise, the ceding nation would not have the authority to make the transfer.

In International Law a cession of sovereignty is much like a transfer of title to land by deed in the United States. In most cases, the nations involved enter into a treaty that defines the area ceded and sets forth the conditions upon which the transfer is made. Once the conditions of the treaty have been met, the change of sovereignty is complete. The old sovereign relinquishes all power and authority over the territory and its inhabitants, and a like power and authority are assumed by the new sovereign. A transfer of sovereignty by cession has no effect upon the private ownership of land in the ceded territory.

Although cessions of territory may be made under a variety of circumstances, International Law has in the past made no distinction as to their validity. For example, the international community has regarded a cession made as part of a treaty of peace—in reality, a forced cession—as being just as valid as one made voluntarily. It has also made no difference to the international community whether the cession was the result of a treaty of sale, as in the case of the Louisiana Purchase; of an exchange, as in the case of Great Britain giving Helgoland to Germany in exchange for certain African territory belonging to the latter; or of a gift, as in the case of Britain giving Horseshoe Reef in Lake Erie to the United States. A current example is the cession by gift of Spanish Sahara by Spain to Morocco and Mauritania, which divided the territory and incorporated it into their then-existing states, according to prior understandings.

In more recent times some authorities in the field of International Law have advanced the view that territory could be validly ceded by plebiscite. Although this view is accepted by most theorists, the practice has not been followed with sufficient consistency to say that it has become a part of International Law. It is noted that in the case of Spain's cession of Ifni to Morocco in 1969 consideration was given to the views of the local inhabitants. Although one of President Woodrow Wilson's Fourteen Points was the principle of self-determination, most of the treaties following World War I drew boundaries and transferred territory from sovereign to sovereign without giving the people of the affected territories the opportunity to express their wishes.

A parallel principle, which is followed in many instances but not yet routinely enough to be considered a rule of International Law, is that the residents of ceded territory should be given the option of retaining their former citizenship and allegiance. Those who choose that course, however, may be required to emigrate within a specified time. If the new state did not have the right to make such a stipulation, it might have a territory in which all the residents owed allegiance to another nation. When the United States has acquired territory by cession, it has been generous in allowing residents to retain their old allegiance without losing their right to continue to reside in the ceded territory. Such was the case, for example, in the purchase of the Virgin Islands from Denmark in 1917.

ANNEXATION

Annexation is a form of acquisition that is closely related to cession. Charles Cheney Hyde, an authority on this subject, declares: "Annexation is a process by means of which a State proceeds to acquire sovereignty over a portion or all of the territory of another, with or without its consent, and without the aid of treaty" (*International Law—Chiefly as Interpreted and Applied by the United States*).

As is the case in a cession of territory, a variety of circumstances can lead up to the transfer of sovereignty and they have not generally been taken into consideration in determining the validity of annexation. For example, in the case of annexation following the complete subjugation of a territory in war, the annexing nation may not consider it necessary to resort to the formality of a treaty. Then again, a nation might be powerful enough to annex its neighbor's territory without having to resort to war. This is how Germany annexed Austria in 1938. On the other hand, the residents and government of a territory may want to become part of another nation. The incorporation of the Republic of Texas into the United States is a good example of this method of annexation.

Today, members of the United Nations would have a problem in acquiring territory by annexation or cession. Article 2 of that body's charter forbids the threat or use of force against the territorial integrity or political independence of any state. Therefore, annexation of territory obtained by threats or use of force would appear to be invalid.

PRESCRIPTION AND ACCRETION

Prescription is the process of acquiring sovereignty over a territory simply by maintaining unmolested governmental control over it long enough for the international community to come to the conclusion that title to it is in conformity with international order. Once that undefined period of time has passed, title is confirmed in the occupying nation, whether or not its original occupation was legal. Validation of title by prescription occurs most often when a boundary between two nations has been drawn so as to allot territory to a nation not entitled to it.

When new land is created within the territorial boundaries of a nation, that nation automatically acquires sovereignty over it. The process is called *accretion*. Common examples of the process are the natural formation of new islands within the territorial waters of a nation, the gradual building up of a river bank by natural deposits on it, and the erection of dikes on the ocean shore and the filling of the land behind them.

LOSS OF TERRITORY

The five ways of acquiring territory described above, occupation, cession, annexation, prescription, and accretion, suggest that there are similar methods of losing it. When one state acquires territory, there is usually a corresponding loss by a second state; Antarctica is the outstanding exception. Perhaps there is one method of losing territory that does not correspond to a method of acquiring it: a revolt or civil war that leads to the secession of part of a state.

BOUNDARIES

Boundaries are important in International Law because they are the imaginary lines that mark the limits of the territory within which a nation may exercise supreme and exclusive authority. Not only do they separate the territory of one nation from that of another, but they also separate the territory of a nation from unappropriated areas, such as the high seas, and mark the limits of a nation's territorial sovereignty in the air. They are, therefore, of vital interest to those who serve in aircraft. Water boundaries, which are of primary interest to naval officers and mariners, are governed by special rules and will be discussed in detail in the next chapter.

Although boundary lines may or may not be indicated by visible markings on the surface of the ground, they are always shown on charts and maps. Generally, such aids are reliable, but in areas where the lines are contested, special instructions are usually needed. In any event, it is important to be aware of boundaries and of the fact that the territorial sovereignty they demarcate must be respected.

Throughout the world there are boundary disputes. A dispute of more than one hundred years' standing between the United States and Mexico was resolved on 28 October 1967, when a mutually acceptable boundary for the Chamizal Territory was negotiated. Nationalistic feelings, however, frequently preclude settlement, and the disputes are a source of constant friction between the states concerned. Classic examples of such disputes are those between Peru and Ecuador concerning their common boundary, and between Iraq and Iran concerning the estuary of the Shatt-al-Arab. In many ways the Shatt-al-Arab is indicative of the sensitivity of boundary issues. Conflict over that boundary between Iraq and Iran has erupted many times since the early 1800s, most recently in September 1980.

The continuing question on the maritime boundaries between Canada and the United States is instructive: of the four boundaries, the one that produced the greatest difficulty was that in the Gulf of Maine. The accompanying chart shows the claims, some based on an equidistance principle and others on factors whose existence should cause a departure from that principle. On 29 March 1979 agreement was reached, subject to ratification (which at this writing appears to be quite contentious), between the two neighbors not as to what the boundary should be, but a commitment as to the procedure for reaching a solution. The Canadian secretary of external affairs described that procedure:

> The treaty to submit the delimitation of the maritime boundary in the Gulf of Maine area to binding dispute settlement and the annexed special agreement provide for the submission of the case to a five judge chamber of the International Court of Justice for a final decision on the placement of the boundary. Should the International Court of Justice be unable to function under the formula mutually agreed upon by the Governments of Canada and the United States, the dispute will automatically be referred to a special five member independent International Court of Arbitration.

While the procedure might appear to be intricate, because of the complexity surrounding the resolution, it is undoubtedly one of the better approaches. Settlement of the dispute on that boundary should facilitate agreement on the other three.

Maritime boundaries need not be single lines for all purposes. For example, Australia and Papua New Guinea were faced with resolving the difficulty created by Australia's claim to sovereignty over some small islands

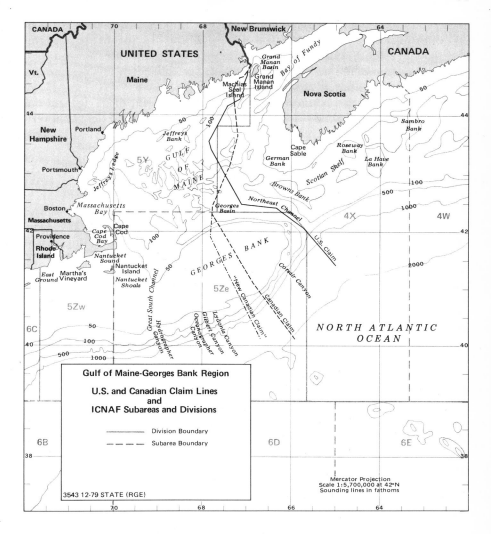

Gulf of Maine-Georges Bank Region

U.S. and Canadian Claim Lines
and
ICNAF Subareas and Divisions

———————— Division Boundary
— — — — Subarea Boundary

3543 12-79 STATE (RGE)

Mercator Projection
Scale 1:5,700,000 at 42°N
Sounding lines in fathoms

that are only 200 yards off the coast of Papua New Guinea. The agreement they reached established a series of boundaries: one for fishing zones, one for territorial seas, one for seabeds, and still another for control of the air space.

SERVITUDES

It has been pointed out that a nation's territory is that part of the globe over which it exercises supreme and exclusive sovereignty. However, the supremacy and exclusiveness of a nation's power over its territory may be subject to a *servitude*.

A servitude limits a nation's territorial supremacy by making a given territory subject to a specified degree of control or use by another sovereign. The privilege enjoyed by the nation for whose benefit the servitude is imposed is often referred to as an *easement*, but that term has no precise meaning in International Law.

Most servitudes are connected with waters—the right of navigation on certain rivers, for example—and they will be discussed in the next chapter. The most common type of servitude in land areas is the granting by treaty of a right-of-way to one nation to build a road or a railroad across the territory of another nation. An example of this is the servitude that allowed landlocked Zambia to build a railroad to Tanzania's major port of Dar es Salaam.

Other types of servitude on land are *negative servitudes*, the most common of which is the demilitarized zone. A negative servitude requires that a nation refrain from certain action, as, for instance, building fortifications on a particular part of its territorial domain. Probably the most famous demilitarized zone was the fifty-kilometer belt east of the Rhine that was imposed upon Germany by the Treaty of Versailles. Equally notorious was Germany's violation of the treaty by beginning to remilitarize this zone in 1936.

LEASES

Somewhat akin to an acquisition of sovereignty over territory and to the imposition of a servitude is the leasing of territory. The United States has on several occasions availed itself of this means to acquire the right to use certain territory belonging to another nation. The leases probably most familiar to naval men are the perpetual one of Guantánamo Bay from Cuba for use as a naval station and the ninety-nine-year one of Caribbean bases from Great Britain. The perpetual lease of the Panama Canal negotiated under the Hay–Bunau-Varilla Treaty of 1903 received intensive international scrutiny in the 1960s and 1970s, and new treaties were negotiated in 1977.

The powers that the United States may exercise within leased areas do not amount to actual sovereignty—this ultimate authority remains in the leasing nation. But very extensive powers may be given by the treaty granting the lease. For instance, the rights granted the United States by the treaty of 1903 were tantamount to sovereignty over the Canal Zone. This was true particularly with regard to any matter that might have posed a threat to the security of the canal. Under the two treaties negotiated in 1977, the Panama Canal Treaty and the Treaty Concerning the Permanent Neutrality and Operation of the Panama Canal (*see* Appendices B and C), the rights under which the United States will operate the canal until 31 December 1999 are more clearly defined and limited.

4   Territory—Water

I am master of the earth but the law is the mistress of the sea.

Emperor Antoninus

The nation that first learns to understand the seas will control them. And the nation that controls the seas will control the world.

G. V. Petrovich

INTRODUCTION

An incident related by Admiral Harry D. Felt, USN, shows that in a rather complex situation he was constantly concerned about how far from the shore the vessels of his task group could operate legally:

> On the morning of July 23, 1954, Task Group 70.2 was carrying out routine operations in the South China Sea. Our group was composed of the USS *Philippine Sea* (CVA-47), my Flagship; USS *Hornet* (CVA-12); and Destroyer Divisions 242 and 321. Shortly after 0900 we received a message that a British Air Cathay airliner was in distress and preparing to ditch twenty miles south of Hainan Island (18-01N, 110-01E). Shortly thereafter, the plane did ditch near Hainan. The Task Group headed for the scene; flight schedules were delayed one-half hour to permit the forces to get closer to the scene, and to permit briefing of the pilots. All pilots were instructed to approach no closer than fifteen miles to Hainan. Two destroyers, the *Benham* and *Ross*, which were detached from the screen to assist in the rescue, were given the same instructions.
>
> A British rescue plane was the first to arrive at the scene of the crash, which proved to be about five miles from the coast of Hainan. Rescue planes commenced picking up survivors and, upon request, we gave permission for our carrier planes to approach inside fifteen miles from the coast in order to observe rescue operations. The *Benham* and *Ross* were directed to proceed past the fifteen-mile line, go inside the twelve-mile limit in order to assist in the rescue, but not to proceed inside the three-mile limit unless so directed. Late that afternoon the search was terminated upon receiving information that all survivors had been rescued.
>
> On the day following, 24 July, we continued our routine operations; that evening we received the information that the Cathay airliner had been shot down by Chinese Communist planes and, further, that there probably were some more survivors, among them United States citizens. We made plans to commence our search for the survivors with utmost despatch.

Search operations involving both our carrier planes and the *Benham* and *Ross* were conducted throughout the 25th and 26th; all ships and planes involved were instructed to stay to sea-ward of the twelve-mile limit. At about 1000 on the 26th a group of our search aircraft (ADs) were attacked by two Chinese Communist LA-7 aircraft at a position fifteen miles from the mouth of the Wan Chuan Ho River, Hainan. Our aircraft shot both of the attacking planes down and they crashed into the sea outside the twelve-mile limit. At no time did our aircraft go within the Chinese Communist twelve-mile limit.

BREADTH OF THE TERRITORIAL SEA

The territorial sea is the belt of ocean beyond but adjacent to the land territory and internal waters of a coastal state. Sovereignty over it is exercised by that state. Although sovereignty extends to the air space over and the bed and subsoil beneath the territorial sea, there are certain limitations to it, as will be noted below. The territorial seas and archipelagic waters of an archipelagic state such as the Philippines are generally synonymous.

Territorial seas are seaward of rivers, most bays, some gulfs, lakes, ports, and roadsteads, all of which are considered to be internal, or national, waters. It is important to note the difference between territorial seas and internal waters, because separate rules govern them. Internal waters are characterized by the fact that the state in which they lie exercises complete sovereignty over them in the same manner that it exercises sovereignty over its land mass. Included is the right to deny their use to foreign ships. By usage, the term *territorial waters*, includes both the territorial sea and internal waters.

Since 1793 when Secretary of State Thomas Jefferson announced to the British and French that the United States adhered to the three-mile limit, the United States has maintained that three miles is the appropriate breadth for a territorial sea. However, international events in the 1960s and 1970s prompted a change in the regime of the oceans, central to which was the redrawing of jurisdictional lines, i.e., extending territorial seas to a breadth of twelve miles. That change was supported by the vast majority of states and is the fulcrum upon which rests the great body of International Law as it pertains to the seas.

To fully understand that body of law it is necessary to look back into history, for the question of the breadth of territorial seas has been tortuous and lack of agreement has spawned sharp disputes and dangerous flash points throughout the world. In brief, to understand the present and be competent to act or react to the variety of situations that can arise at sea, it is necessary to be aware of the past.

HISTORICAL COMMENT

From the time of the Roman Empire until approximately the fifteenth century various states laid claim to vast ocean areas. These claims were cyclical, were generally ill defined, and the reasons for making them were not clear. There does not appear to have been any consensus or uniform practice regarding such claims.

By the fifteenth century states had begun to abandon extensive claims and substitute claims only to waters contiguous to their coasts. During the following century the term *territorial seas* began to emerge when the publicist Alberico Gentili, in his text *De Jure Belli,* published in 1598, advanced the proposition that a sovereign could legitimately treat waters adjacent to his state in the same way he treated his land territory. The genesis of this concept appears to have been based on control over piracy and other acts that might threaten the security of a sovereign. That same concept applies today when we speak of protecting the peace, good order, or security of the coastal state.

By the seventeenth century, the content, purpose, and breadth of territorial seas had become clearly defined. What emerged was the three-mile limit. In his work *De dominio maris,* published in 1702, the Dutch publicist Cornelis van Bynkershoek, gave his rationale for that limit:

> Wherefore on the whole it seems a better rule that the control of the land over the sea extend as far as cannon will carry; for that is as far as we seem to have both command and possession. I should have to say in general terms that the control from the land ends where the power of man's weapons ends.

At that time cannon shot carried approximately three miles. Thus, many authorities believe that the three-mile rule was predicated on Bynkershoek's idea. There is evidence, however, that it may not have had anything to do with the range of cannon shot, but originated from the line of sight from the shoreline which, at sea level, is approximately three miles. If that were the case, the two different approaches supported each other by coincidence to produce the same result: the three-mile limit.

If the three-mile limit was based on the range of cannon shot, why did the United States and many other maritime states adhere to it when weapons capable of traveling vast distances were developed? The answer is simple: because it had been found practical and acceptable. Obviously, the fact that a cannon used to shoot only three miles had no bearing on the validity of the rule; nor did the distance that a modern weapon could shoot. For example, in World War II English and Germans guns fired, as a matter of routine, across the eighteen-mile-wide English Channel. If the range of cannon shot were today the determinant for the breadth of territorial seas, how could it be applied?

Suffice it to say that during the eighteenth and nineteenth centuries the great preponderance of opinion and practice supported the three-mile limit. It is also clear that the three-mile breadth of territorial seas was a product of the collective thinking of important maritime states; other countries either had concerns of more importance to them or had no interest in the use of the oceans. The United States, a growing maritime power, adopted the three-mile limit in 1793 when, as noted above, Thomas Jefferson informed the British and French of that decision. Part of the text of that communication, dated 3 November 1793, indicates that Jefferson did not accept the three-mile limit without reservations; nor was he prepared to state what distance, in the final analysis, was best for the United States. He wrote:

> The President of the United States, thinking that, before it shall be finally decided to what distance from our seashores the territorial protection of the United States shall be exercised, it will be proper to enter into friendly conferences and explanations with the powers chiefly interested in the navigation of the seas on our coasts, and relying that convenient occasions may be taken for these hereafter, finds it necessary in the meantime to fix provisionally on some distance for the present government of these questions. You are sensible that very different opinions and claims have been heretofore advanced on this subject. The greatest distance to which any respectable assent among nations has been at any time given, has been the extent of the human sight, estimated at upwards of twenty miles, and the smallest distance, I believe, claimed by any nation whatever, is the utmost range of a cannon ball, usually stated at one sea league. Some intermediate distances have also been insisted on, and that of three sea leagues has some authority in its favor. The character of our coast, remarkable in considerable parts of it for admitting no vessels of size to pass near the shores, would entitle us, in reason, to as broad a margin of protected navigation as any nation whatever. Reserving, however, the ultimate extent of this for future deliberation, the President gives instructions to the officers acting under his authority to consider those heretofore given them as restrained for the present to the distance of one sea league or three geographic miles from the seashores. This distance can admit of no opposition, as it is recognized by treaties between some of the powers with whom we are connected in commerce and navigation, and is as little, or less, than is claimed by any of them on their own coasts. (Jefferson's notes of 3 November 1793 to French Minister E.G. Genet and British Foreign Minister G. Hammond.)

As can be seen, even during a period of relative stability there was not international uniformity in acceptance of the three-mile limit.

While the rationale that prompted a departure from Jefferson's note above is not clear, by act of 5 June 1794 the United States gave its unqualified support to the three-mile limit; records indicate that it was the first state to make the limit a part of its domestic law. This unqualified support served us well in what remained of the eighteenth century and in the nineteenth. With a large degree of hindsight it can be said that Jefferson's provisional adherence to the three-mile limit would have served us well during the turbulent changes of the twentieth century.

During this century, particularly since World War II, the rule has been under severe attack by many states for a variety of reasons. Its challengers were in general agreement that the minimum breadth of a territorial sea should be three miles; disagreement centered on what its maximum breadth should be. The nature and scope of that disagreement and its eventual settlement are described in the following paragraphs and chapters.

INCONSISTENT PRACTICE AS TO BREADTH AND PURPOSE

After World War II, some coastal states began to press for extension and many new states emerged from colonial status. Territorial-sea claims became increasingly disparate. However, the seeds for weakening the three-mile limit were sown in 1930 when forty-eight governments met at The Hague primarily for the purpose of establishing a uniform breadth of the territorial sea. They failed to achieve that objective and criticism of the three-mile limit increased. In 1958 and 1960 at Geneva, the world community tried again to reach agreement, but those conferences also failed. The fact that there was no uniformity produced friction and sometimes confrontation between governments. A few examples will suffice.

In 1954, Ecuador, Peru, and Chile proclaimed a form of jurisdiction which, in literal, but not necessarily practical, terms, appeared to extend territorial seas two hundred miles out into the open sea. As a result, several privately owned U.S. and other tuna boats, which were fishing more than twelve miles from the coasts of those countries, were apprehended and charged with violating territorial waters. These arrests and subsequent fines evoked strong protests from the U.S. government. The following report demonstrates the seriousness with which such incidents are viewed:

> Peruvian ships fired upon and seized an American fishing boat off Peru's coast today.
>
> The White House said President Nixon was studying the matter and Secretary of State William P. Rogers called Peruvian Ambassador Fernando Berckemeyer to the State Department, undoubtedly to protest the incident.
>
> According to U.S. officials the Peruvian gunboats fired on the tuna-fishing vessel MARINER and four sister ships early today at a point about 23 miles off the coast of Peru.
>
> The MARINER and one other fishing boat reportedly were damaged by the gunfire and the MARINER was captured and towed into a Peruvian port.
>
> The White House said that if reports of the incident were correct, "We would of course look on this matter with utmost concern."
>
> Rep. Thomas M. Pelly, R-Wash., said the MARINER and one other vessel were fired on and damaged while in international waters.

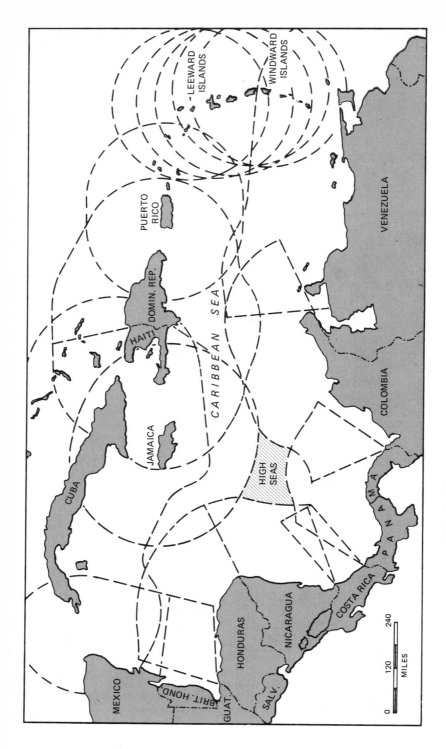

The Caribbean Sea and a Two-Hundred-Mile Territorial Sea

Chairman Edward A. Garmatz, D-Md., of the House Merchant Marine and Fisheries Committee, urged the State Department to "retaliate and get tough." He said "Congress and the American people are getting fed up with these continued acts of piracy."

Sen. George Murphy, R-Calif., wired Nixon, also calling for swift action to protect American fishing fleets. He called the latest incident only the latest of "several years of persistent harassment of United States fishing vessels in open seas" by the Peruvian government.

"This outrageous threat to American lives and property cannot be permitted and I therefore urge you strongly as possible to provide whatever protection, military or otherwise, is necessary to stop the harassment . . ." (*The Evening Star*, Washington, D.C., 14 February 1969.)

The Peruvian press and various spokesmen in Peru also reacted in strong terms in support of their position concerning jurisdiction.

In January and February 1971 units of the Ecuadorian Navy seized twenty-six U.S. tuna clippers some fifty to sixty miles off the coast of Ecuador. This resulted in applying the provisions of the Military Sales Act, which required that military sales to Ecuador be cut off. In response to this act, the government of Ecuador asked the U.S. Military Assistance Group to leave the country.

Many newly independent states or new governments also declared unilaterally that their sovereignty embraced an extensive area of the high seas. Vice Admiral Wallace M. Beakley, USN, relates the U.S. response to one such declaration:

In December 1957, Indonesia proclaimed that all waters in and around the Republic's 3,000 islands were territorial waters of Indonesia. The reason given was that Indonesia was all one land mass and the waters were part of that land mass. This proclamation, if enforced, would obviously hamper world trade over sea routes that have been used by all nations for centuries. This was an extreme violation of the principle of the freedom of the seas. Shortly after the declaration, we sailed the cruiser *Bremerton* through the waters in question en route from Australia to Singapore. I consider this one of the most effective actions that we could have taken to display to Indonesia that the United States could not accede to an act that placed the freedom of the seas in jeopardy.

GENEVA CONFERENCES OF 1958 AND 1960

In June 1956, the International Law Commission of the United Nations considered a draft restatement of the law of territorial seas. Five proposals, ranging from a strict three-mile limitation to the unilateral right of a coastal state to fix the breadth of its own territorial sea, were considered. None of them received a majority vote, and the proposal that was finally accepted did not resolve the problem. It did, however, provide an accurate statement of what the problem was. In the words of the International Law Commission:

1. The Commission recognizes that international practice is not uniform as regards the delimitation of the territorial sea.
2. The Commission considers that international law does not permit an extension of the territorial sea beyond twelve miles.
3. The Commission, without taking any decision as to the breadth of the territorial sea up to that limit, notes on the one hand, that many States have fixed a breadth greater than three miles and, on the other hand, that many States do not recognize such a breadth when that of their own territorial sea is less.
4. The Commission considers that the breadth of the territorial sea should be fixed by an international conference.

In November and December 1956 the United Nations considered the full report of the International Law Commission and, more specifically, the recommendation that the question of the breadth of the territorial sea be referred to an international conference. During that session delegates from some fifty countries took the opportunity to express national views on the breadth of the territorial sea. With certain countries dissenting (*e.g.,* Chile, Ecuador, and Peru), the findings of the International Law Commission were accepted, and it was agreed that a conference on the law of the sea be held. The United Nations fully recognized the complexity of the problem plus the fact that many segments of the law of the sea depended on a satisfactory solution to the question of the breadth of the territorial sea. To meet these issues, the United Nations General Assembly directed that the conferees examine the law of the sea not only from the legal standpoint but also from technical, biological, economic, and political standpoints. The results of the conference were to be embodied in one or more international conventions.

The conference met in Geneva, Switzerland, from 24 February to 27 April 1958. The governments of eighty-six states were represented. The U.S. delegation was headed by Arthur Dean.

No article defining the breadth of the territorial sea was included in the resulting Convention on the Territorial Sea. Thirteen proposals were made, six came to a vote, and none obtained the required two-thirds majority. To indicate the disparity between the proposals, three are given here.

Joint proposal by India and Mexico:

Every state is entitled to fix the breadth of its territorial sea up to a limit of twelve nautical miles measured from the baseline which may be applicable in conformity with Articles 4 and 5 [of the Territorial Sea Convention].

The vote: thirty-nine in favor, thirty-eight against, and eight abstentions.

Proposal by the Soviet Union:

Each state shall determine the breadth of its territorial waters in accordance with established practice within the limit, as a rule, of three to twelve

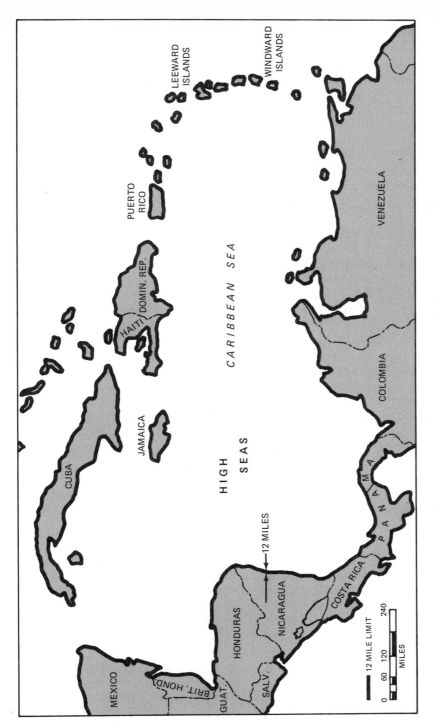

The Caribbean Sea and a Twelve-Mile Territorial Sea

miles, having regard to historical and geographical conditions, economic interests, the interests of the security of the coastal state and the interests of international navigation.

The vote: twenty-one in favor, forty-seven against, and seventeen abstentions.

Proposal by Sweden:

The breadth of the territorial sea shall be fixed by the coastal state but may not exceed six marine miles.

The vote: sixteen in favor, forty-nine against, and four abstentions.

It can be seen that the great majority of states at that time were in agreement that the breadth of the territorial sea should lie somewhere between three and twelve miles. Any claim beyond twelve miles would receive but insignificant sanction.

Faced with the prospect of an inconclusive conference, the U.S. delegation made an extraordinary effort to settle the issue. Had the proposal it made been adopted, it would have constituted a departure from 165 years of traditional adherence to the three-mile limit. The essentials of the proposal were adoption of a six-mile limit plus a six-mile fishing zone, with the proviso that any foreign state that had been fishing regularly in that zone for a period of five years preceding the date of the convention should be allowed to continue to do so. When put to the vote by roll call the result was forty-five for, thirty-three against, and seven abstentions—seven short of the necessary two-thirds majority. Significantly, the U.S. proposal received more votes than any other proposal on the breadth of the territorial sea.

When the various proposals had been considered, the U.S. delegate, Arthur Dean, restated the traditional position of the United States, and emphasized the fact that the U.S. compromise proposal had been made only in an attempt to produce order out of chaos. He said:

My government stands firmly on the view that the three-mile limit is fully established as a principle of International Law and that this principle can only be changed by agreement. If we do not agree, our work here will be a nullity and no statement or proposal or argument will have any effect whatsoever to extend the breadth of the territorial sea beyond three miles.

We have made it clear that in our view there is no obligation on the part of states adhering to the three-mile rule to recognize claims on the part of others to a greater breadth of territorial sea. On that we stand.

In recognition of the obvious need to reach agreement, the conference, in one of its closing sessions, adopted the following resolution:

Considering that, on the basis of the report prepared by the International Law Commission, it [the United Nations Conference on the Law of the Sea] has approved agreements and other instruments on the regime applicable to fishing and the conservation of the living resources of the high seas, the exploration and exploitation of the natural resources of the continental shelf and other matters pertaining to the general regime of the high seas and to the free access of land-locked States to the sea,

Considering that it has not been possible to reach agreement on the breadth of the territorial sea and some other matters which were raised in connexion with this problem.

Recognizing that, although agreements have been reached on the regime applicable to fishing and the conservation of the living resources of the high seas, it has not been possible, in those agreements, to settle certain aspects of a number of inherently complex questions.

Recognizing the desirability of making further efforts, at an appropriate time, to reach agreement on those questions relating to the international law of the sea which have been left unsettled,

Requests the General Assembly of the United Nations to study, at its thirteenth session [1958], the advisability of convening a second international conference of plenipotentiaries for further consideration of the questions left unsettled by the present Conference.

The above request to the General Assembly was approved, and the second Geneva Conference was held in the spring of 1960. Eighty-eight countries participated in the six-week conference. Debate over the breadth of the territorial sea and related fishing rights was long and, in some cases, emotional, but no agreement was reached, despite the fact that many proposals were made and endorsed by various groups of states. A U.S.-Canadian compromise formula for a six-mile territorial sea, coupled with an additional six-mile fishing zone for the exclusive use of the coastal state and recognition of the special interest of the coastal state in the conservation of fisheries beyond jurisdictional waters, received the biggest vote: it was fifty-four for and twenty-eight against—one vote short of the required two-thirds majority.

In the absence of an agreement, the U.S. delegate stated that the United States would adhere to the traditional three-mile limit and would be under no obligation to recognize claims in excess of it.

Why has the United States felt so strongly about a narrow territorial sea? To answer that question, another question has to be asked—if we believe that the high seas must be free, can we accede to large areas of them being under the dominion and absolute control of the different states? Our position does not rest on historical precedent alone, although history has demonstrated repeatedly that unilateral control of large areas of the high seas simply does not work. The principal reasons states give for desiring broader territorial seas are fishing control, security in peace and war, exploitation of the continental shelf, pollution control, and customs matters, all of which can be independent of a narrow territorial sea (*see* Chapter 6). Every extension of a territorial sea produces a corresponding loss to the freedom of the seas and the air above them. Every ship and every aircraft, regardless of nationality, that transits the high seas could, and probably would, suffer inconvenience and higher operating costs as a result of excessive territorial-sea claims. The great trading countries and the developing countries that receive the trade would both suffer accordingly. For the U.S. Navy, unrealistic expansion of the territorial sea means loss of flexibility and maneuverability in carrying out its commitments on the high seas.

Faced with making a choice between advocating a broad territorial sea and sustaining the principle of the freedom of the seas, the United States clearly chose the latter.

Developments since the Geneva Conferences of 1958 and 1960

After the Geneva Conferences on the Law of the Sea of 1958 and 1960, the world community's interest in the oceans increased. The possibility of mining the resources of the deep seabed, the growing need to obtain food from the sea, mounting concern over marine pollution, and intensified scientific research being conducted on the high seas all contributed to this increased interest. Issues arising from these activities had an impact on the question of the breadth of the territorial sea. Clearly, that basic issue had to be resolved, not only in order to simplify resolution of the above problems but also to remove a catalyst for dispute and discord in the world community.

In 1965, at the suggestion of representatives of the Soviet Union, informal bilateral discussions were held in Washington, D.C., for the purpose of exchanging views on whether it would be possible to resolve the question of the breadth of the territorial sea if a new conference were called. The discussions reaffirmed the fact that it was not possible to do so without simultaneously solving the questions of fisheries and straits. Bilateral consultations between the United States and a large number of countries were held during the next few years and showed general acknowledgment of the interrelationship between territorial seas, straits, and fisheries. They also affirmed that, were it possible to hold a world conference limited to those three interrelated problems, the likelihood of successful resolution would be measurably enhanced.

The rationale for holding such a restricted conference was best described in an address by John R. Stevenson, legal adviser of the Department of State, on 18 February 1970:

> While no State in our view is obliged to recognize territorial seas exceeding 3 miles, there is nothing like uniform agreement on this figure. About 30 States claim 3 miles, another 15 between 4 and 10 miles, and about 40 claim 12 miles. Approximately 11 States claim some sort of jurisdiction over the waters

beyond 12 miles, usually fisheries jurisdiction, but in some cases full territorial jurisdiction as far out as 200 miles.

Given this state of affairs, it can readily be seen as the President pointed out in his foreign policy message to Congress today, that it is urgent that international agreement be reached on the breadth of the territorial sea to head off the threat of escalating national claims over the ocean.

In the course of the last two years, the United States has consulted with a large number of nations regarding the desirability of making a new attempt to achieve widespread agreement on the breadth of the territorial sea, and has accelerated the pace of these discussions in the last year.

It appears that there is widespread support for fixing the breadth of the territorial sea at 12 nautical miles. However, the extensión of the territorial sea to 12 miles would place many important international straits, which have high seas areas running through them with a 3-mile limit, within the territorial sea of the coastal State. This would mean that vessels could only traverse these straits in innocent passage; furthermore, there is no established right of innocent passage for aircraft in the airspace over straits within territorial waters. In the view of many countries this is not a satisfactory situation. The freedom of the seas would have a far more restrictive meaning indeed if rights to traverse straits are not clear and secure. A significant number of nations agree that this problem requires solution if a 12-mile territorial sea is to be accepted.

An additional problem directly affected by the breadth of the territorial sea is the conduct of high seas fisheries. Many nations do not believe that mere conservation of such fisheries adequately protects their interests. Large and mobile high seas fleets can move in on an area, seriously overfish the stocks and move on. This can result in economic dislocations in a coastal State, or a region thereof, which is dependent on such fisheries for its livelihood. We believe these economic pressures have contributed significantly to the trend toward expanded unilateral jurisdictional claims and that many nations will insist that these problems be dealt with in conjunction with agreement on the breadth of the territorial sea.

As a result of our consultations we believe the time is right for the conclusion of a new international treaty fixing the limitation of the territorial sea at 12 miles, and providing for freedom of transit through and over international straits and carefully defined preferential fishing rights for coastal States on the high seas. We intend to work closely with the many other nations who share our views in these matters at the U.N. this fall as a matter of high priority.

The Third Law of the Sea Conference

A conference limited to the breadth of the territorial sea, straits, and fisheries, however, was not obtainable because in the winter of 1967 Ambassador Arvid Pardo of Malta called upon the United Nations to adopt a resolution establishing that seabed resources beyond national jurisdiction were for the benefit of all mankind and that an international organization be created to regulate, supervise, and control all seabed activities. In response, the U.N. General Assembly created an ad hoc committee to study issues concerning seabeds. The committee became permanent in 1968 and consisted of forty-two members. It came to the conclusion that the fabric of the law of the sea was so interwoven that seabeds could not be considered in isolation. Furthermore, a number of emerging, developing countries wanted to review the law of the sea in its entirety. The result was a resolution by the General Assembly on 17 December 1970, that a third comprehensive conference on the law of the sea be convened in 1973.

The conference held its first session in New York, 3–15 December 1973, and the breadth of the territorial sea was again debated at length.

As time went by, the shift of countries from three- to twelve-mile claims became more pronounced. In 1968, the Food and Agriculture Organization of the United Nations prepared a synopsis of the varying claims:

3 miles	– 31 states
Between 4 and 10 miles	– 16 states
12 miles	– 46 states
Between 12 and 200 miles	– 12 states
200 miles	– 15 states

In August 1978, the U.S. International Law Association Committee on the Law of the Sea published the following tally:

3 miles	– 20 states
Between 4 and 10 miles	– 9 states
12 miles	– 70 states
Between 12 and 200 miles	– 12 states
200 miles	– 15 states

The listing also showed a total of 69 states claiming a 200-mile fishing or exclusive economic zone.

By the fall of 1980, the Third Conference on the Law of the Sea had held more than nine sessions, many of them filled with exhausting debate and infrequent compromise. At this writing and as noted in the preface, compromises were finally obtained, particularly in the navigation regime as well as those that address other ocean uses related to navigation. These compromises are reflected in the conference's Draft Convention on the Law of the Sea (Informal Text), 28 August 1980, and for general purposes can be characterized as final. Appendices D through L provide the pertinent draft treaty language. The remainder of this chapter, as well as Chapter 5 and Chapter 6, is based in large measure on those provisions.

One of the compromises that will undoubtedly stand, whether or not the conference succeeds and whether or not it gets formal endorsement, is worldwide recognition of a twelve-mile territorial sea. In effect, the twelve-mile territorial sea limit will be recognized as law either by formal collective action in the Law of the Sea Conference, i.e., a treaty, or, failing that, will be generally regarded as customary International Law through the endorsement of that limit by the great majority of states. As of January 1979, seventy-five countries had endorsed a twelve-mile limit.

Other compromises and agreements that bear on the breadth of the territorial sea and the regime of the high seas will be discussed in the following chapters.

MEASUREMENT OF TERRITORIAL SEAS

In order to determine where the outer limit of the territorial sea lies, it is necessary to know where, along the shoreline or base line, the measurement is taken. It begins at the clear line of demarkation between sea and land, which in cases such as the Mississippi River delta area is very difficult to ascertain. From the point of demarkation between sea and land at the low-water line, the territorial sea is measured outwards as marked on an official large-scale chart of the state concerned. Where the coast is dotted with islands and deeply indented, as in Norway, and where long-standing economic interests are involved, the base line may have nothing to do with the low-water mark. In cases such as these, straight base lines joining appropriate points may be used as the starting point for the measurement. They must not depart significantly from the general direction of the coast, and the sea areas lying within them must be sufficiently close to the land mass to be subject to the coastal state's regime over internal waters. The use of straight base lines is further restricted by the fact that one state may not use them in a manner that would cut off from the high seas the territorial sea or exclusive economic zone of another state.

Except for special provisions applying to archipelagoes, waters on the landward side of the base line of the territorial sea are internal waters of the state.

For a river that flows directly into the sea, the base line is a straight line across its mouth between points on the low-tide line of its banks.

ISLANDS

The rules outlined in the preceding section apply to islands. For example, the island of Guam has its own territorial sea. Waters between an island and the coast are considered to be territorial seas if they are between twelve and twenty-four miles wide. The same holds true for the waters on the landward side of rocks and reefs that are visible at high tide. If a rock or shoal is above water at low tide only and it is situated within the breadth of the territorial sea, from the mainland or an island, its low-water line may be used as the base line for measuring the territorial sea. If it is situated outside that breadth, it has no territorial sea of its own.

A lighthouse or other permanent structure built on a submerged rock or shoal is an artificial island and does not have territorial seas. The oil-drilling rigs installed throughout the Gulf of Mexico fall into this category.

ARCHIPELAGOES

Because there is a unique relationship between the water and the islands of an archipelagic state a separate regime has been advanced in the Law of the Sea Conference for measuring the breadth of its territorial sea. Straight base lines known as archipelagic base lines, joining the outermost points of the outermost islands and drying reefs may be used. Both Indonesia and the Philippines are examples of this situation. The precise requirements for establishing an archipelagic territorial sea can be found in Appendix F, Articles 46-51.

BAYS AND GULFS

There has long been a controversy over where the internal waters of bays and gulfs end and territorial seas begin. It once was established that where the entrance to a bay or gulf (a gulf is distinguished from a bay in that it is larger and penetrates deeper into the land) is six miles or less in width, territorial seas commence on a base line drawn between the seaward tangents of the entrance. All waters inside that line are internal waters. In practice and by treaty, the same rule has been applied to bays whose entrance width is ten to twelve miles, and some states have laid claims to much wider bays. If a claim has been of long standing and other states have acquiesced in it, a prescriptive title over the bay can be advanced. So-called historical bays fall into this category. The United States has three such bays: Chesapeake Bay, whose entrance is twelve miles wide; Delaware Bay, with an entrance ten miles wide; and Monterey Bay, with an entrance nineteen miles wide. The Varanger Fjord in Norway, whose entrance is thirty-two miles wide, is also considered an historical bay. Canada has claimed that Hudson Bay, whose entrance is fifty miles wide, should be similarly considered.

There are some bays whose entrance widths exceed the generally accepted rule and whose lack of a prescriptive title prevents them from qualifying as historical. A case in point is the Bay of Fundy, off the Canadian coast. Although its entrance is sixty-five miles wide, the British claimed that it was within the territory of Canada. When an American fishing vessel was seized in those waters in 1852 on the grounds that she had violated the exclusive jurisdiction of the territory of Canada, the Anglo-American

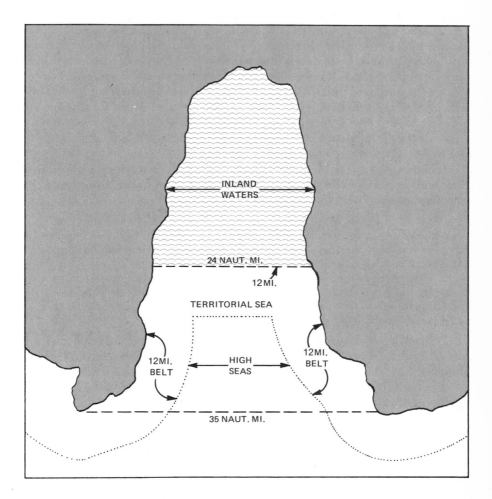

Application of the Twenty-Four-Mile Rule to an Indentation

Claims Commission ruled that the bay was not the territory of the British. The commission declared that, in this case, the word *bay* had "the same meaning as that applied to the Bay of Biscay or the Bay of Bengal over which no nation can have the right to assume sovereignty." That decision still applies.

Within recent years it has been found possible to go from the Atlantic to the Pacific along the northern coast of the Eurasian land mass during the summer months. Thus, it is significant that the Soviet Union apparently takes the position that the four seas—the Kara, Laptev, East Siberian, and

Chukchi—bordering its territory on the north and through which the route passes are territorial bays. It has not made an official claim to that effect, but should it do so and should the world at large acknowledge the claim, those four seas would be considered internal waters of the Soviet Union. In that case, Soviet territorial seas would begin on a line at the northern extremity of the seas in question, and use of the northern route by other states would be hindered, especially since its northern reaches are often impassable on account of ice. The White Sea is now definitely treated as Soviet internal waters, and there is reason to believe that the same principle may apply to the Sea of Okhotsk.

It can be seen that during recent years various countries have followed different practices. The Third Law of the Sea Conference considered the problem and arrived at the following consensus:

> If the distance between the low-water marks of the natural entrance points of a bay does not exceed 24 miles a closing line may be drawn between these two low-water marks, and the waters enclosed thereby shall be considered as internal waters.
>
> Where the distance between the low-water marks of the natural entrance points of a bay exceeds 24 miles a straight base line of 24 miles shall be drawn within the bay in such a manner as to enclose the maximum area of water that is possible with a line of that length.

Provision was also made for use of the semicircular method in determining whether a body of water is a bay or a gulf, and it was pointed out that the status of historical bays would remain unchanged. (*See* Appendix D.)

The conference also provided that islands situated on atolls with fringing reefs could use the seaward low-tide line, i.e., the low-water line of the reef, for measuring the breadth of the territorial sea. From that, it follows that waters inside the lagoon of an atoll are internal waters.

BREAKWATERS AND ROADSTEADS

Breakwaters and piers extending out into the sea at a port are considered integral parts of the port and, as such, are regarded as part of the coast. Territorial seas are adjusted accordingly. Roadsteads used for loading and offloading ships and situated, at least in part, beyond the outer limit of territorial seas, are considered to be part of those seas. The littoral state must make plain what the limits of such roadsteads are.

NEIGHBORING STATES

Where the coasts of two states are opposite or adjacent to each other and such states have not otherwise agreed, territorial seas may not be extended beyond a median line every point of which is equidistant from the base lines that serve to measure the territorial seas of the states concerned. It is interesting to note that while the United States and Canada have sought to resolve differences over their maritime boundaries in the Gulf of Maine, Juan de Fuca Strait, Dixon Entrance between southeastern Alaska and the Queen Charlotte Islands, and in the Arctic area, at the Beaufort Sea, at this writing no settlement has been reached.

The emergence of the 200-mile fishing or exclusive economic zone has created a vast new array of "neighboring" states which, with narrower jurisdictional waters, were not technically opposite or adjacent to one another. For example, with its 200-mile fishery zone, the United States created thirty-seven new maritime boundaries, all of which will have to be negotiated in order to reach agreement on geographic coordinates of jurisdictional boundaries. This new problem exists throughout the world and years will certainly pass before such boundaries become agreed upon and fully identified. This transitional period is likely to pose some unexpected jurisdictional problems for those who use the seas.

RIVERS

Late in 1955, Juan Peron, the dictator of the Argentine Republic, was deposed as a result of a revolution in that country. Feeling was running high, and he quickly sought, and received, asylum aboard a Paraguayan gunboat that was visiting Buenos Aires. Shortly thereafter, with the full knowledge of the new government in Argentina, the gunboat carrying Peron got under way and steamed up the Paraná River to Asunción, the capital of Paraguay. The Paraná River flows through hundreds of miles of Argentine territory before it reaches the border of Paraguay. Why did not the new Argentine government stop the gunboat while she was steaming up the river and seize Peron? The law of asylum was the major reason for the voyage not being interrupted, but the character of the Paraná River also had something to do with it.

Rivers that lie entirely within one country are considered part of that country's territory, and are called *national rivers*. Rivers that form a boundary between two or more countries are known as *international rivers*. If an international river is not navigable, as in the case of the Rio Grande, the territorial boundary lies at its geographical center: if it is navigable, as in the case of the St. Lawrence, the center of the deepest channel marks the boundary. This dividing line is known as the *thalweg*. Why the thalweg is used in determining territorial limits of international rivers was explained by the U.S. Supreme Court: "If the dividing line was to be placed in the center of the stream rather than in the center of the channel, the whole track of navigation might be thrown within the territory of one State to the exclusion of the other."

A country whose boundary is determined by an international river may not, by construction or otherwise, change the river's natural course or the thalweg; nor may it divert or lower the waters of the river, thereby impeding

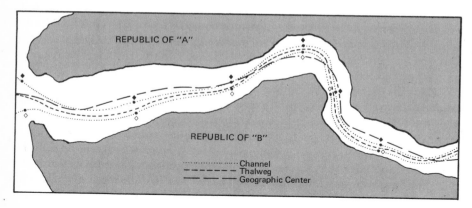

A Thalweg

navigation. If gradual natural action changes the course of a river and thereby creates a new thalweg, the boundary is based on the new thalweg.

Most international rivers are open to all ships. In this respect, they are similar to the high seas, because both are of primary importance to international trade. The same rule is being increasingly applied to rivers that lie in the territory of one state but serve as lines of communication for an interior state. The state in which a river lies may not exercise its sovereignty in a manner that would impede the free flow of traffic to and from the interior state. The Paraná fits this category. Therefore, the government of Argentina did not have the right to stop the Paraguayan gunboat.

In addition to the general rules governing rivers, several of the world's great rivers are further controlled by international treaties and agreements. Among this number are the Rhine, the Congo, the Danube, and the St. Lawrence.

LAKES

Lakes that lie entirely within the boundaries of one country are naturally considered part of that country's territory. Where a lake lies partly in one country and partly in another, the usual procedure is to establish territorial limits by means of a treaty. Should this not be done, the middle line of the lake is generally taken as the dividing line. The Great Lakes are subject to agreements between Canada and the United States: the various treaties regarding them govern not only the territorial limits of each country, but also fix jurisdictional questions, such as admiralty, navigation, and limitations on warships. In the last instance, it is of interest to note that, because of treaty limitations, the USS *Wolverine*, a training carrier on the Great Lakes during World War II, carried no guns. Also, when a captured German submarine was sent to Chicago as a war trophy, her journey to the city was complicated by treaty restrictions on submarines.

USE OF TERRITORIAL SEAS

Thus far we have discussed the physical or geographical aspects of territorial seas; we will now see why territorial seas themselves are important. The law pertaining to territorial seas applies to every ship that sails the seven seas.

Territorial seas are "that part of the sea adjacent to the coast of a given country which is by International Law deemed to be within the sovereignty of that country." When the term *sovereignty*, or *jurisdiction*, is applied in connection with a land mass, it means control subject to but minor servitudes or rights of other countries. When it is used in connection with territorial seas, however, the sovereignty exercised there by the littoral state is subject to certain well-defined limitations. Moreover there are certain rights exercised by the littoral state over the territorial sea which are easily distinguishable from those exercised over the land mass.

Innocent Passage

Ships of all countries enjoy the right of innocent passage through one another's territorial seas; aircraft do not have the same right in the skies above them. Passage can be for the purpose of transit without entering internal waters, or of proceeding to internal waters, or of going to the high seas from internal waters. Passage, which must be continuous and expeditious, is innocent so long as it is not prejudicial to the peace, good order, or security of the coastal state. It includes stopping and anchoring if these actions are incident to ordinary navigation or are necessitated by distress or force majeure.

What would make passage prejudicial to the peace, good order, or security of the coastal state and therefore not innocent? Generally, any threat or use of force against the coastal state. More specifically, exercising with weapons, engaging in intelligence activities, launching or recovering aircraft or any other naval device, willfully polluting to a serious degree, fishing, and conducting research are among the activities that preclude qualification of a passage as innocent. Submarines and other underwater vehicles are required to navigate on the surface and to show their flag.

A coastal state has the right to take whatever steps are necessary to prevent a ship whose passage is not innocent from transiting its territorial sea. Warships, as noted elsewhere in the text, are treated differently.

The *Mayaguez* incident of 12 May 1975 is a vivid example of what can happen when a coastal state acts in the erroneous belief that passage was not innocent. The *Mayaguez*, a U.S. commercial cargo carrier, en route from Hong Kong to Singapore, using the normal steamship route, came within six or seven miles of Poulo Wai Island, which is fifty miles off the coast of Cambodia. At that point she was fired on by a Cambodian gunboat, boarded, and seized by the Cambodians who claimed a twelve-mile territorial sea. When extensive diplomatic initiatives produced no constructive responses, the U.S. Marines and naval destroyers and aircraft were used to effect a release.

A coastal state has the right to make laws and regulations relating to innocent passage through its territorial sea. Article 21 of Appendix D sets forth the specifics of matters upon which a coastal state may rule and requires that the said state give due publicity to such laws and regulations.

When a ship is passing through territorial seas on her way into internal waters, the coastal state has the additional right to take whatever steps are necessary to prevent her from breaking any of the rules that pertain to its internal waters. This is why customs and health inspectors usually board a ship before she enters internal waters. A coastal state may suspend the right of innocent passage in certain areas of its territorial seas if such suspension is considered essential to its national security; adequate publicity must be given to this action.

Coastal states have the right to require ships in innocent passage to use designated sea lanes and traffic-separation schemes. Such separation schemes or sea lanes must take into account the density of traffic and the recommendation of such competent international organizations as the Intergovernmental Maritime Consultative Organization. These provisions apply particularly to tankers, nuclear-powered ships, and cargo ships carrying nuclear material or inherently dangerous or noxious substances.

Certain duties accrue to a coastal state: it must refrain from discriminating in any way against the ships of any state and from imposing on foreign ships any requirement that has the effect of denying or impairing the right of innocent passage. Should any danger to navigation develop, the coastal state concerned must give it appropriate publicity. Further, the only charges it is entitled to levy are nondiscriminatory ones for specific services rendered to a ship.

Flying of Colors

A coastal state may prescribe rules as to the showing of flags and salutes to be rendered by ships passing through its territorial seas. The normal procedure is for a ship to fly her national flag when she is in the territorial seas of another state.

In February 1958, the Indonesian Navy stopped and held the British ship *Moon Breezes* for failure to fly British colors while she was in Indonesian territorial seas. Not all countries enforce the flying of colors in their territorial seas, but the safest procedure is to fly them in such waters.

STRAITS—TRANSIT PASSAGE

In June 1978, the Saudi Arabian government approved the construction of a 750-mile pipeline that will cut across the entire Arabian Peninsula to link oil wells on the Persian Gulf with the Red Sea and establish a major oil transportation route. One of the primary reasons for this decision was fear that Iran might blockade the Strait of Hormuz, thereby crippling Saudi Arabia's ability to export oil by the normal route through the Persian Gulf. (*The Washington Post*, 22 June 1978.)

When armed conflict broke out between Iran and Iraq in September 1980, world attention focused on the Strait of Hormuz and the vital need of the Western World and Japan to keep it open. As of this writing, several nations are discussing the formation of a multilateral naval group to ensure transit. President Carter stated: "Freedom of navigation in the Persian Gulf is of primary importance to the whole international community." (*The Wall Street Journal*, 25 September 1980.)

In 1967 the Gulf of Aqaba and its entrance, the Strait of Tiran, became one of the focal points of dispute between Egypt and Israel. Briefly, in order to interrupt ocean transport to the Israeli port of Elath, at the northern tip of the gulf, the Egyptian government announced that ships destined for Elath would be stopped at the Strait of Tiran. While this action was not the only cause of the Seven-Day War, which started very soon thereafter, it did serve to trigger that conflict.

Article V of the treaty of peace between Egypt and Israel, signed in Washington, D.C., on 26 March 1979, reads:

> The parties consider the Strait of Tiran and the Gulf of Aqaba to be international waterways open to all nations for unimpeded and nonsuspendable freedom of navigation and overflight. The parties will respect each other's right to navigation and overflight for access to either country through the Strait of Tiran and the Gulf of Aqaba.

Because of that provision no longer would the Strait of Tiran be considered a flash point of dispute.

The above examples demonstrate the fact that straits are focal points of navigation and thus their character and regime differ from the territorial sea of a normal coast. Straits, as currently defined, are waters used for international navigation between one area of the high seas or an exclusive economic zone and another area of the high seas or an exclusive economic zone.

It will be recalled that there is an interrelationship between the breadth of the territorial sea and straits, and this is what prompted the U.S. and other delegations to propose at the Third Law of the Sea Conference that there was a need to formulate a regime for straits not based on innocent passage but on a form of freedom of transit. It was noted that, with a twelve-mile territorial sea, many straits less than twenty-four miles wide, which, under the three-mile rule, were considered to be high seas, would become territorial seas. If no recognition were given to the unique characteristics of straits, freedom of navigation therein would depend upon whether or not passage were innocent. For the United States and many others, the need to have assured transit through straits, rather than the possible limitations of innocent passage, was considered to be vital and, indeed, acceptance of a twelve-mile territorial sea was contingent on it.

Speaking in Geneva on 3 August 1971, John R. Stevenson stated that

> the United States believes that straits wider than six miles currently have high seas within them, where States may exercise the freedoms of the high seas. In short, the present rule of international law in virtually all of the straits of concern is freedom of the seas. To achieve widespread international agreement we are prepared to give up high seas freedoms in these international straits in exchange for a limited but vital right. Subject only to the right of free transit, territorial waters in international straits would retain their national character in each and every respect. The new right of free transit would only apply in international straits, using the definition that was adopted at the 1958 Law of the Sea Conference; it would not apply to other territorial or internal waters. Moreover, the right is a narrow one—merely one of transiting the strait, not of conducting any other activities. Should a vessel conduct any other activities that are in violation of coastal State laws and regulations, it would be exceeding the scope of its right, and would be subject to appropriate enforcement action by the coastal State.

Another U.S. delegate, John Norton Moore, noted on 22 July 1974, during the conference's session in Caracas:

> The United States delegation has stated on numerous occasions the central importance that we attach to a satisfactory treaty regime of unimpeded transit through and over straits used for international navigation. Indeed, for states bordering as well as states whose ships and aircraft transit such straits, there could not be a successful Law of the Sea Conference unless this question is satisfactorily resolved. The inadequacies of the traditional doctrine of innocent passage—a concept developed not for transit through straits but for passage through a narrow belt of territorial sea—are well known.
>
> We are appreciative of the strong trend in the debates as well as several proposals recently introduced in this Committee which reflect an understanding of the importance of navigation and overflight through straits for the global flow of trade and communications and for a stable and peaceful world order. These proposals also reflect that there need be no conflict between the interests of states transiting and states bordering straits. While unimpeded transit of straits used for international navigation is vital to achieving a successful treaty, we can and must also protect the interests of states bordering straits. . . .
>
> Unimpeded transit is a right of transit, not a right to engage in activities inimical to the security of these coastal states. It is solely a right of the

transiting ship or aircraft to transit the strait. That is, to enter the strait, pass through or over in the normal mode using customary navigational routes and applicable traffic separation schemes, and then to exit the strait.

The waters in straits that are twenty-four or less miles wide are territorial. If the land on both sides of a strait belongs to one state, then obviously the waters therein belong to that state.

If one state owns one shoreline and another state owns the one opposite, each exercises sovereignty within the limits of its own territorial waters. If the strait is less than twenty-four miles wide, the boundary line is established in the middle of it or in mid-channel. If the strait is wider than twenty-four miles, waters between the two twelve-mile limits are considered to be in the exclusive economic zones of the bordering states.

Obviously the major straits of concern include Gibraltar, Malacca, Dover, and Magellan. Some straits are controlled by particular treaties; the Bosporus, for example, is controlled by the Montreux Convention.

Admiral Harold E. Shear, USN, Commander in Chief, Allied Forces, Southern Europe, at the time of the following incident, tells how a treaty can operate under changing technology and points to what he considers to be some present-day inadequacies:

On 18 July 1976, following initial construction and despite vigorous Western criticism, the Soviet combatant KIEV transited the Turkish Straits from the Black Sea, en route to operations in the Mediterranean and assignment with the northern fleet. Again on 7 February 1978, KIEV transited the Straits into the Black Sea. Finally, on 19 March 1978, KIEV transited the Turkish Straits a third time, en route back to the Soviet northern fleet.

KIEV, a combatant carrying military aircraft which operate from a flight deck, is defined as an aircraft carrier by the West, but as an antisubmarine warfare (ASW) cruiser by the Soviets. Thus, the Soviets attributed to the ship an air capability that is only incidental to its mission.

The Montreux Convention on the Straits signed on 20 July 1936 by, among others, the Soviet Union and Turkey, allows single passage of "capital ships" of greater than 16,000 tons, escorted by not more than two destroyers (Articles 11 and 14, Montreux Convention). While these articles would seem to permit transit of an aircraft carrier, such is not the case since the definition of the term "capital ship" (Annex to the Convention of Montreux, Treaty for the Limitation of Naval Armament, London, 25 March 1936) *specifically excludes* aircraft carriers.

The ASW cruiser designation for the Soviet carrier, along with an armament of SAMs and SSMs, have apparently constituted sufficient grounds for these ships to be categorized as other than aircraft carriers. This appears to have been the approach taken by Turkish authorities who control the straits, and by the NATO Alliance which has acquiesced. The key phrase in this issue lies in the Convention's definition of aircraft carriers ". . . primarily for the purpose of carrying and operating aircraft at sea."

This incident stands as an example of a forty-year-old treaty which has become anachronistic due to such factors as inadequate specificity in the articles and definitions of the original Convention, the then-unforeseen current varieties and utilization of combatant vessels, the pressure and realities of superpower involvement, and perhaps, most basically, of a world and military balance that has evolved into something distinctly different than that present in 1936.

Rights and Obligations regarding Transit Passage of Straits

In general all ships and aircraft enjoy the right of unimpeded transit passage of straits, as understood in the exercise of freedom of navigation and overflight solely for the purpose of continuous and expeditious transit. Specific obligations of transiting ships and aircraft include the obvious requirement that they refrain from any threat or use of force against a state bordering a strait. Except when in distress or restrained by force majeure, ships must adhere to normal navigational standards during transit and comply with the Rules of the Road and international regulations for the prevention, reduction, and control of pollution. Submarines transiting a strait are not required to be on the surface, as they are in innocent passage through a territorial sea. (*See* Appendix E.) No ship, including marine research and hydrographic survey ships, may conduct any research during transit of a foreign strait, unless authorization has been obtained from the bordering state or states.

Civil aircraft are required to apply the Rules of the Air established by the International Civil Aviation Organization; state and military aircraft will normally adhere to the same safety measures and will, specifically, and at all times operate with due regard for the safety of navigation. All aircraft are also required to monitor the internationally designated air-traffic control circuit or distress radio frequency.

States bordering straits have an obligation to refrain from hampering or suspending transit passage. This principle does not preclude their enacting laws and regulations governing ships that exercise the right of transit, and compliance therewith, after they have been given adequate publicity, is mandatory. Laws or regulations may be enacted in the interests of safe navigation, control of traffic, control, reduction, and prevention of pollution, prevention or control of fishing, and matters concerning customs and immigration. A bordering state, however, is under an obligation to ensure that implementation of its restrictions would not have the practical effect of denying or hampering the right of transit passage through the strait. It is also obliged to ensure that such laws do not discriminate in form or in fact amongst foreign ships.

Of particular importance to ships or aircraft entitled to sovereign immunity is the fact that, should they contravene such laws and regulations, their flag state is responsible for any resulting loss or damage to a bordering state.

Passage through Canals

Man-made canals are controlled by agreement between the countries most concerned. In peacetime they are open to the use of all ships, subject to a toll for the transit service. The warships of belligerent countries may use a canal in which they have no title or interest: for example, during the Italian-Ethiopian war Italian warships regularly transited the Suez Canal. A belligerent can, however, deny enemy warships the use of a canal in which it does have title or interest: for example, in both world wars, ships of the Axis powers and their allies were denied the use of both the Panama Canal and the Suez Canal; also, when Egypt was at war with Israel, she denied Israeli ships the use of the Suez Canal.

The provisions of the Treaty Concerning the Permanent Neutrality and Operation of the Panama Canal, signed on 7 September 1977, depart from historical practice. Article I of that treaty reads in part:

> The Republic of Panama declares that the Canal, as an international transit waterway, shall be permanently neutral. . . .

In amplification of that principle, Article II reads in part:

> The Republic of Panama declares the neutrality of the Canal in order that both in time of peace and in time of war it shall remain secure and open to peaceful transit by the vessels of all nations on terms of entire equality, so that there will be no discrimination against any nation, or its citizens or subjects, concerning the conditions or charges of transit, or for any other reason, and so that the Canal, and therefore the Isthmus of Panama, shall not be the target of reprisals in any armed conflict between other nations of the world. . . .

Basically, the above language defines what the parties mean by neutrality, i.e., nondiscriminatory operation of the canal. In addition to indicating that the security of the canal is a vital element of its neutrality, the article contains the basic commitment to keep the canal open. The phrase *in time of peace and in time of war* gives access to all ships for transit including ships of nations at war with either the United States or Panama. Obviously, such provision does not prevent either or both countries from taking legitimate measures against enemy shipping outside the waters of the canal. (For the full text of the treaty, *see* Appendix C.)

On 26 March 1979 Israel and Egypt ended their thirty-year belligerency by signing a treaty of peace. Article V, paragraph 1, of that document incorporates specific provision for use of the Suez Canal:

> Ships of Israel, and cargoes destined for or coming from Israel, shall enjoy the right of free passage through the Suez Canal and its approaches through

the Gulf of Suez and the Mediterranean Sea on the basis of the Constantino-
ple Convention of 1888, applying to all nations. Israeli nationals, vessels and
cargoes, as well as persons, vessels and cargoes destined for or coming from
Israel, shall be accorded nondiscriminatory treatment in all matters connected with usage of the Canal.

Passage through Archipelagic Waters

As stated above, an archipelagic state may draw straight base lines joining
the outermost points of its outermost islands and drying reefs. Those base
lines are used for measuring the various jurisdictions seaward of them,
including the territorial sea.

Waters interior to the above-described base lines are termed *archipelagic
waters*, and control over them is sovereign. This sovereignty, similar to
sovereignty over territorial seas, extends to the air space over them, the
seabed under them, and the resources found there. Within its archipelagic
waters, a state may draw closing lines for the delimitation of internal waters.
Subject to the above general characterization, archipelagic waters differ in
some ways from the territorial sea.

Fisheries that existed before the Third Law of the Sea Conference
defined archipelagic waters shall be recognized and permitted to continue
under bilateral arrangements with the archipelagic state concerned. In like
manner, submarine cables laid by other states may be maintained and
replaced without interference by the archipelagic state, provided that state is
given due notice of repair or replacement.

All ships enjoy the right of innocent passage through archipelagic waters, but the archipelagic state has the right to suspend it without discrimination, upon due notice being given, if such suspension is essential to its
security. Should it so choose, an archipelagic state may designate sea lanes
and air routes to provide the safe, continuous, and expeditious passage of
foreign ships and aircraft through and over its waters. These sea lanes and
air routes include all traffic routes that were used before the sea and air lanes
were instituted. In the interest of safety of transit along designated sea lanes,
traffic-separation schemes may be prescribed for narrow channels through
navigationally obstructed waters.

The institution of both sea lanes and traffic-separation schemes shall
conform in general to international regulations. An archipelagic state is
required to have its plans for such regimes reviewed by the Intergovernmental Maritime Consultative Organization.

The rights and duties of ships and aircraft during their passage and the
corresponding rights and responsibilities of an archipelagic state concerning
such passage are similar to those inherent in innocent passage through the
territorial sea.

THE CONTIGUOUS ZONE

Separate from the territorial sea is a zone that borders, or is contiguous to, the territorial sea. A contiguous zone may not extend more than twenty-four miles from the base line from which the breadth of the territorial sea is measured. Therefore, if a territorial sea is twelve miles wide, so is the contiguous zone. Within its contiguous zone, a coastal state may exercise control to prevent infringement of its customs, fiscal, sanitary, or immigration laws. When a coastal state's customs, fiscal, immigration, or sanitary regulations have been violated within its territory or territorial sea, it may punish the offender in the contiguous zone.

HOT PURSUIT

The doctrine of *hot pursuit* pertains to the situation in which a ship violates the law of a coastal state while in that state's territorial sea, and a coast guard cutter or warship goes out to seize her. The offending craft then tries to escape by making for the open seas and successfully clears the territorial sea. Because the speed differential between the pursued and the pursuer is small, the chase extends for hundreds of miles out to sea before the pursued ship is stopped and seized. It would seem that, by exercising jurisdiction far beyond its territorial seas, the coastal state had violated what has been said about territorial seas and their limits. Nevertheless, the procedure is universally accepted as valid under International Law. It is known as *the right of hot pursuit* and is predicated on the theory that, had it not been for the attempted escape, the arrest would have been effected within the jurisdiction of the coastal state. The logical and accepted conclusion is, therefore, that if the offender were allowed to go free simply because of the proximity of the high seas, the effective administration of justice would be obstructed.

To amplify the above, a coastal state may act not only when a ship has in fact violated its law, but also when it has good reason to believe that a ship has done so. In either event, however, the pursuit must begin while the ship or at least one of her boats is in waters wherein the law or regulation applies. Further, a ship in the contiguous zone, the exclusive economic zone, or on the continental shelf may be pursued only if she has violated the rights for the protection of which the area was established. In the case of a ship engaged in fishing outside the exclusive economic zone and her small boats breaking the fishing law while fishing within the exclusive economic zone the mother ship is considered to be present in the zone, and the right of hot pursuit applies to her.

While it is clear that an offending ship must be in a particular zone at the time of her violation, there is no requirement that the pursuing craft be in the same zone. Pursuit may be begun only after a visual or sound signal to stop has been given in such a way that the offending ship can see or hear it. Other prerequisites for legal hot pursuit are that the pursuit must begin immediately and be hot and continuous. A pursuit that is broken off and rejoined later is not legal hot pursuit. Only ships or aircraft identifiable as being in government service may be used in pursuit.

There is no restriction on the length of a pursuit. However, if the offending ship enters the territorial seas of another country, the right of hot pursuit terminates.

The doctrine of hot pursuit has been broadened to meet technological advances that fit present and future probabilities. First, the law provides that as long as the heat and continuity of pursuit are maintained, other warships or government service craft may relieve the original pursuer. Second, it establishes the right of a state-owned aircraft to order a violating ship to stop her activities and to pursue her, if necessary, out into the high seas. If an aircraft cannot itself make the arrest, it may call on a state-owned ship to join in, or take over, the pursuit and make the arrest.

5

Ships

A ship is born when she is launched and lives so long as her identity is preserved. Prior to her launching she is a mere congeries of wood and iron, an ordinary piece of personal property. . . . In her baptism of launching she receives her name, and from the moment her keel touches the water she is transformed. . . .

Tucker *v.* Alexandroff

INTRODUCTION

In time of peace the high seas are free for the lawful use of all. Lawful use includes maritime commerce, the laying of submarine cables, training exercises by naval surface and air units, fishing, and scientific research. Since the high seas are not under the sovereignty of any state, the preservation of law and order on them falls within the domain of International Law. Until the advent of the technological advances of the present century, virtually the only users of the oceans were men in surface ships. Accordingly a very large segment of International Law is concerned with ships.

RULES OF THE ROAD

From the earliest days of seafaring, the need for order on the seas has been recognized by mariners and, even before there was a community of nations, there had grown up a rudimentary common law designed to bring it about. In later centuries, although there was no treaty governing such matters, most of the maritime nations adopted essentially the same set of navigational rules. To a greater or lesser degree, each maritime state followed the example of England, the pace-setter in this as in other maritime affairs. It was not until 1895, however, that multilateral treaties covering such things pertaining to ships as lookouts, lights to be displayed at night, movements in a meeting or crossing situation, and whistle signals were brought into effect.

Today almost all matters affecting ships are governed by the International Regulations for Preventing Collisions at Sea, 1972. Mariners know this body of law as the International Rules of the Road, or 72 COLREGS, and the following statistics show that their importance cannot be overemphasized.

In 1966, the total world tonnage of merchant ships was 177 million tons; in 1975, it was 342 million tons: in 1950, 550 million tons of cargo were transported across the world's oceans; in 1959, 996 million tons; in 1969, 2,132 million tons; and in 1975, 3,420 million tons.

In recognition of the importance of the Rules of the Road, a federal interagency committee, on which the Navy Department and the Coast Guard are represented, was set up to act on changes to the Rules of the Road recommended by any concerned individual. This committee is also involved in preparing positions on changes for international consideration. Most of the four-year preparatory work for the conference held by the 106 member states of the Intergovernmental Maritime Consultative Organization (IMCO), which drew up the International Rules of the Road, 1972, was done by the above committee.

THE FUNCTION OF IMCO

A brief description of IMCO and its function is pertinent. It is a specialized agency of the United Nations to which all the major shipping nations of the world belong. It was created to provide machinery for cooperation among governments in shipping matters. For example, it developed international safety standards for passenger ships and, following the *Yarmouth Castle* disaster in 1966, those standards were applied more broadly than they had been theretofore.

On 18 March 1967, while nearing the end of a voyage to Milford Haven in Wales, the *Torrey Canyon*, a supertanker of 120,890 deadweight tons capacity, under Liberian registry, foundered in international waters between the Scilly Isles and Land's End, England. The accident resulted in thousands of tons of crude oil being washed up on the resort beaches of southwestern England and northwestern France. So extensive was the damage to the coasts and to fish and wildlife that worldwide attention was focused on the need for measures to prevent such accidents and to minimize ill effects if they should occur.

In the aftermath of the disaster, the United Kingdom called for a meeting of the IMCO Council, the organization's administrative body, in order to study measures that might be taken regarding future incidents. As a result of the meeting, which was held in London, IMCO launched an eighteen-point program for dealing with various technical and legal aspects of marine pollution. The next year the IMCO Assembly, which met in extraordinary session to consider this program, approved certain measures designed to prevent similar accidents and to promote rapid and effective action if they should occur. Most recently, IMCO held two conferences dealing with maritime safety.

The first conference, in February 1978, was concerned with the safety of tankers and the prevention of pollution. It was the result of a U.S. initiative, which in turn followed a series of tanker accidents. The record in 1976 was like a bad dream:

1. In January, the 275,000-ton supertanker, *Olympic Bravery*, the biggest ship ever wrecked, ran aground off the coast of Cuesant Island, near Brittany, and broke up.
2. In October, the 10,000-ton East German tanker, *Bohlen*, sank with the loss of twenty-five lives off Sein Island, also off Brittany. In an operation that cost three lives and millions of dollars, about 8,000 tons of the oil was pumped from the sunken ship.
3. The largest recent spill in American waters occurred in December 1976 when the *Argo Merchant* discharged 180,000 barrels of oil off Nantucket.

In 1977, off the coast of South Africa, two tankers with combined cargoes of 3.1 million barrels collided, creating the potential for a massive spill. Fortunately, both ships were taken into port before any serious damage was done.

As noted, the aim of the 1978 conference was to find ways of improving the safety of tankers and preventing pollution from ships. The conference adopted strengthening protocols to two conventions, the 1973 Marine Pollution Convention and the 1974 Safety of Life at Sea Convention.

The second conference was originally scheduled for late 1978, its purpose being to consider the training and certification of shipboard personnel. In March 1978, however, a vivid example of what might have been lack of training resulted in its being moved up to June. The American-owned 237,000-ton supertanker, *Amoco Cadiz*, registered in Liberia, lost steering control in heavy weather, delayed arranging to be towed, and broke in two on some rocks, again just off the coast of Brittany. This accident resulted in the world's biggest oil spill; damage to French beaches, fish, and wildlife was extensive. In noting the tragedy and the fact that a conference on crew-training was scheduled for June of that year, Roger Kohn, spokesman for IMCO, stated, "Eighty per cent of all accidents at sea are caused by human error."

Its work on setting safety standards in ship construction and in the training of personnel, makes IMCO the recognized U.N. authority in those important fields.

SEA LANES

Continuing expansion in the number, size, variety, and speed of ships has created high density in shipping lanes and at points of convergence off major harbors and in narrow straits. For example, some 750 ships transit the Strait of Dover every day. The establishment of sea traffic lanes, similar to road traffic lanes, would obviously serve to lessen the possibility of collision yet, to date, their establishment has been slowed by mariners' insistence on their time-honored right of freedom to navigate.

The collision between the *Andrea Doria* and the *Stockholm* off Nantucket in July 1956 plus the growing concern of IMCO led to the concept of sea lanes being looked upon with more favor and produced some concrete results. For example, a survey of more than 10,000 ship captains conducted by the navigation institutes of Great Britain, France, and West Germany made it possible for IMCO in 1964 to advise all member states that their ships should use designated sea lanes through the Strait of Dover. Consideration is now being given to the establishment of offshore safety zones near points of convergence in such areas as the Baltic and North seas.

On the initiative of the U.S. Coast Guard, traffic-separation lanes in the approaches to New York Harbor and in Delaware Bay were established in 1967. These lanes and six other U.S. schemes can now be found on charts issued by the National Ocean Survey, a branch of the Department of Commerce. All told, approximately eighty traffic-separation schemes throughout the world have been adopted by IMCO.

Rule 10 of the International Rules of the Road, 1972, provides for the control of vessels operating in or crossing a traffic-separation scheme adopted by IMCO. Use of an adopted scheme is voluntary but a ship that uses such a scheme must comply with Rule 10. Of particular interest is the fact that some countries, France and the United Kingdom, for example, have certain schemes under surveillance and are reporting contraventions of Rule 10 to the flag state of the guilty ship.

APPLICATION OF THE RULES OF THE ROAD

The International Rules of the Road furnish perhaps the best refutation there is for the arguments of those who say that International Law is not concrete or is not enforceable. Ask the insurer or owner of a ship at fault in a collision at sea whether the International Rules are enforceable. His answer will undoubtedly be an emphatic "Yes!" The insurer might add that enforcement of the rules can prove very expensive.

With only minor concessions made to warships because of their peculiar construction, the rules are applicable to vessels of all types—be they rowboats or ocean liners, warships or merchant ships, privately or government-owned, conventionally or nuclear-powered. Every large maritime nation has courts that are empowered to try collision cases coming within their cognizance and to make awards for damages suffered. It makes no difference whether the court be American, British, Japanese, or Russian; it deals in International Law, which is uniformly applied to ships of all nationalities.

The significance of the Rules of the Road to a naval officer is compounded when he is operating with other ships. The incident described below by Rear Admiral L. A. Bryan, USN, demonstrates the heavy responsibility that can be placed in the hands of a commanding officer. The political overtones at the time of the incident are of transitory interest—yet those same overtones might have been the cause of the incident.

During the period of time that I was Commanding Officer of the USS *Northampton*, Flagship of Commander Striking Fleet Atlantic, a good many of our operations took place in Northern European waters. On the occasion in mind, the *Northampton* was the guide of a long column of ships proceeding through restricted waters of the swept channel through the mine fields in the Kattegat. Visibility was good and the sea was calm. A small ship was sighted on the port bow. An initial plot showed that she would pass well clear of the column. However, within a few minutes the contact increased speed and closed the *Northampton* on a collision course. As the range closed, the obvious danger increased; I was able to identify the contact as a Soviet-bloc-country fishing trawler.

I sounded the danger signal when the trawler was approximately 3,000 yards distant. Nothing happened. I sounded it again at a range of approximately 1,800 yards. Again nothing happened. Before the point *in extremis* was reached, I backed full and so notified the column of my reversed engines. All the ships in the column stopped. At this point the trawler, about 800 yards on my port bow, changed course to the right, slowed, and proceeded leisurely down the entire column at about 200 yards distance.

It was my impression throughout that the trawler was well aware of our presence and had no intention of actually causing a collision. There was no question but that the trawler had the inherent right to be where she was and that no breach involving damages could accrue under the International Rules of the Road as written. If her maneuvers were for the purpose of harassing, and I think they were, she certainly succeeded.

Admittedly, an instance of this type is rare, yet when it does happen restraint is manifestly most difficult.

Other such incidents that caught the attention of the world press occurred on 11 and 12 May 1967, when two collisions involving the destroyer USS *Walker* (Commander S. W. McClaran) and Soviet naval ships resulted from what appeared to be harassment by the Soviets. Damage was minor and the *Walker* was able to continue with her task-group operations in the Sea of Japan. In both cases the United States protested, charging harassment and violation of the Rules of the Road.

In October 1971, U.S.-U.S.S.R. consultations were held in Moscow on measures that might be taken by naval ships to reduce the likelihood of incidents such as those described above. The U.S. delegation was headed by John W. Warner, then undersecretary of the navy.

The following words, written on 22 May 1978 by Chief of Naval Operations James L. Holloway III, show what can be achieved by such consultations and negotiations.

Of course, United States naval operations are shaped and controlled by international law, both customary or conventional. One international agreement in particular which has contributed to peace and safety is the Agreement Between the United States of America and the Union of Soviet Socialist Republics for Prevention of Incidents On and Over the High Seas (INCSEA Agreement). . . .

Since the INCSEA Agreement (which is a Navy-to-Navy agreement) was signed in Moscow on 25 May 1972, incidents have decreased to a minimum level. In the INCSEA Agreement, the U.S. and USSR recognize that their freedom to conduct operations on the high seas is based on the principles established under international law. The two nations agree to instruct the commanding officers of their respective ships to observe strictly the letter and spirit of the International Rules of the Road. Specific guidelines are set forth, for situations such as surveillance or when operating near ships restricted in maneuvering ability by flight operations or replenishment, to supplement the Rules of the Road and thereby reduce risk of mutual interference. Special signals have been developed to supplement those in the International Code of Signals which permit the ships to signal their intentions or to warn of potential hazards.

Annual reviews are held to evaluate the effectiveness of the INCSEA Agreement, with the site of the review alternating between capitals. In addition, specific complaints, by either party, are discussed as they arise. Considering the frequent close proximity of operation of ships and aircraft of the two navies, some incidents still are likely to occur, but it cannot be denied that the frequency of such incidents has dropped dramatically and regular channels of communication between the two navies are open and functioning.

Geographic Areas of Application

It is important for the mariner to know that the International Rules of the Road do not apply only on the high seas. Unless a nation prescribes otherwise, they apply in territorial seas and national waters. For example, in the United States, which has adopted a set of Inland Rules that differ in some respects from the International Rules, the boundary between the areas in which the Inland Rules apply and those governed by the International Rules is not the boundary between the territorial seas and the high seas. The boundary between these last two domains is generally fixed with relation to some easily recognizable geographical line. Therefore, there are large water areas under the sovereignty of the United States but subject to the International Rules of the Road. Also, as a matter of convenience, the U.S. Inland Rules apply to certain areas of the high seas adjacent to territorial seas. It is important for the sailor to know that other nations, too, have rules for seas that are subject to their sovereignty. It behooves any sailor bound for the territorial seas or national waters of another country to determine in advance whether that country has its own navigational rules or whether the International Rules of the Road apply.

NUCLEAR POWER PLANTS AT SEA

At 1100 on 17 January 1955, the USS *Nautilus* flashed the message, "Under way on nuclear power." The atom had gone to sea, not as an instrument of destruction but as a form of energy. Since that date, more and more submarines and surface ships have been equipped with nuclear power plants.

Today the law of the sea makes no distinction between nuclear-powered ships and conventionally powered ships. However, when nuclear power first went to sea there were factors in its use that challenged the law as it existed. Atomic power was first used as a devastating explosive with damaging residuals, and people found it difficult to separate the two uses—one to provide propulsion, the other to inflict damage. How could one use be "safe" when the other was so destructive? The thought was also expressed that, even supposing shielding made a nuclear power plant relatively "safe," some radiation must escape and in a harbor or a fishing area such leaks would surely do damage. Furthermore, if a nuclear-powered ship were to be in a collision or to run aground near land, would there not be a risk of contamination or even of an explosion creating a deadly situation? These apprehensions pointed to the central question: should nuclear-powered ships enjoy the same freedom of navigation as ships with conventional power plants? The answer is indicated in the following excerpt from an article entitled "The Atom at Sea," written by Captain Leonard R. Hardy, USN, and published in *JAG Journal*, April 1959:

> A basic concept which must be accepted in any study of the law of nuclear powered ships is that such ships can be designed, built and operated in such a manner that they pose no significant hazard to man and his resources. There is certainly ample evidence to support the validity of that hypothesis. Another necessary hypothesis is that the general use of nuclear power is desirable for man's over-all welfare. In this connection, it is generally conceded that there will ultimately be a crucial shortage of fossil fuels; therefore it is reasonable to assume the desirability of nuclear fuels.

> Based upon the two hypotheses stated above, it is clearly apparent that nuclear powered ships should enjoy the freedom of operation afforded their conventional sisters. There can be no doubt, however, that nuclear fuels may be potentially more dangerous than any other power source which has been used on the seas. The law should, therefore, strike a happy medium. It must provide for virtually complete freedom of action for *safe* nuclear powered ships, but almost complete prohibition against ships which are *not safe*.

WARSHIPS

The U.S. Navy's publication, *Law of Naval Warfare* (NWIP 10-2) says:

> The term 'warships' includes all vessels commissioned as a part of the naval forces of a state and authorized to display the appropriate flag or

pennant as evidence thereof. Such vessels must in addition be commanded by a member of the military forces of a state and must be manned by a crew subject to military discipline.

The Third Law of the Sea Conference arrived at a parallel definition:

"Warship" means a ship belonging to the armed forces of a state bearing the external marks distinguishing such ships of its nationality, under the command of an officer duly commissioned by the government of the state and whose name appears in the appropriate service list or its equivalent, and manned by a crew which is under regular armed forces discipline.

A ship that meets these requirements is therefore classified as a warship and enjoys a particular status in International Law, whether she be in port or on the high seas.

ON THE HIGH SEAS

According to A. P. Higgins, a noted authority on International Law, "warships represent the sovereignty and independence of their State more fully than anything else can represent it on the ocean; they can be met only by their equals there, and equals cannot exercise jurisdiction over equals. The jurisdiction of their own state over them is therefore exclusive under all circumstances and any act of interference with them on the part of a foreign State is an act of war." (*International Law of the Sea.*)

When ships owned or operated by a state and used only on governmental noncommercial service are on the high seas, they are considered to be in the same category as warships and enjoy the same immunity. Most Military Sealift Command (MSC) ships fall within this definition.

Does the above statement mean that a warship on the high seas is free of all restrictions—free to do as she pleases? Clearly not. In this field, as in all others, responsibility accompanies privilege. A U.S. federal court rendered the following rationalization of warships' freedom from foreign interference:

The immunity granted to diplomatic representatives of a sovereign and to its vessels of war . . . can be safely accorded, because the limited numbers and the ordinarily responsible character of the diplomats or agents in charge of the property in question and the dignity and honor of the sovereignty in whose services they are, make abuse of such immunity rare.

It can be seen, therefore, that just as interference with a warship on the high seas is a direct affront to the sovereign in whose service she is employed, the abuse of privilege by a warship is a reflection upon the dignity and honor of that same sovereign. For this reason every nation with a navy attempts, by tradition and regulation, to ensure that its warships comport themselves at all times in a manner that can bring only credit to the nation they represent.

Correlative to the privileges accorded warships are certain duties which the community of nations has imposed upon them. Perhaps the foremost of these today is the obligation to give all possible aid to vessels and aircraft in distress. The Third Law of the Sea Conference reinforced this principle by stating that every state shall require the commanding officers of its ships:

(a) to render assistance to any person found at sea in danger of being lost;
(b) to proceed with all possible speed to the rescue of persons in distress, if informed of their need of assistance, in so far as such action may reasonably be expected of him;
(c) after a collision, to render assistance to the other ship, its crew and its passengers, and where possible, to inform the other ship of the name of his own ship, its port of registry, and the nearest port at which it will call.

Articles 0925 and 1144 of *U.S. Navy Regulations* provide:

1. Insofar as he can do so without serious danger to his ship or crew, the commanding officer or the senior officer present as appropriate shall:
   a. Proceed with all possible speed to the rescue of persons in distress if informed of their need for assistance, insofar as such action may reasonably be expected of him.
   b. Render assistance to any person found at sea in danger of being lost.
2. When so authorized by the senior officer present, a commanding officer may issue such supplies as can be spared to those in distress in the event of a public exigency or calamity, or to vessels in distress.

While this duty is of particular importance to warships, all ships at sea have the same general responsibility, as the following incident indicates:

On 27 October 1978 a U.S. Navy reconnaissance plane caught fire in flight and plunged into the Bering Sea. Upon learning of the crash, many of the Soviet fishing boats in the area sped to the scene. The trawler *Mys Senyavina* rescued the ten survivors, who had been in life rafts for twelve hours, and rushed them to the nearby port of Petropavlovsk-Kamchatski, where they were hospitalized. Upon recovery the crew was returned to the United States.

All coastal states are required to promote effective search and rescue capabilities both on and over the sea and, where appropriate, work out arrangements with neighboring states.

Piracy

Warships have a duty to suppress piracy.

In popular thought, piracy is a thing of the past and the passage of time has lent a bit of romance to Captain Kidd, Morgan, the brothers Barbarossa, and Blackbeard. By 1820 piracy had been to some extent controlled as a result of strong punitive action by legitimate users of the sea. That being the case, it is interesting that nine of the twenty-nine operative articles of the 1958 Geneva Convention on the High Seas deal with piracy and its control.

Apparently, this attention was given to the subject simply because no other international convention had dealt with it and there was considerable controversy among the experts over what constituted piracy. The fact that piracy still existed in some remote areas also served to direct attention to it.

What does constitute piracy? According to Article 15 of the 1958 Convention on the High Seas, piracy consists of any of the following acts:

(1) Any illegal acts of violence, detention or any act of depredation, committed for private ends by the crew or the passengers of a private ship or a private aircraft, and directed:
  (a) On the high seas, against another ship or aircraft, or against persons or property on board such ship or aircraft;
  (b) Against a ship, aircraft, persons or property in a place outside the jurisdiction of any State;
(2) Any act of voluntary participation in the operation of a ship or of an aircraft with knowledge of facts making it a pirate ship or aircraft;
(3) Any act of inciting or of intentionally facilitating an act described in sub-paragraph 1 or sub-paragraph 2 of this article.

While the above definition, reiterated in the negotiating text of the Third Law of the Sea Conference, has been generally acknowledged by the world community, it is considered to be the narrow view of piracy because it restricts it to unlawful acts committed by a private ship (or aircraft) against another ship (or aircraft) for private ends, i.e., robbery or other crimes against the person or property. The broad view postulates that a violent act committed within a ship (or aircraft) can constitute piracy: in other words, in order to be considered piratical, an act does not have to be committed against "another ship (or aircraft)." Furthermore, authorities who favor the broad view are of the opinion that an act committed for other than private ends can constitute piracy. The significance and consequences of accepting the narrow, in lieu of the broad, view came into sharp focus in 1961, when the case of the Portuguese cruise ship *Santa Maria* arose. Admiral Robert L. Dennison, USN, then Commander in Chief, Atlantic Fleet, described the sequence of events as viewed from his headquarters at Norfolk, Virginia:

> The initial report was received at Atlantic Fleet Headquarters in Norfolk late on the afternoon of January 23rd from the United Kingdom's Senior Naval Officer, West Indies, who was at Santa Lucia, where Captain Galvao had put ashore by boat several wounded members of the *Santa Maria*'s crew. The report advised that the cruise ship *Santa Maria*, registered under the Portuguese flag, had been forcibly taken over by a group of about 70 passengers armed with machine guns and grenades. It appeared that piracy might have occurred. The Senior Naval Officer, West Indies, requested that the United States Atlantic Fleet arrange and co-ordinate a search for the ship in areas to the north of Trinidad and advised he would search to the south and east. The ship's schedule called for her to sail from Curaçao, Netherlands

West Indies, to Miami, Florida; however, there was no clear indication where she was bound. A large ocean area had to be searched to cover all possible locations of *Santa Maria*. Many conflicting reports from civil aircraft, merchant ships and other sources had to be investigated in an area of numerous islands and relatively heavy shipping.

Ships and aircraft of the Atlantic Fleet engaged in training maneuvers in Puerto Rican waters were ordered into this extensive search. Instructions at this time to United States ships were to board the vessel to determine if piracy in fact had occurred and, if so, to bring the ship to the nearest United States port, presumably San Juan, using force as necessary.

Expert legal opinions in the United States were unable to support a finding of piracy in international law. Therefore the need no longer existed to determine piracy by boarding and exercising force. Appropriate modifying orders were dispatched to the naval forces involved. The safeguarding of United States nationals embarked and the humanitarian interest for all other passengers and crew members of the ship still remained as a basis for continuing action.

Galvao and his followers had peacefully boarded the *Santa Maria* while she was in port, and, without the assistance of any other ship, seized her when she was at sea. Galvao claimed that his purpose was to overthrow the government of Portugal and that the seizure was symbolic of the coming revolution. No private gain, such as robbery, was envisioned.

From the above it follows that no act of piracy, as defined in the narrow view, had taken place. Yet, it is the author's opinion that Galvao acted without authority, obtained control of the ship by force, changed her course, and left her passengers and crew in suspense as to their fate. It appears that what took place was an essentially hazardous disruption that was representative of likely occurrences at sea and that must be met by the world community. An appropriate approach might be to substitute the criterion of "without due authority" for that of "private ends." Similarly, the requirement that the illegal acts be directed against "another" ship seems too limiting, for it makes a technical point of how the pirates arrived aboard the victim ship. How or where they got on board is of little consequence, as long as their purpose was to take control by use or threat of violence. The primary test of piracy is the act itself and not the mechanics of setting the stage for it. Notwithstanding the rationale in support of the broader view of piracy, the narrow view, as described earlier in this section, is generally settled law and is applicable in cases involving piracy.

An even more acute situation arises when an aircraft is seized in flight. Since 1961 the frequency of the seizure of aircraft in flight in many areas of the world has increased. Characteristically, seizures involve the use of international air space. It is most difficult to determine whether the seizure was made for "private ends" or not. In no case up to the time of publication has "another" aircraft been involved, and it has been difficult to determine whether or not the seizures were made for "private ends." Consequently, it has not been possible to consider any case that has arisen so far as piratical under the present criteria.

The need to modify the definition with regard to aircraft appears to be even greater than the need to modify it with regard to ships. For those bent on piracy, it is clearly better to board the chosen aircraft before it is airborne than to attempt the almost impossible task of intercepting and boarding it in flight. Further, while piracy at sea is dangerous enough, a violent act in the air manifestly creates a greater immediate danger to life and property and is, therefore, more demanding of international control. In regard to the requirement that for an act to constitute piracy it must be committed for "private ends," an airplane is obviously a poor choice of property with which to try to abscond. While in the air, the usurper can maintain control, but once he lands, his problem becomes complex indeed. If his act were automatically qualified as piracy, his problem would be even greater.

Right of Approach or Visit

In order to enable warships to carry out their duty in suppressing piracy, the community of nations recognized that they possess what came to be known as the *right of approach* and could exercise it with regard to the ships of any nation in peace as well as in war. In 1826, Judge Joseph Story of the U.S. Supreme Court, in a famous case involving the seizure of the Portuguese merchantman *Marianna Flora* by the USS *Alligator*, described the right:

> In respect to ships of war, sailing, as in the present case, under the authority of their government, to arrest pirates, and other public offenders, there is no reason why they may not approach any vessels descried at sea, for the purpose of ascertaining their real characters. Such a right seems indispensable for the fair and discreet exercise of their authority.... On the other hand, it is as clear, that no ship is, under such circumstances, bound to lie by, or wait the approach of any other (war) ship.... These principles seem to us the natural result of the common duties and rights of nations, navigating the ocean in time of peace. Such a state of things carries with it very different obligations and responsibilities from those which belong to public war, and is not to be confounded with it.

When a warship, exercising her right of approach, contacts a ship on the high seas, the latter is required only to establish her identity and nationality in the usual manner, which is ordinarily by displaying her flag. If the commanding officer of the warship is not satisfied with this identification and he stops the ship for further verification, he does so at his own risk. He must have justification for taking such direct action. If he does not, his government must make full compensation to the victim. Furthermore, if the ship approached is sailing under a foreign flag, such a violation of the freedom of the seas could be a source of great embarrassment to the naval commander's government.

While today the threat and act of piracy have decreased to a considerable extent, the right of approach by a warship has survived. The occasions for its full exercise are now limited to: (1) acts of interference derived from powers specifically conferred by treaty; (2) a ship suspected of engaging in piracy; (3) a ship suspected of engaging in the slave trade; (4) a ship engaged in unauthorized broadcasting; (5) a ship that is without nationality; and (6) a ship, which though flying a foreign flag or refusing to show her flag, is, in reality, of the same nationality as the warship. However, it might well be argued that when a ship is suspected of interfering with a submarine cable or pipeline, engaging in illicit traffic in narcotics or psychotropic substances, or misusing a national flag, International Law relating to the conduct of major ocean uses should apply. With this in mind, a naval commander might find the right of approach a very useful doctrine.

On 26 February 1959, a party of officers and enlisted men from the USS *Roy O. Hale* boarded a Soviet fishing trawler 120 miles off Newfoundland to investigate the breakage of five submarine cables. All five of the cables were broken within a seventy-two-hour period prior to the boarding; aerial observation had established that the trawler was operating in the area of the breaks during that period. The boarding party was well received aboard the trawler and the investigating officer reported that there were no indications of any intent other than fishing with deep-sea equipment. After a brief search the investigating party returned to the *Hale* and both ships proceeded independently.

The Soviet Union later denied that the trawler was responsible for the breaks and claimed that the U.S. Navy had no right to board her. The United States rejected the Soviet arguments. It pointed out that the Convention for the Protection of Submarine Cables, signed in Paris in 1884 and recognized by both the United States and the Soviet Union as binding, authorized naval ships to examine the official documents of ships suspected of damaging or interfering with cables under the high seas.

However, it is this author's opinion that even if there were no convention of 1884, action by a naval ship under such circumstances should be permitted in order to prevent interference with international submarine cables or pipelines. The basis for such acts is the maintenance of a benefit to the world community and they should, therefore, be recognized as legal. It is contemplated that eventually the law will be broadened to cover any case where a recognized benefit to the world community is involved.

ENTERING FOREIGN TERRITORIAL SEAS AND PORTS

The general rights and obligations of ships in innocent passage and the corresponding rights and duties of coastal states are covered in Chapter 4. Pertinent here is the fact that, when a merchant ship is found not to be in innocent passage, the coastal state is permitted to take the necessary steps in its territorial sea to prevent passage, i.e., the coastal state may seize or arrest the offender. In contrast, warships, possessing an immunity, may not be seized or arrested. Should a warship fail to comply with the laws and regulations of the coastal state concerning passage and, further, disregard a request to comply, the only action a coastal state is permitted to take is to require the warship to leave its territorial waters immediately (*see* Appendix D). In such a situation, the warship's flag state must bear responsibility for any loss or damage to the coastal state resulting from the warship's noncompliance.

Entirely separate from that problem is the right of a warship to enter foreign territorial seas and ports for the purpose of visiting.

It is clearly within the right of any sovereign state to forbid foreign warships to enter any or all of its ports. On the other hand, it is customary for nations to grant access to at least some of their ports to the warships of nations with which they are at peace. Sometimes, the grant of this right is conditional upon reciprocity.

When a warship plans to visit a foreign port, the government of the sending nation usually gets permission for such a visit through diplomatic channels. Today, however, because of its extensive overseas commitments, which make it mandatory for our warships to visit the ports of our allies at frequent intervals, and because of the delays that diplomatic clearance sometimes entails, the United States has entered into "Naval Visits" agreements with nations whose ports are used most often by U.S. warships. Most of these agreements allow port visits after informal notification has been given to the receiving nation through naval, rather than diplomatic, channels. Consequently, warships of the United States enjoy a considerable amount of freedom to use the ports of foreign countries, particularly those joined with us in mutual defense agreements.

In Port

It is in a foreign port that the unique status of a warship is most apparent. Warships in a foreign port have come, by custom, to be accorded so many immunities that some leading authorities on International Law see their privileges as exterritorial. But this view is not accurate. The more logical view is that when a state permits the warship of another nation to enter one of its ports, that permission implies the granting of certain immunities from the territorial sovereignty of the receiving nation. The immunities implied are a part of customary International Law. Some of them are clear and uniform; others are not so clear and have been subjects of controversy between nations. It should be pointed out at this time, however, that military and naval aircraft do not have the same status as warships. Although they may have considerable immunity flowing from the fact that they are property of a sovereign state, they are not representatives of that state, as are warships.

While in a foreign port a warship is not subject to any interference by the authorities of the receiving state. Police or other port authorities are never entitled to board the ship without the permission of her commanding officer. And a commanding officer is never required to submit to a search of his ship. While this is old and well-established law, cases do arise wherein the immunity is questioned. The incident below, described by Rear Admiral A. S. Heyward, Jr., USN, shows how necessary it is for naval officers to know all the ramifications of the immunity of a ship.

> During my tenure as Director, Politico-Military Policy Division, CNO (1958–60), one of our constant tasks was to be alert for any challenge or misunderstanding of the immunity of public ships of the United States. Failure to grant the full benefits of sovereign immunity was not uncommon in the case of MSTS [now called MSC] non-commissioned ships (USNS). It also occurred, in rare cases, to warships.
>
> In one particular case USNS ships followed the merchant ship practice of flying the flag of the country being visited—in this case, France. This was done at the request of the French port authorities. It was recognized by MSTS that this practice was inconsistent with the ships' immunity as clearly expressed in *Navy Regulations*. In collaboration with MSTS, an instruction was drafted requiring USNS ships to fly flags only as authorized by *Navy Regulations*. We then worked with the State Department in promulgating the same directive to all diplomatic posts concerned with MSTS ship visits. Since that time such incidents have decreased.
>
> In another instance one of our destroyers visited a port of one of the Middle East countries. Upon anchoring, the Commanding Officer was told by the local authorities to fly the flag of the country being visited. After some hesitation he complied and then requested instructions from CNO. The answer was clear—take the flag down and proceed to the high seas.

These immunities do not mean that a ship may behave in a lawless manner. Here, too, responsibility is the key to the privilege. Furthermore, by accepting the hospitality of the port, a warship tacitly consents to comply with the harbor regulations with regard to such matters as speed and traffic control, garbage disposal, and health and quarantine restrictions. If a ship's behavior did not meet acceptable standards in these matters, the host country would have valid ground for making a complaint through diplomatic channels.

Asylum

Because of their exemption from the territorial sovereignty of the receiving state, warships have often been looked to as places of asylum by political or other refugees. The right of a warship to grant asylum has consequently often been a source of controversy between nations.

Until 1971, Article 0621, *U.S. Navy Regulations*, providing guidance to commanding officers on granting asylum, had remained virtually unchanged since 1894. The increase in political refugees' requests for asylum, and in particular the case of a Lithuanian sailor who in late November 1970 defected from a Russian ship anchored in U.S. territorial waters, but was denied asylum on a U.S. Coast Guard cutter and returned to the Russian ship, made more detailed guidance necessary. After long and careful discussions between representatives of the departments of State, Defense, and Justice, Article 0940, *U.S. Navy Regulations*, was approved and promulgated:

1. If an official of the Department of the Navy is requested to provide asylum or temporary refuge, the following procedures shall apply:
   a. On the high seas or in territories under exclusive United States jurisdiction (including territorial seas, the Commonwealth of Puerto Rico, territories under United States administration, and possessions):
      (1) At his request, an applicant for asylum will be received on board any naval aircraft or water-borne craft, Navy or Marine Corps activity or station.
      (2) Under no circumstances shall the person seeking asylum be surrendered to foreign jurisdiction or control, unless at the personal direction of the Secretary of the Navy or higher authority. Persons seeking political asylum should be afforded every reasonable care and protection permitted by the circumstances.
   b. In territories under foreign jurisdiction (including foreign territorial seas, territories, and possessions):
      (1) Temporary refuge shall be granted for humanitarian reasons on board a naval aircraft or water-borne craft, Navy or Marine Corps activity or station, only in extreme or exceptional circumstances wherein life or safety of a person is put in imminent danger, such as pursuit by a mob. When temporary refuge is granted, such protection shall be terminated only when directed by the Secretary of the Navy or higher authority.
      (2) A request by foreign authorities for return of custody of a person under the protection of temporary refuge will be reported to the CNO or Commandant of the Marine Corps. The requesting foreign authorities will be informed that the case has been referred to higher authorities for instructions.
      (3) Persons whose temporary refuge is terminated will be released to the protection of the authorities designated in the message authorizing release.
      (4) While temporary refuge can be granted in the circumstances set forth above, permanent asylum will not be granted.
      (5) Foreign nationals who request assistance in forwarding requests for political asylum in the United States will be advised to apply in person at the nearest American Embassy or Consulate.
   c. The Chief of Naval Operations or Commandant of the Marine Corps, as appropriate, will be informed by the most expeditious means of all action taken pursuant to subparagraphs 1a and 1b above, as well as the attendant circumstances. Telephone or voice communications will be

used where possible, but must be confirmed as soon as possible with an immediate precedence message, information to the Secretary of State (for actions taken pursuant to subparagraphs 1b(1) and 1b(5) of this article, also make the appropriate American Embassy or Consular Office an information addressee). If communication by telephone or voice is not possible, notification will be effected by an immediate precedence message, as described above. The Chief of Naval Operations or Commandant of the Marine Corps will cause the Secretary of the Navy and the Deputy Director for Operations of the National Military Command Center to be notified without delay.

2. Personnel of the Department of the Navy shall neither directly nor indirectly invite persons to seek asylum or temporary refuge.

As indicated, requests for asylum can bring into play many factors that must be measured in making a final determination. Rear Admiral William O. Miller, JAGC, USN, when he was Judge Advocate General of the Navy from 1976 to 1978, brought this interplay into sharp focus in the following narrative:

A recent incident in which international law played a role occurred in August of last year. On the evening of 10 August 1977, 101 Haitian nationals were discovered to be *in extremis* in a 40-foot boat. The boat was found to be unseaworthy for any future voyage, and the Haitians were given shelter aboard U.S. Naval Station, Guantánamo Bay, Cuba. First reports indicated that the group had departed Haiti for economic reasons, and that there were no requests for political asylum. Liaison was established quickly with the government of Haiti, which provided assurances that no penalties would be imposed upon the members of the group although their departure had been contrary to Haitian domestic law. Some reluctance nevertheless was displayed by the group when urged to return to Haiti. Again, economic reasons primarily were advanced in support of the group's hesitation, although some political comment also was heard. At length, based upon in-depth interviews conducted with the Haitians by U.S. State Department officials, 97 of the Haitians were determined to be economic refugees and were returned to Haiti without incident. The remaining four Haitians were authorized temporary parole into the United States for consideration of their asylum applications.

The above facts demonstrate an interesting interplay of several different aspects of international law. The starting point was the provision of necessary assistance by the U.S. Navy to the vessel in distress. This action was commensurate with the humanitarian duty under international law to aid persons and vessels in distress at sea. Secondly . . . international law permits a sovereign country to determine who may enter its territory. Criteria for the entry or exclusion of aliens are prescribed by the immigration laws of each country. Under U.S. law, economic "refugees" occupy the same status as most other aliens, and cannot enter the United States without proper documentation. According to the International Convention Relating to the Status of

Refugees, to which the U.S. adheres, an individual must establish a "well-founded fear of being persecuted" in order to merit designation as a political refugee. In the case of the four Haitians, U.S. officials considered that a sufficient showing had been made to justify entry and consideration of their asylum petitions. The right to accord such territorial asylum likewise is rooted in principles of customary international law, *viz.*, the exclusive territorial sovereignty of the state and the right to admit aliens to its territory. Finally, as to the remaining Haitians, the mere fact that an individual is from a country that has been alleged to have a "human rights problem" does not necessarily mean that a specific individual from that country has been or will be the subject of "political" harassment. In that regard, the assurances of the Government of Haiti were considered persuasive.

Modern communications have made it possible for commanding officers to share the burden of determining whether asylum should be granted or not. Since requests for asylum involve delicate political questions, all facts must be communicated, on a priority basis, to the secretary of the navy and the secretary of state.

Ships' Boats

The boats belonging to a warship are entitled to the same exemptions in a foreign port as the warship herself. In order that a boat may be recognized for what she is and accorded the immunities to which she is entitled, she must always display her national ensign during daylight hours.

Personnel

On Board

The officers and crew of a warship while on board in a foreign port are immune from local jurisdiction. If any of them should commit a crime on board, International Law dictates that the disciplining of the offender be left to the authorities of the warship's nation. Likewise, if a local inhabitant should commit a crime while visiting the ship, the national authorities of the visiting warship would have jurisdiction to try him; but under such circumstances it is customary for the ship to surrender the offender to the local authorities for trial by them.

On Shore

When the officers and crew of a warship go ashore on official business, it is customary for local authorities to waive all jurisdiction over them. For their acts on shore these officers and men are answerable only to their naval superiors. It is just as if they were on board their ship.

On the other hand, when officers and men go ashore unofficially for liberty or leave, a different situation is presented. The status of such persons has often been a source of disagreement among nations. Because of the effect that the absence of any member of the crew would have on the fighting effectiveness of his ship, many nations have contended that the exercise of criminal jurisdiction over a warship's personnel by local authorities would constitute interference with the sovereignty of that ship's nation. On the other hand, it can be argued with equal force that, by voluntarily granting liberty to members of her crew, a visiting ship consents to the exercise of criminal jurisdiction over them by the territorial sovereign, which, as we saw earlier, has full authority over all persons and things within the boundaries of its territory. This jurisdiction would obviously include the officers and crew of a visiting warship.

Because of these powerful but conflicting arguments, the law as to the status of the personnel of visiting warships while ashore on other than official business is not settled. However, since the tendency today is for the foreign power to take jurisdiction, that contingency must be taken into consideration when visits are made to foreign ports. For this reason, the United States has attempted to make arrangements, either by treaty or by executive agreement, to specify which sovereign will exercise jurisdiction under varying circumstances. Some of these arrangements will be discussed in Chapter 8. A naval officer whose ship is about to visit a foreign port would be well advised to know and explain to his men to what extent they will be subject to the local jurisdiction of the port while they are on liberty.

The fact that the exercise of jurisdiction over visiting personnel is an ever-present and real problem is clearly indicated in the following case reports described by Rear Admiral William Sheeley, USN.

CASE NO. 1

Recently a destroyer made a rest and recreation visit to an island which belonged to a foreign power. On this particular island there were no United States military installations nor was there any treaty or agreement regarding the exercise of criminal jurisdiction over naval personnel who might visit that island.

Towards the end of the visit, an altercation occurred between crew members and a local uniformed customs official which resulted in a general melee involving several persons. The foreign customs official was hospitalized as a result of his injuries. Shortly after the melee, local authorities requested permission to hold a line-up aboard the destroyer for the purpose of identifying United States naval participants in the fight. The commanding officer of the destroyer permitted the line-up aboard ship. The following day, local authorities requested that suspects be taken to the local hospital for another line-up before the injured customs official. The commanding officer granted permission on the understanding that all men would be returned to the ship. At the hospital a crew member, one B, was identified and taken to the police station where he was formally arrested on a charge of assault. The destroyer subsequently departed leaving B behind for trial under the care of the American Consul.

Trial was held by local authorities; B had the benefit of a locally hired attorney but had no witnesses in his defense. B was sentenced to six months' imprisonment. A retrial was held immediately thereafter, when witnesses from the ship and an attorney from the Office of the Judge Advocate General arrived on the island. B was again found guilty but his sentence was reduced to the payment of a $126.00 fine. The fine was paid immediately and B was returned to the continental United States.

It is pertinent to know that the investigation conducted by the commanding officer of the destroyer indicated that B was not involved in the fight.

CASE NO. 2

At approximately the same time as Case No. 1, another Navy ship made an operational visit to another foreign country. Similar to Case No. 1, there were no United States military installations in this foreign country nor was there any agreement between the United States and the foreign country regarding the exercise of criminal jurisdiction.

In this case a criminal offense was discovered, in which crew members of the ship were considered suspects by the local authorities, after the ship had put to sea. The offense was possible rape and strangulation. The local authorities requested that the ship be returned to port in order to make an investigation. This request was forwarded directly to the Chief of Naval Operations by the United States Naval Attaché and the commanding officer of the ship. The request was also made through diplomatic channels to the State Department. After considering all of the known elements of the case, the Chief of Naval Operations, as a matter of policy toward that particular country, directed the ship to return in order to permit the investigation to take place. The Chief of Naval Operations specified that the interrogation must be carried out on board the ship under the direct supervision of the commanding officer, and further, that the release of United States Naval personnel to the foreign authorities was not authorized.

Upon return to a port of the foreign country, the local authorities did come aboard to interrogate possible witnesses and did so under the direct supervision of the commanding officer who was assisted by a legal officer. At no time did the commanding officer permit any of the witnesses or possible suspects to come under the jurisdiction or control of the foreign authorities. Members of the crew furnished the local investigating authorities with information which led to the arrest of the perpetrator. At the conclusion of the investigation, local authorities determined that no members of the crew were implicated in the crime and the ship departed with all hands aboard.

CONCLUSION

In countries where we *do* have a treaty or agreement pertaining to criminal jurisdiction over personnel of the naval forces, the obligation can exist which would require the commanding officer to turn the suspect over to local authorities for prosecution in the foreign courts. Treaty arrangements vary from country to country, thus it is essential that commanding officers know the commitments made by treaty prior to their visiting such foreign countries.

In countries where we *do not* have treaties or agreements regarding the exercise of criminal jurisdiction over personnel in our naval forces, the present, apparent general rule of International Law applies. That law specifies that where personnel are ashore for liberty or recreation, they come under the jurisdiction of the foreign country and they can therefore be tried in local courts. However, such jurisdiction can only be exercised when the foreign country also has custody or physical control over the suspected person. Thus in those cases where the authorities of the foreign country apprehend naval personnel within their territory for an offense committed within their territory there is no question about the legality of their exercising their right of jurisdiction. In such an event commanding officers should notify the Chief of Naval Operations and the Judge Advocate General as well as the local American Consul and United States Naval Attaché, giving the full facts of the case. Commanding officers should also exert every effort within the law to secure custody of their personnel from the foreign authorities.

Likewise where we *do not* have treaty commitments and a crime has been committed within the foreign territory but the suspect has returned to his ship, foreign authorities no longer have jurisdiction over the suspect. Exclusive jurisdiction over the suspect then rests with the United States Navy. In order for the foreign country to then acquire jurisdiction over the person it is necessary that a request for extradition be made through prescribed diplomatic channels. Then, and only then, should the person be turned over to foreign authorities.

Case No. 1 described above represents the handling of a situation without the knowledge of this law. Case No. 2 represents the correct procedure to follow with knowledge of the law.

It follows then that where there is doubt as to what should be done in a given situation, authority to act should be requested from the Chief of Naval Operations sending an information copy of such request to the Office of the Judge Advocate General.

Shore Patrol

Article 0922 of *U.S. Navy Regulations (1948)* provides:

2. A patrol shall not be landed in any foreign port without first obtaining the consent of the proper local officials. Tact must be used in requesting permission; and, unless it is given willingly and cordially, the patrol shall not be landed. If consent cannot be obtained, the size of liberty parties shall be held to such limits as may be necessary to render disturbances unlikely.

3. Officers and men on patrol duty in a foreign country normally should not be armed. In the United States, officers and men may be armed as prescribed by the senior officer present.

Why is it necessary to obtain permission before landing a shore patrol on foreign territory? After all, it is going to exercise jurisdiction only over

American naval personnel. The answer lies again in territorial sovereignty. As has been previously stated, a nation's power within its boundaries is supreme, and no other nation can exercise any of the prerogatives of a sovereign within those boundaries, unless given permission to do so. Since the exercise of police jurisdiction by a shore patrol is an exercise of one aspect of sovereignty, to land a shore patrol without first securing the permission of the local authorities would be an infringement of sovereignty. Therefore, it is incumbent on officers in charge of a shore patrol in foreign territory carefully to instruct members of the patrol as to the scope of this authority and concerning their relations with foreign nationals and officials. A shore patrol has no *right* to be in foreign territory; it is merely granted permission to be there.

MERCHANT SHIPS
ON THE HIGH SEAS

It has been emphasized that the high seas are beyond the territorial sovereignty of any nation. They are free for the lawful use of any nation or the ships of any nation. But if this is true, how is law and order preserved? The answer lies in a combination of national law and International Law. International Law governs the relations between ships, as in the case of the Rules of the Road; it also requires that every ship lawfully plying the oceans must have a nationality. But the *national* law of the flag-nation governs the internal discipline of a ship on the high seas and also is in effect to a limited extent while the ship is within the territorial waters of a foreign nation.

Obviously, a merchant ship must meet certain prerequisites before she is entitled to fly the flag of a particular state and thus acquire its nationality. This is referred to as *immatriculation*. Generally, each state fixes the conditions for the grant of its nationality. Other states are required to recognize this grant, provided that the granting state discharges its obligation to maintain the public order of the oceans with regard to ships flying its flag. In brief, the state must exercise its jurisdiction and control in administrative, technical, and other matters, which include providing the ship with documents showing her nationality. The primary document is the *registry*, which must be retained aboard. When these requirements have been met, the ship is entitled to fly a national flag; she then possesses the nationality of that flag. Once a vessel has acquired a nationality, she cannot change her flag during a voyage or while she is in a port of call, except in the case of a bona fide transfer of ownership or change of registry. Were a ship to sail under the flags of two or more states, shifting their use at her own convenience, she would be considered a ship without nationality. Ships employed in the service of an intergovernmental organization can and do fly two flags. For

SHIPS

115

example, ships employed by the United Nations on various occasions fly both their national flag and the United Nations flag.

The type of jurisdiction that a nation exercises over its merchant ships has been a source of some disagreement among authorities in this field of law. One argument is that, since a merchant ship is a floating part of a nation's territory, the jurisdiction of national law should extend beyond a nation's physical boundaries. The argument against such extension is that the jurisdiction exercised by a flag-nation over its merchant ships is not a territorial jurisdiction at all: it is a jurisdiction born of necessity and exercised beyond a nation's boundaries over the persons and property of its citizens. It must be recognized—and it will perhaps be brought into clearer focus when we consider jurisdiction over a merchant ship in a foreign port—that the latter school is correct in theory. It is not necessary for this text to become involved with the legal theory as long as the doctrine is understood, and that doctrine is that, while on the high seas, a merchant ship is subject to the jurisdiction of the nation whose flag she flies.

As a principal source of authority, International Law specifies the duties of the flag state in exercising its jurisdiction over merchant ships; the resulting national or domestic law is the most visible result of international flag-state duties, which include:

1. Maintenance of a shipping register that gives the names and particulars of ships flying its flag.
2. Promulgation of domestic law governing administrative, technical, and social matters concerning the ships that fly its flag.
3. Institution of measures to ensure safety at sea, including the seaworthiness of ships, the training and working conditions of crews, the maintenance of communications, and the prevention of collisions.

The following incident, described by Rear Admiral S. H. Evans, USCG, indicates the degree of jurisdiction that a state exercises over its ships:

> On 5 April 1958, the Atomic Energy Commission established a danger area in connection with a nuclear test series to be conducted at the Eniwetok Proving Ground in the Marshall Islands. In order to "avoid any unnecessary delay or interruption of that test activity, and to protect the health and safety of the public," the Atomic Energy Commission issued regulations published in the Code of Federal Regulations which contained the following prohibition:
>
>> No United States citizen or other person who is within the scope of this part shall enter, attempt to enter or conspire to enter the danger area during the continuation of the Hardtack test series, except with the express approval of appropriate officials of the Atomic Energy Commission or the Department of Defense.

On 19 April 1958, the American ketch *Golden Rule* arrived in Honolulu, Hawaii, from the West Coast with the express intent of sailing on into the Eniwetok danger area in defiance of the law. The United States Attorney, Honolulu, being advised by the Coast Guard Captain of the Port of the intent of the master and crew of the *Golden Rule*, as communicated to the Coast Guard, sought and obtained a temporary restraining order preliminary to hearing upon motion for a preliminary injunction restraining the master and crew of the *Golden Rule* from entering, attempting to enter, or conspiring to enter the danger area and from directly or indirectly moving the *Golden Rule* from its anchorage or mooring without permission of the court. Following a hearing in Honolulu Federal District Court on 1 May 1958, the court issued a temporary injunction to the same effect as its restraining order. The master and crew of the *Golden Rule* thereupon in open court announced that despite these court orders they intended to sail their vessel into the danger area. Approximately two hours later they boarded the ketch, slipped the mooring, and headed for sea. The court, being advised of their actions, forthwith issued a warrant for their arrest, and the Coast Guard made the arrest before the vessel got beyond the three-mile limit.

The master and crew of the *Golden Rule* were convicted of contempt of the Federal Court order and were sentenced to sixty days in jail, but were released on one year's probation. Their request for a stay of injunction was denied by the Ninth Circuit Court. They then announced their intentions to attempt to sail again at noon on 4 June 1958. Just prior to sailing time, the master was again arrested and a few hours later a member of the crew sailed the *Golden Rule* but was apprehended by the Coast Guard approximately five miles at sea. The master and crew of the *Golden Rule* were sentenced to sixty days in jail for contempt of court. Upon completion of their confinement, the ketch was sold, and the crew abandoned their attempt to sail into the test area.

Most nations give considerable authority to the masters of their merchant ships. While this authority is never as extensive as that exercised by the commanding officer of a warship, it does usually confer limited power over minor breaches of ship's discipline. Also, a master has, of necessity, the power to detain, and to confine if necessary, any person who has committed a crime on board his ship while on the high seas. Depending on the law of his nation, he may be authorized to detain the person on board either until he reaches a port where there is a consul of his nation or until he again reaches a national port. It is of interest to note that a master is not authorized to perform marriages.

It is clear that when a collision or any other navigational error involving the penal or disciplinary responsibility of the master occurs on the high seas, disciplinary proceedings can be instituted only by the flag state or the state of which the master is a national. The only authority empowered to withdraw a master's certificate is the state that issued it, and that only after due legal process.

Consuls also have limited powers over acts committed on the high seas, the one most commonly exercised being that of accepting custody of a prisoner and making arrangements for his return to a national port for trial. Other consular powers will be considered in more detail when we discuss the status of a merchant ship in the jurisdictional waters of a foreign state.

The procedure for punishing crimes committed at sea varies from nation to nation. Some countries have special courts for the exercise of maritime jurisdiction. Others, including the United States, give authority over such matters to courts of general jurisdiction.

The U.S. Criminal Code provides that U.S. district courts shall have jurisdiction over certain crimes committed within the "special maritime and territorial jurisdiction of the United States." This jurisdiction includes:

> The high seas, any other waters within the admiralty and maritime jurisdiction of the United States and out of the jurisdiction of any particular State, and any vessel belonging in whole or part to the United States or any citizen thereof, or to any corporation created by or under the laws of the United States, or of any State, Territory, District, or possession thereof, when such vessel is within the admiralty and maritime jurisdiction of the United States and out of the jurisdiction of any particular State.

IN TERRITORIAL SEAS

The specific rights and duties of a coastal state and ships in transit through its territorial sea were spelled out in Chapter 4. This section deals with a coastal state's authority to exercise criminal or civil jurisdiction over persons in ships in transit.

When a crime has been committed on board a ship during her passage through territorial seas, the coastal state concerned may exercise criminal jurisdiction on board such ship only when one of the following conditions pertains:
1. The consequences of the crime extend to the coastal state;
2. The crime disturbs the peace of the coastal state or the good order of its territorial sea;
3. The ship's master or a diplomatic agent (consular officer) of the flag state requests the assistance of local authorities;
4. Such a measure is necessary for the suppression of illicit traffic in narcotic or psychotropic substances.

When a ship is passing through a territorial sea after leaving internal waters, the above conditions do not apply. Under those circumstances, the coastal state has the right to arrest or investigate according to its own laws.

When one of the above conditions does obtain, the coastal state shall, if the captain so requests, advise the diplomatic agent of the flag state of the situation before taking any steps and will assist in establishing contact between such agent and the ship's crew. Clearly, in cases of emergency, notification and the taking of measures to arrest might be simultaneous.

When a ship is in passage through a territorial sea and is not leaving internal waters, the coastal state may not stop or divert her for the purpose of exercising civil jurisdiction in relation to a person on board. Nor may the coastal state arrest a ship in passage for the purpose of instituting any civil proceedings, except in regard to obligations or liabilities incurred by the ship in the course of, or for the purpose of, her voyage through the waters of the coastal state.

In Port

Perhaps no doctrine of the International Law that applies to ships is more rigid than that which holds that a merchant ship entering the port of a foreign nation becomes completely subject to that nation's jurisdiction. This fact makes it clear that a flag nation's jurisdiction over its merchant ships is not territorial. If it were territorial, i.e., if a merchant ship were regarded as a floating part of the flag nation, no local authorities would be able to exercise any jurisdiction over acts committed aboard her.

Practical necessities are responsible for a number of customary rules concerning the exercise by local authorities of their jurisdiction over visiting merchant vessels. The community of nations has come to recognize the fact that matters affecting only the internal discipline of a ship are better left to the jurisdiction of the flag nation. For example, if one member of a crew assaults another on board a merchant ship in a foreign port, the public peace of the port is not affected. Furthermore, the departure and operation of the vessel might be seriously affected if the accused, the complaining witness, and other witnesses had to be sent ashore to take part in a criminal trial. For these reasons, it is a rule of customary International Law that port authorities waive the jurisdiction that is unquestionably theirs and leave the settlement of internal disciplinary infractions that occur on board merchant ships in foreign ports to the authorities of the flag nation.

As is the case in so many fields of International Law, this customary law has found its way into the conventional law of nations. The practices of most nations in this regard may be found in bilateral consular conventions. The consular convention between the United States and the United Kingdom, signed on 6 June 1951, is representative:

> Without prejudice to the right of the administrative and judicial authorities of the territory to take cognizance of crimes or offenses committed on board the vessel when she is in the ports or in the territorial waters of the territory and which are cognizable under the local law or to enforce local laws applicable to vessels in ports and territorial waters or persons and property

thereon, it is the common intention of the High Contracting Parties that the administrative and police authorities of the territory should not, except at the request or with the consent of the consular officer,

(a) concern themselves with any matter taking place on board the vessel unless for the preservation of peace and order or in the interests of public health or safety, or

(b) institute prosecutions in respect of crimes or offenses committed on board the vessel unless they are of a serious character or involve the tranquility of the port or unless they are committed by or against persons other than the crew.

Closely related to the situation just discussed is the matter of a ship entering a foreign port with a seaman in detention for a disciplinary infraction that occurred on the high seas. In such cases also it is customary for local authorities to refrain from interfering, and many consular conventions cover specific agreement with respect to them. The above-mentioned convention with the United Kingdom provides:

The administrative and judicial authorities will not interfere with the detention in custody on the vessel of a seaman for disciplinary offenses, provided such detention is lawful under the law of the sending state and is not accompanied by unjustifiable severity or inhumanity.

Asylum

Since a merchant ship is not immune from the territorial sovereignty of the foreign state in which the port is located, it is obvious that to whatever extent the doctrine of asylum exists it does not apply to merchant ships. Furthermore, when a merchant ship enters a foreign port with a fugitive from that nation on board, local authorities are entitled to board her and remove the fugitive. Although some nations have, on occasion, refrained from exercising their undoubted authority in this respect, no rule of International Law, or even considerations of comity, requires that they do so.

6

The High Seas

Mare clausum versus mare liberum.

Grotius

...upon the ocean, in time of peace, all possess an entire equality. It is the common highway of all, appropriated to the use of all, and no one can vindicate to himself a superior or exclusive prerogative there.

Judge Joseph Story

INTRODUCTION

CONFERENCE REPORT

Place: Office of the Chief of Naval Operations, the Pentagon.

Participants: Seven of the top officials of the American Merchant Marine Institute (AMMI); fourteen senior officers from CNO, Cinc-Lant, Key West, and JAG.

Subject: Key West Operating Areas.

Facts: 1. The U.S. Naval Base, Key West, is one of the major operating bases of the U.S. Navy. Among its varied activities the principal one is the training of submarines in attack and evasive tactics; conversely, destroyers, destroyer escorts, and other ships with anti-submarine equipment are trained in searching for, tracking, and destroying submarines. Because there are many ships involved, the operating schedule is tight. Normally the naval units sortie from Key West to the operating areas in the Straits of Florida daily between 0700 and 0900 and return to Key West, after their training, between 1500 and 1700. The Key West channel is narrow, and good seamanship dictates that ships do not pass in the channel.

2. The operating area in the Florida Straits is so situated that its northern limit lies close to the Florida Keys; thus ships in training can commence their operations shortly after leaving the channel. In addition to economy in time and money, the close-in-area is advantageous to submarines and ships of low silhouette because there are only a few navigational aids visible beyond a few miles from the coast.

3. The Key West Operating Area lies directly athwart the shipping lanes through the Florida Straits. The normal westbound shipping track is 2 to 4 miles off the coast, while the normal eastbound shipping track is 8 to 12 miles off the coast.

4. Commercial shipping lines are governed in their activities, in large part, by economic considerations; unnecessary changes in course and speed increase operating expenses. A delay in arriving at a scheduled port of call can

cause the payment of penalties under a cargo contract. A collision at sea might mean the loss of customers and possibly cause bankruptcy.

Problem: Applying the preceding elements to the Key West Operating Area, the opportunity for misunderstanding as to a skipper's intention and the resulting possibility of collision is readily apparent. Proceeding out of or into the harbor, naval ships constantly cross the shipping lanes, and this dangerous situation is present hundreds of times a month. Merchant ships proceeding along the usual shipping tracks frequently enter the Operating Area and interfere with destroyer-submarine exercises. Naval ships in the past have signalled merchant ships to clear the area so as not to interfere with a scheduled exercise. Merchant ships have in the past proceeded across the entrance of the channel, thereby causing naval ships to stop or back down in the channel—a dangerous maneuver in view of the narrow channel and shifting currents and winds. The key problem for the conferees, then, was how to prevent these misunderstandings and to keep these potentially dangerous conditions from occurring in the future.

Agreed Solution: 1. The high seas are free seas and open to the legitimate use of all.

2. Merchant ships and naval ships must adhere strictly to the Rules of the Road.

The application of the agreed solution to the specific problems involved shows that:

(a) No area of the high seas can be denied to the use of others, i.e., the merchant ships do have the right to proceed through a naval operating area. Likewise, naval ships can engage in training exercises wherever they choose on the high seas.

(b) The fact that an area of the seas is congested by commercial shipping and naval activities does not permit deviation from the Rules of the Road. Thus, when naval ships leaving the Key West channel have the right of way, a merchantman must follow the rules as a give-way vessel. Conversely, if the merchantman is the stand-on vessel, the naval ships must react according to the rules obligating a give-way vessel.

(c) During naval exercises a warning may be issued to commercial shipping activities regarding the possible danger; individual ships may be requested to clear the area, but they have no obligation to do so.

Historically, the term *high seas* has meant all seas outside the boundary of any country, or, in other words, all seas that are not the territorial seas or internal waters of any country. There is, however, strong evidence that the vast majority of countries participating in the Third Law of the Sea Conference are of the opinion that for a variety of uses the demarkation of the high seas should be at the seaward limit of the 200-mile exclusive economic zone. There is also evidence that, because it is important to retain freedom of navigation in the exclusive economic zone, the countries involved do not intend to create an exclusive economic zone that is totally national. The reason for this apparent departure from the traditional view of the high seas will be made clearer in this chapter. As of now, the high seas comprise more than 70 per cent of the world's surface, but if they were measured from the outer limit of 200-mile exclusive economic zones, the percentage would be a good deal less. Whatever the boundary of the high seas might be, the world's commerce moves through them without interruption or impediment.

This flow of commerce moves without interruption or impediment because the high seas are free. They are open to the use of all nations, and no state can appropriate them to its own use or occupy them in order to acquire title. They have an established legal status which requires freedom of navigation and freedom of use for all. The rule of International Law that the high seas are free seas has become so fixed that we take it for granted. But, as is the case with any hard-fought-for freedom, it should not be taken for granted. This chapter examines some of the old and new challenges to the freedom of the high seas.

HISTORICAL COMMENT

In Chapter 4 historical comment was made in order to provide a base for understanding the importance of the territorial sea and its breadth. The following comment provides a base for understanding the high seas and how their regime emerged.

One of the results of the great voyages of discovery during the fifteenth and sixteenth centuries was a confusion of claims by European powers as to who owned what land and who had title to certain parts of the ocean. At one time Great Britain claimed title to that part of the Atlantic Ocean which surrounded the British Isles and extended from Norway to Spain. One of the early English kings, Edward III, claimed for himself the title "King of the Seas." Denmark, not to be outdone, staked out claims to all the seas between Greenland, Iceland, and Norway. For many centuries the Italian states claimed the Mediterranean as their private lake. The most extravagant and optimistic claim of title was published as a papal bull in 1494 when Pope Alexander VI neatly partitioned the Atlantic Ocean between Spain and Portugal. Spain received everything to the west of the line and Portugal everything to the east of it. On the basis of the agreement growing out of the papal bull, the Pacific and the Gulf of Mexico were acknowledged as Spain's, while Portugal had to be content with the South Atlantic and the Indian Ocean.

The concept of freedom of the seas, as formulated by Grotius, was not generally accepted until the end of the Napoleonic Wars. By that time, Great

Britain had become supreme on the seas; she had quietly let her claim of sovereignty over parts of the ocean slip into oblivion and had used her navy to open the way for her merchant ships to sail freely over the seven seas. In this endeavor, she, along with the United States, fought piracy wherever it existed. The U.S. Navy, for example, wrote a magnificent chapter in its history in the war with the Barbary pirates.

Both the United States and Great Britain realized that if large slices of the seas were to be considered the territory of a particular state, international commerce could be hampered and restricted to the detriment of all. They therefore advanced the view that the seas should be free and, where necessary, backed their pronouncements with action. Because more and more states acknowledged the validity of this concept of freedom, the high seas are today the free seas.

The concept may work well in peacetime, but what about wartime? Chapter 10 shows that belligerents have certain legal rights in the conduct of naval warfare and that neutral rights of commerce on the high seas are subject to the restrictions created by war.

FREEDOM OF THE HIGH SEAS

When the term *free seas* is used to designate the high seas, it signifies that no state may subject any part of the high seas to its sovereignty. Certain fundamental freedoms pertaining to the high seas are available to all states, whether they have a coastline or not: freedom to navigate, freedom to fish, freedom to lay submarine cables and pipelines, freedom to undertake scientific research, and freedom to fly over (*see* Appendix I). In exercising these freedoms on the high seas, states must have reasonable regard for the rights of others.

It was in the exercise of their freedom to undertake scientific research that, before the Test Ban Treaty was signed, the United States and the United Kingdom carried out tests with nuclear weapons in a remote part of the Pacific Ocean. Among the factors that distinguish such tests from other scientific research and experimentation is the greater danger they create. Consequently, the states involved "fenced off," or temporarily closed, the area of the high seas where their activities took place. Their right to take this action aroused controversy on the grounds that to close any part of the high seas for any reason was a violation of the freedom of the seas. The accused states claimed in rebuttal that it was not unreasonable temporarily to close a part of the high seas where possible harm to humans and living resources was minimal and interference with navigation was transitory, and pointed out that, if a ship did enter the area, the testing, not the ship, was stopped: furthermore, adequate notice of the closing was given.

Control of the High Seas

It is axiomatic that freedom must be regulated if it is to be exercised in the interests of all who are entitled to enjoy it. Pursuant to this axiom, many international conventions and treaties have been concluded on safety of life and traffic at sea, salvage, international signals, fisheries, the laying of cables and pipelines, oil pollution, and the suppression of piracy and the slave trade. As a matter of fact, provision has been made for virtually every matter requiring some measure of international control.

Territorial Seas as Servitude

As was pointed out in Chapter 4, the belt of water around a coastal state is called a territorial sea and it comes within the exclusive jurisdiction of the state concerned. In a *physical* and geographic sense, it is part of the high seas; in a *legal* sense, it is universally recognized that the territorial sea is not part of the high seas. This limitation on the high seas may be described as a servitude imposed by coastal states and recognized by all states. It is not the same as other servitudes on the high seas, because it is absolute in all respects but one—the right of innocent passage. Much confusion has arisen in recent years regarding the servitude represented by territorial seas and other servitudes that a coastal state may impose on an area of the high seas, its bed, or subsoil. In the discussion that follows, it is essential to keep in mind that sovereignty over territorial seas has nothing to do with the authority that a coastal state may exercise over part of the high seas for a particular purpose. This distinction is clearly made by Charles C. Hyde in *International Law*:

> It need constantly be borne in mind, for the sake of clearness of thought and as a means of inspiring general agreement, that the distinction between a right of sovereignty over a particular area (territorial waters) and a right to exercise a preventive or protective jurisdiction (continental shelf, fisheries, self-defense measures etc.) over or within an area that is outside of the national domain is a real one. Failure to heed it inevitably breeds confusion of thinking.

Special-Purpose Controls

When we refer to a control over the high seas established for customs or fishing purposes, for self-defense, or for exploitation of the continental shelf, we are not speaking of an extension of territorial seas. These special-purpose controls over, or servitudes on, the high seas are separate and distinct.

A major or central component of the new regimes emerging from the Third Law of the Sea Conference is the creation or repositioning of jurisdictional lines to determine the prerogatives of states in their use of the seas. During the course of the negotiations, many coastal states, including the United States, made unilateral claims, such as a 200-mile fishing jurisdiction.

The combination of the negotiations at the conference and the unilateral acts of numerous coastal states complemented each other to a considerable degree. Thus, what has been produced is a series of special-purpose controls over precisely delineated activities in large areas of the high seas that are for the benefit of the coastal states, which have changed considerably the regime of the high seas.

Self-Defense

Modern weapons make the right of self-defense a very important aspect of International Law. A state's incontestable right under International Law to take all the defensive measures required to guarantee its existence obviously applies within its own territory. But does a state not have the right to go beyond its territorial seas in order to protect itself? Charles C. Hyde answers that question in the affirmative:

> A State may endeavor to prevent, in times of peace or war, the commission of certain acts by foreign ships or the occupants thereof . . . without claiming that the place where they occur is a part of its domain. . . .
> Although without a sovereign, the high seas is, nevertheless, oftentimes the scene of activities in which a State asserts the right to check or forbid the commission of a particular act. Yet that assertion . . . does not necessarily or commonly purport to be a manifestation of dominion over waters, or of a control over them, but rather an interference with acts sought to be committed thereon. (*International Law.*)

This opinion is upheld in the courts. A case in point is *Cucullu* v. *Louisiana Insurance Company*, where the presiding judge held that:

> Strictly speaking, the authority of a nation cannot extend beyond its own territory. . . . But the right of the nation to protect itself from injury, by preventing its laws from being evaded, is not restrained to this boundary [the territorial sea]. It may watch its coast and seize ships that are approaching it with an intention to violate its laws. It is not obliged to wait until the offense is consummated before it can act. It may guard against injury, as well as punish it.

A state's right of self-defense beyond its territorial waters is generally recognized and adhered to by all states but, because it involves an exercise of control over the high seas, two tests must be met before it can be applied.

The first test requires that the potential act be definitely within the realm of a threat to the security of the state. The difficulty here lies in determining what constitutes a threat to national security. Because of the many types of weapons available today, there is no set rule by which this determination can be made. Each case must be judged on its facts. Immediately before the United States entered World War II, for example, President Roosevelt declared: "Their [German submarines'] very presence in any waters which America deems vital to its defense constitutes an attack."

The second test requires that the measures taken to repel the threat be reasonable. In other words, they may not go beyond the limits of the threat being dealt with. Thus, to continue the example of the German submarines, the order went out to the U.S. Navy to sink such submarines on sight. Note that the U.S. Navy was not ordered to sink *all* ships on sight. In view of the unlimited national emergency which had been declared as a result of the war in Europe and the sinking of U.S. ships, the order did not go beyond the particular threat and was, therefore, a reasonable measure.

The concept of defensive sea areas established during wartime is based on a state's right to act in self-defense upon the high seas. It is pertinent to note that the law involved here does not require the establishment of a defensive sea area—in either peace or war—as a condition of acting in self-defense on or over the high seas. An order establishing a defensive sea area on the high seas may not be couched in terms that would prohibit the entry of ships into the area. Such a prohibition would be an exercise of sovereignty over the high seas.

FISHERIES AND THE EXCLUSIVE ECONOMIC ZONE

Harvesting fish from the seas is one of man's oldest activities: over the centuries it has provided him with food, income, and adventure. It is also one of the few activities in which the participants and the countries they represent have been in direct confrontation with each other over a common resource. Of all the uses of the oceans, it has been the cause of the most numerous and the most sustained conflicts.

Freedom to fish on the high seas has been a part of customary International Law for as long as there have been fisheries. It was reduced to treaty law in 1958 in both the Convention on the High Seas and the Geneva Convention on Fishing and Conservation of the Living Resources of the High Seas.

The decades before the above Geneva Convention on Fishing were marked not only by an increase in the number of international disputes concerning fisheries but by a growing concern for the protection of fish stocks. It became clear that intensive fishing could and did deplete fish stocks to the point where certain important fisheries were lost: the halibut fishery of the northeastern Atlantic and the sardine fishery of the Pacific are examples. Demands that fishing be conducted in a manner to ensure that fish would be available for future generations became the cornerstone upon which the 1958 Geneva Convention on Fishing was built. Its central purpose was conservation of the living resources of the sea. Thus, one of the basic obligations placed upon ratifying countries was to conduct their fisheries, whether on a national, bilateral, or multilateral basis, so as to ensure that fisheries would be maintained at a level that provided for a maximum sustainable annual yield.

The convention also provided mechanisms for international cooperation in fisheries, a compulsory method of settling disputes and, significantly, recognition of the special interest of coastal states in the conservation of fisheries on the high seas off their coasts. This interest, limited to conservation, allowed a coastal state a special-purpose control over an activity on the high seas.

INADEQUACIES OF THE 1958 CONVENTION

The 1958 Convention on Fishing and Conservation of the Living Resources of the High Seas received little general support, as is illustrated by the fact that as late as 1971 only twenty-seven countries had ratified it. Moreover, few of the major fishing countries were among those twenty-seven. Nevertheless, most countries accepted the principles of conservation laid down in the convention and have applied them in innumerable multilateral and bilateral agreements on fisheries. For example, at one point, the United States belonged to nine fisheries conventions, most of which were based on the principles of conservation laid down in the Convention on Fishing. Although many countries applied conservation principles, it was clear that the world community did not consider those laid down in the 1958 Convention on Fishing adequate to meet the overall objectives of the future. Advanced technology has played a major role in the development of this general view, as is clearly indicated in an address delivered in Geneva by Roy Jackson, deputy director general of the United Nations Food and Agriculture Organization (FAO) on 19 March 1971:

> The period since the previous [1958 Law of the Sea] Conference has been one of rapid development of fisheries throughout the world. The production of marine fish (including shellfish) has increased from 27 million tons in 1958 to 56 million tons in 1969. Problems of over-exploitation have become intensified, and this has increased the need for measures for conservation and management. In 1955, when the International Technical Conference on the Conservation of the Living Resources of the Sea met at FAO Headquarters in Rome in preparation for the Conference on the Law of the Sea, virtually all fish stocks outside the North Atlantic and the North Pacific were underexploited, or not exploited at all. Now there are few stocks of the types of fish readily caught and marketed which are not heavily exploited, many by large fleets of long-range vessels capable of fishing anywhere in the world. The number of countries involved in long-range fishing beyond the vicinity of their own coasts is also increasing and includes already, often as a result of bilateral and multilateral assistance programmes, several developing countries. This last trend constitutes an important development since the 1958 Conference.

Besides being a valuable protein resource, fish have proven to be a very valuable economic resource now being obtained from the seas. Gross revenues, worldwide, from the annual harvest of living marine resources have been estimated at approximately twenty billion dollars. As a consequence, more and more countries, both for food and for revenue demanded a share of the world's fisheries. This was particularly true of developing countries that saw large, sophisticated foreign fishing fleets operating—processing, canning, and freezing their catches—off their coasts and frequently depleting stocks that local fishermen had historically fished. These countries were well aware of the fact that the distant-water fleets could move over thousands of miles from one fishery to another, while their own fishermen suffered because they could not move beyond local fishing grounds. In short, a great number of countries came to the conclusion that a coastal state's economic interest had to be recognized as well as its interest in conservation. These factors are the underlying reasons why the 1958 convention was not better supported and why there was a deepening demand for a new regime for high-seas fisheries.

As noted in Chapter 4, some states, particularly in Latin America, claimed complete sovereignty over waters adjacent to their coasts by extending their territorial seas, primarily to obtain full jurisdiction over the fisheries off their coasts. Some authorities espoused a policy of granting a coastal state extensive fisheries jurisdiction but maintaining a narrow territorial sea. Others were of the opinion that, partly for the reasons listed below, an extensive exclusive fisheries zone did not respond to the present and anticipated demands of the world community:

1. Fish will not abide by lines drawn on the ocean.
2. The world demand for protein is so great that living resources should not be allowed to lie unused in national preserves.
3. Countries engaged in distant-water fishing will not accept unilateral extensions of jurisdiction. Developed countries are not the only ones engaged in distant-water activities: an increasing number of developing countries look upon fisheries, both coastal and distant-water, as a primary means of obtaining food and foreign exchange.
4. There is an acknowledged tendency for a jurisdiction created for one purpose to expand to cover other activities and uses of the high seas. This is known as *creeping jurisdiction*, and its final result would be that coastal states had absolute control over vast areas of the oceans. Such a situation would be detrimental to all countries, whether coastal or landlocked, and would interfere not only with fishing but with other ocean uses.

Speaking in Montreal before an international fishery association on 10 May 1967, Wilbert McLeod Chapman, a world expert on fisheries, said:

> It is difficult to completely disassociate special jurisdiction for fisheries purposes from exclusive jurisdiction for all purposes, or sole sovereignty. This can be done easily in the minds of foreign offices and international lawyers of nations who want to do so, but their thoughts may also be easily disregarded in a peaceful world by those nations who do not wish to do so.

Thus the stage was set for a new approach to a fishery regime that would satisfy the inadequacies of the 1958 Convention and meet the needs of coastal states. By 1974 the deliberations of the Third Law of the Sea Conference made it clear that the vast majority of coastal states wanted exclusive control over fisheries out to a distance of 200 miles from their coasts. This area became known as the *exclusive economic zone*. On 11 July 1974, before a plenary session of the Third Law of the Sea Conference, the U.S. representative, John R. Stevenson, indicated his government's general endorsement of a 200-mile economic zone:

> Our willingness and that of many other delegations to accept a 200-mile outer limit for the economic zone depends on the concurrent negotiation and acceptance of correlative coastal state duties.
>
> The coastal state rights we contemplate comprise full regulatory jurisdiction over exploration and exploitation of seabed resources, non-resource drilling, fishing for coastal and anadromous species, and installations constructed for economic purposes.
>
> The rights of other states include freedom of navigation, overflight, and other non-resource uses.
>
> With respect to the zone as a whole, we contemplate coastal state duties to prevent unjustifiable interference with navigation, overflight, and other non-resource uses, and to respect international environmental obligations. With regard to the seabeds and economic installations, this includes respect for international standards to prevent interference with other uses and to prevent pollution. With regard to fishing, this includes a duty to conserve living resources.
>
> For the seabeds, we also contemplate a coastal state duty to observe exploration and exploitation arrangements it enters into.
>
> For fisheries, to the extent that the coastal state does not fully utilize a fishery resource, we contemplate a coastal state duty to permit foreign fishing under reasonable coastal state regulations. These regulations would include conservation measures and provision for harvesting by coastal state vessels up to their capacity and could include the payment of a reasonable license fee by foreign fishermen. We also contemplate a duty for the coastal state and all other fishing states to cooperate with each other in formulating equitable international and regional conservation and allocation regulations for highly migratory species, taking into account the unique migratory pattern of these species within and without the zones.

By the spring of 1979 more than eighty countries were claiming exclusive economic or fisheries zones over a 200-mile belt of national jurisdiction over resources. Although the specific rights and duties established by the enactment of national legislation by these countries were not necessarily identical in scope or purpose, other states raised but few objections, most of them minor. In April 1976, the United States enacted the Fishery Conservation and Management Act, which, based on general acceptability by the world community, unilaterally established a 200-mile fishery zone. The 2.25 million nautical square miles of fishery jurisdiction that the United States thereby acquired equals 95 per cent of all U.S. land territory.

APPLICATIONS OF THE EXCLUSIVE ECONOMIC ZONE

The exclusive economic zone is an area adjacent to the territorial sea and extending 200 miles seaward from the lines that served for measuring the territorial sea. It is a vast area incorporating approximately 36 per cent, or more than one-third, of the world's oceans. Within that zone specific rights and jurisdiction accrue to the coastal state and the rights and freedoms of other states are governed by the regime in its entirety. Its central thrust is economic in character and essentially provides for sovereign rights over resources, both living and nonliving, on and in the ocean floor as well as in superjacent waters. It also has rights over other activities that could have a bearing on its economic exploitation and exploration, such as scientific research, the establishment and use of artificial islands and structures, and control of pollution. *See* Appendix G.

In its exclusive economic zone, a coastal state has the sole right and jurisdiction to authorize and regulate the building and operation of artificial islands and other structures; such installations do not have a territorial sea of their own. It must, however, give notice of the construction of such installations and it is responsible for seeing that when one is abandoned it is removed. To further protect and enhance the safety of navigation and of an installation itself, the state concerned may establish safety zones, which may not exceed 500 meters in radius: all transiting ships must stay outside such zones and while in the area must proceed with the caution dictated by good seamanship. Clearly, no installation may be constructed or operated in recognized sea lanes essential to international navigation.

Although the production of energy from the water, currents, and winds is not yet a reality, a coastal state's rights in its exclusive economic zone specifically include that of controlling such production. Ongoing work in this area promises varying degrees of potential for the United States as well as for other areas of the world. Both thermal and salinity gradients cause movement in the ocean and, therefore, produce energy; tidal power, particularly in Maine and Alaska, and the more exotic wave power found off Oregon and Washington are being investigated; the Gulf Stream off the Florida coast is another likely source; experimental work is under way on the cultivation of several seaweeds that may be convertible to energy; and a device that uses temperature differential to produce electricity is in service in Hawaii.

Just as all present and potential economic activities within its exclusive economic zone come under the jurisdiction and control of the coastal state, noneconomic activities of long-standing usage as a freedom of the high seas are provided a special status in the zone. The most important of the latter is freedom of navigation and overflight. All states enjoy the right to lay sub-marine cables and pipelines. In exercising their continued rights in the exclusive economic zone, all states must have due regard to the rights and duties of the coastal state and must comply with the laws and regulations it establishes to further the purpose and scope of its exclusive economic zone.

CONSERVATION AND USE OF LIVING RESOURCES

In terms of world production the harvesting of fish was growing dramati-cally until it leveled off in the 1970s. The United Nations Food and Agricul-ture Organization provides the following statistics on the growth of total world catch:

1948—19.1 million tons
1958—41.8 million tons
1965—63.9 million tons
1971—70.2 million tons
1977—73.5 million tons

Most of the above tonnages were harvested in exclusive economic zones but they do not include the contemplated harvesting of living resources in the Antarctic such as krill (*see* Chapter 3) and other underexploited resources. Many experts are of the opinion that the world catch of utilized species is at or close to the maximum optimum yield. Without adequate conservation controls, overfishing, as has occurred in the past, could interrupt and im-pede the supply of protein from fish.

The management of fisheries is, by far, the most significant control exercised by a coastal state in its exclusive economic zone. Indeed, when the United States enacted its Fishery Conservation and Management Act of 1976 it restricted controls to fisheries rather than legislate the broader controls in the exclusive economic zone envisioned (as described hereto-fore). Having sovereign rights over fisheries, a coastal state determines not only how much harvesting should be done, but who should do it and under what circumstances. In doing so, it has the obligation, based on the best scientific evidence, to ensure that the living resources are not endangered by overharvesting. Coastal stocks of fish move back and forth between adjacent states or jurisdictions. When there are many neighboring states with relative-ly small coastlines, and, therefore, narrow exclusive economic zones, as is the case in the North Sea and off the west coast of Africa, the need for coopera-tion and coordination is obvious. Consequently, coastal states are required to exchange statistics in order to arrive at common or similar conservation measures, and the best way of doing that it to create subregional or regional organizations.

It is incumbent upon a coastal state that does not have the capacity to harvest the allowable catch in its exclusive economic zone to permit other states to harvest, on terms agreed upon, the particular stock of fish under its control. In 1979, for example, the United States, under bilateral agreements, permitted foreign fishermen to catch surplus mackerel and squid off its Atlantic coast and pollack off its Alaskan coast. If and when the U.S. market for such species becomes more attractive and U.S. fishermen expand their capacity to harvest them, the catch permitted to foreigners will be decreased. Within the limits of good conservation, this principle, known as *optimum utilization*, is followed because it is far better to catch and use excess fish than to allow them to lie fallow and be of no use to mankind.

The Third Law of the Sea Conference drew up the conditions that a coastal state, in implementation of the principle of optimum utilization, could impose on foreign fishermen (*see* Appendix G, Article 62). The conditions are complex and extensive. They include the coastal state's right to board, inspect, arrest, and conduct judicial proceedings, as it deems necessary to ensure compliance with its laws and regulations. Many experts are of the opinion that, by applying the permissible regulations, a coastal state could essentially preclude foreign fishermen from its exclusive economic zone, thereby negating the purpose of optimum utilization.

The U.S. shrimp industry, which for many years fished off the coasts of Mexico and Brazil, has been informed by those states that existing arrangements for U.S. shrimp boats to fish off their coasts in the exclusive economic zone will be terminated. Consequently, unless equitable access under EEZ regulations or reciprocal arrangements can be made, a major and colorful component of the U.S. fishing industry will disappear. William Utz, executive director of the National Shrimp Congress, says of the future of his industry:

> The development of the EEZ [Exclusive Economic Zone] concept worldwide, has, in my judgment, produced a far greater impact than many envisioned and—at least initially—taken a course contrary to which many expected.
>
> Nations with developed fishing industries have the capability to range and harvest resources off the shores of other countries. When a nation with an undeveloped fishing industry excludes those foreign fleets from its EEZ it does not automatically follow that a domestic fishing industry for that country will develop. The typical attitude appears to reflect a belief that exclusion will force the foreign fishing fleets to enter joint ventures under terms very lucrative to the nation controlling the EEZ. The distant-water shrimp fleets have been confronted with just such circumstances in two instances. In both cases, the turn of events has not been beneficial to either party, i.e., the shrimp fleet or the country in question.
>
> Phrased simply and pointedly—one fine day does not make a summer; owning a fishing boat does not make one a fisherman. Controlling a resource does not automatically provide the wealth of that resource; excluding fleets from resources will not force joint ventures. Until nations learn that only when a business deal is truly beneficial to both parties in the short run, with

incentives for greater benefit in the long run, the riches from renewable resources will waste away with the unharvested protein of no benefit to anyone.

The impact of the EEZ on our distant-water shrimp fleets is apparent. What is not apparent, however, is the ultimate impact on our domestic shrimp fleets. The EEZ has provided the domestic U.S. fishing industry an opportunity to manage resources and thereby develop some stability for the industry. The past few years have produced unusually good production years. More and more vessels, however, are moving into the Gulf shrimp fishery—some are new boats out of the yard, some are older boats returning from foreign waters. How all of this will evolve is uncertain at the moment; but, one thing is certain—the fisherman's mode of operation will never be the same as before the EEZ.

Some species of fish are oceanic in range. A fine example is tuna, some species of which migrate between Chile and Southern California, other species speed across the entire Pacific, while others roam the tropical Atlantic and the Gulf of Guinea. Unlike coastal stocks, whose migratory habits are limited, tuna are constantly moving over vast areas. Clearly, it is less than satisfactory for a coastal state to try to manage such fish on a unilateral basis while they are transiting its exclusive economic zone. The probability is that management would be so fragmented by multiple and perhaps contradictory regulations as the fish transited various exclusive economic zones that it would, in effect, be nonexistent. Because of their habits a special regime is required. Before the Seabeds (or Law of the Sea Conference Preparatory) Committee in August 1972, Ambassador Donald L. McKerman identified the arrangements best suited for such species:

> The highly migratory and truly oceanic species can only be properly regulated through international organizations, because of their ocean-wide distribution and vast migrations, the temporary nature of their presence in the waters off any single state, and the well demonstrated economic fact that a viable fishery for such species must also be far ranging.

The negotiating text of the Third Law of the Sea Conference prescribed that both coastal and fishery states in a particular region should cooperate either directly or through appropriate international organizations to ensure conservation and promote optimum utilization of highly migratory species throughout that region, both within and beyond the exclusive economic zone. It provided further that, in regions where there was no international organization, the concerned states should form one. On the other hand, the text of the provisions indicates that the conditions a coastal state may establish for foreign fishermen to fish in its exclusive economic zone under the principle of optimum utilization may be applied in these cases also. It thus appears that, should a particular country, or countries, choose to do so, it could pursue a policy that would create two regimes applicable to highly

migratory species; one emanating from a regional international organization for the area generally beyond the exclusive economic zone, and another
prescribed by a particular coastal state while the fish are within its exclusive
economic zone. At this writing, it appears that most countries are not seeking
a duality of regimes, but one international regime that would manage the
fish throughout their range, both within and beyond 200 miles. The United
States made its position clear by making international (not coastal state)
management of highly migratory species an integral part of the Fishery
Conservation and Management Act of 1976.

One of the most modern and efficient of the U.S. fishing fleets is the
high-capacity and long-range tuna fleet. It operates off the west coast of the
Americas, in the central and southwest Pacific, and in the Atlantic in the Gulf
of Guinea. The United States has been an active participant in two major
international tuna conventions, one dealing with the eastern Pacific, the
other with the Atlantic. Before exclusive economic zones were developed,
the biggest problem the tuna fleet faced was the 200-mile jurisdictional claim
made by Ecuador, Peru, and Chile but not recognized by the United States
or the world community in general. Incidents that occurred during that
period are noted in Chapter 4. With the advent of the exclusive economic
zone, waters that were once considered to be high seas with concomitant
freedom to fish came under a special-purpose control of the coastal state.
That broadened considerably the problem of access to tuna because all
coastal states became involved. A report from the *Wall Street Journal* of 29
November 1978 used the central Pacific to illustrate the changes that were
taking place:

> In the past, anyone who wanted to catch tuna near the islands was free to try.
> But in June 1977, the independent countries and self-governing states of the
> region (there are 10 altogether) decided to hang out the world's biggest "No
> Fishing" sign. By last March, each had declared sovereignty over all re-
> sources—fish, minerals and anything else—for 200 miles in every direction.
>   This doesn't seem like much territory until you realize that each country is
> composed of not one but often hundreds of islands strung out over thousands
> of ocean miles. The Cook Islands, for instance, have a total land area of 149
> square miles, but the group's 15 islands encompass 1.2 million square miles of
> ocean. Added up, the total territory claimed by these "microstates" comes to
> at least six million square miles. "Amazing," says an American diplomat
> passing through Fiji. "There isn't much of the Pacific left."

It follows that at this point the international tuna fisheries conventions
are undergoing the stresses of change resulting from the impact of the new
fisheries regimes. Whether the older conventions will survive or be replaced
is a moot question, as is the future of the U.S. tuna fleet. Many years might
well elapse before international institutions in the various regions are re-
structured. One element is relatively clear: should the regulations for fishing

within the exclusive economic zone under the optimum utilization principle be applied to vessels that follow the highly migratory tuna to the same extent and in the same manner as they are to fishing for coastal stocks, the economics of tuna-vessel operations would become vulnerable and that could foretell unknown directions for the U.S. tuna clipper.

August Felando, president of the American Tunaboat Association, expresses the following views on the future of his industry:

> The short-term impact of the enforcement of the EEZ [Exclusive Economic Zone] will be to reduce capitalization efforts in new tuna vessels for the six countries that presently dominate 90% of the world production of tuna. Fishing effort will increase in areas outside of the EEZ and off countries that do not maintain extensive naval protection of their EEZ. Conservation efforts on a multinational basis will decline for the short term. Regional license arrangements will be utilized to induce and strengthen international tuna conservation efforts, but such arrangements will be adopted only after a long passage of time and after the economics of highly mobile vessel activities become too risky and costly. The market for tuna will continue to increase but change to a "luxury item" or high value and cost product. This will be especially true for Bluefin, Bigeye, Albacore, and within a relatively few years for Yellowfin. A variety of fishing techniques will prevail, however, the purse seine technique will continue to increase its share of production over the longline and baitboat techniques in the Atlantic, Indian and the Eastern Pacific Oceans. There will be a steady increase in the production of Skipjack tuna world-wide, with a corresponding decline because of the decline in sub-surface fishing techniques world-wide, the increase in tuna fishing intensity by surface fishing techniques, and the enforcement of EEZones by nations attempting to unilaterally manage tuna.

Still a third category of fish have characteristics that require a different regime. They are the anadromous stocks; for the United States, salmon is of principal interest. Anadromous fish are spawned in the upper reaches of freshwater streams and, upon reaching a degree of maturity, begin their descent to the ocean. The salmon of Alaska, Washington, and Oregon migrate beyond the western tip of the Aleutians, mingle with Asian salmon, and, after two or three years at sea, return to the streams they left to spawn or to die. Salmon in the Atlantic follow a similar pattern.

Because of these characteristics, the coastal states in whose territories the salmon rivers and streams are located and maintained—maintenance can be expensive, as is the case with the Columbia River in Oregon—have primary interest in and rights over such stocks. Except in the rare case where economic dislocation would occur if it were otherwise, fishing for anadromous stocks is restricted to being conducted only in exclusive economic zones. The above qualification of economic dislocation refers particularly to Japan's long-existing, open-sea salmon fishery in the Bering Sea. In cases such as this, the states concerned are obligated to cooperate to minimize the economic dislocation of a historic open-sea salmon fishery.

THE CONTINENTAL SHELF

In general geographic terms a continental shelf is the underwater extension of the land mass of a littoral country to the outer edge of the continental margin beyond which is the deep seabed. Because of the tremendous wealth of resources, particularly oil and gas, of continental shelves, the question of their legal extent and precise limits has been one of the more difficult issues in negotiations on the Law of the Sea.

As long as the bed of the sea was not technically susceptible to occupation by any state, the general rule was that it was as free as the seas above it. This rule drew part of its strength from the fact that use of the seabed implied a required support from stationary units on the surface of the sea, and such units could interfere with navigation on the free seas. For example, had a bridge been built across the English Channel to the continent of Europe, as was being considered in 1930, its supports, resting in the seabed, would have constituted an obstacle to navigation on the free seas.

In 1945, when President Truman proclaimed that the United States regarded the natural resources of the seabed and subsoil beneath the high seas contiguous to its coasts as subject to its jurisdiction and control, the old law of both the seabed and subsoil began to change. While there were and are varying estimates on amounts, it is manifest that the subsoil of the U.S. continental shelf contains major deposits of oil and gas and, it is claimed, quantities of ores. To extract the oil and gas from the subsoil, American companies installed drilling rigs or derricks in the high seas above the seabed.

Growing out of this major development certain facts and factors became apparent: (1) an area of the seabed and subsoil had been successfully occupied; (2) according to the technology of the 1940s, the only way to get the resources from the subsoil was by the use of oil and gas rigs planted on the ocean floor; (3) the presence of stationary oil or gas rigs could constitute a menace to free navigation; and (4) because continents extend under the sea, littoral nations' claims to subsoil resources should have priority over all others. The right to this priority is based on what is known as the *theory of contiguity*. It is interesting to note that the United States has not claimed any sovereignty, title, or ownership in the continental shelf itself, but directed its jurisdiction and control to the natural resources of the shelf. In exercising control over these resources, however, it created what might, in some instances, be considered physical impediments to navigation—offshore oil rigs. This development may appear to contradict what President Truman said in his proclamation of 1945: "The character as high seas of the waters above the continental shelf and the right to their free and unimpeded navigation are in no way affected."

The factor that created this apparent contradiction was the physical presence of the rigs. Thus an accommodation to provide for the new (offshore rigs) and the old (freedom of navigation) use had to be made. This was accomplished through the mechanism of the 1958 Geneva Convention on the Continental Shelf.

After the Truman proclamation, numerous other coastal states made similar claims to their continental shelves and used similar equipment for extracting oil and gas. Thus, through common practice in the international community, it became recognized that a coastal state had sovereign rights over its continental shelf for the purpose of exploring and exploiting the natural resources thereof. The law that developed was codified in the 1958 Geneva Convention on the Continental Shelf and received wide support in the world community. The exercise of sovereign rights over continental shelves does not alter the legal status of the superjacent waters or the air space above those waters. Nor does it affect the right of all states to lay submarine cables and pipelines across the continental shelf of any state, subject to reasonable measures taken by the coastal state to prevent and control pollution and to protect its own rights concerning exploration and exploitation of the natural resources of its shelf.

A coastal state has the right to install oil rigs or other devices extending to the surface of the high seas in order to exploit the natural resources of its continental shelf. It may also establish safety zones up to a distance of 500 meters around such installations for the mutual protection of shipping and the installation itself. The state concerned is obliged, however, to maintain permanent navigational warning of the presence of zones and installations. Ships of all nationalities must respect such safety zones, provided the coastal state has given due notice of their creation and of the installations they protect. No installation may be established in a recognized sea lane where its presence could interfere with international navigation. Though installations of the type under discussion come under the jurisdiction of the coastal state, they do not have the status of islands and, consequently, do not have territorial seas of their own.

When the Third Law of the Sea Conference met, its provisions incorporated most of the tenets that had developed with the increasing use of continental shelves and had become codified in the 1958 Convention on the Continental Shelf. There were, however, some significant differences. The 1958 Convention described the seaward limit of a shelf as "a depth of 200 metres or, beyond that limit . . . where the depth of the superjacent waters admits to the exploitation of the natural resources of the said areas." The draft articles of the Third Law of the Sea Conference, August 1980, describe the seaward limit as "the natural prolongation of its [a coastal state's] land territory to the outer edge of the continental margin, or to a distance of 200 nautical miles from the baselines from which the breadth of the territorial sea is measured where the outer edge of the continental margin does not extend up to that distance" (*see* Appendix H).

The above extension is obviously a result, in part, of advanced technology permitting greater use of continental-shelf resources; up to the 200-mile line, the coastal state's rights under the provisions governing the continental shelf complement and expand those established for the exclusive economic zone. To meet the requirements of some few states whose shelves are broader than 200 miles, claims not to exceed 350 miles are recognized. The limitations imposed in these special cases can be found in Appendix H, Article 76.

In somewhat the same stage of development as the law of space, the law regarding the continental shelf is still relatively elementary. It is expected, however, that, as technology finds new uses for continental shelves, the law will become more refined and comprehensive. An indication of what can be expected in the future is the navy's project to build a village 500 feet beneath U.S. coastal waters, i.e., on the continental shelf. The purpose is to permit extended underwater living as a step toward solving many marine mysteries. As envisioned, the village would consist of two-story, concrete buildings resting on adjustable pilings to keep them level. Devices for supplying electricity and air have already been developed. If the venture is successful, the door will be open for a vast new utilization of the continental shelf.

Another use of the continental shelf was tested in 1968 when some U.S. investors started digging fill from the shelf in order to create an island on the submerged coral reefs beyond U.S. jurisdictional waters off Florida. They intended to set up huts, and proclaim it as a sovereign country, the Grand Capri Republic.

The issue of whether the continental shelf could be used for such a purpose was joined in a U.S. federal court. Ruling in favor of the government, the judge declared that the disputed territory was not an island but was seabed and, under the Continental Shelf Convention, the United States had all rights to exploit its resources. The court pointed out also that not only would the artificial island constitute an obstacle to navigation on the high seas, but it would destroy the coral, which had aesthetic value (*U.S.* v. *Ray*).

SCIENTIFIC RESEARCH

When Article 2 of the International Law Commission's Convention on the High Seas, drawn up in 1956, enumerated the freedoms that could be exercised on the high seas, it did not specifically include freedom of scientific research. It did, however, note that freedoms, other than those listed, were recognized by the general principles of International Law. Thus, the International Law Commission's commentary on the draft article listed scientific research as one of those unenumerated freedoms of the high seas, as comprehended by the community of states during that period.

By its actions and in its policy statements, the United States has always supported the principle of the freedom of scientific research of the high seas. Indeed, until fairly recently few questions were raised concerning the exercise of that freedom because such scientific research of the high seas was limited and few people appreciated the contributions that knowledge of the oceans, their resources, and their environment could make to the world community. Scientific research of the high seas was conducted without hindrance; it enjoyed the full status of a freedom on the high seas.

In the middle of the twentieth century the situation began to change and it became clear that freedom of scientific research was being challenged. In an address at a regional meeting of the American Society of International Law held in Miami in December 1969, William L. Sullivan, Jr., an expert in the field of ocean research, described what was happening:

> The freedom of scientific research in the oceans was virtually unquestioned only a few years ago. States made few claims to ocean areas which restricted scientific research, and even in the limited areas where the coastal state clearly exercised jurisdiction there was little or no interference with scientific research. Necessary clearances could often be arranged informally by scientific colleagues, and it is safe to say that the formalities of obtaining clearances were sometimes ignored, without appearing to cause concern to officials of the coastal state or anyone else. This situation generally prevailed through the 50s and in large measure continued into the 60s. As that decade drew to a close, however, the scientist found it increasingly difficult to carry out his activities because of restraints imposed by the coastal state, either unilaterally or through international concert. Indications are that this deteriorating situation will get worse before it gets better. In large measure it is caused by coastal-state concern over actual or potential development of ocean resources, whether from the waters themselves or the continental shelf or seabeds.
>
> At the same time the ability of the marine scientist to carry out his research has increased tremendously, and his research has drawn increasing support with a consequent expansion of these activities. The trend is undoubtedly toward more and better research. It is ironic that the technical developments which form the basis of this expansion of research have also led to the increasing activity and interest in the development of the actual or potential resources of the ocean which in turn give rise to the problems facing the marine scientist today. This dichotomy is unfortunately self-reinforcing, for as Dr. Milner B. Schaefer, a renowned expert from Scripps Institution, has observed: "Studies of large scope are extremely important for the development of our increased knowledge of the sea and generate new technology which makes possible more extensive and effective utilization of ocean resources."

THE THIRD LAW OF THE SEA CONFERENCE

Despite some progressive efforts in various specialized international gatherings, including the Intergovernmental Oceanographic Commission, which addressed itself directly to the question of ensuring the freedom of scientific research, the status of scientific research was seriously challenged in the Law of the Sea forum in the 1970s. Part of the problem is the difficulty of distinguishing between commercial exploration or prospecting and pure scientific research. Another facet of the issue is that in many areas of the world there is some suspicion as to what work is being carried out by scientific-research ships. In line with its historic adherence to the concept of freedom of scientific research, the United States and other countries with experience in the conduct of ocean research worked hard to retain a high degree of freedom for that activity. Indicative of this effort were the positions taken by the United States and the United Kingdom in the sessions of the U.N. Seabed Committee held in August 1972. A. A. Archer, the U.K. delegate, stated:

> In conclusion, Mr. Chairman, I must reassert that the objective of all marine research scientists is to improve and increase the knowledge of the marine environment. This knowledge benefits all mankind. Positive encouragement should, therefore, be given to marine science. To provide this encouragement my delegation believes that . . . scientific research should remain as free of regulation as it is at present.

At the same session, on behalf of the U.S. delegation, Donald L. McKernan said in part:

> The sea is a critical component of an ecosystem that reaches every corner of the globe. It produces large quantities of living and non-living resources. Furthermore, it is an efficient and essential means of transportation and communication. Better understanding of the sea is, thus, of vital importance to every nation whether coastal or landlocked, developed or developing.
>
> The United States considers that the quest for knowledge throughout the ocean is not only a necessity for all the important reasons stated above, but in the area beyond the territorial sea, it is also a right which should not be diminished or abridged by the restrictive actions of states, coastal or otherwise, except as recognized by international law. The United States believes that to facilitate the investigative process that makes possible the benefits outlined above, and others as well, it is in the common interest of everyone to accept rules that maintain maximum freedom to conduct scientific research in the ocean.

Unfortunately the great weight of the positions taken by the one hundred developing countries active in the Third Law of the Sea Conference was contrary to that of maximum freedom for scientific research. Those countries believed that a coastal state's interest in the conduct of scientific research within its 200-mile exclusive economic zone was superior to that of any other state or, indeed, of the international community. In brief, their position was that scientific research could be conducted in that area only with the consent of the coastal state. Other delegations, including that of the United States, in an attempt to reach a common ground on the issue, prepared a series of requirements that would be applicable to anyone seeking to conduct scientific research in an exclusive economic zone. These requirements included sharing data and samples with the coastal state, notifying the coastal state in advance of an impending project, and allowing the coastal state's participation in the project. Had this proposal been accepted, access to any area would have been assured because consent of the coastal state would not have been required.

However, the consent issue was not that easily resolved; a compromise suggested in a session of the Law of the Sea Conference held in 1976 required a coastal state's consent for research related to resources but only a state's fulfillment of its obligations for all other research activities. In 1977, this politically attractive, but scientifically difficult, formula was modified in the direction of the developing countries by requiring consent for all research in the exclusive economic zone but allowing it to be withheld only if the research related to resources. Since then efforts to find a reasonable balance between the interests of coastal states and those of the international community have continued. The regime for scientific research that will emerge seems likely, at this writing, to be close to that outlined in Appendix L. That text specifies the right of a coastal state to require consent as a prerequisite to scientific research in its exclusive economic zone; beyond that zone, all states are free to conduct scientific research subject to the generalized duty of promoting international cooperation.

This discussion is an abbreviated treatment of a difficult and contentious issue; more detailed treatment would, however, go beyond the scope and purpose of this text. What is significant is the fact that the close scrutiny that the world community has given to the conduct of scientific research of the oceans during the last decade has resulted in what must be considered dramatic changes. What the future might hold is indicated in the following personal view of Norman A. Wulf, director of the State Department's Office of Marine Science and Technology. Mr. Wulf has been directly involved in deliberations on the conduct of scientific research since the Third Law of the Sea Conference began and has served as U.S. spokesman on this subject since 1977.

> Consent has become the watchword for marine scientists—total unqualified consent for research in the territorial sea, in archipelagos, in straits and restricted consent in the economic zone and on the continental shelf beyond. For the economic zone, consent is required but the coastal state must "in normal circumstances" grant its consent. The phrase "normal circumstances"

refers to the overall state of relations between the researching state and the coastal state. If circumstances are normal, consent must be granted unless the research is "of direct significance" to utilization of resources, involves drilling, the use of explosives or the introduction of harmful substances in which cases the coastal state has discretion to withhold consent. Requests for consent must be submitted six months in advance. Consent of the coastal state shall be presumed if there is no response in four months. Finally, all disputes concerning research must go to binding third party settlement or compulsory conciliation except when both the researcher and the coastal state agree that the research activity is subject to its discretionary consent.

An identical regime applies to research "on the continental shelf" beyond the 200-mile zone except a major qualification applies to the research of "direct significance" to resource utilization. This discretionary right shall apply beyond 200 miles only when the research is to be conducted in an area that the coastal state has designated as an area in which exploitation or exploratory drilling is occurring or is about to occur. Beyond the economic zone or the continental shelf where it extends beyond 200 miles, there are no restrictions on scientific research. Indeed, the likely treaty article on high seas freedoms specifically lists scientific research as one of the enumerated freedoms.

Thus, we see in the outcome of the treaty negotiations on science a steady lessening of coastal state control as one moves from the shoreline seaward. Total control applies in the territorial sea, control subject to several meaningful restrictions applies in the economic zone and no controls over marine science in the area beyond national jurisdiction. Given the vast areas now subject to coastal states control that were formerly free, scientists in particular should hope that it will be a long, long time before there is another conference on the law of the sea.

This regime may have very harsh consequences for research activities within 200 miles of the coast if most coastal states utilize the provisions in the treaty to prevent research. On the other hand, many coastal states may become much more relaxed about research once their control over resources has been universally recognized. The probable future will lie somewhere in between the two extremes. Most countries will create no problems for the research and it will be conducted albeit with much more red tape. Some few countries, however, will utilize the provisions of the text to prevent the research from being conducted. One can only hope that further knowledge of the ways of science and the benefits it can bring forth will limit the number of countries in the latter category.

POLLUTION—PROTECTION OF THE MARINE ENVIRONMENT

For several centuries the high seas were used for the disposal of wastes and little thought was given to the possibility that the procedure might damage the living resources of the oceans as well as the oceans themselves. In brief, pollution of the seas was not considered a major problem. The first to recognize the problem were the London Convention for the Prevention of Oil Pollution of the Seas, held in 1954 and sponsored by the Intergovernmental Maritime Consultative Organization (IMCO), and the 1958 Geneva High Seas Convention, but their provisions were weak on control and enforcement. A major weakness was that only the flag state of an offending ship had the authority to act. Coastal states, the parties most likely to be the victims of oil spills, had no such authority. After the above conventions came into force, public concern over the decreasing quality of the marine environment focused sharp attention on the need to prevent pollution of the high seas. By that time, research had shown that the oceans could tolerate only a certain amount of pollution without having their chemical balances disturbed and their living resources endangered, a situation in which man would be the loser.

How to control pollution in the oceans therefore became one of the major ocean issues of the 1970s, and in 1970 many states took unilateral action. The United States strengthened its laws regulating the activities of U.S. ships at sea, and passed a statute concerning the dumping of pollutants at sea. Canada unilaterally proclaimed a 100-mile pollution zone in the Arctic region, which, when implemented, will require ships of all flags to meet certain standards. Perhaps the event most responsible for the concern was the grounding of the supertanker *Torrey Canyon* off the southwest coast of England in March 1967. The resulting oil spill inundated beaches and marshes in both England and France. Two international results obtained.

The first result was that IMCO called a conference which produced the 1969 Convention on Intervention. This convention specifically recognized the need for coastal states to be able to respond to situations similar to the *Torrey Canyon* disaster:

> Art. I (1) [the coastal state may] take such measures on the high seas as may be necessary to prevent, mitigate, or eliminate grave and imminent danger to their coastline or related interests from pollution or threat of pollution of the sea by oil, following upon a maritime casualty,

and

> Art. III (d) In cases of extreme urgency requiring measures to be taken immediately, the coastal state may take measures rendered necessary by the urgency of the situation, without prior notification or consultation with the flag state.

The second result was to increase the urgency of the effort within the Law of the Sea Conference to negotiate meaningful and enforceable pollution standards. As mentioned in Chapter 5, the *Argo Merchant* disaster in 1976 and the *Amoco Cadiz* grounding in 1978 served as stark reminders of the urgency of the problem and helped shape the thinking of the conference. Finally, in August 1979, the chairman of the Law of the Sea Committee, which was charged with drafting a pollution regime, reported that his committee had reached a consensus on balance of interests and produced a draft text. To show how divergent the thinking was before this consensus was reached, the following views expressed by various delegates at the 1972 session have been picked at random:

Statement made by Ambassador M. Ogiso, delegate of Japan, on 28 July 1972:

It has been proposed by several delegates that, in order to cope with marine pollution effectively, it is essential to allow coastal states to establish a pollution zone beyond their territorial water where coastal states can exercise special authority for the prevention of pollution which could cause damage or injury to the land or marine environment under its exclusive or sovereign authority. We entertain a grave doubt as to the validity and effectiveness of such an approach.

I wish to reiterate that this very idea of partitioning the ocean space for the prevention and control of marine pollution is incompatible with the basic framework as envisaged in these Principles, in which global standards and rules are to be applied to every part of the sea to be observed by every country of our globe. The pollutants would constantly spread in the oceans through tides, currents and winds and protective measures against such pollution cannot be effectively taken if we concentrate on imposing arbitrary measures on one part of the ocean while ignoring completely the other adjacent part. Since our objective should be to reduce the level of contamination of every part of the sea, we must aim at controlling all the sources of marine pollution regardless of whether the original source is located in the middle of the ocean or near the coast. As long as we adhere to a zonal approach there would inevitably be a dichotomy in the mode of control between inside and outside of the zone and the objective of effective control cannot be achieved since the pollutants know no boundaries. It is essential that we should develop a kind of regime in which the same degree of effectiveness of control can be secured globally for the entire ocean. . . .

Statement made by Chen Chih-Fang, delegate of the People's Republic of China, on 2 August 1972:

One of the major differences of opinion on how marine pollution should be prevented and controlled is whether a coastal state has the right of jurisdiction over an area within a given limit, which is adjacent to its territorial sea. Many representatives have in their statements strongly maintained that coastal states have the right to exercise direct jurisdiction and control over areas within given limits, which are adjacent to their territorial seas, for the purpose of preventing, reducing or eliminating the serious harms of pollution. The superpowers, however, have opposed this right of coastal states by using all kinds of pretexts.

On the prevention and control of marine pollution, we think that coastal states, being the direct victims of marine pollution, have the full right as well as necessity to exercise direct jurisdiction and control over areas within given limits, which are adjacent to their territorial seas, in order to protect the health and security of their people and meet the needs of their economic development. The proposals submitted by representatives of many countries at the Sea-Bed Committee with a view to safeguarding the rights of the coastal states are of positive significance to the prevention of marine pollution. Any argument aimed at opposing or weakening such jurisdiction of coastal states is detrimental to the prevention of marine pollution and runs counter to the desire of the peoples of the world to preserve the marine environment and is therefore unacceptable. . . .

Statement made by J. Alan Beesley, representative of Canada, on 20 July 1972:

The first of the three principles [on the rights of coastal states] reads as follows:
A state may exercise special authority in areas of the sea adjacent to its territorial waters where functional controls of a continuing nature are necessary for the effective prevention of pollution which could cause damage or injury to the land or marine environment under its exclusive or sovereign authority.

This principle represents, in our view, the logical extension of the particular interests of the coastal state recognized in the statement of objectives endorsed by the Stockholm Conference. . . . In practical terms this principle signifies that coastal states have or should have the right to establish zones of specialized jurisdiction in areas adjacent to their territorial sea for the prevention of pollution of the coastal environment and the marine environment in general. Every state surely must ultimately have the right to protection under the law against pollution damage within its territory from activities by other states, and to protect that right coastal states should have the right and responsibility to assume necessary maritime jurisdiction beyond traditional limits, taking into account the degree of danger and special circumstances which may be involved. In our view, the Law of the Sea Conference will fail to provide the necessary accommodation of national and international interests if it fails to give effect to this principle.
The second of the principles in question reads as follows:
A coastal state may prohibit any vessel which does not comply with internationally agreed rules and standards or, in their absence, with reasonable national rules and standards of the coastal state in question, from entering waters under its environmental protection authority.

As noted, one of the principles actually endorsed by the Stockholm Conference provided that all states should ensure that their vessels comply with internationally agreed rules and standards relating to ship design and construction, operating procedures and other relevant factors. To give practical effect to this agreed principle, it seems to us essential that the coastal state should have the right to prohibit vessels not complying with internationally agreed rules and standards from entering areas where it exercises jurisdiction for the protection of the environment. Measures will have to be worked out to solve the problems of inspection, but inaction is not acceptable on this issue. Similarly, where internationally agreed rules and standards have not been established, the coastal state must have the right to enforce its own reasonable national rules and standards against all vessels in the areas in question. As the Canadian delegation has pointed out in the past, it has become necessary to modernize the concept of innocent passage and to extend its application to areas adjacent to the territorial sea.

The third principle in question reads as follows:

The basis on which a state should exercise rights or powers, in addition to its sovereign rights or powers, pursuant to its special authority in areas adjacent to its territorial waters, is that such rights or powers should be deemed to be delegated to that state by the world community on behalf of humanity as a whole. The rights and powers exercised must be consistent with the coastal state's primary responsibility for marine environmental protection in the areas concerned: they should be subject to international rules and standards and to review before an appropriate international tribunal.

This principle, of course, reflects the general Canadian approach to the whole range of problems of the law of the sea and to marine pollution in particular. I wish to emphasize, however, that we do not attach any particular importance to terminology for its own sake. I refer to such terms as "custodianship" and "delegation of powers." Such terms should not, in any event, be thought of as suitable for draft treaty articles, but rather as illustrations of our conceptual approach to the problem. What is fundamentally important is that the necessary recognition of the rights of coastal states should also make adequate provision for the vital interests of the international community and that, to attain this end, the rights in question be exercised on the basis of internationally agreed rules and standards and subject to appropriate dispute settlement procedures. Otherwise we could fail not only to protect the interests of the international community but fail as well to achieve an accommodation among conflicting national interests.

Statement made by John R. Stevenson, delegate of the United States, on 2 August 1972:

Finally, pollution from vessels is a subject requiring careful balancing of interests, rights, and obligations among maritime, shipping, and coastal states. Control of such pollution must be by international agreement in order to ensure an acceptable balance. Therefore, while we sympathize with and share the concerns which have produced proposals such as the three principles on the rights of coastal states to which the distinguished representative of Canada, Mr. Beesley, referred in his statement to this Subcommittee on July 20, 1972, we cannot accept that approach. Vesting large discretion and powers in coastal states would not be likely to result in the striking of a proper balance of interests, or in coping with pollution in the open ocean beyond whatever zone of control were established, and it could lead to the type of conflict which it is the main purpose of this Committee and the Law of the Sea Conference to avoid. Moreover, in view of the actions and proposals I have outlined, I believe the needs of coastal states for increased protection against pollution from vessels can and will be met without resort to dangerous methods of self help. I am convinced that temptations to leave the urgent and important problems of marine pollution to coastal states must be resisted. We must recognize and act on the fact that only concerted international action can hope to be adequate to meet the common danger.

Clearly, the views expressed in 1972 did not prove immutable; however, their diversity serves to point up the difficulty in reaching a balance. The committee consensus reached in 1979, which was tantamount to conference consensus, necessitated the laborious writing of forty-five articles spelling out rights and duties (*see* Appendix K). The rights and duties that are of primary concern to the purpose of this text are noted in the following paragraphs.

RIGHTS AND DUTIES

The primary duty of every state is to protect and preserve the marine environment. Implicit in that obligation is the fact that man's activities create the larger polluting effect against the delicate balance of ocean chemistry.

In carrying out the duty noted above, all states are required to use the best practicable means at their disposal, including joint actions with neighboring states, to ensure that pollution arising from incidents or activities under their jurisdiction does not spread beyond the areas where they exercise sovereign rights. This means that they must protect and preserve the marine environment from, among other things, pollution caused by the release through the atmosphere or by dumping of toxic, harmful, and noxious substances from land-based sources; and from pollution by ships, in particular for preventing accidents and dealing with emergencies, ensuring the safety of operations at sea, preventing intentional and unintentional discharges, and regulating the design, construction, equipment, operation, and manning of ships. Pollution from installations and devices used in exploration or exploitation of the resources of seabeds and subsoil is also specifically included, as is pollution from other installations and devices operating in the marine environment.

In carrying out this broad duty to protect the marine environment, all states are required to refrain from unjustifiable interference with activities of other states, and to cooperate on both a global and regional basis in formulating consistent rules, standards, and procedures to meet the threat of pollution. The requirement to cooperate on a regional basis carries with it the need for neighboring states to develop and promote joint contingency plans to respond to pollution accidents. The Campeche incident is a case in point.

On 3 June 1979, an exploratory oil well being drilled fifty miles offshore in Campeche Bay, one of Mexico's richest oil fields, "blew out" and, in the huge explosion that followed, the drilling platform was destroyed by fire. An uncontrolled flow of oil began pouring into the Gulf of Mexico. Attempts to cap the well were hampered by extremely bad weather and the continuing spill was not even partially contained until 18 October 1979. During the intervening four and a half months, more than one hundred million gallons of crude oil poured into the sea. Unfortunately, a slow, steady current, aided by winds, pushed the oil to the northwest, where it first struck Mexican estuaries and beaches and then the coast of Texas. It is the world's worst oil spill to date—far worse than that created by the grounding and breakup of the *Amoco Cadiz* off the coast of France in March 1978. From an economic point of view, Mexican officials estimated a cost of hundreds of millions of dollars in salvage operations, clean-up, and lost crude oil and gas. At this writing, the extent of damage to the coast of Texas and the living resources along it is not known, but property-owners, shrimp-fishing industries, and tourist interests have filed suits totaling approximately $350 million. Some Texans have proposed suing the government of Mexico.

Had the joint contingency planning between Mexico and the United States advanced beyond the preliminary stage when the accident happened, cooperation between the two countries might well have been facilitated and the damage been consequently less. Be that as it may, the articles of the Law of the Sea require such cooperation, and should there be similar disasters in the future, they might be better controlled. Additionally, the dramatic spread of the oil from one country's jurisdictional area to the other places increased emphasis on the need to recognize and understand the importance of ocean currents in planning to protect the marine environment. Currents, like fish, do not necessarily respect jurisdictional lines drawn on charts by man.

RULES APPLICABLE TO SHIPS

States are obliged to establish for ships flying their flag laws for the prevention and control of pollution. These laws must be generally consistent with rules that are accepted internationally as a result of diplomatic conferences or the work of such international organizations as IMCO.

A state may make compliance with particular pollution controls a condition for the entry of foreign ships into its ports and internal waters, or for visits to its offshore terminals. When it does so, it is under obligation not only to advise competent international organizations but to give publicity to the controls so that ships may be aware of them before they attempt entry.

A coastal state may establish national laws for pollution control within its territorial sea, but such laws are not to interfere with or hamper innocent passage.

Within its exclusive economic zone, a coastal state may establish laws for pollution control so long as they are in conformity with generally accepted international rules. If, however, it has reasonable grounds for believing that an area of its exclusive economic zone has characteristics that make it particularly susceptible to pollution, it may resort, through international forums, to special mandatory methods of control. Areas that are normally ice-covered, such as the Arctic, are the most sensitive to pollution. Accordingly, pertinent coastal states have the authority to establish extra-stringent laws and regulations within their exclusive economic zones.

Enforcement of Rules for Ships

States must ensure that ships flying their flag or registered under their law (flag states) comply with international rules for the control of pollution. This requirement includes prohibiting such ships from going to sea unless they can proceed in compliance with applicable international rules and they carry valid certificates showing that the necessary inspections for seaworthiness have been made. Should a ship violate an international rule regarding pollution, her flag state must, without prejudice to the rights of other states, as described below, provide for an immediate investigation and, where appropriate, cause proceedings to be taken against her, regardless of where the violation occurred. A flag state must, at the request of another state, investigate any violation alleged to have been committed by one of its ships. If the evidence is sufficient so to warrant, the flag state then has a duty to conduct the necessary proceedings.

There is a special relationship between a ship voluntarily visiting a foreign port and the state in which that port is situated, commonly referred to as the *port state*. If such a ship is suspected of having violated international rules outside the port state's jurisdictional waters, including its exclusive economic zone, that state may, in the interest of pollution control, inspect her and, if the evidence justifies it, initiate proceedings against her. It is also the duty of the port state to comply with a request from the flag state that it investigate an alleged violation, no matter where it might have occurred. However, should a violation take place in the jurisdictional waters of another state, the port state may initiate proceedings only if requested to do so by the offended state. Contingent on certain safeguards, if a port state ascertains that a visiting ship is in violation of international pollution-control rules relating to seaworthiness and, consequently, constitutes a hazard to the marine environment, it has the right to take administrative measures to prevent that ship from sailing. Should a port state decide to permit such a ship to sail, it may permit her to proceed only as far as the nearest appropriate repair yard.

The authority that a coastal state has over events within its own territorial sea or exclusive economic zone is different from that of port states. In brief, when a foreign ship is voluntarily in the port of a state, that state may take proceedings against the ship for any violation of its national laws, provided they are based on international norms, that occurred within its territorial sea or exclusive economic zone. In contrast, when a foreign ship is navigating in the territorial sea and there are clear grounds for suspecting that she has violated the national laws of the coastal state, that state may order the ship to stop, conduct a physical inspection of the ship relating to the violation, and conduct proceedings, which may result in detention, in accordance with its laws.

When a coastal state has clear grounds for suspecting that a ship navigating in its exclusive economic zone has violated applicable international or national rules, based on international norms, it has the right to require that ship to provide her identification, port of registry, last and next port of call, and other information required to establish whether a violation had occurred. Again, if there was a violation in the exclusive economic zone and it resulted in a substantial discharge causing or threatening significant pollution, the coastal state may order the ship to stop and physically inspect her, if the ship has refused to give information or if there is a variance between the information given and the evident factual situation. In the more damaging case where the discharge from the ship causes major damage or threatens major damage to the coastline or resources of the coastal state, it may, if the evidence warrants it, take action, including detention, in accordance with its laws.

In conformity with the key principles of the 1969 Convention on Intervention, a coastal state has the right to adopt measures and enforce them beyond its territorial sea in response to actual or threatened damage to its coastline or resources from pollution following a maritime casualty.

Immunity and Safeguards for Ships

In the fight against marine pollution, as in other areas, recognition is given again to the official status of warships and other government ships and aircraft engaged in noncommercial service. Because of the immunity vested in them, such ships and aircraft are exempt from the provisions related to pollution noted in this text and in more detail in Appendix K. Nevertheless, each sovereign state is responsible for seeing that ships and aircraft in its service operate and act in a manner consistent, so far as is reasonable and practicable, with the pollution provisions.

In seeking the necessary balance between earlier-noted conflicting interests of various countries, certain safeguards were incorporated into the draft provisions. Among such safeguards are: only officials, ships, and aircraft clearly marked and identifiable as being in government service and authorized to enforce the law may take action against foreign ships; ships engaged in law enforcement may not endanger a foreign ship by creating navigational hazards, taking her to an unsafe port or anchorage, or causing an unreasonable risk to the marine environment; law-enforcement agents may not delay a foreign ship longer than is essential for purposes of investigation or treat her in a discriminatory way. A physical inspection of a foreign ship must be limited to the examination of her pertinent certificates and records. Further inspection may be made only when there are grounds for believing that the ship or her equipment does not correspond substantially with the particulars shown on the above documents or that the certificates and records are not valid. Should the investigation indicate a violation, the ship shall be released promptly, subject to reasonable procedures for bonding. Should it, however, appear that, if the ship were released, she would constitute an unreasonable threat or damage to the marine environment, her release should be refused or made conditional upon her proceeding to the nearest appropriate repair yard.

Within the coming decades, different rules for different types of ships, depending on their ability to harm the marine environment, might well be devised. There might, for example, be special navigation rules for supertankers, liquified natural gas carriers, and ships carrying other extremely hazardous materials that are capable of having catastrophic effects on the marine environment.

At the conclusion of this section on the control and prevention of pollution of the marine environment, the question is whether the world community has reached a balance between the interests of coastal states and those of states more concerned with generally unimpeded navigation. The answer is not easy; it may depend on the perspective of the individual reader.

SEABEDS

As it has done in the case of fisheries, advancing technology has focused attention on one of the world's last frontiers—the deep seabeds and the ocean floor. Until the 1960s little was known about the resources present on the seabeds and in the ocean floor. Even had more been known about them, they could not have been exploited because the necessary technology did not exist.

During that decade, there were two significant developments. First, research technology advanced to a point that indicated the probable presence of significant petroleum and hard-mineral resources in and on the seabeds beyond the 200-meter isobath. It also confirmed the suspicion that there were no commercially harvestable living resources at those depths. Second, major developed countries, with the United States in the lead, began to develop the equipment and technology needed to exploit the resources of the seabeds. The extent of these resources is not yet fully known but several authorities have made estimates. In 1968, in an article entitled "The Political and Legal Problems of Using the Seabed for Peaceful Purposes," S. N. Kibirevskiy reported:

American specialists believe that concentrated on the surface of the sea-bed are 5 billion tons of cobalt, 43 billion tons of aluminum, 100 billion tons of copper, about 1 billion tons of zirconium, 15 billion tons of nickel, and 25 billion tons of magnesium. This does not, of course, exhaust the wealth on the floor of the world ocean. There are some scientists who suggest that the amount of oil, for example, under the seabed and ocean floor is many times that of all the continents and islands put together.

As an example of how far technology had advanced, an American mining company reported in 1971 that it had solved all the technical problems that had prevented it from mining manganese nodules from the seabeds, and was prepared to conduct such mining.

On 17 August 1967, Ambassador Arvid Pardo, then Malta's representative at the United Nations, called for the U.N. to prepare a treaty that would reserve the seabed and ocean floor as the common heritage of mankind, and to carry out that objective, establish a system which would ensure that all countries, regardless of geographic position or economic wealth, would benefit from the resources found there. In response, the U.N. created the Ad Hoc Committee to Study the Peaceful Uses of the Seabed and the Ocean Floor Beyond the Limits of National Jurisdiction (The Seabeds Committee). Within a year, during which the complexity of the issues became known, this committee had become a permanent standing body of the U.N. The Seabeds Committee produced a resolution embodying the principles that should apply to the seabeds and ocean floor. The resolution, passed in December 1970, was adopted by the General Assembly with support by an overwhelming number of the member states. The agreed-upon principles are:

1. The seabed and ocean floor, and the subsoil thereof, beyond the limits of national jurisdiction (hereinafter referred to as the area), as well as the resources of the area, are the common heritage of mankind;
2. The area shall not be subject to appropriation by any means by States or persons, natural or juridical, and no State shall claim or exercise sovereignty or sovereign rights over any part thereof;
3. No State or person, natural or juridical, shall claim, exercise or acquire rights with respect to the area or its resources incompatible with the international régime to be established and the principles of this Declaration;
4. All activities regarding the exploration and exploitation of the resources of the area and other related activities shall be governed by the international régime to be established;
5. The area shall be open to use exclusively for peaceful purposes by all States whether coastal or land-locked, without discrimination, in accordance with the international régime to be established;
6. States shall act in the area in accordance with the applicable principles and rules of international law including the Charter of the United Nations and

the Declaration on Principles of International Law concerning Friendly Relations and Co-operation among States in accordance with the Charter of the United Nations, adopted by the General Assembly on 24 October 1970, in the interests of maintaining international peace and security and promoting international co-operation and mutual understanding;

7. The exploration of the area and the exploitation of its resources shall be carried out for the benefit of mankind as a whole, irrespective of the geographic location of States, whether land-locked or coastal, and taking into particular consideration the interests and needs of the developing countries;

8. The area shall be reserved exclusively for peaceful purposes, without prejudice to any measures which have been or may be agreed upon in the context of international negotiations undertaken in the field of disarmament and which may be applicable to a broader area.
One or more international agreements shall be concluded as soon as possible in order to implement effectively this principle and to constitute a step towards the exclusion of the sea-bed, the ocean floor and the subsoil thereof from the arms race;

9. On the basis of the principles of this Declaration, an international régime applying to the area and its resources and including appropriate international machinery to give effect to its provisions shall be established by an international treaty of a universal character, generally agreed upon. The régime shall, *inter alia*, provide for the orderly and safe development and rational management of the area and its resources and for expanding opportunities in the use thereof and ensure the equitable sharing by States in the benefits derived therefrom, taking into particular consideration the interests and needs of the developing countries, whether land-locked or coastal;

10. States shall promote international co-operation in scientific research exclusively for peaceful purposes:
    (a) By participation in international programmes and by encouraging co-operation in scientific research by personnel of different countries;
    (b) Through effective publication of research programmes and dissemination of the results of research through international channels;
    (c) By co-operation in measures to strengthen research capabilities of developing countries, including the participation of their nationals in research programmes.
    No such activity shall form the legal basis for any claims with respect to any part of the area or its resources;

11. With respect to activities in the area and acting in conformity with the international régime to be established, States shall take appropriate measures for and shall co-operate in the adoption and implementation of international rules, standards and procedures for, *inter alia:*
    (a) Prevention of pollution and contamination, and other hazards to the marine environment, including the coastline, and of interference with the ecological balance of the marine environment;

(b) Protection and conservation of the natural resources of the area and prevention of damage to the flora and fauna of the marine environment;

12. In their activities in the area, including those relating to its resources, States shall pay due regard to the rights and legitimate interests of coastal States in the region of such activities, as well as of all other States, which may be affected by such activities. Consultations shall be maintained with the coastal States concerned with respect to activities relating to the exploration of the area and the exploitation of its resources with a view to avoiding infringement of such rights and interests;

13. Nothing herein shall affect:
    (a) The legal status of the waters superjacent to the area or that of the air space above those waters;
    (b) The rights of coastal States with respect to measures to prevent, mitigate or eliminate grave and imminent danger to their coastline or related interests from pollution or threat thereof resulting from, or from other hazardous occurrences caused by, any activities in the area, subject to the international régime to be established;

14. Every State shall have the responsibility to ensure that activities in the area, including those relating to its resources, whether undertaken by governmental agencies, or non-governmental entities or persons under its jurisdiction, or acting on its behalf, shall be carried out in conformity with the international régime to be established. The same responsibility applies to international organizations and their members for activities undertaken by such organizations or on their behalf.
    Damage caused by such activities shall entail liability;

15. The parties to any dispute relating to the activities in the area and its resources shall resolve such dispute by the measures mentioned in Article 33 of the Charter of the United Nations and such procedures for settling disputes as may be agreed upon in the international régime to be established.

While the Seabeds Committee was developing the above set of principles, a treaty to prohibit the placing of nuclear weapons on the seabed beyond twelve miles from any coast was negotiated. It was approved by the United Nations on 17 November 1970 by a vote of ninety-one to two. Under the terms of the treaty, countries are prohibited from placing on the ocean floor beyond twelve miles from the coast any launching facilities or installations designed for storing, testing, or using nuclear weapons.

When it reconvened in 1971, the Seabeds Committee was faced not only with the task of preparing a seabed regime but of reviewing and recasting, as deemed necessary, the entire body of the law of the sea. Its title then became a misnomer because it was, in fact, the preparatory committee for a Law of the Sea Conference, and not just a seabeds conference. Unlike the 1958 Conference, which had the good fortune of working from draft texts that were more than seven years in preparation by the U.N. International Law

Commission, the Seabeds Committee, by its very nature, was a political body, composed of national delegations with varying levels of knowledge of International Law and ocean uses, and had to operate without benefit of organized texts. That fact plus the fact that 158 countries participated contributed to the marathon life of the Third Law of the Sea Conference and its preparatory Seabeds Committee.

For ten years seabed issues played a dominant role in the conference's negotiations. The conditions under which seabed resources could be exploited, was the most difficult and controversial of all the questions facing the conference. Quite distinct from the basic economic issues is the question of a state's right to begin mining before viable seabed treaty articles have been formulated and accepted. On 14 March 1979 Ambassador-at-Large Elliot L. Richardson addressed that issue:

> Last summer, when passage of the bill [a bill in the U.S. Congress to create a framework for U.S. companies to begin mining before the Law of the Sea Conference reached agreement] appeared imminent, the Chairman of the Group of 77 told the Conference that unilateral action would be viewed by the group as a grave breach of international law. He insisted that the United Nations' "common heritage" resolution overrode any nation's high-seas rights with regard to seabed mining.
>
> My response to the Third World totally disagreed with this charge. I rejected any contention that other states without our consent could alter our high-seas rights through manifestoes, resolutions, and the like. We are convinced that nations retain their rights to mine the deep oceans as one of the freedoms of the seas. On this point there is flat and unbridgeable disagreement which will someday become a major dispute unless we can agree on a new treaty regime that resolves it.

While that thorny issue underlies the fundamental need to reach an accord, economic questions have dominated the proceedings. They are not, in fact, strictly ocean issues but economic developmental issues that have illuminated sharp differences between the views of developed and developing countries. Essentially, the primary interest of the group of developed or industrial countries, including the United States, is reaching a secure source of minerals and giving their industries the opportunity to take part in the exploration and exploitation of seabed resources. Their aim is an international authority whose power to grant licenses to those desirous of mining the seabeds is limited. The primary interest of developing countries, of which there are considerably more than one hundred, is the creation of a new international economic order giving them a chance at a greater share in the world's resources than they have had in the past. Hence, their espousal of a monopolistic international authority whose function would be to exploit seabed resources. A third, small group, consisting of land-based mineral producers, is interested in protecting its markets and prices from the products of deep-seabed mining. The two following quotations indicate the intensity of the debate. In an article entitled "The International Seabed Resource Agency: Negotiations and the New International Economic Order" and published in *International Organization*, Spring, 1977, R.L. Freidheim and N.J. Durch said that the Group of 77 used the Law of the Sea seabed negotiations

> not merely to harass, slow down, or at least stop temporarily a widening of the economic gap, but to create an entirely new system to exploit the nodules that would be a working example of the type of economic system that the developing states considered just.

Referring to an address by Northcutt Ely, an attorney professionally interested in seabed matters, the *Congressional Record*, 14 April 1976, reported:

> In his own view the United Nations Conference on the Law of the Sea, now in its third substantive session in New York City, is dominated by a vast majority of nations dedicated to the formation of a cartel with the authority to control operations and production and provide for exactions by the proposed international authority. If a treaty embodying these views were in existence, "all prospects of deep seabed mining would evaporate," Mr. Ely said. "No mining company, no bank, could put a dime into a venture subject to these hazards."

After the heated confrontation over seabed issues in the preceding eight years, events in the 1979 and 1980 spring and summer sessions of the Third Law of the Sea Conference indicated a movement away from the many interrelated impasses noted above and towards a greater understanding of the need to accommodate opposing views. Developed and developing countries edged towards compromises that would provide a seabed authority and, at the same time, allow individual states or their nationals access to seabed resources under reasonable terms and conditions, including an equitable system for obtaining contracts, financial obligations, and a balance in the comprehensive powers of a seabed authority and its main organs.

The degree of progress accomplished in the 28 July-28 August 1980 session on these issues was such that the U.S. delegation noted in its report on the session:

> The negotiation of new texts dealing with the major outstanding deep seabeds issues constitutes the decisive breakthrough of this session of the Conference. These new texts provide for the decision-making procedures of the Council of the Seabed Authority and related matters, and also contain improvements and clarifications of other texts dealing with the system of exploration and exploitation as well as with financial matters.

This major forward movement on the seabeds issues at the above 1980 session prompted authorities in the field to express a high degree of optimism for the success of the draft treaty in its entirety. Venezuelan Delegate Andrés Aguilar stated, "There is nothing comparable to it in diplomatic history" (*Time*, 8 September 1980), and Canada's J. Alan Beesley, chairman of the drafting committee of the conference, considered it "the most significant achievement in international relations since the U.N. charter. It is indeed a constitution for the seas" (*Time*, 8 September 1980).

With this visible progress as a catalyst, the remaining seabed issues might well be resolved in the final 1981 sessions of the conference. Having said that, it would be less than prudent to underestimate the difficulties in reaching final solutions. There are still serious differences and some of the problems have resisted broadly based solutions. At this juncture, it is to be hoped that participating states would proceed in a spirit of accommodation and reach a treaty acceptable to the great majority of the world community. That community has put too much effort into the process over the last fourteen years to be deterred in this final effort of the conference.

The views of Melvin A. Conant, long an adviser on U.S. law of the sea matters and an acknowledged expert in international resources, are pertinent:

> The task of rewriting a large part of what Western nations regard as long-accepted principles of international "ocean" law has come at a time when great political and social changes are underway in large parts of the community of nations. The strain engendered as well as the hopes raised are mirrored in the LOS Seabed negotiations; what may emerge from this process is a set of new definitions as to how we are to deal with others in matters of international resource development in a time of changing circumstances— but the process is a slow one, and it should be, for very great stakes are involved.

CLOSED SEAS

From an historical perspective, various countries at various times espoused the concept of a highly specialized regime governing closed seas. Most of these so-called closed seas were saltwater seas connected to the mass of the high seas by a strait or other restricted passage. They were further distinguished by the fact that they formed the border between two or more countries, as is the case of the Caribbean and Black seas. In the early 1800s, Norway, Denmark, and Russia claimed that the Baltic Sea was a closed sea in time of war and prohibited ships belonging to any belligerents from using it. They did, however, "permit" all powers to use it during peacetime for legitimate navigation and trade. The majority of states objected to this control over the Baltic Sea and, at the Convention of 1857, that sea was declared to be free.

Similarly, Soviet writers claimed, apparently with the approval of their government, that some of the seas bordering the Soviet Union were closed. Included in this category were the Black Sea and the Baltic Sea. The Soviet "Sea of Peace" campaign concerning the Baltic was essentially a program to neutralize that sea by declaring it out of bounds to the warships of any country that did not border it. There was strong evidence that the Soviet Union regarded the Sea of Okhotsk also as a closed sea; in furtherance of that concept, it announced that as of 1959 Japanese fishing in that sea would be prohibited. Reports also indicated that the Soviet Union had proposed to Japan that the Sea of Japan be declared a closed sea with a definite restriction on its use by the warships of outside powers.

The reasoning behind the closed-sea concept was that the only navigation on such bodies of water was to and from the littoral states; navigation on them was of concern only to those states, which should, therefore, be entitled to regulate their use in their own interests—even to the point of forbidding entry to outsiders both in peace and war. In other words, the states bordering a particular sea could make it a private lake merely by agreement among themselves.

This concept was of particular interest in connection with the Black Sea and the Bosporus, because the Soviet Union is a signatory to the 1936 Montreux Convention, which controls them and does not completely bar the warships of outside powers from the Black Sea. Turkey is charged with the enforcement of the convention, mostly because the Bosporus lies within her territory. The Soviet Union would have liked to have the Montreux Convention amended to give control of the Black Sea and the Bosporus to the powers that border the Black Sea: the Soviet Union, Romania, Turkey, and Bulgaria. If this step were taken, it would effectively advance the concept of the closed sea, because Turkey would then be in a minority position, considering that the other three states involved are members of the Soviet bloc. Turkey successfully resisted all efforts to disturb the commitments of the Montreux Convention and the Black Sea continues to be part of the high, or free, seas, open to the ships of all states.

In treating the question of closed seas, the Third Law of the Sea Conference identified the areas as enclosed or semienclosed, i.e., areas such as gulfs, basins, or seas surrounded by two or more states and connected to the open seas by a narrow outlet or areas consisting entirely or primarily of the territorial seas and exclusive economic zones of two or more states. Among other things, bordering states are required to cooperate with each other in the exercise of their rights and duties. They are also to coordinate the management of fishing and pollution control in the area, and to undertake appropriate joint scientific research. No navigational discrimination against any ship of any flag is included or intended.

OCEAN SECTORS

Another theory advanced at times by different states is the so-called *sector principle*. This was first advanced by the Soviet Union in 1926, and, to a lesser degree, by Canada in asserting claims to the areas between its northern coast and the North Pole. Although it made no absolute claim to full sovereignty over the open water and great ice mass involved, there were indications that the Soviet Union considered the area different from the high seas in general. In 1969 and 1970 Canada made pronouncements regarding unilateral control of the Arctic area 100 miles north of Canada for purposes of preventing pollution. Both the United States and Norway have similar proximity to the North Pole, but neither country has shown any apparent intention of espousing the sector principle or exercising control.

The delegations to the Third Law of the Sea Conference clearly consider that remote and ice-covered sea area unique in some respects. They agreed that the Arctic coastal states had the right to establish and enforce nondiscriminatory laws and regulations for the prevention and control of pollution by ships in their exclusive economic zones where severe climatic conditions and the presence of ice created hazards to navigation. This special authority or control was granted to the pertinent coastal states in recognition of the fact that pollution could cause serious damage or irreversible disturbance to the delicate Arctic ecological balance.

BEYOND THE EXCLUSIVE ECONOMIC ZONE

Some authorities and officials consider the exclusive economic zone to be high seas, others do not, but there is no question about the waters seaward of them. This area of the oceans is open to the use of all states on an equal footing and clearly encompasses the whole gamut of high-seas freedoms, including: (1) freedom of navigation; (2) freedom of overflight; (3) freedom to lay and maintain submarine cables and pipelines; (4) freedom of fishing, subject to the duty of conservation in cooperation with other states; (5) freedom to conduct scientific research; and (6) freedom to construct artificial islands and other installations.

To distinguish the high seas from the exclusive economic zone, all states enjoy within the latter the above-listed freedoms of navigation and overflight and of the laying of submarine cables and pipelines, and other related lawful uses of the sea associated with the operation of ships, aircraft, and submarine cables that are compatible with other provisions of the draft Law of the Sea Treaty. In contrast, the high-seas freedoms of fishing, scientific research, and the construction of artificial islands in an exclusive economic zone require the consent of the coastal state. Enforcement of pollution controls is also vested in the coastal state. Another way to make the distinction is to note that the articles on the high seas (*see* Appendix I) apply to the exclusive economic zone only insofar as they are not incompatible with the sovereign rights and jurisdiction that may be exercised by the coastal state within the exclusive economic zone.

No state may claim sovereignty over any part of the high seas and, in exercising the freedoms of the high seas, all states must give due consideration to the interests of other states. In exercising the freedoms of the high seas all participants are bound by the treaty and conventional law that is applicable. For example, provisions for the control of pollution, agreements relative to fishing, and accommodations to seabed activities all have a bearing on the exercise of the historic but still-valid freedoms of the high seas.

As an instrument of the international community to work towards the maintenance of a high degree of tranquility on the world's oceans, the purpose and function of the immunity of a warship is no clearer than when it is on the high seas.

COMMENTARY

The two previous chapters, "Territory—Water" and "Ships," and this one focus on the present and most probable future state of ocean law as it affects users of the seas. Historical development is included in order to put the new regimes in appropriate perspectives. While the first three editions of this work dealt at length with the high seas and the freedoms inherent in that regime, in this edition necessary emphasis lies elsewhere; the comment herein relates to that phenomenon.

In retrospect, the 1958 Convention on the High Seas simply restated what had been practiced and acknowledged by the world community as the correct rule of law, i.e., that *high seas* meant all parts of the sea that were not included in territorial waters. Undoubtedly the greatest transition effected by the Third Law of the Sea Conference was to change that basic tenet and tilt the international regime in favor of the coastal state. Quite clearly and in contrast to world practice codified in the 1958 Convention on the High Seas, the control of many activities previously recognized as high-seas freedoms now comes under the jurisdiction of a coastal state within its exclusive economic zone. A technical reading of the pertinent articles of the draft Law of the Sea Treaty (*see* Appendices G and I) presents the following:

Article 86 specifies that high-seas rights and duties apply to all parts of the sea that are not included in the exclusive economic zone (EEZ) or territorial waters. Articles 55 and 58 contain a caveat that the provisions of articles that refer to the high seas apply to an EEZ only insofar as they are not incompatible with a coastal state's rights and jurisdiction in its EEZ. The text limits these freedoms in an EEZ to navigation, overflight, and the laying of pipelines and cables.

The above is a brief technical analysis. The reasons for the ambiguity lie in the laudable attempt to reach a compromise, i.e., a balance of interests, between opposing groups of states with widely divergent interests. An example is pertinent.

In April 1978, the Soviet Union's delegate to the Law of the Sea Conference proposed that no coastal state could purport to subject to its sovereignty any part of its EEZ or of any other sea beyond its territorial sea. Had this proposal been approved, the high seas would have begun twelve miles out from any coast. As a counterproposal, Mexico suggested that Article 55 be amended to make it explicit that the EEZ was a part neither of the territorial sea nor of the high seas. Although this proposal was not accepted and the final text of the article contains no direct reference to the character of the EEZ regime, I submit that the EEZ is not part of the high seas but that the balance of rights to be exercised by a coastal state in the EEZ makes those waters closer to being territorial seas than high seas. Not being high seas, no residual high-seas freedoms exist in the area, except as specified in the treaty. The EEZ is best described as *sui generis*, i.e., a one-of-a-kind regime, neither high seas nor territorial sea.

Many experts might well disagree with my assessment that the rights of coastal states make EEZs close to being territorial in character. In May 1974, during the development of the EEZ at the Caracas session of the Law of the Sea Conference, U.S. Ambassador John R. Stevenson said:

> One of the most serious restraints in the history of the law of the sea on the expansion of coastal state jurisdiction over resources has been the concern that this jurisdiction would, with time, become territorial in character.

The same concern was expressed by the Comptroller General in his report to the Congress entitled "Results of the Third Law of the Sea Conference, 1974 to 1976," and dated 3 June 1977:

> The question of the economic zone was raised. Creation of the zone would remove or modify some of the traditional high-seas freedoms, such as fishing, while retaining others, including navigation and overflight. The United States feared that granting rights to coastal states in the zone would erode the status of the high seas and, through extension of various forms of jurisdiction, make the zone the equivalent of a territorial sea. Thus the U.S. delegation proposed a text stating that the regime of the high seas applied to the economic zone except as modified by the provisions of the treaty.

A coastal state's rights and jurisdiction over resources in its EEZ is not the only element that gives a territorial cast to the area. Various forms of jurisdiction over other activities in the EEZ must also be considered.

The regime for the continental shelf defines the area of a shelf; part of that definition is artificial because it provides that even where a geographic shelf is only 15 miles offshore, for example, the coastal state has jurisdiction out to at least 200 miles—the precise area of the EEZ. While acknowledging that in some unusual cases shelf jurisdiction can extend beyond 200 miles, the 200-mile figure is complementary to and additive of the degree of control and jurisdiction the coastal state has over activities in the area.

The draft treaty text on control over pollution of the marine environment treats the oceans as three separate entities: the territorial sea, the EEZ, and the high seas. It specifies that a coastal state has a maximum degree of control in its territorial sea: in its EEZ it has a high degree of control over ships navigating in that area, dependent on the degree of pollution involved; it is significant that only the coastal state can exercise enforcement procedures within the EEZ: on the high seas beyond the EEZ it has no control and prevention of pollution is not keyed to coastal-state control.

In the case of the conduct of scientific research within the EEZ, what was once considered a freedom of the high seas is now subject to the consent of the coastal state.

The new controls and jurisdiction exercised by a coastal state over the variety of ocean users in the EEZ apply not only to economic activities. It is the aggregate of these jurisdictions that constitute a composite core and indicate that emerging territorialization could pose a potential threat to existing freedoms of ocean navigation and communication. To be specific, a coastal state's misapplication of its jurisdiction in the EEZ could have an adverse impact on the freedom of navigation. It is easy to visualize what might happen: a national law regulating inspections in the territorial sea is erroneously applied to a ship in the EEZ, causing interruption of her voyage; a large amount of oil is observed in the EEZ resulting in a public outcry, and the ship closest to it is boarded and brought into port; a ship, mistakenly thought to be conducting scientific research in the EEZ, is intercepted and escorted out of the EEZ. It is also easy to visualize the reaction of some countries if another country were to conduct naval exercises within the former's EEZ; the perception as to what is permissible within the EEZ would most probably not coincide.

All the above possible situations would bring freedom of navigation into question. The following episode cited by David G. Burney, General Counsel, U.S. Tuna Foundation, raises the question of control over fisheries within the EEZ:

> On January 18, 1979, at approximately one o'clock in the morning, two US flag tuna vessels were seized by authorities of the government of Costa Rica approximately 170 miles off the shore of Costa Rica. The vessels were seized for allegedly fishing tuna without the authorization required by Costa Rican law. . . . When seized, one vessel was underway with its lights on; the other vessel was at anchor and the crew was asleep. The vessel which was underway had no fish on board and the other vessel had 45 tons of skipjack tuna on board which had been caught off the coast of Panama.
>
> On January 26, 1979, a Costa Rican lower court ruled, that as presented, the cases against the two seized vessels lacked sufficient merit for trial. The

court ruled that the government of Costa Rica had not presented sufficient evidence to establish a violation of Costa Rican law. However, the court ruled that further evidence might be uncovered by more extensive investigation. The Court ordered the vessels' masters freed after posting bond in excess of $400,000. The basic point of the decision was that the government of Costa Rica had not established that either vessel had engaged in fishing activity in Costa Rican waters.

In February, 1979, a Costa Rican Superior Court, hearing the cases on appeal, decided that there was sufficient merit in the charges and ordered that the matter be tried. This ruling took place after the Executive Branch of the government of Costa Rica had requested that the legislative assembly interpret the Costa Rican law to define "illegal fishing activity" to include the presence in Costa Rican waters of unlicensed fishing vessels without transit permits.

One has to wonder whether control over fisheries within the EEZ can logically be extended to apply to fishing vessels in transit, i.e., navigating through the EEZ.

The multiple applications of jurisdiction that coastal states can exercise within the EEZ could serve as a catalyst for even broader jurisdiction and consequent further erosion of the freedom of the high seas. Should this be the case, a difficult period lies ahead; should it not be the case, then freedom of navigation could provide a stabilizing force in the law.

While there is a degree of pessimism in the above discussion, history dictates to me that over the long term a balanced ocean regime may be achieved. This optimism is based partly on the fact that some of the artificialities noted below may wither in time. They became part of the ocean regimes because the political climate at the time of the Third Law of the Sea Conference was such that the primary interest of the majority of states was to obtain more territory or control or jurisdiction for themselves. This is how the 200-mile limit, so adamantly adhered to for many years by three lonely Latin-American states, captured the world's imagination and became a reality of the 1970s. Ambassador Arvid Pardo, the father of the seabeds, portrayed that political reality when, as the Maltese delegate to the Committee on the Peaceful Uses of the Seabed and the Ocean Floor beyond the Limits of National Jurisdiction, he said in Geneva on 10 August 1972:

> In this well-tried and eminently successful tradition we all understand that the title of our committee is a misnomer and that its real title should be "The United Nations Committee for the First Partition of Ocean Space in the Interests of Coastal States."

The desire for acquisition was so strong that landlocked and otherwise geographically disadvantaged states did not fare well when it came to acquiring what they considered to be a fair share of resources in the EEZs of neighboring coastal states.

Permit the noting of some of the artificialities alluded to above. Perhaps the foremost reality is that geography, living and nonliving resources, ocean processes, ocean traffic, pollution control, and scientific research do not form a logical basis for setting the breadth of the EEZ at 200 miles. But, just as that is a reality, it is also valid that during this era the 200-mile EEZ is a strong political reality. If one were to construct a jurisdictional fishery zone based on the habits and biology of fish, one would see control areas established for particular species: some zones might be 15 miles from the coast, others 215 miles. Aggravating the artificiality is the fact that fish stocks are very unevenly distributed throughout the world: some of the countries in need of protein have few fish off their coasts, while others, such as the United States, have a surplus. The same element of markedly uneven distribution of continental shelf nonliving resources, such as oil, is also true.

Scientific research is just as important 50 miles off a coast as it is 231 miles off a coast. Indeed, similar to pollution control in many respects, the need to study and follow ocean currents has no relation to a 200-mile EEZ. Like fisheries, pollution-control areas should logically be shaped to meet the challenge of currents. Iceland, for example, is most concerned about the ocean area to its west because that is the direction of the Gulf Stream, which would bring pollutants. On that basis, Iceland's pollution zone should be broad indeed to the west and negligible to the east.

The probability is that over the long term the artificialities of the EEZ will eventually be recognized and practical considerations will produce desirable changes. Perhaps the labels will remain the same but the content will differ. In 1978 William T. Burke commented in "Ocean Development and International Law":

> The division of the oceans in large, separate zones, within which a single state has exclusive and nearly comprehensive authority to make decisions, is neither compatible with the nature of the ocean and the processes occurring within it, nor with most of the resource base available in it as well as the need for its investigation and understanding.

The above commentary and critique is not to reflect on the tremendous task that faced the Third Law of the Sea Conference. During most of its life there were few who felt that its task would be completed; that the conferees were successful in balancing interests is a monument to them.

Ambassador Morris D. Busby, Deputy Assistant Secretary of State for Ocean and Fisheries Affairs, looks at the balance sheet of the Third Law of the Sea Conference and concludes:

> Even if a comprehensive LOS [Law of the Sea] Treaty is never signed, the conference has been successful in that it provided a forum for discussion at a time when the potential for conflict was very great indeed. Since 1969, when preparatory meetings leading to the LOS Conference began, tremendous

changes have taken place in the law of the sea. That these changes were accomplished in a peaceful way is perhaps the greatest achievement of the conference to date. Coastal nations have already declared, and are exerting, virtually total jurisdiction over activities within 200 miles of their coasts. As they begin significant development of resources in their zones, they will come into competition with other nations who are using these waters for resource, military, scientific, or navigational purposes. The challenge for the future is to ensure that conflicts are avoided, and that as man makes more and more use of the oceans, it does not become a source of international discord.

Significantly, we are bound to the new order on the oceans; if through reading this text a better understanding is obtained that is all that really matters for the moment.

The seas are ancient, yet they are new.
Their regimes are immutable, yet they are fragile.
They are catalysts for progress, yet platforms for discord.

7

Territory—Air and Space

One small step for man—one giant step for mankind.
Astronaut Neil Armstrong upon setting foot on the moon, 21 July 1969

INTRODUCTION

The almost simultaneous birth of the aircraft and the radio at the beginning of the twentieth century posed perplexing problems for the states of the world in regard to their rights of control over the air space above them. The advent of space vehicles in 1957 accentuated these problems. Because of the different nature of the problems of electronic communications and worldwide meteorological services, in contrast to aerial navigation and space control, the laws relating to meteorology and communications have not followed parallel courses. They must, therefore, be discussed separately.

AIR

As we have seen in the preceding chapters, the law governing land and water developed with the expansion of civilization. Obviously this is not true of the law of the air, for it was not until after the beginning of the twentieth century that man began to use the air for transportation. The first successful power-driven heavier-than-air craft was flown by the Wright brothers, on 17 December 1903. Until that time, there was no need for law to govern the use of air space.

To meet the challenge of providing such law, the world community relied heavily on international agreements. Today, some of these agreements are multilateral, such as the Chicago Civil Aviation Convention of 1944, and others are bilateral arrangements for the international use and operation of a single airport. By 1970, more than 1,000 of these agreements and arrangements had been registered with the International Civil Aviation Organization, a specialized agency of the United Nations. While the above indicates that a system of air law soon began to take shape, it will be seen that it is not yet complete. The interruption caused by two world wars, plus the arrival of jet aircraft, has left some basic legal and political problems unresolved.

Once man began to fly, there was never any question as to who had the right to do so. The appeal was universal. Man had simply conquered another medium and all would share the benefits. Today, all states have the right to fly whether for public or private purposes. Possessing this right, where can man fly?

As long as a pilot flew within his own state's navigable air space and landed within its borders, there was no problem. But when, in July 1909, Louis Blériot took off from Les Barraques, France, crossed the English Channel, and landed at Dover, England, there arose the question of a state's right to use the air space over the territory of another state. Four theories developed.

The Free-Air Theory

The most nearly parallel situation from which a well-developed doctrine could be borrowed was that of the high, or free, seas. They are considered to be the common domain of all states, not subject to the control of any one state. Air should likewise be free. But there is one significant factor that makes an aircraft, no matter how great its altitude, of vital interest to the state over which it is passing—the law of gravity. The theory was also qualified by recognition of the fact that a state has the right to make provisions for its own self-defense and the flight of an aircraft is subordinate to that.

The Complete-Sovereignty Theory

This theory held that a state's sovereignty over the air space above its territory and its territorial sea is absolute and unqualified. As laid down in Roman law, "Whose is the soil, his it is up to the sky."

The Navigable-Air Space or Territorial-Air Theory

Similar to the free-air theory, the navigable-air space theory was based, in part, on the law of the high seas. It held that each state had the right to exercise full sovereignty in the air space above its territorial land and sea up to a certain undefined height. Above that height, the air should be as free as are the high seas.

The Innocent-Passage Theory

As did two of the above theories, this one drew on the relatively stabilized law of the sea. While a coastal state has complete sovereignty over its territorial sea, that sovereignty is subject to the right of innocent passage of all ships. A state has the same sovereignty over the air above both its land mass and its territorial sea, subject to the same right of innocent passage.

THE AERIAL NAVIGATION CONVENTION, 1919

World War I hastened the solution of the problem, because with aircraft in the possession of the belligerents, all states, belligerents and neutrals alike, were quick to assert their right to absolute sovereignty over the air space above their territory. As is often the case, the insistence of many states upon a certain right and their vigorous measures to enforce it evolved into a rule of customary International Law. This customary rule was soon incorporated into The Aerial Navigation Convention of 1919. Perhaps the most important provision of this multilateral treaty was the statement that "every power has complete and exclusive sovereignty over the air space above its territory." A limited right of innocent passage was granted mutually by parties to the treaty, but it was in no sense as broad as the right of innocent passage through territorial seas. The United States was not a party to this convention.

THE CHICAGO CIVIL AVIATION CONFERENCE, 1944

Just as man's proficiency as a flyer did not remain static at the 1919 level, neither did the law that governed his use of air space remain frozen. The development of the law by means of multilateral agreements proceeded apace with the needs of aerial navigation, and in 1944 the Chicago Civil Aviation Conference took place. The agreements that grew out of this conference retained the concept that every state had complete and exclusive sovereignty over its air space, but granted more liberal rights of navigation than did the convention of 1919.

Since, for economic reasons, the states attending the conference were not prepared to grant other states very extensive rights of navigation in their own air space, two separate agreements were drawn up, the International Air Transport Agreement and the International Air Service Transit Agreement. The first of these compacts is commonly known as the Five Freedoms Agreement. While recognizing a state's exclusive sovereignty over the air space above its territory, it provides for the reciprocal grant to scheduled air services of five freedoms:

1. The privilege of flying across the territory of another country without landing;
2. The privilege of landing for non-traffic purposes;
3. The privilege of discharging passengers, mail, and cargo loaded in the territory of the aircraft's nationality;
4. The privilege of embarking passengers, mail, and cargo destined for the territory of the aircraft's nationality;
5. The privilege of taking on passengers, mail, and cargo destined for the territory of any other contracting state, as well as the privilege of landing passengers, mail, and cargo from the same.

Because a relatively small number of states were willing to grant all five of these freedoms, the compromise Two Freedoms Agreement, which more nations were willing to accept, was also adopted. It granted only the first two of the privileges listed above. Because even the Two Freedoms Agreement has not yet been accepted by all states, mostly for economic reasons, the development of universally applicable and definitive rules with regard to rights of aerial navigation remains for the future.

Although it is clearly established that the air space above a state's territory is subject to the exclusive sovereignty of that state, the extent of the right of innocent passage in such air space has not as yet been universally agreed on. For practical purposes, the safe procedure is to assume that there is no right of innocent passage over a land mass or territorial sea and to seek permission to enter. For example, on 10 November 1958 King Hussein of Jordan took off by air from Amman and proceeded across territory of the United Arab Republic, i.e., Syria. Jet fighters of the United Arab Republic intercepted his plane and forced it back to the Jordanian border. In Damascus, a spokesman for the United Arab Republic charged that King Hussein had violated his country's air space by not getting clearance to use it.

In March 1979, Syrian officials radioed a PanAmerican jet airliner bound from New York to Bahrain and ordered it to land in Damascus. The pilot was accused of violating Syrian air space. After several hours on the ground, the plane was permitted to continue on its flight. Nothing more serious than relatively brief delay occurred in either of these cases, but none could dispute the right to exercise the inherent sovereignty.

STATE-OWNED AIRCRAFT

While the Chicago conventions granted a limited right of innocent passage to commercial air carriers, they specifically withheld that right from state-owned aircraft, including military aircraft and those used in customs and police services. The exception grows out of the recognition that military aircraft can constitute a serious threat, particularly when flying, uninvited, over the territory of a foreign state. In the event that permission is not requested and obtained, the offending state receives a quick and strong protest. Such was the case when, in the summer of 1958, U.S. Air Force planes en route from Germany to Lebanon flew over the western tip of Austria. In a note delivered to the U.S. embassy in Vienna, the Austrian Foreign Office said, in essence, that Austria would not tolerate such violations of its territory. The United States sent a note of apology. Another incident, recorded below, is of interest because it shows that the exception might well be expanded to include unmanned balloons whose course is determined by the will of the wind:

> The Soviet Government protested in a note published here today that the United States Air Force is sending balloons equipped with automatic cameras and two-way radios over Russian soil.
>
> The note handed to United States Chargé d'Affaires Richard H. Davis by Deputy Foreign Minister Georgi N. Zarubin charged "gross violation" of Soviet air space and international rights. It did not specify where or when the alleged incidents took place but demanded that they be stopped at once.
>
> The Kremlin has made similar charges in the past, accusing the United States of sending balloons over Russia for aerial reconnaissance. The United States denied the charges, declaring that the balloons were sent up only to collect weather data. (*The Evening Star*, Washington, D.C., 4 September 1958.)

Because of the strict regulations governing military flights into foreign territory, the U.S. Air Force and U.S. Navy keep abreast of foreign regulations regarding the obtaining of clearances for their aircraft to fly across or land in foreign territory and follow them to the letter. As an example, when one of our carrier task groups intends to visit a foreign port, it has to request clearance to fly in some aircraft or operate helicopters after arrival. If the clearance is not received, the planes do not fly. Obtaining the necessary clearances plays a major role in the planning of the Strategic Air Command's far-flung exercises.

An exception to these rules is made in the case of state-owned aircraft in distress: they may land at the nearest airport, regardless of nationality or status of clearance.

State-owned and -operated aircraft involved in commercial ventures, such as many national airlines, are subject to the same general requirements clearly established for state-owned merchant ships used for commercial purposes. In brief, they are subject to the jurisdiction of the country they are visiting. An incident that occurred on 26 August 1979 demonstrated the severity with which that jurisdiction is exercised:

> Ignoring an angry Soviet protest, American authorities continued to hold a Russian jetliner at Kennedy International Airport last night to determine whether the wife of a Russian ballet dancer who defected last week was being forced to return to Moscow.
>
> The silver and blue Aeroflot Ilyushin-62, which had been halted just before takeoff on a taxiway at 5 p.m. Friday, remained grounded outside the Pan American World Airways terminal through the day, blocked by police cars and guarded by Immigration Service and Port Authority police officers. (*The Washington Star*, 26, 27, 28 August 1979.)

On 28 August, after U.S. officials had determined that the passenger did not desire to seek asylum and wanted to return to the Soviet Union, the plane was released for departure.

Military Aircraft

Various international agreements bear on the right of transit of military aircraft:

1. Article 43 of the United Nations charter gives the military aircraft of a member nation the right to transit the air space of another member nation during a U.N. military action.
2. Regional agreements, such as the North Atlantic Treaty, imply consent for military aircraft to use the air space of other members of the pact.
3. Most U.S. base-rights agreements contain a provision permitting the use of other countries' air space and landing fields.
4. The United States has some bilateral overflight agreements that pertain to military aircraft.

Military aircraft do not enjoy the same immunity as warships do in a foreign port (*see* Chapter 5). They have the status of state-owned property, but there are very few recorded instances of interference with visiting military aircraft.

AIRCRAFT AND THE HIGH SEAS

In contrast with the authority a state exercises over aircraft in the air space over its land territory and territorial seas, no authority is exercised over an aircraft's freedom to fly over the high seas. In a pamphlet entitled *International Law and Naval Operations*, published by the Naval War College, Commander Dennis F. McCoy, USN, comments:

> The rule that has evolved for airspace above the high seas is similar to that of the high seas themselves. As a sovereign state may not exercise jurisdiction over the high seas, so assertions of sovereignty in the form of controlling or denying access, exit or transit are improper in the airspace above the high seas. This does not mean that a sovereign is denied all right of action in the airspace above the high seas. On the high seas sovereigns may act in self defense, and may engage in any other reasonable activity that does not unduly interfere with the rights of others to use freely the high seas.

However, as with all freedoms or rights, there is an inherent duty to exercise the right of freedom to fly over the high seas with reasonable regard to the interests of other states. As international air traffic over the high seas grows in scope, frequency, and complexity of routes, it can be expected that the world community will agree, as a matter of mutual convenience, to ever-increasing regulation of the conduct of such flights.

Military and other state-owned aircraft are often used to identify ships and observe activities on the surface of the high seas. This practice is an extension of the lawful establishment of identification in international waters. For example, U.S. Coast Guard planes with conservation agents from the National Marine Fisheries Service aboard frequently fly close to U.S. and foreign fishing vessels operating off the U.S. coast in order to identify them and the species of fish being caught.

The exercise of this lawful practice has many times brought strong protest from the Soviet Union on the ground that it abuses the right to fly over the high seas, interferes with free navigation, and constitutes a hazard to ships and crews. The comments of a number of countries on such Soviet protests indicate that they view the identification procedures used as being in conformance with International Law and practice. Consequently, it can be concluded that such operations are considered reasonable exercises of the right to fly over the high seas and are not incompatible with freedom of navigation on the high seas.

On 25 May 1968 the Department of Defense reported that a Soviet medium jet bomber crashed in the Norwegian Sea after making a low pass close to the USS *Essex*. At the time, the *Essex* was conducting antisubmarine warfare training operations some 200 miles off Norway. On its fourth pass, the aircraft in question came within approximately 20 yards of the port quarter of the *Essex*; after passing the ship, it maintained its low altitude until, some miles distant, its right wing dipped, and it crashed. The United States notified the Soviets of the incident but made no protest.

Air Defense Identification Zones

Self-defense is a sovereign right of all states. If a state is not permitted to inspect rapidly moving aircraft beyond its territorial limits, how can it protect itself against hostile planes? Pearl Harbor taught us that by the time enemy airmen are close to their objective, it may be too late to prevent attack. Obviously, the only effective means of protection lies in the identification and, if necessary, interception of planes before they reach the territory of their objective. This is why the United States established Air Defense Identification Zones over the high seas off its coasts. The zones constitute a protective screen that makes it possible to recognize hostile planes before they reach the United States, and, in practice as well as in theory, they do not interfere with innocent air traffic.

SPACE

When Apollo 11 landed in the South Pacific on 24 July 1969, not only had it made the first manned flight to the moon, but man had compressed the challenges of the future into present opportunities.

Space ventures between 1957, when the Soviet Union launched the first successful satellite, and the Apollo series defined and extended our goals, greatly increased our scientific understanding of the solar system and the earth's environment, and produced applications of space technology that have major economic and social benefits. Current applications of this technology have led to significant progress in communications, meteorology, and navigation. Only 10 per cent of the atmosphere can be kept under surveillance by land- and sea-based weather stations, whereas 100 per cent can be covered by satellite stations. The surveying of the earth's resources from satellites and other as yet unthought-of applications are bound to follow. Through mid-1970, U.S. and Soviet programs, together, included thirty-two manned flights, eighteen of which involved more than one person, and more than four thousand man-hours' experience in space, involving fifty-eight men, eleven walks in space, fifteen space rendezvous, and eight space dockings.

THE REGIME OF SPACE

With the advent of space exploration and use, it became apparent that some system had to be established to guide activities in space. Just as man's relationships on land and at sea are generally governed by laws and practices that have proven workable, so it seemed that his relationships in the new dimension—space—should be governed. International lawyers are still seeking to solve the many-faceted problems of how and to what extent laws for this purpose should be established, but some important steps have already been taken.

Agreed-Upon Space Principles

Through U.N. resolutions and treaties, some important principles for a space regime have been identified and agreed to by the world community. The first of these was incorporated in the Test Ban Treaty, signed 5 August 1963, the parties to which undertook not to test or explode any nuclear weapon at any place under their jurisdiction, in the atmosphere, beyond their territorial limits, including outer space; underwater, including territorial waters; or on the high seas. A resolution passed by the U.N. General Assembly on 24 December 1963, reflected the views of the world community as to how the activities of nations engaged in the exploration and use of space should be governed. Among the operative paragraphs of that resolution were the following:

2. Outer space and celestial bodies are free for exploration and use by all States on a basis of equality and in accordance with international law.
3. Outer space and celestial bodies are not subject to national appropriation by claim of sovereignty, by means of use or occupation, or by any other means.

While a U.N. resolution does not have the same legal force and effect as a treaty, these principles have served as guidelines for space activities and commitments. They have since been incorporated into International Law through the Outer-Space Treaty.

The Outer-Space Treaty

The Outer-Space Treaty was signed by sixty countries on 27 January 1967, in Washington, D.C., and came into force on 10 October 1967. It provides that no celestial body or area in outer space shall be subject to national appropriation. Accordingly, when the U.S. astronauts landed on the moon, no claim to sovereignty on the basis of discovery and occupation was made. The treaty further provides that any exploration in outer space shall be in the interests of all countries, and that International Law and the U.N. charter shall apply. Of military significance are the provisions that prohibit the orbiting and stationing of nuclear and other weapons of mass destruction on celestial bodies, and the establishment of military bases or conducting of military maneuvers on celestial bodies. The treaty declares that the moon and other celestial bodies shall be used exclusively for peaceful purposes, and gives signatories the right to visit each other's facilities on them.

Assistance to and Return of Astronauts

The Agreement on the Rescue of Astronauts, the Return of Astronauts, and the Return of Objects Launched into Outer Space was developed through the United Nations, and signed at simultaneous ceremonies in London, Moscow, and Washington in April 1968; it came into force on 3 December 1969. President Lyndon B. Johnson emphasized the duties imposed on the signatory states:

> Immediately notify the appropriate authorities if they receive information that astronauts have accidentally landed or are in distress;
> Immediately take all possible steps to rescue astronauts who have accidentally landed on their territory and render them all necessary assistance;
> If necessary and if they are in a position to do so, extend assistance in search and rescue operations for astronauts who have alighted on the high seas;
> Safely and promptly return astronauts who have landed either on their territory or on the high seas; and
> Notify the appropriate authorities of space objects which have come down on their territory or on the high seas, and, upon request, take steps to recover and return such objects.

Damage Caused by Space Objects

In 1972 the United Nations was again instrumental in fostering cooperation in the development of a broad regime applicable to the exploration of outer space. Specifically, on 29 March 1972, the Convention on the International Liability for Damage Caused by Space Objects was signed by the United States, and entered into force for the United States on 9 October 1973. This multilateral agreement, ratified by the states most involved in space exploration, sets forth the requirement that a launching state "shall be absolutely liable to pay compensation for damage caused by its space objects on the surface of the earth or to aircraft in flight." It also apportions responsibility in cases of joint launchings. Another significant achievement of this convention was the creation of a commission to deal with claims. With the exception that it does not deal with the claims of a national of a launching state against his own state for damages caused by fallen space objects, the Liability Convention provides a broad regime permitting recovery in almost all cases.

The need for the above treaty was based on the fact that space use was going to produce more and more "space junk," some of which would enter the earth's atmosphere. At this writing, more than 4,500 pieces of obsolete and unused space equipment are orbiting the earth. On average, some 40 such objects per month come in contact with the earth's atmosphere; about one-fourth of them actually survive reentry and strike the earth. One such object, the U.S. Skylab vehicle that was launched in May 1973, received considerable international attention when it began its reentry sequence in 1979. The attention was merited because no one could predict exactly where the major pieces of Skylab, which weighed more than seventy-seven tons and, before it broke up, was the equivalent in size of a nine-story building, would fall. On 11 July 1979 it entered the earth's atmosphere and its fiery components fell harmlessly into the Indian Ocean and on the arid area of Australia. Had it caused injury or damage, the United States, by the terms of the treaty, would have had to accept full liability.

Registration of Space Objects

Another U.N.-sponsored multilateral agreement relative to space exploration entered into force for the United States on 15 September 1976, when it ratified the 1975 Convention on Registration of Objects Launched into Outer Space. This most recent multilateral agreement on outer space provides simply that a launching state must maintain a registry of all objects it launches into outer space and forward the information to the Secretary General of the United Nations. The Soviet Union did not ratify this treaty until 1979, which is interesting in light of the confusion surrounding a Russian satellite alleged to contain nuclear material that impacted in the northern regions of Canada in 1978. Presumably, the requirement to register space objects, coupled with the agreement on liability for damage caused by them, closes the door on the need to protect the people of the world from damage caused by governmental space exploration.

PROGNOSIS FOR A COMPREHENSIVE SPACE REGIME

Since the launching of Sputnik I, legal scholars have been flirting with the idea that the term *outer space* ought to be defined. There have been countless attempts to do this, but none has found broad agreement. Furthermore, the definition of sovereignty, as it applies to exploration in outer space, has also eluded definition, primarily because the space powers take a nationalistic approach to the subject. Nevertheless, as indicated by the above capsule review of existing agreements, some major steps have been taken toward the development of a comprehensive regime for outer space. But, examination of the existing multilateral space treaties indicates that perhaps this development will remain rather limited. Existing agreements do not resolve any of what might be considered the problems unique to space. They deal with issues that derive from broadly established principles of earth-bound International Law. The conventions on registration, liability, and the return of astronauts are remarkably similar to those that deal with the same topics regarding uses of the high seas and the Antarctic.

The problems that remain to be solved are those that are being created by rapidly advancing technology: the ability to catalog information on the earth's resources received and transmitted to earth by remote-sensing satellites, the ability to mine the surface of celestial bodies, and the ability to store and poise weapons in outer space. Furthermore, it is obvious that these technologies are only the vanguard of what man will devise as he moves towards a future in space, and any attempt at the present time to develop a comprehensive regime to regulate anticipated conduct is bound to fall short of its mark: man's technological abilities will most assuredly outpace his legal and regulatory imagination. An analogy often used relates to when the automobile first appeared on the scene. One of our large cities passed an ordinance prohibiting the operation of an automobile unless it were preceded by a policeman on a bicycle. The regime for the automobile that those city fathers created restrained progress. Similarly, a comprehensive legal regime for outer space formulated now would be likely to restrain scientific progress or, more probably, would create a set of laws and agreements that would undoubtedly be observed in their breach.

One has only to scan the newspapers to be aware that scientific imaginations are not in abeyance pending international consensus on a space regime. Wondrous achievements, such as space shuttles and television transmissions from Jupiter, Venus, and Mars, go on apace. Indeed, there has been talk of landing a man on those far-distant bodies. These activities are creating an ever-enlarging body of law which, because it has gone unchallenged, has indeed become workable and useful customary space law.

Concomitantly, in the political arena, there are three major protagonists whose interests in the development of space law differ according to their nationalistic goals.

The first of the protagonists is the United States, which has set a national policy for broad international usage of available technology; it leads the world in establishing bilateral agreements that permit technologically undeveloped states to participate in those of its programs that have the potential for being useful to and used by all nations. These agreements are in the areas of meteorology, navigation, pest control, irrigation, mining, and many others that involve the collection of information by space satellites from terrestrial sources.

The second protagonist is the Soviet Union, which has developed programs to be used solely for the benefit of the communist-aligned states. Its reluctance to participate on a broad scale seems to be based on distrust of the motives of states outside the Soviet bloc.

The third, and certainly influential, protagonist is the large group of states known as the developing nations or the Group of 77. These states, having neither the technology nor the financial base to initiate significant space programs, have taken the position that outer space, as well as the information concerning the earth gained from it through space technology, is the heritage of all mankind and should be shared equally. Furthermore, they claim that no information gleaned from observation of their territories should be used by the technologically advanced states for their own purposes or for those of their allies, unless the state concerned gives permission. These positions are in principle parallel to those the Group of 77 takes relative to Law of the Sea problems such as scientific research and seabed mineral rights. Indeed, when the draft of a proposed moon treaty, prepared under U.N. auspices, came before the general public in 1979, the principal objection to it was the inclusion of the developing countries' thesis that the moon's resources were the heritage of all mankind—a thesis first advanced in the debate on seabeds in the Law of the Sea Conference (*see* Chapter 6).

Perhaps a compromise will eventually be realized, but the development of a comprehensive regime for outer space is not a realistic presumption. Bilateral agreements specific to certain space missions will no doubt continue to be made, and there will probably be multilateral agreements on the use of weaponry in space. However, because of the dynamics of the problems, the most significant body of International Law relative to the exploration of outer space must remain as customary International Law, governed only by the general precepts of the U.N. charter and the principles of reciprocity that govern other forms of unconventional International Law.

How High Is Up?

Just the fact that while the earth rotates it is also traveling around the sun at 66,000 miles an hour emphasizes the essential impracticability of extending sovereignty indefinitely into space. Any given point in space is over a particular state for a period of less than a second. Space is essentially *res communis*—a thing common to all. It cannot be appropriated by a single state. Hence, the question has to be asked, how high is up?

Numerous and, in some cases, imaginative criteria have been advanced for establishing the inner limit of space:

1. Space should begin about fifteen to eighteen miles above the earth because approximately 97 per cent of the earth's atmosphere lies within those parameters.
2. The upward limit of national sovereignty should extend only as high as an airplane that derives its support from the atmosphere can fly.
3. Sovereignty should extend to the point where the gravitational pull of the earth is exceeded by the gravitational pull of the sun.
4. The inner limit of space should begin at the outer limits of the earth's atmosphere, which is estimated to lie somewhere between 150 and 50,000 miles from the earth.
5. The line of demarkation between national sovereignty and space should be at the point of minimum temperature.
6. Space should begin where the release of a falling body would cause it to land within a reasonable distance of the perpendicular to the dropping point at the time of dropping.
7. National sovereignty should extend approximately fifty-three miles because, beyond that point, aerodynamic lift must be replaced by some other force.
8. National sovereignty should extend to the height at which a satellite may be put in orbit, which is estimated to be about ninety miles.

Whether one of the above criteria, or one as yet undefined, will prove to be the governing factor in establishing the lower limit of space cannot now be predicted. It is submitted, however, that, should there be attempts to establish a lower limit, the eventual resolution of the problem will revolve around criteria based on the earth's atmosphere or gravitational influence.

CONCLUSIONS

It is manifest that the exploration of space will increase in scope and intensity and will be of increasingly significant use to man. It is also apparent that, although essential principles have been agreed to, there is not now a comprehensive regime of space. Use of space will produce regulation in the same manner as use of the high seas produced comprehensive regimes. Indeed, the latter may serve as the pattern for the former. The very nature of space and its potential has prompted some concepts that have no precedent in history. One such concept, based on present-day technology, is described by an acknowledged space scholar, Joseph J. Hahn.

> I refer to the fact that the technology is currently available to develop enormous space stations at several points of equal gravitational pull around

the earth. The prospect of such an endeavor prompts the imagination to conjure up the shape of the generations to come. The suggestion is made that with self-contained life-support systems society will begin anew on these space platforms. There could well be yet a further physical and social evolution to the human being. Indeed, the species may take on physiological changes to adapt to the rigors of space environment similar to, but perhaps not so dramatic as, man's evolution from a four-legged to two-legged animal. Accompanying this suggestion is the notion that such a dramatic change will require new and more effective systems of law to deal with societal problems as yet to be envisioned. It is my opinion that it is in these areas that legal scholars will now begin to expand their efforts.

INTERNATIONAL COMMUNICATIONS

Although there is general agreement that a state exercises exclusive sovereignty over the air space above its territory, most states have been willing to surrender a portion of their sovereignty, or at least to accept limitations upon their freedom of action, where radio communications are concerned. The reason, of course, is that without some sort of cooperation among nations in the use of radio frequencies, interference among radio stations would create chaos and no nation would be able to communicate reliably by radio.

The hazards and inconvenience of harmful interference have brought about cooperation in regulating most international facets of radio broadcasting and communication. As far back as 1903 the Berlin Preliminary Radio Conference adopted a provision requiring that a wireless station operate in such a manner as to avoid interference with other stations. The advantage of such regulations is that they are inherently self-enforcing, since the alternative would be loss of the use of radio. The International Radio Regulations now in effect define harmful interference as "any emission, radiation or induction which endangers the functioning of a radio navigation service or of other safety services or seriously degrades, obstructs or repeatedly interrupts a radio-communication service operating in accordance with these Regulations." Therefore, in order to constitute a violation of the regulations, interference must be harmful, as distinguished from merely annoying.

COMMUNICATING FROM FOREIGN TERRITORY

Although states have surrendered some of their sovereignty in the case of radio communications, practically all have guarded zealously their right to control the use of radio within their own territory. Most states prohibit the use of transmitters by foreigners, except under the most carefully controlled conditions. In cases such as American forces stationed in European countries in support of the North Atlantic Treaty Organization, the right to use transmitters is usually included in the pertinent base-rights agreements. If there is no agreement covering the point, special arrangements to use transmitters must be made.

DEVELOPMENT OF INTERNATIONAL REGULATIONS

Since 1903, there has been a series of international conferences dealing with various aspects of radio communications. These conferences dealt with and established rules regarding safety of life at sea, air and marine navigation, aeronautical communications, and broadcasting.

In order to reduce harmful interference, a procedure for the international registration of frequencies was put into effect several years ago. With the passage of years, this procedure has become so elaborate and detailed that it now requires that a request for registration be approved by a five-member international board. The international register is published by the International Telecommunication Union and thus is available for inspection on a worldwide basis. A registered frequency has priority over an unregistered one or one not used in accordance with the details of its registration. International registration of frequencies has brought about a high degree of cooperation in adjusting harmful interference, even during times of international stress.

International regulations have established bands of frequencies for certain types of operations or services. The regulations adopted at the Geneva Radio Conference of 1959 provide that "the frequency 500 kilohertz is the international distress and calling frequency for radio-telegraphy. . . . The frequency 121.5 megahertz is the aeronautical emergency frequency. . . ." Special bands have also been established for maritime mobile, aeronautical mobile, and fixed communications. Certain bands are assigned to navigational aids and others are earmarked for the exclusive use of broadcasting. These various bands have been established in such a manner as to reduce the possibilities of harmful interference.

The International Radio Regulations include also provisions on frequency tolerances, stoppage of telecommunications, secrecy (privacy) of telecommunications, charges for use of telecommunications, priority of government telegrams and telephone calls, use of secret language (codes), false or deceptive distress messages, and the irregular use of call signs.

The United States is a party to a number of bilateral and multilateral agreements on radio communications. Such agreements result from two fundamental characteristics of radio: first, two stations must be on the same frequency to communicate with each other; second, harmful interference is likely to be caused if other stations use the same frequency at the same time. Therefore, there must be agreement on the frequencies to be used and how stations are to operate, and standards with regard to such factors as operational procedures and the characteristics of equipment.

Satellite Communications

Telecommunications is a dynamic field. The advent of communications to and from outer space revolutionized it and opened challenging vistas. It has also added a new dimension to international relations because, if space telecommunications are to function, there must be worldwide cooperation.

Two organizations have been established to operate satellite telecommunications systems on a global basis, namely the International Telecommunications Satellite Organization (INTELSAT) and the International Maritime Satellite Organization (INMARSAT). The former provides telecommunications between earth terminals on land, using satellites as relays. The latter provides a similar service for earth terminals aboard ships.

INMARSAT is based on an international convention and operating agreement that went into effect on 16 July 1979. Its purpose is to provide "the space segment necessary for improving maritime communications, thereby assisting in improving distress and safety of life at sea communications, efficiency and management of ships, maritime public correspondence services and radio determination capabilities." Article 7 of the convention states that the INMARSAT space segment "shall be open for use by ships of all nations," subject to conditions set by the INMARSAT Council, which "shall not discriminate among ships on the basis of nationality."

The International Radio Regulations have designated certain frequency bands for space research and satellite communications. The most important characteristic of satellite communications is their ability to handle large volumes of communications instantaneously, which not only permits the worldwide linking of computers, including shipboard computers, but has virtually unlimited potential for worldwide telephone communications and broadcasting.

METEOROLOGY

As in international communications, cooperation between states in the area of meteorology has improved steadily. All states recognize that the basic tools of meteorology are simultaneous global observations of phenomena and their rapid distribution. The coordination required to make simultaneous observations and to communicate them is manifest. For example, if meteorologists in Belgium are to give an accurate prediction for their area, they must know the weather conditions in Iceland, Morocco, and Poland.

The machinery for effecting this coordination is administered by the World Meteorological Organization (WMO) established in 1951 as an agency of the United Nations. Its purposes are best expressed in Article 2 of the WMO Convention:

a. To facilitate world-wide co-operation in the establishment of networks of stations for the making of meteorological observations or other geophysical observations related to meteorology and to promote the establishment and maintenance of meteorological centres charged with the provision of meteorological services;

b. To promote the establishment and maintenance of systems for the rapid exchange of weather information;

c. To promote standardization of meteorological observations and to ensure the uniform publication of observations and statistics;

d. To further the application of meteorology to aviation, shipping, agriculture, and other human activities; and

e. To encourage research and training in meteorology and to assist in co-ordinating the international aspects of such research and training.

By the middle of the 1970s, WMO was composed of more than 115 member states and territories. The meteorologic service to the world community is excellent and is marked by the fact that no major disputes have arisen. There were gaps in the service, particularly in the Southern Hemisphere, caused by lack of equipment or the absence of a land mass to support equipment, but most of them have been eliminated by the world coverage that highly sophisticated satellites provide.

8 Persons

A case in which a sovereign is understood to cede a portion of his territorial jurisdiction is where he allows troops of a foreign prince to pass through his domain.

Schooner Exchange *v.* McFadden

INTRODUCTION

The preceding chapters set forth the rights and duties of sovereign states with regard to their territory—land, water, and air. In examining these rights and duties with respect to the individuals who are found in this territory, one word is used again and again: *jurisdiction.* Webster defines this word as, "1. The legal power, right, or authority to interpret and apply the law; 2. The authority of a sovereign power to govern or legislate." This second aspect of jurisdiction is the first subject of the following discussion.

PASSPORTS

A passport is the internationally accepted evidence of a person's identity and nationality. It does not give its bearer the right to travel in another country, but it does request that other governments permit him to travel in their territories or within their jurisdiction. It also entitles him to the protection and assistance of his own diplomatic and consular officers abroad. There are six types of passport, only three of which are of interest here: regular, official, and diplomatic.

Regular passports are issued to persons who prove that they are citizens of the state to which they apply for a passport or that they owe permanent allegiance to that state and who are not entitled to receive official or diplomatic passports. They contain a statement of citizenship and a request for all lawful or friendly aid and protection.

Official passports are generally issued to high government officials and subordinate consular officials proceeding abroad for the government on official, but not diplomatic, business. They provide the same identity information as a regular passport, but contain a request for the bearer's safe and free passage and all such aid and protection as would be extended to citizens or subjects of foreign governments in the territory of the bearer.

Diplomatic passports are issued to foreign service officers and other persons involved in diplomatic service. This type of passport serves both as a travel document and as a certification of the official identity of the bearer.

As stated above, a passport only requests a foreign government to permit its bearer to travel in their territories. It does not in itself give any *right* to do such traveling. Every state has the right to decide for itself who may enter its territory. Some countries require that a visitor have a visa, or an entry permit, or a border-crossing permit as well as a passport.

ALIENS AND NATIONALITY

It is not difficult to accept the principle of a state having jurisdiction over its own citizens. But what jurisdiction does a state have over aliens within its territory?

Briefly, a sovereign state has the right to determine who shall and shall not be permitted to enter its territory. Every country has the right to protect its own form of government, its own citizens, and its own social structure and, therefore, to keep out undesirable aliens, such as subversives.

ADMISSION

The criteria for the admission of aliens to, or their exclusion from, a given country are set forth in that country's immigration laws. A number of criteria are used to determine who is undesirable. U.S. immigration laws identify undesirables as those who might, among other things, endanger its form of government, endanger the health of its population, endanger the personal safety of its citizens, its morals, its way of life, and even those who might endanger its economy by, for example, having no means of support and becoming public charges. Another way in which the United States protects its economy is by limiting the number of immigrants in any one year.

STATUS OF ALIENS

Once an alien has been permitted to enter a country, the government of that country may decide to keep him under close supervision and subject him to control stricter than that to which it subjects its own citizens. Aliens are subject to all the laws of the country they enter. Thus, the United States has an Alien Registration Law, which requires all aliens to register with the proper authorities; to keep the immigration authorities informed of their whereabouts by filling out a card at least once a year; and to provide similar information every time they change their place of residence. Generally, however, an alien who has been lawfully admitted to a country enjoys the same civil rights as its citizens and is entitled to protection by its authorities as long as he obeys the laws of the host country. He can be deported if he violates those laws, but only in accordance with lawfully established procedure.

Citizenship by Birth

Acquisition of citizenship at birth is based on two different concepts—*jus soli*, the law of the soil, and *jus sanguinis*, the law of blood relationship. Most European countries adhere to the latter law and confer citizenship accordingly. The United States, Great Britain, and some Latin-American countries determine citizenship primarily by the place of birth. The nationality of children born to parents who are residing in a foreign country may be determined in accordance with the jurisdiction under which they happen to be born, as well as by their parents' nationality. For instance, a child born of German parents in the United States is treated as a U.S. citizen when he is in this country, a German citizen when he is in Germany, and both when he is in most other countries.

A child born of American parents in a foreign country is an American citizen if one of the parents resided in the United States before he was born. When only one parent is a U.S. citizen, that parent must have been physically a resident of the United States for at least ten years. There are special provisions for members of the armed forces stationed overseas.

In case of doubt, the best procedure is to consult the American consul in the country concerned. Not only can he give advice but, more important, he can issue the documents enabling any alien in question to enter the United States. He can register the birth of a child and issue a U.S. birth certificate, which will serve as a step towards proof of U.S. citizenship.

Citizenship by Naturalization

Citizenship may be acquired by voluntary action; namely, naturalization. The wide publicity accorded the U.S. Immigration and Nationality Law (1952), the so-called McCarran Act, has made most of us familiar with this road to citizenship. Admission of aliens to citizenship varies in accordance with each country's ability and desire to absorb new citizens from outside its own borders.

Under U.S. law an alien generally cannot petition for naturalization until he has been a resident of the United States for five years, at least half of which time was spent in the United States and was within the five years immediately preceding the filing of the petition. Aliens married to American citizens need to be residents for only three years. Aliens who have served in U.S. armed forces for a period (or periods) aggregating three years do not have to meet any requirements concerning residence and physical presence in the United States. There are other special provisions facilitating the naturalization of members of the armed forces who have served honorably during certain wars and periods of armed conflict.

Naturalization procedures are simpler for members of the armed forces than they are for other candidates. On the other hand, the law penalizes applicants for naturalization who refuse to serve in, or who desert from, the armed forces of the United States. Wartime deserters and draft dodgers are permanently ineligible to become citizens of the United States and are deemed incapable of holding any office of trust or profit in the United States. An alien who claims exemption from military service on the grounds that he is an alien is permanently disbarred from becoming a citizen of the United States.

LOSS OF NATIONALITY

A section of the U.S. nationality law lists the actions that automatically strip either a native-born or a naturalized citizen of his U.S. nationality, but in a number of decisions, on a case-by-case basis, the Supreme Court has declared this provision unconstitutional. The current trend is towards protecting citizenship: to be deprived of citizenship, a person must voluntarily commit an act that clearly shows his intention to divest himself of his citizenship. Thus, renunciation of nationality, acquisition of foreign nationality, and other acts of allegiance to a foreign sovereign, committed voluntarily, may at present be considered the only certain grounds for loss of citizenship. Citizenship conferred by act of Congress, such as that derived from one or both parents, can, in accordance with a Supreme Court decision, be withdrawn by act of Congress.

U.S. CITIZENS IN FOREIGN COUNTRIES

Sometimes the jurisdiction or control of a sovereign state over all persons residing within its territory comes into conflict with the authority of the state to which a person owes allegiance. For example, a U.S. citizen who resides abroad and is in the employ of a private business remains a U.S. citizen and owes allegiance to the United States unless he takes steps to become a citizen of the country in which he resides. He is subject to the *territorial* jurisdiction of the latter and to the *personal* jurisdiction of the United States. Personal jurisdiction means, for example, that the U.S. government can order him home if the political situation in the country of his residence makes this advisable. As a counterpart to its right over his person, the government, through its diplomatic or consular officers, extends him protection wherever he is.

TRAINING ABROAD

The two conflicting principles of territorial jurisdiction of one sovereign and personal jurisdiction of another are exemplified in the case of a reserve officer residing in a foreign country who desires to undergo periodic training in that country in order to maintain his efficiency and earn points towards promotion and retirement.

One of the principal rights of a sovereign state is that of recruiting and training an armed force to protect and defend its citizens and territory. No state has the right to undertake such activities in another country without the latter's consent. On the other hand, a state retains the right to order its reservists to periodic training duty in accordance with its laws. There would be no problem if reservists were called home for training; however, distance and expense frequently make this impractical. Therefore, the question arises whether a reservist residing abroad may undergo training in that foreign country. The general rule is that, without the permission of the country in which he is residing, he cannot.

In some cases, the required permission is implied. For example, where U.S. personnel are on active duty in a foreign country as a result of a mutual or collective defense agreement (e.g., the North Atlantic Treaty), the training of U.S. reservists is generally permitted because it is in the best interest of both countries. It increases the defense potential of the U.S. forces in the foreign country without increasing the number of *active* duty personnel. Therefore, consent to reserve training in conjunction with active forces can be implied. In other words, a naval reservist residing in Italy may undertake any form of training, even active duty, with U.S. naval forces operating in that country.

In some instances consent of the foreign government is expressly given in base-rights or status-of-forces agreements. Examples are the Military Bases Agreement with the Philippines and the Administrative Agreement with Japan.

Although members of Military Assistance Advisory Groups and of naval missions, as well as military attachés, are assigned to active duty in foreign countries, their presence does not imply that the host country consents to their undergoing reserve training. The reason for this exception is that these groups enjoy special status; their duties involve aid and advice to the foreign government and, in the case of attachés, intelligence matters. In countries with *only* this type of active-duty personnel, express consent must be obtained before any form of reserve training may be undertaken.

The United States has secured the informal consent of most governments in whose territory U.S. reserve personnel reside for training through correspondence courses. In order to avoid violating a country's sovereign rights by sending training material without consent, the chief of naval personnel checks every request for such material.

JURISDICTION OF FOREIGN COURTS

The first aspect of jurisdiction defined in the introduction above is "the legal power, right, or authority to interpret and apply the law." This definition gives the courts of a country the authority to adjudicate all cases, criminal and civil, arising out of acts committed in that country. Some of this jurisdiction is taken for granted. If a visitor to, let us say, France sold his car there and the purchaser refused to pay the full price, the visitor would probably assume that he could sue in a French court for breach of contract. If a tourist were involved in a traffic accident in France and the local authorities charged him with reckless driving, he would probably take it for granted that a French court would have the right to adjudicate the case in accordance with French law. In this situation the French court is said to have *jurisdiction*.

APPLICATION OF FOREIGN LAW

The complicated problems of jurisdiction may be brought into focus by citing a typical situation. An American serviceman stationed abroad wishes to divorce his wife while they are both in the foreign country. If neither of the marriage partners is a citizen of that country, can a foreign court dissolve the marriage in accordance with local laws? Would the United States recognize such a divorce, if granted? The answer depends on the situation. Everyone is familiar with the lack of uniformity in the divorce laws of the various states of the United States and with the conflicting decisions that have been handed down by state courts on the validity of decrees obtained in other states. The laws of countries vary to a much greater degree, and so far there has been no agreement on a formula that could be incorporated in a treaty for recognition of divorce decrees obtained in foreign countries.

CRIMINAL JURISDICTION

Of great interest to members of the armed forces is the question of criminal jurisdiction—that is, the right of foreign countries to try American citizens for offenses committed in their territory. As already mentioned, they generally do have such jurisdiction. Exceptions, especially those of interest to members of the armed forces, will be discussed later on.

Extradition

What happens if somebody commits a crime in one foreign country and escapes to another one before he can be arrested and brought to trial? The answer to this question involves *extradition*.

Webster defines extradition as "the surrender of an alleged criminal by one state . . . or other authority to another having jurisdiction to try the charge." Extradition generally signifies that a state in which a fugitive from justice has taken refuge prefers to surrender him to the authorities of the state where the crime was committed rather than let the crime go unpunished. This is the attitude taken by the United States and Great Britain, who consider crimes as territorial and punishable only where committed.

Other countries, including some in Latin America, indicate a strong preference for trying their own nationals for crimes committed on foreign soil.
Extradition on the part of such countries, when it occurs, indicates a high
regard for the administration of justice in the country demanding surrender
of the fugitive.

Unless a treaty imposes an obligation to extradite, there is, generally, no
duty to surrender fugitives from justice for trial and punishment. Where
there is no treaty, it has been the practice of the United States, based on
decisions of the Supreme Court, to refuse to extradite on the grounds that
the executive branch of government has no power to arrest and surrender in
such cases. Occasionally, fugitives have been surrendered as a matter of
courtesy, but on the basis of strict reciprocity.

Most extradition treaties are bilateral. The only multilateral treaty to
which the United States is a party is the Montevideo Convention of 1933
between the United States and a large number of Latin-American countries.
But even here, practice is not uniform. Several countries, including the
United States, insisted on reservations on several of the provisions, and the
surrender of nationals of the surrendering state is optional.

One of the basic requirements of extradition is that of *double criminality*.
This term means that the crime for which surrender is demanded must be
punishable by *both* the demanding and the surrendering state. In addition,
there must be sufficient evidence of criminality to warrant prosecution by
the state from which extradition is requested, had the act been committed in
its territory. In short, a state is not bound to surrender a fugitive merely on
the demand of another state; there has to be evidence that a crime was
committed and the facts have to point towards the person whose surrender is
demanded.

A troublesome question may arise if a country is asked to surrender one
of its own nationals. The extent of this obligation depends on the provisions
of the treaty under which the demand for extradition is made. Many treaties
contain a clause to the effect that the parties are not bound to surrender
their own nationals. The courts have interpreted such clauses to mean that
U.S. authorities have no right to extradite American citizens. Other treaties
do not cover the matter or, as in the case of the Montevideo Convention,
contain an optional clause.

In some cases the principle of strict reciprocity is applied. The United
States will not surrender Americans to a country that will not surrender its
nationals as a matter of policy or is prohibited from doing so by its own law.
On the other hand, the United States is bound to surrender Americans to a
country that will surrender its nationals—always provided, of course, that all
the facts have been examined in the light of U.S. criminal law.

So-called extraditable offenses are generally enumerated in the extradition treaties, and most of these lists are amended from time to time. The

Montevideo Convention, which does not contain such a listing, requires that, in order to be extraditable, a crime be punishable by the laws of both the demanding and surrendering states and that the minimum penalty for it be imprisonment for one year. Political and purely military offenses are usually expressly excluded from extradition.

EXCEPTIONS TO JURISDICTION

Before discussing the principles governing jurisdiction over armed forces stationed abroad, it must be emphasized again that as a general principle of International Law a sovereign state has exclusive jurisdiction over all persons within its territory.

The rule embodied in the quotation from the *Schooner Exchange* case at the head of this chapter has led to many misunderstandings and misinterpretations. It was at one time considered to express the rule that the United States had exclusive jurisdiction over its own armed forces wherever stationed. This is valid, of course, as far as court-martial jurisdiction is concerned. It is not valid as a principle of International Law. This point was finally clarified by the Supreme Court in the *Wilson* v. *Girard* case: "A sovereign nation has exclusive jurisdiction to punish offenses against its law committed within its borders, unless it expressly or impliedly consents to surrender its jurisdiction." An example of implied consent is where one sovereign permits the troops of another *to pass through* his territory, as stated in the *Schooner Exchange* case.

It is clear that as a general rule every country has the right to determine what measure of jurisdiction it is willing to surrender when it admits foreign troops into its territory in peacetime for any length of time. Only when troops are in transit through a foreign country and when their contacts with the local population are few is there any basis for the application of the principle enunciated in the quotation that opens this chapter.

The most important exceptions to the exclusive jurisdiction of a state over all persons within its territory are embodied in the principles of *sovereign immunity* and *diplomatic immunity*. Diplomatic immunity is discussed in Chapter 2. Sovereign immunity derives from the immunity of the head of a state. While in the territory of another state, the head of a state is immune from criminal and civil jurisdiction for both his public and private actions. This immunity is absolute and is based on long-standing customary International Law. It extends to all official acts of the state itself, its government, or its official representatives, even if the state or the government be named as defendant.

Jurisdiction over Armed Forces

The status of U.S. military forces stationed in foreign countries is of considerable importance, since it directly affects the discipline and morale of uniformed personnel.

During World War II, the Allied countries granted to each other, either by special agreement or by tacit concession, the exclusive right of military jurisdiction over their own armed forces. These arrangements were in the interest of the common war effort and necessary for the maintenance of discipline within the armed forces.

The concept of collective security which has developed since 1945 has brought with it a change in the attitude of countries towards foreign military personnel abroad and their right to trial by their own military courts for any offenses committed on foreign soil, including offenses against the citizens of the host country. There is no doubt, of course, that from the U.S. point of view it is desirable to retain the largest possible measure of military jurisdiction over its own forces. Nor is there any doubt that, without a special grant by the host countries, the United States does not have this exclusive jurisdiction. It has, therefore, attempted to obtain the most favorable jurisdiction provisions in agreements granting it the right to station troops on foreign territory.

Leased-Bases Agreement with Great Britain

In an agreement signed in 1941, Great Britain leased certain bases to the United States in exchange for the transfer of fifty over-age destroyers. The jurisdictional provision of this agreement proved unworkable. The agreement was therefore amended in 1950, and a new article on jurisdiction was substituted for the original one. This detailed and complicated provision gave the United States exclusive jurisdiction over all offenses committed by members of its armed forces in the British colonies concerned in time of war and over any offenses against U.S. interests committed inside the leased bases. In all other cases there is some form of *concurrent jurisdiction*, which means that either one of the two states, the sending state (the United States) or the receiving state (the British colony in which the base is located), may try an offender, the party having the greater interest in a particular case having the primary right.

These generalizations are only a sketchy outline of a long and detailed provision, but the arrangement has worked out well in practice. The results have been so good that the colonial governments of the areas concerned have refused to substitute the comparable provision of the North Atlantic Treaty Organization Status-of-Forces Agreement (NATO SOFA), which is discussed below. Since most of the former colonies and territories in the Caribbean have acquired independence, the 1950 version of the jurisdictional provision of the Leased-Bases Agreement now applies only in Bermuda. An identical provision, however, is contained in the two agreements covering the Long-Range Proving Ground and the Oceanographic Research Stations in the Bahamas. Newfoundland, in which the jurisdictional provision of the Leased-Bases Agreement originally applied, is now a province of Canada and covered by the NATO Status-of-Forces Agreement.

North Atlantic Treaty Status-of-Forces Agreement

The North Atlantic Treaty Status-of-Forces Agreement was a major attempt to define on a multilateral basis the jurisdictional status of military personnel stationed in countries of members of NATO. It was signed by all NATO countries on 19 June 1951, and has been ratified by all signatories except Iceland. Greece and Turkey, which became members of NATO on 15 February 1952, have also ratified the agreement. Germany joined NATO on 5 May 1955, and on 1 July 1963, the Status-of-Forces Agreement, together with a detailed supplementary agreement, came into force for that country. Since France has pulled out of the military aspects of NATO and U.S. forces are no longer stationed in France, the applicability of the agreement in that country is moot, but the principles of SOFA are followed as a matter of practicality.

The agreement has been condemned in some quarters as abandonment of the traditional U.S. position of exclusive jurisdiction over military personnel and as a surrender of the constitutional rights of U.S. military personnel stationed abroad. However, as explained earlier in this chapter, U.S. jurisdiction over military personnel stationed abroad is an exception to the general rule and is based on treaties. Nothing has been surrendered by these agreements; in fact, the United States gained some jurisdiction that it did not have under the general rule. This interpretation does not, of course, mean that U.S. military authorities have court-martial jurisdiction only on the basis of these agreements. The military has jurisdiction over military personnel wherever they may be. But that is jurisdiction over the *person*. Jurisdiction over the *offense* is normally a territorial matter, and part of it is surrendered to the United States by treaty. Thus, host countries have relinquished their primary right to jurisdiction in so-called *inter se* offenses, which is to say offenses committed in the performance of official duty and offenses against other U.S. personnel, civilians and dependents.

How well the formula of the NATO Status-of-Forces Agreement has worked out in practice is evidenced by the fact that it has become the pattern for status-of-forces agreements. Japan led the way by incorporating it into the Administrative Agreement, which combines status-of-forces and facilities, or base-rights, provisions. That agreement was signed on 19 January 1960, and its provision on jurisdiction, identical with the one contained in NATO SOFA, is incorporated in Article XVII. Article IV of the Panama Canal Treaty of 1977 makes provision for the status of U.S. armed forces throughout Panama: an amplifying agreement is modeled after similar status-of-forces arrangements elsewhere.

The same provision is contained in agreements with Australia, 9 May 1963; Nationalist China, 31 August 1965; Korea, 9 July 1966; and the West Indies Federation, 10 February 1961. Although the West Indies Federation was never formed, the agreement was approved and accepted not only by

Great Britain, on behalf of the territories to be included in it, but by the territories themselves, many of which are now independent. The agreement applies in Trinidad and Tobago, Barbados, and the British colonies of Antigua, St. Lucia, and the Turks and Caicos Islands. It used to apply in Jamaica, but does not now because the United States no longer maintains forces there. However, by informal arrangement, Jamaican authorities adhere to this agreement for crew members of visiting U.S. ships. Because of particular circumstances in Spain and the Philippines, status-of-forces agreements being renegotiated with those two countries will probably give them more authority than other host states have.

Efforts are being made to adopt the NATO formula for other agreements still under negotiation. Details of interpretation and slight differences in procedure are usually contained in agreed minutes, which are attached to the agreement and made part of it. Only the NATO Status-of-Forces Agreement is fully reciprocal, all others cover only the status of U.S. forces in the host country. A special arrangement has been made for jurisdiction over Australian forces in the United States. By presidential proclamation, the Friendly Foreign Forces Act of 1944 allows members of the Australian armed forces in the United States to be tried there by their own military courts and entitles Australian military authorities to U.S. assistance in the arrest of offenders, the securing of witnesses at their trials, and judicial help to which U.S. military authorities in other countries are entitled by virtue of status-of-forces agreements.

Civilians

Most status-of-forces agreements grant the United States the right to exercise jurisdiction over all persons subject to U.S. military law. In the past, this included civilians who were accompanying and serving with the armed forces and the dependents of both military and civilian personnel.

In a series of decisions, the Supreme Court of the United States has declared that court-martial jurisdiction over civilians in time of peace is unconstitutional. Therefore, until Congress amends the Constitution or by law establishes civil courts empowered to try civilian employees and dependents for offenses committed overseas, only the foreign courts have the right to try such persons. In cases of certain minor offenses, where U.S. military authorities can take disciplinary action administratively, requests for waiver of jurisdiction over civilians are made. And in all cases civilians enjoy the protection and safeguards that apply to military personnel, and U.S. military authorities will render the same assistance and support.

The decisions of the Supreme Court declaring court-martial jurisdiction over civilians in time of peace unconstitutional do not affect the right of U.S. authorities to exercise such jurisdiction in time of war. For the purpose of applying the Uniform Code of Military Justice, the Korean conflict, although not a declared war, was considered to be a war. During that conflict, the U.S. Court of Military Appeal ruled that the phrase *time of war* could be applied only to wars declared by Congress and, thus, removed from court-martial jurisdiction civilians who committed offenses in Vietnam.

Article VII of NATO Status-of-Forces Agreement

The simplest way to illustrate how the jurisdictional provisions of the NATO Status-of-Forces Agreement, Article VII, works may be by giving concrete examples. It should be remembered that the provisions in question are reciprocal and whatever applies to U.S. troops in foreign countries applies with equal force to foreign military personnel from NATO countries in the United States.

Assume that a sailor stationed in Italy, one of the North Atlantic Treaty Organization countries, commits a crime. If his offense were punishable by U.S. law *only*, as treason and sabotage against the United States would be, then the United States would have exclusive jurisdiction. In this instance, he would be tried by court-martial and could not be tried by Italian courts. If his offense were punishable by Italian law *only*, for instance, operating in the black market or violating Italian customs laws, then the Italian civil courts would have jurisdiction and would try him in accordance with Italian law. Exclusive jurisdiction, therefore, rests in the sending state (here, the United States) for offenses punishable by its laws but not by the laws of the receiving state (here, Italy). Similarly, exclusive jurisdiction rests in the receiving state for offenses punishable by its laws but not by those of the sending state.

In all other cases jurisdiction is *concurrent*, which means that either one of the states may try the offender, but not both. The Status-of-Forces Agreement stipulates which state has the primary right to exercise jurisdiction. For offenses that are of more importance to the sending state, its military authorities have the primary right: such offenses include acts committed in the performance of official duty and acts solely against the persons and property of other members of the armed forces of the sending state. For all other offenses, the receiving state has the primary right.

Assume that a U.S. sailor in Italy, while driving a navy vehicle on official duty, injured an Italian civilian: the U.S. military authorities would have the primary right to exercise jurisdiction. Should that sailor have a similar accident when he was off duty and driving a private car, the Italian authorities would have the primary right. If, for some reason, the Italian authorities did not want to try the sailor, they would have to so notify the American authorities. Also, the latter could request the Italian authorities for a *waiver of jurisdiction*. In other words, they could ask that the Italian courts not exercise their right and, instead, allow the U.S. military authorities to try the offender. As a matter of practice, U.S. authorities request a waiver of jurisdiction in *all* cases where servicemen violate foreign law. In some countries, such waivers are considered to be granted automatically. In others, if the authorities intend to try an offender, they must so notify U.S. authorities within a certain period of time. Failure to do so makes the waiver automatic and the case is tried by court-martial.

The Status-of-Forces Agreement entitles a member of the U.S. armed forces who is tried in a foreign court, in accordance with the above provision, to a number of procedural safeguards. These safeguards comprise most of the constitutional rights that U.S. citizens have come to consider inviolable. This protection does not mean, however, that the procedure before a foreign court has to be identical with that of a U.S. court in a similar case. For instance, countries subject to civil law do not have trial by jury, which does not mean that a serviceman's rights would be prejudiced. The United States cannot demand that other countries change their laws, but it does have the right to ensure that its servicemen receive fair and impartial trials, that they are properly defended, and are fully aware of all their rights under the procedure being used.

Extensive procedures have been established to safeguard all the rights of U.S. servicemen subject to trial by foreign courts. However, since this aspect of jurisdiction may—and probably will—at some time be of concern to seagoing officers, detailed directives on the subject are available at all commands. A serviceman who comes in conflict with foreign law is entitled to the aid and advice of representatives of his command from the time the offense is committed until the end of trial and appeal. He is entitled to counsel at the expense of the U.S government and his trial will be attended by an official observer from his service who, except for offenses such as minor traffic accidents, must be a trained lawyer. The observer reports to the Judge Advocate General and to the commanding officer of the area in which the trial is held whether or not, in his opinion, the trial was fair and whether or not the accused was denied any of the rights to which he was entitled. If the accused should be sentenced to confinement in a foreign jail, regular visits, medical and dental care, where not otherwise available, and similar assistance are provided until he is released from prison.

Statistics maintained by the three services on the exercise of jurisdiction by foreign courts over U.S. servicemen consistently show a large number of waivers. This is evidence of the fact that foreign authorities generally recognize the desirability of trial by court-martial for the maintenance of discipline in the armed forces. Only when its laws have been flagrantly violated does a country insist on punishing the offender.

FOREIGN LAW AND PROCEDURE

A serviceman tried by a foreign court is tried in accordance with the laws of that country. Certain aspects of foreign law and procedure and differences in the interpretation of some terms of status-of-forces agreements have given rise to disputes with foreign authorities and have, in some cases, resulted in reports of trials being unfair, whereas it was only a difference in procedure that gave that impression.

Performance of Official Duty

A term that caused considerable dispute in the Girard case was *performance of official duty*. Girard, an army man, was ordered to guard a machine gun and some field jackets during a break in exercises on a U.S. target range in Japan. While he was doing so, some Japanese civilians came on the range to pick up empty brass shells for sale as scrap. Girard tried to chase them away by shooting empty cartridges from a grenade launcher attached to his rifle. One of these cartridges hit a Japanese woman in the back and killed her. Girard's commanding officer certified that the killing arose out of an act done in the performance of official duty. The Japanese authorities contended that shooting empty cartridges at shell-pickers was not within the scope of Girard's guard duty. Such differences of opinion must, in accordance with the Administrative Agreement, be resolved by a joint United States-Japanese committee. In this case, however, the committee was not able to reach a decision. Because of the strong public feeling in Japan, the U.S. authorities decided to waive their primary right to exercise jurisdiction, in accordance with Article XVII of the Administrative Agreement. The issue before the U.S. Supreme Court was whether this waiver violated the constitutional rights of Girard. The court held that it did not: Girard had no special immunity from Japanese jurisdiction, and whatever immunity was granted by the Administrative Agreement was for the benefit of the United States and could, therefore, be waived by it.

This case clarified the U.S. position on jurisdiction over its armed forces in foreign countries. From the point of view of the present discussion, it also shows how a term, in this case *performance of official duty*, can be interpreted differently. Many countries give that particular term a broad interpretation and grant the United States the right to exercise jurisdiction in many border-line cases. Others, as the Girard case shows, insist on a narrow interpretation, especially when the case is one that arouses public sentiment. In a subsequent case, also in Japan, a sentry on duty shot and killed an innocent passer-by. The United States, aware of Japanese interpretation that such a shooting was not within the scope of his sentry duty, did not press for jurisdiction.

Appeal from an Acquittal

The strict common-law concept of double jeopardy, namely that no man can be tried twice for the same offense, makes the prosecution's appeal from an acquittal unconstitutional. Under the U.S. system of law, a retrial on appeal would be considered a new trial. In many countries subject to civil law, and especially in Japan, a trial is not completed until the last legal resort has been exhausted or the time for availing oneself of this resort has passed. As a result, appeals to higher courts are part of the same trial and not new trials. In a capital offense, a trial is not completed until the case has been decided by the supreme court or until the period of time set by law for filing appeal to that court has elapsed without appeal by either side. Under Japanese law and also under the criminal procedure of most civil-law countries, the prosecution as well as the defense has the right to appeal. Sentence on appeal may be reduced, increased, or reversed. This last means that not only may a convicted offender be acquitted, but also, unfortunately, that the court may impose a sentence, including confinement, on a defendant who has been acquitted. From the point of view of common law, this would be intolerable. However, since servicemen in a foreign country are tried in accordance with the laws of that country, such a procedure does not deprive a U.S. serviceman of the safeguards guaranteed under status-of-forces agreements and must be accepted as a legal concept unknown to common law. Whether U.S. authorities will ever be able to persuade foreign authorities to refrain, as a matter of policy and in deference to the U.S. concept of double jeopardy, from lodging appeals from acquittals when U.S. offenders are involved is hard to predict.

Combined Civil and Criminal Action

Another procedural concept of civil law that is unknown to common law, as practiced in the United States, is the combination of civil and criminal law action in negligence cases. This procedure entitles an injured party to bring criminal action against the person who caused the damage. The action is brought in the name of the state; the injured party is represented by counsel, who joins the prosecutor in bringing arguments against the defendant. This joint civil-criminal action determines the issue of negligence, including the presence or absence of criminal negligence. Damages are assessed later in a purely civil action, whereas the criminal aspect is confined to fixing the penalty, if any. This joint action is frequently the only way in which liability can be established, and thus the only way in which the injured party can collect damages. In most cases, the injured party is interested only in satisfactory financial settlement and not in criminal prosecution. Expeditious settlement of claims will therefore frequently avoid criminal charges.

Trial in absentia

Also unknown to the U.S. system of law, but quite common in countries subject to civil law, is *trial in absentia*, that is, trial in the absence of the accused. The purpose of such trials is to clear a court's dockets, and countries that conduct trials in absentia maintain that an accused has no right to complain because he voluntarily removed himself from the jurisdiction of the court. From the U.S. point of view, this form of trial violates a number of the accused's rights, such as confrontation, compulsory process to obtain witnesses, possibly also the right to counsel, interpreter, notice of charges against him, and so forth. This form of procedure becomes important to a serviceman who is due to be transferred or discharged. In this case, it is the practice of military commands to inform the accused that, if he leaves the country, he will be tried in his absence. If he appoints counsel to represent him, the trial is not in absentia in the strict legal sense. But by waiving his right to be heard and to be confronted by his witnesses, the accused forgoes some of the rights that would aid his defense. In many countries an accused may request a new trial after a true trial in absentia. Should he be sentenced to confinement in such a trial, he need not serve his sentence unless he returns to that country.

Claims

For members of the armed forces stationed in foreign countries, the rapid settlement of claims for damages caused by military personnel is of the utmost importance. Settlement procedure is not uniform in all countries, since some status-of-forces agreements contain detailed provisions for settlements.

Foreign Claims Act

The Foreign Claims Act recognizes that, in the interest of maintaining friendly foreign relations, it is important that claims be settled. In this act, Congress authorized the settlement of legitimate claims by inhabitants of foreign countries who suffer damages through acts of U.S. military forces or their members. Detailed procedure for the settlement of foreign claims is contained in Chapter XXII of the *Manual of the Judge Advocate General*. All commanding officers are authorized to appoint foreign claims commissions and to settle claims in accordance with that procedure, except in countries where different procedures have been established by international agreement.

Claims under Status-of-Forces Agreements

In NATO countries and other countries that have status-of-forces agreements, the settlement of claims follows procedures spelled out in the applicable agreement.

Claims arising out of acts committed in the performance of official duty are considered and settled or adjudicated by the authorities of the receiving state, in accordance with its laws and regulations. Claims are submitted to the receiving state, which determines the amount to be paid and pays the claimant directly. The sending state must reimburse the receiving state for an agreed portion of the settlement (75 per cent in NATO countries), and the receiving state bears the balance.

The most common claims are those that arise out of acts not committed in the performance of official duty and for which there is not adequate insurance. They are dealt with as follows: the receiving state considers the claim and assesses compensation "in a fair and just manner, taking into account all the circumstances of the case, including the conduct of the injured persons." It then prepares a report on the claim and submits it to the authorities of the sending state. The sending state decides whether or not to offer an ex-gratia payment, and if so, what it will be. If the claimant accepts this offer in full settlement of the claim, the sending state makes payment directly and informs the authorities of the receiving state that it has done so. If the offer is rejected, the injured may sue in the local courts.

In considering claims submitted for ex-gratia payment, the authorities of the sending state follow the procedure and regulations set forth in the Foreign Claims Act referred to above.

Naval Missions and Military Assistance Advisory Groups

A discussion of jurisdiction over members of the armed forces would be incomplete without brief mention of two categories of military personnel who enjoy privileged status: members of missions and of Military Assistance Advisory Groups, which are established by special agreements. While mission agreements do not contain jurisdiction provisions, as do status-of-forces agreements, they do provide that "personnel of a mission shall be governed by the disciplinary regulations of the United States armed forces." This has been interpreted to mean that such personnel are subject to court-martial jurisdiction only, and not to the jurisdiction of the host country.

Military Assistance Advisory Groups are established in foreign countries pursuant to mutual security legislation and agreements. Their primary purpose is the supervision of military aid and the transfer and use of military equipment. Countries that have consented to the establishment of Military Assistance Advisory Groups have agreed that the members of the groups will be attached to the diplomatic mission, will work under its direction, and will enjoy a status equivalent to that of members of the diplomatic mission of corresponding rank. Under this provision the chiefs of Military Assistance Advisory Groups and the chiefs of the army, navy, and air force sections enjoy full diplomatic immunity. The status of other members of such missions depends on the size of the group and the rank of each of its members.

The distinction between members of a Military Assistance Advisory Group and members of a mission has, for all practical purposes, been more or less wiped out. Most U.S. military missions were established in Latin-American countries, where they were also Military Assistance Advisory

Groups. These two types of groups have now been combined into "military groups," which carry out the functions of both and operate under the direction of the chief of the diplomatic mission concerned. Military personnel attached to this type of group are rarely involved in trials by foreign courts.

9   Armed Conflict and Protection of War Victims

Let war be so carried on that no other object
may seem to be sought but the acquisition of peace.

Cicero

GENERAL

Vice Admiral William L. Rodgers, USN, former battleship commander, president of the Naval War College, and commander in chief of the Asiatic Fleet, wrote a good deal about the practicalities of the law of armed conflict. In 1924 he wrote that the rules of war

> fulfill a double object, as towards the individual enemy these restrictive rules are humane; as towards one's own organized forces in the field these restrictives promote discipline and efficiency, and so help to shorten war through earlier and more complete victory over the hostile state.... Provincial armies are inefficient because they permit and even rely on pillage and personal violence. Thus these so-called humane rules are advantageous simultaneously to both sides. Were it not so, they would have less chance of being observed.

About the same time he commented:

> Combatant forces desire the limitation on the exercise of belligerent power in humanitarian interest because they themselves as individuals share the views of the general public as to avoidance of the infliction of suffering having no influence on the outcome of the war. But combatants have two reasons for such limitations additional to those governing the general public. First, because combatants themselves are the first to feel the horrors of war, and second, because both in victory and defeat, cruelty and license towards individuals and wanton damage and destruction of property tend to destruction of discipline and make the national forces less efficient instruments in the execution of national will. By the impressment of humanitarian principles upon the mass of men under arms and their education therein during peace, the military forces are rendered more efficient and also the popular desire for amelioration of the sufferings of war will slowly be assisted to accomplishment.

These points are still valid and are reflected in the Geneva Conventions for the Protection of War Victims, 1949, in Protocols I and II additional to those conventions, 1977, and in national and military policies of most states participating in the negotiations that produced those treaties.

In negotiating the above-mentioned protocols and in the Conference on Certain Conventional Weapons, 1979–1980, delegations operated on the premise that rules formulated in peacetime are not likely to endure unless they are practical and the value that they would have in times of conflict can be demonstrated. They were aware that humanitarian proposals that were not likely to be observed by combatants or in times of high national emotion and stress were not only unrealistic but dangerous, because they gave combatants and civilians alike a false sense of security. The efficacy of the new protocols cannot be determined until the extent of adherence to their terms and their spirit has been tested in the crucible of war.

DEFINITIONS

The broadest, traditional definition of the word *war* is "armed, physical contest between nations." A modern definition is "a legal condition of armed hostility between states." The latter may be a more accurate definition because, although war generally involves acts of violence, a state of war may legally exist before or after the use of force. After World War II, for example, the United States was "at war" with Japan and Germany for many years after the shooting ended. The Treaty of Peace with Japan did not come into force until 1952.

Perhaps the two most important changes in the concept of war as a state of hostilities were the provisions of the 1928 Kellogg-Briand Peace Pact (or Pact of Paris), which essentially codified the customary law, and the 1945 United Nations charter. By the former, the United States and sixty-four other nations renounced war as an instrument of national policy. In approving the U.N. charter, almost all nations promised to "refrain in their international relations from the threat or use of force against the territorial integrity or political independence of any state, or in any other manner inconsistent with the purposes of the United Nations." Hence, aggressive war, as such, has been eliminated from among the lawful means of conducting international relations. Yet, the use of armed force has not ceased.

Use of armed force pursuant to a decision or recommendation of the United Nations, in accordance with Article 42 of its charter, is not "war" in the strict technical sense. The conflict in Korea provides an example of such a use of U.N. armed force. The nations that were involved in that conflict have been careful to avoid the word *war* in connection with the hostilities in Korea. Instead, the action has been termed *armed conflict* or *police action*. Nevertheless, to those who fought in Korea, it was as real a war as any in our history. In fact, U.S. courts have held that for all practical purposes the Korean conflict was a war. The same was true of the Vietnam conflict. It may seem strange that the courts should be called upon to make such a decision, but when a conflict is not war, as defined by International Law, only they, by applying domestic law, can decide whether or not so-called war clauses in contracts and insurance policies are applicable. They must also decide whether a "conflict" is a "war" within the meaning of certain provisions of the Uniform Code of Military Justice.

As a result of the evolving limitations of "war," the term *armed conflict* has come into common use, and is now generally understood to mean hostilities between states at least one of which has resorted to the use of armed force. It may also mean hostilities between a state and organized, disciplined, and uniformed groups, most often within the state, such as organized resistance movements.

THE LAW OF ARMED CONFLICT

Although it may seem incongruous, armed conflict must be considered to be in the framework of International Law. Many textbooks on International Law used to treat the International Law of Peace and the International Law of War as separate from one another. This division of subject matter suggests that there are two separate areas of the law and is misleading. In the last four decades, there has been a gradual change in many of the concepts of war and peace. The result is a twilight zone, which is neither peace nor war in the traditional meaning of those terms. It can no longer be said that the moment two countries engage in war a different set of rules comes into force. Furthermore, the law of armed conflict is only one group of principles guiding the nations in times of conflict.

The law of armed conflict is of obvious interest to the naval officer since it governs the actual conduct of hostilities, as distinguished from such issues as whether hostilities should have been begun or should continue, whether one of the belligerents was guilty of aggression, or whether one of the belligerents was exercising its right of self-defense. It is now generally recognized that the law of armed conflict applies in all international armed conflicts, regardless of their legality. This principle is expressed in Article 2, which is common to all four Geneva Conventions of 1949: "[The Conventions apply to] all cases of declared war or any other armed conflict which may arise between two or more of the High Contracting Parties, even if the state of war is not recognized by one of them."

Protocol I extends the application of this international humanitarian law of armed conflict to the modern phenomenon known as *wars of national liberation*. These revolutions, as defined by Article 1(4) of the protocol, are

> armed conflicts in which peoples are fighting against colonial domination and alien occupation and against racist regimes in the exercise of their right of self-determination, as enshrined in the Charter of the United Nations and the Declaration on Principles of International Law concerning Friendly Relations and Co-operation among States in accordance with the Charter of the United Nations.

In practical terms, this provision was adopted to respond to the situations in the Middle East and South Africa as they existed at the time of the Protocol I negotiations, 1974–1977. It is probably not as broadly applicable as might appear at first glance. This is so in part because Protocol I applies to such wars only if an authority representing the liberation group, i.e., a regional intergovernmental body such as the Organization of American States or the Organization of African Unity, makes a declaration assuming all the obligations as well as the rights of the protocol. It is highly doubtful that such a thing would ever happen. Nevertheless, Article 96 of Protocol I makes it clear that, if such a declaration should be made, the liberation movement would not be favored over a state's combatants nor could it acquire rights without assuming corresponding obligations, including full application of the law of armed conflict.

Consequently these provisions of Protocol I cannot be read, as some have suggested, as reintroducing into the law of armed conflict the old concept of "just war," which allowed opposing combatants to be treated unequally, according to the cause for which they were fighting. Further, the record of the negotiations makes it clear that Protocol I does not apply to civil strife caused, for example, by secessionist groups, riots, isolated acts of violence, or fighting by a group that does not control a significant amount of territory or is not able to conduct sustained military operations.

BACKGROUND

The sources of International Law are discussed in Chapter 1—written and unwritten rules, treaties, agreements, and customary law. The law of armed conflict is part of that same pattern of development. Nations have long recognized the need to codify the rules of war. One attempt was made in the United States during the Civil War by Francis Lieber, a professor at Columbia College. His *Instructions for the Government of Armies of the United States in the Field*, most of which is a codification of the laws and customs of war existing at that time, was promulgated by President Abraham Lincoln on 24 April 1863 as binding on the armed forces of the United States. The *Lieber Code*, which the book came to be called, stimulated a major international attempt at codification, i.e., the Hague Peace Conference of 1899. At that conference, a number of conventions on the rules and laws of war were reduced to writing. In 1907, another conference at The Hague revised the rules and made them more detailed. The rules that emerged from these two conferences are known, collectively, as the Law of The Hague.

Two points about the Hague conventions are particularly noteworthy. First, they recognized that the total avoidance of war should be their ultimate goal. Second, they recognized that war was sometimes unavoidable and had to be accepted as a regrettable but legitimate means of settling disputes between nations. In view of the latter reality, the best that could be hoped for was general acceptance of humanitarian rules of warfare. As a result, Article 1 of the First Hague Convention provides: "With a view to obviate as far as possible recourse to force in the relations between States, the Contracting Powers agree to use their best efforts to ensure the pacific settlement of international disputes." The convention then provides for mediation through the good offices of other parties to the convention and for arbitration by a special commission. Compared with current agreements designed to avoid war, this convention appears to have made a rather feeble and ineffective attempt, which was defective particularly in regard to the enforcement of arbitration.

Nevertheless, the rules of warfare embodied in the Hague conventions give an interesting example of the interrelation between written and unwritten International Law. The preamble to the second convention respecting the Laws and Customs of War on Land provides:

> Until a more complete code of the laws of war has been issued, the High Contracting Parties deem it expedient to declare that, in cases not included in the Regulations adopted by them, the inhabitants and the belligerents remain under the protection and the rule of the principles of the law of nations, as they result from the usages established among civilized peoples, from the laws of humanity, and the dictates of the public conscience.

This preamble shows that the nations at the Hague conferences did not intend to codify all the laws of war. Even the parties to these conventions were to use customary International Law to supplement the codified rules. The codification's continuing applicability is established in Article 1(2) of Protocol I.

The codified rules were initially made largely ineffective by the general participation clause, which is a part of all the Hague conventions: "the provisions contained in the Regulations referred to in Article 1, as well as in the present Convention, do not apply except between Contracting Powers, and then only if all the belligerents are parties to the Convention." The conventions thereby made themselves inapplicable in any war in which one of the participants had not ratified them.

Certain of the belligerent countries in World War II had not ratified or adhered to these conventions. Therefore, some defendants in war crimes trials at the end of the war claimed that they could not be prosecuted for violating the laws of war embodied in these conventions. The judges rejected this defense on the grounds that by 1939 the rules in question represented customary International Law and were recognized by all civilized nations. This view has long been held by the United States, and it is now accepted almost worldwide that the Hague rules are binding upon all nations as customary International Law.

The law of armed conflict relating to the protection of war victims has experienced a similar growth. Inspired by the sight of 40,000 wounded or dead Austrian, French, and Piedmontese soldiers abandoned after the twelve-hour battle at Solferino, Italy, in June 1859, and of the thousands more who died because there was no organized medical care, Henri Dunant, a Swiss philanthropist, called upon the local population for help. Later he publicized the horrors of Solferino in a book wherein he suggested the setting-up of voluntary relief societies, whose work should be based on an international humanitarian treaty. In 1863, four Genevese citizens joined him in establishing a private committee, which became the International Committee of the Red Cross (the ICRC). Prompted by that initiative, the Swiss Federal Government convened a diplomatic conference in Geneva in 1864, which drafted the first Convention for the Amelioration of the Condition of the Wounded in Armies in the Field. This convention was renegotiated in 1906, 1929, and 1949. The resulting four Geneva Conventions of 1949 for the Protection of War Victims are together known as the Law of Geneva and must be distinguished from the Law of The Hague, which deals principally with weapons and methods of warfare. Because of the role the ICRC plays in protecting war victims, its structure and activities under the Law of Geneva are of importance and are described below.

ADHERENCE

It is a popular misconception that the rules of war are of but marginal value, that they are out of date, and that they should be revised. At the beginning of this book, it was stressed that International Law is a living law. Like the common law of the United States, it is subject to change and adaptation to new developments, political or technical. Thus, it was revised as recently as 1977, and efforts to expand its application are ongoing as this is written. In no field of law is this dynamism more characteristic than in that of armed conflict, because war itself has been completely revolutionized by technical developments.

Yet, in spite of revisions of the law, the written policy of the U.S. Department of Defense (DoD Directive 5100.77) has since 1974 been to ensure that:

1. The law of war and the obligations of the U.S. Government under that law are observed and enforced by the U.S. Armed Forces.
2. A program, designed to prevent violations of the law of war, is implemented by the U.S. Armed Forces.
3. Alleged violations of the law of war, whether committed by or against U.S. or enemy personnel, are promptly reported, thoroughly investigated, and, where appropriate, remedied by corrective action.

4. Violations of the law of war alleged to have been committed by or against allied military or civilian personnel shall be reported through appropriate command channels for ultimate transmission to appropriate agencies of allied governments.

The same directive requires that the armed forces of the United States "comply with the law of war in the conduct of military operations and related activities in armed conflict, however such conflicts are characterized" and "institute and implement programs to prevent violations of the law of war to include training and dissemination [of the law]."

It has been said that the law of armed conflict hurts military commanders and prevents them from successfully completing their missions. In fact, it has just the opposite purpose and effect. It is consistent with and reinforces such military principles and doctrines as accuracy of targeting, concentration of effort, maximization of military advantage, conservation of resources, minimization of collateral damage, and economy of force. Both the law and the principles and doctrines cited have as their goal the efficient application of military force against military objectives. The use of excessive or misdirected force is not only costly and inefficient, it may also waste scarce resources. It could even involve a violation of the law of armed conflict, which would have counterproductive political consequences. Conduct that violates the law often has only marginal military advantages at best and, at worst, can be highly dysfunctional; for example, attacks against civilian populations. Experience has shown that disobedience or simple neglect of the law detracts from, and in some cases prevents, the accomplishment of a mission, while contributing nothing to overall military and political objectives.

Thus, respect for the law of armed conflict generally serves the self-interest of everyone. Self-interest is reciprocal. If country X does not abide by the law, the chances increase that its enemy will not, and the conflict will get worse for all. If country X wants its prisoners of war to be treated humanely, it must treat enemy prisoners humanely.

Individuals, as well as states, have an interest in the law of armed conflict because it not only imposes certain obligations on combatants, but it grants them certain rights. The most important of these rights is *military privilege*, which allows combatants to engage in combatant acts—killing and destroying property authorized by the laws of war, for examples—which, if not committed by recognized combatants in armed conflict, would be unlawful and punishable as common criminal acts. When captured, a combatant is held as a prisoner of war, not as a common criminal prisoner, and he cannot be punished for any act he committed as a combatant, as long as it was in conformity with the laws of war.

THE INTERNATIONAL COMMITTEE OF THE RED CROSS

The International Committee of the Red Cross (ICRC) has been a cornerstone in the effective development and functioning of the law of armed conflict. It is and always has been an independent private institution, neutral in politics, ideology, and religion. Headquartered in Geneva, the ICRC is composed of no more than twenty-five Swiss nationals. In its role as a neutral institution, it endeavors to ensure that the victims of war, civil war, and internal disturbances, whether civilians or members of armed forces, receive protection and assistance. It also promotes the understanding and dissemination of the Conventions' provisions. The ICRC, in cooperation with governments and experts in the field, is also active in developing international humanitarian law. The protocols for the protection of war victims drawn up in 1977 are a product of that cooperative effort.

The ICRC transmits donations, in cash and in kind, to suffering people in every part of the world. During World War II, it paid 11,000 visits to prisoner-of-war and civilian internment camps, forwarded to and distributed in those camps relief whose total value was 3.5 billion Swiss francs, and provided civilian populations in occupied territories with relief amounting to 500 million Swiss francs. Since the end of World War II, the ICRC has visited civilian and military prisoners held in some one thousand camps, prisons, and hospitals in many countries, aided war victims in various parts of the world, and distributed relief supplies valued at 1 billion Swiss francs to victims of numerous conflicts.

The ICRC also operates the Central Tracing Agency and the International Tracing Service. The Central Tracing Agency, which is headquartered in Geneva, has a card-index comprising forty-five million entries, representing fifteen million individual cases, containing any information obtained on prisoners of war, civilian internees, and persons released or repatriated, mainly on the basis of names it receives. It traces civilians and servicemen displaced during conflicts and informs their families. It draws up captivity and death certificates. When normal means of communication are cut off, it transmits messages between civilians and between prisoners and their families.

The International Tracing Service, headquartered in Arolsen, West Germany, is today the most important center of information concerning persons deported or otherwise displaced during World War II, whether in Germany or in countries that were occupied by German troops. Its index contains twenty-five million cards, and it has received well over two million inquiries since its establishment.

PROTECTION OF WAR VICTIMS

The purpose of most of the rules of war is to prevent or alleviate the suffering of persons not actually involved in the fighting. Those rules, based on the principle of humanity, have been revised again and again to keep pace with the developments of modern warfare. The Hague Rules annexed to the Conventions on the Laws and Customs of War on Land, 1899 and 1907, contain a chapter on the treatment of prisoners of war which is still in effect between the parties thereto, inasmuch as the Third Geneva Convention of 1949 specifically provided for its inclusion.

The treatment of the sick and wounded in the armed forces of belligerents has also long been governed by customary rules as well as by treaties. In World War II whole countries were conquered and occupied and sizable populations were mistreated, exterminated, or forcibly removed from their homes and country. These actions forced civilized nations to recognize the need for strict rules to prevent such things from happening again. For this reason, the Geneva Conference of 1949, for the first time, codified rules of humane warfare designed to protect the civilian population in time of war.

Protection of war victims is now covered by the four Geneva Conventions of 12 August 1949, which came into force for the United States on 6 February 1956, and the Protocols of 1977. These agreements are:

Convention for the Amelioration of the Condition of the Wounded and Sick in Armed Forces in the Field (commonly known as the First Convention).

Convention for the Amelioration of the Condition of Wounded, Sick, and Shipwrecked Members of Armed Forces at Sea (commonly known as the Second Convention).

Convention Relative to the Treatment of Prisoners of War (commonly known as the Third Convention).

Convention Relative to the Protection of Civilian Persons in Time of War (commonly known as the Fourth Convention).

Protocol Additional to the Geneva Conventions of 12 August 1949, and relating to the Protection of Victims of International Armed Conflicts (Protocol I).

Protocol Additional to the Geneva Conventions of 12 August 1949, and relating to the Protection of Victims of Non-International Armed Conflicts (Protocol II).

The texts of these agreements have been widely disseminated and may be found, for example, as appendices to the U.S. Navy's *Law of Naval Warfare* (NWIP 10-2).

The principles of the 1949 conventions were applied in the Korean and Vietnam conflicts, although not all the participants complied fully, by any means. In the Korean conflict, application of the conventions was accomplished by notification of adherence to the ICRC by the parties to the conflict, since the conventions were not in force when the Korean conflict began on 25 June 1950.

There is not room in this text to discuss in detail these agreements and all their provisions, but the broad implications of each are examined briefly. Provisions that are important to naval officers are examined in more detail.

All four conventions of 1949 contain the following article:

> The High Contracting Parties undertake, in time of peace as in time of war, to disseminate the text of the present Convention as widely as possible in their respective countries, and, in particular, to include the study thereof in their programmes of military and, if possible, civil instruction, so that the principles thereof may become known to the entire population, in particular to the armed fighting forces, the medical personnel and the chaplains.

The Convention Relative to the Treatment of Prisoners of War provides that:

> Any military or other authorities, who in time of war assume responsibilities in respect of prisoners of war, must possess the text of the Convention and be specially instructed as to its provisions.

Similar provisions are contained in Protocol I.

All officers should be familiar with the provisions of these agreements because U.S. personnel may have the misfortune of falling into enemy hands as prisoners of war, possibly in a wounded or sick condition. Knowledge of the rights and duties involved in such cases will obviously be of the greatest value to all concerned, especially to those responsible for and in charge of any of the persons protected by these agreements.

The 1949 conventions have by now been ratified by or are acceded to by almost all nations. The 1977 protocols to the conventions are now in force, at this writing eleven nations being parties to Protocol I. Although all the major military powers are parties to the 1949 conventions, none has yet become a party to either protocol. Neither of the protocols contains a "general participation clause," which might makes its provisions ineffective, were one of the belligerents not a party to them. On the contrary, all four conventions of 12 August 1949 state:

> Although one of the Powers in conflict may not be a party to the present Convention, the Powers who are parties thereto shall remain bound by it in their mutual relations. They shall furthermore be bound by the Convention in relation to the said Power, if the latter accepts and applies the provisions thereof.

Protocol I contains a similar provision.

APPLICATION OF THE GENEVA CONVENTIONS IN THE VIETNAM CONFLICT

One of the questions raised by the Vietnam conflict was whether it was the type of action to which the Geneva Conventions of 1949 were applicable. The following discussion shows that it was.

Of significance is the fact that all the parties to the conflict were parties to the conventions. Furthermore, the conventions were intended to give maximum protection in any type of conflict. They apply to all cases of declared war and to "any other armed conflict which may arise between two or more of the High Contracting Parties, even if the state of war is not recognized by one of them." The minimum standards of protection established for armed conflict "not of an international character occurring in the territory of one of the High Contracting Parties" are to assure protection in civil war, insurrection, and so forth. Both of these articles are common to all four conventions. The nature and extent of involvement of both North Vietnam and the United States should leave no doubt that the protection provided for international armed conflict did apply, not just the minimum protection established for internal conflicts.

More difficult to answer is the question, who was entitled to the protection of the conventions? It must be remembered that a great variety of people were fighting against South Vietnam, among them North Vietnamese troops, guerrillas, terrorists, even civilians, many of whom, from the South Vietnamese point of view, were insurgents. As will be seen, the Prisoner of War Convention clearly defines who is entitled to be treated as a prisoner of war, and requires that in case of doubt a competent tribunal must determine the status of those involved. The screening of all persons captured by the United States and South Vietnam, and the establishment of a tribunal to decide their status, were among the problems that had to be solved.

PRISONERS OF WAR

Although the four Geneva conventions and the 1977 protocols are of the utmost importance in ensuring humane treatment for victims of war, the Prisoner of War Convention, which covers every detail of prisoner-of-war life from the moment of capture through to release, and Protocol I have special significance to members of the armed forces.

Treatment as a prisoner of war is a right to which large and generally well-defined categories of participants in armed conflict are entitled under Protocol I. These participants include not only members of armed forces, but civilians who work with and for armed forces under conditions where they could fall into the hands of the enemy: for example, civilian crews of military aircraft and crews of merchant ships. Not normally entitled to prisoner-of-war status are spies, saboteurs, and mercenaries. Under Protocol I, military advisers are not considered to be mercenaries nor are foreign members of the armed forces of a party to the conflict. In addition, Protocol I extends prisoner-of-war status to guerrillas, even those who do not meet all the requirements of Article 4 of the Third Convention, if they carry their arms openly during military engagements and when they are visible to the enemy while "engaged in a military deployment preceding the launching of an attack in which they are to participate." The U.S. view is that it would be very difficult for a guerrilla to qualify just by carrying his arms openly, as required. U.S. opinion is that prisoner-of-war status for a guerrilla would be valid only in occupied territory or in wars of national liberation, and, further, that the phrase concerning military deployment refers to any movement towards a place from which an attack is to be launched, such as an assembly area, an approach march, or infiltration to an assembly area.

Commandos, paratroops, and similar forces are entitled to treatment as prisoners of war as long as they belong to the organized armed services of one belligerent and wear a uniform, even if they operate singly. When a member of an armed force is found behind enemy lines, the wearing of a uniform has long been considered of utmost importance in determining his status. Thus, under Protocol I, if a person wearing the uniform of his armed forces is captured in enemy territory while engaged in espionage or sabotage he is not considered to be a spy and is entitled to prisoner-of-war status.

Article 5 of the Prisoner of War Convention stipulates that persons whose right to be treated as prisoners of war is in doubt must be protected until their status has been determined by a "competent tribunal."

Prisoners of war are legally in the hands of the enemy power or state, and not in the hands of the individual or unit that captured them. Responsibility for their treatment rests with the capturing power. Questioning of prisoners has become a matter of especially great concern as a result of experiences in the Korean and Vietnam conflicts. A prisoner of war is required to give only his name, rank, serial number, and date of birth as provided in the Prisoner of War Convention. Members of all armed forces carry Geneva Convention Identification Cards, which show the above information, for presentation in the event of their being taken prisoner. It hardly need be mentioned, however, that, since time immemorial, prisoners of war have been sources of information for the enemy and ever-new methods of questioning have been devised. Article 17 of the Convention states:

> No physical or mental torture, nor any other form of coercion, may be inflicted on prisoners of war to secure from them information of any kind whatever. Prisoners of war who refuse to answer may not be threatened, insulted or exposed to unpleasant or disadvantageous treatment of any kind.

Even this strict prohibition will not prevent some powers from using every conceivable means of coercing prisoners of war into giving information. This fact was, in effect, officially recognized by the president of the United States, when in 1955 he issued a "Code of Conduct for Members of the Armed Forces of the United States," whose purpose was to impress on military personnel the importance of withholding information in the face of even the most uncivilized forms of questioning.

THE CODE OF CONDUCT

The Code of Conduct was formulated with the provisions of the Prisoner of War Convention in mind. Even in captivity, where he has to abide by the disciplinary regulations of his captor, a U.S. serviceman is still a U.S. serviceman and subject to the regulations and orders of his service. Compare Article 17 of the convention and Article V of the code. The former states that a prisoner is not obliged to give any information other than name, rank, service number, and date of birth. Until 1976, Article V of the code allowed a prisoner to give that much information. Now, the Code of Conduct, having been extensively reviewed since the return of prisoners of war from Vietnam, has been amended to require, in parallel to the convention, giving name, rank, service number, and date of birth. These data provide positive prisoner identification, and a prisoner who fails to give them forfeits his right to be treated as a prisoner of war. The Code of Conduct was changed in recognition of the reality that any prisoner of war can be coerced into giving more information and that some prisoners took the words "is bound to give only" to mean that they were restricted to giving only that information, even though the old language of Article V also required that a prisoner "evade answering further questions to the utmost of his ability." Thus the change was intended to encourage a prisoner to adopt "successive lines of resistance," and to prevent one who had been coerced into giving more information than he felt he should from feeling "broken." This "rebound" technique, which has been very successful, allows a prisoner to "bounce back," continue to resist, and provide as little information as possible during subsequent interrogations.

The convention also protects prisoners of war against torture or any other form of coercion. Article V of the code amplifies Article 85 of the Third Convention, which guarantees that a prisoner who is prosecuted by his captors for offenses committed before his capture, even if he is convicted, is entitled to the protection of this convention, that is, to full prisoner-of-war status. The nations of the Communist bloc have entered a reservation to this provision. They do not recognize the right of a combatant *convicted* of an "offense" committed in the prosecution of the conflict to be treated as a prisoner of war. Upon conviction, such a combatant forfeits the protections of the Geneva Conventions.

In Protocol I an effort has been made to overcome such reservations by omitting the requirement that the law of armed conflict be observed as a condition for granting or denying prisoner-of-war status, and specifically stating that violations of that law "shall not deprive a combatant of his right to be a combatant or . . . a prisoner of war," unless he fails to distinguish himself from civilians.

Protocol I provides also that all persons in the "power of a Party to the conflict" who are accused of war crimes or crimes against humanity are entitled to fundamental due process and human-rights guarantees.

The Code of Conduct does not impose on a captured serviceman any obligation that would hurt his status under the Prisoner of War Convention or put him under obligation to act in violation of his duties under this convention. It explains his duties towards his country and his service in the framework of what he is entitled to under International Law, as expressed in the provisions of the Third Convention.

Another provision of the code is of interest. Article III imposes on a captured serviceman the duty to make every effort to escape. Escape does not violate the Third Convention, which recognizes that every prisoner will attempt to escape and enumerates the circumstances under which escape is considered legal. That convention further states that, when an attempt to escape is not successful, a prisoner, even one who has made previous attempts to escape, is subject to disciplinary punishment only. It further states that offenses committed to facilitate escape, except murder of or injury to a guard or a person attempting to recapture, are punishable by disciplinary action only. The same holds true for offenses committed to help others to escape. Each duty cited by the code is consistent with the provisions of the Prisoner of War Convention.

Under provisions of the Third Convention, captured medical personnel and chaplains are not to be considered prisoners of war but "retained personnel." As such, they should receive, as a minimum, the benefits and protections afforded by that convention to prisoners of war generally. Their privileged status does not give them latitude to act contrary to the Code of Conduct. They are subject to that code and responsible for their actions even while fulfilling their duties as retained personnel. However, they may perform their medical and spiritual duties without the restrictions placed on prisoners of war by the code and by the Third Convention. Thus, retained personnel may encounter competing priorities. For example, a doctor may have many opportunities to escape as he moves freely among prisoners of war; yet he may determine that he has an obligation to continue ministering to the sick and wounded rather than take advantage of those opportunities. In such a case, there would be no conflict between the code and the convention because the moral duty of retained personnel to minister to the needs of prisoners of war is to be inferred from the code.

The incident of the USS *Pueblo* raised the question of when the Code of Conduct applies. As indicated by U.S. protests, the seizure of the *Pueblo* and detention of her crew were illegal under International Law. Consequently, the crew members were entitled to immediate release and could not be considered as prisoners of war. In spite of its references to the Prisoner of War Convention, does the code apply to U.S. servicemen illegally detained and subjected to torture and indignities, as investigation following the crew's release established to have been the case? The prevailing view is that the code applies in all instances where servicemen find themselves in the hands of a hostile power. The code is intended as a standard of conduct applicable when the normal processes of command and discipline cannot obtain because of lack of communications or conditions of confinement. But it is not a penal code and violations of its provisions can be punished only if they also constitute offenses under the Uniform Code of Military Justice.

REPATRIATION

One provision of the Prisoner of War Convention, as was discovered during the Korean conflict, might be open to different interpretations. Article 118 provides that "prisoners of war shall be released and repatriated without delay after the cessation of active hostilities." Does this mean that prisoners of war *must* be repatriated, even forcibly, without regard to their own wishes?

The view of the United States is that this provision requires only that every prisoner of war be offered an unrestricted opportunity to go home, and does not prohibit a capturing nation from granting asylum to prisoners who request it because they fear prosecution, or even execution, in their home country on account of their political beliefs or activities. Because the question has not arisen since some members of the U.S. armed forces chose to remain in Communist China after the Korean conflict, the views of other nations on this point are not yet clear. In any event, the obligation to repatriate at the close of hostilities cannot legally be modified or qualified by using prisoners of war as bargaining chips in settling other issues.

SICK, WOUNDED, AND SHIPWRECKED

The first two Geneva Conventions of 1949, for "The Amelioration of the Condition of the Wounded and Sick in Armed Forces in the Field" and for "The Amelioration of the Condition of Wounded, Sick, and Shipwrecked Members of Armed Forces at Sea," as supplemented by Protocol I, are complementary and will, therefore, be discussed together.

The purpose of these conventions is to ensure to the sick and wounded of the armed forces the most humane treatment possible under wartime conditions. Protocol I extends them to include, in addition to the armed forces, civilians who either are in need of medical assistance or care, or who are in peril at sea as a result of misfortune affecting them or the ship or aircraft carrying them, and who refrain from any act of hostility.

Less-than-humane experiences in World War II made it necessary to add to the general statement guaranteeing protection and respect without distinction or discrimination as well as humane care and treatment. The addi-

tions explicitly prohibited murder, extermination, torture, physical mutila-
tion, medical, scientific or biological experiments, removal of tissue or
organs for transplantation, willful neglect, or willful exposure to contagion
or infection. When members of armed forces who are sick, wounded, or
shipwrecked fall into enemy hands, they are entitled to prisoner-of-war
status as well as to the above guarantees of humane treatment.

MEDICAL FACILITIES, MEDICAL AIRCRAFT, AND HOSPITAL SHIPS

To make treatment and care of the sick and wounded possible at all
times, the agreements specify that military and certain civilian medical units
and establishments shall be immune from attack.

This provision applies to hospitals as well as to hospital ships and medical
vehicles. When a hospital falls into enemy hands, its personnel are free to
continue to care for the wounded and sick, if the capturing party has not
made adequate provisions. By the terms of the convention, hospital ships are
immune and may not be captured: when they fall into enemy hands while in
port, they may not be detained. The immunity granted to hospital ships
extends not only to those belonging to the governments of the belligerent
powers but also to those made available by neutral powers and recognized
relief societies, such as the International Committee of the Red Cross. Even
lifeboats and small coastal rescue craft belonging to neutrals and relief
societies are exempt from capture, where military operations permit. A
qualification here was necessary because during a major naval engagement,
it might be impossible to guarantee absolute protection to small rescue craft
moving in and out among large naval ships. Small craft are of such importance in the speedy rescue of the shipwrecked, however, that their protection was included along with that of large hospital ships.

Protocol I makes perhaps its most significant advance in humanitarian
law by providing useful protections to medical aircraft. Article 24 eliminates
the strangling provisions of the 1949 conventions, which limited protection
for medical aircraft to those "flying at heights, times and on routes specifically agreed upon between the belligerents concerned." The requirement for
agreed flight plans, which were almost never achieved, has been replaced by
a more rational regime that takes into account the relative dangers to the
aircraft and abuse of protected status within three distinct areas: areas
controlled by friendly forces, areas in the contact zone, and areas where
control is not clear; it also provides immunity for medical aircraft operating
over enemy-controlled areas. Article 25 explicitly frees medical aircraft
from the requirement to file flight plans in land areas under the physical
control of friendly forces and sea areas not controlled by adversary forces.
Medical evacuation by air from rear areas is thus generally protected without
formality. Medical evacuation by air from a battle area, however, particular-

ly within range of enemy surface-to-air missiles, is less secure. Accordingly, notification of flight plans and display of the distinctive emblem and signals discussed below are recommended precautions. Although medical flights are forbidden over enemy or enemy-occupied territory, and thus can legitimately be attacked, Protocol I details less drastic measures than shooting down to be taken where there are no agreed flight plans or prescribed corridors, particularly in encircled areas, at beachheads, and in established airheads.

An important factor in the protection of hospitals, hospital ships, and medical aircraft is that they must be recognizable as such. The agreements therefore require that they shall be clearly marked with a distinctive emblem which, except in a few Moslem countries, is a red cross on a white background. Emblems need to be much larger than they used to be because tests made by the International Committee of the Red Cross have shown, for example, that the old-sized emblems on ambulances are not distinguishable beyond three hundred meters and the armband prescribed by Articles 40 and 41 of the First Convention is not recognizable beyond sixty meters. Their size is left in the discretion of the competent commander who may direct such size as is appropriate and consistent with the tactical situation. The emblem on a battle aid station need only be large enough for patrols or assault infantry to identify it, whereas the emblem on the roof of a hospital or sides and deck of a hospital ship must be large enough to be recognized by aircraft and distant submarines. Article 42 of the First Convention gives commanders and the competent authorities of a party to the conflict the discretion to determine, "insofar as military considerations permit," which medical units and establishments are to display the distinctive emblem. This discretion is allowed because, under some tactical circumstances, concealment is preferable to recognition. Tactical commanders may direct the removal or camouflage of the distinctive emblem if, in the exercise of sound discretion, they determine that the requirements of concealment outweigh those of recognition and possible attack.

There are detailed provisions regarding markings for all hospital ships, lifeboats, and coastal rescue craft, and the obligation is imposed upon the parties concerned to make them visible and recognizable at night. In addition, the protection of hospital ships is conditioned upon notification to the adversary parties of the names and descriptions of these ships. The immunity from capture granted to hospital ships extends to their medical personnel and crews, even if there are no sick or wounded on board.

Annex I to Protocol I also provides for a number of signals to be used exclusively by medical units and transports. This is done to extend through technological means the range at which medical units and transports are recognizable. The signals include rapidly flashing blue lights, a distinctive radio signal, the secondary surveillance radar system IFF (Identification

Friend or Foe) used worldwide for air-traffic control and military identification, flags, and flares. Provision is also made for the development of even more modern devices, such as acoustic underwater and laser signals.

Medical establishments, units, and transports, including hospital ships and medical aircraft, lose the protection granted them if they are used for acts injurious to the enemy, for example, to shield military objectives from attack.

The agreements, however, provide that the establishments do not lose their protection because their personnel are armed for their own defense and that of the sick and wounded. An additional important exception is provided for hospital ships: the carrying of medical personnel and equipment in excess of the normal requirements of the ship does not deprive her or her personnel of protection. Since this provision does not apply to medical aircraft, aircraft carrying mixed loads of patients and equipment or personnel not associated with a medical mission may not be designated or marked as medical aircraft and are therefore subject to attack.

Hospital ships may not possess or use secret codes for their communications, and medical personnel employed for coding and decoding of operational messages are considered to be engaged in activity "outside their humanitarian duties." Similarly, medical aircraft "shall not be used to collect or transmit intelligence data and shall not carry any equipment intended for such purposes." But, in recognition of the safety role played by some modern aviation electronic systems, such as IFF (Identification Friend or Foe), their use is not prohibited. However, even in the face of clear violations of the duty to refrain from actions harmful to the enemy, protection does not cease unless due warning of the violation remains unheeded.

In order to prevent abuses by hospital ships, belligerents have certain rights of control, including the right to search them. These rights, now an integral part of the Geneva Convention of 1949, were first accepted in the Hague Conventions (Number III of 1899 and Number X of 1907). The following experience, related by Admiral H. P. Smith, USN, provides a good illustration:

> In about May of 1945, I was Senior Officer Present of naval forces in the forward areas, including the Volcano and Mariana Islands. I had task units at Guam and Saipan, and I was in command at Iwo Jima. One of my duties was to provide blockade forces in the Bonins, just to the north of Iwo. One evening the destroyer *Roe*, on patrol off Futami Ko (the harbor of Chichi Jima), made contact with a Japanese hospital ship. The hospital ship was correctly lighted, and was proceeding on a normal route to Futami Ko. The destroyer closed the hospital ship, identified her, but didn't attempt to hinder her movements. By the time the *Roe* reported the incident to me, the hospital ship was already in Futami Ko.
>
> I then reported my intention to the Commander-in-Chief, Pacific, in Guam to exercise the privilege accorded in Article 4 of the Hague Convention

to divert the hospital ship, on her departure from Chichi Jima, to Iwo Jima, where I would conduct an examination.

I was immediately directed by the Commander-in-Chief not to undertake the action in view of the fact that every effort was being made to avoid any incident regarding hospital vessels, which might lead to a reprisal against our own. Within a matter of a few days after this exchange of despatches, one of our hospital ships, off Okinawa, was bombed with damage to the ship and personnel casualties.

About a month later, aircraft identified a Japanese hospital ship proceeding to Marcus Island. On this occasion, I was directed by the Commander-in-Chief to send a destroyer to intercept the hospital ship on her emergence from Marcus and conduct an inspection to see that the ship was not violating International Law in any respect. The destroyer *Case* intercepted the ship. An inspection party, headed by the executive officer, was well received aboard the hospital ship, and allowed to make a thorough inspection. He found everything in perfect order. The ship had nothing aboard except a full load of hospital cases evacuated from Marcus Island.

MEDICAL AND RELIGIOUS PERSONNEL

To balance the large measure of protection and the many immunities granted to those entrusted with the care of the wounded and sick, the Geneva Convention requires that protected persons refrain from any acts injurious to the enemy, and that medical establishments and hospital ships be used only to carry out their humanitarian missions.

CIVILIANS

Before Protocol I went into force, civilian populations were protected from the dangers of war by customary International Law: Hague Regulations on Land Warfare of 1907 and the Fourth Geneva Convention of 1949. Most of the Hague Regulations and the Fourth Convention apply only to civilians in the hands of a power hostile to them, for example, the inhabitants of occupied territory. The Convention on Protection of Civilians is concerned with responsibilities of a belligerent toward its own civilian population with regard to the establishment of hospital and safety zones to protect the wounded, sick, aged, children, and expectant mothers from the effects of war.

This convention deals mainly with the occupation of defeated nations by the victor and the rights and duties of the occupant and residents of occupied areas. American military government in occupied areas is primarily the responsibility of the army. During and after World War II, however, the navy was responsible for governing the Pacific islands formerly administered by Japan, until these islands were put under the trusteeship system of the United Nations. Most of the provisions contained in this convention have long been recognized as the duties of an occupying power. The deportation or transfer of the entire population of an occupied area is now explicitly prohibited. However, evacuation of civilian populations for their protection or for more imperative military reasons is still permitted.

Another controversial issue, much in the limelight during the Nuremberg trials, has been settled by Article 34 of this convention, which prohibits the taking of hostages. This provision answered the much-disputed question of whether a belligerent had the right to execute hostages if the population was warned by the belligerent that the commission of certain specified acts would lead to execution, and this warning failed to restore order. Execution of hostages as a last resort was considered lawful even during World War II. Now, however, even the taking of hostages is absolutely prohibited.

In contrast to the stringent responsibility imposed on belligerents to protect the civilian population in time of war, there are well-established rights of control which are necessary for the security of a nation and its armed forces. Such is the case with internment. The convention has detailed provisions regarding internment camps and all facets of their operations. These provisions parallel those made for prisoner of war camps and their administration and discipline.

Protocol I codifies and considerably expands the customary rules and treaty provisions protecting civilians still in territory controlled by their own side or in the immediate vicinity of a battle, expands the protection provided by civil-defense operations, and further encourages relief operations for civilians affected by armed conflict. It also expands the rights of civilians, including journalists, in the hands of a party to the conflict. It affects, however, only civilians on land. Thus, civilians involved in air-to-air, air-to-sea, sea-to-air, land-to-sea, and sea-to-sea situations have no more protection than they did under the old law.

PROTECTIONS FROM ATTACK

Perhaps the most significant advances in the law contained in Protocol I and the ones of greatest practical effect on combatants are the provisions of Articles 48-60, which are for the protection of all civilians against the effects of hostilities. Many of them require military personnel to make important decisions that may affect civilian lives and property as well as the outcome of the conflict. They are, therefore, treated here in some detail.

The material that follows is based on a Department of Defense sectional analysis prepared to accompany the protocol when the president submits it for the advice and consent of the U.S. Senate.

The basic rule of Protocol I is that parties to a conflict should always distinguish between a civilian population and military objectives to the extent that this is practical and possible, and "direct their operations only against military objectives." A civilian is anyone who is not a member of an "armed force," or a member of a militia or volunteer corps on active duty, or part of a levy. Any person whose status is in doubt shall be considered to be a civilian and, if captured, treated as a prisoner of war, at least until his status is established by competent authority. The practical impact of this rule is to require commanders and other responsible combatants to act on the basis of the best information available to them at the time they take their actions, and not on the basis of speculation that they might, for example, be guerrillas or other combatants. A person's behavior, location, and appearance will all be relevant factors in deciding whether or not he is a civilian. The U.S. view is that such determinations are not to be made on the basis of hindsight, for to do so would be to require the impossible of the combatant and foster disregard for these new and useful rules.

The presence of a few combatants within a civilian population does not deprive that population of its civilian character. For example, the presence in a community of a small number of sailors on leave would not make that entire community vulnerable to attack. In balance, however, parties to a conflict are obliged to refrain from using civilians to shield military forces from attack, and civilians are obliged to refrain from acting as a shield for military forces.

Article 51 of Protocol I amplifies the customary international rule that has long provided general protection for civilian populations in wartime. *General protection* means that civilians are to be spared the dangers of war as much as reasonably possible under the circumstances; it is not the same as the *special protection* that belligerents owe to medical personnel, the sick, wounded, and shipwrecked, and captured women and children. Civilians are not to be made the objects of deliberate attack, although they may suffer collateral injury as a result of attacks on combatant personnel and other military objectives. Especially prohibited are attacks or threats of attack whose primary purpose is to induce terror among a civilian population. Note that it is not producing terror that is forbidden, but attacking or threatening to attack civilians for the *purpose* of producing terror. As a practical matter, a certain amount of terror will be produced whenever military objectives in the vicinity of civilians are attacked.

Civilians lose their immunity from deliberate attack when they take direct part in hostilities. Whereas members of the armed forces may be attacked whether they are engaged in combat or not, civilians are subject to deliberate attack only "for such time" as they take a direct part in hostilities. Clearly, civilians who try to kill, injure, or capture enemy persons or damage enemy material are taking a direct part in hostilities. The same would be true of a civilian who was acting as a member of a weapons crew. A civilian providing intelligence information to combat units, such as an artillery spotter or member of a ground observer corps, would also be subject to attack while he was carrying out that function. On the other hand, civilians providing indirect support to the armed forces, such as workers in defense plants, would not be subject to deliberate, individual attack, although they might have assumed the risk of incidental injury as a result of attacks on their places of work.

Indiscriminate attacks are prohibited. These are defined as attacks not directed at a military objective, attacks launched by a method that makes such direction impossible, and attacks whose effects cannot be limited as required elsewhere in the protocol. This rule prohibits the use of "blind" weapons, which do not have any reasonable assurance of hitting only a military objective, and thus pose an unacceptable risk of injury to "innocent civilians": attaching antipersonnel bombs to free-floating balloons or using long-range missiles with only rudimentary guidance systems would be examples of this type of weapon. Other weapons prohibited by the protocol include those, other than nuclear weapons, that might be expected to cause excessive civilian damage and losses in relation to the expected military advantage, or those whose effects on the environment would be widespread, long-term, and severe. This rule does not prohibit the use of such weapons against military objectives in areas not occupied by civilians.

An attack treating a number of military objectives as one objective is forbidden if the objectives are in a city, town, village, refugee camp, or similar "concentration of civilians," if that concentration of civilians is endangered by the attack. This rule does not apply to a city or village whose civilian population has been evacuated. Nor does it apply if the military objectives in a village are, for example, hopelessly intermingled with the civilian population, either deliberately, in violation of the rules, or through neglect.

The governing rule for these types of situations is known as the *rule of proportionality*. Article 51 (5(b)) of Protocol I prohibits an attack that "may be expected to cause incidental loss of civilian life, injury to civilians, damage to civilian objects, or a combination thereof, which would be excessive in relation to the concrete and direct military advantage anticipated." This rule recognizes that, under modern conditions, civilians are often endangered by legitimate military operations and that civilian casualties and damage are inevitable—although regrettable—in war. It simply states that civilian damage and losses should not be out of proportion to the military advantage to be reasonably anticipated from an attack. It is not required that the effects of bombardments and other attacks be strictly limited to the target. It is required that persons preparing to launch an attack proceed only if, on the basis of the information available at the time, they can determine that the attack will not cause excessive civilian damage and loss. Civilian losses and damage must be balanced against expected military advantage.

The term *concrete and direct military advantage* means an honest expectation that the attack will make a relevant contribution to the attainment of the purposes of the military operation involved. The concept of military advantage involves a variety of considerations, including the security of the attacking force. Civilian losses and damage are to be weighed against the military value of the military operation taken as a whole, and not only the value of the particular attack that happened to produce the civilian damage.

The general protection of civilian populations against the effects of armed conflict is not to be abused by parties to a conflict. Article 51 (7), therefore, forbids the use of civilians to shield, favor, or impede a military operation, to give a military objective immunity from attack, or to block a road in order to prevent its use by the enemy. On the other hand, this rule does not prohibit measures to restrict the movement of civilians so as to avoid their interference with military movements, nor does it prohibit ordering their evacuation if their security or some imperative military reason so demands.

To complement these rules, Article 57, which is titled "Precautions in Attack," relates to all acts of violence against an enemy, whether in offense or in defense, and specifies some of the precautions that must be taken to avoid injury to civilian persons and damage to civilian objects. Commanders and staff officers who order and plan an attack must first perform three duties: verify that the target is a lawful one to attack; minimize civilian casualties; and ensure that any unavoidable civilian damage will be proportionate to the military advantage to be gained. An attack that is under way must be suspended if it appears that continued action would be unlawful. The duty to call off such an attack falls on any officer with appropriate authority, and not only on the initiating commander, who would probably not be on the scene. A civilian population must be given "effective advance warning" of any attack that might affect it, "unless circumstances do not permit."

When several military objectives offer similar military advantages, the one selected for attack should be that which would involve the least danger to civilian lives and civilian objects. Article 57 also reaffirms the accepted principle of the laws of air and naval warfare that the parties to conflicts in the air and at sea should "take all reasonable precautions to avoid losses of civilian lives and damage to civilian objects." *Reasonable* means that which is practicable, taking into account all circumstances, including those relevant to the success of military operations.

STATUS OF OBJECTS

Civilian objects, which are defined as all things that are not military objectives, are given restricted protection compared with that afforded civilian populations in general. Article 52 of Protocol I forbids making civilian objects targets of attack or reprisal. On the other hand, objects which, by "their nature, location, purpose, or use make an effective contribution to military action and whose total or partial destruction, capture, or neutralization, in the circumstances ruling at the time, offers a definite military advantage" do not enjoy the protection afforded civilian objects. This is a broad definition, which goes considerably beyond strictly military objects such as tanks, weapons, and fortifications. It authorizes attacks upon activities providing administrative and logistic support to military operations, e.g., transportation and communications systems, or industrial plants producing equipment and material for combat forces. While military objectives must make an "effective contribution to military action," this does not require a direct connection with combat operations, such as is implied in the direct "participation in hostilities" language of Article 51(3). Civilian objects thus receive *less* protection against deliberate attack than civilian persons. The term *military action* includes logistic, administrative, and training activities, which are only indirectly related to combat action. To be a military objective, an object must both "make an effective contribution to [enemy] military action," and its destruction, capture, or neutralization must offer a definite military advantage to the attacker. The term *military advantage* involves a variety of considerations, including the security of the attacking force. It is not necessary that the military value of the object to the enemy be related to the advantage anticipated by the attacker from the destruction, capture, or neutralization of the object. It would thus be permissible to bombard objects supporting the enemy forces for the purpose of deceiving the enemy as to the location of an impending ground attack, or in order to pressure the enemy to negotiate a settlement to the conflict. Whether a definite military advantage would result from an attack must be judged in light of the advantage anticipated from the whole military operation of which the attack is a part, not from isolated or particular parts of that operation. The term *neutralization* refers to a military action which denies an object to the enemy without capturing or destroying it. For example, a specific area of land may be a military objective if, because of its location, nature, or use, its total or partial destruction, capture, or neutralization would offer a definite military advantage in the circumstances ruling at the time. Such an area of land might, for example, be neutralized by planting land mines on or around it, thus denying it to the enemy. In cases of doubt as to whether an object normally dedicated to civilian purposes is being used to make an effective contribution to military action, "it shall be presumed not to be so used." There is compliance with this rule whenever a commander or other person responsible for planning, deciding upon, or executing an attack concludes, on the basis of the information reasonably available to him at the time, that the object is a military objective as defined.

Articles 53-56 deal with types of civilian objects which, for their intrinsic value or because of the danger that damage to them would entail, should be protected: cultural objects, places of worship, objects indispensable to the survival of the civilian population, the natural environment, and works and installations containing dangerous forces, such as dams, dykes, and nuclear electrical generating stations. Article 53 and other rules of war forbid the use of cultural buildings in support of a military effort, acts of violence against them, and the direction of reprisals against them. It does.not forbid the infliction of incidental damage to these objects in the course of lawful military operations. Any of these buildings that, contrary to the law, are used in support of a military effort, lose their special immunity from acts of hostility and may be attacked directly.

Earlier rules provided that it was permissible to starve a hostile belligerent, armed or unarmed, in order to speed his subjection. Article 54 of Protocol I for the first time formally forbids the deliberate starvation of a civilian population as a means of waging war and provides specific rules for the special protection of food and other things indispensable to civilian survival.

The special protection that Article 56 provides for certain dams, dykes, and nuclear electrical generating stations applies only if an attack might release floodwaters or radioactive material, thereby producing "severe losses among the civilian population." The article would not apply to a dam, dyke, or station in a sparsely populated region where relatively few civilian casualties might be expected, nor would it apply to infantry assaults and other attacks that did not create a danger of release. Military objectives near protected dams, dykes, and stations are also protected if attack on them would create a reasonably foreseeable risk of releasing dangerous forces. Circumstances that would cause these objects to lose their special protection are set forth in the article.

10

Land, Aerial, and Naval Warfare

In any armed conflict, the right of the Parties to the conflict to choose methods or means of warfare is not unlimited.

It is prohibited to employ weapons, projectiles and material and methods of warfare of a nature to cause superfluous injury or unnecessary suffering.

It is prohibited to employ methods or means of warfare which are intended, or may be expected, to cause widespread, long-term and severe damage to the natural environment.

Article 35 of Protocol I additional to
the 1949 Geneva Conventions
for the Protection of War Victims, 1977

INTRODUCTION

The preceding chapter dealt with certain principles of law governing warfare and the obligation of nations at war and the personnel of their armed forces to abide by them. It also considered in detail the efforts made to reduce the suffering of the sick, wounded, and shipwrecked, of prisoners of war, and of other categories of persons who are victims of war. The present chapter deals with the specific law governing weapons and methods of warfare, on land, in the air, and on the sea.

Just as modern warfare has become increasingly complex, so has much of the law of armed conflict. However, in both there are the essentials that must be understood whether or not detailed knowledge and expertise are required.

The laws concerning warfare can be divided into two groups. The first group consists of restrictions from the Law of The Hague on the conduct of the war itself; for example, prohibitions on the use of certain weapons, such as poison. The second group consists of rules from the Law of Geneva for protecting persons who are not involved in the actual conduct of war: obvious examples are civilians, sick, wounded, and shipwrecked members of the armed forces and prisoners of war, as discussed in the preceding chapter.

GENERAL PRINCIPLES

In the past, rules of warfare cited three basic principles: chivalry, military necessity, and humanity. The first of these has little relevance today except as it is collaterally reflected in specific prohibitions against the use of poison;

against dishonorable or treacherous conduct; and against the misuse of enemy flags, uniforms, and flags of truce. Military necessity and humanity are, however, fundamental. The principle of humanity is the basis for all the obligations that International Law now imposes on belligerents for the purpose of checking the use of more violence than is actually necessary for the accomplishment of legitimate military purposes. Complementing the principle of humanity is the principle of military necessity, which permits the use of such regulated force as is not forbidden by International Law and is indispensable for securing the submission of the enemy with the least possible expenditure of human and material resources. A U.S. Air Force pamphlet, *International Law—The Conduct of Armed Conflict and Air Operations* (No. 110-31), points out that this concept has four constraints: "(i) that the force used is capable of being and is in fact regulated by the user; (ii) that the use of force is necessary to achieve as quickly as possible the partial or complete submission of the adversary; (iii) that the force used is no greater in effect on the enemy's personnel or property than needed to achieve his prompt submission (economy of force); and (iv) that the force used is not otherwise prohibited." It is noted that the above is not the nineteenth-century German doctrine of Kriegsraison, which asserted that any measure, even a violation of the laws of war, could be justified by "military necessity." The war crimes trials that followed World War II established the fact that "military necessity" is not an acceptable defense for lawlessness in the conduct of war. There are limits, and these are the rules to be discussed hereafter.

Rules of warfare are designed to restrain belligerents from the unrestricted use of force. As the regulations annexed to the Hague Convention on the Laws and Customs of War on Land state, "the right of belligerents to adopt means of injuring the enemy is not unlimited." All limitations on the conduct of war imposed by treaties or by customary law should be viewed in the light of this principle, which is recodified in Protocol I as quoted at the beginning of this chapter. The rules exist for the protection of belligerents. Failure to abide by them may lead to total war with all of its devastation. It certainly results in savagery and brutality, thereby impeding the restoration of peace and friendly relations between nations which must, at some point, accompany or follow the conclusions of hostilities.

WEAPONS AND METHODS OF WARFARE

In the following discussions the rules of warfare are treated in the three physical environments where they are applicable; however, each discussion deals with the same two separate subsets of rules; i.e., (1) the weapons of warfare, and (2) the methods of using those weapons.

The two key general legal principles applicable to weapons and methods of warfare are military necessity and proportionality. Military necessity protects the right to use any degree or means of permissible force required to achieve the objective sought. Proportionality is a well-recognized legal limitation on weapons and methods of warfare which requires that injury or damage to legally protected interests not be disproportionate to the legitimate military advantages to be secured.

Air Force pamphlet No. 110-31 identifies the limitations or constraints:

(1) The nature, degree, extent and duration of individual injuries involved in the prohibition against unnecessary suffering;
(2) Excessive incidental injury to protected civilian persons or damage to civilian objects; and
(3) Uncontrollable effects against one's own combatants, civilians or property.

The principle of proportionality forbids the use of weapons, projectiles, and material and methods of warfare of a nature to cause superfluous injury or unnecessary suffering. This rule is firmly established in customary law and was reaffirmed in Protocol I. A military commission that met in St. Petersburg, Russia, in 1868 stated that "the employment of arms which uselessly aggravate the sufferings of disabled men or render their death inevitable" would not help in the weakening of enemy military forces, and that is the only legitimate objective of war. Which weapons or methods of warfare cause unnecessary suffering, and hence are unlawful is most frequently determined by the practice of states. All weapons cause suffering. The critical factor is whether the suffering is needless or disproportionate to the military advantages secured by the weapon, and not the degree of suffering itself.

Some international agreements give substance to the principle by specifying that certain weapons or methods of warfare may not be used. For example, International Law has condemned dumdum, or expanding, bullets because they inevitably cause death. Usage and practice have also led to the outlawing of projectiles filled with glass or other materials that are difficult to detect medically; of any substance in projectiles that tends unnecessarily to inflame the wounds they cause; of irregularly shaped bullets; and the scoring of the surface or filing-off of the ends of the hard cases of bullets, both of which actions cause bullets to expand upon contact and aggravate the wounds they cause.

The rule against unnecessary suffering applies also to the manner in which a weapon or method of warfare is used against combatants or enemy military objectives. It prohibits the infliction of suffering for its own sake or for indulgence in cruelty.

The principle of proportionality applied to weapons that can affect civilian populations is reflected in the rule prohibiting the use of indiscriminate weapons. Air Force pamphlet No. 110-31 defines an indiscriminate weapon as one whose inherent characteristics make it "incapable of being directed at specific military objectives" or one "of a nature to necessarily cause disproportionate injury to civilians or damage to civilian objects." The circumstances under which a weapon may or may not be considered unlawful because of its effects are described in that same pamphlet:

> The existing law of armed conflict does not prohibit the use of weapons whose destructive force cannot strictly be confined to the specific military objective. Weapons are not unlawful simply because their use may cause incidental casualties to civilians and destruction of civilian objects. Nevertheless, particular weapons or methods of warfare may be prohibited because of their indiscriminate effects. Upon occasion, a prohibition is confirmed by the practice of states in refraining from the use of a weapon because of recognition of excessive injury or damage to civilians or civilian objects which will necessarily be caused by the weapon. The extent to which a weapon discriminates between military objectives and protected persons and objects depends usually on the manner in which the weapon is employed rather than on the design qualities of the weapon itself. Where a weapon is designed so that it can be used against military objectives, its employment in a different manner, such as against the civilian population, does not make the weapon itself unlawful. Indiscriminate weapons are those incapable of being controlled, through design or function, and thus they can not, with any degree of certainty, be directed at military objectives. For example, in World War II German V-I rockets, with extremely primitive guidance systems yet generally directed toward civilian populations, and Japanese incendiary balloons without any guidance systems were regarded as unlawful. Both weapons were, as deployed, incapable of being aimed specifically at military objectives. Use of such essentially unguided weapons could be expected to cause unlawful excessive injury to civilians and damage to civilian objects. Attempting to avoid or minimize injury to civilians or damage to civilian objects is fully consistent with, and strongly reinforced by, the traditional military doctrine of economy of force. The United States, in order to avoid excessive collateral injury or damage and acquire maximum military advantage, has historically stressed the importance of accuracy in aerial weapons. In addition, some weapons, though capable of being directed only at military objectives, may have otherwise uncontrollable effects so as to cause disproportionate civilian injuries or damage. Biological warfare is a universally agreed illustration of such an indiscriminate weapon. Uncontrollable effects, in this context, may include injury to the civilian population of other states as well as injury to an enemy's civilian population. Uncontrollable refers to effects which escape in time or space from control of the user so as to necessarily create risks to civilian persons or objects excessive in relation to the military advantage anticipated.

Distinction must be made between unlawful weapons and unlawful uses of weapons. According to Air Force pamphlet No. 110-31:

> The international law of armed conflict is generally characterized as prohibitive law forbidding certain manifestations of force, rather than posi-

tive law authorizing other such manifestations. The prohibitions may relate to a specific weapon or be expressed in one of the generic principles of warfare: to avoid unnecessary suffering and to maintain proportionality. A weapon may be illegal *per se* if either international custom or treaty has forbidden its use under all circumstances. An example is poison to kill or injure a person. On the other hand, any weapon may be used unlawfully, such as when it is directed at civilians and not at a military objective. In the first example, the question of how the weapon is used is irrelevant because the use of the weapon itself is prohibited; in the second example, the manner of employment is critical. . . . The distinction between the legality of a weapon, apart from its possible use, and the limitations placed upon the use of an otherwise lawful weapon, is frequently overlooked, despite its importance. Any weapon may be put to an unlawful use.

Therefore, the distinction between a weapon itself and the manner in which or the objective against which it is used is important. Many times, when use of an illegal weapon is claimed, it turns out that the illegality lies, not in the weapon itself, but in the way it was used or the persons against whom it was directed.

The principles governing the conduct of warfare of concern to naval officers are those that provide for the immunity of civilians and the separation of military and civilian activities. Protocol I has established a number of specific rules governing the conduct of such hostilities as bombardment. Appendix M, which is an extract from Air Force pamphlet No. 110-31, although written in the context of aerial bombardment, clearly sets forth and discusses the rules that must be followed and the actions that must be taken in planning and executing naval air and shore bombardment.

WAR ON LAND

CHEMICAL AND BIOLOGICAL WEAPONS

The use of poison as a weapon is prohibited as a matter of customary International Law codified in Article 23(a) of the 1907 Hague Regulations. Poisons are biological or chemical substances which, when they are ingested, enter the lungs or bloodstream, or touch the skin, even in small quantities, cause death or permanent disability. The long-standing prohibition against them is based on their uncontrollable character, the inevitability of their causing death or permanent disability, and the traditional belief that their use is treacherous.

The use of poison gas in World War I resulted in more than 1,000,000 casualties and more than 100,000 deaths. That shocking example led to the Geneval Gas Protocol of 1925, which reaffirmed the prohibition against poison gas; most nations, now including the United States and the other major military powers, are parties to that protocol. Many of these nations, again including the United States, have made their adherence to this protocol subject to a so-called *first use* reservation, which means that they will use such weapons only in retaliation against their prior use by other belligerents. Ratification of the protocol by the United States was delayed until 1975 because of disagreement as to whether it applied to chemical herbicides, tear gas, other nontoxic gases, and other chemical and biological weapons. The U.S. position on that question is summarized in a 1976 change to Field Manual No. 27-10:

> Concerning chemical weapons, the United States considers the Geneva Protocol of 1925 as applying to both lethal and incapacitating chemical agents. Incapacitating agents are those producing symptoms that persist for hours or even days after exposure to the agent has terminated. It is the position of the United States that the Geneva Protocol of 1925 does not prohibit the use in war of either chemical herbicides or riot control agents, which are those agents of a type widely used by governments for law enforcement purposes because they produce, in all but the most unusual circumstances, merely transient effects that disappear within minutes after exposure to the agent has terminated. In this connection, however, the United States has unilaterally renounced, as a matter of national policy, certain uses in war of chemical herbicides and riot control agents. The policy and provisions of Executive Order No. 11850 do not, however, prohibit or restrict the use of chemical herbicides or riot control agents by U.S. armed forces either (1) as retaliation in kind during armed conflict or (2) in situations when the United States is not engaged in armed conflict. Any use in armed conflict of herbicides or riot control agents, however, requires Presidential approval in advance.
>
> The use in war of smoke and incendiary material is not prohibited or restricted by the Geneva Protocol of 1925.

Some chemicals have a high capability for destroying plants. Thus, they can limit the production of food or defoliate vegetation used either as a raw material, such as trees for pulp, or as a cover, such as trees for camouflage. These agents kill or inhibit the growth of plants; regulate or inhibit plant growth, sometimes causing plant death; and dry up plant foliage. The policy of the United States is to renounce the first use of herbicides in wartime except "under regulations applicable to their domestic use, for control of vegetation within U.S. bases and installations or around their immediate defensive perimeters." By executive order, they may be used only with the advance approval of the president. However, it is the U.S. view that there is no international rule prohibiting their use and the 1925 Geneva Gas Protocol does not restrain the use of chemical herbicides, as such.

Riot-control agents are chemicals, such as sprays and gases, that have no harmful effects other than temporarily disabling the person to whom they are applied. U.S. policy regarding their use in war is set forth in Executive Order 11850:

> The United States renounces, as a matter of national policy . . . first use of riot control agents in war except in defensive military modes to save lives such as:
>
> (a) Use of riot control agents in riot control situations in areas under direct and distinct U.S. military control, to include controlling rioting prisoners of war.
> (b) Use of riot control agents in situations in which civilians are used to mask or screen attacks and civilian casualties can be reduced or avoided.
> (c) Use of riot control agents in rescue missions in remotely isolated areas, of downed aircrews and passengers, and escaping prisoners.
> (d) Use of riot control agents in rear echelon areas outside the zone of immediate combat to protect convoys from civil disturbances, terrorists and paramilitary organizations.

Wartime use of riot-control agents requires presidential approval. This executive order does not change the U.S. position that neither the Geneva Gas Protocol nor any rule in International Law restricts the use of riot-control agents, as such.

Biological weapons and methods of warfare are prohibited by International Law whether they are directed against persons, animals, or plants. The indiscriminate and uncontrollable nature of such weapons has resulted in their condemnation by the international community. The fact that states have refrained from using them in warfare has confirmed this rule.

The United States considers bacteriological methods of warfare to include not only biological weapons but also toxins, which, although not living organisms and therefore susceptible of being characterized as chemical agents, are generally produced from biological agents. In addition the United States and the Soviet Union have, since 1975, been parties, along with more than eighty other nations, to the 1972 Biological Weapons Convention. That convention prohibits the development, production, stockpiling, acquisition by other means, or retention of microbial or other biological agents, and of toxins, whatever their origin or method of production, of types and in quantities that have no justification for prophylactic, protective, or other peaceful purposes; it also prohibits weapons, equipment, or means of delivery designed to use such agents and toxins for hostile purposes or in armed conflict. Thus biological weapons have been effectively outlawed.

The arms-control treaty concerning environmental modifications prohibits the states that are parties thereto from making military or other hostile use of any environmental modification that has widespread, long-lasting, or severe effects. The term *environmental modification* refers to any technique for changing, through the deliberate manipulation of natural processes, the dynamics, composition, or structure of the earth, including its biota, lithosphere, hydrosphere, and atmosphere, or of outer space. Earthquakes, changes in weather or climate patterns, in ocean currents, or in the state of the ozone layer or ionosphere, and an upset in the ecological balance of a region are some of the effects that could be produced by environmental modification. The term *widespread* is defined as "encompassing an area on the scale of several hundred square kilometers"; *long-lasting* is defined as "lasting for a period of months, or approximately a season"; and *severe* is defined as "involving serious or significant disruption or harm to human life, natural and economic resources or other assets."

Entering into force on 5 October 1978, this U.N. treaty has, at this writing, twenty-eight parties, including the United States and the Soviet Union.

NUCLEAR WEAPONS

Many of the rules of war go back a long way in history, but there is only recent history when it comes to nuclear weapons. These massive weapons have been available for more than thirty years but no customary rule restricting their use has as yet developed. Until the nations reach formal agreement on this point, it cannot be said that their use would violate International Law. This conclusion is strengthened by the fact that discussions and plans for restricting the use of nuclear weapons turn on the question of disarmament, rather than on illegality of use. Current international negotiations concerning prohibitions or restrictions on the use of weapons that may be deemed to be excessively injurious or to have indiscriminate effects deal only with conventional, nonnuclear weapons.

World concern over nuclear weapons and their potential for mass destruction is demonstrated by the following developments in the arms-control arena: the 1963 Limited Nuclear Test Ban Treaty and the 1968 Nuclear Non-Proliferation Treaty, to each of which more than one hundred countries have become parties; the 1969 treaty establishing Latin America as a nuclear-free zone; the 1971 Seabed Arms Control Treaty, to which more than sixty nations have become parties; and the 1959 Antarctic Treaty and 1967 Outer Space Treaty, both of which demilitarize areas to which no armaments have yet been introduced. Such concern is also shown by the bilateral arms-control agreements between the United States and the Soviet Union, which restrict nuclear weapons and reduce the chances for an accidental nuclear exchange: the 1963 Hotline Agreement and its 1971 modernization; the 1971 "Accidents Measures" agreement; the 1972 Anti-Ballistic Missile treaty and its 1974 protocol; the 1973 agreement on the Prevention of Nuclear War; the 1974 Threshold Test Ban treaty and protocol; the 1976 Treaty on Underground Nuclear Explosion for Peaceful Purposes (the last two have not been ratified by the United States); and SALT I. Because of their effects, nuclear weapons, like chemical weapons, may be used by the armed forces of the United States only if and when authorized by the president.

The negotiations that led to the adoption in 1977 of Protocol I and Protocol II expressly did not deal with nuclear weapons, and the rules established in Protocol I relevant to the use of weapons were not intended to have any effect on and do not regulate or prohibit the use of nuclear weapons.

CONVENTIONAL WEAPONS

The use of aircraft, ships, guns, rockets, and guided missiles by land, sea, and air forces against combatants and other lawful military objectives is clearly permissible under International Law. This view is confirmed by the extensive practice of nations in wars during the twentieth century, and even earlier in the cases of guns and rockets. The manner in which weapon-delivery systems are used in warfare is regulated by the principles and rules of International Law discussed in this and the preceding chapter.

Blast and Fragmentation Weapons

The use of explosives and fragmentation particles such as those contained in projectiles, mines, bombs, rockets, missiles, and hand grenades is not prohibited under the law of armed conflict, provided a military purpose is apparent and suffering is incidental to the military necessities involved. Extensive use of such weapons in armed conflict in this and past centuries confirms the general rule. Cluster bombs and fuel-air explosives, recent developments in warfare, are only refinements of fragmentation and blast munitions, respectively. Blast and fragmentation weapons must be designed in a manner to ensure that they do not violate the prohibition against unnecessary suffering. Explosive devices with fragments, such as plastic or glass, are prohibited because it is not easy to detect the fragments and they make the treatment of wounds unnecessarily difficult.

Incendiary Weapons

Weapons such as incendiary ammunition, flamethrowers, napalm, and other incendiary agents are widely used in armed conflict. Although they evoke intense international concern and there have been attempts to ban their use, practice indicates that they are still regarded as lawful in situations that require their use. Conventional incendiary weapons are most often used against such targets as pillboxes, tanks, vehicles, and fortifications, and combatants in their vicinity. They are useful in support of ground troops in close contact with enemy forces. Such uses of incendiary weapons are justified by their military effectiveness, as demonstrated during both world wars and the Korean, Vietnam, and other conflicts. However, attempts have been made to compare incendiary weapons with prohibited means of chemical warfare, partly because burns are difficult to treat.

The possibility of fire spreading beyond the immediate target area has also raised concern about uncontrollable or indiscriminate effects on civilian populations or civilian objects. There is currently in negotiation within the U.N. Conference on Specific Conventional Weapons a proposal for an international ban on the use of air-delivered napalm and other incendiaries against military targets within a concentration of civilians. Some countries are urging a ban on any use of incendiaries, including use against combatants or other military objectives.

The manner in which incendiary weapons are used is subject to the other rules regulating armed force. In particular, the potential of fire to spread must be considered in relation to the rules protecting civilians and civilian objects. For example, incendiaries should not be used in urban areas if other equally effective weapons are available.

Delayed-Action Weapons

Land mines, whether dropped by aircraft or rocket or laid by hand, and other delayed-action weapons are not currently prohibited, provided they do not have inherent characteristics that cause unnecessary suffering. The manner of use of such weapons, however, is regulated by the rules of armed conflict. Mines in the nature of booby traps are frequently used unlawfully; for example, when they are attached to the sick and wounded, dead bodies, and medical facilities, which are under the protection of International Law. Also illegal are portable booby traps in the form of fountain pens, watches, and trinkets, which unfairly risk injury to civilians likely to be attracted to the objects. These customary prohibitions are being considered for codification in the U.N. Conference on Specific Conventional Weapons. The conference will probably adopt them and extend the ban to internationally protected emblems, graves, children's toys, food, drink, civilian kitchen utensils and appliances, religious objects, historic monuments, and animals or their carcasses.

Of course, the precautions that must be taken in the use of all weapons to avoid or minimize incidental civilian casualties apply to delayed-action weapons. Mines must not be used to prevent the rescue or protection of the sick and wounded or to deny other humanitarian protections. The U.N. Conference on Specific Conventional Weapons is attempting to extend these customary rules to prohibit the indiscriminate use, on land, of mines and booby traps. Such extension would require the recording and later disclosure of the location of minefields, mines, and booby traps. Similarly, it would prohibit the use of land mines, however delivered, except in areas containing military objectives and if the mines are self-neutralizing. It would also allow the use of mines and booby traps in populated areas only if they are on or close to the enemy or an enemy military objective and civilians have been warned by signs, sentries, or fences. These new restrictions are likely to be adopted in the near future.

NEW WEAPONS

In Article 36, Protocol I establishes an explicit requirement to determine the legality of new weapons before they are used. When a new weapon is being developed, a decision must be made as to whether its use would, in some or in all circumstances, be prohibited by International Law. As has been seen, most regulations concerning weapons are not total prohibitions, but place selective restrictions on their use. These restrictions are now more complex than ever before.

The United States and the Soviet Union are attempting to develop the basis for a multilateral arms-control treaty that would prohibit the development, production, stockpiling, and use of radiological weapons. Such weapons would use radioactive material whose natural decay would cause damage or injury.

These two countries are also negotiating a limit on antisatellite (ASAT) systems. Both use satellites for a wide variety of purposes. They use them in such key military roles as warning, reconnaissance, communications, and navigation, as well as for such civilian functions as meteorology, civil communications, and scientific exploration. Photo-reconnaissance satellites are important in verifying arms-control agreements. Because of the growing importance of both civilian and military satellites, the prospect of systems that threaten them gives rise to serious concern. Unrestrained development of antisatellite systems by one side would be likely to lead to the development of such systems by the other. It would also call into question the ability of satellites to carry out their missions in time of conflict. The goal of the antisatellite negotiations is to prevent such an arms race in space and to limit the threat.

An ASAT agreement would expand the protection of satellites that existing arms-control agreements provide. The Outer Space Treaty of 1967 bans the deployment in space of nuclear and other weapons of mass destruction. The Anti-Ballistic Missile Treaty of 1972 prohibits interference with technical means of verification, including photo-reconnaissance satellites. An ASAT agreement could supplement these agreements by, for example, prohibiting attacks on satellites and placing limits on, among other things, the number of systems for attacking satellites.

Neither of the weapons noted in this section can today be considered illegal because there are no rules of customary or treaty International Law prohibiting them or their use.

AERIAL WARFARE

Generally speaking, the rules for war on land heretofore described apply to aerial warfare. There are, however, certain rules that relate only to aircraft.

Air Force pamphlet No. 110-31 summarizes the customary law governing military and civil aircraft in aerial warfare:

> During armed conflict, enemy military aircraft or missiles may be attacked and destroyed in airspace anywhere outside of neutral jurisdiction. Enemy military aircraft may be captured anywhere outside of neutral jurisdiction. Prize procedure is not used for such captured aircraft because their ownership immediately passes to the captor's government by virtue of capture.
> . . .
> Attacks against aircraft may be made by any method or weapon, not otherwise prohibited, including air to air or ground to air missiles, and explosive or incendiary projectiles. The use of incendiary projectiles, limited in some uses on land, was expressly recognized as not prohibited against aircraft by the 1923 Draft Hague Rules of Air Warfare. Ramming techniques including the use of suicide squadrons are also not prohibited.
> The law of armed conflict clearly forbids the killing or wounding of an enemy who, in good faith, surrenders or is otherwise *hors de combat*. Surrenders in air combat are not generally offered. If surrender is offered, usually no way exists to enforce the surrender. However, surrenders have been made on occasion. If surrender is offered in good faith so that circumstances do not preclude enforcement, then surrender must be respected. Although relatively rare, surrenders by defecting troops on military aircraft offer valuable intelligence and psychological opportunities, and should not be discouraged.
> Disabled enemy aircraft in air combat are frequently pursued to destruction because of the impossibility in verifying its true status and inability to enforce surrender. Although disabled, the aircraft may or may not have lost its means of control. Moveover, it still may represent a valuable military asset. If an aircraft in distress is clearly *hors de combat* (out of conflict), from the information known to the attacking force at the time, then its destruction offers no military advantage, and the attack should be broken off to permit possible evacuation by crew or passengers. If the aircraft is a support or civil aircraft it is particularly important that this rule be observed. If the distressed aircraft lands, the same protection applies if the aircraft is clearly out of the conflict, and further attack is prohibited against otherwise protected persons (wounded and sick, civilians, etc.) who do not offer resistance.

The rescue of downed airmen is clearly a combatant activity and is not protected under International Law. Rescue efforts may be accompanied by the use of armed force and resisted with armed force. However, when an aircraft is disabled and its occupants escape by parachute, they should not be attacked as they descend, because such a practice would have the military disadvantage of discouraging airmen from abandoning disabled aircraft. Persons descending from an aircraft for hostile purposes, such as paratroopers or those who appear to be bound upon hostile missions, are not protected. A person who continues to resist as he descends from a disabled aircraft may be attacked. Downed enemy airmen from aircraft in distress are subject to immediate capture and may be attacked if they resist or escape or are behind their own lines. Otherwise they should be afforded a reasonable opportunity to surrender. Their status as prisoners of war and the protection to which they are entitled begins when they surrender or are captured.

An aircraft in flight that is identified as civilian may be attacked only if it represents a valid military objective, such as when there is an immediate military threat. Unauthorized entry into a zone where flight is restricted might, in some conflicts, be deemed an immediate military threat. Wherever encountered, enemy civil aircraft are subject to verification of their status and instructions to preclude their involvement. The requirement to respect neutral jurisdiction remains valid in any event.

Attacks on civil aircraft on the ground are governed by the rules of what constitutes a legitimate military objective, as well as the rules and principles that apply to aerial bombardment. If they are engaged in airlift, they might, depending on the circumstances, qualify as important military objectives.

Civil aircraft entitled to protection include nonmilitary state aircraft and state-owned airliners. The principle of law and humanity that protects civilians and civilian objects from being objects of attack, as such, protects civil aircraft in flight, because civil aircraft are presumed to be transporting civilians. Such aircraft are not subject to attack unless it has been determined that they constitute valid military targets. A civil aircraft in the vicinity of military operations, including air operations, may be attacked before its identity as a civil aircraft is known. As a practical matter, the degree of protection afforded to civil aviation and the potential military threat represented varies in direct proportion to the intensity of the conflict. Difficulties have been avoided in the past by civil aircraft keeping clear of areas of hostile air activity and by parties to a conflict refraining from attacking civil aircraft. A state may establish a flight-restriction zone from which civil aircraft are excluded and provide notice that it has done so to the International Civil Aviation Organization.

An immediate military threat may occur when a civil aircraft initiates an attack. It may also exist when there is reasonable suspicion of hostile intent and the aircraft disregards signals or warnings to land or proceed to a designated place, or approaches an adversary's territory or armed forces without permission.

The 1923 Draft Hague Rules made nonmilitary aircraft flying within the jurisdiction of their own state subject to attack unless they landed as soon as possible on approach of enemy military aircraft. The rules also made them subject to attack if they flew within the jurisdiction of the enemy or in the immediate vicinity thereof, outside the jurisdiction of their own state, or in the immediate vicinity of the military operations of the enemy by land or sea. Otherwise they are protected, although subject to capture. During World War II, civil aircraft, particularly civil airliners, were not generally regarded as proper objects of attack by either the Allies or Axis powers. A recognized authority on World War II practice noted:

There was . . . an appreciable volume of international air traffic in being during the second world war. It suffered but little, on the whole, as a result of belligerent action. This was largely because the Air Forces of the States at war had more urgent tasks to perform.

Practice since World War II shows that states have increasingly recognized the necessity of avoiding attacks on civil aircraft. Hence, with the exception of terrorist attacks, which are soundly condemned, there have been few attacks on such craft.

International Law does not prohibit the use of civil aircraft for military purposes. However, in high-intensity conflicts care must be taken not to attempt to cloak such aircraft in civilian immunity. Parties to a conflict must be able to distinguish between aircraft being used, for example, for public transportation on an airline and those being used for military purposes. The objective is to ensure effective protection for civil aircraft.

Respect for neutrality extends to neutral aircraft, whether military or civil, during periods of armed conflict, However, an attack against a neutral aircraft in flight would not be prohibited by the law of armed conflict if the aircraft was over nonneutral territory and it initiated the attack.

The extent to which enemy civil aircraft are subject to capture, confiscation, or condemnation is unsettled in practice and specific treaty law. Although a right of capture may be admitted, states do not generally exercise or attempt to exercise it outside the territorial jurisdiction under their control.

PERFIDY AND RUSES

There are some useful ruses that may be used in aerial warfare but there are also a number of unlawful uses of deceit. The rules governing both derive from a few treaty provisions applicable to land and naval warfare and from the practice of nations.

The Hague Regulations of 1907 provide that "it is especially forbidden . . . to kill or wound treacherously individuals belonging to the hostile nation or army . . . to make improper use of a flag of truce, of the national flag or of the military insignia and uniform of the enemy, as well as the distinctive badges of the Geneva Convention." They also provide that "ruses of war and the employment of measures necessary for obtaining information about the enemy and the country are considered permissible."

Perfidy or treachery intended to kill, injure, or capture has been prohibited in armed conflict in order to strengthen the trust that combatants should have in International Law. Perfidy tends to destroy the basis for restoration of peace and causes a conflict to degenerate into savagery. Articles 37-39 of Protocol I are explicit in the codification involving perfidy. Air Force pamphlet No. 110-31 gives a number of useful examples of the operation of rules concerning perfidy and ruses:

LAWFUL RUSES:

a. Article 24 of the 1907 Hague Regulations confirms the general rule that ruses of war not constituting perfidy are lawful. Among the permissible ruses are surprises, ambushes, feigning attacks, retreats, or fights; simulation of quiet and inactivity; use of small forces to simulate large units; transmission of false or misleading radio or telephone messages (not involving protection under international law such as internationally recognized signals of distress); deception by bogus orders purported to have been issued by the enemy commander; use of the enemy's signals and passwords; feigned communication with troops or reinforcements which have no existence; and resort to deceptive supply movements. Also included are the deliberate planting of false information, moving of landmarks, putting up of dummy guns and vehicles, laying of dummy mines, erection of dummy installations and airfields, removal of unit identifications from uniforms, and use of signal deceptive measures.

b. The following examples provide guidelines for lawful ruses:

(1) The use of aircraft decoys. Slower or older aircraft may be used as decoys to lure hostile aircraft into combat with faster and newer aircraft held in reserve. The use of aircraft decoys to attract ground fire in order to identify ground targets for attack by more sophisticated aircraft is also permissible.

(2) Staging air combats. Another lawful ruse is the staging of air combat between two properly marked friendly aircraft with the object of inducing an enemy aircraft into entering the combat in aid of a supposed comrade.

(3) Imitation of enemy signals. No objection can be made to the use by friendly forces of the signals or codes of an adversary. The signals or codes used by enemy aircraft or by enemy ground installations in contact with their aircraft may properly be employed by friendly forces to deceive or mislead an adversary. However, misuse of distress signals or distinctive signals internationally recognized as reserved for the exclusive use of medical aircraft would be perfidious.

(4) Use of flares and fires. The lighting of large fires away from the true target area for the purpose of misleading enemy aircraft into believing that the large fires represent damage from prior attacks and thus leading them to the wrong target is a lawful ruse. The target marking flares of the enemy may also be used to mark false targets. However, it is an unlawful ruse to fire false target flare indicators over residential areas of a city or town which are not otherwise valid military objectives.

(5) Camouflage use. The use of camouflage is a lawful ruse for misleading and deceiving enemy combatants. The camouflage of a flying aircraft must not conceal national markings of the aircraft, and the camouflage must not take the form of the national markings of the enemy or that of objects protected under international law.

(6) Operational ruses. The ruse of the "switched raid" is a proper method of aerial warfare in which aircraft set a course, ostensibly for a particular target, and then, at a given moment, alter course in order to strike

another military objective instead. This method was utilized success-fully in World War II to deceive enemy fighter intercepter aircraft.

CIRCUMSTANCES MAY MAKE A LAWFUL RUSE UNLAWFUL:

Deception of the adversary is generally a permissible method of warfare if it does not involve treachery, or the violation of any expressed or implied agreement requiring truth between combatants. However, prevailing cir-cumstances may make an otherwise lawful ruse unlawful. For example, it is an unlawful ruse to place ground lights or landing flares around naturally or artifically dangerous places in order to lure enemy aircraft to land if civil and neutral aircraft are likely to respond. However, if circumstances were such that only enemy military aircraft would respond as was the case in World War II, then such a ruse would be permissible. Another unlawful ruse is mislead-ing or luring an attacking force into attacking civilian objects or the civilian population in the mistaken belief that military objectives were being attacked.

PERFIDY AND UNLAWFUL RUSES:

a. Examples. The following are examples of conduct which constitute per-fidy when carried out in order to commit or resume hostilities.
   (1). The Feigning of a Situation of Distress Through the Misuse of an Internationally Recognized Protective Sign. Since situations of dis-tress occur during times of armed conflict, as well as peace, and frequently suggest that the persons involved are hors de combat, feigning distress or death, wounds or sickness in order to resume hostilities constitutes perfidy in ground combat. However, a sick or wounded combatant does not commit perfidy by calling for and receiving medical aid even though he may intend immediately to resume fighting. Nor do medical personnel commit perfidy by rendering such aid. In aerial warfare, it is forbidden to improperly use internationally recognized distress signals to lure the enemy into a false sense of security and then attack. Feigning distress for the purpose of escape has always been permissible in air warfare. With respect to internationally recognized signals, this principle was fully recognized in 1923. Article 10 of the Hague Rules for The Control of Radio in Times of War states: "The perversion of radio distress signals and distress messages prescribed by international conventions to other than their normal, legitimate purposes constitutes a violation of the laws of war and renders the perpetrator personally responsible under international law." Thus, the use of false or misleading distress signals and messages is restricted.
   (2) The Feigning of a Ceasefire, of a Humanitarian Negotiation, or of a Surrender. An example is the treacherous raising of a white flag. The white flag has traditionally indicated a desire to communicate with the enemy and may indicate more particularly, depending upon the situa-tion, a willingness to surrender. It raises expectations that the particu-lar struggle is at an end or close to an end since the only proper use of the flag of truce or white flag in international law is to communicate to

the enemy a desire to negotiate. Thus, the use of a flag of truce or white flag in order to deceive or mislead the enemy, or for any other purpose than to negotiate or surrender, has long been recognized as an act of treachery. This rule is codified in Article 23(f), HR. Similarly international law prohibits pretending to surrender or requesting quarter in order to attack the enemy because of the obligation of combatants who are hors de combat or have surrendered. A false broadcast to the enemy that an armistice has been agreed upon has been widely recognized to be treacherous. The language set out above expressed in terms of cease-fire, humanitarian negotiation or surrender, expresses the customary and conventional law in this area.

(3) The Disguising of Combatants in Civilian Clothing. Since civilians are not lawful objects of attack, as such, in armed conflict, it follows that disguising combatants in civilian clothing in order to commit hostilities constitutes perfidy. This is analogous to other situations where combatants attempt to disguise their intentions behind the protections afforded by the law of armed conflict in order to engage in hostilities.

b. The Misuse of Specified Signs, Signals and Emblems Which are Internationally Recognized. The Geneva Conventions of 1949, as well as earlier conventions, contain various provisions concerning distinctive emblems for medical functions or for safety zones. It is accordingly forbidden to make use of the protective sign of the red cross (red crescent, red lion and sun) or signs for safety zones (oblique red bands on a white ground) in cases other than provided for in agreements establishing these signs. The 1954 Hague Convention Relative To The Protection Of Cultural Property prescribes also a distinctive emblem for the protection of specific property which should not be misused. The United Nations also has a distinctive sign. In view of the responsibilities of the United Nations, particularly the Security Council under Article 24 of the UN Charter, UN representatives may be present near the scene of future conflicts. Accordingly, prohibitions concerning improper use of its distinctive signs, emblems and signals should be observed.

The following are examples of improper use of the medical emblems: (i) using a hospital or other building marked with a red cross or equivalent insignia as an observation post, military office or depot; (ii) using distinctive signs, emblems or signals for cloaking acts of hostilities, such as firing from a building or other protected installation or means of medical transport; (iii) using protected means of medical transport, such as hospital ships, trains or airplanes, to facilitate the escape of able-bodied combatants; (iv) displaying protective emblems on vehicles, trains, ships, airplanes, or other modes of transportation or other buildings containing ammunition or other military non-medical supplies.

c. Misuse of Enemy Flags, Insignia and Uniform. Article 23(f) of the Hague Regulations forbids "improper use . . . of the national flag, or of the military insignia and uniform of the enemy." Improper use of an enemy's flags, military insignia, national markings and uniforms involves use in actual attacks. This clarification is necessary because disputes arose concerning the meaning of the term "improper" during World War II. A reciprocal advantage is secured from observing this rule. It is clear, however, that this article does not change or affect the law concerning whether a combatant is entitled to PW status. That question is a separate question determined by the 1949 GPW, as well as other applicable international law.

d. Assassination. Article 23(b) HR, quoted previously, prohibits the killing or wounding treacherously of individuals belonging to a hostile nation or army, whether they are combatants or civilians. This article has been construed as prohibiting assassination, proscription or outlawry of an enemy, or putting a price upon an enemy's head, as well as offering a reward for any enemy "dead or alive." Obviously it does not preclude lawful attacks by lawful combatants on individual soldiers or officers of the enemy.

NAVAL WARFARE

GENERAL PRINCIPLES

It is important to grasp the significance of one major distinction between land warfare and armed conflict at sea: land warfare is carried on almost exclusively in the territory of one of the belligerents, while sea warfare is, for the most part, fought on the high seas, which are not within the sovereignty of either belligerent but are open to lawful use by all nations of the world. There is bound to be some conflict between the interests of the belligerents, whose purpose is the destruction of one another's naval power and maritime commerce, and the legitimate interests of neutrals, who seek to carry on their ordinary commerce with each other and, to the extent permitted by International Law, with the belligerents. This conflict has resulted in the formulation of rules governing the relations between belligerents and neutrals in naval warfare.

In most respects the general principles of the law of naval warfare are not materially different from those applicable to land or aerial warfare. The prohibitions against weapons that cause unnecessary suffering, such as dumdum bullets and poisons, are applicable to warfare at sea as well as on land. The complementary principles of humanity and military necessity apply equally to war at sea, as does the principle of chivalry, at least to the extent that it is still valid.

In war at sea, private enemy property—and under certain circumstances the private property of neutrals—is subject to confiscation by belligerent warships and military aircraft. In land warfare, such property is generally required to be left undisturbed by the contending military forces. The influence of this difference is seen throughout the law of naval warfare, which allows belligerent warships—and, in some instances, military aircraft—to exercise certain rights that are unheard of in land warfare. Since these rights cannot be exercised by vessels other than the *warships* of a *belligerent*, it is important to understand what these two italicized terms mean.

The U.S. Navy's publication, *Law of Naval Warfare*, says: "The term 'warships' includes all vessels commissioned as a part of the naval forces of a State and authorized to display the appropriate flag or pennant as evidence thereof. Such vessels must in addition be commanded by a member of the military forces of a State and must be manned by a crew subject to military discipline" (NWIP 10-2, Article 500 c).

It may be somewhat inexact to state that a nation is a belligerent when it is in an actual state of war with some other nation. In cases of civil war or insurrection, a question often arises as to whether or not the contending factions are belligerents. That question is more political than legal, however, and the answer to it depends on a recognition of belligerency by other nations. For example, in the American Civil War, the belligerency of the Confederacy was recognized by most nations, and the exercise of belligerent rights by Southern warships was therefore not in violation of International Law. It is enough to remember here that a naval officer in command at sea always has orders from his government to guide him.

The two episodes described below illustrate the importance of the definitions made above, for both involved an assertion of the right to exercise belligerent rights. The first incident occurred in May 1917, when a captured Dutch vessel with a German naval prize crew on board, captured another Dutch vessel, the *Koningin Emma*. The latter was stranded while being taken into a German port. The Dutch government protested the capture of the *Koningin Emma* on the grounds that the capturing vessel was not a warship. The German government apologized and compensated the owners of the *Koningin Emma*. This incident illustrates the point that the mere fact that a naval prize crew is put aboard a captured vessel does not convert that vessel into a warship.

The second incident is described in the words of Commander E. B. Hayes, USNR (Inactive), formerly Director, Admiralty Division, Office of the Judge Advocate General of the Navy:

> On 6 November 1941, the USS *Omaha* and USS *Somers*, on neutrality patrol in the South Atlantic, sighted a vessel disguised as the SS *Willmoto* of Philadelphia, apparently taking evasive action. The *Willmoto* was hailed and, upon giving unsatisfactory answers, was ordered to heave to. A boarding party was dispatched from the *Omaha*, and upon approaching the *Willmoto*, it was noted that the international flag signal Foxtrot Mike had been hoisted, meaning, "I am sinking. Send boats to take off passengers and crew." The crew had lowered life boats and were abandoning ship and explosive detonations within the vessel were heard. The *Omaha's* motor launch came alongside and the Officer-in-Charge ascertained that the *Willmoto* actually was the German merchant vessel M/S *Odenwald* of Hamburg. She was being scuttled.

The Officer-in-Charge forced the German crew back aboard the ship. An examination by the members of the boarding party resulted in the conclusion that the vessel, though leaking somewhat, probably would remain afloat, and the boarding party eventually found out how to operate the pumps and control the water and to start the engines. Thereafter, with additional personnel from the *Omaha*, the boarding crew sailed the merchant vessel to Puerto Rico, escorted by the *Omaha* and *Somers*. She arrived in Puerto Rico on 17 November 1941. The *Odenwald* carried a full cargo of rubber, rubber truck tires, and other strategic commodities.

Since we were then at peace with Germany, the *Odenwald* could not be taken in prize, and under the Neutrality Act of 1939 the only assessable penalty for using the American flag was denial of entrance to ports of the United States and its territorial waters for three months. Therefore, it was decided to file a salvage claim against the vessel on behalf of the officers and men who boarded and saved her. A substantial salvage award was made. The case presents a situation where the general maritime law of salvage was invoked to obtain possession of the ship and her cargo, which could not have been taken in prize.

Vessels and Aircraft Exempt from Attack

Hospital ships and aircraft, when marked as required by the Geneva Convention of 1949, may never be made the objects of attack in naval warfare. Similarly exempt are vessels traveling under a safe-conduct granted by the belligerents, including, for example, those used for exchanging prisoners of war and for carrying out religious, scientific, or philanthropic missions, and small fishing vessels and boats engaged in local coastal trade and not taking part in hostilities. The following incident, related by Rear Admiral William D. Irvin, USN, took place in World War II and is illustrative of the heavy responsibility that can lie upon a naval officer:

> The question of immunity from attack in the case of a surface vessel and a submarine in time of war is one which may confront the submarine commanding officer.
>
> There is no issue over the particulars of designation of a vessel as a hospital ship. The procedures for doing so are clear and well recognized. There is little likelihood of mistaken identity when the vessel so designated is proceeding on her mission at sea, *i.e.* alone, well lighted at night, and well marked in daylight. Conversely, there is no set procedure provided for de-classifying a vessel once designated as immune and here there can be some measure of difficulty. A decision based on knowledge of International Law became our task during the war.
>
> My command, USS *Nautilus*, was returning to base at the end of a patrol. Traversing the sea lanes from the Marianas to Japan, we encountered a convoy headed for Japan.

Submarines were provided with manuals which carried the silhouette and pertinent particulars of all known enemy shipping. It was the practice to utilize a part of each periscope observation to describe the salient features of the target. Her bow, masts, kingposts, superstructure, stacks, stern, hull form and any other distinctive points were covered. The fire control party, by means of the manual, endeavored to identify the target.

In this instance, our position with respect to the convoy made one particular vessel, which was well into the formation, the best target for us. On first observation she was identified as the *America Maru*. She was most distinctive, having raked masts and stack, a bow and a stern contour which were somewhat unique, in toto, an outstanding ship in appearance.

Each succeeding observation seemed to confirm the identity, in fact, there was no other ship listed whose silhouette closely approached that of this target, and she had been designated by the Japanese at an earlier date as a hospital ship. No cancellation of this designation was known to us.

The decision as to whether this was a ship immune from attack had to be made.

As the law was interpreted, the target would enjoy immunity only in the case she was proceeding alone, not in the organization of a convoy nor under the escort of combatant vessels, be properly illuminated, and marked as required by the convention. She did not meet any of these criteria and the decision was made to continue with the attack. She was treated as a legitimate target under the warfare instructions we were executing, and she was sunk in the action.

The Geneva Convention of 1949 specifies that hospital ships shall at all times be respected and shall in no case be attacked or captured. On the other hand, it states that, in order to enjoy this protection, hospital ships must have all their exterior surfaces painted white. It also requires that dark red crosses, as large as possible, be painted and displayed at all times on each side of the hull. Apparently, the ship involved in the incident described above was not painted white, or marked, or illuminated.

STRATAGEMS AND TREACHERY

It is not illegal for a naval commander to use such ruses as false colors or disguises of outward appearance in order to entice an enemy warship or aircraft into action. Before going into action, however, he must always show his own warship's true colors. It is illegal to use a red cross or equivalent emblems for the purpose of obtaining advantage over an enemy.

Mines and Torpedoes

Prohibitions against the use of certain types of sea mines and torpedoes are found in Hague Convention Number VIII (1907). That convention forbids the laying of unanchored, automatic contact mines, unless they will become harmless within one hour after the person laying them ceases to control them. If an anchored mine does not become inert when it breaks loose from its mooring, its use is forbidden by the Hague Convention. Automatic minefields may not be laid off enemy coasts and ports solely for the purpose of intercepting commercial shipping, and precautions must be taken for the security of peaceful shipping. Torpedoes must become harmless after they have missed their target.

In his article "Legal Aspects of Arms Control Measures Concerning Missile-Carrying Submarines and Anti-Submarine Warfare," MIT Press, 1973, the distinguished international lawyer and judge on the International Court of Justice, R. R. Baxter, appraised Hague Convention VIII (1907) as follows:

> The Convention does not apply by its literal terms to [bottom] acoustic and magnetic mines. Since the only restrictions on the purpose of mine-laying under the terms of the treaty is that they may not be laid for the "sole object" of intercepting commercial shipping, the use of mines against submarines [and surface combatants] is not precluded. There is no firm requirement in the Convention of adequate notice to commercial shipping. The Convention thus puts no obstacle in the way of mining of the high seas and of the territorial seas and internal waters of the belligerents against submarines and warships or, for that matter, against merchant ships, enemy and neutral. The objections that have been raised to the establishment of war zones and the laying of mine fields in the high seas or territorial seas are based on the effect of these activities on the shipping of neutral states, rather than on any impact they may have upon the navies of the contending states.

Article 611, Note 3, of the U.S. Navy's publication NWIP 10-2 points out:

> Although these provisions [of Hague Convention VIII] date from 1907, they remain the only codified rules with respect to the deployment of mines and torpedoes. Their purpose was to ensure to the maximum extent practicable the safety of peaceful shipping. This purpose, despite the experiences of WW I and WW II, continues to be valid. New technological developments have created weapons systems obviously not contemplated by the drafters of these rules, such as [bottom] magnetic and acoustic mines. The above-stated general purpose must be considered in arriving at any extrapolation of the Hague Rules to serve as a guide to lawful conduct with respect to such weapons or with respect to any other situations not specifically covered by the rules.

In recent years mines have been used offensively: in 1971 by India to impede seaborne resupply from West Pakistan to East Pakistan (now Bangladesh); in 1972 by the United States to blockade the entrances to North Vietnamese ports, as a measure of collective self-defense; and in 1974 by the Khmer Rouge to block access via the Mekong River to the Cambodian capital city of Phnom Penh.

The mining of North Vietnamese ports in 1972 is instructive of the modern application of the rules governing the use of mines. The following precautions for the security of peaceful shipping were taken by the United States: in an address on 3 May the president announced details of the mining; notices were issued to all mariners; a letter was sent to the U.N. Security Council; and bilateral approaches were made through diplomatic channels to countries concerned. Each of these communications detailed the protective measures taken, which included the facts that delayed-activation mines only were to be used so that ships in Vietnamese harbors had three days in which to leave, and U.S. and Republic of Vietnam warships were to notify every ship approaching the internal and claimed territorial waters of North Vietnam. In addition, no mines were laid in international waters and the mining did not bar access to or departure from neutral coasts.

It can be seen that sea mines can be used so that only military targets are subject to attack, unnecessary suffering is avoided, and the risk of incidental damage to noncombatant objects and noncombatants is minimized. The laying of mines is a nonescalating form of warfare, the intensity, area, time, and duration of which can be precisely determined by all naval components. Indeed, it calls for a minimum use of force, since the opponent has the choice of bringing about his own destruction by challenging an announced minefield or avoiding it by keeping clear of the mines.

The use of torpedoes, like that of all other weapons, is governed by rules of engagement. In specifying the conditions under which a weapon may be used, these limitations take into consideration its characteristics. Very specific guidelines have been established, for example, for the use of acoustic torpedoes, to ensure that they can accomplish their mission in a legal manner.

Submarines

Surface combatant warships have been used in armed conflict for centuries, and there is no question as to the legality of their use under International Law. Obviously, they can be used unlawfully, as when they are disguised as hospital ships. Submarines are relatively new and, although they have had profound effects on naval warfare, no special rules governing their conduct in warfare have as yet been developed. Whenever their status has been brought up at international conferences, it has been agreed that they should be governed by the rules that apply to surface ships. Yet, that law does not regulate, except in incidental respects, combat between warships, whether surface or underwater. In attacks on valid military and naval targets, submarines are entitled to take full advantage of their ability to strike without warning by means of stealthy, submerged approaches. This phase of their operations has never been subject to criticism, but they have provoked great controversy in their role as commerce-destroyers.

Although maritime warfare directed against commerce is legal, some means of pursuing it are illegal. In particular, there has been widespread condemnation of Germany's practice, adopted in both world wars, of setting up large operational zones and making submarine attacks without warning on *all* vessels, neutral or otherwise, found in those zones. In the Nuremberg war crimes trials, Admirals Erich Raeder and Karl Doenitz were convicted of violating International Law in this respect. On the other hand, whether unrestricted submarine warfare against an *enemy's* merchant marine, as practiced by Axis and Allies alike in World War II, is in violation of International Law is still an unsettled point.

Generally, a submarine must follow the rules of warfare applicable to surface ships. Among these rules is the requirement of the London Protocol of 1936 that before a merchant vessel can be sunk, the belligerent warship must give warning and place the victim's crew and ship's papers in a place of safety. The fact that both sides in World War II claimed that they adopted unrestricted warfare in retaliation for illegal acts of warfare by the other side has made if difficult to analyze the legality of the practices used in that war.

The difficulty is complicated by the fact that merchant vessels were armed, convoyed, and ordered to fire upon, or ram, submarines on sight. Furthermore, almost all nations integrated merchant vessels into the warning net of naval intelligence. Were these acts sufficient to integrate merchant vessels into the belligerent naval forces and thus make them liable to attack without warning? Submariners argue with force and a great deal of logic that this was the case. They maintain that these factors, coupled with the peculiar characteristics of submarines—in particular their vulnerability when surfaced—made their actions legal.

Another aspect of submarine operations has raised some questions: intelligence activities, particularly within territorial waters. During the 1970s there were accounts of submarines engaged in covert intelligence-gathering in periods of armed conflict. When conducted in international space, air space, or on the high seas, reconnaissance is recognized as a lawful activity. However, when it is conducted within the territory or territorial waters of an enemy a different situation arises. Although there is no treaty law on the subject, analogy to the law of espionage on land allows some conclusions to be drawn.

Espionage is the clandestine collection or transmission of intelligence gathered inside the territory of an adversary. The law of armed conflict has always considered it lawful to obtain that necessary information but has permitted a state that is the object of such operations to take measures against them under their own laws, including subjecting captured spies, whether civilian or military, to trial and punishment. However, members of the armed forces who are captured in their own uniform during such operations are *not* spies and cannot be treated as such; they must be treated as prisoners of war. These rules are codified in Article 46 of Protocol I. By analogy, then, in periods of armed conflict, uniformed members of armed forces engaged in aerial or submerged intelligence operations, even if they are in enemy territorial waters or air space, are not engaged in spying and, on capture, must be treated as lawful combatants.

MEASURES DIRECTED AGAINST COMMERCE

One of the accepted means of reducing an enemy to submission in war is to block his trade with other countries so that he cannot receive the arms, munitions, food, and other products he needs to carry on. In several wars of the last century, economic measures of this type had results almost as significant as those of operations against enemy military and naval forces. In the American Civil War, the federal blockade of the southern coast was so stringent that it virtually starved the Confederacy to death. Another pertinent example is the vigorous submarine warfare carried on by the United States against the Japanese in World War II, which practically isolated the Japanese islands from their primary sources of raw materials in Southeast Asia.

Blockade

One of the permissible ways of shutting off an enemy's trade is the imposition of a blockade. Traditionally, a blockade was a cordon of ships stationed off the entrance to an enemy port or off his coast for the purpose of preventing vessels of all nationalities from entering or leaving. Although the purpose of a blockade remains the same today, advances in weapons and ship and aircraft design have caused a change in methods.

To make a blockade legal, the primary requirement is that it be effective. An effective blockade is one where it is probable that a ship attempting to breach it will be captured. In the days of sail this requirement meant that a force of ships had to hover close enough to the blockaded port or coast to be able to sight and capture blockade-runners day or night—the traditional "close-in" blockade. Today, however, effectiveness does not require such measures. Radar, aircraft, and satellites have extended enormously the area of effective search and no longer do blockading ships depend on the vagaries of the wind to pursue a blockade-runner. In addition, advances in weapons, as well as the advent of the submarine and the airplane, have made it extremely dangerous for a blockading force to hover practically immobile close to the blockaded area. Today, therefore, a distant force, supplemented by whatever search assistance is needed, may suffice to establish an effective blockade.

The penalties for breaching or attempting to breach a blockade are liability to capture by a belligerent warship and condemnation by a prize court. The vulnerability of a blockade-runner to capture begins with the commencement of a voyage intended to end in the blockaded area and does not terminate until the voyage is completed.

With these considerations in mind, the German use of submarines as commerce-destroyers in two world wars can be viewed as long-distance blockading enforced by submarines, since the purposes were the same: to interdict the enemy's commerce in enemy ships and neutral commerce with the enemy. The ultimate aims of surface and submarine blockades are the same: destruction of an offending vessel, by gunfire or torpedo, respectively. Since the United States used the same techniques against Japan during World War II as the Germans used against the Allies, it can no longer assert that submarine-enforced blockades are illegal. There is evidence, however, from the Nuremberg trials that an opposing view might be more appropriate. For example, the Nuremberg Tribunal did not try anyone for the terror bombing of London and Coventry because the Allies subsequently bombed Dresden; however, that certainly does not mean that bombing undefended cities is legitimate.

Blockades have continued to be used in the years since 1945. In the Korean conflict, the U.N. naval forces successfully used a relatively close-in blockade of both coasts of North Korea. During the last two weeks of the Indo-Pakistani war in 1971, the Indian Navy maintained a long-distance blockade of more than 180 miles of East Pakistan's coastline to prevent resupply of the Pakistani Army or its escape to sea.

During the Vietnam conflict, South Vietnam, with the assistance of U.S. Navy and Coast Guard vessels, maintained a defensive blockade of her own coast to prevent infiltration by small craft of enemy personnel, weapons, and supplies through her territorial waters. These craft were visited and searched, and on occasion captured or sunk. Such actions can be justified as a proper exercise of domestic police power consistent with International Law and with her authority to blockade her enemy's coast to prevent the same infiltration.

In 1972 the United States mined North Vietnamese harbors to interdict the delivery of seaborne weapons and supplies to North Vietnam. The purpose of the mining was the same as that of a blockade. Under the circumstances there prevailing, a blockade on the high seas enforced by naval vessels and aircraft would have been justified by the traditional law of blockade.

Quarantine

In the early 1960s intelligence information indicated that Soviet long-range missiles were being introduced to Cuba. Their presence there constituted a ready threat to the security of many countries in the Western Hemisphere and, to meet it, the Organization of American States decided to

take protective actions. One of the steps taken under the leadership of the
United States was the institution of an interdiction, or *quarantine*. As
announced and put into practice by the participating states, the quarantine
was a limited and selective form of naval blockade directed against the
delivery of offensive weapons. Its application is clearly described by Commander N. Mikhalevsky, USN, who was commanding officer of the USS
Joseph P. Kennedy, Jr., the destroyer that made the first intercept under its
procedures:

> On the afternoon of 25 October 1962 the USS *Joseph P. Kennedy, Jr.*,
> received orders from the Task Force Commander to intercept the SS *Marucla*
> by first light of the following day, board her and search her for prohibited
> materials. The USS *John R. Pierce* was already in the immediate vicinity and
> was keeping the *Marucla* under surveillance. En route to the rendezvous, I
> assembled and briefed the ship's boarding party. The ship's visit and search
> bill, pertinent NWPs [Naval Warfare Publications] and President John F.
> Kennedy's proclamation, which specifically enumerated the prohibited mate-
> rials, were carefully reviewed.
>
> In view of the significance of what we were about to do, I decided to retain
> full control of any "armed action." The boarding party would go unarmed. If
> anyone on the SS *Marucla* succeeded in drawing anyone of the boarding party
> into some sort of an incident, it could have worldwide repercussions. The
> boarding party would be provided with a walkie talkie for immediate com-
> munications in case of any trouble or language difficulty. Our plan called for
> no outward display of hostility, with no guns trained, but with the crew at
> general quarters, ready for action. Although I am fluent in both Russian and
> French, and this we knew to be a Soviet chartered Lebanese ship where at
> least one or both languages might be useful, I did not feel this to be sufficient
> justification for me to leave my ship and depart from the established ship's
> organization which called for the executive officer to head the boarding
> party. Lieutenant-Commander K. C. Reynolds, my executive officer, perhaps
> due to an historical sense, or perhaps as a result of his tour of duty on board
> the Sixth Fleet flagship, the USS *Springfield*, suggested that the boarding party
> wear service dress whites. We had made up our minds that this operation was
> to be carried out with all the grace and finesse we could muster. It was going to
> be a pacific boarding. We were going to "speak softly" and not use the "big
> stick" unless provoked.
>
> At first light on 26 October, the USS *Joseph P. Kennedy, Jr.*, was on the port
> quarter a few thousand yards from the SS *Marucla*, the *John R. Pierce* was on
> her starboard quarter. Captain S. H. Moore, Commander Destroyer Division
> 102, the on the scene commander, whose flagship was the *Kennedy*, issued the
> order to proceed with the boarding as previously directed. It was 0600 local
> time; I broke the flag hoist CODE OSCAR NOVEMBER and paralleled by
> flashing light "Request you stop" followed by "I intend to board you, request
> you advise me when your sea ladder is ready." The SS *Marucla* stopped as
> requested and at about 0630 sent a message by light stating "We are ready to

receive you, port side." Our whaleboat left the starboard side and proceeded to the USS *Pierce* to pick up their executive officer, Lieutenant Commander G. Osborne, who was to be a member of the boarding party. The whaleboat then proceeded to the *Marucla*, circled her to observe her close up from all sides and then came alongside to port. We observed, from a few hundred yards, the members of the boarding party precariously climb the long sea ladder strung along the port side of the merchantman.

As I learned later, the boarding officer, after introducing himself and announcing the purpose of his visit, proceeded with his party to the Master's cabin. The radioman with the walkie talkie stayed on deck at a predetermined spot where I could see him at all times. The Master of the *Marucla* turned out to be a very polite gentleman, well informed both as to current events and his rights and responsibilities under international law. Our pacific approach paid off.

The Master's awareness of the situation was evidenced by his familiarity with the President's proclamation. A copy of *Navocean* Number 30, advising of the quarantine was on his desk. Lieutenant-Commanders Reynolds and Osborne examined the ship's papers. Lieutenant-Commander Osborne's experience in the merchant marine greatly aided in ascertaining the correctness, adequacy, and veracity of the documents which appeared to be in good order. Sequence of ports of call logically matched the sequence of loading and the ship's loading plan, configuration of holds and type of gear loaded. After examining the papers, Lieutenant-Commander Reynolds requested that a certain hold be opened for inspection. Cargo in this hold was checked against the loading plan and shipping manifests. Ensign Mass, from the *Kennedy*, who could read Russian, confirmed the Russian markings and nature of the cargo against the shipping manifests. At the end of about two hours, Lieutenant-Commander Reynolds advised me by walkie talkie that, in his opinion, there were no prohibited materials on board. The cargo consisted of such items as trucks, automotive parts and sulfur. After consultation with Commander Destroyer Division 102, the SS *Marucla* was cleared to resume her voyage to Cuba via Providence Channel. Lieutenant-Commander Reynolds made the appropriate entries in the SS *Marucla* log and the boarding party returned to the *Kennedy*. The inspection of the SS *Marucla* was greatly facilitated by the nature of the prohibited materials since the ship was fully loaded and a search from top to bottom would have been physically impossible without entering port and unloading. We maintained surveillance of the SS *Marucla* until our action was approved by the Task Force Commander who then ordered us to terminate our surveillance and return to our assigned stations in the quarantine.

Although this limited use of force did not fit into the doctrines of the law of blockade, it met the tests of both necessity and proportionality. It clearly was necessary because of the severe immediate nuclear threat to the national security of the Americas. And it was proportional because the force that was used was probably the least that could have been effective. In addition, it was approved by the Organization of American States as a measure of collective self-defense, by the silence of other nations, and by the agreement between President John F. Kennedy and Premier Nikita Khrushchev.

Pacific Blockade

A measure that must be distinguished from the blockade as used by belligerents is *pacific blockade*. It is used only in time of peace, usually by a group of maritime states, to coerce a state to end a disturbance or comply with a treaty obligation. The only ships that the blockading power may seize are those flying the flag of the state being blockaded; thus, third-party states are not obliged to honor such a blockade. The legality of pacific blockade is questionable under the terms of the United Nations charter, whether such action is taken by a single power or several powers acting in concert, unless taken pursuant to authorization of the Security Council.

Contraband

Another permissible means of warfare against maritime commerce is the control and capture of contraband. Article 631a of the U.S. Navy's publication *Law of Naval Warfare* (NWIP 10-2) states:

> Contraband consists of all goods which are destined for an enemy and which may be susceptible of use in war. Contraband goods are divided into two categories: absolute and conditional. Absolute contraband consists of goods which are used primarily for war (or goods whose very character makes them destined to be used in war). Conditional contraband consists of goods which are equally susceptible of use either for peaceful or for warlike purposes.

Contraband lists published by belligerents guide naval commanders in determining whether a particular cargo consists of absolute contraband, conditional contraband, or so-called free goods.

Absolute contraband may be seized by a belligerent warship or aircraft, if it is destined to territory under control of the enemy. It is immaterial whether the shipment is direct or requires transshipment, either by water or overland. Conditional contraband is subject to seizure if it is destined for the use of an enemy government or enemy armed forces. The same rules as to transshipment apply here as to absolute contraband. Free goods are not subject to seizure under any circumstances.

The law as to absolute and conditional contraband was developed at a time when armies were relatively small and only a low percentage of a nation's population was affected by the existence of a state of war. Under modern conditions of warfare, the distinctions have very little significance. The present practice of most nations in time of war is for the government to take control of the distribution of all products—food, fuel, raw materials, and so forth. From these resources the government meets defense needs first, and then those of the civilian population as best it can. Under these conditions, the distinction between absolute and conditional contraband is largely meaningless and "free goods" have virtually disappeared. The published contraband lists of World War II proved this to be so, because they included on either the absolute or conditional list practically every item that can be imagined.

In World War II a system was developed to make it possible for neutral merchant ships to operate only when they complied with Allied contraband controls. Known as the *navicert* system, it provided clearance certificates, issued by naval authorities, to neutral ships whose cargoes, routes, and destinations were approved. Later, during the Cuban missile crisis, *clearcerts* were issued to ships that were not carrying prohibited material.

Visit and Search

How does the commander of a belligerent warship determine that a merchant ship is carrying contraband and is therefore subject to capture? The answer lies in the belligerent's right of visit and search.

One of the rights a belligerent warship has is to visit any merchantman she encounters upon the high seas. This right is exercised in the following manner. The merchantman is signaled to stop, and one or two officers are sent over in a small boat. They board her and examine her papers to determine her registry, ports of departure and destination, the nature of her cargo and employment, and other facts deemed essential. If this examination satisfies them that she is not liable to capture, they will make an entry of the visit in her log and depart, allowing her to proceed. If, on the other hand, the ship's papers arouse suspicion as to their authenticity or suggest that her cargo, destination, or employment would subject her to capture, a search of her may be made. In earlier times it was required that this search be made on the spot. However, since merchant ships today are so large and the manner of their loading is so different from what it used to be, it is now customary to require the ship to accompany the warship to port so that the search may be conducted thoroughly and in safety.

If the ship's papers or the search reveal that she is liable to capture, she is sent in for adjudication by prize court. It is important to emphasize at this point that the boarding officer is not expected to make a judicial determination of the liability of the ship or cargo to capture. This is the function of the prize court. All the boarding officer is expected to do is to determine whether there is substantial reason to believe that the ship may be liable to capture. Although the prize court may subsequently find that his suspicions did not justify confiscation of the vessel, the boarding officer will have acted properly if the results of his visit and search furnished *probable* cause for capture.

Suppose, however, that a merchant ship, upon becoming aware that a belligerent warship intends to visit her, either resists the approach or tries to flee. In this case, the warship may act forcibly, and, if absolutely necessary, may sink her. An enemy merchantman's right to resist visit is recognized by International Law, and the consequences of such an act are the risks of damage and loss that the captain chooses to take. A neutral does not have this right. Forcible resistance or flight by a neutral merchant ship may be treated by a belligerent warship as a suspicious circumstance justifying her capture.

Although both neutral and enemy merchant ships are subject to visit and search by a belligerent warship, the captures that may follow have different legal effects. If the captured ship belongs to the enemy, the very act of capture removes any right of ownership the enemy may have in her. In case of military necessity, the prize may be destroyed when she cannot be sent or escorted into port for adjudication. This action, however, should be avoided, if possible, because the prize may be carrying neutral cargo, which, unless it is contraband, is exempt from capture, even when in enemy bottoms. If the captured ship belongs to a neutral, however, the act of capturing does not in itself vest title in the capturing nation. The title remains in trust with the captor until there has been adjudication in a prize court. Destruction of a neutral prize is therefore lawful only under the most unusual circumstances. For example, destruction would be authorized if the ship could not be sent or escorted into port and her release were absolutely impossible.

RIGHTS AND DUTIES OF NEUTRALS

Before discussing the rights and duties of neutrals, a few words about neutrality are appropriate. In Chapter 2 a distinction was made between *neutrality* and *neutralization.* Neutrality is the condition of a state or government that refrains from taking part, directly or indirectly, in a war between other powers; also, it is a condition of immunity from invasion or use by belligerents. This definition covers the two sides of neutrality—more commonly referred to as "the rights and duties of neutrals."

A few thoughts come to mind when one tries to apply this definition to well-known actions of World War II, the Korean and Vietnamese conflicts, and even present defense activities all over the world. Is true neutrality, as defined above, still possible when the nations of the world are divided into large factions whose ideologies are opposed to each other? Neutrality does not demand that nations not participating in an armed conflict should be indifferent to the issues of the belligerents. The sympathies of neutrals may well lie entirely with one side, and a neutral does not violate his duties as long as he does not commit any unneutral *acts* that might aid the side he favors. It has been said that in view of the worldwide commitments of almost all nations in mutual defense organizations, it will be practically impossible to remain strictly neutral in any future armed conflict. There are, however, nations which by tradition have successfully maintained neutrality throughout even modern total war. Switzerland and Sweden are examples. On the other hand, it should be remembered that these nations are not members of any regional defense organizations, even in time of peace.

Neutrality is a concept that has been drastically changed by the charter of the United Nations. When notified of a threat to or a breach of peace, or an act of aggression, as in the case of Korea, the Security Council may call on its members to take measures short of force to restore international peace and security. Nations that take part in military action pursuant to a resolution of the United Nations are not "belligerents" in the strict sense of International Law. Since they cannot be said to be neutral, the question arises as to what their status actually is. It is now generally recognized that countries engaged in military action pursuant to a call of the United Nations and its organs, are "unneutral" only insofar as they comply with the request of the United Nations. A state that refrains from taking part in hostilities between other nations but renders assistance to one side has been called a *qualified neutral*.

Some of the general principles of neutrality can be summarized here. Inviolability of neutral territory is a basic principle, but it was extensively violated by Germany in both world wars. The duty of a neutral not to supply the military forces of one of the belligerents is an important principle of neutrality, but it does not apply to private commercial transactions. The prohibition against recruiting and forming combatant corps in neutral territory is still another principle of neutrality, as is the duty of a neutral state to intern military personnel who have entered its territory. Space does not permit going into the details of the rights and duties of military personnel interned in neutral countries. Under the Geneva Convention of 1949 for the protection of prisoners of war, such persons are, at least, assured the same treatment as prisoners of war. The neutral countries may, however, if they choose, grant them more favorable treatment. Interned Allied personnel in Sweden during World War II were afforded many privileges.

When a state adopts the policy of neutrality, it assumes certain obligations toward the belligerents. As long as it fulfills these obligations impartially, it has certain rights that are entitled to respect by the belligerents. A great many of the rights and duties of both neutrals and belligerents are concerned with measures directed against commerce, a number of which may appropriately be set forth here.

International Law forbids a belligerent's making use of neutral territory—territorial or internal waters, harbors, ports, or air space—for hostile acts, such as visit and search of merchant vessels and attacks upon the opposing belligerent. It also forbids a belligerent's making use of neutral territory as a base from which to sally forth and make hostile raids or captures beyond the territory of the neutral. Corresponding to this restraint on a belligerent is the obligation of the neutral to ensure that no belligerent use is made of its territory. If the neutral is unable to enforce its obligation, it must make reparation to the injured belligerent or neutral.

Most of the restrictions upon belligerent use of neutral ports and harbors are covered in Hague Convention XIII of 1907, the highlights of which are:

(1) Belligerent warships may remain in a neutral's territorial sea, ports, or roadsteads for no more than 24 hours. The neutral may extend this period for a reasonable period because of weather or urgent repairs. [*See* (5) below.] If the belligerent warship does not leave when required, it must be interned along with its crew.

(2) No more than three warships of the same belligerent power may be in the same port or roadstead together. When warships of opposing belligerents are in the same port, the order of their leaving is that of entry, and after the departure of a belligerent warship at least 24 hours must elapse before a warship belonging to the other belligerent can depart.

(3) Belligerent warships may not increase their supplies of war material or armaments in a neutral port.

(4) Food and fuel may be obtained to a limited extent.

The wording of rule (4) is so loose that much controversy has arisen over its exact meaning. Most neutrals have interpreted the provision concerning fuel to permit the furnishing of only enough fuel to allow the warship to reach the nearest friendly belligerent port.

(5) Belligerent warships may carry out only such repairs as are absolutely necessary to render them *seaworthy*. No repairs are permitted which would add in any manner to their *fighting force*.

(6) A prize may be brought into a neutral port only because of unseaworthiness, stress of weather, or want of fuel or provisions. It must leave as soon as the circumstances which justified its entry are at an end. If a prize crew violates these rules, the neutral must release the vessel and its crew and intern the prize crew.

The terms *seaworthy* and *fighting force* as used in (5) above, are sufficiently ambiguous to suggest that controversies have arisen in their interpretation. The following incident, related by Rear Admiral Thomas C. Ragan, USN, illustrates how one such controversy arose and was settled:

> Information was received in the latter part of 1944, concerning a German submarine which entered a port of neutral Spain and requested to make certain repairs. I do not recall that our government knew how the damage had been incurred or the nature and extent of the repairs requested. The question arose, however, as to the extent, without protesting unneutral service, to which we could acquiesce in repairs to submarines under the generally accepted practice with respect to belligerent warships.

The Navy was most vitally concerned with antisubmarine warfare and was consulted as to the position our government should take. At the time, I was on duty in the Central Division of Naval Operations and the problem was given to that division.

There was little time for research, but, insofar as could be determined, there was no precedent to apply. Existing rules of International Law gave no definite answer. What did "seaworthy" mean when referring to a submarine? Did it include "under-seaworthiness"? True, an interned enemy submarine would be virtually as good as a "kill"—but there were other factors to be considered as well. The position taken would probably be with us for a long, long time. It was recommended, after debating all aspects of the problem, that repairs which did not affect the ability of the submarine to submerge, such as to improve or renew such submerging ability, should be recognized as a proper neutral duty or right in extension of the principle applying to belligerent surface warships.

The recommended position was accepted.

ENFORCEMENT OF THE LAW OF ARMED CONFLICT

In the years since World War II, a frequent criticism of International Law has been that the laws of armed conflict are meaningless because there is no way of enforcing them. If this criticism is based on the fact that there is no single, all-powerful tribunal that can impartially try and punish offenders, whether losers or victors, the point is well made. On the other hand, there are other methods of enforcing the law of armed conflict, and in many cases they have been quite effective.

Probably the most effective means of enforcing the laws of war at the political level is the wronged nation's publication of the facts with a view to influencing world opinion against the offender. Some people have scoffed at this procedure as a means of enforcement, but the fact remains that it has been effective. Germany's reaction to world opinion after she sank the *Lusitania* without warning provides a good example. Primarily as a result of the sharp protests of neutrals, who were shocked at her lawless conduct, Germany acknowledged her liability and issued instructions to her submarine commanders not to sink merchant ships without warning and without providing for the safety of crews and passengers.

Where the laws of war have been breached, protest and demands for punishment, as well as for compensation, are also effective means. It was on this basis that the commanding officer of a U.S. submarine was punished by the United States when his submarine sank an enemy hospital ship.

Reprisals between belligerents are acts, otherwise illegal, that are permitted to a belligerent in reaction to illegal acts of warfare committed by an enemy. They may not be taken merely for revenge, but may be used to induce compliance with the laws of war, and they must cease as soon as they have achieved their objective. An example is the arming of merchant vessels in reprisal for unrestricted submarine warfare. It should be pointed out that measures of reprisal against prisoners of war and civilian populations are prohibited by the Geneva Convention.

The final method of enforcing the laws of war is punishment. It is a popular misconception that war crimes trials originated at Nuremberg following World War II. This erroneous belief is probably the result of the large amount of publicity that surrounded them. Some of the defendants were tried for war crimes, such as the violation of the laws of warfare, but the offenses that received the most notoriety and elicited the greatest amount of controversy were the so-called crimes against humanity and crimes against peace.

It has always been an obligation—one that most civilized belligerents have honored—for states to punish their own nationals who violate the laws of armed conflict. Most violations of the laws of war are also violations of domestic law. Belligerents have the same right on the same grounds to try enemy nationals, whether members of the armed forces or civilians, who fall under their control as prisoners of war or through occupation of enemy territory. War crimes trials and the publicity that accompanies them obviously have possibilities as effective deterrents against violation of the laws of war.

The obligation for a state to punish its own nationals who violate the laws of armed conflict raises the need for commanding officers to know command and individual responsibilities. For example, a commander who orders a subordinate to commit an illegal act is held responsible for that act. In some circumstances, a subordinate is responsible for an act he is ordered to commit, and a superior may be responsible for a subordinate's act even though it is not the result of his direct orders.

In the most publicized case of the Vietnam conflict, an army platoon commander, First Lieutenant William L. Calley, Jr., was tried by court-martial and convicted of the premeditated murder of about one hundred Vietnamese civilians. Part of Calley's defense was that he was carrying out the orders of his company commander. This defense was rejected by the appellate courts that considered his conviction on the grounds that the order to "waste" the victims was illegal "upon even cursory evaluation by a man of ordinary sense and understanding." The basic rule is that a superior may not lawfully order one of his subordinates to violate the law of armed conflict. Therefore, when a subordinate obeys an order that is a clear violation of the law of armed conflict, such as killing or torturing a prisoner, the result can be conviction by court-martial of both the subordinate and the superior.

The law requires that before an individual may be held criminally responsible for an act, he must bear some measure of personal responsibility for its commission. It may be impossible for a military commander to know what is occurring in all parts of his command at all times. Consequently, it would be unfair to hold him responsible for a violation of the law of armed conflict about which he knew nothing and could not reasonably have been expected to know anything. However, because of a commander's disciplinary powers over his subordinates, he presumably has the power—and certainly the responsibility—to stop violations of the law of armed conflict of which he has knowledge. Therefore, a military commander who knows that his subordinates are violating the law of armed conflict and fails to take action to suppress such violations may be convicted by court-martial for the acts of his subordinates.

It is manifest that the most effective way to minimize the frequency of violations of the law of armed conflict is to focus on prevention. This can be done best by educating and training members of the armed forces, particularly those who are likely to be exposed to situations where violations can easily occur.

In Chapter 12 the enforcement of International Law in general is examined. The combination of what is described therein plus these brief comments on the subject should provide the reader with a relatively broad perspective on the mechanisms and directions that operate so as to further and enhance the enforcement of the law.

11

Collective Security—International Organizations

That objective [of the North Atlantic Treaty Organization] is to assist . . . in achieving the primary purpose of the United Nations—the maintenance of international peace and security. The Treaty is designed to do so by making clear the determination of the parties collectively to preserve their common heritage of freedom and to defend themselves against aggression.
Joint Communique by the North Atlantic Council, September 1949.

INTRODUCTION

At 0400, Sunday, 25 June 1950, Korean time, armed forces from North Korea commenced an unprovoked assault against the territory of Korea.

Speaking on that same date before the Security Council of the United Nations, the U.S. representative to that council said:

> This is clearly a threat to international peace and security. As such, it is of grave concern to my Government. It is a threat which must inevitably be of grave concern to the governments of all peace- and freedom-loving nations.
>
> A full-scale attack is now going forward in Korea. It is an invasion upon a state which the United Nations itself, by action of its General Assembly, has brought into being. It is armed aggression against a government elected under United Nations supervision.
>
> Such an attack strikes at the fundamental purposes of the United Nations charter. Such an attack openly defies the interest and authority of the United Nations. Such an attack, therefore, concerns the vital interest which all the members of the United Nations have in the organization. (Department of State Bulletin XXIII, 1950.)

The Security Council responded to this anouncement by passing a resolution which called upon the authorities of North Korea to cease hostilities and to withdraw their armed forces to the thirty-eighth parallel. It asked the U.N. Commission on Korea to observe the withdrawal and report on the execution of this resolution, and called "upon all members to render every assistance to the United Nations in the execution of this resolution and to refrain from giving assistance to the North Korean authorities." The same day, in support of the resolution, the president of the United States ordered

U.S. sea and air forces to give the Korean government troops cover and support.

Two days later, the Security Council passed another resolution, asking members of the United Nations to "furnish such assistance to the Republic of Korea as may be necessary, to repel the armed attack and to restore international peace and security in the area." Fifty-three of the fifty-nine members of the United Nations heeded the call and assisted the government of the Republic of Korea in some form or other to repel the attack made upon its territory.

Never before had sovereign states responded to the request of a supervisory international organization that they help to maintain peace in the world.

THE UNITED NATIONS

HISTORICAL BACKGROUND

Attempts to form an international organization for the peaceful settlement of disagreements between nations are not new. After almost every war, efforts have been made to find ways and means of avoiding another war. As an outgrowth of World War I, the League of Nations was established. This was the first world organization aimed at preserving peace through worldwide cooperation on political, economic, and social problems. The United States did not join it: other nations, after having joined it, withdrew. The league failed in its main objective, the preservation of peace. In 1946, it was dissolved and the United Nations took over its assets and functions. However, the league cannot be dismissed as a total failure. Indeed, it provided the United Nations with valuable experience in the voluntary association of states for the purpose of fostering peace by cooperation in political, economic, and social areas.

The principles of the United Nations are embodied in the Declaration of Principles, known as the Atlantic Charter, signed by President Roosevelt and Prime Minister Churchill on 14 August 1941, several months before the United States entered World War II. They were accepted in the Declaration by United Nations, signed by twenty-six nations on 1 January 1942, and later adhered to by twenty-one more countries. Although this declaration was a pledge of solidarity in the prosecution of the war and does not contain any reference to forming an international organization for the purpose of avoiding war, it is considered the cornerstone of the United Nations as we know it today.

The first declaration on the forming of an international organization was issued after the Moscow Conference of 30 October 1943. The United States, Great Britain, the Soviet Union, and China participated in this declaration, which stated that the participants at the conference jointly recognized the necessity of establishing at the earliest practicable date a general international organization, based on the principle of the sovereign equality of all peace-loving states, and open to membership by all such states, large and small, for the maintenance of international peace and security.

Representatives of the same four powers met at Dumbarton Oaks in the late summer of 1944 and drew up what are known as the Dumbarton Oaks Proposals. As the name indicates, this document was not the draft of a charter, but a general outline for formulating a charter. It did not contain any recommendations for voting procedures; these were decided upon at the Yalta Conference of February 1945, and finally embodied in the charter of the United Nations.

Fifty nations met in San Francisco on 25 April 1945 and the charter of the United Nations was signed on 26 June of that year. The U.S. Senate, led by the bipartisan team of Senators Thomas Connally and Arthur H. Vandenberg, approved it with only two dissenting votes. On 24 October 1945, the charter came into effect through deposit of instruments of ratification by the requisite number of states. Thus, 24 October is now celebrated throughout the world as United Nations Day.

CHARTER

What is the charter of the United Nations? It is a multilateral treaty; it does not purport to set up a super state or super government. The fact that the preamble starts with "We the peoples of the United Nations" does not mean that the charter is a constitution for a union or government of all the people in the United Nations. That it is a multilateral treaty becomes clear in the conclusion of the preamble: "Accordingly, our respective Governments, through representatives assembled in the City of San Francisco . . . have agreed . . . ."

The purposes of the United Nations are set forth in Article 1 of the charter as well as in the preamble. Article 1 lists the following purposes:

1. To maintain international peace and security, and to that end: to take effective collective measures for the prevention and removal of threats to the peace.
2. To develop friendly relations among nations.
3. To achieve international cooperation in solving international problems of an economic, social, cultural, or humanitarian character.
4. To be a center for harmonizing the actions of nations in the attainment of these common ends.

Article 2 of the charter cites seven principles for the achievement of the above purposes:

1. The Organization is based on the principle of the sovereign equality of all its Members.

2. All Members . . . shall fulfill in good faith the obligations assumed by them in accordance with the present Charter.
3. All Members shall settle their international disputes by peaceful means.
4. All Members shall refrain in their international relations from the threat or use of force.
5. All Members shall give the United Nations every assistance in any action it takes in accordance with the present Charter.
6. The Organization shall ensure that states which are not Members of the United Nations act in accordance with these Principles so far as may be necessary for the maintenance of international peace and security.
7. Nothing contained in the present Charter shall authorize the United Nations to intervene in matters which are essentially within the domestic jurisdiction of any state.

From the above it is clear that the maintenance of international peace and security is the prime purpose of the United Nations. This aim is stated in the Preamble, in the Purposes, and in the Principles.

The charter distinguishes between original members, namely those who participated at the San Francisco Conference, or who signed the Declaration by United Nations in 1942, and then signed and ratified the charter, and members admitted later. Membership is open to all peace-loving states that accept the obligations contained in the charter. By the end of 1978 there were more than 150 member nations. New members are admitted by decision of the General Assembly upon recommendation of the Security Council.

Article 7 of the charter lists the following bodies as the principal organs of the United Nations: the General Assembly, the Security Council, the Economic and Social Council, the Trusteeship Council, the International Court of Justice, and the Secretariat. The first two organs, the General Assembly and the Security Council, being the most important and most powerful, are described below.

General Assembly

The General Assembly consists of all the members of the United Nations, each member having one vote. Decisions on important questions are made by a two-thirds majority vote; on other questions, they are made by a simple majority vote. Article 18 of the charter enumerates the matters considered to be "important questions," and they include recommendations with respect to the maintenance of international peace and security, election of non-permanent members of the Security Council, and admission of new members to the United Nations.

Security Council

The Security Council, intended to be the ever-present policeman, is organized quite differently from the General Assembly. For one thing, it is organized so that it can function continuously, whereas the General Assembly meets but once a year. Therefore, each member of the council must be represented at all times at the seat of the United Nations in New York.

The Security Council consists of permanent and nonpermanent members. The five permanent members are enumerated in Article 23: the United States, the United Kingdom, France, the Soviet Union, and China. The ten nonpermanent members are elected by the General Assembly to a two-year term. Election is by a two-thirds majority vote, because the selection of nonpermanent members for the Security Council is considered an "important question."

One of the most interesting aspects of the Security Council's operations is its voting procedure. It is known as the Yalta Formula, which, after long debate, was embodied in Article 27 of the charter. Each of the fifteen members has one vote and decisions are made on the basis of a majority vote of not less than nine. In procedural matters, nine affirmative votes are decisive. In all other matters, however, the nine affirmative votes must include concurring votes by the permanent members. Therefore, nonprocedural matters can be decided only by the agreement of all five permanent members and the concurrence of four nonpermanent members. Procedural matters involve which items have precedence on the agenda and administrative matters of like import.

The Yalta Formula is based on the premise that, if the Security Council is to carry out its responsibility in the framework of the United Nations, agreement among the Big Five is essential to any action.

The word *veto* is not used in the charter of the United Nations. Under the voting procedure in the Security Council, the dissenting vote of one permanent member blocks any contemplated action, and this dissenting vote has become known as "the veto." *Veto* is a Latin word meaning "I forbid." The president of the United States can block legislation approved by both houses of Congress by refusing to sign it. He vetoes it. In the Security Council, a disagreeing permanent member has the same power and exercises it by casting a dissenting vote. A negative vote is a veto only in the event that a resolution receives at least nine affirmative votes and then fails solely because of a permanent member's negative vote.

The practice of the Security Council has established that a permanent member's abstention from voting does not constitute a veto. Voluntary absence of a permanent member from a meeting of the Security Council is considered to be the same as abstention. It, therefore, does not prevent action by the council, nor does it make such action illegal, as the Soviet Union has claimed. The generally accepted interpretation is based on the provision of the charter that requires the Security Council to be able to function continuously. If, by his absence, a permanent member could prevent the

Security Council from taking action, a walkout would make the above requirement of the charter meaningless.

The importance of interpreting the absence of a permanent member as abstention from a vote, rather than as a veto, was highlighted by the action of the Security Council on the Korean question. Since the Soviet Union is a permanent member and the council's action was directed against communist aggression, it seemed logical to assume that the Soviet Union would veto the proposed resolutions to assist Korea. The Soviet representative did not take that action because he was not present at the time the resolutions were considered. In protest against the membership of Nationalist China, the Soviet Union boycotted all meetings of the Security Council from January 1950 until 1 August 1950, when the Soviet representative took over the presidency of the Security Council. Thereafter, two resolutions condemning aggression in Korea were vetoed by the Soviet Union.

Statistics show that the Soviet Union has blocked Security Council action more than one hundred times by casting a negative vote. Other permanent members have used the procedure much less frequently.

Although both the Security Council and the General Assembly are charged with maintaining international peace and security, the importance of the Security Council lies in its power to *act*. The General Assembly may only discuss, consider, and recommend. The powers of the Security Council are defined in several provisions of the charter. Article 39 states:

> The Security Council shall determine the existence of any threat to the peace, breach of the peace, or act of aggression and shall make recommendations, or decide what measures shall be taken in accordance with Articles 41 and 42, to maintain or restore international peace and security.

Article 41 outlines "measures not involving the use of armed force," including "complete or partial interruption of economic relations" and "the severance of diplomatic relations." Should these measures prove inadequate, Article 42 provides that the Security Council may take such action by air, sea, or land forces as "may be necessary to maintain or restore international peace and security. Such action may include demonstrations, blockade, and other operations by air, sea, or land forces of Members of the United Nations." The charter puts members of the United Nations under obligation to place at the organization's disposal armed forces to carry out the actions decided upon by the Security Council.

Notwithstanding the power of the Security Council to take action in case of aggression, Article 51 of the charter specifically recognizes the right of members to act in self-defense, individually or collectively. Members are required to inform the Security Council immediately of any action they take in self-defense, and such action in no way diminishes the responsibility and authority of the Security Council to take the measures necessary to maintain or restore international peace and security.

Pacific Settlement of Disputes and Regional Arrangements

The charter declares that the parties to any dispute "the continuance of which is likely to endanger the maintenance of international peace and security" shall *first of all* seek a solution by peaceful means. Some of these means are enumerated in the charter and include resort to regional arrangements. In Article 52, the charter recognizes the right of members to conclude such arrangements as long as their activities are consistent with its purposes and principles.

The Security Council has the right to investigate any dispute of the nature described above and make recommendations for its settlement. It uses regional organizations for that purpose and may even use them for enforcement measures. But these organizations cannot initiate enforcement action without the approval of the Security Council. As previously stated, however, this prohibition does not affect the exercise of the right of collective self-defense under Article 51 of the charter.

From the above, the importance of regional organizations in the framework of the United Nations is quite evident. Since the United Nations came into existence, regional organizations and collective defense treaties linking the majority of the nations of the world have been concluded.

REGIONAL ORGANIZATIONS—COLLECTIVE DEFENSE

The terms *regional organization* and *collective defense* may seem to be one and the same thing when they are used side by side. Technically speaking, they are not. However, most arrangements and pacts have the characteristics of both.

Regional organizations are "arrangements" recognized by Chapter VIII of the charter of the United Nations. They embrace all problems common to the parties thereto, political, technical, cultural, or educational; in short, the same problems that the United Nations itself deals with. As in the case of the parent body, regional organizations have as their goals the maintenance of international peace and security, and they recognize the right of self-defense. The word *regional* does not necessarily mean that the territories of all parties to an organization must lie within the region embraced by the pact. It is sufficient that the parties have common interests in the region. For example, the United States has extensive interests in the North Atlantic Treaty area.

Collective defense pacts serve the prime purpose of collective self-defense, as recognized by Article 51 of the United Nations charter. This right, however, is inherent and exists regardless of the charter. Therefore, membership in a collective defense organization is not dependent upon membership in the United Nations.

Procedures for the pacific settlement of disputes between members of a regional organization usually precede action by the Security Council of the United Nations, but the Security Council may at any time investigate any dispute that may lead to international friction. If the regional organization has not taken any action with regard to settlement, the Security Council may direct it to do so. Since collective self-defense is based on the inherent right of self-defense, such action may be taken without prior appeal to the United Nations. Members of the United Nations are, however, obliged to report to the Security Council any measures they take.

How closely regional organizations and collective security pacts are linked to the United Nations can be seen from the text of their charters or defense agreements. These documents refer specifically to the obligations of the individual countries under the charter of the United Nations and state that their purposes coincide with those of the United Nations.

This giant network of organizations and treaty commitments presents probably the most ambitious step ever taken by the free nations to prevent war and to secure peace. The overall result for the nations thus linked together is a mutual guarantee of territorial integrity and the maintenance of peace and security. Regional defense agreements, considered as a whole, embody the principle of universal collective security proclaimed by the United Nations.

The keystone of the collective defense system is the provision that if one' member state is attacked, the other member states will come to its assistance. What obligation does this provision impose on all the parties to the agreement? Does an attack upon one member *automatically* involve all the others in war? The answer is no. Until collective action is decided upon by the collective organization empowered to do so, each state must decide on the immediate measures it deems necessary to fulfill its obligation to aid the attacked state. The attacked state will, of course, immediately respond with military action. Other states may offer assistance in the form of providing arms and equipment, or the breaking of commercial and political relations with the attacking state, or they may take the ultimate step of using their own armed forces to assist the attacked state. The fact that an attack on even the smallest nation belonging to a regional organization will result in collective and individual action by all members of that organization makes the successful outcome of aggression doubtful. Regional pacts, therefore, are a strong deterrent to aggression.

Ever since the Monroe Doctrine was promulgated in 1823, the problems of the states of the Western Hemisphere have been considered so closely interrelated as to be virtually common to all. Declarations and treaties between the American states have set an example for regional solidarity.

Treaties presently in force in the Western Hemisphere embody the underlying principles of declarations and resolutions made at regional conferences over the last few decades.

In the community of American states the dual purpose of regional organization and collective defense clearly exists. It is embodied in the Inter-American Treaty of Reciprocal Assistance (the Rio Pact) of 2 September 1947 (*see* Appendix O) and the Organization of American States, whose charter was signed at Bogotá, Colombia, on 30 April 1948. Canada is not a member of either the Rio Pact or the Organization of American States.

Rio Pact

As its full title implies, the Rio Pact is a collective defense treaty. However, it not only makes provision for assistance in the case of attack from the outside, but also provides for consultation on measures to resist subversive activities from outside and for settlement of disputes among its members, through the Organization of American States. Peaceful settlement of any dispute within the regional organization must precede referral to the Security Council of the United Nations. Measures, short of force, are in general the same as those contemplated by the charter of the United Nations. Article 10 of the pact specifically states that the obligations it imposes in no way impair the member countries' obligations under the charter of the United Nations.

Organization of American States

The Organization of American States is fashioned generally after the United Nations charter. Its principles and purposes, along the same lines as those of the United Nations, are more explicit and more detailed. For instance, whereas the United Nations charter states that members will refrain from the threat or use of force, its charter condemns wars of aggression and declares that no rights accrue to an aggressor state if it wins such a war. Since the American states have long agreed on a great many problems not yet ripe for settlement on a worldwide scale, the organization's charter embodies principles of International Law not found in the charter of any other organization.

The Organization of American States was instrumental in settling disputes between Costa Rica and Nicaragua and between Haiti and the Dominican Republic. It also provided the cohesive force for the American states at the time of the Cuban missile crisis in 1962.

North Atlantic Treaty

The North Atlantic Treaty (*see* Appendix P) was signed in Washington, D.C., on 4 April 1949 and became effective on 24 August of the same year.

The following countries were original parties to this treaty: Belgium, Denmark, Iceland, Italy, France, Luxembourg, Netherlands, Norway, Portugal, Great Britain, Canada, and the United States. Article 10 permits the parties, by unanimous agreement, to invite participation by any other European state in a position to further the principles of the treaty. Thus, Greece and Turkey became members of the North Atlantic Treaty Organization in 1951 and West Germany in 1955.

This treaty, patterned after the Rio Pact, stresses that its mission is within the framework of the United Nations. The organization is, however, entirely different from the Organization of American States. Although maintenance of international peace and security, pacific settlement of disputes among members, and political and economic collaboration for the development of better international understanding are among its principles and purposes, its prime purpose is collective defense. Articles 3 and 5 both state that an armed attack against one member shall be considered an armed attack against all members, and provide for measures necessary to meet such an attack.

Mutual Defense Assistance

Article 3 of the North Atlantic Treaty endorses the principle of mutual aid, which has been the basis of U.S. foreign policy for the past three decades. Under it, the United States has provided friendly foreign nations with arms and equipment in order to develop their "individual and collective capacity to resist armed attack." Based on this principle, legislation for foreign military assistance has been enacted. This aid is extended not only to North Atlantic Treaty countries, but also to every country in the U.S. mutual defense system. The amount and type of the aid depends on the need, specified in each instance by an agreement between the United States and the country concerned. These agreements are amended or modified as the requirements change. One vital point should be borne in mind: the United States is under no obligation to strengthen the defense capability of a particular country unless such aid also strengthens the *collective* capability of the United States. In other words, the value of the aided country to the defense of the treaty area as a whole is a prime consideration.

The obligation to provide assistance is mutual. Other countries besides the United States have an obligation to contribute to the common defense and they do. For example, U.S. armed forces are now stationed all over the world, and other countries are contributing to collective and mutual defense by making areas available for the establishment of U.S. bases.

The success of the North Atlantic Treaty Organization in the area of mutual defense has prompted its members to expand its activities to mutual economic and political areas.

Southeast Asia Collective Defense Treaty

The Southeast Asia Collective Defense Treaty was signed in Manila on 8 September 1954. The following countries are parties to it: the United States, Great Britain, Australia, New Zealand, France, the Philippines, and Thailand. When this treaty was concluded, the parties involved proclaimed the Pacific Charter, which is not like that of either the United Nations or the Organization of American States. A proclamation of principles and purposes similar to the Atlantic Charter, it restates and subscribes to the principles of the United Nations.

The Southeast Asia Collective Defense Treaty is based on the inherent right of collective self-defense. The commitments of the signatories to give assistance in the case of armed attack are not, however, as strong as are those in the North Atlantic Treaty. There is no provision that an armed attack on one party to the treaty constitutes an armed attack on all of them. Article IV says: "Each Party recognizes that aggression by means of armed attack in the treaty area against any of the Parties . . . would endanger its own peace and safety, and agrees that it will in that event act to meet the common danger in accordance with its constitutional processes."

The war in Vietnam created so much strain within the alliance that, while the treaty is still in force, it is, at this writing, essentially dormant. Significantly, the United States has other security agreements with most members of the alliance.

Other Regional Organizations

There are other regional organizations formed primarily for collective security and political purposes. ANZUS binds the United States, Australia, and New Zealand. The United States is not a member of and does not participate in the activities of three other important regional organizations: the Arab League, whose membership comprises most of the Arab world; the Warsaw Pact, an alliance of the iron-curtain countries; and, lastly, the Balkan Pact, comprised of Yugoslavia, Greece, and Turkey.

The Central Treaty Organization was formed in 1955 by Turkey, Iran, the United Kingdom, and Pakistan, the United States serving as a partial member. When the government of Iran fell in February 1979, the subsequent revolutionary government withdrew from the treaty, followed shortly by Pakistan, reducing the scope of the organization to a shell.

BILATERAL AGREEMENTS

A discussion of U.S. defense commitments would not be complete without the inclusion of two bilateral agreements: the Defense Agreement with Spain and the Security Treaty with Japan.

Spain

In view of the strategic importance of the Iberian Peninsula to the defense of the North Atlantic Treaty countries and the desire of Spain to align herself with the Western Powers, the United States undertook to explore the possibility of defense commitments with her on a bilateral basis. These efforts resulted in the Defense Agreement and Mutual Defense Assistance Agreement, both concluded in Madrid on 26 September 1953. The latter follows the pattern established by other mutual defense assistance agreements and is mainly concerned with the transfer of military supplies and equipment and their effective use by Spain for common defense purposes.

The Defense Agreement, however, is entirely different from the collective defense agreements discussed above. Although its stated purpose is that of maintaining international peace and security, it does not mention the charter of the United Nations; this is because Spain did not become a member of that organization until December 1955. The preamble to the Defense Agreement simply recognizes the danger the Western World faces, and expresses the desire of Spain and the United States to participate in agreements for self-defense. There is no provision that an attack upon one of the parties shall be considered an attack upon the other, or that attack upon one shall be considered a danger to the peace and security of the other. Both countries recognize, however, the fact that they may be faced with situations that make friendly cooperation advisable. They therefore agreed that the United States would contribute to Spain's defense capability and Spain would make its military facilities available to the United States. That agreement expired on 26 September 1968, and, after extensive consultations and negotiations, a new agreement of friendship and cooperation and a detailed agreement on the use of military facilities in Spain came into force on 26 September 1970. In 1976 the two countries negotiated a treaty that covered essentially the same substantive areas of cooperation as were set forth in the agreements of 1970.

Japan

It will be recalled that, upon its defeat in World War II, Japan was completely demilitarized. Consequently, she could not join in a mutual defense treaty. She and the United States, therefore, concluded the Security Treaty, which came into force on 28 April 1952, simultaneously with the Peace Treaty, which restored Japan's sovereignty.

The Security Treaty recognized Japan's inability to defend herself and, as a provisional measure, made it the duty of the United States to keep armed forces in and about Japan "so as to deter armed attack" upon her. This obligation was to cease "whenever in the opinion of the Governments of the United States of America and Japan there shall have come into force such United Nations arrangements or such alternative individual or collective security dispositions as will satisfactorily provide for the maintenance by the United Nations or otherwise of international peace and security in the Japan area." This moral obligation of the victorious state to provide for the defense of the vanquished state until she could do so herself is a new and interesting concept in International Law.

After the ratification of the treaty, Japan made tremendous strides in rebuilding her defense forces. Consequently, it became apparent that responsibility for her own security should be returned to her. Japan's status as a coequal with the United States in matters of mutual defense is reflected in the Secutrity Treaty between the two countries that was signed in Washington, D.C., on 19 January 1960 (*see* Appendix Q) and renewed in 1970.

COMMUNIST ATTITUDE TOWARDS COLLECTIVE DEFENSE

A few observations on the attitude of communist countries, especially the Soviet Union, toward the collective defense network of the Western Powers may be of interest.

There can be no disagreement on the validity of regional security organizations because the United Nations explicitly recognizes and encourages them. However, the Soviet Union maintained for a long time that collective defense agreements such as the North Atlantic Treaty Organization constituted violations of the principles of the United Nations charter. Starting with the generally recognized principle of individual and collective self-defense, as accepted in Article 51 of the charter, the Soviet Union argued that self-defense did not arise until an actual attack had taken place: collective defense agreements, therefore, could only be poorly disguised agreements for the preparation of aggressive war.

As was pointed out in the discussion of the principle of self-defense, a state is not obliged to defer defensive action until an actual attack has taken place. Given the range and effectiveness of modern weapons, a state must, of necessity, be permitted to prepare itself against possible attack. If it were prohibited from making an agreement on collective defense until it was attacked, the probabilities are that such an agreement would be of little, if any, value. No one disputes today that the right of collective self-defense includes the right to agree *in advance* on what collective action will be taken in the event of an attack. Only thus can the principle of collective self-defense provide sufficient deterrence effectively to secure international peace. The communist countries changed their position on this point and, in May 1955, formed a collective defense alliance of their own, the Warsaw Pact, which parallels the North Atlantic Treaty Organization.

SPECIALIZED AGENCIES

In addition to regional international organizations dealing with mutual security, there is a variety of other international organizations, the more important of which merit brief mention insofar as they relate to the oceans. Such organizations are usually referred to as "specialized agencies" of the United Nations.

The International Oceanographic Commission, a subordinate body of the United Nations Educational, Scientific, and Cultural Organization, is headquartered in Paris. It serves as the focal point for the acquisition of knowledge about the oceans through scientific research. At its annual meetings, the world's foremost oceanographers meet for the purpose of increasing and coordinating ocean research for the benefit of all countries.

Within the Food and Agriculture Organization, headquartered in Rome, there is a large fisheries department which is guided by the Committee on Fisheries, membership in which is open to all members of the Food and Agriculture Organization. The committee is concerned with the development and conservation of fisheries throughout the world, with emphasis on assisting developing countries to meet their expanding needs for protein from the oceans.

Some of the activities of the Intergovernmental Maritime Consultative Organization, headquartered in London, have been described elsewhere in this text. Established in 1948, its primary functions are consultative and advisory. All aspects of maritime safety come under its purview.

The primary function of the World Meteorological Organization, with headquarters in Geneva, is to study the factors that control weather, including the interaction between the atmosphere and the oceans.

In addition to the ocean-oriented international organizations connected with the United Nations there are other multilateral organizations, whose primary purpose is focused on the oceans and their resources. Of importance to those who use the seas are the international fishery commissions, established under treaty, whose function is the conservation of various fisheries throughout the world, and the various organizations concerned with pollution and the environmental aspects of particular bodies of water, such as the Mediterranean.

THE EUROPEAN ECONOMIC COMMUNITY

The European Economic Community is still another type of international organization, its primary purpose being the economic integration of the nine European countries that comprise its membership. The member countries have granted to a body known as the European Commission certain competences that normally flow only from sovereignty. For instance, they permit it to enter into negotiations on international fisheries and even to conclude bilateral and multilateral fishery arrangements in its own name and right, on behalf of its member nations. The United States has a fisheries agreement with the European Commission, rather than with its member states. The European Economic Community, through its commission, is a member in full standing of the North Atlantic Fisheries Organization, and recently participated in the negotiation of the Convention for Antarctic Marine Living Resources.

Regional economic-integration organizations are a new, unique, and very important type of international organization which will have a profound impact on international affairs in the coming years.

12 International Instruments— Enforcement

A treaty is a contract between independent nations, depending for the enforcement of its provisions on the interests and honor of the governments which are parties to it. If these fail, its infractions become the subject of international negotiations and reclamations, as far as the injured chooses to seek redress, which may in the end be enforced by actual war.
Edye *v.* Robertson

INTERNATIONAL INSTRUMENTS

The first chapter of this text touched briefly on some of the sources of International Law: (1) the great body of customary law which develops slowly through the ages and finds written expression in the work of publicists and in codifications; (2) the decisions of international and national courts and other law-making bodies; and (3) treaties, agreements, and conventions. Into this last category fall also the less formal instruments of international diplomacy, such as exchanges of notes, protocols, and minutes of understanding. Collectively, the instruments are referred to as *international instruments.*

Treaty law, frequently referred to as "particular International Law," is distinguished from customary, or general, International Law by the fact that the former is binding only upon the states that are parties to the treaty concerned, whereas the latter is binding upon all states.

The greatest advances in the creation of International Law during the last century have come from the use of international instruments. Customary law, evolving from uniform and constant usage, is slow in the making and does not readily meet the economic and political needs of an ever-changing society of states. Consequently, the world community now relies heavily on the use of international instruments, which provide a more convenient and definite method of creating new law. As noted in Chapter 7, the expanding body of air and space law is an excellent example of the extensive use of treaties.

While the word *treaty* (frequently used as a synonym for international instruments as a whole) conveys the popular concept of a binding instrument between two or more countries, the types of agreements mentioned above can be considered to be equally binding. There are many more international instruments of various forms than there are ratified treaties. As a matter of fact, even an oral agreement between heads of states, their foreign ministers, or other bona fide representatives, can create binding obligations and duties between states.

Who Can Make International Instruments

Sovereign states have the inherent right to conduct foreign relations. They have, therefore, the capacity, collectively, to create International Law and to assume binding obligations imposed by treaties and other international instruments.

Some self-governing colonies, protectorates, and international organizations, like the United Nations, also have the capacity to enter into agreements, although their right to do so is usually limited. Of particular interest to a naval officer is the fact that, while he is in command, he may make agreements binding on his country, such as a temporary truce to bury the dead and care for the wounded.

Treaties are considered to be binding under the rule of customary International Law, which states that they must be executed. This rule, in turn, rests upon the principle of good faith, which underlies the entire body of International Law. Good faith, of course, is applicable not only in relations between great powers; it is a vital part of living with a neighbor, whether that neighbor be a foreign state or the man across the street.

Duration of International Instruments

Most treaties and other international instruments include a clause stating the duration for which they are to be effective; methods for renewal, amendment, and revision are also usually incorporated. If there is no clause giving a specific duration, the instrument is considered to be effective indefinitely. If methods of revision or amendment are provided, the consent of all the signatories is usually required for both procedures.

Some authorities propose that treaties, particularly political ones, be concluded with the tacit understanding or reservation that they will be binding only as long as the circumstances that surrounded their making remain unchanged. If the initial circumstances changed, then the treaties would automatically lapse. Needless to say, if that principle were accepted, the entire body of treaty law would be undermined, because no one would be able to determine whether a treaty was binding or not at any given time. For example, circumstances have certainly changed since Russia sold Alaska to the United States, yet both countries adhere strictly to the provisions of the treaty that establish the boundary line separating Alaska and the Aleutians from Siberia. The majority of states have on numerous occasions rejected the faulty principle of conditional treaty obligation and have reaffirmed the basic rule that an international instrument can be changed or abrogated only by the consent of the parties to it.

CREATION OF AN INTERNATIONAL INSTRUMENT

Obviously, an international treaty or agreement is not consummated by a sudden decision on the part of the contracting states; its exact scope must be spelled out in precise language. While two or more countries may agree in principle to do a certain thing, it takes a long time to translate principles into specific written commitments. This procedure applies when solutions to domestic problems must be reduced to writing. In 1967 the Pennsylvania Railroad and New York Central Railroad companies agreed in principle to merge their assets and form one company. However, it took well over two years to draw up the contracts embodying the specific terms of the agreement. Almost any daily newspaper contains a news item reporting the delays encountered in hammering out a contract between a labor union and a particular company. Several months pass before the contract is in a form acceptable to both parties. With these examples in mind, it may be easier to visualize the difficulties involved in negotiating agreements between sovereign states.

When two or more countries want to make an agreement between themselves, they intend that it not only reflect national interests, but they also want it to be an international instrument that is agreeable to both and will stand the test of time. The goal of such efforts is a *particular constitution* that will bind them together in a specific area of their relations. For example, when the United States signs a fisheries agreement with Japan, both parties want that agreement to be a particular constitution governing that specific relationship. Perhaps the most notable particular constitution is the treaty of friendship between Portugal and Great Britain; is was signed in the fifteenth century and remains valid today.

Final clauses of a compact generally set forth the procedures for its entering into force, the requirement for ratification, eligibility for accession, and the languages considered as authentic texts. It can take a long time for a multilateral convention to go into force because most states are inclined to move at a measured pace in arriving at a decision whether to ratify or not. For example, it took an average of five and one-half years for the necessary twenty-two states to ratify the four Law of the Sea Conventions of 1958 and bring the individual conventions into force.

At this writing (the summer of 1980), the delegates to the Third Law of the Sea Conference have yet to reach a consensus on its final clauses. Obviously, a key question is how many states will be required to ratify before the convention can come into force and be binding on the world community. Experience shows that it might be many years before the requisite number of states ratify. (The draft Law of the Sea articles of September 1980 indicate sixty.)

MILITARY AGREEMENTS

Since the close of World War II there has been a great expansion in the number of U.S. military bases in foreign territory. The agreements involved are known as *base-rights agreements*. Naval officers should be familiar with the way the United States goes about obtaining such agreements.

For example, the planning staff of the Office of the Chief of Naval Operations determines that it would be advantageous to establish a U.S. base at a particular port in Turkey (and Turkey agrees in principle). The chief of naval operations (CNO) then forwards the proposal to the Joint Chiefs of Staff (JCS), one of whose major functions is to integrate and supervise all strategic planning. They, therefore, examine the CNO's decision in conjunction with strategic proposals for that area submitted by the army and the air force. If the JCS concur with the proposal and find that it fits in with the overall strategic plan, they so notify the CNO. Upon receipt of this approval, the Office of the Chief of Naval Operations, in close coordination with the army and the air force, begins to work out the physical requirements of the base: the air force might want to put in a fighter strip and the army might want a repair facility for automotive equipment. When the basic requirements have been agreed upon, the following step-by-step procedure has to be followed before the final agreement is signed:

1. An inspection team is sent to Turkey, with the consent of the Turkish government, to examine the port in question. The team is concerned particularly with the suitability of the port and the availability of land to meet the requirements that the new base must satisfy.
2. The results of this on-site inspection are analyzed. The analysts must be satisfied that the physical characteristics of the port and its surrounding land meet the agreed-upon requirements, and, conversely, that the requirements fit the physical characteristics of the port. When these two controlling factors are integrated, the result represents, in essence, the basis upon which the U.S. government will approach the Turkish government. By now, the United States knows what it will require in the way of land, rights, and other privileges, and Turkey knows what it can expect in return.
3. A rough draft of the proposed agreement is then drawn up—it might be prepared by the CNO, by the CinC, U.S. Naval Forces, Europe, (because the country involved is within his area), or by the International Law Division of the Judge Advocate General's office (JAG). It sets out the physical requirements of the base, and proposes articles concerning

jurisdiction over persons, claims, mail, commissary arrangements, financial matters, and so forth. The draft is then circulated throughout the interested agencies of the three services for comment and revision, and conferences are held to air differences of opinion and to find mutually satisfactory answers to them. At these conferences, the Navy Department has in attendance a representative of the CNO for matters of policy, representatives of technical commands for technical matters, and a legal officer from the International Law Division, JAG, for legal matters. When complete agreement is reached among the services, a smooth draft of the proposed agreement is drawn up and forwarded to the Department of State via the Department of Defense. An accompanying letter requests the Secretary of State to open discussions with the Turkish government on the subject of the proposed naval base.

4. At this stage in the proceedings the representatives of the services meet with Department of Defense and Department of State representatives to examine the political and economic factors involved in the proposed agreement. When accord is reached, the draft agreement is forwarded to the American ambassador in Ankara. Simultaneously, a team of negotiators from the Departments of State and Defense is readied to go to Ankara to conduct the actual negotiations under the control of the ambassador. Since the agreement is of primary interest to the navy, the negotiating team may include several naval officers. It is because negotiations of this nature call for special qualifications that a certain number of officers from the offices of the CNO and JAG attend postgraduate schools for training in International Law and diplomacy.

5. When the ambassador notifies the Departments of State and Defense that the Turkish government is ready to begin talks, the negotiating team, after a final briefing, goes to Ankara to start conversations with representatives of the Turkish government.

The agreement reached might be an annex to an umbrella-type agreement previously negotiated between the United States and Turkey, authorizing the United States to establish specified bases and facilities; it might be a government-to-government agreement or memorandum of understanding; or it might be an agreement executed between the two navies.

In the course of negotiations, it is not unusual for impasses to arise over particular points which eventually must be agreed upon. This development is to be expected, because both sides are striving to further their own national interests, while remaining within the framework of the agreement in principle.

Suppose, for example, it is agreed that a dock is to be built at the proposed naval base. The U.S. position is that the Turkish Navy should build it with its money and men, and the Turkish government's position is that it should be built with U.S. money and manpower. Obviously, if both governments remain inflexible, the dock will never be built. The job of the negotiators is to find a formula within the spirit of the agreement that will make it possible for the dock to be built under conditions acceptable to both contracting governments. The variations between the two opposing positions are innumerable. The U.S. team may propose that the Turks furnish the manpower and the United States the money, or vice versa. The Turks may offer the counterproposal that manpower and costs be split fifty-fifty, or that the material be furnished by one and the manpower and costs be split to reflect that furnishing of material. Eventually the negotiators agree on a formula, and the clauses incorporating it are forwarded to both governments for their approval. If the results are acceptable, the negotiators go on to the next point. If the results are not acceptable to their respective governments, the negotiators must keep on trying until mutual agreement is reached.

When full accord is reached, the agreement in its final form, written in both languages, is duly signed by the authorized representative of each government, and it becomes a binding contract between the two countries.

ENFORCEMENT

In the section on the creation of an international instrument, we stated that, upon signature, the two countries had entered into a binding contract or agreement. This brings into focus the immediate issue: how binding is an agreement between countries? In the internal or domestic law of practically all countries, a contract between persons and between corporations is binding because courts are available to enforce the law of contracts. The same thesis does not always apply to international agreements. Therefore, on what basis can an agreement be said to be binding? The question can be broadened by stating an oft-spoken idea: the whole body of International Law is good in concept but it is of no significance because it cannot be enforced.

The preceding eleven chapters have provided indications that International Law is enforceable, perhaps not in its entirety, but nevertheless it is enforceable. What makes it enforceable? What agencies or methods provide International Law with vitality and validity? What makes the states of the world tend to stay within its rules?

Before examining various methods of enforcement, it is instructive to note the graphic presentation of the problem in the following excerpt from a lecture delivered at the Naval War College on 20 August 1958 by Richard R. Baxter, of the Harvard University Law School, and subsequently a justice on the International Court of Justice:

To many, it seems incredible that a body of rules purporting to govern the conduct of nations but providing no sanctions or punishment for their violation should be called law at all. It is not altogether fair to speak of international law as a sanctionless body of law, for the great numbers of cases in which damages have been awarded and paid and in which individuals have been punished for criminal violations of the law of nations bear witness to the contrary. The single category of cases in which civil damages have been most commonly granted are those arising out of wrongs done by States to aliens. Criminal penalties, leaving aside such exceptional offenses as piracy, have been reserved for violations of the law of war, which resemble the normal crimes punishable under national legal systems to such a degree that some countries have even tried war criminals under their ordinary penal codes. Yet a third type of satisfaction exists in international law—the apology or rendering of honors or other admission of violation of the law. One should not scoff at these symbolic acts. They constitute outward and visible signs of what should be the correct relationships between the parties and the proper principle of law to be applied in the future.

But, you justifiably object, what force is there to compel a State to pay the damages which have been assessed against it, or to render up its nationals for trial by a foreign court, or to admit the impropriety or illegality of its conduct in a particular case? Admittedly, there is no international sheriff armed with power to see that judgments are enforced or that the parties appear before an international tribunal in the first place. But it is easy to overemphasize the importance of the sanction. A superior court has no forceful means at its disposal to compel obedience to its mandate by a subordinate court. If a court directs a command to the executive which goes unheeded, what means has it of compelling that obedience? You may remember the words attributed to President Jackson: "Well, John Marshall has made his decision, now let him enforce it!" A comparative statistical analysis of the number of divisions available to the Pope and to the United States Supreme Court would not be difficult to make. And if a hillbilly called to high political office voices contempt for the law of the land and allows the mob to rule within his jurisdiction, can the sanction of employing loyal troops solve this problem of subversion? Sanctions, as we commonly think of them, seem to belong to the normal day-to-day enforcement of the law. The great edifice of our constitutional system is held together not by the fear of duress if the law be violated, but by a common devotion and loyalty to the law by those charged with its making and its application.

Moreover, as I mentioned some minutes ago, it is not the law alone, in the form of a fear of criminal penalty or or of civil damages, which secures compliance with law. Morality, taboos, social pressure, the views of the community, and religion are amongst the forces allied with the threat of penalty or damages in securing compliance with law.

It would thus appear that the sanction behind the sanction in national law is the sense of the community *that it should be governed by the rule of law*. It is that basic sanction which is very largely lacking in the international sphere. It is not altogether absent, however, for if it were the world would be in a state of anarchy. The extent of the conviction in favor of subjection to law varies from country to country, from international relationship to international relationship, from legal principle to legal principle, and from case to case. With many countries of the world, the United States has a vast network of agreements, which are carried out on a routine basis, although differences of views as to interpretation may arise from time to time. The United States can carry on discussions with Great Britain or France or Switzerland or Japan in terms of international law, and both parties can make themselves understood. We—and I speak here of a responsibility all Americans bear through our senators—are, on the other hand, unwilling to concede to the International Court of Justice compulsory jurisdiction over disputes with those States with which we have the closest affinities of law, tradition, interest, and security. In their public pronouncements, our principal ministers are fiercely dedicated to the rule of law and in steadfast opposition to international sin. In its actual conduct in particular cases, this country frequently shows itself as zealous to preserve its sovereignty—which is a polite way of saying being a law unto itself—as other major powers.

PACIFIC PROCEDURES

World Opinion

World opinion plays an important role in the enforcement of International Law. Writing in 1908, Secretary of State Elihu Root made this point effectively by drawing an analogy between the community of nations and the small neighborhood community familiar to everyone:

> Why is it that nations are thus continually yielding to arguments with no apparent compulsion behind them, and before the force of such arguments abandoning purposes, modifying conduct, and giving redress for injuries? A careful consideration of this question seems to lead to the conclusion that the difference between municipal and international law, in respect of the existence of forces compelling obedience, is more apparent than real, and that there are sanctions for the enforcement of international law no less real and substantial than those which secure obedience to municipal law.
>
> It is a mistake to assume that the sanction which secures obedience to the laws of the state consist exclusively or chiefly of the pains and penalties imposed by the law itself for its violation. It is only in exceptional cases that men refrain from crime through fear of fine or imprisonment. *In the vast majority of cases men refrain from criminal conduct because they are unwilling to incur in the community in which they live the public condemnation and obloquy which would follow a repudiation of the standard of conduct prescribed by that community for its members* (emphasis supplied).

In this same connection President Taft declared that

either the utilitarian spirit, or perhaps a real conscience in all nations, has ultimately brought about a sanction for what we call international law, with-

out any power to enforce it, but simply from the general public opinion of all
the peoples of the world. Begun by individuals, reasoned from their own
consciences and from their own sense of justice, without any power to enforce
their opinions, and finally but reluctantly adopted by nations by common
consent, the history of the growth of international law may well command our
admiration, our wonder, and our hope for a growth in the scope and sanction
of such law in the future that should make us all optimists.

Speaking to the American Bar Association in October 1955, Herman
Phleger, at one time the legal adviser to the Department of State, stated:

> We would be naive to think that peace can be assured by words of
> agreement. Behind those words there must be good faith, and resolution, and
> dedication to the cause of peace. It behooves us all to add our moral and
> material support to these efforts to preserve peace.
>
> International law has been described as law without a constitution. In the
> absence of effective juridical sanction, world opinion—aptly described in the
> Declaration of Independence as "a decent respect of the opinions of man-
> kind"—remains the most effective means of preventing aggressive war.

These observations apply today just as they did in 1908 and earlier, but
with increased meaning. Advances in world communications and the public
forum available in the United Nations have broadened the scope of understanding throughout the world. A departure by any state from the normal
conduct of international relations receives immediate attention. If the conduct is contrary to International Law, the guilty state is soundly condemned
by the community of states. In November 1979 when Iranian students in
Tehran violated the immunity of the U.S. embassy there and seized as
hostages more than sixty Americans, the world community, through individual petitions and declarations and collectively through the United Nations, condemned Iran. Clearly, release of the hostages on 20 January 1981
was prompted in large part by the increasing isolation of Iran in the world
community. Similarly, when an individual sees that his conduct brings down
on him uniform disfavor in his own community, his strong tendency is to
alter or modify his conduct so that he may receive the approval of his fellow
men. World opinion today produces the same result in the world community; it is a valid sanction or method of enforcing International Law.

Mutuality of Interest

The fact that International Law is not necessarily enforced or supported
by a concrete and superior power does not mean that the world community
could not, if it so desired, create a superior authority with power to enforce
the rules of International Law. Several efforts in this direction have already
been noted in this text—the defunct League of Nations and the present
United Nations within the limits of its charter.

Until a superior authority such as the United Nations is given the power
to act for the *entire* society of states, the effectiveness and enforcement of

International Law will depend in large measure upon mutuality of interest among states. The nations find it to their individual interest to take measures to prevent, for example, the spread of disease and the misuse of habit-forming drugs. Since they realize that a joint effort is much more satisfactory than several independent efforts, they have bound themselves together to control these dangers. A state that did not enter such a relationship would bring hardship on itself because it could not alone control the dangers as effectively as can be done by joint actions of all the states. It follows then that mutuality of interest and convenience make it worthwhile for states to obey the law.

Each state tends to obey the rules of International Law in anticipation that other states will do the same thing. While deviation from International Law might yield momentary advantages to one state, in the long run it would be counterproductive if it served to encourage other states to depart from the accepted mode of behavior. Such a development would be contrary to the long-term interest of all states in establishing a stable pattern of interstate relations. Therefore, even when observing the obligations of International Law seems to be temporarily disadvantageous, the inclination is to observe it in the expectation that other states will reciprocate and comply with it even when doing so causes them to be similarly disadvantaged.

Like world opinion, mutuality of interest does not stem from any concrete superior power; yet it is an effective instrument in the enforcement of International Law.

Nondecisional Procedures

Nondecisional procedures for the pacific settlement of disputes include diplomatic negotiation, good offices, mediation, and conciliation. They are based on voluntary participation by the states that are parties to the dispute, and they are nondecisional because accord is not necessarily reached. The primary purpose of these procedures is to bring the contesting states together to examine the International Law in question as a step towards reaching a settlement. In diplomatic negotiations and enquiries, only the contesting states participate; in good offices, mediation, and conciliation, a third state acts as a neutral agent, or go-between, to help the disputing states to reach agreement. An example is the agreement reached between Argentina and Chile in January 1979 to submit their highly emotional dispute over the Beagle Channel to mediation by a representative of the pope.

Although nondecisional procedures are frequently used to good effect, their very name shows that they lack an essential element—the requirement to come to a decision.

Decisional Procedures

Whereas nondecisional procedures give no assurance that a settlement will be reached, decisional procedures of arbitration and adjudication contain that assurance. As is the case with nondecisional procedures, arbitration and adjudication depend on the disputing states' consent to participate. They imply that the disputants will accept the decision or judgment as binding, regardless of what it might be. Decisional procedures are occasionally incorporated into treaties and other international instruments. Obviously, they provide ready machinery for the rapid settlement of disputes. Furthermore, the judgments are not influenced by political factors because, in the hands of experienced jurists, the state with the stronger legal case will win, no matter what its size or power.

Sovereign states are sometimes reluctant to commit themselves to settlement by arbitration and adjudication, particularly when the dispute is in the areas of politics and sovereignty. There have, however, been several instances of states agreeing to the settlement of disputes through compulsory procedures. At this writing (summer 1980), Canada and the United States are trying to settle their long-standing dispute over the maritime boundary in the Gulf of Maine either by submission of the case to the International Court of Justice or by arbitration (see Chapter 3). On a multilateral basis, while the delegates to the Third Law of the Sea Conference agree that parties to the convention should seek peaceful means of resolving disputes over the use of the oceans, they are wrestling with the question of which possible disputes will be settled by adjudication or arbitration. At this time, it is clear that many issues will be subject to decisional procedures—such a mandatory system of settling disputes, as envisioned in the draft Law of the Sea treaty, is a significant contribution to the rule of law.

Speaking at the Naval War College's International Law Seminar in 1955, Leo Gross, of the Fletcher School of Law and Diplomacy, stressed the difficulties involved in settling disputes by arbitration and adjudication:

> The Soviet Union has been consistently unwilling to agree to the arbitration or adjudication of any dispute. Thus both the Soviet Union and Communist Hungary declined to submit to the jurisdiction of the International Court of Justice in the proceedings which the United States attempted to institute on 3 March 1954 in regard to the treatment in Hungary of an American aircraft and crew. The Court, by orders of 12 July 1954, found that in view of this refusal it could take no further steps upon the American applications.
>
> Some 32 states, of whom 30 are members of the United Nations, have accepted the jurisdiction of the International Court of Justice as compulsory for legal disputes concerning:
> a. The interpretation of a treaty;
> b. Any question of International Law;
> c. The existence of any fact which, if established, would constitute a breach of International Law;
> d. The nature or extent of the reparation to be made for the breach of an international obligation.
> Compulsory jurisdiction, in this context, means that a dispute may be

brought before and decided by the Court by means of a unilateral application by one of the parties, provided that both parties have accepted the jurisdiction of the Court. To guard against any extensive use of the compulsory jurisdiction of the Court, the states which consented to this compulsory jurisdiction for the four classes of disputes, have attached reservations to their declarations of acceptance. The legal as well as the political effect of such reservations is to restrict the consent given and thus to exclude certain types of disputes from the compulsory jurisdiction of the Court. The reservations usually exclude disputes arising out of war or out of matters which are within the domestic jurisdiction of States. The United States made the latter reservation in unusually strong terms by stipulating that it is for the United States, and by implication not for the Court, to decide whether or not a concrete dispute arises out of a matter which is essentially within the domestic jurisdiction of the United States.

The International Court of Justice will, however, accept a case in which one of the parties takes the position that the issue is domestic and, therefore, beyond its jurisdiction. Such was the situation on 29 November 1979, when the United States brought action against Iran for the seizure of hostages and of the embassy premises in Tehran. Before the action began, Iran denied that the court had authority. Nevertheless, the court proceeded and passed judgment, even though Iran send no representatives to the proceedings. The unanimous decision handed down on 15 December 1979 included the comment:

By not appearing in the present proceedings, the government of Iran, by its own choice, deprives itself of the opportunity of developing its own argument before the Court.

On the merits of the case, the International Court of Justice found in part:

There is no more fundamental prerequisite for the conduct of relations between states than the inviolability of diplomatic envoys and embassies, so that throughout history, nations of all creeds and cultures have observed reciprocal obligations for that purpose. The obligations to assure personal safety of diplomats and their freedom from persecution are essential, unqualified and inherent in their representative character and their diplomatic function.

The court directed that Iran

should ensure the immediate release, without any exception, of all persons of United States nationality who are or have been held in the embassy of the United States of America or in the ministry of foreign affairs in Tehran.

It further found that Iran

should immediately ensure that the premises of the United States Embassy, chancery and consulates be restored to the possession of the United States authorities under their exclusive control [and protect them].

Despite the fact that the decision was not directly binding on Iran because of its reservation, the action of the International Court of Justice laid the legal and moral groundwork for any other actions that might be found necessary. One further action was taken on 7 April 1980 when the United States broke diplomatic relations with Iran.

Obviously, when states opt to create impediments to the jurisdiction of the International Court of Justice, the settlement of international disputes is hindered. On the other hand, all states want to have the highest degree of control over their own destiny. No common medium for facilitating compulsory international decisional procedures and lessening the fears of individual states has yet been found. The principle of the rule of law dictates that such a medium be found.

National Law

In the Constitution of the United States, Congress is given the power "to define and punish Piracies and Felonies committed on the high seas, and Offenses against the Law of Nations." The word *define* is here synonymous with *legislate* and the word *punish* is synonymous with *judicial proceedings*, and Congress has seen fit to legislate into federal law many of the rules of International Law. In fact, if U.S. federal law on foreign relations, ships, and the high seas were to be examined, it would be found that most of it contains some facet of International Law. When statutes are drafted and enacted by Congress, they are applicable within the United States just as is any law that deals with a local or national problem. If someone disobeys such a law, he is subject to trial and punishment before a federal court. Note that this is a compulsory procedure. When a defendant is brought into a federal court, there is no question of prior consent or voluntary acceptance of jurisdiction. The law of the United States is backed by the power necessary to make it effective.

In other sovereign states also International Law is translated into national or federal law. Once a provision of International Law becomes national statutory law, national courts enforce it. In proceedings before national courts throughout the world there is a common enforcement of International Law based, not on acquiescence, but on the legal authority of the nation concerned.

When a case involving International Law is brought before a national court, the law applied may come from the great body of customary International Law or, if appropriate, from a treaty. The comment of the U.S. Supreme Court in the *Paquete Habana* case, already quoted in Chapter 1, is worth repetition:

> Where there is no treaty, and no controlling executive or legislative act or judicial decision, resort must be had to the customs and usages of civilized nations; and, as evidence of these, to the works of jurists and commentators,

who by years of labor, research, and experience, have made themselves peculiarly well acquainted with the subjects of which they treat. Such works are resorted to by judicial tribunals, not for the speculations of their authors concerning what the law ought to be, but for trustworthy evidence of what the law really is.

It follows, then, that the translation of International Law into national law by specific legislation is *not* a prerequisite to the enforcement of International Law by national courts.

Measures of Self-Help

All the preceding methods of enforcing International Law are known as *pacific procedures*. The following, identified as measures of self-help, are in an entirely different category; they involve the threat or use of force as a means of enforcing International Law. An injured state resorts to them when a dispute cannot be solved by pacific procedures.

Intervention

The theory of intervention was concisely stated by Leo Gross in his lecture quoted in part above:

> The term intervention has a variety of meanings. It may mean any kind of action, usually in the territory of another state, which a Government takes in order to assure the fulfillment by that State of the duties which that state owes to the intervening Government. Notably they comprise the duty within the State's territory to protect the integrity and inviolability of other States and the duty to treat aliens in accordance with the international standard. Intervention of this kind involves the application of force and has been resorted to on numerous occasions.
>
> The right to resort to intervention as a measure of self-help has recently been severely criticized by the International Court of Justice in the Corfu Channel Case. . . . After its ships were damaged in the Corfu Channel on 22 October 1946, the British Government on 12 and 13 November 1946 dispatched some minesweepers to the area which it will be recalled, was within the territorial waters of Albania. Although Albania protested, the minesweeping operation was nevertheless carried out in order to secure the *corpora delicti*. The Albanian Government charged that the British Government had thereby violated its sovereignty. The British Government justified its action, first, as an application of the theory of intervention and, secondly, as a method of self-protection or self-help. The Court rejected both arguments.
>
> On this point judgment was given unanimously. Referring to the defense based on the theory of intervention, the Court said:
>
> "The Court can only regard the alleged right of intervention as the manifestation of a policy of force, such as has, in the past, given rise to most serious abuses and such as cannot, whatever be the present defects in International Organization, find a place in International Law. Intervention is

perhaps still less admissible in the particular form it would take here; for, from the nature of things, it would be reserved for the most powerful States, and might easily lead to perverting the administration of international justice itself."

And referring to the defense based on the theory of self-protection or self-help, the Court said:

"The Court cannot accept this defense either. Between independent States, respect for territorial sovereignty is an essential foundation of international relations. The Court recognizes that the Albanian Government's complete failure to carry out its duties after the explosions, and the dilatory nature of its diplomatic notes, are extenuating circumstances for the action of the United Kingdom Government. But to ensure respect for International Law, of which it is the organ, the Court must declare that the action of the British Navy constituted a violation of Albanian sovereignty." (Corfu Channel Case, International Court of Justice, April 1949).

On this point judgment was accordingly given unanimously in favor of Albania. There is probably solid ground for the Court's view that intervention as a form of self-help has been abused in the past and that by its very nature it is the kind of proceeding which is open to more powerful states for use against weak or weaker States.

Reprisals

The use of reprisals to enforce International Law was noted in Chapter 10. To expand that discussion, the authoritative statement of Leo Gross is again relevant:

Self-help may also take the form of reprisal. The difference between intervention, as defined above, and reprisal is not very sharp. The latter is generally defined as an action by an injured State against a wrong-doing state. In taking this action a State is usually resorting to measures which, looked at by themselves, are contrary to International Law. They are nevertheless permitted if and only to the extent that they have been provoked by another State's violation of International Law. In order to be lawful, in addition to the justification, reprisals must satisfy two further conditions: first, they must have been preceded by a request for redress (*Sommation*) which has been unavailing; and, secondly, they must be proportionate to the offense.

In actual practice, particularly in case of wartime reprisals, these conditions are not always fulfilled. Usually there is a protest against the offense and a request for redress. If these remain unheeded, States feel free to take reprisals, provided, of course, that they are in a position to do so. Here the element of power, as pointed out by the International Court of Justice in the Corfu Channel Case, becomes of decisive significance. The element of proportionality between offense and reprisal is perhaps not generally accepted. . . .

Two observations are in order at this point: the first is that disputes involving the question of the legality of reprisals rarely come before international tribunals for adjudication. The second is that, in the absence of an authoritative decision, each state involved in this sort of incident determines for itself the facts, the applicable law and the extent and nature of the reprisals which it deems appropriate. Of course, such unilateral determinations lack legal force and in particular, are not in any sense binding upon the other State or States involved.

It can be concluded from the above statement that, as a method of enforcing International Law, reprisals are inherently faulty because they rest on a unilateral decision by a single state or allied states. The reprisal may be out of proportion to the initial wrongdoing. If this is the case, it only increases and broadens the dispute. However, when correctly used—and in proportion to the wrongdoing—threats of reprisals are a strong deterrent to any state that contemplates a breach of International Law. In this context, reprisals constitute an effective procedure of enforcement.

Reprisals are frequently confused with another, less-used form of self-help known as *retorsion*. As Lieutenant Commander Bruce Harlow, USN, wrote:

> *Retorsion* consists of legal but deliberately unfriendly acts with a retaliatory or coercive purpose. A common form of retorsion consists of increases in tariff rates against a country which discriminates against the products of the state taking the retorsive action. Another example is the traditional "Showing of the Flag." Though frequently called "retaliation in kind" because of the practice of states of replying to legal, but discourteous or unfriendly acts, with acts of the same character, retorsion is not limited to retaliation by the same or similar response.
>
> The point to bear in mind, in considering the law of retorsion, is that the acts thereunder must be legal without regard to the conduct of the state towards which the action is directed. ("The Legal Use of Force . . . Short of War," U.S. Naval Institute *Proceedings*, November 1966)

War

When International Law has been violated and no pacific procedure of enforcement has been of any avail to the injured country, that country may turn to intervention or reprisal in order to right the wrong. In the event that these measures of self-help do not result in compliance with International Law, there is one last resort: war or the threat of war, the ultimate sanction or measure that a country may take. Like intervention or reprisal, it has the inherent weakness of being a unilateral decision usually backed by superior physical power.

Unfortunately, the threat of war has also been used as a primary instrument of national policy. This device can be likened to a property-owner threatening to take physical action against a neighbor who indicates that he will continue to trespass. In both cases—neighbor against neighbor and state against state—the threat of physical conflict acts as a deterrent; it is the enforcement of law by threat of maximum injury. War itself is simply the execution of that threat.

It is not the purpose of this text to examine in detail the use of war as a means of enforcement. Suffice it to say that war has been so used in the past. In his address quoted above, Herman Phleger provided a succinct outline of the problem:

> One of the paradoxes of our time is that while the overwhelming majority of mankind abhors war, it has not been possible as yet to achieve a just and lasting peace. [It has been estimated that between 1496 BC and AD 1861 there were a total of 3,130 years of war.] The prospect, in this atomic age, that the next war might result in annihilating mankind points to the urgency of finding a solution for this problem.

> While undue optimism is to be avoided, and the failures are fresh in our memory, it is worthy of note that significant progress has been made in the past 60 years in the concept of collective security and the renunciation of aggressive war. We should not permit the failures to obscure the successes, for, if we are to build a system of collective security that will be effective in the future, it must be upon the foundations that have been laid since the beginning of this century.

> Indeed, if we compare the situation today with that of a scant 50 years ago, the progress has been significant.

> Fifty years ago war was accepted as a perfectly legitimate instrument of national policy. Learned writers in the field of International Law asserted its legality. Collective efforts were largely confined to ameliorating the harsh conditions of war—agreeing on the rules of the game, so to speak. The Hague Conventions on land and naval warfare, the Red Cross Convention, and the later Geneva Conventions regulating the treatment of prisoners of war represented efforts of the world community to make war endurable, since its abolition seemed impossible.

Today, states have renounced war as an instrument of national policy. Leo Gross says:

> For centuries States have employed war as an instrument of national policy with varying success. They have, for good reason, renounced war as an instrument of policy, for in the twentieth century war tends to escape the hands of statesmen and run its course. The task of diplomacy, then, is to make this renunciation effective, through the United Nations if possible, through other media if necessary. As this task is progressively achieved, international law will increasingly become an effective basis for the peaceful coexistence of States. The alternative is co-destruction which for the first time seems to have become a substantial possibility.

It would be less than realistic to suggest that war, as an instrument of policy that has been used by all the countries of the world, is now a matter of history. Wars are in progress at this writing, but there are signs that the world community is turning more and more to peaceful procedures for settling disputes. Among the many severe disputes that arose in the 1960s and 1970s and were settled by arbitration or agreement are: the Rann of Kutch dispute between India and Pakistan; a territorial dispute between Argentina and Chile; a dispute between Indonesia and The Netherlands regarding West Irian; a dispute over the North Sea Continental Shelf; an Anglo-French dispute over the boundary of the English Channel; and a dispute between Egypt and Israel.

CONCLUSION

It can be seen that there is little similarity between the enforcement of International Law and the enforcement of national law. It can be seen also that, although there are gaps and processes are not always smooth, International Law is enforceable and has, for the most part, been enforced. In an article entitled "Fancies vs. Facts," the noted scholar, Arthur Larson, comments:

> It is a misconception that even though it is clear that power or the threat of power in the form of diplomacy is not solving current disputes, nations cannot bring themselves to accept settlement of their important disputes by peaceful means such as arbitration and adjudication. The actual fact of history is that nations have repeatedly submitted important controversies involving high interests and high public excitement to peaceful settlement. During the nineteenth century 177 major disputes between nations were resolved by arbitration, including seventy-nine to which the United States was a party. It will not do to explain this away by saying that nations only submit unimportant issues to arbitration. No type of controversy between nations is more emotion-packed than a boundary dispute, a dispute over territory. Yet Norway, to give one example of an international adjudication, gave up East Greenland to Denmark as the result of a court decision. In the last few years, boundary disputes important enough to provoke armed conflict between Nicaragua and Honduras, and between Cambodia and Thailand, have been settled in the World Court. As a matter of fact, adjudication or arbitration is frequently, if not usually, the only way that a hotly contested boundary argument can be settled. The reason is that no government can make a diplomatic settlement giving away the sacred soil of the motherland without political disaster at home, but a judicial settlement, reaching the same result, can be accepted, as it was in these cases, without the losing government falling.
>
> Another misconception is that since there is no world government with overwhelming military power to enforce law, nations will not pay any attention to judicial and arbitral decisions that they do not like. The fact is that the Permanent Court of International Justice never had one of its decisions disobeyed. And in the case of its successor, the International Court of Justice, there is only one record of disobedience in a contentious case. Among the hundreds, if not thousands, of other decisions, arbitral, judicial, mixed claims

commissions, and the like, there is no more than the tiniest handful of cases in which the question of non-compliance has ever been raised. (*Foreign Service Journal*, September 1967.)

In his book *Digest of International Law*, 1940, G. E. Hackworth states:

Whatever be the sanction upon which the enforcement of international law rests, its effectiveness increases as the nations of the world find it not only to their benefit but also to the benefit of the community of nations to conduct their relations according to certain generally accepted standards possible of performance and at the same time fair and reasonable.

These "accepted standards" are the rules of International Law. All nations have the choice of broadening and strengthening them. Today the world appears to have made that choice, particularly in view of the destructiveness of modern war.

Is there any real alternative?

Conspectus

The following report on the execution of the orders set forth below is intended to provide the reader with an outline of the practical application of a number of the principles in the foregoing text.

ORDERS
To: Battle Group Commander Yankee
When ready for sea, get under way, proceed to Naples, Italy, and report to Commander Sixth Fleet. En route attached nuclear-powered submarine will remain within ultra high frequency range of main body. Flight ops and destroyer exercises in accordance my Op-Order 7-80. When detached by Commander Sixth Fleet, proceed and report to Commander Seventh Fleet at established rendezvous. When released by Commander Seventh Fleet, proceed to Norfolk and report to type commanders. Liberty ports and logistic support as per my Op-Order.

In compliance with the above orders, the battle group, consisting of one carrier, one submarine, and a squadron of destroyers, got under way from Norfolk on the afternoon of 20 May. While proceeding down Lynnhaven Roads, fog set in and all ships sounded fog signals in accordance with U.S. Rules for Inland Waters (Chapter 5). Upon entering international waters, the fog gradually lifted and the battle group executed a cruising formation. Precisely at sunset, all ships lighted their navigational lights (Chapter 5). The first few days of the cruise were uneventful, except that the officer in tactical command (OTC) was not pleased with the conduct of the shakedown exercises; however, indications were that performance would improve considerably and be satisfactory before they entered the Mediterranean. On the night of 23 May, weather reports (Chapter 7) indicated a major disturbance to the northeast of the formation, and all ships battened down for heavy weather. At 0300Z on the twenty-fourth an SOS was received via the international distress frequency (Chapter 7). The ship in distress was a freighter, and she was at a point bearing 050 degrees true from the formation, 100 miles distant. She reported hatch covers ripped off and taking water. The OTC immediately dispatched a destroyer to proceed at best possible speed to render assistance and effect rescue, if necessary (Chapter 5). Upon arrival at the scene, the commanding officer of the destroyer put aboard personnel and they assisted in covering the open hatches and pumping the water out of the affected compartments. Upon completion of her mission, the destroyer returned to the formation, and the freighter proceeded to her destination.

On the morning of the twenty-fifth, the battle group was within 150 miles of the Azores and expected to pass them fifteen miles to the north, en route to Gibraltar. One of the scheduled exercises was a test of the submarine's ability to keep the battle group under surveillance throughout the day without being detected. As the exercise began, the OTC specifically warned the submarine that she would have to surface if she entered the territorial sea of the Azores (Chapter 4). Search planes from the carrier were likewise warned not to enter the territorial limit of the Azores (Chapter 7). When the exercise ended, the submarine reported that she had been able to maintain contact with the battle group more than 73 per cent of the allotted time. There were no violations of the territorial sea or air of the Azores.

On the morning of the twenty-sixth, the battle group executed a drone-firing formation. During the third firing run, the exercise was interrupted because a Danish merchantman was bearing down on the formation. The OTC maneuvered his group until she was clear of the firing range, then ordered the exercise to continue (Chapter 6).

Toward the end of the exercise, the battle group commander received a message relaying the information that the Portuguese authorities had given permission for one of the carrier planes to make a courier run in to Lisbon (Chapter 7). This clearance was requested by the staff before the group left Norfolk, because clearances for aircraft flights frequently take time. The pilot of the plane was instructed to remain overnight in Lisbon and rendez-vous with the carrier the following morning.

The transit through the Strait of Gibraltar, during which the submarine was submerged, was uneventful (Chapter 4). The Spanish authorities had notified all shipping that survey work, dangerous to navigation, would be in progress two and one-half miles south of Tarifa, Spain, during the period of transit (Chapter 4). Accordingly, the OTC ordered the screening destroyers on the port side of the formation to form column astern of the formation. As it passed Tarifa, the group saw several moored barges; upon clearing the strait, it re-formed and entered the Mediterranean.

One major exercise was held in the Mediterranean before the group went in to Naples. This was an air-defense drill, for which the Sixth Fleet furnished both combat air patrol and enemy aircraft. It proved to be an excellent exercise, because the numerous commercial airliners criss-crossing the Mediterranean provided an opportunity to test the abilities of the ships' combat information centers to distinguish between exercise and nonexercise aircraft (Chapter 5). It also provided good experience for the air controllers and pilots in ensuring safe separation between exercise aircraft and the commercial airliners. No exercises were held the day before entering Naples; all ships used that time for field day and for giving personnel final instructions on their conduct ashore in a foreign port (Chapters 5 and 8).

A division officer, with the assistance of the staff legal officer, gave one of his men advice on a personal problem. The sailor wanted permission to marry an Italian girl whom he had met on a prior cruise, and needed advice on how to make arrangements for the wedding with the local authorities in Naples, to send his wife back to the United States, and to get immigration papers for her as soon as possible (Chapter 8).

With the exception of two incidents ashore, the visit to Naples was satisfactory. The first incident was a reported brawl in a cafe, which resulted in damage to equipment. From the available facts, it appeared that the fight was instigated by three U.S. servicemen, two of whom were permanently assigned to North Atlantic Treaty Organization forces stationed in Italy (Chapter 11) and the third, a nonrated man, was attached to one of the visiting destroyers. The two men permanently assigned to duty in Italy were in the custody of the Italian police, but the third man had eluded capture. These facts were presented by the Italian police to the officer of the deck of the destroyer to which the man was assigned. The police requested that when the man returned to the ship he be turned over to their custody. The officer of the deck acknowledged this report and informed the police that he had already returned to the ship. The man was transferred to the U.S. naval command in Naples until the matter of waiver of jurisdiction had been decided (Chapter 8). In the second incident, a ship's mailman, while driving the ship's vehicle on official duty (Chapter 8) to the U.S. mail center in Naples, struck and partially destroyed a fruit vendor's wagon. The Sixth Fleet's foreign claims commission went into action and was able to pay the vendor for the damage before Battle Group Yankee left Naples (Chapter 8).

At the completion of the four-day visit, the battle group got under way with units of the Sixth Fleet to participate in classified operations in the eastern Mediterranean. As part of the exercise, two of the destroyers were designated to proceed through the Dardanelles and the Bosporus to visit Turkish ports on the Black Sea. Both ships were ordered to comply fully with the provisions of the Montreux Convention (Chapters 4 and 6). These operations lasted eleven days, at the end of which Battle Group Yankee was detached and ordered to report to Commander, Seventh Fleet, in the Pacific. The battle group transited the Suez Canal without incident (Chapter 4). As it entered the Red Sea, the narrow entrances to the Gulf of Aqaba were clearly visible (Chapter 4). One day out of Suez, it received orders to proceed to Bombay, India, for a courtesy call and logistics. Provision was made for the submarine to meet the port's strict requirements for nuclear-powered ships (Chapter 6). The arrival of Battle Group Yankee in Bombay produced some confusion, when the captains of two of the ships tried to wave off the pilot boat in order to proceed independently into port. The actions of the men in the pilot boat made it obvious that there was a misunderstanding. As a consequence, both ships stopped and the Indian pilots told their captains that under the federal law of India pilots were mandatory for the Bombay channel. After some debate, the pilots were accepted on board and the two ships proceeded to their assigned berths (Chapter 4).

The naval attaché (Chapter 2) arranged with the Indian naval authorities for officers from the U.S. ships to visit the Indian warships in the harbor.

Upon completion of the courtesy call to Bombay, the battle group put to sea and, enroute to the Persian Gulf, conducted antisubmarine-warfare exercises. On the morning of the third day of the exercises, one of the ASW search planes had engine trouble and made a forced landing at a small airstrip on the coast of Saudi Arabia (Chapter 7). The local officials assisted in finding a mechanic, and the plane rejoined the task group late in the afternoon.

When the exercise was over, all unit COs participated in a critique held in the flagship off Bahrain. Some officers asked permission to visit Baghdad but, inasmuch as they did not have passports, the request was refused (Chapter 8).

Upon departure from Bahrain, Battle Group Yankee steamed out of the Persian Gulf. The following evening, in response to the hail of a coastal dhow, one of the destroyers stopped and sent her boat over. It was learned that some six hours earlier the dhow was overtaken by another ship and stopped. Then, while the crew was held at gunpoint, her entire cargo, including a shipment of pearl oysters, was transferred to the intercepting ship, which then departed at full speed down the Gulf of Oman. The dhow's crew believed the pirate had come from the east coast of Africa. Continuing passage, the battle group searched without success for the pirate, but it notified local shipping and interested authorities of the incident (Chapter 5).

The battle group transited the Arabian Sea and rounded the southern tip of India en route to Singapore. As it passed through the 200-mile exclusive economic zone of Sri Lanka, it observed vessels from several different countries fishing. Whether the fishermen were there by agreement with Sri Lanka or were, in fact, poaching was not clear (Chapter 6). Entrance into and transit through the Malacca Strait were uneventful but the traffic in the area was heavy and the traffic-separation schemes proved again their value as navigational safety measures (Chapter 5). As arranged, the battle group went in to Singapore for fuel and a two-day recreation visit. Upon arrival, a staff officer made an official request through the military attaché for permission to operate helicopters in the waterfront area (Chapter 7); permission was granted. Permission to land a U.S. shore patrol was also requested of the local authorities and, when the details of cooperation between the Singapore police and the patrol had been worked out, permission was granted (Chapter 5). With the exception of one incident, the visit proved to be most successful and friendly. A member of the carrier's crew had been seen stealing some articles from a store display. In the dark, he escaped his pursuers and got back to the ship in the last liberty boat. Shortly thereafter, the local police came to the carrier's quarterdeck and asked that the man be turned over to them for trial and punishment. The officer of the deck told them that, since the man was aboard, jurisdiction belonged to the United States and the man would be tried by U.S. court-martial aboard ship (Chapters 5 and 8). The court-martial was held at sea, and the accused was found guilty and punished accordingly.

Upon departing Singapore and while en route across the South China Sea to the Pacific Ocean, a freighter going in the opposite direction and flying the flag of Taiwan passed close aboard. She dipped her colors, but the battle group was ordered not to acknowledge the dip (Chapter 2). As directed, the battle group proceeded directly to a rendezvous at sea with the Seventh Fleet commander. Thereafter, a series of conferences was held between the staffs of the Seventh Fleet and of Battle Group Yankee on the subject of experimental antisubmarine-warfare tactics then being developed by the Seventh Fleet.

At the conclusion of the last conference, Battle Group Yankee proceeded towards the Philippines. Twice, destroyers were sent out to investigate and obtain the names and destinations of stray merchant ships in the area (Chapter 5). As a navigational exercise, the group steamed between the Philippine Islands (Chapter 4) and out into the Pacific through the Makassar Strait. Some ten miles out at sea, calls and best wishes were exchanged with some Philippine Navy ships that were practicing for a coming coastal patrol exercise. The task group commander notified all units that they would proceed directly to the Panama Canal. During the transit of the Trust Territory of the Pacific Islands (Chapter 2) and the area where the danger zones for the U.S. nuclear tests had once been established (Chapter 6), the weather held fair, and no untoward incidents occurred.

Heavy traffic at the entrance to the Panama Canal (Chapter 4) delayed transit for a few hours, but the experienced Panama Canal pilots moved the ships through at a good speed. Upon departure from the Panama Canal Zone, the task group split up, each ship being assigned to visit a different port in Central America. During these visits, one ship reported that two men had come aboard requesting asylum for political reasons. Inasmuch as there was no apparent and ready threat to their personal safety, the commanding officer refused the request (Chapter 5). Another ship reported that two new oil rigs had been installed off Yucatán (Chapter 6). All ships rendezvoused off the eastern tip of Cuba, an operation that was complicated by the presence of a great number of fishing vessels from many different countries (Chapter 6). Upon forming up, Battle Group Yankee proceeded up the Strait of Florida and, taking full advantage of a fair current in the Gulf Stream, reported back to Norfolk in order to resume its regular duties with the U.S. Atlantic Fleet.

Only one matter marred the homecoming; when the battle group commander reported in to Norfolk, he was informed that the government of the

Philippines had sent a diplomatic communication to Washington informing the U.S. government that it had found a large amount of oil pollution within its 200-mile zone shortly after Battle Group Yankee had transited the area. It noted that other ships that had been in the area were being investigated and requested the cooperation of the United States (Chapters 5 and 6).

Appendices

A The Antarctic Treaty of 1959

The Governments of Argentina, Australia, Belgium, Chile, the French Republic, Japan, New Zealand, Norway, the Union of South Africa, the Union of Soviet Socialist Republics, the United Kingdom of Great Britain and Northern Ireland, and the United States of America,

Recognizing that it is in the interest of all mankind that Antarctica shall continue forever to be used exclusively for peaceful purposes and shall not become the scene or object of international discord;

Acknowledging the substantial contributions to scientific knowledge resulting from international cooperation in scientific investigation in Antarctica;

Convinced that the establishment of a firm foundation for the continuation and development of such cooperation on the basis of freedom of scientific investigation in Antarctica as applied during the International Geophysical Year accords with the interests of science and the progress of all mankind;

Convinced also that a treaty ensuring the use of Antarctica for peaceful purposes only and the continuance of international harmony in Antarctica will further the purposes and principles embodied in the Charter of the United Nations;

Have agreed as follows:

ARTICLE I

1. Antarctica shall be used for peaceful purposes only. There shall be prohibited, *inter alia*, any measures of a military nature, such as the establishment of military bases and fortifications, the carrying out of military maneuvers, as well as the testing of any type of weapons.
2. The present Treaty shall not prevent the use of military personnel or equipment for scientific research or for any other peaceful purpose.

ARTICLE II

Freedom of scientific investigation in Antarctica and cooperation toward that end, as applied during the International Geophysical Year, shall continue, subject to the provisions of the present Treaty.

ARTICLE III

1. In order to promote international cooperation in scientific investigation in Antarctica, as provided for in Article II of the present Treaty, the Contracting Parties agree that, to the greatest extent feasible and practicable:
   (a) information regarding plans for scientific programs in Antarctica shall be exchanged to permit maximum economy and efficiency of operations;
   (b) scientific personnel shall be exchanged in Antarctica between expeditions and stations;
   (c) scientific observations and results from Antarctica shall be exchanged and made freely available.
2. In implementing this Article, every encouragement shall be given to the establishment of cooperative working relations with those Specialized Agencies of the United Nations and other international organizations having a scientific or technical interest in Antarctica.

ARTICLE IV

1. Nothing contained in the present Treaty shall be interpreted as:
   (a) a renunciation by any Contracting Party of previously asserted rights of or claims to territorial sovereignty in Antarctica;
   (b) a renunciation or diminution by any Contracting Party of any basis of claim to territorial sovereignty in Antarctica which it may have whether as a result of its activities or those of its nationals in Antarctica, or otherwise;
   (c) prejudicing the position of any Contracting Party as regards its recognition or non-recognition of any other State's right of or claim or basis of claim to territorial sovereignty in Antarctica.
2. No acts or activities taking place while the present Treaty is in force shall constitute a basis for asserting, supporting or denying a claim to territorial sovereignty in Antarctica or create any rights of sovereignty in Antarctica. No new claim, or enlargement of an existing claim, to territorial sovereignty in Antarctica shall be asserted while the present Treaty is in force.

ARTICLE V

1. Any nuclear explosions in Antarctica and the disposal there of radioactive waste material shall be prohibited.
2. In the event of the conclusion of international agreements concerning the use of nuclear energy, including nuclear explosions and the disposal

of radioactive waste material, to which all of the Contracting Parties whose representatives are entitled to participate in the meetings provided for under Article IX are parties, the rules established under such agreements shall apply in Antarctica.

ARTICLE VI

The provisions of the present Treaty shall apply to the area south of 60° South Latitude, including all ice shelves, but nothing in the present Treaty shall prejudice or in any way affect the rights, or the exercise of the rights, of any State under international law with regard to the high seas within that area.

ARTICLE VII

1. In order to promote the objectives and ensure the observance of the provisions of the present Treaty, each Contracting Party whose representatives are entitled to participate in the meetings referred to in Article IX of the Treaty shall have the right to designate observers to carry out any inspection provided for by the present Article. Observers shall be nationals of the Contracting Parties which designate them. The names of observers shall be communicated to every other Contracting Party having the right to designate observers, and like notice shall be given of the termination of their appointment.
2. Each observer designated in accordance with the provisions of paragraph 1 of this Article shall have complete freedom of access at any time to any or all areas of Antarctica.
3. All areas of Antarctica, including all stations, installations and equipment within those areas, and all ships and aircraft at points of discharging or embarking cargoes or personnel in Antarctica, shall be open at all times to inspection by any observers designated in accordance with paragraph 1 of this Article.
4. Aerial observation may be carried out at any time over any or all areas of Antarctica by any of the Contracting Parties having the right to designate observers.
5. Each Contracting Party shall, at the time when the present Treaty enters into force for it, inform the other Contracting Parties, and thereafter shall give them notice in advance, of
   (a) all expeditions to and within Antarctica, on the part of its ships or nationals, and all expeditions to Antarctica organized in or proceeding from its territory;
   (b) all stations in Antarctica occupied by its nationals; and

(c) any military personnel or equipment intended to be introduced by it into Antarctica subject to the conditions prescribed in paragraph 2 of Article I of the present Treaty.

ARTICLE VIII

1. In order to facilitate the exercise of their functions under the present Treaty, and without prejudice to the respective positions of the Contracting Parties relating to jurisdiction over all other persons in Antarctica, observers designated under paragraph 1 of Article VII and scientific personnel exchanged under subparagraph 1(b) of Article III of the Treaty, and members of the staffs accompanying any such persons, shall be subject only to the jurisdiction of the Contracting Party of which they are nationals in respect of all acts or omissions occurring while they are in Antarctica for the purpose of exercising their functions.
2. Without prejudice to the provisions of paragraph 1 of this Article, and pending the adoption of measures in pursuance of subparagraph 1(e) of Article IX, the Contracting Parties concerned in any case of dispute with regard to the exercise of jurisdiction in Antarctica shall immediately consult together with a view to reaching a mutually acceptable solution.

ARTICLE IX

1. Representatives of the Contracting Parties named in the preamble to the present Treaty shall meet at the City of Canberra within two months after the date of entry into force of the Treaty, and thereafter at suitable intervals and places, for the purpose of exchanging information, consulting together on matters of common interest pertaining to Antarctica, and formulating and considering, and recommending to their Governments, measures in furtherance of the principles and objectives of the Treaty, including measures regarding:
   (a) use of Antarctica for peaceful purposes only;
   (b) facilitation of scientific research in Antarctica;
   (c) facilitation of international scientific cooperation in Antarctica;
   (d) facilitation of the exercise of the rights of inspection provided for in Article VII of the Treaty;
   (e) questions relating to the exercise of jurisdiction in Antarctica;
   (f) preservation and conservation of living resources in Antarctica.
2. Each Contracting Party which has become a party to the present Treaty by accession under Article XIII shall be entitled to appoint representatives to participate in the meetings referred to in paragraph 1 of the present Article, during such time as that Contracting Party demonstrates its interest in Antarctica by conducting substantial scientific research

activity there, such as the establishment of a scientific station or the despatch of a scientific expedition.

3. Reports from the observers referred to in Article VII of the present Treaty shall be transmitted to the representatives of the Contracting Parties participating in the meetings referred to in paragraph 1 of the present Article.

4. The measures referred to in paragraph 1 of this Article shall become effective when approved by all the Contracting Parties whose representatives were entitled to participate in the meetings held to consider those measures.

5. Any or all of the rights established in the present Treaty may be exercised as from the date of entry into force of the Treaty whether or not any measures facilitating the exercise of such rights have been proposed, considered or approved as provided in this Article.

ARTICLE X

Each of the Contracting Parties undertakes to exert appropriate efforts, consistent with the Charter of the United Nations, to the end that no one engages in any activity in Antarctica contrary to the principles or purposes of the present Treaty.

ARTICLE XI

1. If any dispute arises between two or more of the Contracting Parties concerning the interpretation or application of the present Treaty, those Contracting Parties shall consult among themselves with a view to having the dispute resolved by negotiation, inquiry, mediation, conciliation, arbitration, judicial settlement or other peaceful means of their own choice.

2. Any dispute of this character not so resolved shall, with the consent, in each case, of all parties to the dispute, be referred to the International Court of Justice for settlement; but failure to reach agreement on reference to the International Court shall not absolve parties to the dispute from the responsibility of continuing to seek to resolve it by any of the various peaceful means referred to in paragraph 1 of this Article.

ARTICLE XII

1. (a) The present Treaty may be modified or amended at any time by unanimous agreement of the Contracting Parties whose representatives are entitled to participate in the meetings provided for under Article IX. Any such modification or amendment shall enter into

force when the depositary Government has received notice from all such Contracting Parties that they have ratified it.

(b) Such modification or amendment shall thereafter enter into force as to any other Contracting Party when notice of ratification by it has been received by the depositary Government. Any such Contracting Party from which no notice of ratification is received within a period of two years from the date of entry into force of the modification or amendment in accordance with the provisions of subparagraph 1(a) of this Article shall be deemed to have withdrawn from the present Treaty on the date of the expiration of such period.

2. (a) If after the expiration of thirty years from the date of entry into force of the present Treaty, any of the Contracting Parties whose representatives are entitled to participate in the meetings provided for under Article IX so requests by a communication addressed to the depositary Government, a Conference of all the Contracting Parties shall be held as soon as practicable to review the operation of the Treaty.

(b) Any modification or amendment to the present Treaty which is approved at such a Conference by a majority of the Contracting Parties there represented, including a majority of those whose representatives are entitled to participate in the meetings provided for under Article IX, shall be communicated by the depositary Government to all the Contracting Parties immediately after the termination of the Conference and shall enter into force in accordance with the provisions of paragraph 1 of the present Article.

(c) If any such modification or amendment has not entered into force in accordance with the provisions of subparagraph 1(a) of this Article within a period of two years after the date of its communication to all the Contracting Parties, any Contracting Party may at any time after the expiration of that period give notice to the depositary Government of its withdrawal from the present Treaty; and such withdrawal shall take effect two years after the receipt of the notice by the depositary Government.

ARTICLE XIII

1. The present Treaty shall be subject to ratification by the signatory States. It shall be open for accession by any State which is a Member of the United Nations, or by any other State which may be invited to accede to the Treaty with the consent of all the Contracting Parties whose representatives are entitled to participate in the meetings provided for under Article IX of the Treaty.

2. Ratification of or accession to the present Treaty shall be effected by each State in accordance with its constitutional processes.
3. Instruments of ratification and instruments of accession shall be deposited with the Government of the United States of America, hereby designated as the depositary Government.
4. The depositary Government shall inform all signatory and acceding States of the date of each deposit of an instrument of ratification or accession, and the date of entry into force of the Treaty and of any modification or amendment thereto.
5. Upon the deposit of instruments of ratification by all the signatory States, the present Treaty shall enter into force for those States and for States which have deposited instruments of accession. Thereafter the Treaty shall enter into force for any acceding State upon the deposit of its instrument of accession.
6. The present Treaty shall be registered by the depositary Government pursuant to Article 102 of the Charter of the United Nations.

ARTICLE XIV

The present Treaty , done in the English, French, Russian and Spanish languages, each version being equally authentic, shall be deposited in the archives of the Government of the United States of America, which shall transmit duly certified copies thereof to the Governments of the signatory and acceding States.

B Panama Canal Treaty of 1977

Note: In addition to the basic Panama Canal treaties set forth herein and in Appendix C, there are numerous subsidiary agreements, annexes, and protocols concerning the implementation and understandings reached between the two governments. They are not included in this text.

The United States of America and the Republic of Panama,

Acting in the spirit of the Joint Declaration of April 3, 1964, by the Representatives of the Governments of the United States of America and the Republic of Panama, and of the Joint Statement of Principles of February 7, 1974, initialed by the Secretary of State of the United States of America and the Foreign Minister of the Republic of Panama, and

Acknowledging the Republic of Panama's sovereignty over its territory,

Have decided to terminate the prior Treaties pertaining to the Panama Canal and to conclude a new Treaty to serve as the basis for a new relationship between them and, accordingly, have agreed upon the following:

ARTICLE I

ABROGATION OF PRIOR TREATIES AND ESTABLISHMENT OF A NEW RELATIONSHIP

1. Upon its entry into force, this Treaty terminates and supersedes:
   (a) The Isthmian Canal Convention between the United States of America and the Republic of Panama, signed at Washington, November 18, 1903;
   (b) The Treaty of Friendship and Cooperation signed at Washington, March 2, 1936, and the Treaty of Mutual Understanding and Cooperation and the related Memorandum of Understandings Reached, signed at Panama, January 25, 1955, between the United States of America and the Republic of Panama;
   (c) All other treaties, conventions, agreements and exchanges of notes between the United States of America and the Republic of Panama concerning the Panama Canal which were in force prior to the entry into force of this Treaty; and
   (d) Provisions concerning the Panama Canal which appear in other treaties, conventions, agreements and exchanges of notes between the United States of America and the Republic of Panama which were in force prior to the entry into force of this Treaty.

2. In accordance with the terms of this Treaty and related agreements, the Republic of Panama, as territorial sovereign, grants to the United States of America, for the duration of this Treaty, the rights necessary to regulate the transit of ships through the Panama Canal, and to manage, operate, maintain, improve, protect and defend the Canal. The Republic of Panama guarantees to the United States of America the peaceful use of the land and water areas which it has been granted the rights to use for such purposes pursuant to this Treaty and related agreements.
3. The Republic of Panama shall participate increasingly in the management and protection and defense of the Canal, as provided in this Treaty.
4. In view of the special relationship established by this Treaty, the United States of America and the Republic of Panama shall cooperate to assure the uninterrupted and efficient operation of the Panama Canal.

ARTICLE II

RATIFICATION, ENTRY INTO FORCE, AND TERMINATION

1. This Treaty shall be subject to ratification in accordance with the constitutional procedures of the two Parties. The instruments of ratification of this Treaty shall be exchanged at Panama at the same time as the instruments of ratification of the Treaty Concerning the Permanent Neutrality and Operation of the Panama Canal, signed this date, are exchanged. This Treaty shall enter into force, simultaneously with the Treaty Concerning the Permanent Neutrality and Operation of the Panama Canal, six calendar months from the date of the exchange of the instruments of ratification.
2. This Treaty shall terminate at noon, Panama time, December 31, 1999.

ARTICLE III

CANAL OPERATION AND MANAGEMENT

1. The Republic of Panama, as territorial sovereign, grants to the United States of America the rights to manage, operate, and maintain the Panama Canal, its complementary works, installations and equipment and to provide for the orderly transit of vessels through the Panama Canal. The United States of America accepts the grant of such rights and undertakes to exercise them in accordance with this Treaty and related agreements.
2. In carrying out the foregoing responsibilities, the United States of America may:
   (a) Use for the aforementioned purposes, without cost except as provided in this Treaty, the various installations and areas (including the

Panama Canal) and waters, described in the Agreement in Implementation of this Article, signed this date, as well as such other areas and installations as are made available to the United States of America under this Treaty and related agreements, and take the measures necessary to ensure sanitation of such areas;

(b) Make such improvements and alterations to the aforesaid installations and areas as it deems appropriate, consistent with the terms of this Treaty;

(c) Make and enforce all rules pertaining to the passage of vessels through the Canal and other rules with respect to navigation and maritime matters, in accordance with this Treaty and related agreements. The Republic of Panama will lend its cooperation, when necessary, in the enforcement of such rules;

(d) Establish, modify, collect and retain tolls for the use of the Panama Canal, and other charges, and establish and modify methods of their assessment;

(e) Regulate relations with employees of the United States Government;

(f) Provide supporting services to facilitate the performance of its responsibilities under this Article;

(g) Issue and enforce regulations for the effective exercise of the rights and responsibilities of the United States of America under this Treaty and related agreements. The Republic of Panama will lend its cooperation, when necessary, in the enforcement of such rules; and

(h) Exercise any other right granted under this Treaty, or otherwise agreed upon between the two Parties.

3. Pursuant to the foregoing grant of rights, the United States of America shall, in accordance with the terms of this Treaty and the provisions of United States law, carry out its responsibilities by means of a United States Government agency called the Panama Canal Commission, which shall be constituted by and in conformity with the laws of the United States of America.

(a) The Panama Canal Commission shall be supervised by a Board composed of nine members, five of whom shall be nationals of the United States of America, and four of whom shall be Panamanian nationals proposed by the Republic of Panama for appointment to such positions by the United States of America in a timely manner.

(b) Should the Republic of Panama request the United States of America to remove a Panamanian national from membership on the Board, the United States of America shall agree to such request. In that event, the Republic of Panama shall propose another Panamanian national for appointment by the United States of America to such position in a timely manner. In case of removal of a Panamanian member of the Board at the initiative of the United States of America, both parties will consult in advance in order to reach agreement concerning such removal, and the Republic of Panama shall propose another Panamanian national for appointment by the United States of America in his stead.

(c) The United States of America shall employ a national of the United States of America as Administrator of the Panama Canal Commission, and a Panamanian national as Deputy Administrator, through December 31, 1989. Beginning January 1, 1990, a Panamanian national shall be employed as the Administrator and a national of the United States of America shall occupy the position of Deputy Administrator. Such Panamanian nationals shall be proposed to the United States of America by the Republic of Panama for appointment to such positions by the United States of America.

(d) Should the United States of America remove the Panamanian national from his position as Deputy Administrator, or Administrator, the Republic of Panama shall propose another Panamanian national for appointment to such position by the United States of America.

4. An illustrative description of the activities the Panama Canal Commission will perform in carrying out the responsibilities and rights of the United States of America under this Article is set forth at the Annex. Also set forth in the Annex are procedures for the discontinuance or transfer of those activities performed prior to the entry into force of this Treaty by the Panama Canal Company or the Canal Zone Government which are not to be carried out by the Panama Canal Commission.

5. The Panama Canal Commission shall reimburse the Republic of Panama for the costs incurred by the Republic of Panama in providing the following public services in the Canal operating areas and in housing areas set forth in the Agreement in Implementation of Article III of this Treaty and occupied by both United States and Panamanian citizen employees of the Panama Canal Commission: police, fire protection, street maintenance, street lighting, street cleaning, traffic management and garbage collection. The Panama Canal Commission shall pay the Republic of Panama the sum of ten million United States dollars ($10,000,000) per annum for the foregoing services. It is agreed that every three years from the date that this Treaty enters into force, the costs involved in furnishing said services shall be reexamined to determine whether adjustment of the annual payment should be made because of inflation and other relevant factors affecting the cost of such services.

6. The Republic of Panama shall be responsible for providing, in all areas comprising the former Canal Zone, services of a general jurisdictional nature such as customs and immigration, postal services, courts and licensing, in accordance with this Treaty and related agreements.

7. The United States of America and the Republic of Panama shall establish a Panama Canal Consultative Committee, composed of an equal number of high-level representatives of the United States of America and the Republic of Panama, and which may appoint such subcommittees as it may deem appropriate. This Committee shall advise the United States of America and the Republic of Panama on matters of policy affecting the Canal's operation. In view of both Parties' special interest in the continuity and efficiency of the Canal operation in the future, the Committee shall advise on matters such as general tolls policy, employment and training policies to increase the participation of Panamanian nationals in the operation of the Canal, and international policies on matters concerning the Canal. The Committee's recommendations shall be transmitted to the two Governments, which shall give such recommendations full consideration in the formulation of such policy decisions.

8. In addition to the participation of Panamanian nationals at high management levels of the Panama Canal Commission, as provided for in paragraph 3 of this Article, there shall be growing participation of Panamanian nationals at all other levels and areas of employment in the aforesaid commission, with the objective of preparing, in an orderly and efficient fashion, for the assumption by the Republic of Panama of full responsibility for the management, operation and maintenance of the Canal upon the termination of this Treaty.

9. The use of the areas, waters and installations with respect to which the United States of America is granted rights pursuant to this Article, and the rights and legal status of United States Government agencies and employees operating in the Republic of Panama pursuant to this Article, shall be governed by the Agreement in Implementation of this Article, signed this date.

10. Upon entry into force of this Treaty, the United States Government agencies known as the Panama Canal Company and the Canal Zone Government shall cease to operate within the territory of the Republic of Panama that formerly constituted the Canal Zone.

ARTICLE IV

PROTECTION AND DEFENSE

1. The United States of America and the Republic of Panama commit themselves to protect and defend the Panama Canal. Each Party shall act, in accordance with its constitutional processes, to meet the danger resulting from an armed attack or other actions which threaten the security of the Panama Canal or of ships transiting it.

2. For the duration of this Treaty, the United States of America shall have primary responsibility to protect and defend the Canal. The rights of the

United States of America to station, train, and move military forces within the Republic of Panama are described in the Agreement in Implementation of this Article, signed this date. The use of areas and installations and the legal status of the armed forces of the United States of America in the Republic of Panama shall be governed by the aforesaid Agreement.

3. In order to facilitate the participation and cooperation of the armed forces of both parties in the protection and defense of the Canal, the United States of America and the Republic of Panama shall establish a Combined Board comprised of an equal number of senior military representatives of each Party. These representatives shall be charged by their respective governments with consulting and cooperating on all matters pertaining to the protection and defense of the Canal, and with planning for actions to be taken in concert for that purpose. Such combined protection and defense arrangements shall not inhibit the identity or lines of authority of the armed forces of the United States of America or the Republic of Panama. The Combined Board shall provide for coordination and cooperation concerning such matters as:

   (a) The preparation of contingency plans for the protection and defense of the Canal based upon the cooperative efforts of the armed forces of both Parties;

   (b) The planning and conduct of combined military exercises; and

   (c) The conduct of United States and Panamanian military operations with respect to the protection and defense of the Canal.

4. The Combined Board shall, at five-year intervals throughout the duration of this Treaty, review the resources being made available by the two Parties for the protection and defense of the Canal. Also, the Combined Board shall make appropriate recommendations to the two Governments respecting projected requirements, the efficient utilization of available resources of the two Parties, and other matters of mutual interest with respect to the protection and defense of the Canal.

5. To the extent possible consistent with its primary responsibility for the protection and defense of the Panama Canal, the United States of America will endeavor to maintain its armed forces in the Republic of Panama in normal times at a level not in excess of that of the armed forces of the United States of America in the territory of the former Canal Zone immediately prior to the entry into force of this Treaty.

ARTICLE V

PRINCIPLE OF NON-INTERVENTION

Employees of the Panama Canal Commission, their dependents and designated contractors of the Panama Canal Commission, who are nationals of the United States of America, shall respect the laws of the Republic of Panama and shall abstain from any activity incompatible with the spirit of this Treaty. Accordingly, they shall abstain from any political activity in the Republic of Panama as well as from any intervention in the internal affairs of the Republic of Panama. The United States of America shall take all measures within its authority to ensure that the provisions of this Article are fulfilled.

ARTICLE VI

PROTECTION OF THE ENVIRONMENT

1. The United States of America and the Republic of Panama commit themselves to implement this Treaty in a manner consistent with the protection of the natural environment of the Republic of Panama. To this end, they shall consult and cooperate with each other in all appropriate ways to ensure that they shall give due regard to the protection and conservation of the environment.
2. A Joint Commission on the Environment shall be established with equal representation from the United States of America and the Republic of Panama, which shall periodically review the implementation of this Treaty and shall recommend as appropriate to the two Governments ways to avoid or, should this not be possible, to mitigate the adverse environmental impacts which might result from their respective actions pursuant to the Treaty.
3. The United States of America and the Republic of Panama shall furnish the Joint Commission on the Environment complete information on any action taken in accordance with this Treaty which, in the judgment of both, might have a significant effect on the environment. Such information shall be made available to the Commission as far in advance of the contemplated action as possible to facilitate the study by the Commission of any potential environmental problems and to allow for consideration of the recommendation of the Commission before the contemplated action is carried out.

ARTICLE VII

FLAGS

1. The entire territory of the Republic of Panama, including the areas the use of which the Republic of Panama makes available to the United States of America pursuant to this Treaty and related agreements, shall be under the flag of the Republic of Panama, and consequently such flag always shall occupy the position of honor.

2. The flag of the United States of America may be displayed, together with the flag of the Republic of Panama, at the headquarters of the Panama Canal Commission, at the site of the Combined Board, and as provided in the Agreement in Implementation of Article IV of this Treaty.
3. The flag of the United States of America also may be displayed at other places and on some occasions, as agreed by both Parties.

ARTICLE VIII

PRIVILEGES AND IMMUNITIES

1. The installations owned or used by the agencies or instrumentalities of the United States of America operating in the Republic of Panama pursuant to this Treaty and related agreements, and their official archives and documents, shall be inviolable. The two Parties shall agree on procedures to be followed in the conduct of any criminal investigation at such locations by the Republic of Panama.
2. Agencies and instrumentalities of the Government of the United States of America operating in the Republic of Panama pursuant to this Treaty and related agreements shall be immune from the jurisdiction of the Republic of Panama.
3. In addition to such other privileges and immunities as are afforded to employees of the United States Government and their dependents pursuant to this Treaty, the United States of America may designate up to twenty officials of the Panama Canal Commission who, along with their dependents, shall enjoy the privileges and immunities accorded to diplomatic agents and their dependents under international law and practice. The United States of America shall furnish to the Republic of Panama a list of the names of said officials and their dependents, identifying the positions they occupy in the Government of the United States of America, and shall keep such list current at all times.

ARTICLE IX

APPLICABLE LAWS AND LAW ENFORCEMENT

1. In accordance with the provisions of this Treaty and related agreements, the law of the Republic of Panama shall apply in the areas made available for the use of the United States of America pursuant to this Treaty. The law of the Republic of Panama shall be applied to matters or events which occurred in the former Canal Zone prior to the entry into force of this Treaty only to the extent specifically provided in prior treaties and agreements.

2. Natural or juridical persons who, on the date of entry into force of this Treaty, are engaged in business or non-profit activities at locations in the former Canal Zone may continue such business or activities at those locations under the same terms and conditions prevailing prior to the entry into force of this Treaty for a thirty-month transition period from its entry into force. The Republic of Panama shall maintain the same operating conditions as those applicable to the aforementioned enterprises prior to the entry into force of this Treaty in order that they may receive licenses to do business in the Republic of Panama subject to their compliance with the requirements of its law. Thereafter, such persons shall receive the same treatment under the law of the Republic of Panama as similar enterprises already established in the rest of the territory of the Republic of Panama without discrimination.

3. The rights of ownership, as recognized by the United States of America, enjoyed by natural or juridical private persons in buildings and other improvements to real property located in the former Canal Zone shall be recognized by the Republic of Panama in conformity with its laws.

4. With respect to buildings and other improvements to real property located in the Canal operating areas, housing areas or other areas subject to the licensing procedure established in Article IV of the Agreement in Implementation of Article III of this Treaty, the owners shall be authorized to continue using the land upon which their property is located in accordance with the procedures established in that Article.

5. With respect to buildings and other improvements to real property located in areas of the former Canal Zone to which the aforesaid licensing procedure is not applicable, or may cease to be applicable during the lifetime or upon termination of this Treaty, the owners may continue to use the land upon which their property is located, subject to the payment of a reasonable charge to the Republic of Panama. Should the Republic of Panama decide to sell such land, the owners of the buildings or other improvements located thereon shall be offered a first option to purchase such land at a reasonable cost. In the case of non-profit enterprises, such as churches and fraternal organizations, the cost of purchase will be nominal in accordance with the prevailing practice in the rest of the territory of the Republic of Panama.

6. If any of the aforementioned persons are required by the Republic of Panama to discontinue their activities or vacate their property for public purposes, they shall be compensated at fair market value by the Republic of Panama.

7. The provisions of paragraphs 2–6 above shall apply to natural or juridical persons who have been engaged in business or non-profit activities at locations in the former Canal Zone for at least six months prior to the date of signature of this Treaty.

8. The Republic of Panama shall not issue, adopt or enforce any law, decree, regulation, or international agreement or take any other action which purports to regulate or would otherwise interfere with the exercise on the part of the United States of America of any right granted under this Treaty or related agreements.
9. Vessels transiting the Canal, and cargo, passengers and crews carried on such vessels shall be exempt from any taxes, fees, or other charges by the Republic of Panama. However, in the event such vessels call at a Panamanian port, they may be assessed charges incident thereto, such as charges for services provided to the vessel. The Republic of Panama may also require the passengers and crew disembarking from such vessels to pay such taxes, fees and charges as are established under Panamanian law for persons entering its territory. Such taxes, fees and charges shall be assessed on a nondiscriminatory basis.
10. The United States of America and the Republic of Panama will cooperate in taking such steps as may from time to time be necessary to guarantee the security of the Panama Canal Commission, its property, its employees and their dependents, and their property, the Forces of the United States of America and the members thereof, the civilian component of the United States Forces, the dependents of members of the Forces and the civilian component, and their property, and the contractors of the Panama Canal Commission and of the United States Forces, their dependents, and their property. The Republic of Panama will seek from its Legislative Branch such legislation as may be needed to carry out the foregoing purposes and to punish any offenders.
11. The Parties shall conclude an agreement whereby nationals of either State, who are sentenced by the courts of the other State, and who are not domiciled therein, may elect to serve their sentences in their State of nationality.

ARTICLE X

EMPLOYMENT WITH THE PANAMA CANAL COMMISSION

1. In exercising its rights and fulfilling its responsibilities as the employer, the United States of America shall establish employment and labor regulations which shall contain the terms, conditions and prerequisites for all categories of employees of the Panama Canal Commission. These regulations shall be provided to the Republic of Panama prior to their entry into force.
2. (a) The regulations shall establish a system of preference when hiring employees, for Panamanian applicants possessing the skills and qual-

ifications required for employment by the Panama Canal Commission. The United States of America shall endeavor to ensure that the number of Panamanian nationals employed by the Panama Canal Commission in relation to the total number of its employees will conform to the proportion established for foreign enterprises under the law of the Republic of Panama.

(b) The terms and conditions of employment to be established will in general be no less favorable to persons already employed by the Panama Canal Company or Canal Zone Government prior to the entry into force of this Treaty, than those in effect immediately prior to that date.

3. (a) The United States of America shall establish an employment policy for the Panama Canal Commission that shall generally limit the recruitment of personnel outside the Republic of Panama to persons possessing requisite skills and qualifications which are not available in the Republic of Panama.

(b) The United States of America will establish training programs for Panamanian employees and apprentices in order to increase the number of Panamanian nationals qualified to assume positions with the Panama Canal Commission, as positions become available.

(c) Within five years from the entry into force of this Treaty, the number of United States nationals employed by the Panama Canal Commission who were previously employed by the Panama Canal Company shall be at least twenty percent less than the total number of United States nationals working for the Panama Canal Company immediately prior to the entry into force of this Treaty.

(d) The United States of America shall periodically inform the Republic of Panama, through the Coordinating Committee, established pursuant to the Agreement in Implementation of Article III of this Treaty, of available positions within the Panama Canal Commission. The Republic of Panama shall similarly provide the United States of America any information it may have as to the availability of Panamanian nationals claiming to have skills and qualifications that might be required by the Panama Canal Commission, in order that the United States of America may take this information into account.

4. The United States of America will establish qualification standards for skills, training and experience required by the Panama Canal Commission. In establishing such standards, to the extent they include a requirement for a professional license, the United States of America, without prejudice to its right to require additional professional skills and qualifications, shall recognize the professional licenses issued by the Republic of Panama.

5. The United States of America shall establish a policy for the periodic rotation, at a maximum of every five years, of United States citizen employees and other non-Panamanian employees, hired after the entry into force of this Treaty. It is recognized that certain exceptions to the said policy of rotation may be made for sound administrative reasons, such as in the case of employees holding positions requiring certain nontransferable or nonrecruitable skills.

6. With regard to wages and fringe benefits, there shall be no discrimination on the basis of nationality, sex, or race. Payments by the Panama Canal Commission of additional remuneration, or the provision of other benefits, such as home leave benefits, to United States nationals employed prior to entry into force of this Treaty, or to persons of any nationality, including Panamanian nationals who are thereafter recruited outside of the Republic of Panama and who change their place of residence, shall not be considered to be discrimination for the purpose of this paragraph.

7. Persons employed by the Panama Canal Company or Canal Zone Government prior to the entry into force of this Treaty, who are displaced from their employment as a result of the discontinuance by the United States of America of certain activities pursuant to this Treaty, will be placed by the United States of America, to the maximum extent feasible, in other appropriate jobs with the Government of the United States in accordance with United States Civil Service regulations. For such persons who are not United States nationals, placement efforts will be confined to United States Government activities located within the Republic of Panama. Likewise, persons previously employed in activities for which the Republic of Panama assumes responsibility as a result of this Treaty will be continued in their employment to the maximum extent feasible by the Republic of Panama. The Republic of Panama shall, to the maximum extent feasible, ensure that the terms and conditions of employment applicable to personnel employed in the activities for which it assumes responsibility are no less favorable than those in effect immediately prior to the entry into force of this Treaty. Non-United States nationals employed by the Panama Canal Company or Canal Zone Government prior to the entry into force of this Treaty who are involuntarily separated from their positions because of the discontinuance of an activity by reason of this Treaty, who are not entitled to an immediate annuity under the United States Civil Service Retirement System, and for whom continued employment in the Republic of Panama by the Government of the United States of America is not practicable, will be provided special job placement assistance by the Republic of Panama for employment in positions for which they may be qualified by experience and training.

8. The Parties agree to establish a system whereby the Panama Canal Com-

mission may, if deemed mutually convenient or desirable by the two Parties, assign certain employees of the Panama Canal Commission, for a limited period of time, to assist in the operation of activities transferred to the responsibility of the Republic of Panama as a result of this Treaty or related agreements. The salaries and other costs of employment of any such persons assigned to provide such assistance shall be reimbursed to the United States of America by the Republic of Panama.

9. (a) The right of employees to negotiate collective contracts with the Panama Canal Commission is recognized. Labor relations with employees of the Panama Canal Commission shall be conducted in accordance with forms of collective bargaining established by the United States of America after consultation with employee unions.

   (b) Employee unions shall have the right to affiliate with international labor organizations.

10. The United States of America will provide an appropriate early optional retirement program for all persons employed by the Panama Canal Company or Canal Zone Government immediately prior to the entry into force of this Treaty. In this regard, taking into account the unique circumstances created by the provisions of this Treaty, including its duration, and their effect upon such employees, the United States of America shall, with respect to them:

   (a) determine that conditions exist which invoke applicable United States law permitting early retirement annuities and apply such law for a substantial period of the duration of the Treaty;

   (b) seek special legislation to provide more liberal entitlement to, and calculation of, retirement annuities than is currently provided for by law.

ARTICLE XI

PROVISIONS FOR THE TRANSITION PERIOD

1. The Republic of Panama shall reassume plenary jurisdiction over the former Canal Zone upon entry into force of this Treaty and in accordance with its terms. In order to provide for an orderly transition to the full application of the jurisdictional arrangements established by this Treaty and related agreements, the provisions of this Article shall become applicable upon the date this Treaty enters into force, and shall remain in effect for thirty calendar months. The authority granted in this Article to the United States of America for this transition period shall supplement, and is not intended to limit, the full application and effect of the rights and authority granted to the United States of America elsewhere in this Treaty and in related agreements.

2. During this transition period, the criminal and civil laws of the United States of America shall apply concurrently with those of the Republic of Panama in certain of the areas and installations made available for the use of the United States of America pursuant to this Treaty, in accordance with the following provisions:

(a) the Republic of Panama permits the authorities of the United States of America to have the primary right to exercise criminal jurisdiction over United States citizen employees of the Panama Canal Commission and their dependents, and members of the United States Forces and civilian component and their dependents, in the following cases:

    (i) for any offense committed during the transition period within such areas and installations, and

    (ii) for any offense committed prior to that period in the former Canal Zone.

The Republic of Panama shall have the primary right to exercise jurisdiction over all other offenses committed by such persons, except as otherwise provided in this Treaty and related agreements or as may be otherwise agreed.

(b) Either Party may waive its primary right to exercise jurisdiction in a specific case or category of cases.

3. The United States of America shall retain the right to exercise jurisdiction in criminal cases relating to offenses committed prior to the entry into force of this Treaty in violation of the laws applicable in the former Canal Zone.

4. For the transition period, the United States of America shall retain police authority and maintain a police force in the aforementioned areas and installations. In such areas, the police authorities of the United States of America may take into custody any person not subject to their primary jurisdiction if such person is believed to have committed or to be committing an offense against applicable laws or regulations, and shall promptly transfer custody to the police authorities of the Republic of Panama. The United States of America and the Republic of Panama shall establish joint police patrols in agreed areas. Any arrests conducted by a joint patrol shall be the responsibility of the patrol member or members representing the Party having primary jurisdiction over the person or persons arrested.

5. The courts of the United States of America and related personnel, functioning in the former Canal Zone immediately prior to the entry into force of this Treaty, may continue to function during the transition period for the judicial enforcement of the jurisdiction to be exercised by the United States of America in accordance with this Article.

6. In civil cases, the civilian courts of the United States of America in the Republic of Panama shall have no jurisdiction over new cases of a private

civil nature, but shall retain full jurisdiction during the transition period
to dispose of any civil cases, including admiralty cases, already instituted
and pending before the courts prior to the entry into force of this Treaty.

7. The laws, regulations, and administrative authority of the United States
of America applicable in the former Canal Zone immediately prior to the
entry into force of this Treaty shall, to the extent not inconsistent with this
Treaty and related agreements, continue in force for the purpose of the
exercise by the United States of America of law enforcement and judicial
jurisdiction only during the transition period. The United States of
America may amend, repeal or otherwise change such laws, regulations
and administrative authority. The two Parties shall consult concerning
procedural and substantive matters relative to the implementation of this
Article, including the disposition of cases pending at the end of the
transition period and, in this respect, may enter into appropriate agreements by an exchange of notes or other instrument.

8. During this transition period, the United States of America may continue
to incarcerate individuals in the areas and installations made available for
the use of the United States of America by the Republic of Panama
pursuant to this Treaty and related agreements, or to transfer them to
penal facilities in the United States of America to serve their sentences.

ARTICLE XII

A SEA-LEVEL CANAL OR A
THIRD LANE OF LOCKS

1. The United States of America and the Republic of Panama recognize that
a sea-level canal may be important for international navigation in the
future. Consequently, during the duration of this Treaty, both Parties
commit themselves to study jointly the feasibility of a sea-level canal in the
Republic of Panama, and in the event they determine that such a waterway is necessary, they shall negotiate terms, agreeable to both Parties, for
its construction.

2. The United States of America and the Republic of Panama agree on the
following:
    (a) No new interoceanic canal shall be constructed in the territory of the
    Republic of Panama during the duration of this Treaty, except in
    accordance with the provisions of this Treaty, or as the two Parties
    may otherwise agree; and
    (b) During the duration of this Treaty, the United States of America
    shall not negotiate with third States for the right to construct an
    interoceanic canal on any other route in the Western Hemisphere,
    except as the two Parties may otherwise agree.

3. The Republic of Panama grants to the United States of America the right to add a third lane of locks to the existing Panama Canal. This right may be exercised at any time during the duration of this Treaty, provided that the United States of America has delivered to the Republic of Panama copies of the plans for such construction.

4. In the event the United States of America exercises the right granted in paragraph 3 above, it may use for that purpose, in addition to the areas otherwise made available to the United States of America pursuant to this Treaty, such other areas as the two Parties may agree upon. The terms and conditions applicable to Canal operating areas made available by the Republic of Panama for the use of the United States of America pursuant to Article III of this Treaty shall apply in a similar manner to such additional areas.

5. In the construction of the aforesaid works, the United States of America shall not use nuclear excavation techniques without the previous consent of the Republic of Panama.

ARTICLE XIII

PROPERTY TRANSFER AND ECONOMIC PARTICIPATION BY THE REPUBLIC OF PANAMA

1. Upon termination of this Treaty, the Republic of Panama shall assume total responsibility for the management, operation, and maintenance of the Panama Canal, which shall be turned over in operating condition and free of liens and debts, except as the two Parties may otherwise agree.

2. The United States of America transfers, without charge, to the Republic of Panama all right, title and interest the United States of America may have with respect to all real property, including non-removable improvements thereon, as set forth below:

   (a) Upon the entry into force of this Treaty, the Panama Railroad and such property that was located in the former Canal Zone but that is not within the land and water areas the use of which is made available to the United States of America pursuant to this Treaty. However, it is agreed that the transfer on such date shall not include buildings and other facilities, except housing, the use of which is retained by the United States of America pursuant to this Treaty and related agreement, outside such areas.

   (b) Such property located in an area or a portion thereof at such time as the use by the United States of America of such area or portion thereof ceases pursuant to agreement between the two Parties.

   (c) Housing units made available for occupancy by members of the Armed Forces of the Republic of Panama in accordance with paragraph 5(b) of Annex B to the Agreement in Implementation of Article IV of this Treaty at such time as such units are made available to the Republic of Panama.

(d) Upon termination of this Treaty, all real property and non-removable improvements that were used by the United States of America for the purposes of this Treaty and related agreements and equipment related to the management, operation and maintenance of the Canal remaining in the Republic of Panama.

3. The Republic of Panama agrees to hold the United States of America harmless with respect to any claims which may be made by third parties relating to rights, title and interest in such property.

4. The Republic of Panama shall receive, in addition, from the Panama Canal Commission a just and equitable return on the national resources which it has dedicated to the efficient management, operation, maintenance, protection and defense of the Panama Canal, in accordance with the following:

(a) An annual amount to be paid out of Canal operating revenues computed at a rate of thirty hundredths of a United States dollar ($0.30) per Panama Canal net ton, or its equivalency, for each vessel transiting the Canal after the entry into force of this Treaty, for which tolls are charged. The rate of thirty hundredths of a United States dollar ($0.30) per Panama Canal net ton, or its equivalency, will be adjusted to reflect changes in the United States wholesale price index for total manufactured goods during biennial periods. The first adjustment shall take place five years after entry into force of this Treaty, taking into account the changes that occurred in such price index during the preceding two years. Thereafter, successive adjustments shall take place at the end of each biennial period. If the United States of America should decide that another indexing method is preferable, such method shall be proposed to the Republic of Panama and applied if mutually agreed.

(b) A fixed annuity of ten million United States dollars ($10,000,000) to be paid out of Canal operating revenues. This amount shall constitute a fixed expense of the Panama Canal Commission.

(c) An annual amount of up to ten million United States dollars ($10,000,000) per year, to be paid out of Canal operating revenues to the extent that such revenues exceed expenditures of the Panama Canal Commission including amounts paid pursuant to this Treaty. In the event Canal operating revenues in any year do not produce a surplus sufficient to cover this payment, the unpaid balance shall be paid from operating surpluses in future years in a manner to be mutually agreed.

ARTICLE XIV

SETTLEMENT OF DISPUTES

In the event that any question should arise between the Parties concerning the interpretation of this Treaty or related agreements, they shall make every effort to resolve the matter through consultation in the appropriate committees established pursuant to this Treaty and related agreements, or, if appropriate, through diplomatic channels. In the event the Parties are unable to resolve a particular matter through such means, they may, in appropriate cases, agree to submit the matter to conciliation, mediation, arbitration, or such other procedure for the peaceful settlement of the dispute as they may mutually deem appropriate.

DONE at Washington, this 7th day of September, 1977, in duplicate, in the English and Spanish languages, both texts being equally authentic.

For the Republic of Panama: For the United States of America:

OMAR TORRIJOS HERRERA   JIMMY CARTER

Head of Government of   *President of the*
the Republic of Panama   *United States of America*

C Treaty Concerning the Permanent Neutrality and Operation of the Panama Canal (1977)

The United States of America and the Republic of Panama have agreed upon the following:

ARTICLE I

The Republic of Panama declares that the Canal, as an international transit waterway, shall be permanently neutral in accordance with the regime established in this Treaty. The same regime of neutrality shall apply to any other international waterway that may be built either partially or wholly in the territory of the Republic of Panama.

ARTICLE II

The Republic of Panama declares the neutrality of the Canal in order that both in time of peace and in time of war it shall remain secure and open to peaceful transit by the vessels of all nations on terms of entire equality, so that there will be no discrimination against any nation, or its citizens or subjects, concerning the conditions or charges of transit, or for any other reason, and so that the Canal, and therefore the Isthmus of Panama, shall not be the target of reprisals in any armed conflict between other nations of the world. The foregoing shall be subject to the following requirements:

(a) Payment of tolls and other charges for transit and ancillary services, provided they have been fixed in conformity with the provisions of Article III (c);

(b) Compliance with applicable rules and regulations, provided such rules and regulations are applied in conformity with the provisions of Article III (c);

(c) The requirement that transiting vessels commit no acts of hostility while in the Canal; and

(d) Such other conditions and restrictions as are established by this Treaty.

ARTICLE III

1. For purposes of the security, efficiency and proper maintenance of the Canal the following rules shall apply:
   (a) The Canal shall be operated efficiently in accordance with conditions of transit through the Canal, and rules and regulations that shall be just, equitable and reasonable, and limited to those necessary for safe navigation and efficient, sanitary operation of the Canal;
   (b) Ancillary services necessary for transit through the Canal shall be provided;
   (c) Tolls and other charges for transit and ancillary services shall be just, reasonable, equitable and consistent with the principles of international law;
   (d) As a pre-condition of transit, vessels may be required to establish clearly the financial responsibility and guarantees for payment of reasonable and adequate indemnification, consistent with international practice and standards, for damages resulting from acts or omissions of such vessels when passing through the Canal. In the case of vessels owned or operated by a State or for which it has acknowledged responsibility, a certification by that State that it shall observe its obligations under international law to pay for damages resulting from the act or omission of such vessels when passing through the Canal shall be deemed sufficient to establish such financial responsibility;
   (e) Vessels of war and auxiliary vessels of all nations shall at all times be entitled to transit the Canal, irrespective of their internal operation, means of propulsion, origin, destination or armament, without being subjected, as a condition of transit, to inspection, search or surveillance. However, such vessels may be required to certify that they have complied with all applicable health, sanitation and quarantine regulations. In addition, such vessels shall be entitled to refuse to disclose their internal operation, origin, armament, cargo or destination. However, auxiliary vessels may be required to present written assurances, certified by an official at a high level of the government of the State requesting the exemption, that they are owned or operated by that government and in this case are being used only on government non-commercial service.
2. For the purposes of this Treaty, the terms "Canal," "vessel of war," "auxiliary vessel," "internal operation," "armament" and "inspection" shall have the meanings assigned them in annex A to this Treaty.

ARTICLE IV

1. The United States of America and the Republic of Panama agree to maintain the regime of neutrality established in this Treaty, which shall

be maintained in order that the Canal shall remain permanently neutral, notwithstanding the termination of any other treaties entered into by the two Contracting Parties.

2. A correct and authoritative statement of certain rights and duties of the parties under the foregoing is contained in the statement of understanding issued by the government of the United States of America on October 14, 1977, and by the government of the Republic of Panama on October 18, 1977, which is hereby incorporated as an integral part of this treaty, as follows:

3. Under the treaty concerning the permanent neutrality and operation of the Panama Canal (the neutrality treaty), Panama and the United States have the responsibility to assure that the Panama Canal will remain open and secure to ships of all nations. The correct interpretation of this principle is that each of the two countries shall, in accordance with their respective constitutional processes, defend the canal against any threat to the regime of neutrality, and consequently shall have the right to act against any aggression or threat directed against the canal or against the peaceful transit of vessels through the canal.

4. This does not mean, nor shall it be interpreted as, a right of intervention of the United States in the internal affairs of Panama. Any United States action will be directed at insuring that the canal will remain open, secure, and accessible, and it shall never be directed against the territorial integrity or political independence of Panama.

ARTICLE V

After the termination of the Panama Canal Treaty, only the Republic of Panama shall operate the Canal and maintain military forces, defense sites and military installations within its national territory.

ARTICLE VI

1. In recognition of the important contributions of the United States of America and of the Republic of Panama to the construction, operation, maintenance, and protection and defense of the Canal, vessels of war and auxiliary vessels of those nations shall, notwithstanding any other provisions of this Treaty, be entitled to transit the Canal irrespective of their internal operation, means of propulsion, origin, destination, armament or cargo carried. Such vessels of war and auxiliary vessels will be entitled to transit the Canal expeditiously.

2. In accordance with the statement of understanding mentioned in Article VI above: the neutrality treaty provides that the vessels of war and auxiliary vessels of the United States and Panama will be entitled to

transit the canal expeditiously. This is intended, and it shall so be interpreted, to assure the transit of such vessels through the canal as quickly as possible, without any impediment, with expedited treatment, and in case of need or emergency, to go to the head of the line of vessels in order to transit the canal readily.

3. The United States of America, so long as it has responsibility for the operation of the Canal, may continue to provide the Republic of Colombia toll-free transit through the Canal for its troops, vessels and materials of war. Thereafter, the Republic of Panama may provide the Republic of Colombia and the Republic of Costa Rica with the right of toll-free transit.

ARTICLE VII

1. The United States of America and the Republic of Panama shall jointly sponsor a resolution in the Organization of American States opening to accession by all nations of the world the Protocol to this Treaty whereby all the signatories will adhere to the objectives of this Treaty, agreeing to respect the regime of neutrality set forth herein.

2. The Organization of American States shall act as the depositary for this Treaty and related instruments.

ARTICLE VIII

This Treaty shall be subject to ratification in accordance with the constitutional procedures of the two Parties. The instruments of ratification of this Treaty shall be exchanged at Panama at the same time as the instruments of ratification of the Panama Canal Treaty, signed this date, are exchanged. This Treaty shall enter into force, simultaneously with the Panama Canal Treaty, six calendar months from the date of the exchange of the instruments of ratification.

DONE at Washington, this 7th day of September, 1977, in the English and Spanish languages, both texts being equally authentic.

For the Republic of Panama: For the United States of America:

OMAR TORRIJOS HERRERA   JIMMY CARTER

Head of Government of   *President of the*
the Republic of Panama   *United States of America*

ANNEX A

1. "Canal" includes the existing Panama Canal, the entrances thereto and the territorial seas of the Republic of Panama adjacent thereto, as defined

on the map annexed hereto (Annex B), and any other interoceanic waterway in which the United States of America is a participant or in which the United States of America has participated in connection with the construction or financing, that may be operated wholly or partially within the territory of the Republic of Panama, the entrances thereto and the territorial seas adjacent thereto.

2. "Vessel of war" means a ship belonging to the naval forces of a State, and bearing the external marks distinguishing warships of its nationality, under the command of an officer duly commissioned by the government and whose name appears in the Navy List, and manned by a crew which is under regular naval discipline.

3. "Auxiliary vessel" means any ship, not a vessel of war, that is owned or operated by a State and used, for the time being, exclusively on government noncommercial service.

4. "Internal operation" encompasses all machinery and propulsion systems, as well as the management and control of the vessel, including its crew. It does not include the measures necessary to transit vessels under the control of pilots while such vessels are in the Canal.

5. "Armament" means arms, ammunitions, implements of war and other equipment of a vessel which possesses characteristics appropriate for use for warlike purposes.

6. "Inspection" includes on-board examination of vessel structure, cargo, armament and internal operation. It does not include those measures strictly necessary for admeasurement, nor those measures strictly necessary to assure safe, sanitary transit and navigation, including examination of deck and visual navigation equipment, nor in the case of live cargoes, such as cattle or other livestock, that may carry communicable diseases, those measures necessary to assure that health and sanitation requirements are satisfied.

PROTOCOL TO THE TREATY CONCERNING THE PERMANENT NEUTRALITY AND OPERATION OF THE PANAMA CANAL

Whereas the maintenance of the neutrality of the Panama Canal is important not only to the commerce and security of the United States of America and the Republic of Panama, but to the peace and security of the Western Hemisphere and to the interests of world commerce as well;

Whereas the regime of neutrality which the United States of America and the Republic of Panama have agreed to maintain will ensure permanent access to the Canal by vessels of all nations on the basis of entire equality; and

Whereas the said regime of effective neutrality shall constitute the best protection for the Canal and shall ensure the absence of any hostile act against it;

The Contracting Parties to this Protocol have agreed upon the following:

ARTICLE I

The Contracting Parties hereby acknowledge the regime of permanent neutrality for the Canal established in the Treaty Concerning the Permanent Neutrality and Operation of the Panama Canal and associate themselves with its objectives.

ARTICLE II

The Contracting Parties agree to observe and respect the regime of permanent neutrality of the Canal in time of war as in time of peace, and to ensure that vessels of their registry strictly observe the applicable rules.

ARTICLE III

This Protocol shall be open to accession by all States of the world, and shall enter into force for each State at the time of deposit of its instrument of accession with the Secretary General of the Organization of American States.

D   Territorial Sea and Contiguous Zone

Note: Appendices D through L are from the "Draft convention on the Law of the Sea (Informal Text)," dated 28 August 1980, of the Third Conference on the Law of the Sea. As recorded in the text and noted in the preface, it is expected that the articles contained therein will remain substantially unchanged. The whole draft convention is not included because some sections are (a) not germane to navigation and related issues, and (b) still open to negotiation in the concluding sessions of the conference.

PART II

SECTION 1. GENERAL

Article 2
Legal status of the territorial sea, of the air space
over the territorial sea and of its bed and subsoil

1. The sovereignty of a coastal State extends beyond its land territory and internal waters, and in the case of an archipelagic State, its archipelagic waters, over an adjacent belt of sea described as the territorial sea.
2. This sovereignty extends to the air space over the territorial sea as well as to its bed and subsoil.
3. The sovereignty over the territorial sea is exercised subject to this Convention and to other rules of international law.

SECTION 2. LIMITS OF THE TERRITORIAL SEA

Article 3
Breadth of the territorial sea

Every State has the right to establish the breadth of its territorial sea up to a limit not exceeding 12 nautical miles, measured from baselines determined in accordance with this Convention.

Article 4
Outer limit of the territorial sea

The outer limit of the territorial sea is the line every point of which is at a distance from the nearest point of the baseline equal to the breadth of the territorial sea.

Article 5
Normal baseline

Except where otherwise provided in this Convention, the normal baseline for measuring the breadth of the territorial sea is the low-water line along the coast as marked on large-scale charts officially recognized by the coastal State.

Article 6
Reefs

In the case of islands situated on atolls or of islands having fringing reefs, the baseline for measuring the breadth of the territorial sea is the seaward low-water line of the reef, as shown by the appropriate symbol on official charts.

Article 7
Straight baselines

1. In localities where the coastline is deeply indented and cut into, or if there is a fringe of islands along the coast in its immediate vicinity, the method of straight baselines joining appropriate points may be employed in drawing the baseline from which the breadth of the territorial sea is measured.
2. Where because of the presence of a delta and other natural conditions the coastline is highly unstable, the appropriate points may be selected along the furthest seaward extent of the low-water line and, notwithstanding subsequent regression of the low-water line, such baselines shall remain effective until changed by the coastal State in accordance with this Convention.
3. The drawing of such baselines must not depart to any appreciable extent from the general direction of the coast, and the sea areas lying within the lines must be sufficiently closely linked to the land domain to be subject to the régime of internal waters.
4. Straight baselines shall not be drawn to and from low-tide elevations, unless lighthouses or similar installations which are permanently above sea level have been built on them or except in instances where the drawing of baselines to and from such elevations has received general international recognition.
5. Where the method of straight baselines is applicable under paragraph 1 account may be taken, in determining particular baselines, of economic interests peculiar to the region concerned, the reality and the importance of which are clearly evidenced by a long usage.
6. The system of straight baselines may not be applied by a State in such a manner as to cut off from the high seas or the exclusive economic zone the territorial sea of another State.

Article 8
Internal waters

1. Except as provided in Part IV, waters on the landward side of the baseline of the territorial sea form part of the internal waters of the State.
2. Where the establishment of a straight baseline in accordance with article 7 has the effect of enclosing as internal waters areas which had not previously been considered as such, a right of innocent passage as provided in this Convention shall exist in those waters.

Article 9
Mouths of rivers

If a river flows directly into the sea, the baseline shall be a straight line across the mouth of the river between points on the low-tide line of its banks.

Article 10
Bays

1. This article relates only to bays the coasts of which belong to a single State.
2. For the purposes of this Convention, a bay is a well-marked indentation whose penetration is in such proportion to the width of its mouth as to contain land-locked waters and constitute more than a mere curvature of the coast. An indentation shall not, however, be regarded as a bay unless its area is as large as, or larger than, that of the semi-circle whose diameter is a line drawn across the mouth of that indentation.
3. For the purposes of measurement, the area of an indentation is that lying between the low-water mark around the shore of the indentation and a line joining the low-water mark of its natural entrance points. Where, because of the presence of islands, an indentation has more than one mouth, the semi-circle shall be drawn on a line as long as the sum total of the lengths of the lines across the different mouths. Islands within an indentation shall be included as if they were part of the water area of the indentation.
4. If the distance between the low-water marks of the natural entrance points of a bay does not exceed 24 nautical miles a closing line may be drawn between these two low-water marks, and the waters enclosed thereby shall be considered as internal waters.
5. Where the distance between the low-water marks of the natural entrance points of a bay exceeds 24 nautical miles a straight baseline of 24 nautical miles shall be drawn within the bay in such a manner as to enclose the maximum area of water that is possible with a line of that length.
6. The foregoing provisions do not apply to so-called "historic" bays, or in any case where the system of straight baselines provided for in article 7 is applied.

Article 11
Ports

For the purpose of delimiting the territorial sea, the outermost permanent harbour works which form an integral part of the harbour system are regarded as forming part of the coast. Off-shore installations and artificial islands shall not be considered as permanent harbour works.

Article 12
Roadsteads

Roadsteads which are normally used for the loading, unloading, and anchoring of ships, and which would otherwise be situated wholly or partly outside the outer limit of the territorial sea, are included in the territorial sea.

Article 13
Low-tide elevations

1. A low-tide elevation is a naturally formed area of land which is surrounded by and above water at low tide but submerged at high tide. Where a low-tide elevation is situated wholly or partly at a distance not exceeding the breadth of the territorial sea from the mainland or an island, the low-water line on that elevation may be used as the baseline for measuring the breadth of the territorial sea.
2. Where a low-tide elevation is wholly situated at a distance exceeding the breadth of the territorial sea from the mainland or an island, it has no territorial sea of its own.

Article 14
Combination of methods for determining baselines

The coastal State may determine baselines in turn by any of the methods provided for in the foregoing articles to suit different conditions.

Article 15
Delimitation of the territorial sea between States
with opposite or adjacent coasts

Where the coasts of two States are opposite or adjacent to each other, neither of the two States is entitled, failing agreement between them to the contrary, to extend its territorial sea beyond the median line every point of which is equidistant from the nearest points on the baselines from which the breadth of the territorial seas of each of the two States is measured. The above provision does not apply, however, where it is necessary by reason of historic title or other special circumstances to delimit the territorial seas of the two States in a way which is at variance therewith.

Article 16
Charts and lists of geographical co-ordinates

1. The baselines for measuring the breadth of the territorial sea determined in accordance with articles 7, 9 and 10, or the limits derived therefrom, and the lines of delimitation drawn in accordance with articles 12 and 15, shall be shown on charts of a scale or scales adequate for determining them. Alternatively, a list of geographical co-ordinates of points, specifying the geodetic datum, may be substituted.
2. The coastal State shall give due publicity to such charts or lists of geographical co-ordinates and shall deposit a copy of each such chart or list with the Secretary-General of the United Nations.

SECTION 3. INNOCENT PASSAGE IN THE TERRITORIAL SEA

SUBSECTION A. RULES APPLICABLE TO ALL SHIPS

Article 17
Right of innocent passage

Subject to this Convention, ships of all States, whether coastal or landlocked, enjoy the right of innocent passage through the territorial sea.

Article 18
Meaning of passage

1. Passage means navigation through the territorial sea for the purpose of:
   (a) Traversing that sea without entering internal waters or calling at a roadstead or port facility outside internal waters; or
   (b) Proceeding to or from internal waters or a call at such roadstead or port facility.
2. Passage shall be continuous and expeditious. However, passage includes stopping and anchoring, but only in so far as the same are incidental to ordinary navigation or are rendered necessary by *force majeure* or distress or for the purpose of rendering assistance to persons, ships or aircraft in danger or distress.

Article 19
Meaning of innocent passage

1. Passage is innocent so long as it is not prejudicial to the peace, good order or security of the coastal State. Such passage shall take place in conformity with this Convention and with other rules of international law.
2. Passage of a foreign ship shall be considered to be prejudicial to the peace, good order or security of the coastal State, if in the territorial sea it engages in any of the following activities:

(a) Any threat or use of force against the sovereignty, territorial integrity or political independence of the coastal State, or in any other manner in violation of the principles of international law embodied in the Charter of the United Nations;

(b) Any exercise or practice with weapons of any kind;

(c) Any act aimed at collecting information to the prejudice of the defence or security of the coastal State;

(d) Any act of propaganda aimed at affecting the defence or security of the coastal State;

(e) The launching, landing or taking on board of any aircraft;

(f) The launching, landing or taking on board of any military device;

(g) The embarking or disembarking of any commodity, currency or person contrary to the customs, fiscal, immigration or sanitary regulations of the coastal State;

(h) Any act of wilful and serious pollution, contrary to this Convention;

(i) Any fishing activities;

(j) The carrying out of research or survey activities;

(k) Any act aimed at interfering with any systems of communication or any other facilities or installations of the coastal State;

(l) Any other activity not having a direct bearing on passage.

Article 20
Submarines and other underwater vehicles

In the territorial sea, submarines and other underwater vehicles are required to navigate on the surface and to show their flag.

Article 21
Laws and regulations of the coastal State
relating to innocent passage

1. The coastal State may adopt laws and regulations, in conformity with the provisions of this Convention and other rules of international law, relating to innocent passage through the territorial sea, in respect of all or any of the following:

(a) The safety of navigation and the regulation of marine traffic;

(b) The protection of navigational aids and facilities and other facilities or installations;

(c) The protection of cables and pipelines;

(d) The conservation of the living resources of the sea;

(e) The prevention of infringement of the fisheries regulations of the coastal State;

(f) The preservation of the environment of the coastal State and the prevention, reduction and control of pollution thereof;

(g) Marine scientific research and hydrographic surveys;

(h) The prevention of infringement of the customs, fiscal, immigration or sanitary regulations of the coastal State.

2. Such laws and regulations shall not apply to the design, construction, manning or equipment of foreign ships unless they are giving effect to generally accepted international rules or standards.

3. The coastal State shall give due publicity to all such laws and regulations.

4. Foreign ships exercising the right of innocent passage through the territorial sea shall comply with all such laws and regulations and all generally accepted international regulations relating to the prevention of collisions at sea.

Article 22
Sea lanes and traffic separation schemes
in the territorial sea

1. The coastal State may, where necessary having regard to the safety of navigation, require foreign ships exercising the right of innocent passage through its territorial sea to use such sea lanes and traffic separation schemes as it may designate or prescribe for the regulation of the passage of ships.

2. In particular, tankers, nuclear-powered ships and ships carrying nuclear or other inherently dangerous or noxious substances or materials may be required to confine their passage to such sea lanes.

3. In the designation of sea lanes and the prescription of traffic separation schemes under this article the coastal State shall take into account:
   (a) The recommendations of the competent international organization;
   (b) Any channels customarily used for international navigation;
   (c) The special characteristics of particular ships and channels; and
   (d) The density of traffic.

4. The coastal State shall clearly indicate such sea lanes and traffic separation schemes on charts to which due publicity shall be given.

Article 23
Foreign nuclear-powered ships and ships carrying nuclear
or other inherently dangerous or noxious substances

Foreign nuclear-powered ships and ships carrying nuclear or other inherently dangerous or noxious substances shall, when exercising the right of innocent passage through the territorial sea, carry documents and observe special precautionary measures established for such ships by international agreements.

Article 24
Duties of the coastal State

1. The coastal State shall not hamper the innocent passage of foreign ships through the territorial sea except in accordance with this Convention. In

particular, in the application of this Convention or of any laws or regulations adopted under this Convention, the coastal State shall not:

(a) Impose requirements on foreign ships which have the practical effect of denying or impairing the right of innocent passage; or

(b) Discriminate in form or in fact against the ships of any State or against ships carrying cargoes to, from or on behalf of any State.

2. The coastal State shall give appropriate publicity to any dangers to navigation, of which it has knowledge, within its territorial sea.

Article 25
Rights of protection of the coastal State

1. The coastal State may take the necessary steps in its territorial sea to prevent passage which is not innocent.

2. In the case of ships proceeding to internal waters or a call at a port facility outside internal waters, the coastal State also has the right to take the necessary steps to prevent any breach of the conditions to which admission of those ships to internal waters or such a call is subject.

3. The coastal State may, without discrimination amongst foreign ships, suspend temporarily in specified areas of its territorial sea the innocent passage of foreign ships if such suspension is essential for the protection of its security, including weapons exercises. Such suspension shall take effect only after having been duly published.

Article 26
Charges which may be levied upon foreign ships

1. No charge may be levied upon foreign ships by reason only of their passage through the territorial sea.

2. Charges may be levied upon a foreign ship passing through the territorial sea as payment only for specific services rendered to the ship. These charges shall be levied without discrimination.

SUBSECTION B. RULES APPLICABLE TO MERCHANT SHIPS AND GOVERNMENT SHIPS OPERATED FOR COMMERCIAL PURPOSES

Article 27
Criminal jurisdiction on board a foreign ship

1. The criminal jurisdiction of the coastal State should not be exercised on board a foreign ship passing through the territorial sea to arrest any person or to conduct any investigation in connexion with any crime committed on board the ship during its passage, save only in the following cases:

(a) If the consequences of the crime extend to the coastal State;

(b) If the crime is of a kind to disturb the peace of the country or the good order of the territorial sea;

(c) If the assistance of the local authorities has been requested by the captain of the ship or by a diplomatic agent or consular officer of the flag State; or

(d) If such measures are necessary for the suppression of illicit traffic in narcotic drugs or psychotropic substances.

2. The above provisions do not affect the right of the coastal State to take any steps authorized by its laws for the purpose of an arrest or investigation on board a foreign ship passing through the territorial sea after leaving internal waters.

3. In the cases provided for in paragraphs 1 and 2, the coastal State shall, if the captain so requests, notify a diplomatic agent or consular officer of the flag State before taking any steps, and shall facilitate contact between such agent or officer and the ship's crew. In cases of emergency this notification may be communicated while the measures are being taken.

4. In considering whether or in what manner an arrest should be made, the local authorities shall pay due regard to the interests of navigation.

5. Except as provided in Part XII or with respect to violations of laws and regulations adopted in accordance with Part V, the coastal State may not take any steps on board a foreign ship passing through the territorial sea to arrest any person or to conduct any investigation in connexion with any crime committed before the ship entered the territorial sea, if the ship, proceeding from a foreign port, is only passing through the territorial sea without entering internal waters.

Article 28
Civil jurisdiction in relation to foreign ships

1. The coastal State should not stop or divert a foreign ship passing through the territorial sea for the purpose of exercising civil jurisdiction in relation to a person on board the ship.

2. The coastal State may not levy execution against or arrest the ship for the purpose of any civil proceedings, save only in respect of obligations or liabilities assumed or incurred by the ship itself in the course or for the purpose of its voyage through the waters of the coastal State.

3. Paragraph 2 is without prejudice to the right of the coastal State, in accordance with its laws, to levy execution against or to arrest, for the purpose of any civil proceedings, a foreign ship lying in the territorial sea or passing through the territorial sea after leaving internal waters.

SUBSECTION C. RULES APPLICABLE TO WARSHIPS AND OTHER GOVERNMENT SHIPS OPERATED FOR NON-COMMERCIAL PURPOSES

Article 29
Definition of warships

For the purposes of this Convention, "warship" means a ship belonging to the armed forces of a State bearing the external marks distinguishing such ships of its nationality, under the command of an officer duly commissioned by the Government of the State and whose name appears in the appropriate service list or its equivalent, and manned by a crew which is under regular armed forces discipline.

Article 30
Non-observance by warships of the laws and
regulations of the coastal State

If any warship does not comply with the laws and regulations of the coastal State concerning passage through the territorial sea and disregards any request for compliance which is made to it, the coastal State may require it to leave the territorial sea immediately. ˙

Article 31
Responsibility of the flag State for damage caused by
a warship or other government ship operated for
non-commercial purposes

The flag State shall bear international responsibility for any loss or damage to the coastal State resulting from the non-compliance by a warship or other government ship operated for non-commercial purposes with the laws and regulations of the coastal State concerning passage through the territorial sea or with the provisions of this Convention or other rules of international law.

Article 32
Immunities of warships and other government ships
operated for non-commercial purposes

With such exceptions as are contained in subsection A and in articles 30 and 31, nothing in this Convention affects the immunities of warships and other government ships operated for non-commercial purposes.

Section 4. Contiguous Zone

Article 33
Contiguous zone

1. In a zone contiguous to its territorial sea, described as the contiguous zone, the coastal State may exercise the control necessary to:
   (a) Prevent infringement of its customs, fiscal, immigration or sanitary regulations within its territory or territorial sea;
   (b) Punish infringement of the above regulations committed within its territory or territorial sea.
2. The contiguous zone may not extend beyond 24 nautical miles from the baselines from which the breadth of the territorial sea is measured.

E

Straits Used for International Navigation

Note: These articles are from the "Draft convention of the Law of the Sea (Informal Text)," dated 28 August 1980, of the Third Conference on the Law of the Sea.

PART III
SECTION 1. GENERAL

Article 34
Legal status of waters forming straits
used for international navigation

1. The régime of passage through straits used for international navigation established in this Part shall not in other respects affect the status of the waters forming such straits or the exercise by the States bordering the straits of their sovereignty or jurisdiction over such waters and their air space, bed and subsoil.
2. The sovereignty or jurisdiction of the States bordering the straits is exercised subject to this Part and to other rules of international law.

Article 35
Scope of this Part

Nothing in this Part shall affect:
 (a) Any areas of internal waters within a strait, except where the estab-lishment of a straight baseline in accordance with article 7 has the effect of enclosing as internal waters areas which had not previously been considered as such;
 (b) The status of the waters beyond the territorial seas of States border-ing straits as exclusive economic zones or high seas; or
 (c) The legal régime in straits in which passage is regulated in whole or in part by long-standing international conventions in force specifically relating to such straits.

Article 36
High seas routes or routes through exclusive economic
zones through straits used for international navigation

This Part does not apply to a strait used for international navigation if a high seas route or a route through an exclusive economic zone of similar convenience with respect to navigational and hydrographical characteristics exists through the strait.

SECTION 2. TRANSIT PASSAGE

Article 37
Scope of this section

   This section applies to straits which are used for international navigation between one area of the high seas or an exclusive economic zone and another area of the high seas or an exclusive economic zone.

Article 38
Right of transit passage

1. In straits referred to in article 37, all ships and aircraft enjoy the right of transit passage, which shall not be impeded, except that, if the strait is formed by an island of a State bordering the strait and its mainland, transit passage shall not apply if a high seas route or a route in an exclusive economic zone of similar convenience with respect to navigational and hydrographical characteristics exists seaward of the island.
2. Transit passage is the exercise in accordance with this Part of the freedom of navigation and overflight solely for the purpose of continuous and expeditious transit of the strait between one area of the high seas or an exclusive economic zone and another area of the high seas or an exclusive economic zone. However, the requirement of continuous and expeditious transit does not preclude passage through the strait for the purpose of entering, leaving or returning from a State bordering the strait, subject to the conditions of entry to that State.
3. Any activity which is not an exercise of the right of transit passage through a strait remains subject to the other applicable provisions of this Convention.

Article 39
Duties of ships and aircraft during their passage

1. Ships and aircraft, while exercising the right of transit passage, shall:
   (a) Proceed without delay through or over the strait;
   (b) Refrain from any threat or use of force against the sovereignty, territorial integrity or political independence of States bordering straits, or in any other manner in violation of the principles of international law embodied in the Charter of the United Nations;
   (c) Refrain from any activities other than those incident to their normal modes of continuous and expeditious transit unless rendered necessary by *force majeure* or by distress;
   (d) Comply with other relevant provisions of this Part.
2. Ships in transit shall:
   (a) Comply with generally accepted international regulations, procedures and practices for safety at sea, including the International Regulations for Preventing Collisions at Sea;

(b) Comply with generally accepted international regulations, procedures and practices for the prevention, reduction and control of pollution from ships.

3. Aircraft in transit shall:
   (a) Observe the Rules of the Air established by the International Civil Aviation Organization as they apply to civil aircraft; State aircraft will normally comply with such safety measures and will at all times operate with due regard for the safety of navigation;
   (b) At all times monitor the radio frequency assigned by the appropriate internationally designated air traffic control authority or the appropriate international distress radio frequency.

Article 40
Research and survey activities

During their passage through straits, foreign ships, including marine scientific research and hydrographic survey ships, may not carry out any research or survey activities without the prior authorization of the States bordering straits.

Article 41
Sea lanes and traffic separation schemes in straits
used for international navigation

1. In conformity with this Part, States bordering straits may designate sea lanes and prescribe traffic separation schemes for navigation in straits where necessary to promote the safe passage of ships.
2. Such States may, when circumstances require, and after giving due publicity thereto, substitute other sea lanes or traffic separation schemes for any sea lanes or traffic separation schemes previously designated or prescribed by them.
3. Such sea lanes and traffic separation schemes shall conform to generally accepted international regulations.
4. Before designating or substituting sea lanes or prescribing or substituting traffic separation schemes, States bordering straits shall refer proposals to the competent international organization with a view to their adoption. The organization may adopt only such sea lanes and traffic separation schemes as may be agreed with the States bordering the straits, after which the States may designate, prescribe or substitute them.
5. In respect of a strait where sea lanes or traffic separation schemes are proposed through the waters of two or more States bordering the strait, the States concerned shall co-operate in formulating proposals in consultation with the organization.
6. States bordering straits shall clearly indicate all sea lanes and traffic separation schemes designated or prescribed by them on charts to which due publicity shall be given.

7. Ships in transit shall respect applicable sea lanes and traffic separation schemes established in accordance with this article.

Article 42
Laws and regulations of States bordering
straits relating to transit passage

1. Subject to the provisions of this section, States bordering straits may adopt laws and regulations relating to transit passage through straits, in respect of all or any of the following:
   (a) The safety of navigation and the regulation of marine traffic, as provided in article 41;
   (b) The prevention, reduction and control of pollution, by giving effect to applicable international regulations regarding the discharge of oil, oily wastes and other noxious substances in the strait;
   (c) With respect to fishing vessels, the prevention of fishing, including the stowage of fishing gear;
   (d) The taking on board or putting overboard of any commodity, currency or person in contravention of the customs, fiscal, immigration or sanitary regulations of States bordering straits.
2. Such laws and regulations shall not discriminate in form or in fact amongst foreign ships or in their application have the practical effect of denying, hampering or impairing the right of transit passage as defined in this section.
3. States bordering straits shall give due publicity to all such laws and regulations.
4. Foreign ships exercising the right of transit passage shall comply with such laws and regulations.
5. The flag State of a ship or aircraft entitled to sovereign immunity which acts in a manner contrary to such laws and regulations or other provisions of this Part shall bear international responsibility for any loss or damage which results to States bordering straits.

Article 43
Navigation and safety aids and other improvements and
the prevention, reduction and control of pollution

   User States and States bordering a strait should by agreement cooperate:
   (a) In the establishment and maintenance in a strait of necessary navigation and safety aids or other improvements in aid of international navigation; and
   (b) For the prevention, reduction and control of pollution from ships.

Article 44
Duties of States bordering straits

States bordering straits shall not hamper transit passage and shall give appropriate publicity to any danger to navigation or overflight within or over the strait of which they have knowledge. There shall be no suspension of transit passage.

SECTION 3. INNOCENT PASSAGE

Article 45
Innocent passage

1. The régime of innocent passage, in accordance with section 3 of Part II, shall apply in straits used for international navigation:
   (a) Excluded under article 38, paragraph 1, from the application of the régime of transit passage; or
   (b) Between an area of the high seas or an exclusive economic zone and the territorial sea of a foreign State.
2. There shall be no suspension of innocent passage through such straits.

F   Archipelagic States

Note: These articles are from the "Draft convention on the Law of the Sea (Informal Text)," dated 28 August 1980, of the Third Conference on the Law of the Sea.

PART IV

Article 46
Use of terms

For the purposes of this Convention:
(a) "Archipelagic State" means a State constituted wholly by one or more archipelagos and may include other islands;
(b) "Archipelago" means a group of islands, including parts of islands, interconnecting waters and other natural features which are so closely interrelated that such islands, waters and other natural features, form an intrinsic geographical, economic and political entity, or which historically have been regarded as such.

Article 47
Archipelagic baselines

1. An archipelagic State may draw straight archipelagic baselines joining the outermost points of the outermost islands and drying reefs of the archipelago provided that within such baselines are included the main islands and an area in which the ratio of the area of the water to the area of the land, including atolls, is between 1 to 1 and 9 to 1.
2. The length of such baselines shall not exceed 100 nautical miles, except that up to 3 per cent of the total number of baselines enclosing any archipelago may exceed that length, up to a maximum length of 125 nautical miles.
3. The drawing of such baselines shall not depart to any appreciable extent from the general configuration of the archipelago.
4. Such baselines shall not be drawn to and from low-tide elevations, unless lighthouses or similar installations which are permanently above sea level have been built on them or where a low-tide elevation is situated wholly or partly at a distance not exceeding the breadth of the territorial sea from the nearest island.
5. The system of such baselines shall not be applied by an archipelagic State in such a manner as to cut off from the high seas or the exclusive economic zone the territorial sea of another State.

6. The archipelagic State shall clearly indicate such baselines on charts of a scale or scales adequate for determining them. The archipelagic State shall give due publicity to such charts and shall deposit a copy of each such chart with the Secretary-General of the United Nations.

7. If a certain part of the archipelagic water of an archipelagic State lies between two parts of an immediately adjacent neighbouring State, existing rights and all other legitimate interests which the latter State has traditionally exercised in such waters and all rights stipulated under agreement between those States shall continue and be respected.

8. For the purposes of computing the ratio of water to land under paragraph 1, land areas may include waters lying within the fringing reefs of islands and atolls, including that part of a steep-sided oceanic plateau which is enclosed or nearly enclosed by a chain of limestone islands and drying reefs lying on the perimeter of the plateau.

Article 48
Measurement of the breadth of the territorial sea, the contiguous zone, the exclusive economic zone and the continental shelf

The breadth of the territorial sea, the contiguous zone, the exclusive economic zone and the continental shelf shall be measured from the baselines drawn in accordance with article 47.

Article 49
Legal status of archipelagic waters, of the air space
over archipelagic waters and of their bed and subsoil

1. The sovereignty of an archipelagic State extends to the waters enclosed by the baselines, described as archipelagic waters, regardless of their depth or distance from the coast.

2. This sovereignty extends to the air space over the archipelagic waters, the bed and subsoil thereof, and the resources contained therein.

3. This sovereignty is exercised subject to this Part.

4. The régime of archipelagic sea lanes passage established in this Part shall not in other respects affect the status of the archipelagic waters, including the sea lanes, or the exercise by the archipelagic State of its sovereignty over such waters and their air space, bed and subsoil, and the resources contained therein.

Article 50
Delimitation of internal waters

Within its archipelagic waters, the archipelagic State may draw closing lines for the delimitation of internal waters, in accordance with articles 9, 10 and 11.

Article 51
Existing agreements, traditional fishing rights
and existing submarine cables

1. Without prejudice to article 49, archipelagic States shall respect existing
agreements with other States and shall recognize traditional fishing
rights and other legitimate activities of the immediately adjacent neighbouring States in certain areas falling within archipelagic waters. The
terms and conditions of the exercise of such rights and activities, including the nature, the extent and the areas to which they apply, shall, at the
request of any of the States concerned, be regulated by bilateral agreements between them. Such rights shall not be transferred to or shared
with third States or their nationals.
2. Archipelagic States shall respect existing submarine cables laid by other
States and passing through their waters without making a landfall.
Archipelagic States shall permit the maintenance and replacement of
such cables upon receiving due notice of the location of such cables and
the intention to repair or replace them.

Article 52
Right of innocent passage

1. Subject to article 53 and without prejudice to article 50, ships of all States
enjoy the right of innocent passage through archipelagic waters, in
accordance with section 3 of Part II.
2. The archipelagic State may, without discrimination in form or in fact
amongst foreign ships, suspend temporarily in specified areas of its
archipelagic waters the innocent passage of foreign ships if such suspension is essential for the protection of its security. Such suspension shall
take effect only after having been duly published.

Article 53
Right of archipelagic sea lanes passage

1. An archipelagic State may designate sea lanes and air routes thereabove,
suitable for the continuous and expeditous passage of foreign ships and
aircraft through or over its archipelagic waters and the adjacent territorial sea.
2. All ships and aircraft enjoy the right of archipelagic sea lanes passage in
such sea lanes and air routes.
3. Archipelagic sea lanes passage is the exercise in accordance with this
Convention of the rights of navigation and overflight in the normal mode
solely for the purpose of continuous, expeditious and unobstructed
transit between one part of the high seas or an exclusive economic zone
and another part of the high seas or an exclusive economic zone.

4. Such sea lanes and air routes shall traverse the archipelagic waters and the adjacent territorial sea and shall include all normal passage routes used as routes for international navigation or overflight through the archipelagic waters and, within such routes, so far as ships are concerned, all normal navigational channels, provided that duplication of routes of similar convenience between the same entry and exit points shall not be necessary.

5. Such sea lanes shall be defined by a series of continuous axis lines from the entry points of passage routes to the exit points. Ships and aircraft in archipelagic sea lanes passage shall not deviate more than 25 nautical miles to either side of such axis lines during passage, provided that ships and aircraft shall not navigate closer to the coasts than 10 percent of the distance between the nearest points on islands bordering the sea lane.

6. An archipelagic State which designates sea lanes under this article may also prescribe traffic separation schemes for the safe passage of ships through narrow channels in such sea lanes.

7. An archipelagic State may, when circumstances require, after giving due publicity thereto, substitute other sea lanes or traffic separation schemes for any sea lanes or traffic separation schemes previously designated or prescribed by it.

8. Such sea lanes and traffic separation schemes shall conform to generally accepted international regulations.

9. In designating or substituting sea lanes or prescribing or substituting traffic separation schemes, an archipelagic State shall refer proposals to the competent international organization with a view to their adoption. The organization may adopt only such sea lanes and traffic separation schemes as may be agreed with the archipelagic State, after which the archipelagic State may designate, prescribe or substitute them.

10. The archipelagic State shall clearly indicate the axis of the sea lanes and the traffic separation schemes designated or prescribed by it on charts to which due publicity shall be given.

11. Ships in transit shall respect applicable sea lanes and traffic separation schemes established in accordance with this article.

12. If an archipelagic State does not designate sea lanes or air routes, the right of archipelagic sea lanes passage may be exercised through the routes normally used for international navigation.

Article 54
Duties of ships and aircraft during their passage, research and survey activities, duties of the archipelagic State and laws and regulations of the archipelagic State relating to archipelagic sea lanes passage

Articles 39, 40, 42 and 44 apply *mutatis mutandis* to archipelagic sea lanes passage.

G Exclusive Economic Zone

Note: These articles are from the "Draft convention on the Law of the Sea (Informal Text)," dated 28 August 1980, of the Third Conference on the Law of the Sea.

PART V

Article 55
Specific legal régime of the exclusive economic zone

The exclusive economic zone is an area beyond and adjacent to the territorial sea, subject to the specific legal régime established in this Part, under which the rights and jurisdictions of the coastal State and the rights and freedoms of other States are governed by the relevant provisions of this Convention.

Article 56
Rights, jurisdiction and duties of the coastal State in the exclusive economic zone

1. In the exclusive economic zone, the coastal State has:
   (a) sovereign rights for the purpose of exploring and exploiting, conserving and managing the natural resources, whether living or non-living, of the sea-bed and subsoil and the superjacent waters, and with regard to other activities for the economic exploitation and exploration of the zone, such as the production of energy from the water, currents and winds;
   (b) jurisdiction as provided for in the relevant provisions of this Convention with regard to:
      (i) the establishment and use of artificial islands, installations and structures;
      (ii) marine scientific research;
      (iii) the protection and preservation of the marine environment;
   (c) other rights and duties provided for in this Convention.
2. In exercising its rights and performing its duties under this Convention in the exclusive economic zone, the coastal State shall have due regard to the rights and duties of other States and shall act in a manner compatible with the provisions of this Convention.
3. The rights set out in this article with respect to the sea-bed and subsoil shall be exercised in accordance with Part VI.

Article 57
Breadth of the exclusive economic zone

The exclusive economic zone shall not extend beyond 200 nautical miles from the baselines from which the breadth of the territorial sea is measured.

Article 58
Rights and duties of other States in the exclusive economic zone

1. In the exclusive economic zone, all States, whether coastal or land-locked, enjoy, subject to the relevant provisions of this Convention, the freedoms referred to in article 87 of navigation and overflight and of the laying of submarine cables and pipelines, and other internationally lawful uses of the sea related to these freedoms such as those associated with the operation of ships, aircraft and submarine cables and pipelines, and compatible with the other provisions of this Convention.
2. Articles 88 to 115 and other pertinent rules of international law apply to the exclusive economic zone in so far as they are not incompatible with this Part.
3. In exercising their rights and performing their dutites under this Convention in the exclusive economic zone, States shall have due regard to the rights and duties of the coastal State and shall comply with the laws and regulations adopted by the coastal State in accordance with the provisions of this Convention and other rules of international law in so far as they are not incompatible with this Part.

Article 59
Basis for the resolution of conflicts regarding the attribution of rights and jurisdiction in the exclusive economic zone

In cases where this Convention does not attribute rights or jurisdiction to the coastal State or to other States within the exclusive economic zone, and a conflict arises between the interests of the coastal State and any other State or States, the conflict should be resolved on the basis of equity and in the light of all the relevant circumstances, taking into account the respective importance of the interests involved to the parties as well as to the international community as a whole.

Article 60
Artificial islands, installations and structures in the exclusive economic zone

1. In the exclusive economic zone, the coastal State shall have the exclusive right to construct and to authorize and regulate the construction, operation and use of:
   (a) Artificial islands;

(b) Installations and structures for the purposes provided for in article 56 and other economic purposes;

(c) Installations and structures which may interfere with the exercise of the rights of the coastal State in the zone.

2. The coastal State shall have exclusive jurisdiction over such artificial islands, installations and structures, including jurisdiction with regard to customs, fiscal, health, safety and immigration regulations.

3. Due notice must be given of the construction of such artificial islands, installations or structures, and permanent means for giving warning of their presence must be maintained. Any installations or structures which are abandoned or disused must be entirely removed.

4. The coastal State may, where necessary, establish reasonable safety zones around such artificial islands, installations and structures in which it may take appropriate measures to ensure the safety both of navigation and of the artificial islands, installations and structures.

5. The breadth of the safety zones shall be determined by the coastal State, taking into account applicable international standards. Such zones shall be designed to ensure that they are reasonably related to the nature and function of the artificial islands, installations or structures, and shall not exceed a distance of 500 metres around them, measured from each point of their outer edge, except as authorized by generally accepted international standards or as recommended by the competent international organization.

6. All ships must respect these safety zones and shall comply with generally accepted international standards regarding navigation in the vicinity of artificial islands, installations, structures and safety zones. Due notice shall be given of the extent of safety zones.

7. Artificial islands, installations and structures and the safety zones around them may not be established where interference may be caused to the use of recognized sea lanes essential to international navigation.

8. Artificial islands, installations and structures have no territorial sea of their own and their presence does not affect the delimitation of the territorial sea, the exclusive economic zone or the continental shelf.

Article 61
Conservation of the living resources

1. The coastal State shall determine the allowable catch of the living resources in its exclusive economic zone.

2. The coastal State, taking into account the best scientific evidence available to it, shall ensure through proper conservation and management measures that the maintenance of the living resources in the exclusive economic zone is not endangered by over-exploitation. As appropriate, the

coastal State and competent international organizations, whether subregional, regional or global, shall co-operate to this end.

3. Such measures shall also be designed to maintain or restore populations of harvested species at levels which can produce the maximum sustainable yield, as qualified by relevant environmental and economic factors, including the economic needs of coastal fishing communities and the special requirements of developing States, and taking into account fishing patterns, the interdependence of stocks and any generally recommended subregional, regional or global minimum standards.

4. In taking such measures the coastal State shall take into consideration the effects on species associated with or dependent upon harvested species with a view to maintaining or restoring populations of such associated or dependent species above levels at which their reproduction may become seriously threatened.

5. Available scientific information, catch and fishing effort statistics, and other data relevant to the conservation of fish stocks shall be contributed and exchanged on a regular basis through competent international organizations, whether subregional, regional or global, where appropriate and with participation by all States concerned, including States whose nationals are allowed to fish in the exclusive economic zone.

Article 62
Utilization of the living resources

1. The coastal State shall promote the objective of optimum utilization of the living resources in the exclusive economic zone without prejudice to article 61.

2. The coastal State shall determine its capacity to harvest the living resources of the exclusive economic zone. Where the coastal State does not have the capacity to harvest the entire allowable catch, it shall, through agreements or other arrangements and pursuant to the terms, conditions and regulations referred to in paragraph 4, give other States access to the surplus of the allowable catch having particular regard to the provisions of articles 69 and 70, especially in relation to the developing States mentioned therein.

3. In giving access to other States to its exclusive economic zone under this article, the coastal State shall take into account all relevant factors, including, *inter alia*, the significance of the living resources of the area to the economy of the coastal State concerned and its other national interests, the provisions of articles 69 and 70, the requirements of developing States in the subregion or region in harvesting part of the surplus and the need to minimize economic dislocation in States whose nationals have habitually fished in the zone or which have made substantial efforts in research and identification of stocks.

4. Nationals of other States fishing in the exclusive economic zone shall comply with the conservation measures and with the other terms and conditions established in the regulations of the coastal State. These regulations shall be consistent with this Convention and may relate, *inter alia*, to the following:
  (a) Licensing of fishermen, fishing vessels and equipment, including payment of fees and other forms of remuneration, which, in the case of developing coastal States, may consist of adequate compensation in the field of financing, equipment and technology relating to the fishing industry;
  (b) Determining the species which may be caught, and fixing quotas of catch, whether in relation to particular stocks or groups of stocks or catch per vessel over a period of time or to the catch by nationals of any State during a specified period;
  (c) Regulating seasons and areas of fishing, the types, sizes and amount of gear, and the numbers, sizes and types of fishing vessels that may be used;
  (d) Fixing the age and size of fish and other species that may be caught;
  (e) Specifying information required of fishing vessels, including catch and effort statistics and vessel position reports;
  (f) Requiring, under the authorization and control of the coastal State, the conduct of specified fisheries research programmes and regulating the conduct of such research, including the sampling of catches, disposition of samples and reporting of associated scientific data;
  (g) The placing of observers or trainees on board such vessels by the coastal State;
  (h) The landing of all or any part of the catch by such vessels in the ports of the coastal State;
  (i) Terms and conditions relating to joint ventures or other co-operative arrangements;
  (j) Requirements for training personnel and transfer of fisheries technology, including enhancement of the coastal State's capability of undertaking fisheries research;
  (k) Enforcement procedures.
5. Coastal States shall give due notice of conservation and management regulations.

Article 63
Stocks occurring within the exclusive economic zones of two or more coastal States or both within the exclusive economic zone and in an area beyond and adjacent to it

1. Where the same stock or stocks of associated species occur within the exclusive economic zones of two or more coastal States, these States shall

seek either directly or through appropriate subregional or regional organizations to agree upon the measures necessary to co-ordinate and ensure the conservation and development of such stocks without prejudice
to the other provisions of this Part.

2. Where the same stock or stocks of associated species occur both within the
exclusive economic zone and in an area beyond and adjacent to the zone,
the coastal State and the States fishing for such stocks in the adjacent area
shall seek either directly or through appropriate subregional or regional
organizations to agree upon the measures necessary for the conservation
of these stocks in the adjacent area.

Article 64
Highly migratory species

1. The coastal State and other States whose nationals fish in the region for
the highly migratory species listed in annex I shall co-operate directly or
through appropriate international organizations with a view to ensuring
conservation and promoting the objective of optimum utilization of such
species throughout the region, both within and beyond the exclusive
economic zone. In regions where no appropriate international organization exists, the coastal State and other States whose nationals harvest
these species in the region shall co-operate to establish such an organization and participate in its work.

2. The provisions of paragraph 1 apply in addition to the other provisions
of this Part.

Article 65
Marine mammals

Nothing in this Part restricts the right of a coastal State or the competence of an international organization, as appropriate, to prohibit, limit or
regulate the exploitation of marine mammals more strictly than provided
for in this Part. States shall co-operate with a view to the conservation of
marine mammals and in the case of cetaceans shall in particular work
through the appropriate international organizations for their conservation,
management and study.

Article 66
Anadromous stocks

1. States in whose rivers anadromous stocks originate shall have the primary
interest in and responsibility for such stocks.

2. The State of origin of anadromous stocks shall ensure their conservation
by the establishment of appropriate regulatory measures for fishing in all
waters landwards of the outer limits of its exclusive economic zone and

for fishing provided for in paragraph 3 (b). The State of origin may, after consultations with other States referred to in paragraphs 3 and 4 fishing these stocks, establish total allowable catches for stocks originating in its rivers.

3. (a) Fisheries for anadromous stocks shall be conducted only in waters landwards of the outer limits of exclusive economic zones, except in cases where this provision would result in economic dislocation for a State other than the State of origin. With respect to such fishing beyond the outer limits of the exclusive economic zone, States concerned shall maintain consultations with a view to achieving agreement on terms and conditions of such fishing giving due regard to the conservation requirements and needs of the State of origin in respect of these stocks.

   (b) The State of origin shall co-operate in minimizing economic dislocation in such other States fishing these stocks, taking into account the normal catch and the mode of operations of such States, and all the areas in which such fishing has occurred.

   (c) States referred to in subparagraph (b), participating by agreement with the State of origin in measures to renew anadromous stocks, particularly by expenditures for that purpose, shall be given special consideration by the State of origin in the harvesting of stocks originating in its rivers.

   (d) Enforcement of regulations regarding anadromous stocks beyond the exclusive economic zone shall be by agreement between the State of origin and the other States concerned.

4. In cases where anadromous stocks migrate into or through the waters landwards of the outer limits of the exclusive economic zone of a State other than the State of origin, such State shall co-operate with the State of origin with regard to the conservation and management of such stocks.

5. The State of origin of anadromous stocks and other States fishing these stocks shall make arrangements for the implementation of the provisions of this article, where appropriate, through regional organizations.

Article 67
Catadromous species

1. A coastal State in whose waters catadromous species spend the greater part of their life cycle shall have responsibility for the management of these species and shall ensure the ingress and egress of migrating fish.

2. Harvesting of catadromous species shall be conducted only in waters landwards of the outer limits of exclusive economic zones. When conducted in exclusive economic zones, harvesting shall be subject to this article and the other provisions of this Convention concerning fishing in these zones.

3. In cases where catadromous fish migrate through the exclusive economic zone of another State or States, whether as juvenile or maturing fish, the management, including harvesting, of such fish shall be regulated by agreement between the State mentioned in paragraph 1 and the State or States concerned. Such agreement shall ensure the rational management of the species and take into account the responsibilities of the State mentioned in paragraph 1 for the maintenance of these species.

Article 68
Sedentary species

This part does not apply to sedentary species as defined in article 77, paragraph 4.

Article 69
Right of land-locked States

1. Land-locked States shall have the right to participate, on an equitable basis, in the exploitation of an appropriate part of the surplus of the living resources of the exclusive economic zones of coastal States of the same subregion or region, taking into account the relevant economic and geographical circumstances of all the States concerned and in conformity with the provisions of this article and of articles 61 and 62.
2. The terms and modalities of such participation shall be established by the States concerned through bilateral, subregional or regional agreements taking into account, *inter alia*:
    (a) the need to avoid effects detrimental to fishing communities or fishing industries of the coastal State;
    (b) the extent to which the land-locked State, in accordance with the provisions of this article, is participating or is entitled to participate under existing bilateral, subregional or regional agreements in the exploitation of living resources of the exclusive economic zones of other coastal States;
    (c) the extent to which other land-locked States and States with special geographical characteristics are participating in the exploitation of the living resources of the exclusive economic zone of the coastal State and the consequent need to avoid a particular burden for any single coastal State or a part of it;
    (d) the nutritional needs of the populations of the respective States.
3. When the harvesting capacity of a coastal State approaches a point which would enable it to harvest the entire allowable catch of the living resources in its exclusive economic zone, the coastal State and other States concerned shall co-operate in the establishment of equitable arrangements on a bilateral, subregional or regional basis to allow for participation of developing land-locked States of the same subregion or region in

the exploitation of the living resources of the exclusive economic zones of coastal States of the subregion or region, as may be appropriate in the circumstances and on terms satisfactory to all parties. In the implementation of this provision the factors mentioned in paragraph 2 shall also be taken into account.

4. Developed land-locked States shall, under the provisions of this article, be entitled to participate in the exploitation of living resources only in the exclusive economic zones of developed coastal States of the same subregion or region having regard to the extent to which the coastal State, in giving access to other States to the living resources of its exclusive economic zone, has taken into account the need to minimize detrimental effects on fishing communities and economic dislocation in States whose nationals have habitually fished in the zone.

5. The above provisions are without prejudice to arrangements agreed upon in subregions or regions where the coastal States may grant to land-locked States of the same subregion or region equal or preferential rights for the exploitation of the living resources in the exclusive economic zones.

Article 70
Right of States with special geographical characteristics

1. States with special geographical characteristics shall have the right to participate, on an equitable basis, in the exploitation of an appropriate part of the surplus of the living resources of the exclusive economic zones of coastal States of the same subregion or region, taking into account the relevant economic and geographical circumstances of all the States concerned and in conformity with the provisions of this article and of articles 61 and 62.

2. For the purposes of this Convention, "States with special geographical characteristics" means coastal States, including States bordering enclosed or semi-enclosed seas, whose geographical situation makes them dependent upon the exploitation of the living resources of the exclusive economic zones of other States in the subregion or region for adequate supplies of fish for the nutritional purposes of their populations or parts thereof, and coastal States which can claim no exclusive economic zones of their own.

3. The terms and modalities of such participation shall be established by the States concerned through bilateral, subregional or regional agreements taking into account, *inter alia*:

    (a) the need to avoid effects detrimental to fishing communities or fishing industries of the coastal State;

    (b) the extent to which the State with special geographical characteristics, in accordance with the provisions of this article, is participating or is entitled to participate under existing bilateral, subregional or regional agreements in the exploitation of living resources of the exclusive economic zones of other coastal States;

(c) the extent to which other States with special geographical characteristics and land-locked States are participating in the exploitation of the living resources of the exclusive economic zone of the coastal State and the consequent need to avoid a particular burden for any single coastal State or a part of it;

(d) the nutritional needs of the populations of the respective States.

4. When the harvesting capacity of a coastal State approaches a point which would enable it to harvest the entire allowable catch of the living resources in its exclusive economic zone, the coastal State and other States concerned shall co-operate in the establishment of equitable arrangements on a bilateral, subregional or regional basis to allow for participation of developing States with special geographical characteristics of the same subregion or region in the exploitation of the living resources of the exclusive economic zones of coastal States of the subregion or region, as may be appropriate in the circumstances and on terms satisfactory to all parties. In the implementation of this provision the factors mentioned in paragraph 3 shall also be taken into account.

5. Developed States with special geographical characteristics shall, under the provisions of this article, be entitled to participate in the exploitation of living resources only in the exclusive economic zones of developed coastal States of the same subregion or region having regard to the extent to which the coastal State, in giving access to other States to the living resources of its exclusive economic zone, has taken into account the need to minimize detrimental effects on fishing communities and economic dislocation in States whose nationals have habitually fished in the zone.

6. The above provisions are without prejudice to arrangements agreed upon in subregions or regions where the coastal States may grant to States with special geographical characteristics of the same subregion or region equal or preferential rights for the exploitation of the living resources in the exclusive economic zones.

Article 71
Non-applicability of articles 69 and 70

The provisions of articles 69 and 70 shall not apply in the case of a coastal State whose economy is overwhelmingly dependent on the exploitation of the living resources of its exclusive economic zone.

Article 72
Restrictions on transfer of rights

1. Rights provided under articles 69 and 70 to exploit living resources shall not be directly or indirectly transferred to third States or their nationals by lease or licence, by establishing joint ventures or in any other manner

which has the effect of such transfer unless otherwise agreed upon by the States concerned.

2. The foregoing provision does not preclude the States concerned from obtaining technical or financial assistance from third States or international organizations in order to facilitate the exercise of the rights pursuant to articles 69 and 70, provided that it does not have the effect referred to in paragraph 1.

Article 73
Enforcement of laws and regulations of the coastal State

1. The coastal State may, in the exercise of its sovereign rights to explore, exploit, conserve and manage the living resources in the exclusive economic zone, take such measures, including boarding, inspection, arrest and judicial proceedings, as may be necessary to ensure compliance with the laws and regulations adopted by it in conformity with this Convention.

2. Arrested vessels and their crews shall be promptly released upon the posting of reasonable bond or other security.

3. Coastal State penalties for violations of fisheries regulations in the exclusive economic zone may not include imprisonment, in the absence of agreements to the contrary by the States concerned, or any other form of corporal punishment.

4. In cases of arrest or detention of foreign vessels the coastal State shall promptly notify, through appropriate channels, the flag State of the action taken and of any penalties subsequently imposed.

Article 74[1]
Delimitation of the exclusive economic zone
between States with opposite or adjacent coasts

1. The delimitation of the exclusive economic zone between States with opposite or adjacent coasts shall be effected by agreement in conformity with international law. Such an agreement shall be in accordance with equitable principles, employing the median or equidistance line, where appropriate, and taking account of all circumstances prevailing in the area concerned.

2. If no agreement can be reached within a reasonable period of time, the States concerned shall resort to the procedures provided for in Part XV.

---

[1]The question of the location in this Convention of the definition of the median or equidistance line as included in article 74, paragraph 4, of the ICNT/Rev.1, could be left for consideration in the Drafting Committee. Article 74, paragraph 4, of the ICNT/Rev.1 reads as follows:

For the purposes of this Convention, "median or equidistance line" means the line every point of which is equidistant from the nearest points of the baselines from which the breadth of the territorial sea of each State is measured.

3. Pending agreement as provided for in paragraph 1, the States concerned, in a spirit of understanding and co-operation, shall make every effort to enter into provisional arrangements of a practical nature and, during this transitional period, not to jeopardize or hamper the reaching of the final agreement. Such arrangements shall be without prejudice to the final delimitation.
4. Where there is an agreement in force between the States concerned, questions relating to the delimitation of the exclusive economic zone shall be determined in accordance with the provisions of that agreement.

Article 75
Charts and lists of geographical co-ordinates

1. Subject to this Part, the outer limit lines of the exclusive economic zone and the lines of delimitation drawn in accordance with article 74 shall be shown on charts of a scale or scales adequate for determining them. Where appropriate, lists of geographical co-ordinates of points, specifying the geodetic datum, may be substituted for such outer limit lines or lines of delimitation.
2. The coastal State shall give due publicity to such charts or lists of geographical co-ordinates and shall deposit a copy of each such chart or list with the Secretary-General of the United Nations.

H   Continental Shelf

Note: These articles are from the "Draft convention on the Law of the Sea (Informal Text)," dated 28 August 1980, of the Third Conference on the Law of the Sea.

PART VI

Article 76
Definition of the continental shelf

1. The continental shelf of a coastal State comprises the sea-bed and subsoil of the submarine areas that extend beyond its territorial sea throughout the natural prolongation of its land territory to the outer edge of the continental margin, or to a distance of 200 nautical miles from the baselines from which the breadth of the territorial sea is measured where the outer edge of the continental margin does not extend up to that distance.
2. The continental shelf of a coastal State shall not extend beyond the limits provided for in paragraphs 4 to 6.
3. The continental margin comprises the submerged prolongation of the land mass of the coastal State, and consists of the sea-bed and subsoil of the shelf, the slope and the rise. It does not include the deep ocean floor with its oceanic ridges or the subsoil thereof.
4. (a) For the purposes of this Convention, the coastal State shall establish the outer edge of the continental margin wherever the margin extends beyond 200 nautical miles from the baselines from which the breadth of the territorial sea is measured, by either:
      (i) A line delineated in accordance with paragraph 7 by reference to the outermost fixed points at each of which the thickness of sedimentary rocks is at least 1 per cent of the shortest distance from such point to the foot of the continental slope; or
      (ii) A line delineated in accordance with paragraph 7 by reference to fixed points not more than 60 nautical miles from the foot of the continental slope.
   (b) In the absence of evidence to the contrary, the foot of the continental slope shall be determined as the point of maximum change in the gradient at its base.
5. The fixed points comprising the line of the outer limits of the continental shelf on the sea-bed, drawn in accordance with paragraph 4 (a) (i) and (ii), either shall not exceed 350 nautical miles from the baselines from which the breadth of the territorial sea is measured or shall not

exceed 100 nautical miles from the 2,500 metre isobath, which is a line connecting the depth of 2,500 metres.

6. Notwithstanding the provisions of paragraph 5, on submarine ridges, the outer limit of the continental shelf shall not exceed 350 nautical miles from the baselines from which the breadth of the territorial sea is measured. This paragraph does not apply to submarine elevations that are natural components of the continental margin, such as its plateaux, rises, caps, banks and spurs.

7. The coastal State shall delineate the seaward boundary of its continental shelf where that shelf extends beyond 200 nautical miles from the baselines from which the breadth of the territorial sea is measured by straight lines not exceeding 60 nautical miles in length, connecting fixed points, such points to be defined by co-ordinates of latitude and longitude.

8. Information on the limits of the continental shelf beyond the 200 nautical mile exclusive economic zone shall be submitted by the coastal State to the Commission on the Limits of the Continental Shelf set up under annex II on the basis of equitable geographical representation. The Commission shall make recommendations to coastal States on matters related to the establishment of the outer limits of their continental shelf. The limits of the shelf established by a coastal State on the basis of these recommendations shall be final and binding.

9. The coastal State shall deposit with the Secretary-General of the United Nations charts and relevant information, including geodetic data, permanently describing the outer limits of its continental shelf. The Secretary-General shall give due publicity thereto.

10. The provisions of this article are without prejudice to the question of delimitation of the continental shelf between adjacent or opposite States.

Article 77
Rights of the coastal State over the continental shelf

1. The coastal State exercises over the continental shelf sovereign rights for the purpose of exploring it and exploiting its natural resources.

2. The rights referred to in paragraph 1 are exclusive in the sense that if the coastal State does not explore the continental shelf or exploit its natural resources, no one may undertake these activities without the express consent of the coastal State.

3. The rights of the coastal State over the continental shelf do not depend on occupation, effective or notional, or on any express proclamation.

4. The natural resources referred to in this Part consist of the mineral and other non-living resources of the sea-bed and subsoil together with living organisms belonging to sedentary species, that is to say, organisms which,

at the harvestable stage, either are immobile on or under the sea-bed or are unable to move except in constant physical contact with the sea-bed or the subsoil.

Article 78
Legal status of the superjacent waters and air space
and the rights and freedoms of other States

1. The rights of the coastal State over the continental shelf do not affect the legal status of the superjacent waters or of the air space above those waters.
2. The exercise of the rights of the coastal State over the continental shelf must not infringe, or result in any unjustifiable interference with navigation and other rights and freedoms of other States as provided for in this Convention.

Article 79
Submarine cables and pipelines on the continental shelf

1. All States are entitled to lay submarine cables and pipelines on the continental shelf, in accordance with the provisions of this article.
2. Subject to its right to take reasonable measures for the exploration of the continental shelf, the exploitation of its natural resources and the prevention, reduction and control of pollution from pipelines, the coastal State may not impede the laying or maintenance of such cables or pipelines.
3. The delineation of the course for the laying of such pipelines on the continental shelf is subject to the consent of the coastal State.
4. Nothing in this Part affects the right of the coastal State to establish conditions for cables or pipelines entering its territory or territorial sea, or its jurisdiction over cables and pipelines constructed or used in connexion with the exploration of its continental shelf or exploitation of its resources or the operations of artificial islands, installations and structures under its jurisdiction.
5. When laying submarine cables or pipelines, States shall pay due regard to cables or pipelines already in position. In particular, possibilities of repairing existing cables or pipelines shall not be prejudiced.

Article 80
Artificial islands, installations and structures
on the continental shelf

Article 60 applies *mutatis mutandis* to artificial islands, installations and structures on the continental shelf.

Article 81
Drilling on the continental shelf

The coastal State shall have the exclusive right to authorize and regulate drilling on the continental shelf for all purposes.

Article 82
Payments and contributions with respect to the exploitation
of the continental shelf beyond 200 nautical miles

1. The coastal State shall make payments or contributions in kind in respect of the exploitation of the non-living resources of the continental shelf beyond 200 nautical miles from the baselines from which the breadth of the territorial sea is measured.
2. The payments and contributions shall be made annually with respect to all production at a site after the first five years of production at that site. For the sixth year, the rate of payment or contribution shall be 1 per cent of the value or volume of production at the site. The rate shall increase by 1 per cent for each subsequent year until the twelfth year and shall remain at 7 per cent thereafter. Production does not include resources used in connexion with exploitation.
3. A developing State which is a net importer of a mineral resource produced from its continental shelf is exempt from making such payments or contributions in respect of that mineral resource.
4. The payments or contributions shall be made through the Authority, which shall distribute them to States Parties to this Convention, on the basis of equitable sharing criteria, taking into account the interests and needs of developing States, particularly the least developed and the land-locked amongst them.

Article 83
Delimitation of the continental shelf between States
with opposite or adjacent coasts

1. The delimitation of the continental shelf between States with opposite or adjacent coasts shall be effected by agreement in conformity with international law. Such an agreement shall be in accordance with equitable principles, employing the median or equidistance line, where appropriate, and taking account of all circumstances prevailing in the area concerned.
2. If no agreement can be reached within a reasonable period of time, the States concerned shall resort to the procedure provided for in Part XV.
3. Pending agreement as provided for in paragraph 1, the States concerned, in a spirit of understanding and co-operation, shall make every

effort to enter into provisional arrangements of a practical nature and, during this transitional period, not to jeopardize or hamper the reaching of the final agreement. Such arrangements shall be without prejudice to the final delimitation.

4. Where there is an agreement in force between the States concerned, questions relating to the delimitation of the continental shelf shall be determined in accordance with the provisions of that agreement.

Article 84
Charts and lists of geographical co-ordinates

1. Subject to this Part, the outer limit lines of the continental shelf and the lines of delimitation drawn in accordance with article 83 shall be shown on charts of a scale or scales adequate for determining them. Where appropriate, lists of geographical co-ordinates of points, specifying the geodetic datum, may be substituted for such outer limit lines or lines of delimitation.

2. The coastal State shall give due publicity to such charts or lists of geographical co-ordinates and shall deposit a copy of each such chart or list with the Secretary-General of the United Nations.

Article 85
Tunnelling

This Part does not prejudice the right of the coastal State to exploit the subsoil by means of tunnelling, irrespective of the depth of water above the subsoil.

I

High Seas

Note: These articles are from the "Draft convention on the Law of the Sea (Informal Text)," dated 28 August 1980, of the Third Conference on the Law of the Sea.

PART VII

SECTION 1. GENERAL

Article 86
Application of the provisions of this Part

The provisions of this Part apply to all parts of the sea that are not included in the exclusive economic zone, in the territorial sea or in the internal waters of a State, or in the archipelagic waters of an archipelagic State. This article does not entail any abridgement of the freedoms enjoyed by all States in the exclusive economic zone in accordance with article 58.

Article 87
Freedom of the high seas

1. The high seas are open to all States, whether coastal or land-locked. Freedom of the high seas is exercised under the conditions laid down by this Convention and by other rules of international law. It comprises, *inter alia*, both for coastal and land-locked States;
   (a) Freedom of navigation;
   (b) Freedom of overflight;
   (c) Freedom to lay submarine cables and pipelines, subject to Part VI;
   (d) Freedom to construct artificial islands and other installations permitted under international law, subject to Part VI;
   (e) Freedom of fishing, subject to the conditions laid down in section 2;
   (f) Freedom of scientific research, subject to Parts VI and XIII.
2. These freedoms shall be exercised by all States, with due consideration for the interests of other States in their exercise of the freedom of the high seas, and also with due consideration for the rights under this Convention with respect to activities in the Area.

Article 88
Reservation of the high seas for peaceful purposes

The high seas shall be reserved for peaceful purposes.

Article 89
Invalidity of claims of sovereignty over the high seas

No State may validly purport to subject any part of the high seas to its sovereignty.

Article 90
Right of navigation

Every State, whether coastal or land-locked, has the right to sail ships under its flag on the high seas.

Article 91
Nationality of ships

1. Each State shall fix the conditions for the grant of its nationality to ships, for the registration of ships in its territory, and for the right to fly its flag. Ships have the nationality of the State whose flag they are entitled to fly. There must exist a genuine link between the State and the ship.
2. Each State shall issue to ships to which it has granted the right to fly its flag documents to that effect.

Article 92
Status of ships

1. Ships shall sail under the flag of one State only and, save in exceptional cases expressly provided for in international treaties or in this Convention, shall be subject to its exclusive jurisdiction on the high seas. A ship may not change its flag during a voyage or while in a port of call, save in the case of a real transfer of ownership or change of registry.
2. A ship which sails under the flags of two or more States, using them according to convenience, may not claim any of the nationalities in question with respect to any other State, and may be assimilated to a ship without nationality.

Article 93
Ships flying the flag of the United Nations,
its specialized agencies
and the International Atomic Energy Agency

The preceding articles do not prejudice the question of ships employed on the official service of the United Nations, its specialized agencies or the International Atomic Energy Agency, flying the flag of the organization.

Article 94
Duties of the flag State

1. Every State shall effectively exercise its jurisdiction and control in administrative, technical and social matters over ships flying its flag.

2. In particular every State shall:
   (a) Maintain a register of shipping containing the names and particulars of ships flying its flag, except those which are excluded from generally accepted international regulations on account of their small size; and
   (b) Assume jurisdiction under its internal law over each ship flying its flag and its master, officers and crew in respect of administrative, technical and social matters concerning the ship.
3. Every State shall take such measures for ships flying its flag as are necessary to ensure safety at sea with regard, *inter alia*, to:
   (a) The construction, equipment and seaworthiness of ships;
   (b) The manning of ships, labour conditions and the training of crews, taking into account the applicable international instruments;
   (c) The use of signals, the maintenance of communications and the prevention of collisions.
4. Such measures shall include those necessary to ensure:
   (a) That each ship, before registration and thereafter at appropriate intervals, is surveyed by a qualified surveyor of ships, and has on board such charts, nautical publications and navigational equipment and instruments as are appropriate for the safe navigation of the ship;
   (b) That each ship is in the charge of a master and officers who possess appropriate qualifications, in particular in seamanship, navigation, communications and marine engineering, and that the crew is appropriate in qualification and numbers for the type, size, machinery and equipment of the ship;
   (c) That the master, officers and, to the extent appropriate, the crew are fully conversant with and required to observe the applicable international regulations concerning the safety of life at sea, the prevention of collisions, the prevention, reduction and control of marine pollution, and the maintenance of communications by radio.
5. In taking the measures called for in paragraphs 3 and 4 each State is required to conform to generally accepted international regulations, procedures and practices and to take any steps which may be necessary to secure their observance.
6. A State which has clear grounds to believe that proper jurisdiction and control with respect to a ship have not been exercised may report the facts to the flag State. Upon receiving such a report, the flag State shall investigate the matter and, if appropriate, take any action necessary to remedy the situation.
7. Each State shall cause an inquiry to be held by or before a suitably qualified person or persons into every marine casualty or incident of navigation on the high seas involving a ship flying its flag and causing loss of life or serious injury to nationals of another State or serious damage to

shipping or installations of another State or to the marine environment. The flag State and the other State shall co-operate in the conduct of any inquiry held by that other State into any such marine casualty or incident of navigation.

Article 95
Immunity of warships on the high seas

Warships on the high seas have complete immunity from the jurisdiction of any State other than the flag State.

Article 96
Immunity of ships used only on government non-commercial service

Ships owned or operated by a State and used only on government non-commercial service shall, on the high seas, have complete immunity from the jurisdiction of any State other than the flag State.

Article 97
Penal jurisdiction in matters of collision

1. In the event of a collision or any other incident of navigation concerning a ship on the high seas, involving the penal or disciplinary responsibility of the master or of any other person in the service of the ship, no penal or disciplinary proceedings may be instituted against such person except before the judicial or administrative authorities either of the flag State or of the State of which such person is a national.
2. In disciplinary matters, the State which has issued a master's certificate or a certificate of competence or licence shall alone be competent, after due legal process, to pronounce the withdrawal of such certificates, even if the holder is not a national of the State which issued them.
3. No arrest or detention of the ship, even as a measure of investigation, shall be ordered by any authorities other than those of the flag State.

Article 98
Duty to render assistance

1. Every State shall require the master of a ship sailing under its flag, in so far as he can do so without serious danger to the ship, the crew or the passengers:
   (a) To render assistance to any person found at sea in danger of being lost;
   (b) To proceed with all possible speed to the rescue of persons in distress, if informed of their need of assistance, in so far as such action may reasonably be expected of him;
   (c) After a collision, to render assistance to the other ship, its crew and its passengers and, where possible, to inform the other ship of the name

of his own ship, its port of registry and the nearest port at which it will call.

2. Every coastal State shall promote the establishment, operation and maintenance of an adequate and effective search and rescue service regarding safety on and over the sea and, where circumstances so require, by way of mutual regional arrangements co-operate with neighbouring States for this purpose.

Article 99
Prohibition of the transport of slaves

Every State shall take effective measures to prevent and punish the transport of slaves in ships authorized to fly its flag and to prevent the unlawful use of its flag for that purpose. Any slave taking refuge on board any ship, whatever its flag, shall, *ipso facto*, be free.

Article 100
Duty to co-operate in the repression of piracy

All States shall co-operate to the fullest possible extent in the repression of piracy on the high seas or in any other place outside the jurisdiction of any State.

Article 101
Definition of piracy

Piracy consists of any of the following acts:
(a) Any illegal acts of violence, detention' or any act of depredation, committed for private ends by the crew or the passengers of a private ship or a private aircraft, and directed:
  (i) On the high seas, against another ship or aircraft, or against persons or property on board such ship or aircraft;
  (ii) Against a ship, aircraft, persons or property in a place outside the jurisdiction of any State;
(b) Any act of voluntary participation in the operation of a ship or of an aircraft with knowledge of facts making it a pirate ship or aircraft;
(c) Any act of inciting or of intentionally facilitating an act described in subparagraphs (a) or (b).

Article 102
Piracy by a warship, government ship
or government aircraft whose crew has mutinied

The acts of piracy, as defined in article 101, committed by a warship, government ship or government aircraft whose crew has mutinied and taken control of the ship or aircraft are assimilated to acts committed by a private ship.

Article 103
Definition of a pirate ship or aircraft

A ship or aircraft is considered a pirate ship or aircraft if it is intended by the persons in dominant control to be used for the purpose of committing one of the acts referred to in article 101. The same applies if the ship or aircraft has been used to commit any such act, so long as it remains under the control of the persons guilty of that act.

Article 104
Retention or loss of the nationality
of a pirate ship or aircraft

A ship or aircraft may retain its nationality although it has become a pirate ship or aircraft. The retention or loss of nationality is determined by the law of the State from which such nationality was derived.

Article 105
Seizure of a pirate ship or aircraft

On the high seas, or in any other place outside the jurisdiction of any State, every State may seize a pirate ship or aircraft, or a ship taken by piracy and under the control of pirates, and arrest the persons and seize the property on board. The courts of the State which carried out the seizure may decide upon the penalties to be imposed, and may also determine the action to be taken with regard to the ships, aircraft or property, subject to the rights of third parties acting in good faith.

Article 106
Liability for seizure without adequate grounds

Where the seizure of a ship or aircraft on suspicion of piracy has been effected without adequate grounds, the State making the seizure shall be liable to the State the nationality of which is possessed by the ship or aircraft, for any loss or damage caused by the seizure.

Article 107
Ships and aircraft which are entitled
to seize on account of piracy

A seizure on account of piracy may only be carried out by warships or military aircraft, or other ships or aircraft clearly marked and identifiable as being on government service and authorized to that effect.

Article 108
Illicit traffic in narcotic drugs or psychotropic substances

1. All States shall co-operate in the suppression of illicit traffic in narcotic drugs and psychotropic substances by ships on the high seas contrary to international conventions.

2. Any State which has reasonable grounds for believing that a vessel flying its flag is engaged in illicit traffic in narcotic drugs or psychotropic substances may request the co-operation of other States to suppress such traffic.

Article 109
Unauthorized broadcasting from the high seas

1. All States shall co-operate in the suppression of unauthorized broadcasting from the high seas.
2. Any person engaged in unauthorized broadcasting from the high seas may be prosecuted before the court of the flag State of the vessel, the place of registry of the installation, the State of which the person is a national, any place where the transmissions can be received or any State where authorized radio communication is suffering interference.
3. On the high seas, a State having jurisdiction in accordance with paragraph 2 may, in conformity with article 110, arrest any person or ship engaged in unauthorized broadcasting and seize the broadcasting apparatus.
4. For the purposes of this Convention, "unauthorized broadcasting" means the transmission of sound radio or television broadcasts from a ship or installation on the high seas intended for reception by the general public contrary to international regulations, but excluding the transmission of distress calls.

Article 110
Right of visit

1. Except where acts of interference derive from powers conferred by treaty, a warship which encounters on the high seas a foreign ship, other than a ship entitled to complete immunity in accordance with articles 95 and 96, is not justified in boarding her unless there is reasonable ground for suspecting:
   (a) That the ship is engaged in piracy;
   (b) That the ship is engaged in the slave trade;
   (c) That the ship is engaged in unauthorized broadcasting and the warship has jurisdiction under article 109;
   (d) That the ship is without nationality; or
   (e) That, though flying a foreign flag or refusing to show its flag, the ship is, in reality, of the same nationality as the warship.
2. In the cases provided for in paragraph 1, the warship may proceed to verify the ship's right to fly its flag. To this end, it may send a boat, under the command of an officer, to the suspected ship. If suspicion remains after the documents have been checked, it may proceed to a further examination on board the ship, which must be carried out with all possible consideration.

3. If the suspicions prove to be unfounded, and provided that the ship boarded has not committed any act justifying them, it shall be compensated for any loss or damage that may have been sustained.
4. These provisions shall apply *mutatis mutandis* to military aircraft.
5. These provisions shall also apply to any other duly authorized ships or aircraft clearly marked and identifiable as being on government service.

Article 111
Right of hot pursuit

1. The hot pursuit of a foreign ship may be undertaken when the competent authorities of the coastal State have good reason to believe that the ship has violated the laws and regulations of that State. Such pursuit must be commenced when the foreign ship or one of its boats is within the internal waters, the archipelagic waters, the territorial sea or the contiguous zone of the pursuing State, and may only be continued outside the territorial sea or the contiguous zone if the pursuit has not been interrupted. It is not necessary that, at the time when the foreign ship within the territorial sea or the contiguous zone receives the order to stop, the ship giving the order should likewise be within the territorial sea or the contiguous zone. If the foreign ship is within a contiguous zone, as defined in article 33, the pursuit may only be undertaken if there has been a violation of the rights for the protection of which the zone was established.
2. The right of hot pursuit shall apply *mutatis mutandis* to violations in the exclusive economic zone or on the continental shelf, including safety zones around continental shelf installations, of the laws and regulations of the coastal State applicable in accordance with this Convention to the exclusive economic zone or the continental shelf, including such safety zones.
3. The right of hot pursuit ceases as soon as the ship pursued enters the territorial sea of its own country or of a third State.
4. Hot pursuit is not deemed to have begun unless the pursuing ship has satisfied itself by such practicable means as may be available that the ship pursued or one of its boats or other craft working as a team and using the ship pursued as a mother ship are within the limits of the territorial sea, or, as the case may be, within the contiguous zone or the exclusive economic zone or above the continental shelf. The pursuit may only be commenced after a visual or auditory signal to stop has been given at a distance which enables it to be seen or heard by the foreign ship.
5. The right of hot pursuit may be exercised only by warships or military aircraft, or other ships or aircraft clearly marked and identifiable as being on government service and specially authorized to that effect.

6. Where hot pursuit is effected by an aircraft:
   (a) The provisions of paragraphs 1 to 4 shall apply *mutatis mutandis*;
   (b) The aircraft giving the order to stop must itself actively pursue the ship until a ship or aircraft of the coastal State, summoned by the aircraft, arrives to take over the pursuit, unless the aircraft is itself able to arrest the ship. It does not suffice to justify an arrest outside the territorial sea that the ship was merely sighted by the aircraft as an offender or suspected offender, if it was not both ordered to stop and pursued by the aircraft itself or other aircraft or ships which continue the pursuit without interruption.
7. The release of a ship arrested within the jurisdiction of a State and escorted to a port of that State for the purposes of an inquiry before the competent authorities may not be claimed solely on the ground that the ship, in the course of its voyage, was escorted across a portion of the exclusive economic zone or the high seas, if the circumstances rendered this necessary.
8. Where a ship has been stopped or arrested outside the territorial sea in circumstances which do not justify the exercise of the right of hot pursuit, it shall be compensated for any loss or damage that may have been thereby sustained.

Article 112
Right to lay submarine cables and pipelines

1. All States shall be entitled to lay submarine cables and pipelines on the bed of the high seas beyond the continental shelf.
2. Article 79, paragraph 5, applies to such cables and pipelines.

Article 113
Breaking or injury of a submarine cable or pipeline

Every State shall adopt the laws and regulations necessary to provide that the breaking or injury by a ship flying its flag or by a person subject to its jurisdiction of a submarine cable beneath the high seas done wilfully or through culpable negligence, in such a manner as to be liable to interrupt or obstruct telegraphic or telephonic communications, and similarly the breaking or injury of a submarine pipeline or high-voltage power cable, shall be a punishable offence. This provision shall apply also to conduct calculated or likely to result in such breaking or injury. However, it shall not apply to any break or injury caused by persons who acted merely with the legitimate object of saving their lives or their ships, after having taken all necessary precautions to avoid such break or injury.

Article 114
Breaking or injury by owners of a submarine cable or
pipeline of another submarine cable or pipeline

Every State shall adopt the laws and regulations necessary to provide
that, if persons subject to its jurisdiction who are the owners of a cable or a
pipeline beneath the high seas, in laying or repairing that cable or pipeline,
cause a break in or injury to another cable or pipeline, they shall bear the cost
of the repairs.

Article 115
Indemnity for loss incurred in avoiding injury
to a submarine cable or pipeline

Every State shall adopt the laws and regulations necessary to ensure that
the owners of ships who can prove that they have sacrificed an anchor, a net
or any other fishing gear, in order to avoid injuring a submarine cable or
pipeline, shall be indemnified by the owner of the cable or pipeline, provided that the owner of the ship has taken all reasonable precautionary
measures beforehand.

SECTION 2. MANAGEMENT AND CONSERVATION OF THE
LIVING RESOURCES OF THE HIGH SEAS

Article 116
Right to fish on the high seas

All States have the right for their nationals to engage in fishing on the
high seas subject to:
  (a) Their treaty obligations;
  (b) The rights and duties as well as the interests of coastal States provided
       for, *inter alia*, in article 63, paragraph 2, and articles 64 to 67; and
  (c) The provisions of this section.

Article 117
Duty of States to adopt with respect to their nationals measures
for the conservation of the living resources of the high seas

All States have the duty to take, or to co-operate with other States in
taking, such measures for their respective nationals as may be necessary for
the conservation of the living resources of the high seas.

Article 118
Co-operation of States in the management
and conservation of living resources

States shall co-operate with each other in the management and conservation of living resources in the areas of the high seas. States whose nationals

exploit identical resources, or different resources in the same area, shall enter into negotiations with a view to adopting the means necessary for the conservation of the living resources concerned. They shall, as appropriate, co-operate to establish subregional or regional fisheries organizations to this end.

Article 119
Conservation of the living resources
of the high seas

1. In determining the allowable catch and establishing other conservation measures for the living resources in the high seas, States shall:
   (a) Adopt measures which are designed, on the best scientific evidence available to the States concerned, to maintain or restore populations of harvested species at levels which can produce the maximum sustainable yield, as qualified by relevant environmental and economic factors, including the special requirements of developing States, and taking into account fishing patterns, the interdependence of stocks and any generally recommended subregional, regional or global minimum standards;
   (b) Take into consideration the effects on species associated with or dependent upon harvested species with a view to maintaining or restoring populations of such associated or dependent species above levels at which their reproduction may become seriously threatened.
2. Available scientific information, catch and fishing effort statistics, and other data relevant to the conservation of fish stocks shall be contributed and exchanged on a regular basis through competent international organizations, whether subregional, regional or global, where appropriate and with participation by all States concerned.
3. States concerned shall ensure that conservation measures and their implementation do not discriminate in form or in fact against the fishermen of any State.

Article 120
Marine mammals

Article 65 also applies to the conservation and management of marine mammals in the high seas.

J Régime of Islands

Enclosed or Semi-Enclosed Seas

Right of Access of Land-Locked States to and from the Sea and Freedom of Transit

Note: These articles are from the "Draft convention on the Law of the Sea (Informal Text)," dated 28 August 1980, of the Third Conference on the Law of the Sea.

PART VIII. RÉGIME OF ISLANDS

Article 121
Régime of islands

1. An island is a naturally formed area of land, surrounded by water, which is above water at high tide.
2. Except as provided for in paragraph 3, the territorial sea, the contiguous zone, the exclusive economic zone and the continental shelf of an island are determined in accordance with the provisions of this Convention applicable to other land territory.
3. Rocks which cannot sustain human habitation or economic life of their own shall have no exclusive economic zone or continental shelf.

PART IX. ENCLOSED OR SEMI-ENCLOSED SEAS

Article 122
Definition

For the purposes of this Convention, "enclosed or semi-enclosed sea" means a gulf, basin, or sea surrounded by two or more States and connected to the open seas by a narrow outlet or consisting entirely or primarily of the territorial seas and exclusive economic zones of two or more coastal States.

Article 123
Co-operation of States bordering enclosed or semi-enclosed seas

States bordering enclosed or semi-enclosed seas should co-operate with each other in the exercise of their rights and duties under this Convention. To this end they shall endeavour, directly or through an appropriate regional organization:
  (a) To co-ordinate the management, conservation, exploration and exploitation of the living resources of the sea;
  (b) To co-ordinate the implementation of their rights and duties with respect to the protection and preservation of the marine environment;
  (c) To co-ordinate their scientific research policies and undertake where appropriate joint programmes of scientific research in the area;
  (d) To invite, as appropriate, other interested States or international organizations to co-operate with them in furtherance of the provisions of this article.

PART X. RIGHT OF ACCESS OF LAND-LOCKED STATES
TO AND FROM THE SEA AND FREEDOM OF TRANSIT

Article 124
Use of terms

1. For the purposes of this Convention:
  (a) "Land-locked State" means a State which has no sea-coast;
  (b) "Transit State" means a State, with or without a sea-coast, situated between a land-locked State and the sea through whose territory "traffic in transit" passes;
  (c) "Traffic in transit" means transit of persons, baggage, goods and means of transport across the territory of one or more transit States, when the passage across such territory, with or without transshipment, warehousing, breaking bulk or change in the mode of transport, is only a portion of a complete journey which begins or terminates within the territory of the land-locked State;
  (d) "Means of transport" means:
    (i) Railway rolling stock, sea, lake and river craft and road vehicles;
    (ii) Where local conditions so require, porters and pack animals.
2. Land-locked States and transit States may, by agreement between them, include as means of transport pipelines and gas lines and means of transport other than those included in paragraph 1.

Article 125
Right of access to and from the sea and freedom of transit

1. Land-locked States shall have the right of access to and from the sea for the purpose of exercising the rights provided for in this Convention including those relating to the freedom of the high seas and the common heritage of mankind. To this end, land-locked States shall enjoy freedom of transit through the territory of transit States by all means of transport.
2. The terms and modalities for exercising freedom of transit shall be agreed between the land-locked States and the transit States concerned through bilateral, subregional or regional agreements.
3. Transit States, in the exercise of their full sovereignty over their territory, shall have the right to take all measures necessary to ensure that the rights and facilities provided for in this Part for land-locked States shall in no way infringe their legitimate interests.

Article 126
Exclusion of application of the most-favoured-nation clause

Provisions of this Convention, as well as special agreements relating to the exercise of the right of access to and from the sea, establishing rights and facilities on account of the special geographical position of land-locked States, are excluded from the application of the most-favoured-nation clause.

Article 127
Customs duties, taxes and other charges

1. Traffic in transit shall not be subject to any customs duties, taxes or other charges except charges levied for specific services rendered in connexion with such traffic.
2. Means of transport in transit and other facilities provided for and used by land-locked States shall not be subject to taxes or charges higher than those levied for the use of means of transport of the transit State.

Article 128
Free zones and other customs facilities

For the convenience of traffic in transit, free zones or other customs facilities may be provided at the ports of entry and exit in the transit States, by agreement between those States and the land-locked States.

Article 129
Co-operation in the construction
and improvement of means of transport

Where there are no means of transport in the transit States to give effect to the freedom of transit or where the existing means, including the port installations and equipment, are inadequate in any respect, transit States and the land-locked States concerned may co-operate in constructing or improving them.

Article 130
Measures to avoid or eliminate delays or other difficulties
of a technical nature in traffic in transit

1. Transit States shall take all appropriate measures to avoid delays or other difficulties of a technical nature in traffic in transit.
2. Should such delays or difficulties occur, the competent authorities of the transit States and of land-locked States shall co-operate towards their expeditious elimination.

Article 131
Equal treatment in maritime ports

Ships flying the flag of land-locked States shall enjoy treatment equal to that accorded to other foreign ships in maritime ports.

Article 132
Grant of greater transit facilities

This Convention does not entail in any way the withdrawal of transit facilities which are greater than those provided for in this Convention and which are agreed between States Parties to this Convention or granted by a State Party. This Convention also does not preclude such grant of greater facilities in the future.

K   Protection and Preservation of the Marine Environment

Note: These articles are from the "Draft convention on the Law of the Sea (Informal Text)," dated 28 August 1980, of the Third Conference on the Law of the Sea.

PART XII

SECTION 1. GENERAL PROVISIONS
Article 192
General obligation

States have the obligation to protect and preserve the marine environment.

Article 193
Sovereign right of States to exploit
their natural resources

States have the sovereign right to exploit their natural resources pursuant to their environmental policies and in accordance with their duty to protect and preserve the marine environment.

Article 194
Measures to prevent, reduce and control pollution
of the marine environment

1. States shall take all necessary measures consistent with this Convention to prevent, reduce and control pollution of the marine environment from any source using for this purpose the best practicable means at their disposal and in accordance with their capabilities, individually or jointly as appropriate, and they shall endeavour to harmonize their policies in this connexion.
2. States shall take all necessary measures to ensure that activities under their jurisdiction or control are so conducted that they do not cause damage by pollution to other States and their environment, and that pollution arising from incidents or activities under their jurisdiction or

control does not spread beyond the areas where they exercise sovereign rights in accordance with this Convention.

3. The measures taken pursuant to this Part shall deal with all sources of pollution of the marine environment. These measures shall include, *inter alia*, those designed to minimize to the fullest possible extent:

   (a) Release of toxic, harmful or noxious substances, especially those which are persistent:
       (i) from land-based sources;
       (ii) from or through the atmosphere;
       (iii) by dumping;

   (b) Pollution from vessels, in particular measures for preventing accidents and dealing with emergencies, ensuring the safety of operations at sea, preventing intentional and unintentional discharges, and regulating the design, construction, equipment, operation and manning of vessels;

   (c) Pollution from installations and devices used in exploration or exploitation of the natural resources of the sea-bed and subsoil, in particular measures for preventing accidents and dealing with emergencies, ensuring the safety of operations at sea, and regulating the design, construction, equipment, operation and manning of such installations or devices;

   (d) Pollution from other installations and devices operating in the marine environment, in particular measures for preventing accidents and dealing with emergencies, ensuring the safety of operations at sea, and regulating the design, construction, equipment, operation and manning of such installations or devices.

4. In taking measures to prevent, reduce or control pollution of the marine environment, States shall refrain from unjustifiable interference with activities in pursuance of the rights exercised and duties performed by other States in conformity with this Convention.

5. The measures taken in accordance with this Part shall include those necessary to protect and preserve rare or fragile ecosystems as well as the habitat of depleted, threatened or endangered species and other forms of marine life.

Article 195
Duty not to transfer damage or hazards or transform
one type of pollution into another

In taking measures to prevent, reduce and control pollution of the marine environment, States shall act so as not to transfer, directly or indirectly, damage or hazards from one area to another or transform one type of pollution into another.

Article 196
Use of technologies or introduction
of alien or new species

1. States shall take all necessary measures to prevent, reduce and control pollution of the marine environment resulting from the use of technologies under their jurisdiction or control, or the intentional or accidental introduction of species, alien or new, to a particular part of the marine environment, which may cause significant and harmful changes thereto.
2. This article does not affect the application of this Convention regarding the prevention, reduction and control of pollution of the marine environment.

SECTION 2. GLOBAL AND REGIONAL CO-OPERATION

Article 197
Co-operation on a global or regional basis

States shall co-operate on a global basis and, as appropriate, on a regional basis, directly or through competent international organizations, in formulating and elaborating international rules, standards and recommended practices and procedures consistent with this Convention, for the protection and preservation of the marine environment, taking into account characteristic regional features.

Article 198
Notification of imminent or actual damage

When a State becomes aware of cases in which the marine environment is in imminent danger of being damaged or has been damaged by pollution, it shall immediately notify other States it deems likely to be affected by such damage, as well as the competent international organizations.

Article 199
Contingency plans against pollution

In the cases referred to in article 198, States in the area affected, in accordance with their capabilities, and the competent international organizations shall co-operate, to the extent possible, in eliminating the effects of pollution and preventing or minimizing the damage. To this end, States shall jointly develop and promote contingency plans for responding to pollution incidents in the marine environment.

Article 200
Promotion of studies, research programmes
and exchange of information and data

States shall co-operate, directly or through competent international organizations, for the purpose of promoting studies, undertaking programmes of scientific research and encouraging the exchange of information and data acquired about pollution of the marine environment. They shall endeavour to participate actively in regional and global programmes to acquire knowledge for the assessment of the nature and extent of pollution, the exposure to it, its pathways, risks and remedies.

Article 201
Scientific criteria and regulations

In the light of the information and data acquired pursuant to article 200 States shall co-operate, directly or through competent international organizations, in establishing appropriate scientific criteria for the formulation and elaboration of rules, standards and recommended practices and procedures for the prevention, reduction and control of pollution of the marine environment.

SECTION 3. TECHNICAL ASSISTANCE

Article 202
Scientific and technical assistance to developing States

States shall directly or through competent international organizations:
(a) Promote programmes of scientific, educational, technical and other assistance to developing States for the protection and preservation of the marine environment and the prevention, reduction and control of marine pollution. Such assistance shall include, *inter alia*:
  (i) Training of their scientific and technical personnel;
  (ii) Facilitating their participation in relevant international programmes;
  (iii) Supplying necessary equipment and facilities;
  (iv) Enhancing the capacity of developing States to manufacture such equipment;
  (v) Developing facilities for and advice on research, monitoring, educational and other programmes;
(b) Provide appropriate assistance, especially to developing States, for the minimization of the effects of major incidents which may cause serious pollution of the marine environment;

(c) Provide appropriate assistance, especially to developing States, concerning the preparation of environmental assessments.

Article 203
Preferential treatment for developing States

Developing States shall, for purposes of the prevention, reduction and control of pollution of the marine environment or the minimization of its effects, be granted preference by international organizations in:
(a) The allocation of appropriate funds and technical assistance; and
(b) The utilization of their specialized services.

SECTION 4. MONITORING AND ENVIRONMENTAL ASSESSMENT

Article 204
Monitoring of the risks or effects of pollution

1. States shall, consistent with the rights of other States, endeavour, as far as practicable, directly or through the competent international organizations, to observe, measure, evaluate and analyse, by recognized methods, the risks or effects of pollution of the marine environment.
2. In particular, States shall keep under surveillance the effects of any activities which they permit or in which they engage to determine whether these activities are likely to pollute the marine environment.

Article 205
Publication of reports

States shall publish reports of the results obtained pursuant to article 204 or provide at appropriate intervals such reports to the competent international organizations, which should make them available to all States.

Article 206
Assessment of potential effects of activities

When States have reasonable grounds for expecting that planned activities under their jurisdiction or control may cause substantial pollution of, or significant and harmful changes to, the marine environment, they shall, as far as practicable, assess the potential effects of such activities on the marine environment and shall communicate reports of the results of such assessments in the manner provided in article 205.

SECTION 5. INTERNATIONAL RULES AND NATIONAL
LEGISLATION TO PREVENT, REDUCE AND CONTROL
POLLUTION OF THE MARINE ENVIRONMENT

Article 207
Pollution from land-based sources

1. States shall adopt laws and regulations to prevent, reduce and control pollution of the marine environment from land-based sources including rivers, estuaries, pipelines and outfall structures, taking into account internationally agreed rules, standards and recommended practices and procedures.
2. States shall take other measures as may be necessary to prevent, reduce and control pollution of the marine environment from land-based sources.
3. States shall endeavour to harmonize their national policies at the appropriate regional level.
4. States, acting especially through competent international organizations or diplomatic conference, shall endeavour to establish global and regional rules, standards and recommended practices and procedures to prevent, reduce and control pollution of the marine environment from land-based sources, taking into account characteristic regional features, the economic capacity of developing States and their need for economic development. Such rules, standards and recommended practices and procedures shall be re-examined from time to time as necessary.
5. Laws, regulations, measures, rules, standards and recommended practices and procedures referred to in paragraphs 1, 2 and 4 respectively shall include those designed to minimize, to the fullest extent possible, the release of toxic, harmful or noxious substances, especially persistent substances, into the marine environment.

Article 208
Pollution from sea-bed activities

1. Coastal States shall adopt laws and regulations to prevent, reduce and control pollution of the marine environment arising from or in connexion with sea-bed activities subject to their jurisdiction and from artificial islands, installations and structures under their jurisdiction, pursuant to articles 60 and 80.
2. States shall take other measures as may be necessary to prevent, reduce and control such pollution.
3. Such laws, regulations and measures shall be no less effective than international rules, standards and recommended practices and procedures.

4. States shall endeavour to harmonize their national policies at the appropriate regional level.
5. States, acting especially through competent international organizations or diplomatic conference, shall establish global and regional rules, standards and recommended practices and procedures to prevent, reduce and control pollution of the marine environment arising from or in connexion with sea-bed activities subject to their jurisdiction and from artificial islands, installations and structures under their jurisdiction referred to in paragraph 1. Such rules, standards and recommended practices and procedures shall be re-examined from time to time as necessary.

Article 209
Pollution from activities in the Area

1. International rules, standards and recommended practices and procedures shall be established in accordance with the provisions of Part XI* to prevent, reduce and control pollution of the marine environment from activities in the Area. Such rules, standards and recommended practices and procedures shall be re-examined from time to time as necessary.
2. Subject to the relevant provisions of this section, States shall adopt laws and regulations to prevent, reduce and control pollution of the marine environment from activities in the Area undertaken by vessels, installations, structures and other devices flying their flag or of their registry or operating under their authority as the case may be. The requirements of such laws and regulations shall be no less effective than the international rules, standards, recommended practices and procedures referred to in paragraph 1.

Article 210
Dumping

1. States shall adopt laws and regulations to prevent, reduce and control pollution of the marine environment by dumping.
2. States shall take other measures as may be necessary to prevent, reduce and control such pollution.
3. Such laws, regulations and measures shall ensure that dumping is not carried out without the permission of the competent authorities of States.
4. States, acting especially through competent international organizations or diplomatic conference, shall endeavour to establish global and regional rules, standards and recommended practices and procedures to prevent, reduce and control pollution of the marine environment by dumping. Such rules, standards and recommended practices and procedures shall be re-examined from time to time as necessary.

*Seabed Area articles, which are not included herein.

5. Dumping within the territorial sea and the exclusive economic zone or onto the continental shelf shall not be carried out without the express prior approval of the coastal State, which has the right to permit, regulate and control such dumping after due consideration of the matter with other States which by reason of their geographical situation may be adversely affected thereby.

6. National laws, regulations and measures shall be no less effective in preventing, reducing and controlling pollution of the marine environment by dumping than global rules and standards.

Article 211
Pollution from vessels

1. States, acting through the competent international organization or general diplomatic conference, shall establish international rules and standards for the prevention, reduction and control of pollution of the marine environment from vessels and promote the adoption, in the same manner, wherever appropriate, of routing systems designed to minimize the threat of accidents which might cause pollution of the marine environment, including the coastline and related interests of coastal States. Such rules and standards shall, in the same manner, be re-examined from time to time as necessary.

2. States shall adopt laws and regulations for the prevention, reduction and control of pollution of the marine environment from vessels flying their flag or of their registry. Such laws and regulations shall at least have the same effect as that of generally accepted international rules and standards established through the competent international organization or general diplomatic conference.

3. States which establish particular requirements for the prevention, reduction and control of pollution of the marine environment as a condition for the entry of foreign vessels into their ports or internal waters or for calling at their off-shore terminals shall give due publicity to such requirements and shall communicate them to the competent international organization. Whenever such requirements are established in identical form by two or more coastal States in an endeavour to harmonize policy, the communication shall indicate which States are participating in such co-operative arrangements. Every State shall require the master of a vessel flying its flag or of its registry, when navigating within the territorial sea of a State participating in such co-operative arrangements, to furnish, upon the request of that State, information as to whether it is proceeding to a State of the same region participating in such co-operative arrangements and, if so, to indicate whether it complies with the port entry requirements of that State. The provisions of this article shall be without prejudice to the continued exercise by a vessel of its right of innocent passage or to the application of article 25, paragraph 2.

4. Coastal States may, in the exercise of their sovereignty within their territorial sea, adopt laws and regulations for the prevention, reduction and control of marine pollution from foreign vessels, including vessels exercising the right of innocent passage. Such laws and regulations shall, in accordance with section 3 of Part II, not hamper innocent passage of foreign vessels.

5. Coastal States, for the purpose of enforcement as provided for in section 6, may in respect of their exclusive economic zones adopt laws and regulations for the prevention, reduction and control of pollution from vessels conforming to and giving effect to generally accepted international rules and standards established through the competent international organization or general diplomatic conference.

6. Where international rules and standards referred to in paragraph 1 are inadequate to meet special circumstances and where coastal States have reasonable grounds for believing that a particular, clearly defined area of their respective exclusive economic zones is an area where, for recognized technical reasons in relation to its oceanographical and ecological conditions, as well as its utilization or the protection of its resources, and the particular character of its traffic, the adoption of special mandatory measures for the prevention of pollution from vessels is required, coastal States, after appropriate consultations through the competent international organization with any other States concerned, may for that area, direct a communication to the competent international organization, submitting scientific and technical evidence in support, and information on necessary reception facilities. The organization shall, within 12 months after receiving such a communication, determine whether the conditions in that area correspond to the requirements set out above. If the organization so determines, the coastal State may, for that area, adopt laws and regulations for the prevention, reduction and control of pollution from vessels, implementing such international rules and standards or navigational practices as are made applicable through the competent international organization for special areas. Coastal States shall publish the limits of any such particular, clearly defined area, and laws and regulations applicable therein shall not become applicable in relation to foreign vessels until 15 months after the submission of the communication to the competent international organization. Coastal States, when submitting the communication for the establishment of a special area within their respective exclusive economic zones, shall at the same time, notify the competent international organization if it is their intention to adopt additional laws and regulations for that special area for the prevention, reduction and control of pollution from vessels. Such additional laws and regulations may relate to discharges or navigational practices but shall not require foreign vessels to observe design, construction, manning or equipment standards other than generally accepted interna-

tional rules and standards and shall become applicable in relation to foreign vessels 15 months after the submission of the communication to the competent international organization, and provided the organization agrees within 12 months after submission of the communication.

7. The international rules and standards referred to in this article should include *inter alia* those related to prompt notification to coastal States, whose coastlines or related interests may be affected by incidents, including maritime casualties, which involve discharges or probability of discharges.

Article 212
Pollution from or through the atmosphere

1. States shall, within the air space under their sovereignty or with regard to vessels or aircraft flying their flag or of their registry, adopt laws and regulations to prevent, reduce and control pollution of the marine environment from or through the atmosphere, taking into account internationally agreed rules, standards and recommended practices and procedures, and the safety of air navigation.

2. States shall take other measures as may be necessary to prevent, reduce and control such pollution.

3. States, acting especially through competent international organizations or diplomatic conference, shall endeavour to establish global and regional rules, standards and recommended practices and procedures to prevent, reduce and control such pollution.

SECTION 6. ENFORCEMENT

Article 213
Enforcement with respect to land-based
sources of pollution

States shall enforce their laws and regulations adopted in accordance with article 207 and shall adopt laws and regulations and take measures necessary to implement applicable international rules and standards established through competent international organizations or diplomatic conference for the protection and preservation of the marine environment from land-based sources of marine pollution.

Article 214
Enforcement with respect to pollution
from sea-bed activities

States shall enforce their laws and regulations adopted in accordance with article 208 and shall adopt laws and regulations and take measures necessary to implement applicable international rules and standards established through competent international organizations or diplomatic conference for the protection and preservation of the marine environment from pollution arising from sea-bed activities subject to their jurisdiction and from artificial islands, installations and structures under their jurisdiction, pursuant to articles 60 and 80.

Article 215
Enforcement with respect to pollution
from activities in the Area

Enforcement of international rules, standards and recommended practices and procedures established to prevent, reduce and control pollution of the marine environment from activities in the Area pursuant to Part XI shall be governed by the provisions of that Part.

Article 216
Enforcement with respect to dumping

1. Laws and regulations adopted in accordance with this Convention and applicable international rules and standards established through competent international organizations or diplomatic conference for the prevention, reduction and control of pollution of the marine environment by dumping shall be enforced:
    (a) by the coastal State with regard to dumping within its territorial sea or its exclusive economic zone or onto its continental shelf:
    (b) by the flag State with regard to vessels and aircraft flying its flag or of its registry;
    (c) by any State with regard to acts of loading of wastes or other matter occurring within its territory or at its off-shore terminals.
2. This article does not impose on any State an obligation to institute proceedings when such proceedings have already been commenced by another State in accordance with this article.

Article 217
Enforcement by flag States

1. States shall ensure compliance with applicable international rules and standards established through the competent international organization or diplomatic conference and with their laws and regulations adopted in accordance with this Convention for the prevention, reduction and control of pollution of the marine environment, by vessels flying their flag or of their registry and shall adopt laws and regulations and take other measures necessary for their implementation. Flag States shall provide

for the effective enforcement of such rules, standards, laws and regulations, irrespective of where the violation occurred.

2. States shall, in particular, take appropriate measures in order to ensure that vessels flying their flags or of their registry are prohibited from sailing, until they can proceed to sea in compliance with the requirements of international rules and standards referred to in paragraph 1 for the prevention, reduction and control of pollution from vessels, including the requirements in respect of design, construction, equipment and manning of vessels.

3. States shall ensure that vessels flying their flags or of their registry carry on board certificates required by and issued pursuant to international rules and standards referred to in paragraph 1. Flag States shall ensure that their vessels are periodically inspected in order to verify that such certificates are in conformity with the actual condition of the vessels. These certificates shall be accepted by other States as evidence of the condition of the vessel and regarded as having the same force as certificates issued by them, unless there are clear grounds for believing that the condition of the vessel does not correspond substantially with the particulars of the certificates.

4. If a vessel commits a violation of rules and standards established through the competent international organization or general diplomatic conference, the flag State, without prejudice to articles 218, 220 and 228 shall provide for immediate investigation and where appropriate institute proceedings in respect of the alleged violation irrespective of where the violation occurred or where the pollution caused by such violation has occurred or has been spotted.

5. Flag States in conducting an investigation of the violation may request the assistance of any other State whose co-operation could be useful in clarifying the circumstances of the case. States shall endeavour to meet the appropriate request of flag States.

6. Flag States shall, at the written request of any State, investigate any violation alleged to have been committed by their vessels. If satisfied that sufficient evidence is available to enable proceedings to be brought in respect of the alleged violation, flag States shall without delay institute such proceedings in accordance with their laws.

7. Flag States shall promptly inform the requesting State and the competent international organization of the action taken and its outcome. Such information shall be available to all States.

8. Penalties provided for by the laws and regulations of flag States for their own vessels shall be adequate in severity to discourage violations wherever the violations occur.

Article 218
Enforcement by port States

1. When a vessel is voluntarily within a port or at an off-shore terminal of a State, that State may undertake investigations and, where warranted by the evidence of the case, institute proceedings in respect of any discharge from that vessel in violation of applicable international rules and standards established through the competent international organization or general diplomatic conference, outside the internal waters, territorial sea, or exclusive economic zone of that State.

2. No proceedings pursuant to paragraph 1 shall be instituted in respect of a discharge violation in the internal waters, the territorial sea or exclusive economic zone of another State unless requested by that State, the flag State, or the State damaged or threatened by a discharge violation, or unless the violation has caused or is likely to cause pollution in the internal waters, territorial sea or exclusive economic zone of the State instituting the proceedings.

3. When a vessel is voluntarily within a port, or at an off-shore terminal, that State shall, as far as practicable, comply with requests from any State for investigation of a discharge violation of international rules and standards referred to in paragraph 1, believed to have occurred in, caused, or threatened damage to the internal waters, territorial sea or exclusive economic zone of the State making such a request, and likewise, shall, as far as practicable, comply with requests from the flag State for investigation of such a violation, irrespective of where the violation occurred.

4. The records of the investigation carried out by a port State pursuant to the provisions of this article shall be transferred to the flag State or to the coastal State at their request. Any proceedings initiated by the port State on the basis of such an investigation, subject to the provisions of section 7, may be suspended at the request of a coastal State, when the violation has occurred within the internal waters, territorial sea or exclusive economic zone of that State and the evidence and records of the case and any bond posted with the authorities of the port State shall be transferred to the coastal State. Such transfer shall preclude the continuation of proceedings in the port State.

Article 219
Measures relating to seaworthiness
of vessels to avoid pollution

Subject to the provisions of section 7, States which have ascertained, upon request or on their own initiative, that a vessel within their ports or at their off-shore terminals is in violation of applicable international rules and standards relating to seaworthiness of vessels and thereby threatens damage to the marine environment shall, as far as practicable, take administrative measures to prevent the vessel from sailing. Such States may permit the vessel to proceed only to the nearest appropriate repair yard and upon rectification of the causes of the violation, shall permit the vessel to continue immediately.

Article 220
Enforcement of coastal States

1. When a vessel is voluntarily within a port or at an off-shore terminal of a State, that State may, subject to the provisions of section 7, institute proceedings in respect of any violation of its laws and regulations adopted in accordance with this Convention or applicable international rules and standards for the prevention, reduction and control of pollution from vessels when the violation has occurred within the territorial sea or the exclusive economic zone of that State.

2. Where there are clear grounds for believing that a vessel navigating in the territorial sea of a State has, during its passage therein, violated laws and regulations of that State adopted in accordance with this Convention or applicable international rules and standards for the prevention, reduction and control of pollution from vessels, that State, without prejudice to the application of the relevant provisions of section 3 of Part II, may undertake physical inspection of the vessel relating to the violation and may, when warranted by the evidence of the case, institute proceedings, including detention of the vessel, in accordance with its laws, subject to the provisions of Section 7.

3. Where there are clear grounds for believing that a vessel navigating in the exclusive economic zone or the territorial sea of a State has, in the exclusive economic zone, violated applicable international rules and standards or laws and regulations of that State conforming and giving effect to such international rules and standards for the prevention, reduction and control of pollution from vessels, that State may require the vessel to give information regarding the identification of the vessel and its port of registry, its last and next port of call and other relevant information required to establish whether a violation has occurred.

4. Flag States shall adopt laws and regulations and take other measures so that their vessels comply with requests for information pursuant to paragraph 3.

5. Where there are clear grounds for believing that a vessel navigating in the exclusive economic zone or the territorial sea of a State has, in the exclusive economic zone, violated applicable international rules and standards or laws and regulations of that State conforming and giving effect to such international rules and standards for the prevention, reduction

and control of pollution from vessels and the violation has resulted in a substantial discharge causing or threatening significant pollution of the marine environment, that State may undertake physical inspection of the vessel for matters relating to the violation if the vessel has refused to give information or if the information supplied by the vessel is manifestly at variance with the evident factual situation and if the circumstances of the case justify such inspection.

6. Where there is clear objective evidence that a vessel navigating in the exclusive economic zone or the territorial sea of a State has, in the exclusive economic zone, committed a violation of applicable international rules and standards or laws and regulations of that State conforming and giving effect to such international rules and standards for the prevention, reduction and control of pollution from vessels, resulting in a discharge causing major damage or threat of major damage to the coastline or related interests of the coastal State, or to any resources of its territorial sea or exclusive economic zone, that State may, subject to the provisions of section 7, provided that the evidence so warrants, institute proceedings, including detention of the vessel, in accordance with its laws.

7. Notwithstanding the provisions of paragraph 6, whenever appropriate procedures have been established either through the competent international organization or as otherwise agreed, whereby compliance with requirements for bonding or other appropriate financial security has been assured, the coastal State if bound by such procedures shall allow the vessel to proceed.

8. The provisions of paragraphs 3, 4, 5, 6 and 7 apply correspondingly in respect of national laws and regulations adopted pursuant to article 211, paragraph 6.

Article 221
Measures relating to maritime casualties
to avoid pollution

1. Nothing in this Part shall prejudice the right of States, pursuant to international law, both customary and conventional, to take and enforce measures beyond the territorial sea proportionate to the actual or threatened damage to protect their coastline or related interests, including fishing, from pollution or threat of pollution following upon a maritime casualty or acts relating to such a casualty, which may reasonably be expected to result in major harmful consequences.

2. For the purposes of this article, "maritime casualty" means a collision of vessels, stranding or other incident of navigation, or other occurrence on board a vessel or external to it resulting in material damage or imminent threat of material damage to a vessel or cargo.

Article 222
Enforcement with respect to pollution
from or through the atmosphere

States shall enforce, within the air space under their sovereignty or with regard to vessels or aircraft flying their flag or of their registry, their laws and regulations adopted in accordance with article 212, paragraph 1, and with other provisions of this Convention and shall adopt laws and regulations necessary and take other measures to implement applicable international rules and standards established through competent international organizations or diplomatic conference to prevent, reduce and control pollution of the marine environment from and through the atmosphere, in conformity with all relevant international rules and standards concerning the safety of air navigation.

SECTION 7. SAFEGUARDS

Article 223
Measures to facilitate proceedings

In proceedings instituted pursuant to this Part, States shall take measures to facilitate the hearing of witnesses and the admission of evidence submitted by authorities of another State, or by the competent international organization, and shall facilitate the attendance at such proceedings of official representatives of the competent international organization or of the flag State, or of any State affected by pollution arising out of any violation. The official representatives attending such proceedings shall have such rights and duties as may be provided under national laws and regulations or international law.

Article 224
Exercise of powers of enforcement

The powers of enforcement against foreign vessels under this Part may only be exercised by officials or by warships, military aircraft or other ships or aircraft clearly marked and identifiable as being on government service and authorized to that effect.

Article 225
Duty to avoid adverse consequences
in the exercise of the powers of enforcement

In the exercise under this Convention of their powers of enforcement against foreign vessels, States shall not endanger the safety of navigation or otherwise create any hazard to a vessel, or bring it to an unsafe port or anchorage, or expose the marine environment to an unreasonable risk.

Article 226
Investigation of foreign vessels

1. States shall not delay a foreign vessel longer than is essential for purposes of the investigations provided for in articles 216, 218 and 220. Any physical inspection of a foreign vessel shall be limited to an examination of such certificates, records or other documents as the vessel is required to carry by generally accepted international rules and standards or of any similar documents which it is carrying. Following such an examination, an inspection of the vessel may be undertaken only when there are clear grounds for believing that the condition of the vessel or its equipment does not correspond substantially with the particulars of those documents or when the contents of such documents are not sufficient to confirm or verify a suspected violation or when the vessel is not carrying valid certificates and records. If the investigation indicates a violation of applicable laws and regulations or international rules and standards for the protection and preservation of the marine environment, release shall be made promptly subject to reasonable procedures such as bonding or other appropriate financial security. Without prejudice to applicable international rules and standards relating to the seaworthiness of vessels, the release of a vessel may, whenever it would present an unreasonable threat of damage to the marine environment, be refused or made conditional upon proceeding to the nearest appropriate repair yard. In situations where release has been refused or made conditional, the flag State of the vessel must be promptly notified, and may seek release of the vessel in accordance with the provisions of Part XV.
2. States shall co-operate to develop procedures for the avoidance of unnecessary physical inspection of vessels at sea.

Article 227
Non-discrimination of foreign vessels

   In exercising their rights and carrying out their duties under this Part, States shall not discriminate in form or in fact against vessels of any other State.

Article 228
Suspension and restrictions on
institution of proceedings

1. Proceedings to impose penalties in respect of any violation of applicable laws and regulations or international rules and standards relating to the prevention, reduction and control of pollution from vessels committed by a foreign vessel beyond the territorial sea of the State instituting proceedings shall be suspended upon the taking of proceedings to im-

pose penalties under corresponding charges by the flag State within six months of the first institution of proceedings, unless those proceedings relate to a case of major damage to the coastal State or the flag State in question has repeatedly disregarded its obligations to enforce effectively the applicable international rules and standards in respect of violations committed by its vessels. The flag State shall in due course make available to the first State instituting proceedings a full dossier of the case and the records of the proceedings, whenever the flag State has requested the suspension of proceedings in accordance with the provisions of this article. When proceedings by the flag State have been brought to a conclusion, the suspended proceedings shall be terminated. Upon payment of costs incurred in respect of such proceedings, any bond posted or other financial security provided in connexion with the suspended proceedings shall be released by the coastal State.

2. Proceedings to impose penalties on foreign vessels shall not be instituted after the expiry of three years from the date on which the violation was committed, and shall not be taken by any State in the event of proceedings having been instituted by another State subject to the provisions set out in paragraph 1.

3. The provisions of this article are without prejudice to the right of the flag State to take any measures, including proceedings to impose penalties, according to its laws irrespective of prior proceedings by another State.

Article 229
Institution of civil proceedings

Nothing in this Convention affects the institution of civil proceedings in respect of any claim for loss or damage resulting from pollution of the marine environment.

Article 230
Monetary penalties and the observance of
recognized rights of the accused

1. Monetary penalties only may be imposed with respect to violations of national laws and regulations or applicable international rules and standards for the prevention, reduction and control of pollution of the marine environment, committed by foreign vessels beyond the territorial sea.

2. Monetary penalties only may be imposed with respect to violations of national laws and regulations or applicable international rules and standards for the prevention, reduction and control of pollution of the marine environment, committed by foreign vessels in the territorial sea, except in the case of a wilful and serious act of pollution in the territorial sea.

3. In the conduct of proceedings in respect of such violations committed by a foreign vessel which may result in the imposition of penalties, recognized rights of the accused shall be observed.

Article 231
Notification to flag States
and other States concerned

States shall promptly notify the flag State and any other State concerned of any measure taken pursuant to section 6 against foreign vessels, and shall submit to the flag State all official reports concerning such measures. However, with respect to violations committed in the territorial sea, the foregoing obligations of the coastal State apply only to such measures as are taken in proceedings. The consular officers or diplomatic agents, and where possible the maritime authority of the flag State, shall be immediately informed of any such measures.

Article 232
Liability of States arising
from enforcement measures

States shall be liable for damage or loss attributable to them arising from measures taken pursuant to section 6 when such measures were unlawful or exceeded those reasonably required in the light of available information. States shall provide for recourse in their courts for actions in respect of such damage or loss.

Article 233
Safeguards with respect to straits
used for international navigation

Nothing in sections 5, 6 and 7 affects the legal régime of straits used for international navigation. However, if a foreign ship other than those referred to in section 10 has committed a violation of the laws and regulations referred to in article 42, paragraph 1 (a) and (b), causing or threatening major damage to the marine environment of the straits, the States bordering the straits may take appropriate enforcement measures and if so shall respect *mutatis mutandis* the provisions of this section.

SECTION 8. ICE-COVERED AREAS

Article 234
Ice-covered areas

Coastal States have the right to adopt and enforce non-discriminatory laws and regulations for the prevention, reduction and control of marine pollution from vessels in ice-covered areas within the limits of the exclusive economic zone, where particularly severe climatic conditions and the presence of ice covering such areas for most of the year create obstructions or exceptional hazards to navigation, and pollution of the marine environment could cause major harm to or irreversible disturbance of the ecological balance. Such laws and regulations shall have due regard to navigation and the protection and preservation of the marine environment based on the best available scientific evidence.

SECTION 9. RESPONSIBILITY AND LIABILITY

Article 235
Responsibility and liability

1. States are responsible for the fulfilment of their international obligations concerning the protection and preservation of the marine environment. They shall be liable in accordance with international law.
2. States shall ensure that recourse is available in accordance with their legal systems for prompt and adequate compensation or other relief in respect of damage caused by pollution of the marine environment by natural or juridical persons under their jurisdiction.
3. With the objective of assuring prompt and adequate compensation in respect of all damage caused by pollution of the marine environment, States shall co-operate in the implementation of existing international law and the further development of international law relating to responsibility and liability for the assessment of and compensation for damage and the settlement of related disputes, as well as, where appropriate, development of criteria and procedures for payment of adequate compensation such as compulsory insurance or compensation funds.

SECTION 10. SOVEREIGN IMMUNITY

Article 236
Sovereign immunity

The provisions of this Convention regarding the protection and preservation of the marine environment do not apply to any warship, naval auxiliary, other vessels or aircraft owned or operated by a State and used, for the time being, only on government non-commercial service. However, each State shall ensure by the adoption of appropriate measures not impairing operations or operational capabilities of such vessels or aircraft owned or operated by it, that such vessels or aircraft act in a manner consistent, so far as is reasonable and practicable, with this Convention.

SECTION 11. OBLIGATIONS UNDER OTHER CONVENTIONS
ON THE PROTECTION AND PRESERVATION
OF THE MARINE ENVIRONMENT

Article 237
Obligations under other conventions
on the protection and preservation
of the marine environment

1. The provisions of this Part are without prejudice to the specific obliga-
    tions assumed by States under special conventions and agreements con-
    cluded previously which relate to the protection and preservation of the
    marine environment and to agreements which may be concluded in
    furtherance of the general principles set forth in this Convention.
2. Specific obligations assumed by States under special conventions, with
    respect to the protection and preservation of the marine environment,
    should be carried out in a manner consistent with the general principles
    and objectives of this Convention.

L Marine Scientific Research

Note: These articles are from the "Draft convention on the Law of the Sea (Informal Text)," dated 28 August 1980, of the Third Conference on the Law of the Sea.

PART XIII

SECTION 1. GENERAL PROVISIONS

Article 238
Right to conduct marine scientific research

All States, irrespective of their geographical location, and competent international organizations have the right to conduct marine scientific research subject to the rights and duties of other States as provided for in this Convention.

Article 239
Promotion of marine scientific research

States and competent international organizations shall promote and facilitate the development and conduct of marine scientific research in accordance with this Convention.

Article 240
General principles for the conduct
of marine scientific research

In the conduct of marine scientific research the following principles shall apply:
(a) Marine scientific research shall be conducted exclusively for peaceful purposes;
(b) Such research shall be conducted with appropriate scientific methods and means compatible with this Convention;
(c) Such research shall not unjustifiably interfere with other legitimate uses of the sea compatible with this Convention and shall be duly respected in the course of such uses;
(d) Such research shall comply with all relevant regulations adopted in conformity with this Convention including those for the protection and preservation of the marine environment.

Article 241
Marine scientific research activities not
constituting the legal basis for any claim

Marine scientific research activities shall not constitute the legal basis for any claim to any part of the marine environment or its resources.

SECTION 2. GLOBAL AND REGIONAL CO-OPERATION

Article 242
Promotion of international co-operation

1. States and competent international organizations shall, in accordance with the principle of respect for sovereignty and jurisdiction and on the basis of mutual benefit, promote international co-operation in marine scientific research for peaceful purposes.
2. In this context, without prejudice to the rights and duties of States under this Convention, a State, in the application of this Part, shall provide, as appropriate, other States with a reasonable opportunity to obtain from it, or with its co-operation, information necessary to prevent and control damage to the health and safety of persons and the environment.

Article 243
Creation of favourable conditions

States and competent international organizations shall co-operate, through the conclusion of bilateral and multilateral agreements, to create favourable conditions for the conduct of marine scientific research in the marine environment and to integrate the efforts of scientists in studying the essence of and the interrelations between phenomena and processes occurring in the marine environment.

Article 244
Publication and dissemination
of information and knowledge

1. States and competent international organziations shall, in accordance with this Convention, make available by publication and dissemination through appropriate channels information on proposed major programmes and their objectives as well as knowledge resulting from marine scientific research.
2. For this purpose, States, both individually and in co-operation with other States and with competent international organizations, shall actively promote the flow of scientific data and information and the transfer of knowledge resulting from marine scientific research especially to developing States, as well as the strengthening of the autonomous marine

scientific research capabilities of developing States through, *inter alia*, programmes to provide adequate education and training of their technical and scientific personnel.

SECTION 3. CONDUCT AND PROMOTION OF MARINE SCIENTIFIC RESEARCH

Article 245
Marine scientific research
in the territorial sea

Coastal States, in the exercise of their sovereignty, have the exclusive right to regulate, authorize and conduct marine scientific research in their territorial sea. Marine scientific research therein shall be conducted only with the express consent of and under the conditions set forth by the coastal State.

Article 246
Marine scientific research in the exclusive
economic zone and on the continental shelf

1. Coastal States, in the exercise of their jurisdiction, have the right to regulate, authorize and conduct marine scientific research in their exclusive economic zone and on their continental shelf in accordance with the relevant provisions of this Convention.
2. Marine scientific research in the exclusive economic zone and on the continental shelf shall be conducted with the consent of the coastal State.
3. Coastal States shall, in normal circumstances, grant their consent for marine scientific research projects by other States or competent international organizations in their exclusive economic zone or on their continental shelf to be carried out in accordance with this Convention exclusively for peaceful purposes and in order to increase scientific knowledge of the marine environment for the benefit of all mankind. To this end, coastal States shall establish rules and procedures ensuring that such consent will not be delayed or denied unreasonably.
4. Normal circumstances may exist in spite of the absence of diplomatic relations between the coastal State and the researching State for the purposes of applying paragraph 3.
5. Coastal States may however in their discretion withhold their consent to the conduct of a marine scientific research project of another State or competent international organization in the exclusive economic zone or on the continental shelf of the coastal State if that project:
   (a) is of direct significance for the exploration and exploitation of natural resources, whether living or non-living;

(b) involves drilling into the continental shelf, the use of explosives or the introduction of harmful substances into the marine environment;

(c) involves the construction, operation or use of artificial islands, installations and structures referred to in articles 60 and 80;

(d) contains information communicated pursuant to article 248 regarding the nature and objectives of the project which is inaccurate or if the researching State or competent international organization has outstanding obligations to the coastal State from a prior research project.

6. Notwithstanding the provisions of paragraph 5, coastal States may not exercise their discretion to withhold consent under subparagraph (a) of the above-mentioned paragraph in respect of marine scientific research projects to be undertaken in accordance with the provisions of this Part on the continental shelf, beyond 200 nautical miles from the baselines from which the breadth of the territorial sea is measured, outside those specific areas which coastal States may at any time publicly designate as areas in which exploitation or detailed exploratory operations focused on those areas are occurring or will occur within a reasonable period of time. Coastal States shall give reasonable notice of the designation of such areas, as well as any modifications thereto, but shall not be obliged to give details of the operations therein.

7. The provisions of paragraph 6 are without prejudice to the rights of coastal States over the continental shelf as established in article 77.

8. Marine scientific research activities referred to in this article shall not unjustifiably interfere with activities undertaken by coastal States in accordance with their sovereign rights and jurisdiction as provided for in this Convention.

Article 247
Marine scientific research projects
undertaken by, or under the auspices of,
international organizations

A coastal State which is a member of an international organization or has a bilateral agreement with such an organization, and in whose exclusive economic zone or on whose continental shelf the organization wants to carry out, directly or under its auspices, a marine scientific research project, shall be deemed to have authorized the project to be carried out in conformity with the agreed specifications if that State approved the detailed project when the decision was made by the organization for the undertaking of this project, or is willing to participate in it, and has not expressed any objection within four months of notification of the project by the organization to the coastal State.

Article 248
Duty to provide information
to the coastal State

States and competent international organizations which intend to under-take marine scientific research in the exclusive economic zone or on the continental shelf of a coastal State shall, not less than six months in advance of the expected starting date of the marine scientific research project, provide that State with a full description of:

(a) the nature and objectives of the project;
(b) the method and means to be used, including name, tonnage, type and class of vessels and a description of scientific equipment;
(c) the precise geographical areas in which the project is to be conducted;
(d) the expected date of first appearance and final departure of the research vessels, or deployment of the equipment and its removal, as appropriate;
(e) the name of the sponsoring institution, its director, and the person in charge of the project; and
(f) the extent to which it is considered that the coastal State should be able to participate or to be represented in the project.

Article 249
Duty to comply with certain conditions

1. States and competent international organizations when undertaking marine scientific research in the exclusive economic zone or on the continental shelf of a coastal State shall comply with the following conditions:

    (a) ensure the right of the coastal State, if it so desires, to participate or be represented in the marine scientific research project, especially on board research vessels and other craft or scientific research installations, when practicable, without payment of any remuneration to the scientists of the coastal State and without obligation to contribute towards the costs of the project;
    (b) provide the coastal State, at its request, with preliminary reports, as soon as practicable, and with the final results and conclusions after the completion of the research;
    (c) undertake to provide access for the coastal State, at its request, to all data and samples derived from the marine scientific research project and likewise to furnish it with data which may be copied and samples which may be divided without detriment to their scientific value;
    (d) if requested, provide the coastal State with an assessment of such data, samples and research results or provide assistance in their assessment or interpretation;

(e) ensure, subject to paragraph 2, that the research results are made internationally available through appropriate national or international channels, as soon as feasible;

(f) inform the coastal State immediately of any major change in the research programme;

(g) unless otherwise agreed, remove the scientific research installations or equipment once the research is completed.

2. This article is without prejudice to the conditions established by the laws and regulations of the coastal State for the exercise of its discretion to grant or withhold consent pursuant to article 246, paragraph 5, including requiring prior agreement for making internationally available the research results of a project of direct significance for the exploration and exploitation of natural resources.

Article 250
Communications concerning marine
scientific research projects

Communications concerning the marine scientific research projects shall be made through appropriate official channels unless otherwise agreed.

Article 251
General criteria and guidelines

States shall seek to promote through competent international organizations the establishment of general criteria and guidelines to assist States in ascertaining the nature and implications of marine scientific research.

Article 252
Implied consent

States or competent international organizations may proceed with a marine scientific research project upon the expiry of six months from the date upon which the information required pursuant to article 248 was provided to the coastal State unless within four months of the receipt of the communication containing such information the coastal State has informed the State or organization conducting the research that:

(a) it has withheld its consent under the provisions of article 246; or

(b) the information given by the State or competent international organization in question regarding the nature or objectives of the project does not conform to the manifestly evident facts; or

(c) it requires supplementary information relevant to conditions and the information provided for under articles 248 and 249; or

(d) outstanding obligations exist with respect to a previous marine scientific research project carried out by that State or organization, with regard to conditions established in article 249.

Article 253
Suspension or cessation of marine
scientific research activities

1. Coastal States shall have the right to require the suspension of any marine
   scientific research activities in progress within its exclusive economic zone
   or on its continental shelf if:
   (a) the research activities are not being conducted in accordance with the
       information communicated as provided under article 248 upon
       which the consent of the coastal State was based; or
   (b) the State or competent international organization conducting the
       research activities fails to comply with the provisions of article 249
       concerning the rights of the coastal State with respect to the marine
       scientific research project.
2. Coastal States shall have the right to require the cessation of any marine
   scientific research activities in case of any non-compliance with the provisions of article 248 which amounts to a major change in the research
   project or the research activities.
3. Coastal States may also require cessation of marine scientific research
   activities if any of the situations contemplated in paragraph 1 are not
   rectified within a reasonable period of time.
4. Following notification by the coastal State of its decision to order suspension or cessation, States or competent international organizations authorized to conduct marine scientific research activities shall terminate the
   research activities that are subject of such a notification.
5. An order of suspension under paragraph 1 shall be lifted by the coastal
   State and the marine scientific research activities allowed to continue
   once the researching State or competent international organization has
   complied with the conditions required under articles 248 and 249.

Article 254
Rights of neighbouring land-locked and
geographically disadvantaged States[6]

1. States and competent international organizations which have submitted
   to a coastal State a project to undertake marine scientific research referred to in article 246, paragraph 3, shall give notice to the neighbouring
   land-locked and geographically disadvantaged States of the proposed
   research project. Those States or competent international organizations
   shall notify the coastal State of such notice given to the land-locked and
   geographically disadvantaged States.
2. After the consent has been given for such a proposed marine scientific
   research project by the coastal State concerned, in accordance with article

[6]The terms "geographically disadvantaged States" and "States with special geographic
characteristics" (used in article 70), should be harmonized by the Conference.

246 and other relevant provisions of this Convention, States and competent international organizations undertaking such a project, shall provide the neighbouring land-locked and geographically disadvantaged States, at their request and when appropriate, with relevant information as specified in articles 248 and 249, paragraph 1 (f).

3. The neighbouring land-locked and geographically disadvantaged States referred to above, shall, at their request, be given the opportunity to participate, whenever feasible, in the proposed marine scientific research project through qualified experts appointed by them and not objected to by the coastal State, in accordance with the conditions governing the project as agreed upon, in conformity with the provisions of this Convention, between the coastal State concerned and the State or competent international organizations conducting the marine scientific research.

4. States and competent international organizations referred to in paragraph 1 of this article, shall provide the above-mentioned land-locked and geographically disadvantaged States, at their request, the information and assistance specified in article 249, paragraph 1 (d), subject to the provisions of article 249, paragraph 2.

Article 255
Measures to facilitate marine scientific research
and assist research vessels

States shall endeavour to adopt reasonable rules, regulations and procedures to promote and facilitate marine scientific research, conducted in accordance with this Convention, beyond their territorial sea and, as appropriate, to facilitate, subject to the provisions of their laws and regulations, access to their harbours and promote assistance for marine scientific research vessels, which comply with the relevant provisions of this Part.

Article 256
Marine scientific research in the Area

All States, irrespective of their geographical location, as well as competent international organizations, have the right, in conformity with the provisions of Part XI, to conduct marine scientific research in the Area.

Article 257
Marine scientific research in the water column
beyond the exclusive economic zone

All States, irrespective of their geographical location, as well as competent international organizations, have the right, in conformity with this Convention, to conduct marine scientific research in the water column beyond the limits of the exclusive economic zone.

SECTION 4. LEGAL STATUS OF
SCIENTIFIC RESEARCH INSTALLATIONS OR
EQUIPMENT IN THE MARINE ENVIRONMENT

Article 258
Deployment and use

The deployment and use of any type of scientific research installations or equipment in any area of the marine environment shall be subject to the same conditions as are prescribed in this Convention for the conduct of marine scientific research in any such area.

Article 259
Legal status

The installations or equipment referred to in this section do not possess the status of islands. They have no territorial sea of their own, and their presence does not affect the delimitation of the territorial sea, the exclusive economic zone or the continental shelf.

Article 260
Safety zones

Safety zones of a reasonable width not exceeding a distance of 500 metres may be created around scientific research installations in accordance with the relevant provisions of this Convention. All States shall ensure that such safety zones are respected by their vessels.

Article 261
Non-interference with shipping routes

The deployment and use of any type of scientific research installations or equipment shall not constitute an obstacle to established international shipping routes.

Article 262
Identification markings and warning signals

Installations or equipment referred to in this section shall bear identification markings indicating the State of registry or the international organization to which they belong and shall have adequate internationally agreed warning signals to ensure safety at sea and the safety of air navigation, taking into account rules and standards established by competent international organizations.

SECTION 5. RESPONSIBILITY AND LIABILITY

Article 263
Responsibility and liability

1. States and competent international organizations shall be responsible for ensuring that marine scientific research, whether undertaken by them or on their behalf, is conducted in accordance with this Convention.
2. States and competent international organizations shall be responsible and liable for the measures they take in contravention of this Convention in respect of marine scientific research conducted by other States, their natural or juridical persons or by competent international organizations, and shall provide compensation for damage resulting from such measures.
3. States and competent international organizations shall be responsible and liable pursuant to article 235 for damage caused by pollution of the marine environment arising out of marine scientific research undertaken by them or on their behalf.

SECTION 6. SETTLEMENT OF DISPUTES AND INTERIM MEASURES

Article 264
Settlement of disputes

Disputes relating to the interpretation or application of the provisions of this Convention with regard to marine scientific research shall be settled in accordance with section 2 of Part XV.*

Article 265
Interim measures

Pending settlement of a dispute in accordance with section 2 of Part XV, the State or competent international organization authorized to conduct a marine scientific research project shall not allow research activities to commence or continue without the express consent of the coastal State concerned.

*Settlement of Disputes articles, which are not included herein.

M

The Conduct of Armed Conflict

Extract from U.S. Air Force pamphlet No. 110-31

"General Restrictions on Aerial Bombardment: Principle of Immunity of Civilians:

a. Protection of the Civilian Population/Civilian Objects

    (1) Immunity of Civilians. The civilian population and individual civilians enjoy general protection against dangers arising from military operations. To give effect to this protection, the following rules must be observed.

        (a) The civilian population as such, as well as individual civilians, shall not be made the object of attack. Acts or threats of violence which have the primary object of spreading terror among the civilian population are prohibited.

        (b) Civilian objects shall not be made the object of attack. Civilian objects are all objects which are not military objectives. In case of doubt whether an object which is normally dedicated to civilian purposes, such as a house or other dwelling or a school, is being used to make an effective contribution to military action, it shall be presumed not to be so used.

        (c) Civilians enjoy the protection afforded by law unless and for such time as they take a direct part in the hostilities.

        (d) The presence or movements of the civilian population or individual civilians shall not be used to render certain points or areas immune from military operations. In particular in attempts to shield military objectives from attack, or to shield, favor or impede military operations. Parties to a conflict must not direct the movement of the civilian population or individual civilians in attempts to shield military objectives from attack or to shield military operations.

    (2) Discussion. The foregoing confirms the principle that the civilian population, individual civilians, and civilian objects are not lawful objects of attack, as such, during armed conflict. Attacks primarily intended to terrorize the civilian population instead of destroying or neutralizing military objectives are also prohibited. Civilian objects

also enjoy general immunity from attack and include all objects which are not military objectives. Objects normally dedicated to civilian purposes, such as a house, dwelling or school are in case of doubt presumed not be military objectives. Location as well as prior uses are important factors in determining whether objects are military objectives. Thus, dwellings located within a heavily contested contact zone need not be presumed to be civilian objects. Traditionally, sophisticated transportation systems are used heavily for military purposes in intense conflicts. Their status as military objectives is readily apparent. This general protection of civilian objects is entirely consistent with traditional military doctrine since civilian objects are not, by definition, making an effective contribution to enemy military action, and their destruction or neutralization offers no definite military advantage. Incidental civilian injury or damage is discussed subsequently.

(a) Nonparticipation in Hostilities. Civilian immunity requires a corollary obligation on the part of civilians not to take a direct part in hostilities. This very strict condition means they must not become combatants. For example, taking a direct part in hostilities covers acts of war intended by their nature and purpose to strike at enemy personnel and material. Thus a civilian taking part in fighting, whether singly or as a member of a group, loses the immunity given civilians.

(b) Requirement to Distinguish. The requirement to distinguish between combatants and civilians, and between military objectives and civilian objectives, imposes obligations on all the parties to the conflict to establish and maintain the distinctions. This is true whatever the legal status of the territory on or over which combatant activity occurs. Inherent in the principle protecting the civilian population, and required to make that protection fully effective, is a requirement that civilians not be used to render areas immune from military operations. Civilians may not be used to shield a defensive position, to hide military objectives, or to screen an attack. Neither may they be compelled or induced to leave their homes or shelters in order to disrupt the movement of an adverse party. A party to a conflict which chooses to use its civilian population for military purposes violates its obligations to protect its own civilian population. It cannot complain when inevitable, although regrettable, civilian casualties result. In addition to geographical proximity, civilian casualties result when civilians are functionally used in war activities, as for example, in building bridges or working in munitions factories.

b. Attacks Against Military Objectives

   (1) Requirement That Military Operations be Directed at Military Objectives. In order to insure respect and protection for the civilian population and civilian objects the parties to the conflict must at all times distinguish between the civilian population and combatants and between civilian objects and military objectives and accordingly direct their operations only against military objectives. Insofar as objects are concerned, military objectives are limited to those objects which by their own nature, location, purpose, or use make an effective contribution to military action and whose total or partial destruction, capture, or neutralization in the circumstances ruling at the time offers a definite military advantage.

   (2) Discussion. This rule confirms the basic legal requirement that any aerial bombardment be directed specifically against a military objective. Prior to the introduction of aerial warfare, "military objectives" were often defined to include only such targets as combatant troops, defended or fortified places, military depots, and the like. Since the advent of hostilities waged from the air, the scope of lawful "military objectives" has been enlarged. Previous attempts in Hague IX, and the 1923 Draft Hague Rules to define a military objective for purposes of bombardment have not always been followed in actual practice, particularly in World War II. Many objects, including an adversary's military encampments, his armament, such as military aircraft, tanks, antiaircraft emplacements, and troops in the field, are military objectives beyond any dispute. Controversy exists over whether, and the circumstances under which other objects, such as civilian transportation and communications systems, dams and dikes can be classified properly as military objectives. The inherent nature of the object is not controlling since even a traditionally civilian object, such as a civilian house, can be a military objective when it is occupied and used by military forces during an armed engagement. A key factor in classification of objects as military objectives is whether they make an effective contribution to an adversary's military action so that their capture, destruction, or neutralization offers a definite military advantage in the circumstances ruling at the time. The requirement that attacks be limited to military objectives results from several requirements of international law. The mass annihilation of enemy people is neither humane, permissible, nor militarily necessary. The Hague Regulations prohibit destruction or seizure of enemy property "unless such destruction or seizure be imperatively demanded by the necessities of war." Destruction as an end in itself is a violation of international law, and there must be some reasonable

connection between the destruction of property and the overcoming of enemy military forces. Various other prohibitions and the Hague Regulations and Hague Convention IX further support the requirement that attacks be directed only at military objectives.

c. Precautions in Attack
(1) Precautions Required:
  (a) In conducting military operations, constant care must be taken to spare the civilian population, civilians, and civilian objects.
  (b) With respect to attacks, the following precautions must be taken.
    (1) Those who plan or decide upon an attack must:
      (a) Do everything feasible to verify that the objectives to be attacked are neither civilians nor civilian objects and are not subject to special protection but are military objectives and that it is permissible to attack them;
      (b) Take all feasible precautions in the choice of means and methods of attack with a view to avoiding, and in any event to minimizing incidental loss of civilian life, injury to civilians, and damage to civilian objects; and
      (c) Refrain from deciding to launch any attack which may be expected to cause incidental loss of civilian life, injury to civilians, damage to civilian objects, or a combination thereof, which would be excessive in relation to the concrete and direct military advantage anticipated.
        (i) An attack must be cancelled or suspended if it becomes apparent that the objective is not a military one, or that it is subject to special protection or that the attack may be expected to cause incidental loss of civilian life, injury to civilians, damage to civilian objects, or a combination thereof which would be excessive in relation to the concrete and direct military advantage anticipated:
        (ii) Effective advance warning shall be given of attacks which may affect the civilian population unless circumstances do not permit.
    (c) When a choice is possible between several military objectives for obtaining a similar military advantage, the objective to be selected shall be that which may be expected to cause the least danger to civilian lives and to civilian objects.
(2) Particular Precautionary Measures. Since states have not always separated military activities from civilian activities, a geographical and functional mixture of combatants and civilians and military objectives and civilian objects often results. The requirement for precautionary measures recognizes this reality. Precautionary measures

are not a substitute for the general immunity of the civilian population, but an attempt to give effect to the immunity of civilians and the requirements of military necessity. Dangers to civilian populations in a given situation vary according to the military objective attacked, configuration of terrain, type of weapons used, meteorological conditions, the presence of civilians at the scene or in the immediate vicinity and a particular combatant's ability and mastery of bombardment techniques as well as the level of the conflict and the type of resistance to be encountered during the attack. Permissible bombardment techniques vary according to such factors. Thus, what is needed is:

(a) Identification of Military Objective. Initially, those who plan or decide upon an attack must do everything feasible, under the particular circumstances at the time, to verify that military objectives are in fact being attacked and not civilians or civilian objects. Sound target intelligence also enhances military effectiveness by insuring that the risks undertaken are militarily worthwhile. It is also a matter of conservation of vital resources. Economy of force, concentration of effort and maximization of military advantage support such efforts.

(b) Incidental Civilian Casualties. Civilian casualties are to be avoided to the greatest extent possible. However, international law has long recognized that civilian casualties and damage to civilian objects, although regrettable, do occur in armed conflict. They result from several factors. First, military objectives may not be segregated from civilian population centers, civilians, or civilian objects. Second, civilians may be used for military purposes. Sometimes taking a direct part in hostilities and other times being used unlawfully in an attempt to shield military objectives from attack. Third, objects designed for civilian purposes may be used for military purposes and become military objectives. Fourth, combatants themselves may not fulfill their strict obligation to identify themselves as combatants and thus create risks that what appear to be civilians are in fact combatants. Fifth, care is not taken by combatants to avoid civilian casualties. In spite of precautions, incidental civilian casualties and damage to civilian objects are inevitable during armed conflict. Attacks are not prohibited against military objectives even though incidental injury or damage to civilians will occur, but such incidental injury to civilians or damage to civilian objects must not be excessive when compared to the concrete and direct military advantage anticipated. Careful balancing of interests is required between the potential military advantage and the degree of incidental injury or damage in order to preclude situations raising issues of indiscriminate attacks violating general civilian protections. An attack efficiently carried out in accordance with the principle of economy of force against a military airfield or other military installations would doubtless not raise the issue. On the other hand, attacks against objects used predominantly by the civilian population in urban areas, even though they might also be military objectives, are likely to raise the issue. Those who plan or decide upon an attack must, in the selection of both the place to be attacked and in their choice of weapons or methods of attack, take all feasible precautions to avoid or minimize incidental injury to civilians or damage to civilian objects. They must refrain from launching an attack if injury or damage would be excessive or disproportionate compared with the military advantage anticipated. Traditional military doctrines, such as economy of force, concentration of effort, target selection for maximization of military advantage, avoidance of excessive collateral damage, accuracy of targeting, and conservation of resources all reinforce observance of this requirement.

(c) Cancellation or Suspension of Attacks. Target intelligence may be found to be faulty before the attack is started or completed. Accordingly, attacks must be cancelled or suspended if it is apparent that a given target is not a military objective, or that it is under the special protection of international law. An example of special protection is a hospital protected under the 1949 Geneva Conventions. Cancellation or suspension is also required when excessive incidental injury or damage to persons or objects under the general or special protection of international law is apparent. The taking of effective military action in accordance with traditional military doctrines also supports this requirement.

(d) Warning Requirement. The requirement of warning, when circumstances permit, is longstanding and is derived from both Hague Conventions IV and IX. During World War II, practice was lax on warnings because of the heavily defended nature of the targets attacked as well as because of attempts to conceal targets. More recently, increased emphasis has been placed on the desirability and necessity of prior warnings. Nevertheless, the practice of states recognizes that warnings need not always be given. General warnings are more frequently given than specific warnings, lest the attacking force or the success of its mission be jeopardized. Warnings are relevant to the protection of the civilian population and need not be given when they are unlikely to be affected by the attack.

d. Works and Installations Containing Dangerous Forces. . . . [special rules apply regarding the attack of dams, dikes and nuclear electric generating stations, since] there are clearly special concerns that destruction of such objects may unleash forces causing widespread havoc and injury far beyond any military advantage secured or anticipated. Target selection of such objects is accordingly a matter of national decision at appropriate high policy levels.

e. Prohibition of Attacks on Undefended Areas

   (1) Text: The attack or bombardment, by whatever means, of towns, villages, dwellings, or buildings which are undefended is prohibited.

   (2) Discussion: States desired early to formulate more specific rules furthering the general principle of civilian immunity. The Brussels Conference in 1874 barred the bombardment of unfortified cities or towns, reaffirming the concept of walled cities. In 1899, and again in 1907, the Hague Conference adopted rules prohibiting attacks on undefended cities, towns, villages, or dwellings. The term "by whatever means" was added to cover air bombardment. An international legal scholar at the time wrote regarding this prohibition:

> A place cannot be said to be undefended when means are taken to prevent an enemy from occupying it. The price of immunity from bombardment is that the place shall be left open for the enemy to enter.

But cities behind enemy lines and not open to occupation may contain military objectives. The application of this undefended rule to aerial warfare, where the object of the attack was not to occupy the city but to achieve some specific military advantage by destroying a particular military objective, caused disagreements in the past. In the US view, it has been recognized by the practice of nations that any place behind enemy lines is a defended place because it is not open to unopposed occupation. Thus, although such a city is incapable of defending itself against aircraft, nonetheless if it is in enemy held territory and not open to occupation, military objectives in the city can be attacked.

One guide as to what the undefended test meant under modern conditions of air warfare is found in Hague IX which regulates naval bombardment. Hague IX, after asserting in Article I the prohibition of attacks on undefended ports, towns, villages, dwellings, or buildings, notes in Article 2 that:

> Military works, military or naval establishments, depots or arms or war materiel, workshops or plants which could be utilized for the needs of the hostile fleet or army, and the ships of war in the harbour, are not, however, included in this prohibition. . . .

A party to a conflict may declare, as undefended, inhabited localities which are near or in areas where land forces are in contact when the localities are open for occupation by an adverse party. Bombardment in such a locality would be unlawful, if the following conditions were met and maintained: (1) no armed forces or other combatants present, (2) no mobile weapons or mobile military equipment present, (3) no hostile use of fixed military establishments or installations, (4) no acts of warfare by the authorities or the population, and (5) no activities in support of military operations.

Separation of Military Activities:

a. Discussion. As a corollary to the principle of general civilian immunity, the parties to a conflict should, to the maximum extent feasible, take necessary precautions to protect the civilian population, individual civilians, and civilian objects under their authority against the dangers resulting from military operations. Accordingly, they should endeavor to remove civilians from the proximity of military objectives and to avoid locating military objectives within or near densely populated areas. It is incumbent upon states, desiring to make protection of their own civilian population fully effective, to take appropriate mesures to segregate and separate their military activities from the civilian population and civilian objects. Substantial military advantages may in fact be acquired by such separation. Examples of specific rules designed to enhance civilian protections include:

(1) The obligation of combatants to carry arms openly, wear uniforms (fixed distinctive emblems) or distinguish themselves in their military activities from the civilian population (See Article I, HR: Article 4, GPW).

(2) The provision for identifying protected medical personnel and objects and prohibitions on misuse of distinctive emblems (see Articles 38-44, GWS; 41-45, GWS SEA: Articles 18-22, GC).

(3) The provisions for identifying by distinctive and visible signs, buildings dedicated to religion, art, science or charitable purposes, historic monuments, hospitals, or other places where wounded and sick are collected, and for prohibiting their use for military purposes (Article 27, HR).

(4) The provision for locating medical units in such a manner that attacks against military objectives cannot imperil their safety (See Article 19, GWS).

(5) The provision for removing combatants and mobile military equipment and desisting from hostile acts in declared nondefended localities.

(6) The obligation not to use the presence or movement of civilians to shield military objectives from attack or impede military operations.

b. Result of Failure to Separate Military Activities. The failure of states to segregate and separate their own military activities, and particularly to avoid placing military objectives in or near populated areas and to remove such objectives from populated areas, significantly and substantially weakens effective protection for their own population. A party to a conflict which places its own citizens in positions of danger by failing to carry out the separation of military activities from civilian activities necessarily accepts, under international law, the results of otherwise lawful attacks upon valid military objectives in their territory.

c. Protection Gained Through Separation. Existing international law recognizes and encourages the right of states to separate military activities from population centers in order to gain effective protection during armed conflict. Both the 1923 Draft Hague Rules and the 1949 Geneva Conventions as well as Protocol I, recognize the right of states, by agreement, to create safety zones or demilitarized zones. Doubtless the creation of such zones would be one of the most effective measures to enhance protection of one's own civilian population, and if the conditions required to make a zone were fulfilled and maintained, virtually all civilian casualties would be avoided in this zone.

Special Protection. In addition to the general international law rules protecting civilians and civilian populations, specific protections are applicable to certain facilities.

a. Wounded and Sick, Medical Units and Hospitals and Medical Means of Transport. The law of armed conflict has traditionally provided special protection to the wounded and sick and to persons, facilities and transports caring for wounded and sick. The following persons and objects must be respected and protected from attack pursuant to the 1949 Geneva Conventions [and Protocol I].

(1) Hospitals and other fixed or mobile medical establishments.
(2) Medical personnel and chaplains.
(3) Medical transport.
(4) Medical aircraft.
(5) Hospital ships and, to the extent possible, sick bays of warships.
(6) Wounded, sick and shipwrecked. The protection accorded to the foregoing persons and objects means they must not knowingly be attacked, fired upon, or unknowingly be attacked, fired upon, or unnecessarily prevented from discharging their proper function. The accidental injury of such personnel, or damage to objects, due to their presence among or in proximity to military targets actually attacked, by fire directed against the latter, gives no just cause for complaint.

b. Special Hospital and Neutralized Zones. The Geneva Conventions of 1949 provide for protected or safety zones established by agreement between the parties to the conflict. Safety zones established under the Geneva Conventions of 1949, or by other agreement among parties to a conflict, are immune from bombardment in accordance with the terms of the agreement.

c. Religious, Cultural, and Charitable Buildings and Monuments. Buildings devoted to religion, art, or charitable purposes as well as historical monuments may not be made the object of aerial bombardment. Protection is based on their not being used for military purposes. Combatants have a duty to indicate such places by distinctive and visible signs. When used by the enemy for military purposes, such buildings may be attacked if they are under the circumstances, valid military objectives. Lawful military objectives located near protected buildings are not immune from aerial attack by reason of such location but, insofar as possible, necessary precautions must be taken to spare such protected buildings along with other civilian objects.

d. Prisoner of War Camps. Prisoners of war and prisoner of war camps enjoy a protected status under the law. PWs may not be the object of attack, detained in combat zones or used to render areas immune from military operations. Parties to a conflict must convey to all other nations concerned all useful information regarding the geographical location of their PW camps. Wherever military considerations permit, PW camps are identified during the daytime by the letters "PW" or "PG" placed so as to be clearly visible from the air. Parties to a conflict may also agree upon any other system of markings. However, only PW camps may be so marked, and the use of PW camp markings for other purposes is prohibited. PWs are required to have shelters against air bombardment and other hazards of war to the same extent as the civilian population.

N Multilateral Treaty on Principles Governing the Activities of States in the Exploration and Use of Outer Space, including the Moon and other Celestial Bodies

Done at Washington, London, and Moscow January 27, 1967;
Ratification advised by the Senate of the United States of America
*   April 25, 1967;*
Ratified by the President of the United States of America May 24, 1967;
Ratification of the United States of America deposited at Washington, London, and
*   Moscow October 10, 1967;*
Proclaimed by the President of the United States of America October
*   10, 1967;*
Entered into force October 10, 1967.

BY THE PRESIDENT OF THE UNITED STATES OF AMERICA

A PROCLAMATION

WHEREAS the Treaty on Principles Governing the Activities of States in the Exploration and Use of Outer Space, including the Moon and Other Celestial Bodies, was signed at Washington, London, and Moscow on January 27, 1967 in behalf of the United States of America, the United Kingdom of Great Britain and Northern Ireland, and the Union of Soviet Socialist Republics and was signed at one or more of the three capitals in behalf of a number of other States;

WHEREAS the text of the Treaty, in the English, Russian, French, Spanish, and Chinese languages, as certified by the Department of State of the United States of America, is word for word as follows:

Treaty on Principles Governing the Activities of States in the
*   Exploration and Use of Outer Space, Including the*
*   Moon and Other Celestial Bodies*

The States Parties to this Treaty,

Inspired by the great prospects opening up before mankind as a result of man's entry into outer space,

Recognizing the common interest of all mankind in the progress of the exploration and use of outer space for peaceful purposes,

Believing that the exploration and use of outer space should be carried on for the benefit of all peoples irrespective of the degree of their economic or scientific development,

Desiring to contribute to broad international co-operation in the scientific as well as the legal aspects of the exploration and use of outer space for peaceful purposes,

Believing that such co-operation will contribute to the development of mutual understanding and to the strengthening of friendly relations between States and peoples,

Recalling resolution 1962 (XVIII), entitled "Declaration of Legal Principles Governing the Activities of States in the Exploration and Use of Outer Space," which was adopted unanimously by the United Nations General Assembly on 13 December 1963,

Recalling resolution 1884 (XVIII), calling upon States to refrain from placing in orbit around the Earth any objects carrying nuclear weapons or any other kinds of weapons of mass destruction or from installing such weapons on celestial bodies, which was adopted unanimously by the United Nations General Assembly on 17 October 1963,

Taking account of United Nations General Assembly resolution 110 (II) of 3 November 1947, which condemned propaganda designed or likely to provoke or encourage any threat to the peace, breach of the peace or act of aggression, and considering that the aforementioned resolution is applicable to outer space,

Convinced that a Treaty on Principles Governing the Activities of States in the Exploration and Use of Outer Space, including the Moon and Other Celestial Bodies, will further the Purposes and Principles of the Charter of the United Nations,

Have agreed on the following:

Article I

The exploration and use of outer space, including the moon and other celestial bodies, shall be carried out for the benefit and in the interests of all countries, irrespective of their degree of economic or scientific development, and shall be the province of all mankind.

Outer space, including the moon and the other celestial bodies, shall be free for exploration and use by all States without discrimination of any kind, on a basis of equality and in accordance with international law, and there shall be free access to all areas of celestial bodies.

There shall be freedom of scientific investigation in outer space, including the moon and other celestial bodies, and States shall facilitate and encourage international co-operation in such investigation.

Article II

Outer space, including the moon and other celestial bodies, is not subject to national appropriation by claim of sovereignty, by means of use or occupation, or by any other means.

Article III

States Parties to the Treaty shall carry on activities in the exploration and use of outer space, including the moon and other celestial bodies, in accordance with international law, including the Charter of the United Nations, in the interest of maintaining international peace and security and promoting international co-operation and understanding.

Article IV

States Parties to the Treaty undertake not to place in orbit around the Earth any objects carrying nuclear weapons or any other kinds of weapons of mass destruction, install such weapons on celestial bodies, or station such weapons in outer space in any other manner.

The moon and other celestial bodies shall be used by all States Parties to the Treaty exclusively for peaceful purposes. The establishment of military bases, installations and fortifications, the testing of any type of weapons and the conduct of military maneuvers on celestial bodies shall be forbidden. The use of military personnel for scientific research or for any other peaceful purposes shall not be prohibited. The use of any equipment or facility necessary for peaceful exploration of the moon and other celestial bodies shall also not be prohibited.

Article V

States Parties to the Treaty shall regard astronauts as envoys of mankind in outer space and shall render to them all possible assistance in the event of accident, distress, or emergency landing on the territory of another State Party or on the high seas. When astronauts make such a landing, they shall be safely and promptly returned to the State of registry of their space vehicle.

In carrying on activities in outer space and on celestial bodies, the astronauts of one State Party shall render all possible assistance to the astronauts of other States Parties.

States Parties to the Treaty shall immediately inform the other States Parties to the Treaty or the Secretary-General of the United Nations of any phenomena they discover in outer space, including the moon and other celestial bodies, which could constitute a danger to the life or health of astronauts.

Article VI

States Parties to the Treaty shall bear international responsibility for national activities in outer space, including the moon and other celestial bodies, whether such activities are carried on by governmental agencies or by non-governmental entities, and for assuring that national activities are carried out in conformity with the provisions set forth in the present Treaty. The activities of non-governmental entities in outer space, including the moon and other celestial bodies, shall require authorization and continuing supervision by the appropriate State Party to the Treaty. When activities are carried on in outer space, including the moon and other celestial bodies, by an international organization, responsibility for compliance with this Treaty shall be borne both by the international organization and by the States Parties to the Treaty participating in such organization.

Article VII

Each State Party to the Treaty that launches or procures the launching of an object into outer space, including the moon and other celestial bodies, and each State Party from whose territory or facility an object is launched, is internationally liable for damage to another State Party to the Treaty or to its natural or juridical persons by such object or its component parts on the Earth, in air space or in outer space, including the moon and other celestial bodies.

Article VIII

A State Party to the Treaty on whose registry an object launched into outer space is carried shall retain jurisdiction and control over such object, and over any personnel thereof, while in outer space or on a celestial body. Ownership of objects launched into outer space, including objects landed or constructed on a celestial body, and of their component parts, is not affected by their presence in outer space or on a celestial body or by their return to the Earth. Such objects or component parts found beyond the limits of the State Party to the Treaty on whose registry they are carried shall be returned to that State Party, which shall, upon request, furnish identifying data prior to their return.

Article IX

In the exploration and use of outer space, including the moon and other celestial bodies, States Parties to the Treaty shall be guided by the principle of co-operation and mutual assistance and shall conduct all their activities in outer space, including the moon and other celestial bodies, with due regard to the corresponding interests of all other States Parties to the Treaty. States Parties to the Treaty shall pursue studies of outer space, including the moon and other celestial bodies, and conduct exploration of them so as to avoid their harmful contamination and also adverse changes in the environment of the Earth resulting from the introduction of extraterrestrial matter and, where necessary, shall adopt appropriate measures for this purpose. If a State Party to the Treaty has reason to believe that an activity or experiment planned by it or its nationals in outer space, including the moon and other celestial bodies, would cause potentially harmful interference with activities of other States Parties in the peaceful exploration and use of outer space, including the moon and other celestial bodies, it shall undertake appropriate international consultations before proceeding with any such activity or experiment. A State Party to the Treaty which has reason to believe that an activity or experiment planned by another State Party in outer space, including the moon and other celestial bodies, would cause potentially harmful interference with activities in the peaceful exploration and use of outer space, including the moon and other celestial bodies, may request consultation concerning the activity or experiment.

Article X

In order to promote international co-operation in the exploration and use of outer space, including the moon and other celestial bodies, in conformity with the purposes of this Treaty, the States Parties to the Treaty shall consider on a basis of equality any requests by other States Parties to the Treaty to be afforded an opportunity to observe the flight of space objects launched by those States.

The nature of such an opportunity for observation and the conditions under which it could be afforded shall be determined by agreement between the States concerned.

Article XI

In order to promote international co-operation in the peaceful exploration and use of outer space, States Parties to the Treaty conducting activities in outer space, including the moon and other celestial bodies, agree to inform the Secretary-General of the United Nations as well as the public and the international scientific community, to the greatest extent feasible and practicable, of the nature, conduct, locations and results of such activities. On receiving the said information, the Secretary-General of the United Nations should be prepared to disseminate it immediately and effectively.

Article XII

All stations, installations, equipment and space vehicles on the moon and other celestial bodies shall be open to representatives of other States Parties to the Treaty on a basis of reciprocity. Such representatives shall give reasonable advance notice of a projected visit, in order that appropriate consultations may be held and that maximum precautions may be taken to assure safety and to avoid interference with normal operations in the facility to be visited.

Article XIII

The provisions of this Treaty shall apply to the activities of States Parties to the Treaty in the exploration and use of outer space, including the moon and other celestial bodies, whether such activities are carried on by a single State Party to the Treaty or jointly with other States, including cases where they are carried on within the framework of international inter-governmental organizations.

Any practical questions arising in connection with activities carried on by international inter-governmental organizations in the exploration and use of outer space, including the moon and other celestial bodies, shall be resolved by the States Parties to the Treaty either with the appropriate international organization or with one or more States members of that international organization, which are Parties to this Treaty.

Article XIV

1. This Treaty shall be open to all States for signature. Any State which does not sign this Treaty before its entry into force in accordance with paragraph 3 of this article may accede to it at any time.

2. This Treaty shall be subject to ratification by signatory States. Instruments of ratification and instruments of accession shall be deposited with the Governments of the United States of America, the United Kingdom of Great Britain and Northern Ireland and the Union of Soviet Socialist Republics, which are hereby designated the Depositary Governments.

3. This Treaty shall enter into force upon the deposit of instruments of ratification by five Governments including the Governments designated as Depositary Governments under this Treaty.

4. For States whose instruments of ratification or accession are deposited subsequent to the entry into force of this Treaty, it shall enter into force on the date of the deposit of their instruments of ratification or accession.

5. The Depositary Governments shall promptly inform all signatory and acceding States of the date of each signature, the date of deposit of each instrument of ratification of and accession to this Treaty, the date of its entry into force and other notices.

6. This treaty shall be registered by the Depositary Governments pursuant to Article 102 of the Charter of the United Nations.

Article XV

Any State Party to the Treaty may propose amendments to this Treaty. Amendments shall enter into force for each State Party to the Treaty accepting the amendments upon their acceptance by a majority of the States Parties to the Treaty and thereafter for each remaining State Party to the Treaty on the date of acceptance by it.

Article XVI

Any State Party to the Treaty may give notice of its withdrawal from the Treaty one year after its entry into force by written notification to the Depositary Governments. Such withdrawal shall take effect one year from the date of receipt of this notification.

Article XVII

This Treaty, of which the English, Russian, French, Spanish and Chinese texts are equally authentic, shall be deposited in the archives of the Depositary Governments. Duly certified copies of this Treaty shall be transmitted by the Depositary Governments to the Governments of the signatory and acceding States.

O Inter-American Treaty of Reciprocal Assistance (Rio Pact)

Between the UNITED STATES OF AMERICA
and OTHER AMERICAN REPUBLICS
- Opened for signature at Rio de Janeiro September 2, 1947
- Ratification advised by the Senate of the United States of America
  December 8, 1947
- Ratified by the President of the United States of America
  December 12, 1947
- Ratification of the United States of America deposited with
  the Pan American Union December 30, 1947
- Proclaimed by the President of the United States of America
  December 9, 1948
- Entered into force December 3, 1948

BY THE PRESIDENT OF THE UNITED STATES OF AMERICA

A PROCLAMATION

WHEREAS an inter-American treaty of reciprocal assistance was formulated at the Inter-American Conference for the Maintenance of Continental Peace and Security and was signed on September 2, 1947 at Rio de Janeiro by the respective Plenipotentiaries of the Governments of the United States of America, Argentina, Bolivia, Brazil, Chile, Colombia, Costa Rica, Cuba, the Dominican Republic, El Salvador, Guatemala, Haiti, Honduras, Mexico, Panama, Paraguay, Peru, Uruguay, and Venezuela, and on October 15, 1948 by the Plenipotentiary of the Government of Nicaragua;

WHEREAS the aforesaid treaty, being in the Portuguese, Spanish, French, and English languages, as certified by the Secretary General of the Inter-American Conference for the Maintenance of Continental Peace and Security, is word for word as follows:

In the name of their Peoples, the Governments represented at the Inter-American Conference for the Maintenance of Continental Peace and Security, desirous of consolidating and strengthening their relations of friendship and good neighborliness, and

Considering:

That Resolution VIII of the Inter-American Conference on Problems of War and Peace,[1] which met in Mexico City, recommended the conclusion of a treaty to prevent and repel threats and acts of aggression against any of the countries of America;

That the High Contracting Parties reiterate their will to remain united in an inter-American system consistent with the purposes and principles of the United Nations, and reaffirm the existence of the agreement which they have concluded concerning those matters relating to the maintenance of international peace and security which are appropriate for regional action;

That the High Contracting Parties reaffirm their adherence to the principles of inter-American solidarity and cooperation, and especially to those set forth in the preamble and declarations of the Act of Chapultepec, all of which should be understood to be accepted as standards of their mutual relations and as the juridical basis of the Inter-American System;

That the American States propose, in order to improve the procedures for the pacific settlement of their controversies, to conclude the treaty concerning the "Inter-American Peace System" envisaged in Resolutions IX and XXXIX of the Inter-American Conference on Problems of War and Peace;[2]

That the obligation of mutual assistance and common defense of the American Republics is essentially related to their democratic ideals and to their will to cooperate permanently in the fulfillment of the principles and purposes of a policy of peace;

That the American regional community affirms as a manifest truth that juridical organization is a necessary prerequisite of security and peace, and that peace is founded on justice and moral order and, consequently, on the international recognition and protection of human rights and freedoms, on the indispensable well-being of the people, and on the effectiveness of democracy for the international realization of justice and security,

Have resolved, in conformity with the objectives stated above, to conclude the following Treaty, in order to assure peace, through adequate means, to provide for effective reciprocal assistance to meet armed attacks against any American State, and in order to deal with threats of aggression against any of them:

Article 1

The High Contracting Parties formally condemn war and undertake in their international relations not to resort to the threat or the use of force in

[1] Treaties and Other International Acts Series 1543; 60 Stat. 1831.
[2] *Report of the Delegation of the United States of America to the Inter-American Conference on Problems of War and Peace, Mexico City, Mexico, February 21-March 8, 1945*, Department of State publication 2497, p. 107.

any manner inconsistent with the provisions of the Charter of the United Nations[1] or of this Treaty.

Article 2

As a consequence of the principle set forth in the preceding Article, the High Contracting Parties undertake to submit every controversy which may arise between them to methods of peaceful settlement and to endeavor to settle any such controversy among themselves by means of the procedures in force in the Inter-American System before referring it to the General Assembly or the Security Council of the United Nations.

Article 3

1. The High Contracting Parties agree that an armed attack by any State against an American State shall be considered as an attack against all the American States and, consequently, each one of the said Contracting Parties undertakes to assist in meeting the attack in the exercise of the inherent right of individual or collective self-defense recognized by Article 51 of the Charter of the United Nations.

2. On the request of the State or States directly attacked and until the decision of the Organ of Consultation of the Inter-American System, each one of the Contracting Parties may determine the immediate measures which it may individually take in fulfillment of the obligation contained in the preceding paragraph and in accordance with the principle of continental solidarity. The Organ of Consultation shall meet without delay for the purpose of examining those measures and agreeing upon the measures of a collective character that should be taken.

3. The provisions of this Article shall be applied in case of any armed attack which takes place within the region described in Article 4 or within the territory of an American State. When the attack takes place outside of the said areas, the provisions of Article 6 shall be applied.

4. Measures of self-defense provided for under this Article may be taken until the Security Council of the United Nations has taken the measures necessary to maintain international peace and security.

Article 4

The region to which this Treaty refers is bounded as follows: beginning at the North Pole; thence due south to a point 74 degrees north latitude, 10 degrees west longitude; thence by a rhumb line to a point 47 degrees 30 minutes north latitude, 50 degrees west longitude; thence by a rhumb line to a point 35 degrees north latitude, 60 degrees west longitude; thence due south to a point in 20 degrees north latitude; thence by a rhumb line to a point 5 degrees north latitude, 24 degrees west longitude; thence due south

[1] Treaty Series 993; 59 Stat. 1031.

to the South Pole; thence due north to a point 30 degrees south latitude, 90 degrees west longitude; thence by a rhumb line to a point on the Equator at 97 degrees west longitude; thence by a rhumb line to a point 15 degrees north latitude, 120 degrees west longitude; thence by a rhumb line to a point 50 degrees north latitude, 170 degrees east longitude; thence due north to a point in 54 degrees north latitude; thence by a rhumb line to a point 65 degrees 30 minutes north latitude, 168 degrees 58 minutes 5 seconds west longitude; thence due north to the North Pole.

Article 5

The High Contracting Parties shall immediately send to the Security Council of the United Nations, in conformity with Articles 51 and 54 of the Charter of the United Nations, complete information concerning the activities undertaken or in contemplation in the exercise of the right of self-defense or for the purpose of maintaining inter-American peace and security.

Article 6

If the inviolability or the integrity of the territory or the sovereignty or political independence of any American State should be affected by an aggression which is not an armed attack or by an extracontinental or intracontinental conflict, or by any other fact or situation that might endanger the peace of America, the Organ of Consultation shall meet immediately in order to agree on the measures which must be taken in case of aggression to assist the victim of the aggression or, in any case, the measures which should be taken for the common defense and for the maintenance of the peace and security of the Continent.

Article 7

In the case of a conflict between two or more American States, without prejudice to the right of self-defense in conformity with Article 51 of the Charter of the United Nations, the High Contracting Parties, meeting in consultation shall call upon the contending States to suspend hostilities and restore matters to the *status quo ante bellum*, and shall take in addition all other necessary measures to reestablish or maintain inter-American peace and security and for the solution of the conflict by peaceful means. The rejection of the pacifying action will be considered in the determination of the aggressor and in the application of the measures which the consultative meeting may agree upon.

Article 8

For the purposes of this Treaty, the measures on which the Organ of Consultation may agree will comprise one or more of the following: recall of chiefs of diplomatic missions; breaking of diplomatic relations; breaking of consular relations; partial or complete interruption of economic relations or of rail, sea, air, postal, telegraphic, telephonic, and radiotelephonic or radiotelegraphic communications; and use of armed force.

Article 9

In addition to other acts which the Organ of Consultation may characterize as aggression, the following shall be considered as such:

a. Unprovoked armed attack by a State against the territory, the people, or the land, sea or air forces of another State;

b. Invasion, by the armed forces of a State, of the territory of an American State, through the trespassing of boundaries demarcated in accordance with a treaty, judicial decision, or arbitral award, or, in the absence of frontiers thus demarcated, invasion affecting a region which is under the effective jurisdiction of another State.

Article 10

None of the provisions of this Treaty shall be construed as impairing the rights and obligations of the High Contracting Parties under the Charter of the United Nations.

Article 11

The consultations to which this Treaty refers shall be carried out by means of the Meetings of Ministers of Foreign Affairs of the American Republics which have ratified the Treaty, or in the manner or by the organ which in the future may be agreed upon.

Article 12

The Governing Board of the Pan American Union may act provisionally as an organ of consultation until the meeting of the Organ of Consultation referred to in the preceding Article takes place.

Article 13

The consultations shall be initiated at the request addressed to the Governing Board of the Pan American Union by any of the Signatory States which has ratified the Treaty.

Article 14

In the voting referred to in this Treaty only the representatives of the Signatory States which have ratified the Treaty may take part.

Article 15

The Governing Board of the Pan American Union shall act in all matters concerning this Treaty as an organ of liaison among the Signatory States which have ratified this Treaty and between these States and the United Nations.

Article 16

The decisions of the Governing Board of the Pan American Union referred to in Articles 13 and 15 above shall be taken by an absolute majority of the Members entitled to vote.

Article 17

The Organ of Consultation shall take its decisions by a vote of two-thirds of the Signatory States which have ratified the Treaty.

Article 18

In the case of a situation or dispute between American States, the parties directly interested shall be excluded from the voting referred to in two preceding Articles.

Article 19

To constitute a quorum in all the meetings referred to in the previous Articles, it shall be necessary that the number of States represented shall be at least equal to the number of votes necessary for the taking of the decision.

Article 20

Decisions which require the application of the measures specified in Article 8 shall be binding upon all the Signatory States which have ratified this Treaty, with the sole exception that no State shall be required to use armed force without its consent.

Article 21

The measures agreed upon by the Organ of Consultation shall be executed through the procedures and agencies now existing or those which may in the future be established.

Article 22

This Treaty shall come into effect between the States which ratify it as soon as the ratification of two-thirds of the Signatory States have been deposited.

Article 23

This Treaty is open for signature by the American States at the city of Rio de Janeiro, and shall be ratified by the Signatory States as soon as possible in accordance with their respective constitutional processes. The ratifications shall be deposited with the Pan American Union, which shall notify the

Signatory States of each deposit. Such notification shall be considered as an exchange of ratifications.

Article 24

The present Treaty shall be registered with the Secretariat of the United Nations through the Pan American Union, when two-thirds of the Signatory States have deposited their ratifications.

Article 25

This Treaty shall remain in force indefinitely, but may be denounced by any High Contracting Party by a notification in writing to the Pan American Union, which shall inform all the other High Contracting Parties of each notification of denunciation received. After the expiration of two years from the date of the receipt by the Pan American Union of a notification of denunciation by any High Contracting Party, the present Treaty shall cease to be in force with respect to such State, but shall remain in full force and effect with respect to all the other High Contracting Parties.

Article 26

The principles and fundamental provisions of this Treaty shall be incorporated in the Organic Pact of the Inter-American System.

In witness whereof, the undersigned Plenipotentiaries, having deposited their full powers found to be in due and proper form, sign this Treaty on behalf of their respective Governments, on the dates appearing opposite their signatures.

Done in the city of Rio de Janeiro, in four texts respectively in the English, French, Portuguese and Spanish languages, on the second of September nineteen hundred forty-seven.

RESERVATION OF HONDURAS:

The Delegation of Honduras, in signing the present Treaty and in connection with Article 9, section (b), does so with the reservation that the boundary between Honduras and Nicaragua is definitively demarcated by the Joint Boundary Commission of nineteen hundred and one, starting from a point in the Gulf of Fonseca, in the Pacific Ocean, to Portillo de Teotecacinte and, from this point to the Atlantic, by the line that His Majesty the King of Spain's arbitral award established on the twenty-third of December of nineteen hundred and six.

(Signatures of Representatives of:

THE DOMINICAN REPUBLIC	COSTA RICA
GUATEMALA	PERU
EL SALVADOR	BOLIVIA
PANAMA	COLOMBIA
PARAGUAY	MEXICO
VENEZUELA	HAITI
CHILE	URUGUAY
HONDURAS	THE UNITED STATES OF AMERICA
CUBA	ARGENTINA
	BRAZIL)

WHEREAS the Senate of the United States of America, by their resolution of December 8, 1947, two-thirds of the Senators present concurring therein, did advise and consent to the ratification of the aforesaid treaty;

WHEREAS the aforesaid treaty was duly ratified by the President of the United States of America on December 12, 1947, in pursuance of the aforesaid advice and consent of the Senate;

WHEREAS it is provided in Article 22 of the aforesaid treaty that the treaty shall come into effect between the States which ratify it as soon as the ratifications of two-thirds of the Signatory States have been deposited;

WHEREAS, according to notifications received by the Government of the United States of America from the Pan American Union, instruments of ratification of the aforesaid treaty have been deposited by two-thirds of the Signatory States as follows: the Dominican Republic on November 21, 1947; the United States of America on December 30, 1947; Panama on January 12, 1948; Colombia on February 3, 1948; Honduras on February 5, 1948; El Salvador on March 15, 1948; Brazil on March 25, 1948; Haiti on March 25, 1948; Paraguay on July 28, 1948; Uruguay on September 28, 1948; Venezuela on October 4, 1948; Nicaragua on November 12, 1948; Mexico on November 23, 1948; and Costa Rica on December 3, 1948;

WHEREAS, according to a notification received by the Government of the United States of America from the Pan American Union, the requirements of the aforesaid Article 22 have been fulfilled and the aforesaid treaty came into effect on December 3, 1948;

NOW, THEREFORE, be it known that I, Harry S. Truman, President of the United States of America, do hereby proclaim and make public the aforesaid inter-American treaty of reciprocal assistance to the end that the said treaty and each and every article and clause thereof may be observed and fulfilled with good faith, on and from the third day of December, one thousand nine hundred forty-eight, by the United States of America and by the citizens of the United States of America and all other persons subject to the jurisdiction thereof.

IN TESTIMONY WHEREOF, I have hereunto set my hand and caused the Seal of the United States of America to be affixed.

DONE at the city of Washington this ninth day of December in the year of our Lord one thousand nine hundred forty-eight and of the Independence of the United States of America the one hundred seventy-third.

[SEAL]   HARRY S. TRUMAN
By the President:
   ROBERT A. LOVETT
      Acting Secretary of State

P North Atlantic Treaty

Between the UNITED STATES OF AMERICA AND OTHER GOVERNMENTS

- Signed at Washington April 4, 1949
- Ratification advised by the Senate of the United States of America
  July 21, 1949
- Ratified by the President of the United States of America
  July 25, 1949
- Instrument of Ratification of the United States of America
  deposited at Washington July 25, 1949
- Proclaimed by the President of the United States of America
  August 24, 1949
- Entered into force August 24, 1949

BY THE PRESIDENT OF THE UNITED STATES OF AMERICA

A PROCLAMATION

WHEREAS the North Atlantic Treaty was signed at Washington on April 4, 1949 by the respective Plenipotentiaries of the United States of America, the Kingdom of Belgium, Canada, the Kingdom of Denmark, France, Iceland, Italy, the Grand Duchy of Luxembourg, the Kingdom of the Netherlands, the Kingdom of Norway, Portugal, and the United Kingdom of Great Britain and Northern Ireland;

WHEREAS the text of the said Treaty, in the English and French languages, is word for word as follows:

NORTH ATLANTIC TREATY

The Parties to this Treaty reaffirm their faith in the purposes and principles of the Charter of the United Nations and their desire to live in peace with all peoples and all governments.

They are determined to safeguard the freedom, common heritage and civilization of their peoples, founded on the principles of democracy, individual liberty and the rule of law.

They seek to promote stability and well-being in the North Atlantic area.

They are resolved to unite their efforts for collective defense and for the preservation of peace and security.

They therefore agree to this North Atlantic Treaty:

Article 1

The Parties undertake, as set forth in the Charter of the United Nations, to settle any international disputes in which they may be involved by peaceful means in such a manner that international peace and security, and justice, are not endangered, and to refrain in their international relations from the threat or use of force in any manner inconsistent with the purposes of the United Nations.

Article 2

The Parties will contribute toward the further development of peaceful and friendly international relations by strengthening their free institutions, by bringing about a better understanding of the principles upon which these institutions are founded, and by promoting conditions of stability and well-being. They will seek to eliminate conflict in their international economic policies and will encourage economic collaboration between any or all of them.

Article 3

In order more effectively to achieve the objectives of this Treaty, the Parties, separately and jointly, by means of continuous and effective self-help and mutual aid, will maintain and develop their individual and collective capacity to resist armed attack.

Article 4

The Parties will consult together whenever, in the opinion of any of them, the territorial integrity, political independence or security of any of the Parties is threatened.

Article 5

The Parties agree that an armed attack against one or more of them in Europe or North America shall be considered an attack against them all; and consequently they agree that, if such an armed attack occurs, each of them, in exercise of the right of individual or collective self-defense recognized by Article 51 of the Charter of the United Nations, will assist the Party or Parties so attacked by taking forthwith, individually and in concert with the other Parties, such action as it deems necessary, including the use of armed force to restore and maintain the security of the North Atlantic area.

Any such armed attack and all measures taken as a result thereof shall immediately be reported to the Security Council. Such measures shall be terminated when the Security Council has taken the measures necessary to restore and maintain international peace and security.

Article 6

For the purpose of Article 5 an armed attack on one or more of the Parties is deemed to include an armed attack on the territory of any of the Parties in Europe or North America, on the Algerian departments of France, on the occupation forces of any Party in Europe, on the islands under the jurisdiction of any Party in the North Atlantic area north of the Tropic of Cancer or on the vessels or aircraft in this area of any of the Parties.

Article 7

This Treaty does not affect, and shall not be interpreted as affecting, in any way the rights and obligations under the Charter of the Parties which are members of the United Nations, or the primary responsibility of the Security Council for the maintenance of international peace and security.

Article 8

Each Party declares that none of the international engagements now in force between it and any other of the Parties or any third state is in conflict with the provisions of this Treaty, and undertakes not to enter into any international engagement in conflict with this Treaty.

Article 9

The Parties hereby establish a council, on which each of them shall be represented, to consider matters concerning the implementation of this Treaty. The council shall be so organized as to be able to meet promptly at any time. The council shall set up such subsidiary bodies as may be necessary; in particular it shall establish immediately a defense committee which shall recommend measures for the implementation of Articles 3 and 5.

Article 10

The Parties may, by unanimous agreement, invite any other European state in a position to further the principles of this Treaty and to contribute to the security of the North Atlantic area to accede to this Treaty. Any state so invited may become a party to the Treaty by depositing its instrument of accession with the Government of the United States of America. The Government of the United States of America will inform each of the Parties of the deposit of each such instrument of accession.

Article 11

This Treaty shall be ratified and its provisions carried out by the Parties in accordance with their respective constitutional processes. The instruments of ratification shall be deposited as soon as possible with the Government of the United States of America, which will notify all the other signatories of each deposit. The Treaty shall enter into force between the states which have ratified it as soon as the ratifications of the majority of the signatories, including the ratifications of Belgium, Canada, France, Luxembourg, the Netherlands, the United Kingdom and the United States, have been deposited and shall come into effect with respect to other states on the date of the deposit of their ratifications.

Article 12

After the Treaty has been in force for ten years, or at any time thereafter, the Parties shall, if any of them so requests, consult together for the purpose of reviewing the Treaty, having regard for the factors then affecting peace and security in the North Atlantic area, including the development of universal as well as regional arrangements under the Charter of the United Nations for the maintenance of international peace and security.

Article 13

After the Treaty has been in force for twenty years, any Party may cease to be a party one year after its notice of denunciation has been given to the Government of the United States of America, which will inform the Governments of the other Parties of the deposit of each notice of denunciation.

Article 14

This Treaty, of which the English and French texts are equally authentic, shall be deposited in the archives of the Government of the United States of America. Duly certified copies thereof will be transmitted by that Government to the Governments of the other signatories.

In witness whereof, the undersigned Plenipotentiaries have signed this Treaty.

Done at Washington, the fourth day of April, 1949.

(Signatures of the Representatives of:

THE KINGDOM OF BELGIUM
CANADA
THE KINGDOM OF DENMARK
FRANCE
ICELAND
ITALY
THE GRAND DUCHY OF LUXEMBOURG
THE KINGDOM OF THE NETHERLANDS
THE KINGDOM OF NORWAY
PORTUGAL
THE UNITED KINGDOM OF GREAT BRITAIN AND
   NORTHERN IRELAND
THE UNITED STATES OF AMERICA)

I CERTIFY THAT the foregoing is a true copy of the North Atlantic Treaty signed at Washington on April 4, 1949 in the English and French languages, the signed original of which is deposited in the archives of the Government of the United States of America.

IN TESTIMONY WHEREOF, I, DEAN ACHESON, Secretary of State of the United States of America, have hereunto caused the seal of the Department of State to be affixed and my name subscribed by the Authentication Officer of the said Department, at the city of Washington, in the District of Columbia, this fourth day of April, 1949.

[SEAL]

DEAN ACHESON
Secretary of State

By M. P. CHAUVIN
Authentication Officer
Department of State

WHEREAS the Senate of the United States of America by their resolution of July 21, 1949, two-thirds of the Senators present concurring therein, did advise and consent to the ratification of the said Treaty;

WHEREAS the said Treaty was duly ratified by the President of the United States of America on July 25, 1949, in pursuance of the aforesaid advice and consent of the Senate.

WHEREAS it is provided in Article 11 of the said Treaty that the Treaty shall enter into force between the states which have ratified it as soon as the ratifications of the majority of the signatories, including the ratifications of Belgium, Canada, France, Luxembourg, the Netherlands, the United Kingdom, and the United States, have been deposited;

WHEREAS instruments of ratification were deposited with the Government of the United States of America on May 3, 1949 by Canada; on June 7, 1949 by the United Kingdom of Great Britain and Northern Ireland; on June 16, 1949 by the Kingdom of Belgium; on June 27, 1949 by the Grand Duchy of Luxembourg; on July 8, 1949 by the Kingdom of Norway; on July 25, 1949 by the United States of America; on August 1, 1949 by Iceland; on August 12, 1949 by the Kingdom of the Netherlands; and on August 24, 1949 by the Kingdom of Denmark, France, Italy, and Portugal;

AND WHEREAS, pursuant to the aforesaid provisions of Article 11 of the said Treaty, the Treaty entered into force on August 24, 1949;

NOW, THEREFORE, be it known that I, Harry S. Truman, President of the United States of America, do hereby proclaim and make public the North Atlantic Treaty to the end that the same and each and every article and clause thereof shall be observed and fulfilled with good faith, on and after August 24, 1949 by the United States of America and by the citizens of the United States of America and all other persons subject to the jurisdiction thereof.

IN TESTIMONY WHEREOF, I have caused the Seal of the United States of America to be hereunto affixed.

DONE at the city of Washington this twenty-fourth day of August in the year of our Lord one thousand nine hundred forty-nine and of the Independence of the United States of America the one hundred seventy-fourth.

[SEAL]   HARRY S. TRUMAN.

By the President:
DEAN ACHESON
Secretary of State

Q Security Treaty between the United States of America and Japan

The United States of America and Japan,

Desiring to strengthen the bonds of peace and friendship traditionally existing between them, and to uphold the principles of democracy, individual liberty, and the rule of law,

Desiring further to encourage closer economic co-operation between them and to promote conditions of economic stability and well being in their countries,

Reaffirming their faith in the purposes and principles of the charter of the United Nations, and their desire to live in peace with all peoples and all governments,

Recognizing that they have the inherent right of individual or collective self-defense as affirmed in the charter of the United Nations,

Considering that they have a common concern in the maintenance of international peace and security in the Far East,

Having resolved to conclude a treaty of mutual co-operation and security,

Therefore agree as follows:

Article I

The parties undertake, as set forth in the Charter of the United Nations, to settle any international disputes in which they may be involved by peaceful means in such a manner that international peace and security and justice are not endangered and to refrain in their international relations from the threat or use of force against the territorial integrity or political independence of any state, or in any other manner inconsistent with the purposes of the United Nations.

The parties will endeavor in concert with other peace-loving countries to strengthen the United Nations so that its mission of maintaining international peace and security may be discharged more effectively.

Article II

The parties will contribute toward the further development of peaceful and friendly international relations by strengthening their free institutions, by bringing about a better understanding of the principles upon which these institutions are founded, and by promoting conditions of stability and well being. They will seek to eliminate conflict in their international economic policies and will encourage economic collaboration between them.

Article III

The parties, individually and in co-operation with each other, by means of continuous and effective self-help and mutual aid, will maintain and develop, subject to their constitutional provisions, their capacities to resist armed attack.

Article IV

The parties will consult together from time to time regarding the implementation of this treaty, and, at the request of either party, whenever the security of Japan or international peace and security in the Far East is threatened.

Article V

Each party recognizes that an armed attack against either party in the territories under the administration of Japan would be dangerous to its own peace and safety and declares that it would act to meet the common danger in accordance with its constitutional provisions and processes.

Any such armed attack and all measures taken as a result thereof shall be immediately reported to the Security Council of the United Nations in accordance with the provisions of Article 51 of the Charter. Such measures shall be terminated when the Security Council has taken the measures necessary to restore and maintain international peace and security.

Article VI

For the purpose of contributing to the security of Japan and the maintenance of international peace and security in the Far East, the United States of America is granted the use by its land, air and naval forces of facilities and areas in Japan.

The use of these facilities and areas as well as the status of United States armed forces in Japan shall be governed by a separate agreement, replacing the administrative agreement under Article III of the security treaty between the United States of America and Japan, signed at Tokyo on February 28, 1952, as amended, and by such other arrangements as may be agreed upon.

Article VII

This treaty does not affect and shall not be interpreted as affecting in any way the rights and obligations of the parties under the Charter of the United Nations or the responsibility of the United Nations for the maintenance of international peace and security.

Article VIII

This treaty shall be ratified by the United States of America and Japan in accordance with their respective constitutional processes and will enter into force on the date on which the instruments of ratification thereof have been exchanged by them in Tokyo.

Article IX

The security treaty between the United States of America and Japan signed at the city of San Francisco on September 8, 1951, shall expire upon the entering into force of this treaty.

Article X

This treaty shall remain in force until in the opinion of the governments of the United States of America and Japan there shall have come into force such United Nations arrangements as will satisfactorily provide for the maintenance of international peace and security in the Japan area.

However, after the treaty has been in force for 10 years, either party may give notice to the other party of its intention to terminate the treaty, in which case the treaty shall terminate one year after such notice has been given.

In witness whereof the undersigned plenipotentiaries have signed this treaty.

Done in duplicate at Washington in the English and Japanese languages, both equally authentic, this 19th day of January, 1960.

For the United States of America:

Christian A. Herter, Secretary of State; Douglas MacArthur, II, American Ambassador to Japan; J. Graham Parsons, Assistant Secretary of State for Far Eastern Affairs.

For Japan:

Nobusuke Kishi, Prime Minister; Aiichiro Fujiyama, Foreign Minister; Mitsujiro Ishii, member House of Representatives and chairman of the executive board, Liberal Democratic Party; Tadashi Adachi, president of the Japan Chamber of Commerce and Industry; Koichiro Asakai, Ambassador of Japan to the United States.

AGREED MINUTE TO THE TREATY OF
MUTUAL CO-OPERATION AND SECURITY

Japanese plenipotentiary:

While the question of the status of the islands administered by the United States under Article 3 of the treaty of peace with Japan has not been made a subject of discussion in the course of treaty negotiations, I would like to emphasize the strong concern of the government and people of Japan for the safety of the people of these islands since Japan possesses residual sovereignty over these islands. If an armed attack occurs or is threatened against these islands, the two countries will of course consult together closely under Article IV of the treaty of mutual co-operation and security. In the event of an armed attack, it is the intention of the government of Japan to explore with the United States measures which it might be able to take for the welfare of the islanders.

United States plenipotentiary:

In the event of an armed attack against these islands, the United States Government will consult at once with the government of Japan and intends to take the necessary measures for the defense of these islands, and to do its utmost to secure the welfare of the islanders.

Glossary

This glossary is intended to serve as a ready reference to terms used in this book, whether or not they are defined in the text, and to aid the reader in reviewing the material contained therein.

ABROGATION—The destruction or annulment of a law by an act of legislative power, by constitutional authority, or by usage.

ACCRETION—Gradual and imperceptible accumulation of land by natural causes, as out of the sea or a river.

ADHERENCE—A state's entry into an existing treaty with respect to specifically agreed parts only.

ADJUDICATION—The giving or pronouncing of a judgment or decree; also the judgment given.

AGENT—A diplomatic agent is a person employed by a sovereign to manage his affairs or those of his state at the court of a foreign government.

AMBASSADOR—A public officer, clothed with high diplomatic powers, commissioned to transact the international business of one government at the court of another.

AMENDMENT—A modification or alteration to a law or treaty.

ANNEXATION—The incorporation of newly acquired territory into a national domain.

ARBITRATION—The submission of a disputed matter to selected parties whose decision is substituted for the judgment of a court.

ASYLUM—Refuge; protection from the hand of justice.

AUTHORITY—Legal or rightful power.

BELLIGERENCY—The status of de facto statehood attributed to a body of insurgents, by which their hostilities are legalized.

BELLIGERENT—A nation engaged in lawful war.

BLOCKADE—Measures to obstruct or cut off commerce with an enemy.

CAUSE—A ground of action; a suit of action in a court; a case.

CESSION—The transfer of territory by one state or government to another.

CHARGÉ D'AFFAIRES—(French: Person in charge of affairs) The title of a diplomatic representative who does not have the title or dignity of a minister but may be charged with the functions and offices of the latter.

CITIZENSHIP—The status of a person who owes allegiance to a country and is entitled to enjoy that country's full civil rights.

CODIFICATION—The process of collecting and arranging laws into a complete system of positive law.

COMBATANT—A person taking an active part in fighting.

COMITY—Courtesy, respect; willingness to grant a privilege, not as a matter of right, but out of deference and good will.

COMMONWEALTH—A republican form of government in which the welfare and rights of all the people are the main considerations; a loose federation of sovereign states.

CONDEMNATION—The judgment or sentence of a prize court declaring that a vessel was lawfully seized at sea and may be treated as a prize.

CONSPECTUS—A brief survey or outline of a subject; a synopsis.

CONSUL—An officer appointed by a sovereign state to watch over its subjects and commercial interests in a foreign country.

CONSULAR CONVENTION—An agreement or treaty between two countries establishing the rights and duties of their respective consuls.

CONSULAR COURTS—Courts held by the consuls of one country within the territory of another, under authority given by treaty for the settlement of civil and, in some instances, criminal cases.

CONTIGUOUS ZONE—Adjoining zone.

CONTINENTAL SHELF—The extension of a littoral country's land mass into and under the sea.

CONTRABAND—Goods, such as arms and ammunition, which, by International Law, cannot be furnished or carried by a neutral nation to a belligerent nation.

CONVENTION—A pact or agreement between states in the nature of a treaty.

DE FACTO—(Latin: By fact) Actually; in fact; in reality; in contrast to de jure.

DE JURE—(Latin: By law) Legal, rightful, legitimate.

DEPENDENCY—A territory distinct from the country in which the supreme sovereign power resides, but subject to such laws and regulations as the sovereign may think proper to prescribe.

DEPOSITION—Testimony, usually in writing, given under oath but not in open court, and intended for use in an action in court.

DOMICILE—The place where a man has his true, fixed, and permanent home and principal establishment, and to which whenever he is absent he has the intention of returning.

DOUBLE CRIMINALITY—A principle applied in extradition proceedings under which a crime must be punishable in the country in which it was committed as well as in the country demanding the surrender of a fugitive from justice.

EMBARGO—A proclamation or order, usually issued in time of war or threatened hostilities, prohibiting the departure of ships or goods from the ports of the issuing state.

EMBASSY—The residence or office of an ambassador; sometimes, the functions, business, or position of an ambassador.

ENCLAVE—A tract or territory enclosed within foreign territory.

ENVOY—A public minister of the second class, whose rank is next after an ambassador.

EXCLAVE—A part of a country that is separated from the main part and surrounded by politically alien territory.

EXCLUSIVE ECONOMIC ZONE—The area, not to extend beyond 200 miles, adjacent to the territorial sea, in which a coastal state enjoys sovereign rights over both living and nonliving resources and other economic activities and additionally, jurisdiction over certain other activities.

EXECUTIVE AGREEMENT—An agreement between two nations, signed by representatives of the executive departments of the parties.

EXEQUATUR—(Latin: Let it be executed) A certificate issued by one state to a consul of another, recognizing his official character and authorizing him to fulfill his duties.

EX GRATIA—(Latin: Out of grace) Gratuitous; done out of good will rather than out of obligation.

EXTERRITORIALITY—The privilege of persons, such as ministers, who, though temporarily resident in a foreign state, are not subject to its laws.

EXTRADITION—The surrender of a criminal by a state in which he has taken refuge to the state in which the crime was committed.

EXTRATERRITORIALITY—The operation of laws upon persons who are not in the enacting state. The term is often used in the same sense as exterritoriality.

FORCE MAJEURE—(French: Major force) Superior or irresistible force.

FORUM—(Latin: Public place) A court of justice or judicial tribunal.

GENERAL PARTICIPATION CLAUSE—A clause providing that a treaty shall be effective only in a war in which all belligerents are parties to the treaty.

GOOD OFFICES—The offer of one nation to act as intermediary in a dispute between two other nations.

GUERRILLA—A member of a body of armed men not regularly or organically connected with an army.

HIGH SEAS—The seas that are beyond the boundary of any country.

HIGH SEAS, FREEDOM OF THE—A status that requires freedom of navigation and free use for all.

HOSTILITIES—A state of open war; actual fighting.

IMMATRICULATION—The process by which a merchant ship acquires a nationality.

IMMUNITY—Exemption from the jurisdiction or particular areas of jurisdiction of a foreign state.

IN ABSENTIA—(Latin: In absence) A term applied particularly to a proceeding in which an accused person cannot or does not appear in court.

INCHOATE TITLE—Imperfect title; incomplete title.

INNOCENT PASSAGE—The right of the vessels of one nation to navigate peacefully through the territorial sea of another nation.

INSURGENT—One who rises in revolt against constituted authorities.

INSURRECTION—A rebellion, or rising, of citizens or subjects in resistance to their government.

INTER ALIA—(Latin: Among other things or matters).

INTERVENTION—Interference by one state in the affairs of one or more other states.

IPSO FACTO—(Latin: By the fact itself).

JUDICIAL DETERMINATION—Determination by decision of a court of justice.

JURISDICTION—The legal power, right, or authority to hear or determine a cause; authority of a sovereign power to govern and to legislate.

JURISDICTION, CIVIL—The right and authority to hear and determine a cause in an action involving civil matters such as contracts and torts.

JURISDICTION, CONCURRENT—The right of several different tribunals to deal with the same subject matter.

JURISDICTION, CRIMINAL—The right and authority to hear and determine causes in criminal actions.

JURISDICTIONAL IMMUNITIES—Freedom from jurisdiction, as defined above, of a court.

JUS SANGUINIS—(Latin: The law of blood) The determination of citizenship based on the citizenship of parents.

JUS SOLI—(Latin: The law of the soil) The determination of citizenship based on the place of birth.

LAW, CODIFIED—The laws embodied in a complete system of positive law, in a code.

LAW, COMMON—A system of law developed in England and comprising the body of principles and rules that derived their authority solely from usage and custom, or from the judgment and decrees of the courts upholding such usage and custom.

LAW, CUSTOMARY—Law developed by long custom and usage, in contrast to enacted law.

LAW, DOMESTIC—The law in effect within a country.

LAW, INTERNATIONAL—A system of rules governing relations between sovereign nations.

LAW, MUNICIPAL—Same as domestic law.

LAW OF PRIOR DECISION—Law based on the decisions of courts, in contrast to enacted law.

LAW, TREATY—The system of rules of International Law embodied in treaties.

LAW, UNWRITTEN—Same as customary law.

LAW, WRITTEN—Same as codified law.

LEGATION—The place of business or official residence of a diplomatic minister; an embassy.

LIBEL—A complaint or similar pleading in an admiralty cause.

LITTORAL STATE—A state adjacent to a shore.

MANDATE—An authoritative command; an order.

MANDATES UNDER THE LEAGUE OF NATIONS—Former colonies and territories of countries defeated in World War I and "mandated" to other countries for administration under the League of Nations.

MEDIATION—A form of intervention intended to persuade disputing states to settle their differences.

MINISTER—The general term for a diplomatic representative sent by one state to another.

MINUTES OF UNDERSTANDING—The official records of proceedings which provide agreed interpretation of certain provisions of a treaty or agreement discussed at a meeting.

NATIONALITY—The political status of a person regarding the country to which he owes allegiance.

NEUTRAL—A person or state not taking an active part in hostilities when others are at war.

NEUTRALITY—The status of a nation which takes no part in a war between other nations.

NEUTRALIZATION—A permanent state of neutrality, usually imposed by treaty.

NEUTRALIZED STATE—A state that is permanently neutral.

NONCOMBATANT—A person connected with an armed force for purposes other than fighting, such as medical or religious care; sometimes used to denote an entire civilian population.

NOTES—Formal diplomatic or official written communications.

PACIFIC SETTLEMENT—Peaceful settlement.

PACT—An international agreement.

PERSONA NON GRATA—(Latin: Not acceptable person) A person not acceptable to the court or government to which it is proposed to accredit him as ambassador or minister; a person who, after accreditation, becomes unacceptable and is so declared.

PLEBISCITE—The vote of the entire population of a country or area expressing choice for or against a proposed law; an expression of choice as to sovereignty.

PLENIPOTENTIARY—A diplomatic agent invested with full powers.

POLLUTION OF THE MARINE ENVIRONMENT—The introduction by man, directly or indirectly, of substances or energy into the marine environment, including estuaries, which results or is likely to result in harm to living resources and marine life, hazards to human health, hindrance to legitimate marine activities, impairment of the quality of sea water, and reduction of amenities.

PREAMBLE—A clause at the beginning of a constitution, statute, or treaty explaining the reasons for its enactment and its objectives.

PRESCRIPTIVE TITLE—A title acquired by long-continued use.

PRIZE—A ship or cargo, belonging to a belligerent, captured at sea by another belligerent.

PROTECTORATE—A state that has transferred the management of its international affairs to a stronger state.

PROTOCOL—A document serving as the opening of a diplomatic transaction.

PUBLICIST—A writer in the field of public law, such as International Law.

QUARANTINE—An interdiction or restraint imposed by one country on another country's activities on the high seas.

RATIFICATION—A government's official approval or sanction of a treaty.

RECOGNITION—The formal acknowledgement by one country of the independence and sovereignty of another.

REDRESS—Satisfaction for an injury sustained.

REGIME—(French: System of government or of administration) A system of rules and regulations.

REGIONAL ORGANIZATION—An organization embracing the nations of a certain geographical region or having interests in that region.

REPRISAL—A measure, otherwise illegal, taken by one state to suppress illegal actions by another.

RES COMMUNIS—(Latin: A thing common to all) Something enjoyed by everyone and not subject to exclusive acquisition.

RETORSION—The taking of legal measures in retaliation for legally permissible but cruel, unfair, harassing, or otherwise objectionable, acts.

SAFE-CONDUCT—A guarantee that a ship or diplomatic agent may proceed in safety on a designated voyage.

SALVAGE—Compensation allowed to persons by whose assistance a ship or its cargo has been saved from impending danger or, in cases of shipwreck, has been recovered.

SANCTION—(1) Solemn or ceremonious ratification; confirmation. (2) Penalty or punishment imposed as a means of enforcing obedience to law.

SERVITUDE—A right by which a thing is subject to certain use or enjoyment by another person.

SOVEREIGN—A person or state in which independent or supreme authority is vested.

STRATAGEM—A deception, either by words or actions, designed to obtain an advantage over an enemy; a ruse. Stratagems are legal, whereas treacherous acts are illegal.

SUCCESSION—The taking over by one state of the rights and sovereign duties of another.

SUZERAIN—A state which exercises political control over another state.

TERRITORIAL SEA—The belt of water immediately adjacent to a state's land mass and subject to its sovereignty.

TERRITORY—The area of land over which a sovereign exercises jurisdiction.

THALWEG—(German: Road through a valley) The middle of the deepest part of the channel of a river or stream.

TRANSIT PASSAGE—A right, exercised by all ships, to enter a strait for the sole purpose of continuous and expeditious transit of the strait.

TREACHERY—An act of deceit or perfidy.

TREATY—An agreement between two or more independent states.

TREATY, BILATERAL—(Latin: Two-sided) Agreement between two sovereign states.

TREATY, MULTILATERAL—(Latin: Many-sided) An agreement between a number of sovereign states.

TRIBUNAL—A judicial court.

TRIBUNAL, INTERNATIONAL—An international court usually established by treaty.

TRUSTEESHIP, INTERNATIONAL—A system by which countries whose inhabitants are not sufficiently advanced for self-government, are administered by other countries responsible to the United Nations.

VETO—(Latin: I forbid) The non-approval of an act or a resolution in the Security Council of the United Nations by the decisive negative vote of one of its permanent members.

VISA—An official endorsement made on a passport, denoting that the passport has been examined and its bearer may enter the country that issued the endorsement.

WARSHIP—A ship belonging to the armed forces of a state and bearing the external marks distinguishing such ships of her nationality, under the command of an officer duly commissioned by the government of the state and whose name appears in the appropriate service list or its equivalent, and manned by a crew that is under the discipline of regular armed forces.

WHITE BOOK—An official report of government affairs.

WHITE PAPER—A government report on any subject, usually not as extensive as a White Book.

Bibliography

BOOKS

Alexander, L. M. *The Law of the Sea.* Ohio State University Press, 1967.

Barabolya, P. D., and Associates. *Manual of International Maritime Law.* Moscow, 1966.

Bassett, Frank E., Cdr., USN, and Smith, Richard A., Cdr., RN. *Farwell's Rules of the Nautical Road.* 5th ed. Naval Institute Press, 1977.

Baxter, R. R. *The Law of International Waterways.* Cambridge, Mass., 1964.

Brierly, J. L. *The Law of Nations—An Introduction to the International Law of Peace.* 5th ed. Oxford, 1955.

Briggs, Herbert W. *The Law of Nations.* 2nd. ed. New York, 1952.

Bruel, E. *International Straits.* 2 vols. London, 1947.

Burke, W. T. *Ocean Sciences, Technology and the Future International Law of the Sea.* Ohio State University Pamphlet No. 2, January 1966.

———. *International Legal Problems of Scientific Research in the Oceans.* Ohio State University Press, 1967.

Chapman, W. M. *The Ocean Challenge to Industry.* New York, 1965.

Christol, Carl Q. *The International Law of Outer Space.* Vol. 55, International Law Studies, U.S. Naval War College, 1966.

Christy, F. T., Jr., and Scott, A. *The Common Wealth in Ocean Fisheries.* Baltimore, 1965.

Colombos, C. J. *The International Law of the Sea.* 6th ed. London, 1967.

Commission on Marine Science, Report, Engineering and Resources. *Our Nation and the Sea.* Washington, D.C., 1969.

Cooley, Richard A. *Politics and Conservation.* New York, 1963.

Cooper, John C. *The Right to Fly.* New York, 1947.

Corbett, Percy E. *Law and Diplomacy.* Princeton University Press, 1959.

Crosswell, M. C. *Protection of International Personnel Abroad.* New York, 1952.

Dodd, Joseph W. *Criminal Jurisdiction under the United States-Philippines Military Bases Agreement.* The Hague, 1968.

Draper, G. I. A. D. *The Red Cross Conventions.* London, 1958.

Eichelberger, C. M., and Christy, F. T., Jr. *Comments on International Control of the Sea's Resources.* Ohio State University Press, 1967.

Fenwick, Chas. G. *International Law.* 3rd ed. New York, 1948.

Ferguson, J. H. *Manual of International Law for the Use of Navies, Colonies and Consulates.* 2 vols. London, 1884.

Final Record of the Diplomatic Conference of Geneva of 1949. 4 vols. Berne, 1949.

Franklin, Carl M. *The Law of the Sea: Some Recent Developments.* Vol. 53, International Law Studies, 1959–1960. U.S. Naval War College, 1961.

Friedmann, W. *The Future of the Oceans.* New York, 1971.

Gamble, J. K., Jr. *Law of the Sea: Neglected Issues.* Law of the Sea Institute, University of Hawaii, 1979.

Garcia-Amador, F. V. *The Exploitation and Conservation of the Resources of the Sea.* Leyden, 1959.

Gentili, Alberico. *De Jure Belli Libri Tres*. 1598.

Goodrich, M. L., and Hambro, E. *Charter of the United Nations: Commentary and Documents*. 2nd ed. Boston, 1949.

Gould, Wesley L. *An Introduction to International Law*. New York, 1957.

Greenspan, Morris. *The Modern Law of Land Warfare*. University of California Press, 1959.

Gross, Leo. *Introduction to International Law*. U.S. Naval War College Pamphlet, 1955.

Hackworth, G. E. *Digest of International Law*. 8 vols. Washington, D.C., 1940–1943.

Henkin, L. *Law of the Sea's Mineral Resources*. New York, 1968.

Hull, Roger H., and Novogrod, John C. *Law and Vietnam*. New York, 1968.

Hurewitz, J. C. *Diplomacy in the Near and Middle East, A Documentary Record 1935–1956*. 2 vols. Princeton, N.J., New York, Toronto, London, 1956.

Jessup, Philip C. *The Law of Territorial Waters and Maritime Jurisdiction*. New York, 1927.

——. *A Modern Law of Nations—An Introduction*. New York, 1948.

Johnson, Douglas M. *The International Law of Fisheries*. Yale University Press, 1965.

Kelsen, H. *Principles of International Law*. New York, 1952.

——. *Collective Security and International Law*. Vol. 49, International Law Studies, U.S. Naval War College, 1954.

Knight, Gary. *The Law of the Sea; Cases, Documents, and Readings*. Louisiana State University Law Center, 1980.

Lauterpacht, Hersch. *The Development of International Law by the Permanent Court of International Justice*. London, New York, 1934.

——. *Recognition in International Law*. Cambridge, 1947.

Law of Land Warfare. Department of the Army Field Manual FM 27-10, July, 1956.

Law of Naval Warfare. Naval Warfare Information Publication 10-2, Department of the Navy, 1959.

Lissitzyn, O. J. *The International Court of Justice*. New York, 1951.

Logue, J. J. *The Fate of the Oceans*. Villanova University Press, 1972.

MacChesney, Brunson. *Situations, Documents and Commentary on Recent Developments in the International Law of the Sea*. Vol. 51, International Law Situations and Documents. U.S. Naval War College, 1956.

McDougal, Myres S., and Burke, William T. *The Public Order of the Oceans. A Contemporary International Law of the Sea*. Yale University Press, 1962.

——, and Feliciano, Florentino P. *Law and Minimum World Order—The Legal Regulation of International Coercion*. Yale University Press, 1961.

——, and Associates. *Studies in World Public Order*. Yale University Press, 1964.

McGonigle, R. M., and Zacher, M. W. *Pollution, Politics, and International Law—Tankers at Sea*. University of California Press, 1979.

McNair, A. D. *The Law of Treaties: British Practice and Opinions*. New York, 1938.

——. *The Law of the Air*. 2nd ed. London, 1953.

Mallison, W. T., Jr. *Studies in the Law of Naval Warfare: Submarines in General and Limited War*. Vol. 58, International Law Studies, 1966. U.S. Naval War College, 1968.

Masterson, W. E. *Jurisdiction in Marginal Seas with Special Reference to Smuggling*. New York, 1929.

Mouton, M. W. *The Continental Shelf*. The Hague, 1952.

O'Connell, D. P. *The Influence of Law on Sea Power*. Naval Institute Press, 1976.

Oda, S. *The United Nations and Ocean Exploration.* The Hague, 1969.

———. *International Control of Sea Resources.* Leyden, 1963.

Oppenheim, L. *International Law.* 2 vols. (vol. 1: 8th ed., vol. 2: 7th ed.) London, New York, Toronto, 1952 and 1955.

Oxman, B. H. *The Preparation of Article 1 of the Convention on the Continental Shelf.* U.S. Department of Commerce, Washington, D. C., 1968.

Pictet, Jean S. *Commentary on the Geneva Conventions of 1949.* 4 vols. Geneva, 1952–1960.

Poulantzas, N. M. *The Right of Hot Pursuit in International Law.* Series A., No. 5, 1969. Institute of International Law, University of Utrecht.

Reference Guide to the Articles Concerning the Law of the Sea adopted by the International Law Commission at its 8th Session. U.N. Publication A/C.6/L.378, 25 October 1956.

Reiff, Henry. *The United States and the Treaty Law of the Sea.* University of Minnesota Press, 1959.

Riesenfeld, S. A. *Protection of Coastal Fisheries under International Law.* Washington, D.C., 1942.

Schwarzenberger, George. *A Manual of International Law.* 5th ed. New York, Washington, D.C., 1967.

———. *The Legality of Nuclear Weapons.* Library of World Affairs.

Shalowitz, Aaron L. *Shore and Sea Boundaries.* U.S. Department of Commerce, Washington, D.C., 1962.

Shawcross and Beaumont. *Air Law.* 2nd rev. ed. London, 1951.

Smith, Herbert A. *The Law and Custom of the Sea.* London, 1948.

Snee, Joseph M., and Pye, Kenneth. *Status of Forces Agreements and Criminal Jurisdiction.* New York, 1957.

———. *NATO Agreements on Status: Travaux Préparatoires.* Vol. 54, International Law Studies, 1961. U.S. Naval War College, 1966.

Spaight, J. M. *Air Power and Air Right.* 3rd rev. ed. London, 1947.

———. *Aircraft in Peace and the Law.* London, 1919.

Stambuk, George. *American Military Forces Abroad. Their Impact on the Western State System.* Ohio State University Press, 1963.

Stanger, Roland J. *Criminal Jurisdiction over Visiting Forces.* Vol. 52, International Law Studies, 1957–1958. U.S. Naval War College, 1965.

Starke, J. G. *An Introduction to International Law.* 4th ed. London, 1958.

———. *Introduction to International Law.* 6th ed. London, 1967.

Stone, J. *Legal Controls of International Conflicts. A Treatise on the Dynamics of Disputes and War-Law.* London, New York, 1954.

Stowell, E. C., *Intervention in International Law.* Washington, D.C., 1921.

Stuart, G. H. *American Diplomatic and Consular Practice.* 2nd ed. New York, 1952.

Svarlein, Oscar. *An Introduction to International Law.* New York, 1955.

Swarztrauber, Sayre A., Capt., USN. *The Three-Mile Limit of Territorial Seas.* Naval Institute Press, 1972.

Tate, William H. *A Mariner's Guide to the Rules of the Road.* Naval Institute Press, 1976.

Tucker, Robert W. *The Law of War and Neutrality at Sea.* Vol. 50, International Law Studies. U.S. Naval War College, 1955.

United Nations Conference on the Law of the Sea, February 24 to April 27, 1958, Official Documents, 7 vols.: U.N. Publication 58.4; Vol. 1: Preparatory Documents; Vol. 2: Plenary Meetings; Vol. 3: First Committee, Territorial Sea and

Contiguous Zone; Vol. 4: High Seas—General Regime; Vol. 5: High Seas—Fishing, Conservation of Living Resources; Vol. 6: Continental Shelf; Vol. 7: Question of Free Access to the Sea of Land-Locked Countries.

United Nations Yearbook, 1946–1947.

Verzijl, J. H. *International Law in Historical Perspective.* Vol. IV. University of Utrecht, 1971.

Volkov, A. A. *Maritime Law.* Jerusalem, 1971.

Watson, L. B. *Index to the Geneva Conventions of 1949 for the Protection of War Victims.* Navy Judge Advocate General Pamphlet, 1957.

Westlake, J. *International Law.* 2 vols. Cambridge, 1904, 1907.

Wheaton, H. *Elements of International Law.* 8th ed. Oxford, 1936.

Whiteman, Marjorie M. *Digest of International Law.* 16 vols. (14 complete). Washington, D.C., 1963– .

Wilson, Robert R. *The International Law Standard in Treaties of the United States.* Cambridge, Mass., 1953.

ARTICLES AND PAPERS

NOTE: For more extensive research on issues pertaining to the law of the sea, readers are referred to the numerous articles appearing in various periodicals from institutions and disciplines with an interest in the oceans and international affairs. For fuller development of the issues involved and the sequence of Law of the Sea Committee and then Conference problems and actions, two complementary sources are recommended: (1) The series of articles by J. Stevenson and B. Oxman, and then B. Oxman, on various sessions of the committee and conference as reported in *The American Journal of International Law* between 1974 and 1980; (2) The extensive reports of the U.N. on the proceedings of the Committee on the Peaceful Uses of the Seabed and the Ocean Floor Beyond the Limits of National Jurisdiction and of the Third Conference on the Law of the Sea.

Acheson, Dean. "Clarification of U.S. Position on Antarctic Claims." *Department of State Bulletin* 16 (1947): 3.

Alexander, L. M. "National Jurisdiction and the Use of the Sea." *Natural Resources Journal* 8 (1968): 373.

———. "Geography and the Law of the Sea." *Annals of the Association of American Geographers* 58 (1968): 177.

Anderson, W. R., Cdr., USN. "The Arctic as a Sea Route of the Future." *National Geographic Magazine,* April 1959.

Ball, Milner S. "The Law of the Sea, Federal-State Relations and the Extension of the Territorial Sea." The Dean Rusk Center for International and Comparative Law, 1978.

Barkenbus, Jack N. "How to Make Peace on the Seabed." *Foreign Policy,* Number 25, Winter 1976–77.

Baxter, R. R. "North Atlantic Treaty Status of Forces Agreement." *International and Comparative Law Quarterly* 7 (1958): 72.

———. "Introduction to International Law" (Naval War College Lecture, August 1958). *Naval War College Review* 11: 4.

Becker, Loftus. "The Control of Space." *Department of State Bulletin* 39 (1958): 416.
———. "Major Aspects of the Problems of Outer Space." *Department of State Bulletin* 38 (1958): 962.
———. "The Breadth of the Territorial Sea and Fisheries Jurisdiction." *Department of State Bulletin* 40 (1959): 369.
———. "U.S. Foreign Policy and the Development of the Law of Outer Space—A Symposium on Space Law." *JAG Journal* 13, February 1959.
Benitez, R. C., Cdr., USN, and Yeager, Philip B. "The Law of the Sea and the Naval Officer." *U.S. Naval Institute Proceedings,* December 1956: 1271.
Bosma, John T. "The Alternate Futures of Naval Force, Ocean Development and International Law." *The Journal of Marine Affairs,* Vol. 5, 1978.
Brittin, B. H. "International Law Aspects of the Acquisition of the Continental Shelf of the United States." *U.S. Naval Institute Proceedings,* December 1948: 1541.
———. "Article 3, Regime of the Territorial Sea." *American Journal of International Law* 50 (1956): 934.
———. "Piracy—A Modern Conspectus." *U.S. Naval Institute Proceedings,* May 1965: 71.
Brock, John R., Capt., USN. "Legality of Warning Areas as used by the United States." *JAG Journal* 21 (1966/67): 69.
———. "Archipelago Concept of Limits of Territorial Seas." *Naval War College Review* 19 (1966): 34.
Burke, W. T. "Law of the Sea." *Oceanology International* 3 (1968): 38.
———. "Law, Science, and the Ocean." Law of the Sea Institute, University of Rhode Island, Occasional Paper No. 3, August 1969.
———. "Some Thoughts on Fisheries and a New Conference on the Law of the Sea." Natural Resources Public Policy Seminar, University of Washington, November 1970.
Buzan, Barry. "A Sea of Troubles? Sources of Dispute in the New Ocean Regime." *Adelphi Papers #143.* The International Institute for Strategic Studies, London, 1978.
Cagle, Malcolm W., Cdr., USN. "Gulf of Aqaba—a Trigger for Conflict." *U.S. Naval Institute Proceedings,* January 1959: 75.
Campbell, John C. "The United States in World Affairs 1945–1947." *United Nations Yearbook,* 1946–47.
Carroz, J.E. "International Fisheries Bodies and the Apportionment of the Yield from the Living Resources of the Sea." Law of the Sea Institute, University of Rhode Island, 1970.
Chapman, W. M. "Who owns the Sea?" *Oceanology International* 2 (1967): 24.
———. "The Law of the Sea and Public Policy." University of California Engineering and Physical Science Extension Series, July 1968: 112.
———. "The Theory and Practice of International Fishery Development—Management." *San Diego Law Review* 7, July 1970.
Christy, E. T., Jr. "New Dimensions for Transnational Marine Resources." *The American Economic Review* 40, May 1970.
———. "Fisheries Goals and the Rights of Property." *Transactions of the American Fisheries Society* 98 (1969): 367.
———. "Fisheries and the New Conventions on the Law of the Sea." *San Diego Law Review* 7, July 1970.

Clark, John E., RAdm, USN: "Programming for Space Defense—A Symposium on Space Law." *JAG Journal* 13, February 1959.

Clift, A. Denis. "U.S. Oceanic Programs and Policy." *Naval War College Review*, January 1971.

Clingan, Thomas A. "The Changing Global Pattern of Fisheries Management." *Lawyer of the Americas, University of Miami Journal of International Law*, Winter 1978.

Committee Print. "The Third U.N. Law of the Sea Conference." Senate Commerce Committee, U.S. Government Printing Office, June 1978.

Comptroller General of the U.S. "The Law of the Sea Conference—Status of the Issues, 1978." General Accounting Office, 9 March 1979.

Cooper, John C. "High Altitude Flight and National Sovereignty." *International Law Quarterly* 4, (1951): 411.

———. "Space above the Sea—A Symposium on Space Law." *JAG Journal* 13, February 1959.

Craemer, R.A. "Title to the Deep Seabed: Prospects for the Future." *Harvard International Law Journal* 9, (1968): 205.

Craven, J. P. "Sea Power and the Seabed." *U.S. Naval Institute Proceedings*, April 1966: 36.

Cuban Crisis, *Department of State Bulletin*, Special Issue, 1 November 1962.

Danzig, A. "Who shall own the Riches of the Sea? *Vista* 3, (1968): 10.

Darmen, R. "The Law of the Sea: Rethinking U.S. Interests." *Foreign Affairs* 56 (1978): 373.

Dean, Arthur H. "The Geneva Conference on the Law of the Sea: What was accomplished?" *American Journal of International Law* 52, (1958): 607.

Dembling, Paul C. "National Coordination for Space Exploration—A Symposium on Space Law." *JAG Journal* 13, February 1959.

Department of State. Selected Documents 6B and 6C of September 1977 and January 1978. *Documents Associated With the Panama Canal Treaties. The Meaning of the New Panama Canal Treaties.*

Downy, W. G., Jr. "Training in the Geneva Conventions of 1949." *American Journal of International Law* 46, (1952): 154.

Doyle, Jas. H., Jr., LCdr., USN, and Robertson, Horace B., LCdr, USN. "Our Status of Forces Agreements." *U.S. Naval Institute Proceedings*, March 1958: 87.

———. "Radio Active Waste Disposal." *JAG Journal* 13, April 1959.

Dulles, John Foster. "Foundations of Peace." *Department of State Bulletin* 39, (1958): 378.

———."The Rule of Law in Peace." *Department of State Bulletin* 40 (1959): 255.

Eichelberger, C. M. "The United States and the Sea." *Saturday Review*, October 14, 1967.

———. "The United Nations and the Bed of the Sea." *San Diego Law Review* 8, (1969): 339.

Eisenhower, Dwight D. "Statement on Antarctica." *Department of State Bulletin* 38 (1958): 910.

"Final Environmental Impact Statement for a Possible Regime for Conservation of Antarctic Living Marine Resources." Department of State, June 1978.

Fisheries Jurisdiction (Judgment), 1974. International Court of Justice Reports 3, 26.

Fiske, C. O., LCdr. and Mrs. "Territorial Claims in the Antarctic." *U.S. Naval Institute Proceedings*, January 1959: 92.

Fitzmaurice, Sir Gerald. "The Law and Procedure of the International Court of Justice 1951–1954. Points of Substantive Law." British Yearbook of International Law 1, 1954.

Forman, Benjamin. "International Law of Piracy." *JAG Journal* 15 (1961): 143.

Friedman, A. G., and Williams, C. A. "The Group of 77 at the United Nations: An Emergent Force in the Law of the Sea." *San Diego Law Review*, 16, 1979.

Frosch, R. A. "Marine Mineral Resources: National Security and National Jurisdiction." *Naval War College Review* 21 (October 1968): 53.

Gilbert, DeWitt. "Fisheries Loom Larger on the International Scene." *National Fisherman Yearbook*, Issue 51 (1971): 3.

Greenwald, Gerald B. "L N G Transportation Safety." Address before the Committee on Maritime and Transport Law. International Bar Association, Sydney, Australia, 12 September 1978.

Gross, Leo. "Geneva Conference on the Law of the Sea and the Right of Innocent Passage through the Gulf of Aqaba." *American Journal of International Law* 53, (1959): 564.

Hahn, Joseph John. "Development Toward A Regime for Control of Remote Sensing from Outer Space." *Journal of International Law and Economics*, Vol. 12. George Washington University, 1979.

Haight, G. M., Cdr., USN. "The Geneva Conventions in the Shadow of War." *U.S. Naval Institute Proceedings*, September 1968: 43.

Hardy, Leonard R., Capt., USN. "The Atom at Sea." *JAG Journal* 13, April 1959.

Harlow, Bruce A., LCdr., USN. "Legal Use of Force—Short of War." *U.S. Naval Institute Proceedings*, November 1966: 88.

———. "Contemporary Principles of the International Law of the Sea." *JAG Journal* 20, (1967): 27.

———. "Legal Aspects of Claims to Jurisdiction in Coastal Waters." *JAG Journal* 23, (1968): 81.

Harris, Leo J. "Diplomatic Privileges and Immunities: A new Regime is soon to be adopted by the United States." *American Journal of International Law* 62, (1968): 98.

Hearn, Wilfred A., Capt., USN. "Special Aspects of Jurisdiction at Sea." *U.S. Naval War College Review* 10, February 1958.

Henkin, L. "Changing Law for the Changing Seas." *American Assembly*, Columbia University (1968): 69.

Herrington, W. "Panel: Ocean Strategy for the United States Conference of the Law of the Sea Institute." University of Rhode Island, June 1969: 472.

Herter, Christian. "The Rule of Law among Nations." *Department of State Bulletin* 37 (1957): 223.

Hollick, Ann. "U.S. Oceans Policy: The Truman Proclamations." *Virginia Journal of International Law*, Vol. 17, Fall 1976.

Hooker, W. S., and Savasten, D. H. "The Geneva Conventions of 1949: Application in the Vietnam Conflict." *Virginia Journal of International Law* 5, (1965): 243.

International Law Association Committee on the Law of the Sea. "The Establishment and Implementation of the 200-Mile Exclusive Economic Zone." Interim Report, 15 August 1978.

Irwin, Wallace, Jr. "Nationalism and the United Nations." *Department of State Bulletin* 38 (1958): 863.

"Island of Palmas Case, The." *American Journal of International Law* 22, (1928): 867.

Jessup, Philip C. "Sovereignty in Antarctica." *American Journal of International Law* 41, (1947): 117.

"Judgment and Sentences of the International Military Tribunal (Nuremberg)." *American Journal of International Law* 41, (1947): 172.

Kallay, Thomas, Lt., USNR, "U.S. Warships in Foreign Ports." *JAG Journal* 21, (1967): 105.

———. "Visit to a Foreign Port—the Warship's Crew Ashore." *JAG Journal* 21, (1967): 145.

Kent, H. S. K. "The Historical Origin of the Three-Mile Limit." *American Journal of International Law* 48, (1953): 537.

Kerr, A. A., LCdr., USN. "International Law and the Future of Submarine Warfare." *U.S. Naval Institute Proceedings,* October 1955: 1105.

Kibirevskiy, S. N. "The Political and Legal Problems of Using the Seabed for Peaceful Purposes." *Morskoy Sbornik* No. 7 (1968): 70.

Kunz, Josef L. "Austria's Permanent Neutrality." *American Journal of International Law* 50 (1956): 418.

Lissitzyn, O. J. "The Treatment of Aerial Intruders in Recent Practice and International Law." *American Journal of International Law* 47, (1953): 559.

———. "Soviet Interpretation of International Law." *Naval War College Review* 10, (February 1958).

———. "The American Position on Outer Space and Antarctica." *American Journal of International Law* 53, (1959): 126.

Loring, David C. "The United States-Peruvian Fisheries Dispute." *Stanford Law Review* 23, February 1971.

McCory, Dennis F., Cdr., JAGC, USN. "International Law and Naval Operations." The Naval War College Center for Advanced Research, May 1977.

McDevitt, Joseph B., Capt., USN. "The U.N. Charter and the Cuban Quarantine." *JAG Journal* 17 (1963): 71.

McDougal, Myres S., and Burke, Wm. T. "Crisis in the Law of the Sea—Perspective versus National Egoism." *Yale Law Journal* 63, 1954: 67.

———, and Schlei, Norbert H. "The Hydrogen Bomb Tests in Perspective: Lawful Methods for Security." *Yale Law Journal* 64 (1955): 648.

———, and Feliciano, Florentino P. "International Coercion and World Public Order—The General Principles of the Law of War." *Yale Law Journal* 67 (1958): 771.

———. "Authority to use Force on the High Seas." *Naval War College Review* 20 (1967): 19.

McKernan, D. L. "International Fisheries Regimes—Current and Future Conference of the Law of the Sea Institute." University of Rhode Island, June 1969: 336.

McWethy, Robert D., Cdr., USN. "Significance of the Nautilus Polar Cruise." *U.S. Naval Institute Proceedings,* May 1958: 32.

Mallison, W. T., Jr. "Limited Naval Blockade or Quarantine Interdiction: National and Collective Defense Claims valid under International Law." *George Washington Law Review* 31 (1962): 335.

———. "The Laws of War and the Juridical Control of Weapons of Mass Destruction in General and Limited War." *George Washington Law Review* 36 (1967): 308.

Marine Science Affairs, Third Report of the President to the Congress on Marine Resources and Engineering Development, January 1969.

Marine Science Affairs, Report of the National Council on Marine Resources and Engineering Development, April 1970.

Maurer, Ely. "Legal Problems regarding Formosa and the Offshore Islands." *Department of State Bulletin* 39 (1958): 1005.

Meeker, Leonard C. "Vietnam and the International Law of Self-Defense." *Department of State Bulletin* 56, (1967): 54.

Munro, Sir Leslie K. "The Nations and the Firmament—A Symposium on Space Law." *JAG Journal* 13, February 1959.

O'Connor, D. M. "The Oceans." *Lawyer of the Americas, University of Miami Journal of International Law* 1 (1969): 93.

Oda, S. "Proposals for Revising the Convention on the Continental Shelf." *Columbia Journal of International Law* 7 (1968): 1.

———. "International Law of the Resources of the Sea." *Recueil des Cours* 2 (1969): 460.

"Ownership of the World's Oceans—A Continuing Debate." *Australian Fisheries*, Sydney, Australia, December 1977.

Oxman, Bernard H. "International Arrangements and the Law of the Sea." *Lawyer of the Americas, University of Miami Journal of International Law*, Winter 1978.

———. "The Antarctic Regime." *University of Miami Law Review*, December 1978.

Pardo, A. "Who shall control the Seabed?" *Foreign Affairs* 47 (1968): 123.

Parks, Larry G., Cdr., USN. "Why study International Law?" *JAG Journal* 19 (1965): 61.

Pell, C. "The Oceans: Man's last Great Resource." *Saturday Review*, 11 October 1969: 19, 62.

Phleger, Herman. "Progress in the Rule of Law." *Department of State Bulletin* 33, (1955): 647.

Pietrowski, R. F., Jr. "Hard Minerals of the Deep Ocean Floor: Implications for American Law and Policy." *William and Mary Law Review*, Fall 1977.

Pirtle, C. E. "Transit Rights and U.S. Security Interests in International Straits: The 'Straits Debate' Revisited." *Ocean Development and International Law*, Vol. 5, Number 4, 1978.

Quigg, Philip W. "Open Skies and Open Space." *Foreign Affairs* 37 (1958): 95.

Ratiner, L. S. "United States Ocean Policy: An Analysis." *Journal of Maritime Law and Commerce* 2, (1971): 243.

Rea, Constance E. "U.S. Security and the New International Economic Order; Ocean Politics and the International Seabed Authority." University of Pittsburgh Center for International Studies, October 1977.

Report to the Congress by the Comptroller General of the U.S. "Results of the Third Law of the Sea Conference 1974 to 1976." 3 June 1977.

Richardson, Elliot L. "Law of the Sea, A Test for the United Nations." *Current Policy Paper* #60, U.S. State Department, March 1979.

———. "U.S. Interests and the Law of the Sea." *Lawyer of the Americas, University of Miami Journal of International Law*, Winter 1978.

Robertson, Horace B., Capt., USN. "A Legal Regime for the Resources of the Seabed and Subsoil of the Deep Sea: A Brewing Problem for International Law Makers." *Naval War College Review* 21 (1968): 536.

Robertson, John W., LCdr., USN. "Blockade to Quarantine in International Law." *JAG Journal* 17 (1963): 87.

Rogers, Wm. P. "International Order under Law." *Department of State Bulletin* 39, (1958): 536.

St. George, W. R., LCdr., USN. "The Navy and the Rules of the Road." *JAG Journal* 12, June 1958.

———. "International Operational Regulations and the Nuclear-powered Ship." *JAG Journal* 13, April 1959.

Schaefer, M. B. "Freedom of Scientific Research and Exploration in the Sea." *Stanford Journal of International Studies,* June 1969.

———. "Some recent Developments concerning Fishing and the Conservation of the Living Resources of the High Seas." *San Diego Law Review* 7 (1970): 34.

Schneider, Jan. "Something Old, Something New; Some Thoughts on Grotius and the Marine Environment." *Virginia Journal of International Law,* Fall 1977.

Scully, R. Tucker. "The Marine Living Resources of the Southern Ocean." *University of Miami Law Review,* December 1978.

Selak, Charles B., Jr. "A Consideration of the Legal Status of the Gulf of Aqaba." *American Journal of International Law* 52 (1958): 660.

Shalowitz, A. L. "Where are our Seaward Boundaries?" *U.S. Naval Institute Proceedings,* June 1957: 616.

Sohn, L. B. "Sovereignty of the Sea." *Geographic Bulletin* No. 3. U.S. Department of State, Washington, D.C., October 1969.

———. "U.S. Policy Toward the Settlement of Law of the Sea Disputes." *Virginia Journal of International Law,* 17, Fall 1976.

Sorenson, Max. "Law of the Sea." *International Conciliation,* Carnegie Endowment for International Peace, November 1958.

Stang, D. P. "The Walls Beneath the Sea." *U.S. Naval Institute Proceedings,* March 1968: 24.

Stevenson, J., and Oxman, B. "The Third U.N. Conference on the Law of the Sea." *American Journal of International Law,* 69, 1975.

Swing, John. "Who Will Own the Oceans?" *Foreign Affairs* 54 (1976): 527.

"The Law of the Sea Conference and Its Aftermath." *Proceedings of the American Society of International Law,* 1977.

"U.S. Policy of Non-Recognition of Communist China." Press Release No. 459, 11 August 1958. *Department of State Bulletin* 39 (1958): 385.

Väyrynen, Raimo. "The Sea-Bed Treaty Reviewed." *The World Today,* The Royal Institute of International Affairs, London, June 1978.

Walker, Wyndham L. "Territorial Waters: The Cannon Shot Rule." *British Yearbook of International Law* 20 (1945): 210.

Ward, Chester, RAdm., USN. "Projecting the Law of the Sea into the Law of Space." *JAG Journal* 11, March 1957.

———. "Space Law as a Way to World Peace—A Symposium on Space Law." *JAG Journal* 19, February 1959.

———. "Freedom of Space." *Navy* 2, July 1959.

Watson, L. B. "The McCarran Act—Aspects of Immigration and Naturalization of Interest to the Serviceman." *JAG Journal* 8, December 1954.

————. "International Law and the Training of Naval Personnel in Foreign Countries." *JAG Journal* 12, September 1958.

————. "Status of Forces Agreement—the Navy's Experience in Italy." *JAG Journal* 12, August 1958.

————. "The Naval Attaché and International Law." *JAG Journal* 17 (1963): 139.

————. "Status of Medical and Religious Personnel in International Law." *JAG Journal* 20 (1965): 41.

Weinstein-Bacal, Stuart. "The Ocean Dumping Dilemma." Vol. 10, Number 3, *Lawyer of the Americas, University of Miami Journal of International Law,* 1978.

Wilson, Robert R. "The Commonwealth as Symbol and Instrument." *American Journal of International Law* 53 (1959): 393.

Yankov, Alexander. "The Law of the Sea Conference at the Crossroads." *Virginia Journal of International Law,* 18, Fall 1977.

Yeager, P. B., and Stark, J. R. "Decatur's Doctrine—A Code for Outer Space." *U.S. Naval Institute Proceedings*, September 1957: 931.

Young, Elizabeth. "Jurisdiction at Sea." *The World Today,* Chatam House, June 1978.

Young, R. "The Legal Regime of the Deep-Sea Floor." *American Journal of International Law* 62 (1968): 641.

Index